AGEING IN SOCIETY

The British Society of Gerontology was established in 1973 to provide a multidisciplinary forum for researchers in the field of ageing. Its members include researchers, teachers, policy makers with interests in both theoretical and applied studies and practitioners. The Society's aims are succinctly expressed as being to encourage the research and study of human ageing and later life, and the application of this knowledge to the improvement of the quality of life.

Also published by Sage Publications in association with the British Society of Gerontology:

Researching Social Gerontology
edited by Sheila M. Peace

AGEING IN SOCIETY

An Introduction to Social Gerontology

2nd edition

edited by
John Bond, Peter Coleman and
Sheila Peace

SAGE Publications
London • Thousand Oaks • New Delhi

First published 1993. Reprinted 1994, 1996, 1998, 1999

SAGE Publications Ltd
6 Bonhill Street
London EC2A 4PU

SAGE Publications Inc
2455 Teller Road
Thousand Oaks, California 91320

SAGE Publications India Pvt Ltd
32, M-Block Market
Greater Kailash – I
New Delhi 110 048

British Library Cataloguing in Publication data

Ageing in Society:Introduction to Social
Gerontology. – 2Rev.ed
  I. Bond, John II. Coleman, Peter G.
  III. Peace, Sheila M.
  305.26

  ISBN 0–8039–8946–6
  ISBN 0–8039–8947–4 (pbk)

Library of Congress catalog card number 93–085814

Typeset by Photoprint, Torquay, Devon
Printed in Great Britain by The Cromwell Press,
Trowbridge, Wiltshire

CONTENTS

List of Figures and Tables   vii
Preface   ix
Acknowledgements   x
List of Contributors   xi

1   Ageing in the Twentieth Century   1
    Peter Coleman, John Bond and Sheila Peace

2   The Study of Ageing   19
    John Bond, Roger Briggs and Peter Coleman

3   Biological Ageing   53
    Roger Briggs

4   Psychological Ageing   68
    Peter Coleman

5   Adjustment in Later Life   97
    Peter Coleman

6   Environment and Behaviour: A health psychology
    perspective   133
    Jeffrey Garland

7   Death, Dying and Bereavement   151
    Moyra Sidell

8   The Sociology of Retirement   180
    Chris Phillipson

9   Living Arrangements of Elderly People   200
    John Bond

10 Intimate Relationships   226
    Dorothy Jerrome

11 Dependency and Interdependency   255
    Malcolm Johnson

12 Poverty and Inequality in Old Age   280
    Alan Walker

13 Images of Ageing   304
    Mike Featherstone and Mike Hepworth

14 Ageing into the Twenty-first Century   333
    John Bond and Peter Coleman

    References   351
    Index   391

LIST OF FIGURES AND TABLES

FIGURES

1.1	Age structure of the projected population 1987–2026, Great Britain	3
3.1	Wild-type survival curve	54
3.2	Rectangular survival curve	55
7.1	Place of death, all causes, England and Wales 1975 and 1987	169
9.1	The percentage of pensioners in county districts of Great Britain, 1991: two highest deciles and the lowest decile	203
9.2	The Chicago School's ecological model of the city	205
9.3	Flow diagram to illustrate the household structure of elderly people showing the likely direction of change at different stages of the lifecycle in later life	214
9.4	Long-term care places in the UK, 1970–1991	216
10.1	Case study of a 'top-heavy' family	232
11.1	Classification matrix – dependency	259
11.2	Dependency ratios, Great Britain, 1901–2021	267
14.1	Population aged 60 years or over, by major world regions, 1960–2020	335
14.2	Projected population of elderly people (in millions) in the UK, 1989–2059	336
14.3	Rectangular survival curve	337

TABLES

1.1	Older people in Britain 1851–2001	4
1.2	Gender structure of the population of older people in Britain, 1991	4
1.3	Percentage of older people within different ethnic groups in Great Britain, 1986–1988	5
3.1	Reported longstanding illness or disability amongst women and men aged 65 years and over	56
3.2	Difficulty with hearing among elderly people	57
3.3	Difficulty with eyesight among elderly people	58
8.1	Male economic activity rates in Britain, 1971–2001	195

8.2   Female economic activity rates in Britain, 1971–2001   196
9.1   Regional distribution of pensionable population in
      Britain, 1991   201
9.2   County districts with the largest and smallest
      proportions of the pensionable population in Britain,
      1991   202
9.3   Tenure and type of housing of older people's homes in
      Britain, 1980, 1985   209
9.4   Age of accommodation and amenities of older people's
      homes in Britain, 1980, 1985   210
9.5   Household structure of elderly people in Britain, 1945–
      1989   213
9.6   Household structure of elderly people by age   213
11.1 Estimates of disabled adults in Great Britain, 1988   269
11.2 Estimates of disabled adults by severity in Great
      Britain, 1988 (000s)   269
11.3 Inability to undertake mobility, self-care and domestic
      tasks in the population 65+, 1985   271
11.4 Depression in UK community samples   272
11.5 Market value of care of elderly, chronically ill and
      physically disabled people, UK, annualised at March
      1992   275
11.6 Domiciliary services for elderly people   276
12.1 Numbers and percentages of people of different ages
      living in or on the margins of poverty in Britain, 1975–
      1989   282
12.2 National differences in disposable income, inequality
      and poverty   291
12.3 Comparison of the sources of pensioners' income and
      total UK household income (percentage)   293

PREFACE

The original idea for a textbook in social gerontology arose during the late 1980s and culminated in the first edition of *Ageing in Society*, in 1990. The textbook was sponsored by the British Society of Gerontology and edited by John Bond and Peter Coleman. Since publication the book has been used widely by a number of courses and a decision was taken in 1992 to adopt the text as a set book for a new undergraduate level Open University course, An Ageing Society, launched in 1994. Subsequently, it was agreed to substantially update and extend the text. A chapter on 'Death, Dying and Bereavement' has been added and all authors were asked not only to incorporate new material in their chapter revisions, but also to pay particular attention to issues of diversity in late life and the influence of class, gender and ethnicity. Sheila Peace, a member of the Open University course team, joined John Bond and Peter Coleman as a third editor to oversee the revisions.

ACKNOWLEDGEMENTS

We would like to thank all the contributors who have worked hard to update, extend and develop their chapters during a comparatively short space of time. This second edition has had the full support of the British Society of Gerontology and in particular we acknowledge the interest of Anthea Tinker and Jill Manthorpe, Chairwomen of the Publications Committee and members of the committee. We would also like to thank all those who have been involved in the production of the first edition: Debbie Buck who word-processed the final manuscript; Barbara Ingman for the production of the figures and diagrams; and Penny Fowler and Senga Bond for their assistance in proof-reading. In relation to the second edition, we would like to mention all those who have supported individual authors in the secretarial work associated with revisions, and in particular Wendy Clarke at the Centre for Health Services Research, University of Newcastle and Serena Stewardson, Antonet Roberts and Janet Vango at the School of Health, Welfare and Community Education at the Open University.

LIST OF CONTRIBUTORS

John Bond is Reader in Social Gerontology and Research Director in the Centre for Health Services Research at the University of Newcastle upon Tyne. He has previously been a Senior Research Officer in the Scottish Health Service where he was employed to undertake a large survey of services for elderly people. In Newcastle he has completed an evaluation of the three experimental NHS nursing homes and is currently working on a multi-centre study of the resource implications to families and personal health and social services of physical and mental frailty in elderly people, and a multi-centre study of the process and outcome of care of elderly people admitted to hospital with acute conditions. He has written a number of articles and papers on ageing and health and with his wife is joint author of an introductory textbook on sociology for health care professionals.

Roger Briggs is Professor of Geriatric Medicine and Deputy Dean of the Faculty of Medicine at the University of Southampton. He has previously worked in the National Health Service in London, Brighton and Leicester, and studied neurochemistry at the Institutes of Psychiatry and Neurology, London. He currently teaches students of medicine, nursing and allied professions (including social work) as well as providing a clinical service as a consultant geriatrician. His interests include basic and applied research in dementia.

Peter Coleman is Professor of Social Gerontology at the University of Southampton, a joint appointment between Geriatric Medicine and Social Work Studies. A psychologist by discipline, he obtained his PhD in London in 1972 on the subject of the functions of reminiscence in later life, and then worked for five years at the Institute of Applied Psychology at Nijmegen in The Netherlands. He teaches social work, medical, psychology and nursing students, and established and continues to run a post-qualifying course in ageing, health and social care. His research interests are in the study of identity processes, biography and meaning in late life. His publications include *Ageing and Reminiscence Processes: Social and Clinical Implications* (1986) and *Life-Span and Change in a Gerontological Perspective* (as co-editor 1985).

Mike Featherstone is Professor of Sociology in the School of Health, Social and Policy Studies at the University of Teeside. He is chairperson for the Centre for the Study of Adult Life. His publications include *Surviving Middle Age* (with Mike Hepworth), *Consumer Culture and Postmodernism*, and numerous articles on the sociology of ageing, sociological theory and the sociology of culture. He is founding editor of the international journal *Theory, Culture & Society*.

Jeffrey Garland is a Consultant Clinical Psychologist with Oxford District Health Authority's Mental Health Unit. Based at Littlemore Hospital he heads the psychology service to the department of the Psychiatry of Old Age. A founder of PSIGE, the special interest group of the British Psychological Society's Division of Clinical Psychology, he has contributed, on service development and carer support, to a number of texts. His current interest is in the development and evaluation of life review therapy.

Mike Hepworth is Reader in Sociology at the University of Aberdeen. He is a member of Age Concern Scotland and a founder member of the Centre for the Study of Adult Life, University of Teesside. His publications on the social imagery of ageing include co-authorship of *Surviving Middle Age* (with Mike Featherstone), and he is currently working on a cultural and interactional analysis of the stigmatised elements of 'deep old age'.

Dorothy Jerrome is a social anthropologist and counsellor at the University of Sussex. Her interest in the ageing process has developed over the last fourteen years, during which she has taught a wide variety of groups – professional, undergraduate and postgraduate, and community-based. She is a founder member of the Sussex Gerontology Network. Her research has concentrated on peer and family relationships in later life. Her publications include *Good Company: An Anthropological Study of Old People in Groups*. She is currently concerned with mental health and therapeutic intervention in later life.

Malcolm Johnson has been Professor of Health and Social Welfare and Director of the Department of Health and Social Welfare at the Open University since 1984. He is now Dean of the School of Health, Welfare and Community Education. Previously a Senior Fellow at the Policy Studies Institute in London, Secretary (Research and Policy) to the Personal Social Services Council – an advisory body to government, and Lecturer in Sociology at the University of Leeds, he has published more than 90 books, monographs, articles and chapters. He has also served on many academic and public bodies including being Convener of the British Sociological Association Medical Sociology Group, Secretary of the British Society of Gerontology, Scientific Adviser to the Department of Health and Social Security, Vice Chairman of the DHSS Working Party which produced *Home Life*, the Code of Practice on Residential Care and Vice Chairman of the Centre for Policy on Ageing. Professor Johnson was the founding editor of the international journal *Ageing and Society*.

Sheila Peace is a Lecturer in the School of Health, Welfare and Community Education at the Open University where she has recently been involved in the production of the undergraduate course An Ageing Society. Prior to this appointment she was Senior Research Officer, and a founder member of CESSA at the University of North London. Since 1975 she has been involved in a wide range of research with older people particularly in the area of residential care. She has worked for MIND and the International Federation on Ageing in Washington DC. A social geographer by discipline, she has written widely on many gerontological issues including environment and ageing and the quality of life of older women. She is co-author of *Private Lives in Public Places* (with Dianne Willcocks and Leonie Kellaher, 1987); editor of *Researching Social Gerontology* (1990); co-author of *Making Sense of Inspection* (with Leonie Kellaher, 1990) and co-author of *Elderly People: Choice, Satisfaction and Participation* (with Isobel Allen and Debra Hogg, 1992).

Chris Phillipson is Professor of Applied Social Studies at the University of Keele. His publications include *Capitalism and the Construction of Old Age* (1982), *The Impact of Pre-Retirement Education* (with Pat Strang, 1983), *A Manifesto for Old Age* (with Joanna Bornat and Sue Ward, 1985), *Ageing and Social Policy* (ed. with Alan Walker, 1986), *Drugs, Ageing and Society* (with Bruce Burns, 1986), *The Sociology of Old Age* (with Graham Fennell and Helen Evers, 1988) *Changing Work and Retirement* (with Frank Laczko, 1991) and *Understanding Elder Abuse* (with Simon Biggs, 1992). His latest research is assessing new developments in social relationships amongst older people.

Moyra Sidell is a Research Fellow in the School of Health, Welfare and Community Education at the Open University. Previously she was a researcher at the University of East Anglia, where she was engaged in studies of day centres for older people and an exploration of confusion in older people for her doctorate. She has recently conducted a study of gender differences in health at older ages and was joint author of K258, Death and Dying and K260, Health and Well-being, both courses in the Diploma in Health and Social Welfare at the Open University.

Alan Walker is Professor of Social Policy and Chairperson of the Department of Sociological Studies at the University of Sheffield. His books include *Disability in Britain* (ed. with Peter Townsend, 1981), *Unqualified and Underemployed* (1982), *Community Care* (ed. 1982), *Social*

Planning (1984), *Ageing and Social Policy* (ed. with Chris Phillipson) and *The Caring Relationship* (with Hazel Qureshi, 1989). He has published numerous articles on retirement and old age. He is currently engaged in research on older people with developmental disabilities and employers' policies towards older workers. He is Chairperson of the EC's Observatory on Ageing and Older People.

1

AGEING IN THE TWENTIETH CENTURY

Peter Coleman, John Bond and Sheila Peace

Interest in the study of human ageing has grown steadily throughout the twentieth century, culminating in recent years in the publication of a wide range of academic books and the development of a number of courses in social gerontology. Introductions to the study of human ageing have typically emphasised changes in demography focusing on 'the ageing of populations'; a trend which has characterised industrial societies throughout the twentieth century but which in recent decades has become a worldwide phenomenon. The increase in the number of older people as a proportion of the population has resulted in the study of human ageing focusing on old age in general and the problems or challenges of old age in particular. The products of much of this academic work have reinforced the predominant negative perceptions of old age present in society; views which are held by lay and professional people alike.

In this first chapter we consider the impact of demographic and social change during the twentieth century on how we define an ageing population. In doing so we highlight different approaches to the interpretation of these data offered by some of the scientific disciplines studying human ageing, and discuss how such interpretations help to shape our attitudes towards old age. This multidisciplinary approach will evolve throughout the subsequent chapters of the book.

DEMOGRAPHIC CHANGES IN THE TWENTIETH CENTURY

The ageing of populations

An unfortunate trend in recent years has been the increasing tendency to depict the growing numbers of older people in the population as a problem. Old age throughout this century has been seen as a 'social problem' (MacIntyre, 1977) and this predominant perspective is evident through the language used by policy makers and health and social service planners. Dramatic terms such as 'disaster', 'burden', 'rising tide' and 'impending crisis' are characteristic of many recent publications.

While there is no denying the poor quality of life experienced by many older people (Townsend, 1989) or the challenge that planners and professionals face in providing health and welfare services for the growing numbers of frail old people, it is disappointing that the joys and triumphs of old age in the latter half of the twentieth century are not promoted with such energy. Perhaps this tendency reflects a perspective from the media that good news is not news.

Throughout the twentieth century the proportion of people aged 60 or over has increased in all countries of the world. This trend started earlier in industrialised countries but countries from the Third World are experiencing the same changes in population structure. In 1960 it was estimated that about half of the world's population aged 60 or over were living in Third World countries. By the year 2000 about two in three of the estimated 600 million people aged 60 or over will be living in Third World countries. The increase in the elderly population will be most marked in Asia, particularly China and India (WHO, 1989). (See Chapter 14.)

The development of 'ageing populations' is due to the convergence of two major trends. The first is the long-term downward trend in the birth rate, so that the proportion of older people is increasingly larger than the proportion of children in the population. In some countries such as China there is a planned policy of limiting families to one child each. The second is the improvement in life expectancy throughout the world. In the United Kingdom life expectancy has risen by more than twenty years this century (OPCS, 1991; Henwood, 1992). In particular this is due to a reduction in child mortality which reflects improvements in public health and medical advances in the prevention of many fatal infectious diseases in childhood. Increases in the life expectancy of older people reflect improvements in the quality of life in the second half of the twentieth century and to a limited extent some of the achievements of medical science. However, future improvements in health and life expectancy are likely to come, as in the past, from changes in the physical and social environment which leads to disease, rather than from improved treatment of diseases once they have occurred (McKeown, 1979).

While the ageing of the population has been evident for much of this century it has only been taken seriously by planners and policy makers in the last two decades. This recent concern reflects a recognition of the changing composition of the older population, itself a reflection of fluctuating birthrates earlier in the century. As Figure 1.1 and Table 1.1 show, there has been a gradual decline in the number of people aged 65–74 years relative to those aged 75–84 years and 85 years and over. As Henwood states: 'in 1991 44 per cent of the elderly population were aged at least 75, compared with less than one third in 1951. By 2041 it is expected that for the first time the proportion of elderly people aged at least 75 will have exceeded fifty per cent' (Henwood, 1992, p. 8). Similar

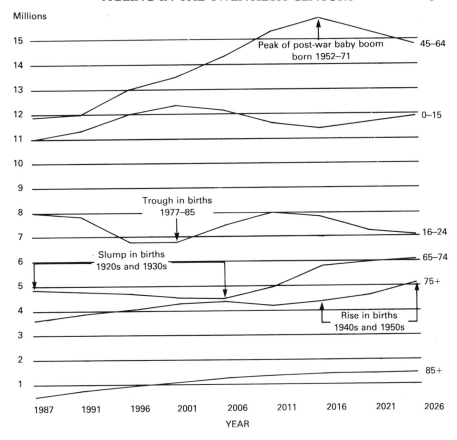

Millions

15 ——————————————— Peak of post-war baby boom ——— 45–64
            born 1952–71
14 —————————————————————————————————
13 —————————————————————————————————
12 —————————————————————————————————— 0–15
11 —————————————————————————————————
10 —————————————————————————————————
9 —————————————————————————————————
            Trough in births
8 ——————— 1977–85 ———————————
7 ——————————————————————————————— 16–24
            · Slump in births ———————————— 65–74
6 |——— 1920s and 1930s ———|
5 ——————————————————————————————— 75+
4 ——————————————————————|
            Rise in births _|
3 —————————— 1940s and 1950s
2 —————————————————————————————————
            85+
1 ———————————————————————————————

1987   1991   1996   2001   2006   2011   2016   2021   2026
                                YEAR

Figure 1.1   *Age structure of the projected population 1987–2026, Great Britain*
Source: Henwood (1992, p. 8)

increases have occurred and are expected in the United States and other industrialised countries (Guralnik et al, 1987). While old age is not synonymous with ill-health, it is the association of advancing age with increasing frailty which creates the concern (see Henwood, 1992). It is estimated that amongst those people aged 85 or over, one in five will have dementia (Jorm, 1990; Kay, 1991) and three in five a limiting longstanding illness (DoH, 1992a).

Gender differences in longevity

An important feature of human ageing is the greater longevity of women than men, a differential which has increased during the twentieth century. Arber and Ginn show that in 'comparing 65-year-olds in 1906 and 1985 a man can now expect to live for another 13 years,

Table 1.1 *Older people in Britain 1851–2001*

					Census date						Prediction	
Number (millions)	1851	1871	1891	1911	1931	1951	1961	1971	1981	1991[1]	2001
65–74	0.7	0.9	1.1	1.5	2.4	3.6	3.9	4.6	5.0	4.9	4.6
75–84	0.3	0.3	0.4	0.5	0.8	1.5	1.8	2.1	2.6	3.0	3.0
85 or over	–	–	0.1	0.1	0.1	0.2	0.3	0.5	0.6	0.8	1.0
Proportion of total population (%)											
65 or over	4.8	4.6	4.8	5.1	7.4	11.0	11.7	13.3	15.1	15.8	15.2
75 or over	1.4	1.1	1.5	1.5	2.0	3.5	4.1	4.8	5.9	7.0	7.1
85 or over	–	–	0.3	0.2	0.2	0.4	0.6	0.9	1.1	1.6	1.8
Total number (millions)	20.8	26.1	33.0	40.8	44.8	48.9	51.3	54.0	54.6	56.1	56.4

[1] The population estimates for mid-1991 are provisional. They are based on early 1991 Census results, and are therefore not comparable with estimates for earlier years which were based on the 1981 Census and will be revised in due course.
Source: Office of Population Censuses and Surveys (1984c, 1993a)

Table 1.2 *Gender structure of the population of older people in Britain, 1991 (thousands)*

	Men	Women	Gender ratio[1]
60–64	1361	1463	107
65–74	2222	2735	123
75–84	1122	1923	171
85 and over	226	654	289

[1] Gender ratio = number of women per hundred men.
Source: Office of Population Censuses and Surveys (1993a)

instead of 11, but a woman can expect another 17 years instead of 12' (1991, p. 9). An examination of sex ratios as age increases highlights the feminisation of later life. Table 1.2 shows the gender structure of the elderly population in Britain in 1991. The gender (sex) ratio of people aged 65–74 is 123 (ie for every 100 men there are 123 women) but this rises to 289 for people aged 85 or over.

This imbalance in the numbers of older men and women has a number of consequences, particularly in terms of marital status and living arrangements. Due to increased longevity, and the tendency for men to marry women younger than themselves, women are more likely to experience widowhood. Fewer women than men remarry following widowhood or divorce and consequently more older women than older men live alone. At present half of women 65 years and over and a fifth of older men live alone (see Chapter 9). In addition, given the predominance of women among the 'very old', they are more likely to live with others and in institutional settings (Bond et al, 1989a; Arber and Ginn, 1991).

Table 1.3 *Percentage of older people within different ethnic groups in Britain, 1986–88*

	45–59	Age group 60 and over	Pensionable age[1]	All ages %
West Indian	20	7	5	100
African	12	3	2	100
Indian	14	5	4	100
Pakistani	11	2	2	100
Bangladeshi	13	2	1	100
Chinese	9	5	4	100
Arab	11	6	4	100
Mixed	6	3	3	100
Other	11	6	5	100
All ethnic minority groups	13	5	4	100
White	17	21	19	100

[1] Men aged 65 years and over; women 60 years and over.
Source: 1986, 1987 and 1988 Labour Force Surveys, cited in Haskey (1990, p. 36)

Ageing amongst different minority ethnic groups

The diversity of our ageing population is also seen in terms of culture, race and ethnic origin (see Young and George, 1991; Blakemore, 1993). With regard to older people from minority ethnic groups in Britain, we are talking about a minority within a minority. A minority within each ethnic group and within the older population as a whole (Table 1.3) (see Haskey, 1990).

Yet as Blakemore and Boneham point out the size of a group may have little to do with the significance of its need (1993). Indeed, the concentration of older people from minority ethnic groups in certain regional and metropolitan areas means that in these areas they do not form a 'small minority'. For example, three-fifths of the Afro-Caribbean population live in Greater London and with other concentrations particularly in the West Midlands (Haskey, 1991). And contrary to what might be imagined given patterns of migration, it is older women who form a majority of older Black and Asian people. With the exception of those from Bangladesh, two-thirds of those over pensionable age are women in both Afro-Caribbean and Asian groups: a figure similar to the majority population.

Blakemore and Boneham also highlight the fact that in the next twenty years there will be a rapid increase in the ageing of minority groups as those who migrated to this country in the 1950s and 1960s reach old age. In addition they show that at present the older population from minority ethnic groups may be under-represented in official statistics as people may have given false information about their age (Blakemore and Boneham, 1993, p. 16).

We still know very little about the lives of older people from minority ethnic groups in Britain (Norman, 1985). Whilst a number of local surveys have begun to highlight the issues for groups within specific areas (Bhalla and Blakemore, 1981; Fenton, 1986; Blakemore and Boneham, 1993), little research has been undertaken nationally (Barker, 1984).

Definitions of old age

Administrative definitions of old age predominate throughout the literature on ageing. The age of 65 as the standard retirement age for men within the UK may still seem a convenient age limit for defining 'old age', 'later life' or what recently has come to be called the 'Third Age' (Laslett, 1989), although fewer and fewer people are actually retiring at this age (Laczko and Phillipson, 1991). It has also been convenient to refer to older people as 'pensioners' since women at the age of 60 and men at the age of 65 are entitled to draw an old age pension. But is the use of chronological age a useful way of defining the later stages of human ageing? Other cultures have used different social definitions of old age such as grandparenthood or physical fitness. For the planners it may be more helpful to relate service needs to functional age. Although the prevalence of disability and physical and mental frailty increases markedly with age many 90-year-old people are as functionally able as people of 50 or 60 (Martin et al, 1988a).

People aged 85 or over, predominantly women, would appear to represent the majority of older people, in the sense that a considerable proportion are physically or mentally frail. But it is important to emphasise the variability in this association between chronological age and disability, an association which is also dependent on factors in earlier life that may have influenced the health of individuals in later life. A lot, too, is unclear. We are not able to predict whether the next generation of older people will be more or less healthy than the present generation. Certainly factors such as the increased prevalence of smoking among younger women, the changing employment patterns of both men and women and general dietary changes in the course of the twentieth century will have their repercussions, but it is difficult to be sure about quite what their impact will be.

Predicting changes in human ageing

It is nevertheless very important for society to look ahead to the situation that awaits people in ten, twenty, thirty, forty or fifty years time. The nature of political processes often makes people very short-sighted, considerations are short term. Yet in planning human services it is essential to look further. In Japan, for example, it is now evident that by the end of the year 2025 about one-fifth of the population will be over the age of 65 and this will be greater than any other country in the world. Presently the proportion of people aged 65 or over is relatively small (only 9 per cent in 1980). The rapid diminution in child mortality after the Second World War when birth rates were very high, followed by lower birth rates when prosperity increased, have contrived to create this rapid demographic change. The Japanese are very concerned about how to manage this transition and rightly so. Will the pension system be adequate for example? Will traditional family care patterns need more external support to survive? It is better to be thinking ahead in time than to be caught unprepared.

Other countries, too, face similar changes. Across the European Community these concerns are being voiced (Nijkamp et al, 1991; Walker, Guillemard and Alber, 1993). The ageing of populations is an international trend in which industrialised countries have most experience but by the middle of the next century this experience will be worldwide. Some degree of planning is therefore essential for all countries.

A longer-term perspective does not only apply to societies and governments. It also applies to individuals. We need to educate individuals to think of their whole life course, to give them a time perspective which does not stop at young adulthood and the acquisition of a job, marriage and the formation of a family. All of us should be thinking beyond this, to middle and later life and to the ultimate point of any life career, death, and to consider the changing roles which we have to negotiate throughout the life course.

Demographic disaster or not?

The view that sees the rising numbers of older people as a disaster and a drain upon resources should be combated with vigour, otherwise it will be a self-fulfilling prophecy. In a society which will have a much more rectangular age distribution with equal numbers of people in each range rather than a pyramidal structure with rapidly declining numbers at the peak, certain adjustments will have to be made. But there is no reason to think that such societies are not viable. Greater changes are likely to occur in the post-industrial society than the ageing of the population. The policies and attitudes of society will need to change to accommodate such changes. People of all ages should be valued not only for their past contribution to society but also for their present and potential contribution.

CHANGES IN THE STRUCTURE OF SOCIAL NETWORKS

Just as societies need to look forward in order to plan effectively for the future, so a historical review assists society in understanding the present. Many people will sense that things have changed but often miss the basis for such change. Of course, in this respect the older we get as individuals the more often we harp back to the 'good old days',

something which the youth of yester-year also found difficult to cope
with. As individuals look backwards at their life experiences they often
appear to see the past through 'rose-tinted spectacles'. This is probably
true of the way that people in general, but also politicians and planners
in particular, view the structure of social networks and the support of
very frail old people.

It is often observed that families do not care for their older relatives as
they used to. Comparison is made with the situation people claim to
remember in the post-war years. Well-documented studies of family life
in this period (Townsend, 1957; Young and Willmott, 1957) describe the
close reciprocal relationships of families and concluded that elderly
people were well integrated in family life. More recent studies of older
people suggest that this situation is not to be found in many places in
modern Britain. For example, Abrams's (1978) survey of older people in
various parts of the country undertaken in the late 1970s showed quite
substantial numbers expressing loneliness. Over half the men and one
third of women who were living alone were not only lonely but 'shaken'
by the extent of their loneliness. Yet in recent years notions of family
care have certainly been central to government policy on supporting
elderly people at home in the community (DHSS, 1982; Rossiter and
Wicks, 1982; Secretaries of State for Health et al, 1989).

Where does the truth lie about the family life of old people? More
recent historical analysis shows us that the position of old people within
the family in England has always been rather ambivalent, and it is no
more true that older people now live more isolated lives, than it is that
older people occupied a more respected position in the past (Laslett,
1977; Wall, 1984). What is true, however, is that the family itself has
changed and continues to change, not only in terms of size and structure
but also in terms of the gendered roles of men and women which
underpin our ideas about the family (see Chapter 10 for further
discussion of the family).

Changes in family size

Throughout the post-war period the size of families has changed
markedly. There are now far fewer children per person of pensionable
age in the 1990s than there were twenty or thirty years ago. This reflects
changes in family size which occurred much earlier this century when
family size decreased quite sharply. Victorian and Edwardian families
were typically large – six, seven or eight children per family was quite
normal – and older people alive during the post-war period had borne
their children in those times.

If we consider only those aged 75 or over in 1960, to take a specific
point in time, we can see that they had brought up children in the era
before the First World War. Not only did they have many children, but
they were likely to have more surviving children than previous

generations, because of improvements in public hygiene, medical treatment and living conditions at the end of the nineteenth century. It is true that many of their sons would have been killed during the awful carnage of the First World War, but this also had the consequence that there were later more single daughters available to care for their elderly relatives. In retrospect, we can see that the post-war years were advantageous for older people in some ways. Also, the solidarity of working-class people was a positive product of urbanisation. In earlier periods of history there was probably less contact between families because travel was not so easy between the rural communities.

The situation only twenty-five years later is a very different one. Those who were over the age of 75 in the 1980s had their children in the period after the First World War and typically had smaller families. Indeed, nearly one in three surviving elderly people aged 75 or over have no surviving children. Wicks (1989) has estimated the ratio of people aged 75 or over to women a generation younger and has shown that in 1901 there were 2.77 women for every person of pensionable age. In 1986 this ratio was 0.84. If 'family' care is predominantly care by women, what does this mean for future caring relationships?

Changes in family structure

In addition to a decline in the size of families, the actual structure of the family has influenced the availability of family support. Geographical mobility has increased markedly in the post-war years. Few people live in the same area as they were born or brought up. Again, according to Abrams (1978), of those older people who did have children, 40 per cent did not have one living within six miles. (Bond reviews the living arrangements of elderly people in Chapter 9.) The increasing participation of women in the work force has made it much harder for the typically one available daughter or daughter-in-law to provide support to older relatives. The impact of divorce cannot be underestimated. It has resulted in the weakening of connections between the generations, where complex patterns of family relationships have often taken the place of simple ties.

All this is not to say that individual bonds of affection and responsibility felt by children toward their parents have diminished or that other forms of intimate relationships have not emerged for many older people. The term 'intimacy at a distance' is now used to express the help given by families who live far apart from their older members. But it does suggest that contacts with other than family members are likely to be relatively more important nowadays – especially contact between peer groups, people of the same age and position in life who also often share similar interests. (Jerrome explores the role of intimate relationships more fully in Chapter 10.) It also has important implications for the concept of community care advocated by successive governments. Care by the community is not always able to be care by the family. (Bond considers the relationship between living arrangements and community care in Chapter 9, and Johnson also considers community care in Chapter 11.)

ATTITUDES TOWARD OLD AGE

Understanding ageing

What effect do the ageing of populations and the changes within some of our major social institutions such as the family have on our attitudes toward old age, as individuals and as members of a wider society? In recent years we have become aware how unnecessarily negative some of our attitudes to older people are. Concern is understandable when one thinks about issues like funding a proper pension system and providing adequate health services, but our attitude should not be only one of concern. Ageing is not only about becoming very frail and needing care. In fact, as already stressed, this is typically only a characteristic of older people at the end of their lives. Negative attitudes only lead to ageism 'which treats older people not as individuals but as a homogeneous group which can be discriminated against' (Scrutton, 1990, p. 13).

There is a widespread interest in developing a greater understanding of ageing. This is reflected in some of the books that have been written for a popular audience such as *A Good Age* (Comfort, 1977), or the telling titles *Ageing for Beginners* (Stott, 1981) and *Look Me in the Eye* (MacDonald and Rich, 1984). All these books reflect, in part, the need for reassurance, to counter a sense of confusion and uncertainty about growing old. Long life should not be something to be afraid of, but an achievement to be enjoyed. New situations which face us as a result of the changing population and family structures should be seen as challenges, not problems.

Central to society's problem-oriented approach to ageing is one of attitudes. Comfort forcibly makes the same point:

> Unless we are old already, then the next 'old people' will be us. Whether we go along with the kind of treatment meted out to those who are now old depends upon how fast society can sell us the kind of pup it sold to them – and it depends more upon that than upon any research. No pill or regimen known or likely, could transform the latter years of life as fully as could a change in our vision of age and a militancy in attaining that change. (Comfort, 1977, p. 13)

An understanding of the basis for our attitudes should help us view the future, if not with optimisim, then with greater awareness.

Old age as a valued period of life?

The claim is sometimes made that older people are no longer as valued or respected as they were in the past. A number of reasons have been put forward in support of this view. The first point that is often made is the demographic one. Since contact with older people is much more frequent nowadays they are no longer so special. Old people have lost their 'rarity' value, the achievement status which was previously obtained merely by reaching the Third Age. Although there is some truth in this observation, numbers probably have little to do with declining levels of respect for older people. People were probably never respected just because they were old but because of the qualities associated with age and experience.

Indeed, we have to beware of the idea that the rising numbers of older people in the population this century is somehow unnatural and abnormal. Furthermore, it is not entirely unprecedented. The researches of social historians (Laslett, 1976) have revealed that there have been 'precursor modern' societies with sizeable numbers of older people in them. The best recorded evidence is available for some of the Italian city states, such as Arezzo and Venice, of the Renaissance period and afterwards, when the proportion of the population aged 65 or over seems to have reached 10 per cent, 'modern' age population structures according to World Health Organization definitions. This probably says something about the standard of living in Italian society at that time. Old age does not appear to have been a notable social problem in Italy during this period. On the contrary, the most revealing records, the artistic works of the period, show striking pictures of older men and women full of character and involvement in the life around them.

Probably the most significant theory to have been developed on historical changes and attitudes to old age is the so-called modernisation theory (Cowgill and Holmes, 1972). This argues that modernisation as a historical process resulted in lowering the status of older people in society. In particular, it explained how respect was lost for old age, and held that the term 'old' acquired a negative connotation as a result of the process of industrialisation. In medieval and Renaissance times, despite the negative image portrayed by Shakespeare's Jacques in *As You Like It* on the last stage of life – 'sans eyes, sans teeth, sans everything', old age had its proper place in the cycle of life, deserving respect especially for the enhancement of qualities of wisdom borne of experience. Indeed, Anglo-Saxon texts in particular portrayed old age as the most favoured period of life and, in fact, rather pitied youth and its follies (Burrow, 1986). According to early versions of modernisation theory, the mass of pre-industrialised societies remained fairly constant in their respectful attitude to the old. As summarised by Fischer such a society was:

> non-literate in its culture, agrarian in its economy, extended in its family structure, and rural in residence. The old were few in number but their authority was very great. Within the extended family the aged monopolised power, within an agrarian economy they controlled the land. A traditional culture surrounded them with an almost magical mystique of knowledge and authority.

Modernisation altered all this in various ways:

> First, the development of modern health technology multiplied the numbers
> of the elderly, and contributed to the ageing of the population and its work
> force. That situation, in turn, created pressures towards retirement, forced
> people out of the most valued and highly regarded roles, deprived them of
> utility, curtailed their income, and lowered their status. Second, modern
> economic technology created new occupations and transformed most of the
> old ones, which also meant loss of jobs, incomes, and status by the aged.
> Third, urbanization attracted the young to the cities thus breaking down the
> extended family in favour of the nuclear conjugal unit. Finally, the growth of
> mass education and literacy meant that 'there can be no mystique of age' and
> no reverence for the aged on account of their superiority of knowledge and
> wisdom. (Fischer, 1978, pp. 20–21)

These two quotes serve to show how within our perceptions of
power, the power of the individual has always been intimately linked to
the power of land, capital and communication systems. Changes within
society and how it defines productivity effect how people of different
ages are perceived. Thus modernisation of itself is not the sole reason for
the devaluation of people as they age. Indeed, examples can also be
given of changing attitudes and declining influence and power in
relation to older people in pre-industrial times (Fischer, 1978). At
present the debate centres on what is the correct interpretation of these
changes. According to Stone (1977) these changes are an indication of
the growth of egalitarianism and individualism rather than the lowering
of respect for older people per se. The end product, though, seems the
same, a loss of respect due to the older person.

In Fischer's account, the displacement of veneration for older people
by contempt as they lost their privileged powers, was followed in its
turn by pity, as older people were seen no longer as the defeated enemy
but as individuals in need of help. One perspective on the current
situation would claim that it is within this set of attitudes of patronising
contempt that we are still entrenched. Certainly the discomfort of mid-
twentieth-century attitudes towards old age is highlighted by the
Churchillian epigram 'All would live long but none would grow old.'

These examples demonstrate clearly the association between the state
of the society in terms of its overall prosperity and how that 'cake is
shared'. We could argue then that in less advantageous times, older
people as a group become marginalised and undervalued, and this
'waxing and waning' is reflected in the ambiguity which many historians
have noted in attitudes towards old people throughout the centuries
(Minois, 1989).

Old age as a difficult period of life?

In Chapter 4 Coleman addresses directly the question of whether for
individuals old age is a particularly difficult period of life. Certainly it is

perceived to be difficult. Evidence for high levels of depression and loneliness are often cited in support of such observations. We have already noted the commonly held view that family relationships are less strong than they were in the past and that this results in greater isolation of older people. The research evidence suggests that there has been a decline in family relationships as a result of changes in family size. But there is a danger of exaggerating the extent to which this has happened, and in creating a false myth about family life in the past. Again, we have to thank the social historians for demonstrating that in English society in particular, many elderly people always seem to have preferred to maintain their own households in old age. Often, for reasons of poverty or disability, this was not possible, but a preferred pattern of life was to live close to but separate from their children. Even widowed people often maintained their own households (Laslett, 1976).

This deeply embedded emphasis on the value of independence in English life has its dark side of course – the greater danger of isolation – but it is not something new. Public criticism of family care of old people has a long history in Britain (Thane, 1985). Take, for example, the following quotation:

> The duty of providing support for parents in old age or infirmity is so strongly enforced by our natural feelings that it is often well performed even among savages and almost always so in a nation deserving the name of civilized. We believe that England is the only European country in which it is neglected. (*Report of the Royal Commission on the Poor Laws*, 1834, quoted in Thane, 1985, p. 11)

Although this was written over 150 years ago, it could have been written today. The aim of the resulting new Poor Law was to encourage greater family responsibility in the care of very frail relatives. So even at this time it was felt that families could do more than they did. Yet, as Thane points out, the beliefs that family attitudes regarding duties owed to the old were in decline were entirely mythical. An obvious index of family neglect of older relatives is their presence in institutions. But over the last three centuries the proportion of older people living in institutions has remained remarkably low and stable. As far as historians can tell, older residents comprised people who were without close kin or community ties (Thomson, 1983). There was, however, the problem in some families of being unable to support their parents because of their own poverty, and this awareness eventually led to the innovative social security legislation at the turn of this century.

A further reason suggested by some, that old age is more difficult now than in the past, relates to the age of death. Documented changes in the survival curve show that deaths in earlier periods of life have drastically diminished, which means that deaths in advanced age have risen sharply. As Briggs shows in Chapter 3, the life expectancy curve has changed its shape to become more rectangular. For the individual this means that the experience of death has come to be concentrated in later

life. Many people will live through to middle age experiencing only the
death of their grandparents among those close to them. Later in middle
age their own parents will die, but it is only in later life that death will be
experienced as a constant pattern as siblings, friends and other
contemporaries die. A statistic worth considering is that of those aged 50
in Britain, only 5 per cent of their cohort will be dead.

This is a very different situation from the one that was customary in
the last century, when death still appeared almost a random occurrence
and the experience of death of people close to one was a common one
through childhood and young adulthood as well as in later life. The
development of a standard pattern of life expectancy must make the
experience of old age different, as the instance of bereavement and the
burden of coping with loss are concentrated on older people. Coleman
and Sidell return to these issues again in Chapters 5 and 7.

A diversity of experience

Understanding the everyday experience of ageing can do much to
change attitudes and increase awareness. One important activity which
has been growing throughout this country, is the interest in oral history,
a recognition of the valuable records older people hold within
themselves and that they hold in virtue of having lived for a long time.
Local projects to write up the history of particular areas of the country
flourish on this basis. In this way we can begin to learn something of the
heterogeneity of older people and the lives of those whose voices often
go unheard, especially older women and older people from minority
ethnic groups (Linton, 1982; Woodberry Down Memories Group, 1989).

The development of pressure groups like the Gray Panthers in the
United States also help contribute to a new awareness of the place of
older people in society, not primarily as individuals needing help but as
people having much to offer and wanting to give. The aim of the Gray
Panthers is explicitly to fight against segregation of the old, shut away
out of harm's way, and to achieve full integration, challenging what they
see around them and to contribute to social movements for the welfare
of the young as well as the old, and to work for peace (Kuhn, 1986). In
Britain, the National Federation of Retirement Pensions Associations
(NFRPA) has also lobbied around the needs for better pension provision
for older people (see Blaikie, 1990).

Yet, in spite of the development of these new role models, ordinary
attitudes expressed toward older people still leave a lot to be desired.
Stereotypes abound of older people as inflexible, hypochondriacal and
self-preoccupied. Such views are also held by professionals, for
example, those who are not prepared to undertake group work with
older people 'because they don't really want to listen to one another', or
refuse the chance of providing therapy, 'because they can't change'.

Stott, in her book *Ageing for Beginners*, cites a number of such examples, including a striking quotation from a fellow journalist writing in the *Guardian*.

> Whenever I pass a group of old men or old women I can hear the keening note in their voices as they list for each other the iniquities of today . . . the elderly are remarkably conformist, no matter how unique each of them might have been in their youth, which is why younger people have difficulty in regarding them as individuals . . . old age has vested interest in decline, a profit motive in refusing to acknowledge improvement . . .' (Tweedie, quoted in Stott, 1981, p. 3)

Stott's reaction is to reject such images, as reflecting the fears and anxieties of the young and the middle-aged. Better, she argues, to cultivate positive images of people ageing well. This is an understandable reaction but also rather escapist. The observations that Tweedie makes do reflect something of reality. What is missing in them is not so much fact, but understanding. There is a lack of sensitivity in the observation, a lack of any real appreciation of how difficult life in old age can be, and why people react the way they do, so wrapped up in themselves or so critical of younger generations. Is it that we find it difficult to empathise with people in life situations that we are not mature enough to comprehend?

Certainly the psychiatrists in Britain who have pioneered the development of specialist mental health services for older people have dispelled the notion of old age as a time of tranquillity. That is a rare state indeed. Adjustment may be a greater task in later life because of the lack of supports available to us in earlier life, and we all have personality flaws that make us liable to fail. In earlier life these are often absorbed in work and the family, in competing and loving, in striving and receiving comfort. In old age we are often left alone without support, without a partner, a job, a role or money to spend. We may face infirmities and considerable isolation. It is no wonder that adjustment difficulties appear enhanced. In fact, of course, many older people are remarkably well adjusted. But because of our lack of imagination, we do not appreciate their achievement. It is a shame that we have to grow old ourselves before we realise.

This point was demonstrated over twenty years ago by Carp (1969). She tested the possibility that behavioural characteristics commonly perceived as those of old age were not in fact specific to the later years of life by comparing a group of 350 older people with a similar number of college students. In the comparison, the students had higher index scores for characteristics such as neurosis, negativism, and un-realistic and unfavourable views of themselves, neglect of personal hygiene, dissatisfaction, social ineptness and drug taking. She also made the point that whereas such symptoms as unusual nervousness, irritability, depression, unaccountable outbursts of rage, personality change, apathy or withdrawal are in the younger person considered clear indications for counselling and psychotherapy, in the older person they often do not arouse interest, but are considered normal and acceptable. It is this kind of discrimination that we must fight against.

We require much greater imagination in our thoughts and feelings about old age. One of the functions of this book is to stimulate such imagination. In the chapters that follow a number of authors from differing disciplines and perspectives critically examine existing ideas about ageing, present some new ideas and at the same time attempt to develop within the reader a critical and questioning eye. The study of human ageing is a challenging field and this book provides just a short introduction. Much remains to be done.

AGEING IN SOCIETY

In this chapter we have chosen to introduce the reader to two dominant themes in social gerontology. The first theme stresses old age as a social problem, emphasising the increasing numbers of older people across the world. The second theme stresses the negative quality of public attitudes to old age. These themes and others will emerge in subsequent chapters of the book but in focusing on only two we wanted to establish within the reader the critical perspective necessary for the successful study of human ageing. By using both historical and life-span perspectives we have highlighted a positive view of human ageing. In the chapters that follow this positive tone will at times be challenged. However, some of the conclusions which will stem from the data presented will, we hope, support our optimism, providing a more balanced view of ageing within our society.

In Chapter 2, Bond, Briggs and Coleman introduce the reader to some of the perspectives used in the study of human ageing by sociologists, clinicians and psychologists. The purpose of this chapter is to emphasise the variety of theoretical ideas available to a student of social gerontology. Biological, psychological and sociological perspectives tend to focus on different aspects of the ageing process. They make different assumptions, use concepts in different ways, pose different questions and arrive at different explanations of the ageing process.

In Chapter 3, Briggs, a physician with a special interest in the health care of elderly people, reviews the major biological changes which are associated with human ageing. He describes the various changes people may experience when they reach the Third Age and summarises the common diseases of old age, emphasising that for the majority of elderly people the experience of morbidity and disability may only be a relatively short one, occurring during the terminal phase of life.

In Chapters 4 and 5, Coleman, a psychologist, provides an insight into some of the psychological perspectives on human ageing. In Chapter 4 he reviews some of the major research findings from studies of age differences in intelligence and cognitive ability, and personality change. He argues that when studying human ageing we should be concerned with the whole life course. In Chapter 5, Coleman looks at adjustment in later life and describes how older people have adjusted to awareness of being in the last stage of life and how they cope with change and loss. He examines the relationship between the social scientist's concept of demoralisation and the psychiatrist's concept of depression within the context of the meaning they have for the elderly individual. In this chapter he also reviews the role of reminiscence in the daily lives of elderly people and its role in therapy.

This clinical theme is taken up by Garland in Chapter 6, where he provides a health psychologist's perspective on environment and behaviour. He reviews the major factors affecting psychological well-being and highlights the significance of stress as a major mismatch between the demands of the environment and the individual's perceived ability to cope. Reflecting the way individuals shape their own environments, Garland reviews the requirements of institutional living and the guidelines for practice in residential and other continuing-care institutions.

Providing a bridge between the psychological and sociological literature, Sidell, in Chapter 7, returns to the often neglected area of death and dying. Building on Coleman's discussion in Chapter 5, she considers both societal and individual attitudes towards ageing and dying, including the influence of cultural and religious beliefs. She reviews the current debates regarding euthanasia and living wills, and discusses how we care for older people who die at home or in institutions. Finally, she considers bereavement, its impact on older people and the support that can be given.

In Chapter 8, Phillipson examines the impact of retirement on individuals and groups from a sociological perspective. He highlights the contradictory feelings often expressed about leaving work and the variety of meanings attached to retirement. In providing an analysis of the future of retirement Phillipson assesses the key issues for social policy.

From a sociological perspective, Bond, in Chapter 9, argues that the geographical location of older people and their living arrangements are strongly influenced by their structural position in society at earlier stages of the life cycle. He describes the living arrangements of older people and discusses how they influence the informal and formal provision of community care. In looking to the future, he questions the need for alternative forms of accommodation which may prevent long-term institutionalisation.

An anthropologist's view of intimate relationships among older people is provided by Jerrome in Chapter 10. Again the significance of relationships throughout the life course is emphasised. Jerrome describes the role of the family in old age and returns to the effects of social change on family relationships and the older person's social network.

Johnson, in Chapter 11, provides a sociological critique of the concepts of dependency and interdependency which reinforce the negative stereotypes of old age. He provides statistical data about the prevalence of 'dependency' emphasising the continuity of experience with other age groups and highlighting the 'independence' of a majority of older people.

In Chapter 12, Walker focuses on the evidence that poverty and inequality remain a substantial part of human ageing. Using comparative, contemporary and historical data on the distribution of income and wealth, he documents the causes of poverty and inequality in old age.

A sociological perspective on the images of ageing is provided by Featherstone and Hepworth in Chapter 13. They develop a theme from this chapter by comparing the images of ageing before the industrial revolution with those which have emerged through the processes of industrialisation and modernisation. They lead into the final chapter in which Bond and Coleman consider the implications of current images of ageing for the twenty-first century.

This introduction to social gerontology and the study of human ageing is a multidisciplinary enterprise. As with all introductions it has been necessary to be selective in the choice of material included. In this first chapter we have begun to highlight something of the diversity of human ageing. Social divisions, such as those based on gender, ethnicity and social class, are important and they have been introduced where appropriate at various points in the book rather than subjected to separate analysis. Finally, in this second edition of *Ageing in Society* all the authors have extended their material and updated their sources in an attempt to keep abreast of the rapidly changing world of social gerontology.

2

THE STUDY OF AGEING

John Bond, Roger Briggs and Peter Coleman

The study of ageing is a multidisciplinary enterprise. Each discipline brings its own theoretical perspectives and methods. The purpose of this chapter is to introduce the reader to this variety of perspectives and to highlight both their different and complementary natures. Biological, psychological and sociological theories of ageing tend to focus on different aspects of the ageing process without necessarily contradicting each other. We show that they make different assumptions, use concepts in different ways, pose different questions and arrive at different explanations of the ageing process. Their perspectives are not right or wrong, simply different.

To illustrate the complementary nature of the different theoretical perspectives we will examine the approaches adopted by each perspective towards the study of mental illness, particularly dementia. The chapter will not only identify differences in biological, psychological and sociological perspectives but will highlight differences in view within each of these broad disciplines. To begin with though, a brief word about theory.

THEORY IN THE STUDY OF AGEING

The word 'theory' often gives rise to difficulties because it is used to describe everything which is not practical. When theory is used, as in psychological or sociological theory, then it refers to a set of conjectures or tentative explanations of reality.

Each one of us uses theory constantly. We carry in our heads our personal theories or models which represent the world about us. To do this we use selected concepts and the relationships between them. It is because we do not all share the same theories that we see the world differently. In other words facts do not speak for themselves; rather facts are interpreted in the light of some particular theory. It is because we have particular ideas about the nature of 'illness', 'old age' or the 'role of women' that we have different views about the way that society should care for sick old people.

Some facts are more generally accepted than others, and this may involve a process of accumulating particular knowledge which produces convergent theory. For example, we now take for granted the fact that the world is spherical. Yet at the time of Columbus' famous voyage it was certainly not taken for granted and the world was believed to be flat by many. It is by testing our hypothetical explanations that we accumulate knowledge and what may begin as scientific facts gradually become accepted into common-sense knowledge. Today we are in a position of uncertainty regarding some of the theories which are evolving about the origins and antecedents of psychiatric illness in old age. It is accepted theory which will influence the kinds of interventions produced and those holding different theories will produce different ideas about what is appropriate. For example, the prevalence of pervasive depression in people aged 65 or over is about 20 per cent (Gurland et al, 1983). A number of theories have been suggested as to the cause of depression in old age. Clinical work has suggested that there are changes in the ageing brain, psychologists have suggested changes in older people's self-concepts and sociologists have suggested changes in the social relationships of older people. These theories have led to pharmacological interventions, psychotherapy and the promotion of day centres and lunch clubs.

We cannot ignore theory, we can only choose from the alternatives. However, theory is not static but dynamic, constantly changing. Theory development therefore is best understood in a historical context, and fashions in the acceptability of different theories can be interpreted equally within a broader political or social context. The acceptability of different explanations of the influence of race on intelligence is a recent example of the fit between theories and the acceptability of broader ideas about the nature of people and society.

The role of theory

It would be a mistake to regard theories as right or wrong. There are, rather, theories which are more or less useful or profitable. No one theory is a completely accurate representation of reality but some provide better insight into a particular phenomenon than do others. The usefulness of any theory depends on how it functions: first, to explain past events; second, to predict future events and, third, to generate new theory.

One function of theory is to provide explanations of what facts already exist about some phenomenon. Often facts appear trivial and disjointed yet they may be linked by some theoretical explanation. One example of this is the similar responses observed (facts) to bereavement, to retirement and to amputation. In all cases they may be explained by response to the loss of something valued. This kind of theorising is possible because of an existing system of relationships connecting different facts. When they are linked theoretically this adds to our understanding of otherwise disparate phenomena. By using theory we are able to summarise specific features which are generalisable beyond the immediate field of study. By the same token, theory should be able to predict future outcomes.

Finally, good theory should lend itself to generating new theory, capable of more parsimonious explanation and prediction. One aspect of this is that good theory should generate testable hypotheses which give rise to empirical testing. Theory therefore should point to areas yet to be explored and indicate which facts to observe while defining them clearly. In this way, new findings and empirical generalisations emerge which are then used to amend existing theory if this is then warranted.

BIOLOGICAL PERSPECTIVES

What is ageing?

We are all so familiar with the human and social effects of ageing and senescence on people around us that most of us do not think of ageing in 'biological' terms. However, just as birth and development can be seen from biological as well as social and psychological viewpoints, so too can senescence and death at the other end of the lifespan – in birds, bees or humans. Most living organisms show an age-related decline in functional capacity which can be studied at various levels ranging from the intact organism, be it plant or animal, through its component organs and their cellular constituents, down to molecular structure.

The terms 'ageing' or 'senescence', which are often used interchangeably, imply decline and deterioration. Thus the growth of children over their initial years is thought of as 'development' rather than ageing, since the changes are beneficial rather than deleterious. Although the culmination of senescent decline is in the death of the individual organism, not all 'cell death' is damaging to the organism as a whole: indeed, it may be 'programmed' as part of the organism's biological economy. For example, the cells on the skin or lining the gut wall of a human have a short lifespan, since as they die they are sloughed off and replaced by new, dividing cells in a constant cycle of regeneration.

Ageing processes have been defined by Maynard-Smith (1962, p. 115) as 'those which render individuals more susceptible as they grow older to the various factors, intrinsic or extrinsic, which may cause death', recognising that death may arise from a decline in the individual organism's ability to maintain its intrinsic function in the face of physiological stress from an extrinsic source such as 'accident' or disease. According to Comfort (1960, p. 8), ageing is 'an increased liability to die, or an increasing loss of vigour, with increasing chronological age, or with the passage of the life cycle'. The four criteria proposed by Strehler (1962) have been widely accepted:

1   Ageing is *universal*, in that it occurs in all members of the population (unlike disease).

2 Ageing is *progressive*, a continuous process.
3 Ageing is *intrinsic* to the organism.
4 Ageing is *degenerative* (as opposed to developmental or 'maturational' changes).

It should be noted that ageing and death are fundamental, intrinsic biological properties of living organisms including humans, and that senescent changes are by definition deleterious. The biologist is concerned with measuring the nature and extent of ageing changes, trying to understand how these changes are caused and controlled, and learning how the effects of ageing can be manipulated or mitigated.

Biological theories of ageing

Programmed ageing
As already discussed, most organisms (including plants) undergo a process of ageing. It is possible that some primitive forms of algae and amoebae may carry on reproducing by simple cell division virtually indefinitely if the environment in which they are maintained is suitable, but more complex cells and organisms appear to have a limited lifespan and reproductive capacity. Natural selection and the process of evolution operate by modifying the characteristics of 'new' members of a species – in other words, it is reproduction and the early part of life which are of biological significance in terms of evolution. Survival into 'old age' is a rare event in the wild, most individuals being removed by accident or predation before the development of senescence. Thus natural selection may have allowed the accumulation of genes which operate to the 'good' of the organism in early life (when most individuals survive) even though these same genes lead to physiological decline later in the lifespan (when few surviving individuals remain to be affected). One could argue that the human being is not 'built' for old age in the industrialised world any more than is the rat for a laboratory – both artificial environments far removed from the world in which natural selection has operated for millennia. Various genetic mech-anisms have been postulated to account for ageing phenomena and the determination of lifespan, and these view ageing as 'programmed'.

Many events during growth, development and reproduction are regulated by 'signals' from nerves or hormone-secreting glands. A key area of the brain in the control of such hormones is the hypothalamus, which is closely related to the pituitary gland. Various 'clock' theories of ageing have suggested that ageing changes are controlled by some kind of pace-maker whose main function is to direct the timetable of development until sexual maturity and reproductive ability are achieved. Thereafter, in the absence of a programme, the functions of the hypothalamus and pituitary become deranged and lead to physio-logical decline. While such 'clock' and 'pace-maker' theories are attractive, at least in highly complex organisms such as mammals, they are difficult to apply to simpler forms of life.

The cells which make up mammals can be thought of as essentially two types: 'fixed' cells, which after development do not divide further and have to serve the organism for the rest of its lifespan (for example, brain cells) and 'dividing' cells which carry on replacing themselves throughout lifespan (for example, skin or gut-wall cells). It should be noted that both types of cell will need to continue to make new molecules such as proteins, a process under genetic control, for the metabolism, function and repair of the cell and, in the case of the dividing cell, for replication. Hayflick and Moorhead (1961) showed that a variety of dividing cells from human tissues were only capable of a certain number of cell divisions: they could not replicate indefinitely when cultured, dying off after a period. A reproducing cell must make accurate copies of itself – too serious an error might be lethal to the cell or transform it to a 'malignant' cell (potentially cancerous). However, it is only through the natural selection of occasional 'good mistakes' that evolution has been able to operate. Thus there must be a balance between expending cellular energy on maintaining accuracy in cell division, and allowing some faulty copies: it has been proposed that the Hayflick *phenomenon* (of limited numbers of cell divisions) is an example of genes 'switching off' the mechanisms which maintain accuracy, thereby conserving energy but allowing errors to accumulate and cause senescence (Kirkwood, 1977).

Unprogrammed ageing
It should be noted that all these theories of 'programmed ageing' rely on the concept that genetic mechanisms are involved and that these mechanisms make evolutionary sense. Other mechanisms involved in ageing may be 'unprogrammed', due to random damage affecting molecules concerned with cell structure, function and metabolism. For example, large molecules like collagen and elastin (the proteins which make up connective tissue such as cartilage) may have their structure and physico-chemical properties changed by a process known as 'cross-linkage'. Similar changes can cross-link the strands of DNA, the molecule which carries genetic information.

Many normal metabolic processes within cells, such as oxygen utilisation, generate toxic by-products known as 'free radicals'. These substances are mopped up by several defence mechanisms which have evolved to protect the cell. However, free radicals may cause damage to membranes which surround cells and also cause breaks in the strands of DNA.

Orgel (1970) pointed out that errors involved in the transfer of genetic information from DNA – in the process of cell replication or the synthesis of proteins – could have serious consequences. Such errors in protein synthesis might themselves lead to further defects in protein synthesis and genetic information processing, introducing yet more error-containing proteins in a vicious cycle of 'error catastrophe' leading to cell death.

Explaining biological ageing

It can be seen that no single theory can explain all the causes of ageing, nor is there any reason why one cause should operate to the exclusion of all others. In general terms, it seems reasonable to suppose that:

1 the fundamental property of 'life' is the replication of genetic material;
2 such replication has an inherent risk of error due to random physico-chemical interactions ('non-programmed'); and
3 the process of natural selection would ensure a balance between catastrophic error and extinction on the one hand and too little error to allow necessary change on the other, so that ageing ('programmed') represents a stable evolutionary strategy.

Finally, we should remember that ageing processes evolved at a time when few animals (or human beings) lived far into their lifespan: in those circumstances, the risk of accidental death or starvation was too high to warrant expending excessive energy on the maintenance of highly accurate, potentially immortal, cells. Rapid and prolific reproduction were more likely to preserve the gene pool, a more important goal than the prevention of senescence in the individual. Now that most of us reach old age, evolution may take humans in a different direction in generations to come.

PSYCHOLOGICAL PERSPECTIVES

In our everyday lives we might think more about the psychological aspects of ageing than we do about biological ageing. However, the study of ageing, within the discipline of psychology, has hitherto played a relatively minor role. Recent emphasis on the interdisciplinary study of ageing and the increased awareness that psychological ageing must be placed within a historical, environmental and biological context, have served to make the study of ageing a model for other areas of psychological research where interdisciplinary links need to be made.

Experimental psychology

Psychology has diverse roots which can still be seen reflected in the different research methods employed by psychologists (Riegel, 1977). It was first cultivated as a laboratory-based science in the second half of the nineteenth century with a focus on analysing human intellectual functioning and ability, 'cognitive' processes by which people gain knowledge or become aware of their environment. Perception, discrimination, memory, learning and reasoning have remained key topics. Although the first proponents of this new science were predominantly Germans, 'experimental psychology' subsequently developed most strongly in the United States and Britain where the findings began to be put to practical use.

The first distinct contribution to the field of ageing is generally credited to Sir Francis Galton (1822–1911), a half-cousin of Darwin. He was concerned above all to find some understanding of the hereditary basis of intelligence, and was particularly involved in measuring individual differences in motor performance and discrimination tasks. But he also launched the first large-scale collection of empirical data across the whole age span.

A major influence on psychology's development was the creation of the intelligence (IQ) test in the first part of the nineteenth century. Again this was the result of an American psychologist named Terman adapting techniques already developed by Binet and Henri in France to analyse more complex performances of judgement and knowledge. The success of the IQ measure as a means of selection gave psychologists a reputation for measuring absolute individual capabilities that has been hard to live down. When, during the Second World War, the occasion arose for testing large groups of young adults with the same instruments used on similar groups in the First World War, the results clearly indicated that a considerable improvement in performance with historical time had taken place, attributable to changes that had occurred in education, communication and welfare. But the full significance of the implications for the dependence of psychological characteristics on social factors was not recognised at the time.

Similarly, the age differences that were observed on psychological tests received little critical examination. The markedly poorer performance by older people on a whole range of tasks was taken at face value, and explained as being due to the apparently inevitable process of biological degeneration. Well before the end of the nineteenth century a picture of psychological ageing as a regressive movement was well established (Labouvie-Vief and Blanchard-Fields, 1982). Cognitive 'disorganisation' was thought to follow the reverse order of development with higher order abilities degenerating first. The model presented of psychological development and ageing was a unitary one, a sequence of growth and rapid build-up of abilities in early life followed by a period of relative stability and then a long period of decline. Within this context the psychological study of ageing was seen as of limited interest and was not surprisingly a rather unpopular field of research. At best, research on older individuals could be seen to provide an additional dimension to investigations on the explanatory power of general theories of cognitive functioning.

More recently as cognitive psychology has developed to take account of people's functioning in the real world as opposed to the laboratory (eg Neisser, 1982), older people's mental functioning has become a more attractive topic to researchers. Closer links are being made between research findings and the practical relevance that they may have (Rabbitt, 1988).

Developmental psychology

On the continent of Europe somewhat different traditions of psychology flourished. The notion of human development received more serious consideration. Whereas in Anglo-American orientations both young and old were compared against an ideal standard of functioning, the young as not yet attaining it and the old as falling away from it, continental philosophers and subsequently psychologists gave more credence to the idea of developmental stages. Thus Jean-Jacques Rousseau (1712–1778) insisted that children should be considered and evaluated by standards independent of those of the successful young adult. Children were not just immature adults but their qualities deserved separate recognition and cultivation.

The idea of human development as a progression in qualitative leaps from one stage to another is best represented in psychology in the work of Jean Piaget (1896–1980) on the cognitive development of children (see Flavell, 1963). He divided this development into separate stages which he termed sensorimotor, pre-operational, concrete operational and formal operational intelligence. Piaget himself did not look beyond childhood, but his methods and interpretations have been used to propose further stages of cognitive development in adulthood.

Thus Riegel (1973) argued that adults come to accept contradictions as a fact of life. Whereas during the stages of concrete and formal operations thought becomes increasingly non-contradictory, the 'mature' adult comes to a new apprehension and an effective use of contradictions in operations and thoughts. Instead of making premature choices between apparently logically incompatible alternatives, the more adult thinker is prepared to endure such tension. Contradictions form the basis for innovative and creative work, and for the discovery of new principles. Therefore the developmental task of being an adult in Riegel's view requires the ability to live with complexity and tolerate a high level of ambiguity. This 'dialectical-operations' stage of cognitive development is achieved through giving greater acknowledgement to the importance of intuitive thought, such as insight and understanding based on hunch, sensing and immediate apprehension rather than reasoning alone.

Ideas on the development of personality
The most well-known contributions to developmental psychology from continental Europe have come in the field of personality study. Whatever one may think of the detail of his theories, Sigmund Freud

(1856–1939) revolutionised thinking about human behaviour by propos-
ing a dynamic model for human motivation and opened up interest in
much broader fields of psychology than cognitive performance alone.
He stressed that people did not always act in rational ways, nor were
they necessarily aware of the bases of their action. Freud and his
immediate followers were not strictly speaking psychologists but
clinicians involved in the treatment of mentally-disturbed people, but in
a short period of time at the turn of the century they produced a wealth
of ideas about human motivation, often conflicting and so broad-ranging
that they have not yet been properly examined.

Freud himself was not interested in ageing and his description of
developmental stages is limited to the very early periods of life. But his
one-time colleague Carl Jung (1875–1961), who broke away from Freud
to establish a rival school of 'psychoanalysis', did give much greater
importance to what he called the second half of life. For him mid-life was
a crucial turning point when the individual was provided with
opportunities for new developments. These were less to do with
involvement in the outside world but more interior processes that he
referred to with the term 'individuation'. A person could achieve a new
balance in personality, a man accepting his 'feminine' as well as
'masculine' aspects for example. Jung laid great stress on the value of
symbolic and religious experience in creating a state of harmony
between the individual and the world around, and derived evidence for
his theories from his wide-ranging knowledge of other cultures and
societies.

Another of Freud's associates Alfred Adler (1870–1937) also came to
stress different aspects of human motivation. Disagreeing with Freud's
stress on the overriding importance of sexuality he proposed that the
prime motivating force in all people's lives is a feeling of inferiority. All
individuals have this feeling to some extent because of the inferior
position they once occupied as children where power and privilege were
exerted by adults. Some feel this more strongly than others, for example
as a result of physical defects or heavy-handed parenting. Adler saw
subsequent developments of an individual's lifestyle as a means of
compensating for feelings of inferiority. In extreme examples this could
take the positive form of remarkable achievements by people with
handicaps, but could also be expressed negatively in excessively self-
assertive behaviour. Adler himself saw the most successful resolution of
problems of inferiority to be in involvement with others, in the
development of 'social interest'.

The relevance to gerontology of Adler's thinking lies in the fact that
feelings of inferiority and loss of self-esteem can become major issues in
late life, as a result, for example, of physical decline, loss of status,
beauty and other attributes. At the same time possibilities for friendship
and close relationships may be diminished. In Adlerian terms rigid,
rejecting attitudes on the part of older people and even disengagement

can be seen as problems resulting from a fear of inferiority. The perspective of an Adlerian approach to therapy is essentially constructive. Inferiority feelings and neurotic lifestyles can be overcome by helping the individual to develop a wider interest in others and cultivate a sense of belonging (Brink, 1979).

Although the early psychoanalysts contributed interesting ideas on personality development, these have proved difficult to investigate in practice. As clinicians they cited their own observations on patients, but these are open to the criticism that they are not independently verifiable observations and refer in any case to a biased sample of people who are not necessarily representative of the general population.

The establishment of acceptable methods of research has remained a major problem for the study of personality development. Although the observations and interpretations of the psychoanalysts can be criticised for their unrepresentative nature, the standard methods of experimental psychology – laboratory-based research on randomly selected individuals – also does not in general provide a suitable basis because of the artificiality of the situations that can be studied in this way. In the last twenty-five years ethology, a branch of zoology dealing with the study of animal behaviour by means of observation in its natural setting, has had a growing impact on the study of human psychology. The challenge is to develop naturalistic methods of observation and systematic recording of human thought, feeling and behaviour. Psychologists have also been learning from the methods of anthropologists who are well experienced in recording activities and customs in different societies.

Erik Erikson's stages of life
Of all the pioneer theorists on personality development the most influential to the study of ageing has been Erik Erikson. His pervasive impact on adult personality research is widely acknowledged (eg Ryff, 1984; McAdams, 1990). In his book *Childhood and Society* (Erikson, 1950) he provided a framework for the whole lifespan in terms of a series of tasks to be fulfilled. Thus the child's, or rather baby's, first psychological task in life is described as developing a sense of trust rather than a sense of mistrust. The ensuing childhood stages are characterised in terms of 'autonomy', 'initiative' and 'industry'. In adolescence the issue is the development of 'ego identity' versus 'identity diffusion' – Erikson is probably best known for his formulation of the concept of 'identity crisis' – and in early adulthood the development of 'intimacy' versus a sense of 'isolation'.

In middle age the issue becomes one of 'generativity', again a word coined by Erikson himself. He describes it as 'primarily the interest in establishing and guiding the next generation'. This can mean a focus on one's own family but it can also include broader interests and concerns in the society in which one lives. The opposite state Erikson calls 'stagnation' for which he offers a succinct illustration. 'Individuals then, often begin to indulge themselves as if they were their own – or one another's – one and only child.' (1950, p. 259)

The task of the last stage of life, old age, for Erikson is to attain 'ego integrity', an assured sense of meaning and order in one's life and in the universe, as against despair and disgust. This involves 'acceptance of one's one and only life cycle as something that had to be and that, by necessity, permitted of no substitutions' (Erikson, 1965, p. 260). Despair may be expressed in a feeling that one has failed and does not have the time to attempt another life or an alternative road to integrity, and also in a disgust with other people, especially the young.

Erikson himself was a Dane who emigrated to the United States, and the influx of many other psychologists from continental Europe, especially following the rise of Nazism, created in the United States a flourishing interest in developmental psychology. In Britain too, notable contributions have been made, most especially by John Bowlby, who demonstrated the catastrophic consequences of maternal deprivation in early life for personality development (Bowlby, 1965). However, Erikson has been one of the few psychodynamic theorists until recently to take an explicit interest in late life. It is no wonder, therefore, that his statements about old age are so often quoted.

Life-span developmental psychology

Erik Erikson can be rightly considered one of the precursors of what has come to be known as life-span developmental psychology (Sugarman, 1986). This appears at present to provide a fruitful context for the study of the psychology of ageing. Although the product of work carried out within this perspective is still small, its influence can be expected to grow (see also Baltes et al, 1980; Datan et al, 1987). In recent years there has also been a revival of interest in the study of whole lives within personality psychology (McAdams, 1990). Erikson is honoured in this tradition for his contribution to 'psychobiography' through his books on Luther and Gandhi.

It is unfortunate in some ways that discussion of the relevance of Erikson's theory to ageing often focuses on the last stage of 'integrity'. His theory is in fact much more sophisticated than brief presentations often imply. It is not the case that at each stage the 'task' is either left unresolved or resolved, thus allowing the way forward to further development. A solution may be only relatively successful, and this will have repercussions on all subsequent stages. Thus major unresolved residues of earlier difficulties can play a salient part in late life, and make the issues somewhat different for each individual according to his or her own past experience. Erikson's ideas in fact should not be seen as a fully worked out theory but more as a model or framework within which to describe psychological development.

The emphasis on the integrity of the lifespan is Erikson's lasting contribution and one that is vital to an understanding of old age. In order to understand people in late life it is necessary to see them in the context of their whole life history with the problems both successfully and unsuccessfully resolved from earlier periods in life. This approach to human development and human ageing contains a number of important implications. The first is that the situations of older individuals will vary according to their histories. The courses of development of different people are likely to diverge the longer they live, and the more experiences they absorb. Rather than growing more alike as we age, we therefore become more unique.

A second important point is that development occurs on a number of different fronts. There is no reason to think that intellectual development, physical development and social development follow the same trajectory. Indeed, the varying importance of different aspects of life may be an essential feature of the life course. Jung expressed a similar thought more poetically: 'we cannot live the afternoon of life according to the program of life's morning, for what in the morning was true will at evening be a lie. Whoever carries into the afternoon the law of the morning . . . must pay with damage to his soul' (Jung, 1972, p. 396). In other words, as each phase of the day, each stage of life has its own characteristics and potentialities which must not be ignored.

A third characteristic of the life-span approach is the recognition of reciprocal influences between the person and the environment. Again, this is a feature of human psychology emphasised by Erikson. An individual's development depends on the right psychosocial circumstances being available, for example in the characteristics of his or her parents and the wider society. This success in turn creates the circumstances for another's successful development. Erikson gave considerable emphasis to the interdependence of the generations with the old needing the young as much as vice versa. This is a very important point as psychology has traditionally put its emphasis on measuring individual characteristics while tending to neglect the environment around.

It must also be admitted that some of these points were already recognised by the first people who gave thought to developing a study of human lifespan in the eighteenth and nineteenth centuries. In particular, they raised the issue of 'cohort differences', that the development of people growing up in a certain period of historical circumstances will differ from those in another, which thus makes invalid 'cross-sectional' comparisons of people of differing ages at the same point in time (Baltes et al, 1977). It is sad in retrospect to realise how these same points were missed by those who exploited the new techniques of psychological measurement developed earlier in this century. Indeed, it is only recently that methods have been developed which provide possible solutions to these theoretical problems. We explore further the relationship between theory and method later in this chapter.

SOCIOLOGICAL PERSPECTIVES

Sociology has provided a number of different perspectives from which to study ageing. Four broad approaches are delineated here: structuralism, symbolic interactionism, ethnomethodology and critical theory. A fuller account of these sociological perspectives is provided by Cuff et al (1990) and the following discussion is based on an account of different sociological perspectives used in the study of health and illness (J. Bond and S. Bond, 1994).

Structuralism

Structuralism as a broad approach is based on the assumption that all our social behaviour, our attitudes and values, are the result of the organisation and structure of society in which we live. A major refinement of this, however, is to view the components of social structure as in consensus with each other or, alternatively, to view them as in conflict.

Structural functionalism – a consensus perspective
All sociological perspectives have in common a focus on the ordered nature of society – that is, a belief that in most situations the range of possible actions is fairly limited and we have a fair idea of how we would behave as well as being able to predict, within limits, the behaviour of others. The notion of order is relevant to situations as diverse as the golden wedding party and the stability of whole societies. It is at the societal extreme that the consensus perspective is situated, based on the assumption that, in the main, societies can be regarded as stable and generally integrated wholes which differ by their cultural and social structural arrangements. This perspective in sociology owes a great deal to an analogy with the natural and biological sciences. When sociology first emerged as a discipline separate from philosophy there was a thrust towards scientific method modelled on the natural sciences. Comte, a French philosopher, believed that sociology was about adapting and applying methods of physical science to social life, to make 'law-like' statements about the determinants of human behaviour and to reshape society by being able to predict and hence control its workings.

The emphasis on societies as integrated wholes was also based in part on the crude analogy between social and biological organisms. The analogy arises from the fact that both social and biological organisms have, on the one hand, a propensity to survive against all odds and, on the other hand, a propensity to decay. Most, if not all, biological organisms are systems made up of a number of distinguishable interrelated parts. Each of these parts affects and responds to changes in other parts of the organism. This analogy does not mean that the social system mirrors the biological system in terms of structure, but that the different parts of the social system are also affected by and respond to changes in other parts of the system. Different parts of the biological system fulfil different functions and roles; hence the sociological analogy, functionalism. Some functions are more essential for the organism's survival than others; so, too, individuals and institutions fulfil a variety of functions and roles. When the human organism loses an eye it adapts to change in circumstances; in the event of heart failure the body eventually dies. The human organism is therefore an open and adaptive system which, however, is not immortal. Likewise, in its simplest form structural functionalism describes society as an adaptive and open system whose different parts function to keep it unified and relatively unchanging.

In the study of ageing the structural functionalist perspective has offered two theories. On the one hand, there is *disengagement theory* which emphasises the phasing out of old people from certain roles in order that society can continue to function. On the other hand, *activity theory* emphasises the need to keep old people active in order to integrate them into society, again so that society can continue to function.

Disengagement theory Disengagement theory was first expounded by Cumming and Henry (1961) in *Growing Old*: 'Disengagement is an inevitable process in which many of the relationships between a person and other members of society are severed and those remaining are altered in quality.' (Cumming and Henry, 1961, p. 211).

As individuals grow older they and society will prepare in advance for the ultimate 'disengagement' which is caused by incapacitating disease or death. The theory states that the process of disengagement is the method by which society prepares for the structure of its members so that when the inevitable arrives it does not disrupt the orderly functioning of society. Three criticisms have been levelled at the theory. First, by implication the theory suggests that disengagement is desirable and therefore condones a policy of indifference towards the problems of older people (Shanas et al, 1965). Second, disengagement is not inevitable and non-engagement in old age reflects the life-long pattern of social interaction for some people. Third, the data presented in *Growing Old* has been incorrectly interpreted since cultural values and the economic structure combine to create a position in which a large proportion of older people are disengaged (Rose, 1965a).

Activity theory Activity theory takes a different perspective in explaining the process of ageing. Havighurst (1963) argued that successful ageing can be achieved by maintaining into old age the activity patterns and values typical of middle age. Happiness in old age is achieved by denying the onset of old age and where the relationships, activities or roles of middle age are lost it is important to replace them with new ones in order to maintain life satisfaction. Indeed, there is a considerable amount of data to suggest that, in North America at least, the level of activity individuals have developed over a lifetime tends to persist into their later years (Riley et al, 1968).

The central criticism of activity theory is its idealistic nature. It would appear unrealistic to expect, for all but a small minority, that people can maintain the level of activity associated with middle age through to old age in view of the limitations imposed by biological changes alone. Activity theory is also unrealistic because the economic, political and social structure of society prevents the older worker from maintaining a major activity of middle age, namely 'productive' employment.

Structuralism – a conflict perspective
Conflict theorists tend to regard themselves as radical critics of the consensus theorists, with their emphasis on maintaining the status quo. As such they are sometimes regarded as political rather than socio-logical, most strongly exemplified in the Marxist perspective.

Marxism is essentially a historical interpretation of the evolution of societies or social systems. It explains social change historically by examining the evolution of modern industrial society from ancient economies based on slavery, through the medieval economy based on serfdom, to the capitalist economy based on waged labour. Marxism is also deterministic in that it predicts the evolution of capitalist society to socialist society. Like other forms of structuralism it is synthetic in its approach to social change, being concerned with the whole of society rather than with specific aspects (Lefebvre, 1968).

Some aspects of Marx's social philosophy are central to his sociological theory (Bottomore and Rubel, 1965). For Marx all societies are *stratified* into distinct *groups* and *classes*. Underlying Marxist theory is the notion that power and authority are linked closely to the economic organisation of society. In capitalistic societies the power of relationships is exemplified by the conflict between owners of capital (*the bourgeoisie*) and the working class (*the proletariat*). The relationship between these two groups is characterised by exploitation.

Marxism sees society as a product of the *conflict* between these two social groups or social classes, and predicts that the struggle will be resolved through revolutionary rather than evolutionary social change. Societies pass through definite stages of development, with each stage containing contradictions and conflicts that lead to social change. But society and history are not seen as external to man. It is through man's own activity as a member of a social class with his distinctive class consciousness that the social and historical world is created and changed.

The main criticisms of Marxist sociological theory have been about the position that only changes in the economic base can change society.

Weber (1930, first published in German in 1904) argued that many factors must come together to produce social change and proposed that it was the religious ideals of Calvinism which transformed people's behaviour and produced capitalism, by turning their religious zeal into economic production through hard work rather than detaching themselves from work to pursue their religious interests.

Weber's other criticism of Marxism was over the derivation of the power available to social groups. He did not agree that power derived solely from economic relations, the relations to private property and the means of production. For Weber, social status or prestige also played an important role in power relationships.

In the study of ageing the conflict perspective is represented by the theory known as the political economy of old age.

The political economy of old age Political economy is understood to be the study of interrelationships between political structure, economic structure and social structure or, more specifically, between government organisations, the labour market, social classes and status groups. The central focus of this perspective is on the interaction between the economic and political structure in society and the way they affect the distribution of resources and social goods (Pratt, 1976). In Britain, Townsend (1981), Walker (1982b) and Walker and Phillipson (1986) have taken a political economy perspective which has as a central concept the idea of structured or structural dependency. Structural dependency describes the development of a dependent status resulting from restricted access to a wide range of social resources, particularly income. This is reflected in the large numbers of elderly people who live in poverty (Townsend, 1979, 1989). A review of secondary data on earnings, incomes and assets, housing circumstances and benefits in kind shows that about one in four elderly people have incomes which are equal to or below the State Poverty Line, ie the supplementary benefit rate appropriate to each family (Walker, 1980; see also Chapter 11). It has long been recognised that elderly people feature in the lower levels of the income distribution because they are usually not in 'productive' work. Society tends to reward present work; it does not reward past work and therefore it does not reward old age. Elderly people are discriminated against by economic and social policies which benefit the young employed and the well-off. Thus, poverty in old age and the dependent status of elderly people are related to low resources and restricted access to resources through the life cycle.

We can illustrate this relationship by considering the effects of retirement on a person's access to resources. Prior to retirement manual workers – the majority of elderly men – experience reduced economic status (Townsend, 1979). Increasingly, early retirement schemes are pushing elderly workers into less skilled jobs and into unemployment. After retirement the inequalities resulting from low pay, unemployment, disability and for women and ethnic minorities, sex and racial discrimination, are carried forward into old age. The decline in the real value of savings and pensions means that the worse-off are the very old. Retirement also restricts access to social resources in the form of a reduction in social relationships once the retiree is away from the world of work (Phillipson, 1982).

The political economy perspective, following the Marxist tradition, has focused analysis and the development of social explanations on class inequality and the relationship between economic production and later life, but equally it is relevant to inequalities between men and women and people from different ethnic groups. Critical gerontologists, to whom we turn below, have commented on the narrowness of this approach, which concentrates on inequalities resulting from poverty and economic disadvantage (Dant, 1988).

Symbolic interactionism

In some ways symbolic interactionism is an embracing term given to a number of characteristics which identify a broad sociological and social psychological perspective. Many of the core ideas in symbolic inter-actionism characterise a rather different frame of reference known as action theory, which evolved from Weber's simple idea that sociologists should proceed to *understand* those they study. This is achieved by attempting to look upon the world as they do; by appreciating how the world looks to them. To this is added learning the ideas, motives and goals which make people act. By learning these things about indi-viduals, the sociologist should gain an understanding of why they act in certain ways in order to achieve particular ends in the face of their individual circumstances as they see them.

This approach, emphasising understanding the individual, is very different from that of structuralism with its emphasis on social structures and facts which exist independently of individual members of society. Although structural functionalist theories are built on the elements of individuals' social action, they are set within the broader social systems which govern individual social actions. The emphasis is therefore on understanding *social action* by reference to social systems rather than of social action as generated through individuals in their particular circumstances. Thus, social action is attractive to a broad range of social theories but is difficult to study empirically while linked to broad social structures rather than small groups. It has been left to those within the broad perspective of social interactionism to translate their theoretical position into empirical studies.

The main ideas of symbolic interactionism were provided by Mead (1964) in Chicago earlier this century, and the major contributions to this perspective have continued to be American. At the heart of Mead's approach is the assumption that there is a difference between animal *reaction* and human *conduct*. Conduct requires the possession of *mind* which is distinctive to the human species. To this is added the concept of *self*. Individuals both undergo experiences and are aware of doing so.

Mead (1964) regards human action as very different from human behaviour. Behaviour is limited to a stimulus–response relationship. The concept of action depends on individuals' ability to plan their actions, reflect on past experience and reflect on themselves in the same way as they look upon other kinds of objects in the environment. It is the capacity for self-consciousness which makes human beings different from animals, and central to this is the ability of the individuals to take the same attitude towards themselves as others take towards them. In this sense the individual becomes an object like any other object; to look upon oneself as an object is to see oneself as others do.

For different individuals the same object will have very different meanings which will depend on such factors as previous experience and current purposes. Individuals will also experience the many different meanings they hold for others, reflected back at them. In order to handle this complexity, individuals construct pictures of themselves according to the general, typical and predominant views of themselves as shown by others. This is carried out largely through the medium of language which Mead refers to as the *significant symbol*. Through such exchanges individuals learn the ways of acting which others expect and the self-consciousness necessary to engage in social life. The meanings of all objects are similarly derived from the social interaction of the individual with other members of society. Such meanings are handled in and modified through an interpretative process used by other people in dealing with the things they encounter.

It is explaining such processes that is the hallmark of symbolic interactionist approaches – providing an understanding of how and why things are as they are, by finding out about the circumstances of people's lives. As Blumer (1969) contends, these circumstances do not exist *in themselves* as stimuli to which the individual reacts. Rather, what constitutes circumstances depends on the purposes, plans and knowledge that the individual has *in mind*. Social action therefore has to be interpreted as the mindful action of individuals initiated to bring about certain purposes.

Symbolic interactionists have also shown how behaviour which from one perspective would be interpreted as totally irrational, from another perspective is a rational response to circumstances. This is associated with an interest in the processes by which members of society define their own circumstances and respective identities. This is encapsulated in a dictum attributed to W.I. Thomas: 'if men define situations as real, they are real in their consequences' (Merton, 1968, p. 475). This definitional approach has had particular applications to what has become to be known as the *labelling theory of deviance*, that is, how members of society come to define and label some of its members as deviant in certain respects and interact with them in such a way that the person takes on the characteristics related to the label. In the study of ageing, labelling theory has been used to explain the way in which elderly people are forced to act out specific roles. Thus, once someone has been labelled old, say they receive a retirement pension, they are expected to act the role of elderly or retired person and not try to seek employment. A further example of labelling theory is included in Chapter 11.

For symbolic interactionists the organisation of social life arises from within society itself and out of the processes of interaction between its members. They do not accept that external factors, such as economic ones, determine the form that society takes, although such factors do exert influence. Such influences will vary, however, depending on how they are perceived and dealt with. While the organisation of social life arises from within, it does not take on any autonomous features like those attributed by structuralist sociologists. To assume that society imposes or determines the action of society's members is incompatible with an interactionist perspective. Neither do the symbolic interactionists regard the structure of society as rigidly adhering to some basic, almost universal structure, as Marxist theory does. Rather, society consists of a relatively loosely articulated array of heterogeneous and overlapping social groups. While the relationships between groups or sub-groups may be characterised as competitive, there is no basic theoretical reason why one group should predominate.

Typically, symbolic interactionists are concerned not with an embracing concept of society but with the way in which individual members of society are engaged in indicating to others who and what they take themselves to be. This is portrayed in the conventional ways in which people communicate their social status, social role and sense of self. Goffman (1971) sought to understand how people come to decide, through social interaction, who they are, and he employs the metaphor of life being just like life on the stage.

Sub-culture theory of ageing   Although interactionist theory underlies a number of studies of ageing and old age there are few interactionist theories specific to the study of ageing. The main contribution is the sub-culture theory of ageing (Rose, 1965b), which postulates that sub-cultures tend to form when members of any group in society, such as elderly people, interact with each other significantly more than they do with other people in society. The development of a sub-culture would be encouraged by elderly people having a positive affinity for each other and their exclusion from interactions to any great extent with other groups in society. In Britain there are a number of factors which contribute to the development of a sub-culture. The influence of compulsory retirement will encourage group affinity, while the decline in family contacts, the development of retirement communities (see Chapter 8) and the explosion in day care will encourage the development of a sub-culture. The strength of some family relationships, particularly in times of ill health and disablement, the continuation in employment and an inbuilt resistance to becoming old might restrict the development of a sub-culture, not to mention structural divisions which make elderly people a heterogeneous group in society. However, changes in the structure of the family and the lack of employment opportunities for older people suggest that sub-cultures may still develop because of the processes of labelling described above.

Phenomenology and ethnomethodology

Like the interactionist perspective, the ethnomethodological perspective has been used widely in recent years as an underlying theoretical perspective in studies of ageing, but has produced no *grand theories* (Mills, 1959) of ageing. To some extent this is because of the very nature of ethnomethodology.

The basic assumptions of ethnomethodology, deriving largely from the phenomenological philosophy of Husserl, are very different from those of other sociological theories. Husserl attempts to describe the ultimate foundations of human experience by 'seeing beyond' the particulars of everyday experiences to describe the 'essences' which underpin them. Only by grasping such essences do we have a foundation for all experiences which enables us to recognise and classify it in an intelligible form. In order to grasp these essences it is necessary for the philosopher to disengage from our usual ideas about the world, to examine the stream of experiences available to us – past, present and future. Phenomenology is about perceiving phenomena in the world as objects or events which are, in essential respects, *common* – the same for others as they are for ourselves. Therefore, the foundations of social life are not within the mind and experience of an individual, but in a commonly lived world of experience. This is a social world known in common with others.

The phenomenological approach was developed in sociology by Schutz and subsequently became known as ethnomethodology (ethno = people, ethnomethodology = the study of people's methods). This approach is particularly concerned with the language used in and used to describe everyday life. The approach is concerned with the basis of common assumptions we all make in order to render comprehensible the routines and activities of our everyday lives. Such order is achieved through what Schutz (1972) has termed our *taken-for-granted assumptions*, in other words our expectations of what should happen in a normal day and how we expect others to act. The social fabric is maintained through the use of *typifications* (Schutz, 1972) – common ways of classifying objects such as tree or elderly woman, events such as buying a loaf of bread, and experiences such as pain or love, but in ways which are capable of being redefined or adapted. One taken-for-granted assumption is that others, by and large, see the world as we do, something which is clearly not always borne out. These elements of everyday life are not only learned through the process of socialisation but are also identified as 'mental tools' which we carry around with us in order that we can adapt our own actions according to the situations in which we find ourselves. Thus, like interactionists, phenomenologists and ethnomethodologists are concerned with how members of a social group perceive, define and classify the ways in which they actually perform their activities, and what meanings they assign to acts occurring in the context of their everyday lives.

Critical social science

The perspective of critical social science is one which encompasses a number of sociological perspectives including post-Marxist perspectives, post-structuralists and postmodernists unified by their criticism of industrial and post-industrial society.

Since the Enlightenment period in the seventeenth and eighteenth centuries Western thought and culture has been dominated by the idea that through science and technology human life in general will be improved. This is clearly evident in modern capitalism, which argues that through economic growth and technological change society will increase wealth to the benefit of everyone.

Critical social science challenges the Enlightenment philosophy suggesting that societies oppress individual members who are unaware that their lives are regulated by such social forces. Marx harnessed this idea within his concept of class consciousness. But it was the classical Marxists like Gramsci who first went beyond Marx's ideas about class and class consciousness suggesting that the state was essentially repressive in order to control opposition to the capitalist system. This was achieved through the control of knowledge and science, social knowledge being subordinated to the needs of capitalism.

Although we might believe that different institutions in society, for example education and health care, are helpful, post-structuralists and postmodernists would argue that we are really being repressed by them. That we may feel perfectly happy with our society and do not feel imprisoned does not negate this view but supports it. It demonstrates how trapped we are within the structure of our ways of thinking.

In everyday life we take most things for granted. This applies equally to the way we structure knowledge as it does to everyday customs. We forget that we did not construct them but inherited them. We acquired them through learning language. Language is one of our most stable institutions (Berger and Berger, 1976) but was created and developed in particular times and places. In order to understand language and the social categories it describes and we take for granted, post-structuralists and postmodernists would argue that we must take a historical perspective. This allows examination of the conditions under which our taken-for-granted ideas were created and developed.

Thus the most significant challenge of critical social science is rooted in the critique of instrumental reason – that is a critique of the effort to explain the natural and social world in order to predict or control it. A critique of instrumental reason exposes the link between knowledge and domination. It shows, for example, how the interests of gerontologists in explaining ageing is linked to a covert strategy of social control by the dominant social group (Gubrium and Silverman, 1989; Baars, 1991). The way that critical theory underpins critical gerontology is illustrated by a recent volume from a group of American gerontologists (Cole, 1992), and in Chapter 13 where Featherstone and Hepworth explore images of ageing.

THEORETICAL APPROACHES TO THE STUDY OF DEMENTIA

In order to show the complementary nature of theoretical perspectives drawn from clinical medicine, psychology and sociology we highlight dementia in old age.

Clinical approaches to dementia

From a biological perspective the first step towards elucidating the nature of a disease is to define the problem. During the nineteenth century, accurate *clinical descriptions* of many diseases of the nervous system appeared, and in 1835 James Cowle Prichard described a syndrome which he called incoherence or senile dementia. He noted 'forgetfulness of recent impressions, while the memory retains a comparatively firm hold of ideas laid up in the recesses from times long past'. The description of the symptoms and clinical signs of a disease, and their progression ('natural history'), enables the classification of diseases and allows the distinction of one from another. 'Dementia' is a 'syndrome' of progressive, global impairment of intellectual function, not a specific disease entity in itself. For example, the dementia which may be caused by infection with syphilis has a different clinical picture and natural history from the inherited disease causing dementia known as Huntington's chorea.

Pathology is that branch of medicine which includes the study of changes in tissues and organs as a result of disease. Early in this century, Alzheimer described abnormal microscopic loops and coils seen in the brain of a patient who died with dementia; this was the first demonstration of a specific brain pathology in any form of insanity apart from that associated with syphilis, and led to the concept of a specific type of dementia known as 'Alzheimer's disease'. The study of the pathology of Alzheimer's disease and senile dementia has been increasingly refined over recent years, since it is more difficult in elderly subjects to distinguish between brain changes due to 'disease' and those due to 'normal ageing'. Similarly, techniques of clinical and psychological assessment have been improved in an attempt to make reliable distinctions during life between Alzheimer's disease and other causes of dementia. However, difficulties remain in clinical diagnosis of dementia during life and in pathological diagnosis, particularly among elderly people. These difficulties are more marked in early, less severe cases, where there is considerable overlap with what may be regarded as 'normal'.

The epidemiology of dementia
Epidemiology is concerned with the occurrence of disease in populations and its control or prevention. In order to establish the prevalence of dementia in a community with any precision, it is obviously important to have sound diagnostic criteria. The difficulties in diagnosis have been alluded to above, but epidemiological research can of itself improve the instruments used to detect disease or to measure change over time. Not only are epidemiological studies necessary for the planning of services and policy-making but they also enable the identification of 'risk factors', which may give clues as to the possible causes of dementia. The most striking risk factor is age, dementia being rare before the age of 60, but suffered by some one-in-five of those aged over 80 (Jorm, 1990; Kay, 1991). There is some *genetic* component of risk, more cases of Alzheimer's disease than expected being found in first-degree relatives of affected subjects and people with Down's syndrome nearly all develop Alzheimer's disease if they live long enough.

Biological explanations of the aetiology of dementia
In the last two decades or so, it has become possible to study the biochemistry of nerve cells and as a result the understanding of neuronal structure and function has increased. In the case of Parkinson's disease, it was discovered that a particular type of nerve cell was involved, which functions by releasing a particular chemical signal known as dopamine. This finding led to the development of a successful treatment using a precursor substance from which dopamine can be synthesised in surviving nerve cells. Similar efforts have been directed at Alzheimer's disease in an attempt to find out which types of nerve cells are involved, their structure and function, and how they pass chemical or electrical signals to other nerve cells. In living patients, it is normally possible to use only rather indirect means of looking at the brain, such as X-ray or similar imaging techniques (which can be used to study function as well as structure), or electrophysiological methods of

recording signals such as the electroencephalogram (EEG). Animal models can be used to study normal brain function or to try to reproduce pathological conditions, but there is no very satisfactory animal model of Alzheimer's disease either occurring naturally or artificially induced in the laboratory.

Treatments for dementia
Ultimately, the hope with any disease is to find its cause and to develop means of prevention or cure. To date, research on dementia has led to greater understanding of the nature of the problem and generated further hypotheses, but as yet the cause is unknown and no pharmacological solution so far is capable of arresting or reversing the progression of the disease. It is sometimes possible to develop drug treatments for a disease without knowing the fundamental cause: Parkinson's disease is a case in point, since treatment ameliorates the symptoms over several years but the underlying death of nerve cells continues for reasons which are unknown. Even where no 'treatment' as such is available for a disease, clinicians still have a role in planning and providing services for the diagnosis and support of sufferers and their carers. Dementia is now the principal cause of admission to long-term institutional care. The practical management of dementia requires psychological and educational skills and raises questions of resource allocation, in addition to the more commonly thought of 'clinical' skills.

Psychological approaches to dementia

A major role of psychologists in the study of dementia has been in developing appropriate cognitive tests used in its detection. For example, it may be difficult to distinguish at a superficial level the reactions of an elderly person who is depressed from one who is demented. Procedures which provide a profile of an individual's mental abilities will help in making a more confident diagnosis. Psychological interest in dementia, however, has recently broadened to include the development and evaluation of different types of therapeutic intervention in addition to the improvement of assessment tools.

A much greater curiosity is also evident in regard to the sufferer's own experience of being demented. Considerable imagination is required to appreciate the impact of crumbling powers of memory and identification upon the individual's feelings of security. A life-span approach can be valuable as we try to understand people's behaviour and the cues to which they respond in terms of habits established earlier in life. There is also the possibility that a study of psychological factors will eventually contribute in significant ways to a total picture of the causation of dementia. If this seems implausible, one should ask oneself why psychology is relevant to understanding the origins of heart disease and cancer, but not brain disease.

Assessment

Issues concerning assessment remain important and will become more so as biological research identifies different types of dementing conditions and especially if ways are found of treating dementia effectively, whether to reverse the condition or to slow down its further progression. Presumably it will be desirable to treat as early in the onset of the condition as possible, and to measure the success of treatment. Whereas crude forms of behavioural assessment may suffice when the behavioural changes are gross, more refined methods will be needed to detect dementia in its early stages and to measure change over time. For example, the most evident early signs of dementia are impairment of memory for recent events, name-finding difficulties and slowing of responses. But even very healthy people complain sometimes of similar problems. Moreover, the increased variability between people's abilities with age makes the detection of a threshold level for early onset of dementia very difficult to achieve. There is a danger of overdiagnosing dementia in persons of limited intelligence or poor education.

There exist a number of different approaches to the assessment of cognitive deterioration. These include taking account of the individual's self-report or the evaluation of someone who knows the subject well. Although important to the total picture and especially to an understanding of the meaning of dementia to the people involved, both of these sources of information are biased by the particular and perhaps idiosyncratic concerns of the informants. Therefore more widely used methods for the detection and measurement of the severity of dementia are so-called 'objective' or 'independent' measures, including observation by a trained individual, rating scales completed by a neutral observer, and actual tests of performance. The last provide the most complete and unbiased picture, but until recently few of such measures were available which tested a broad range of tasks and had sufficient range of scores to allow use with people of varying degrees of dementia. There are now a number of such tests in operation (see Huppert and Tym, 1986), which also take account of the time to perform a task as well as accuracy. It is possible to foresee the increasing application of computerised mental testing in this field.

In addition, application of techniques from experimental psychology are leading to a better understanding of the nature of the various deficits, in memory, use of language and spatial function, which dementing people display (Morris and Kopelman, 1986; Nebes, 1989). One would expect there to be useful comparisons between observations of abnormal behaviour in clinical settings and studies of normal functioning in laboratory settings. Models derived from the latter should have the potential for explaining what is involved in cognitive deterioration. For example, in memory retrieval tasks it has been shown that patients with dementia of the Alzheimer type fail to benefit from more meaningful organisation of material in contrast to elderly people who are depressed. This suggests deficits in the ability to put incoming 'information' in the appropriate 'store'.

Intervention
Efficient provision of help depends upon accurate assessment of need. A hastily formulated view of a situation may lead to an unhelpful response. A consideration of dressing ability provides a simple example of the importance of good assessment. This is a common problem with dementing illness, but can reflect quite different problems, for example the inability to remember what to wear or the inability to work out the right movements to put the clothing on. Simple physical limitations in stretching and bending must also not be overlooked.

Assessment is also important in defining not only the weaknesses, but also the remaining strengths that can be built on. Indeed, one of the major problems in caring for people with dementia is the tendency to neglect what they can do for themselves. Abilities that are not practised soon deteriorate. 'Reality orientation' represents an approach to mentally deteriorated people which deliberately tries to counteract the tendency to shun them but rather to keep them in contact with ordinary daily events, and thus to minimise 'excess' disability. It is discussed further in Chapter 6.

Care also has to be thoughtfully monitored. Standards have often remained poor because of assumptions that dementing people are insensitive to the circumstances in which they live. This is far from the truth. Kitwood has pioneered the systematic collection of data on standards of dementia care and has suggested a variety of indices of well-being, including the ability to experience and express a range of emotions, initiation of social contact and humour, which can be monitored (Kitwood and Bredin, 1992).

Understanding
It is hard to appreciate what it is like to suffer from relatively simple handicaps such as blindness and deafness, let alone a set of disabilities as complex as those resulting from dementia. What is it like to hear people talking but to be unable to make sense of what they are saying, or to understand that someone is cross but not to be able to understand why? The lack of understanding shown by people with dementia and their difficulties in communicating their own needs require that those who try to help them should use their own powers of imagination and empathy to help bridge the gap in understanding. It is a proper concern of psychology not only to describe a person's behaviour patterns, but also to conceptualise the view (or lack of view) of the world which may underlie them.

It is insufficient to characterise dementia purely in terms of cognitive failure. Its impact is more global, more terrifying. Because there is loss of the ability both to remember the past and to develop new knowledge, the onslaught on the person's sense of identity is greater than with other brain traumas (Gilleard, 1984). Close observation and discussion with people in the early stages of dementia show that they have some awareness of what is happening to them (Froggatt, 1988). No easy help is available. Appropriate medication has not been found to favourably effect the course of the condition. Practical support services are not yet required. But it is conceivable that a better understanding of the experience could contribute to a fuller knowledge of ways of retaining and reconstructing the individual's sense of self.

This becomes a more plausible line of investigation if one accepts the possibility that psychological factors, such as loss of self-esteem, are involved in the aetiology of dementia. As some authors, most recently Kitwood (1989), have stressed, there is room for a consideration of social and psychological factors. It is sometimes mistakenly assumed that levels of dementia can be explained in terms of observable pathology of the brain. But post-mortem studies show that the states of the brains of some people with dementia are well within the range of those of mentally well-preserved individuals, while some people become demented with comparatively little accompanying neuropathology. The roles of stress and of personal reactions to stress in the aetiology of dementia have still to be properly considered. Kitwood has also pointed to the 'malignant social psychology' in care situations themselves which may exacerbate the condition (Kitwood, 1990). Resistance to this view is understandable given the horrifying nature of dementia and the comfort that a technical view of dementia provides. It may seem to exclude the threatening possibility of human responsibility for such a disturbing end to a person's life. But the challenge posed by failing mental powers requires imagination, courage and honesty. In understanding dementia we discover much about what it is to be human.

Even if the aetiology of dementia were to be accounted for satisfactorily without recourse to psychosocial factors, it would still be important to take into account life experience. Obtaining the right information may require some degree of detective work on the part of the professional helper by interviewing relatives, friends and neighbours to construct a picture of the important people and events in a person's life. But it is worthwhile if as a result we can find cues which will help elicit a meaningful response. Speaking about the past itself may be an enjoyable activity. The past for an individual with dementia may be much clearer than the present and talking about familiar memories has been shown to be an ideal way of establishing contact for many people (Mills and Walker, 1993, forthcoming). In our use of reminiscence of course we must be as sensitive to individual differences among dementing people as among 'normal' individuals (see Chapter 5).

Investigation of past life may also help explain present behaviour, pointing sometimes to mundane facts (for example, understanding that someone tends to wander in mid-afternoon because that is the time she used to take her dog for a walk), but also sometimes to more serious matters (for example, attacks of panic in circumstances similar to the scene of traumatic events in the individual's past). The work of those life-span psychologists who have tried to make links across periods of an individual's life, in explaining reactions to loss for example, is as relevant to people with dementia as it is to other sections of the elderly population. Miesen, for example, has suggested a link between talk about long-deceased parents, commonly observed in dementing individuals, and need for attachment (Miesen, 1992). The tendency to treat people in this condition as a 'category apart' has to be firmly resisted.

Sociological approaches to dementia

The structuralist approach
Ever since Durkheim (1952, first published in French in 1897) in the middle of the last century attributed suicide to social causes, mental health has been regarded as the appropriate subject matter of sociology. According to Durkheim the behaviour of individuals depends on their social environment and what their society influences them into doing. Therefore, while *individuals* are mentally ill, some sociologists look for reasons not in these individuals themselves but in particular aspects of the social structure in which mentally ill people live.

A structuralist approach to the study of mental health was demonstrated by Hollingshead and Redlich (1958), who sought to show that the incidence and type of mental illness varied as a consequence of position in the social class structure. Thus, while the highest social class contained 3.1 per cent of the population, only 1 per cent of people with a mental illness came from this class. Conversely, they showed that the lowest social class included 17.8 per cent of the population but contributed 36.8 per cent of people with a mental illness. Illness designated as 'neurotic' was concentrated in the higher levels of social class while 'psychotic' types of illness predominated in the lower social classes. This kind of analysis has also been used widely by social epidemiologists interested in the prevalence of dementia and other psychiatric illnesses among older people (Bond, 1987).

The interactionist approach
In contrast with structuralists, sociologists who take an *interactionist* perspective provide rather a different view of mental illness. They begin with no taken-for-granted definition of what mental illness is; they do not see it as something lying with the individual him or herself. Rather it is a *social status* conferred on an individual by other members of society. For interactionists, mental illness is not like some disease within the person which can be universally observed and defined. Being regarded as mentally ill depends on individuals making that definition of others, labelling them and acting towards them as if they were mentally ill. The

definition of mental illness occurs in the process of social interaction. This process can be observed in many geriatric wards where aphasic and deaf elderly patients may be labelled as 'demented' by nursing staff when no formal psychiatric diagnosis has been made by medical staff.

This is in contrast to an understanding of mental illness founded on assumptions about society with a structure which exerts strong influences on individual members and how they behave. Interactionists stress individual actions and perceptions, each person taking account of the actions of others on the basis of the meanings and interpretations they give to them. It is not a case of individuals being governed by and reflecting the structure of their society. Rather, individuals, through social actions, create their society. Individuals have to interpret their world, make sense of it and give meaning to it. Thus 'mental illness' and 'mental patient' are not absolute conditions or objects which exist 'out there'. Interactionists concern themselves in studying the processes by which people go about classifying others as 'mentally ill'.

In social life some people occupying particular roles have more power than others when it comes to labelling people as mentally ill. Szasz (1971) has taken this approach in examining the process of a person becoming so labelled. While most of us would say that we could recognise someone who was mentally ill, it is psychiatrists who are generally accepted as experts in so doing. Psychiatrists have considerable power to declare that someone is sick, requires treatment and should receive a specific kind of institutional care. Such is that power that others are likely to accept their categorisation that someone is mentally ill and to act towards that individual accordingly. In this way individuals become 'mentally ill' not simply on the basis of their behaviour but because they now have a particular label attached to them. If others apply the label it is less likely to stick if it is not supported by a psychiatrist's opinion. Psychiatrists are also able to decide on the label to be given to describe a particular disease entity. In recent years, particularly in North America, there has been a move away from the label 'dementia', which engenders a certain expected way of acting on the part of the patient and other actors, toward the label 'Alzheimer's disease', which engenders a different set of actions, although the actual disease has remained unchanged (Finlinson, 1985).

However, not everyone agrees with such categorisation. Studies based on interactionist assumptions have shown that disagreements occur over the interpretation and meanings given to the behaviour observed. The differentiation of the 'mentally ill' from 'normal' members of society can be contingent upon the particular circumstances of the social situation in which people find themselves. Scheff (1964) examined the psychiatric screening procedures used in a mid-western state in America to decide whether patients should be released. Scheff found that this decision is influenced more by the financial, ideological and political position of the examining psychiatrist than patient factors. The study demonstrated that court-appointed psychiatrists with particular ideological and political views were predisposed to assume that the person was ill from the outset. Within this frame of reference which pre-classifies the patient, psychiatrists then go on to interpret the patient's behaviour and records. Scheff argues that without this prior definition of the person as mentally ill, the patient's records, behaviour and responses to the psychiatrist's tests can be interpreted differently.

On the other side of the coin, interactionists are also concerned with individuals' conception of themselves. This follows from the assumption that individuals have to interpret and give meaning to their own actions as well as make sense of those of others with whom they interact. How individuals act depends on their own self-image and this is constructed largely from their interpretation of how other people react to what they say and do. This has led to studies of the effects of labelling people as mentally ill and how these individuals see themselves. Conferring the label subsequently produces abnormal behaviour because of the way others act towards people so labelled, which in turn produces actions by them which they recognise that others expect of them.

The ethnomethodological approach

The ethnomethodological approach assumes that the social world is constantly being created by members of society which for them is unproblematic because it is regarded as the result of society's members using their own common sense. Society is created by its members using their taken-for-granted knowledge about how the world works and how they can deal with it in acceptable ways. The concern of ethnomethodologists is to study and explain how it is that society's members actually accomplish the social world which they created through commonly accepted, albeit sophisticated methods. Of major importance is language: we accomplish social encounters largely through conversation. Individuals have learned methods for doing so and ethnomethodologists are interested in how they have achieved such methods.

Ethnomethodologists would be unlikely to study mental illness as such; they would be more likely to have as their concern the society-building methods people use which may have relevance to mental illness. The assumptions of ethnomethodology are used in a study of Alzheimer's disease as 'biographical work' (Gubrium and Lynott, 1985; Gubrium, 1986). The way that friends and relatives construct diverse individual biographies of Alzheimer's disease sufferers are described. In the analysis biography is treated as a practical activity of those friends and relatives and is not so much the presentation of the facts of the sufferer's life as it is the descriptive product of retrospective and prospective biographical activity. The ethnomethodological study, by examining these biographies, highlights the social processes which have been part of the production and reproduction of the individual biographies.

In this kind of analysis Alzheimer's disease is not the focus of analysis but a means to an end. It is used as a code for rendering meaningful (chronologically and substantively) the general, age-related problems of later life. By itself, the code tells us little about the meaningful articulation of the problems of later life; it informs us only of an end product, what the troubles recognisably become. In social support groups, 'chapels' of the Alzheimer's Disease and Related Disorders Association, Gubrium and Lynott found that biographical work by the friends and relatives of sufferers revealed the pervasively social character of the disease, the diverse nature of their related experiences and how much it brings people together who attempt to make sense of their experiences.

Critical theory and the study of dementia
Critical theorists hold a very different view of contemporary society to other theorists. Like ethnomethodologists they would not be specifically interested in the study of dementia. Their purpose in considering dementia would be to use it as a general example of the processes whereby our society is being made ever more repressive.

Both postmodernists and post-structuralists approach mental illness in a similar way to that of the interactionists. Rather than explain mental illness in terms of labelling theory, however, which we have seen requires the legitimation of a label by others who act as agents of social control, postmodernists and post-structuralists charge that mental illness is nothing more than a response to a situation that contravenes typical symbolism. They argue that because a person fails or refuses to be limited by a particular portrayal of reality, he or she is identified as mad and sequestered from the rest of society. Madness, by this definition, simply pertains to someone who refuses to accept symbolic repression (Murphy, 1988).

By taking a historical perspective we can explain this response to social reality. The practice of calling people 'witches' has been replaced by calling them 'mad'. It performs the same functions, namely stigmatising and controlling people who are a problem for others. The historical perspective also helps us understand why we incarcerate people who are 'mentally ill' in isolated institutions. Foucault (1973, first published in French in 1963) has suggested that this practice owes much to the fact that there were places available in which to contain people following the eradication of leprosy from Europe in the middle ages. This kind of practice continues today using surplus isolation hospitals and, more recently, wards surplus to requirement in hospitals for people with dementia. These current practices may be of equal historical significance in understanding the portrayal of the social reality of old age.

Understanding dementia

This description demonstrates the different approaches to the study of dementia used by clinicians, psychologists and sociologists. Different disciplines approach the subject from different perspectives, as do the different approaches within individual scientific disciplines. As a result they use different conceptual frameworks, carry out different kinds of studies and use different methods to collect and analyse data, which provides the basis of their theory. None of them are more correct than any other: they simply represent different ways of studying and interpreting the same phenomenon. Thus different biological, clinical, psychological and sociological approaches are complementary, each area fertilising the other. They each have a different contribution to make in the understanding of dementia.

THEORY AND METHOD IN THE STUDY OF HUMAN AGEING

There is a close relationship between theory and method in any scientific discipline. This is no less the case in the study of human ageing. Just as biological, psychological and sociological perspectives provide different views of ageing, make different theoretical assumptions and ask different questions, they also use different methods. Within psychology and sociology different perspectives are often committed to using particular research strategies to define, generate, collect and to interpret empirical data. Thus 'methods and theory are inescapably connected' (Smith, 1975, p. 27) irrespective of the degree to which that theory is made explicit. Method means here not merely the practical considerations of which data-collection techniques to use, but fundamental considerations such as whether to study causes or functions, whether to describe phenomena or explain them, or whether to determine the meaning of a phenomenon or examine the relationship between various variables. There is not space to outline here the variety of methods used in the study of ageing. Some of these are explored in greater detail in *Researching Social Gerontology* (Peace, 1990). But we will focus on a major methodological decision which faces all students of human ageing: whether to use a cross-sectional or longitudinal design.

Cross-sectional and longitudinal studies

A major research activity of the biological sciences has been the study of declining physiological effectiveness during ageing. Senescence brings about changes in the structure and function of many organs including the brain and nervous system, the heart, lungs and circulation, bone, muscle and skin. In psychology, attention has focused on changes in intelligence and personality, while sociology has been concerned with changes in the process of retirement, among others. In order to measure change, two approaches have been used.

In cross-sectional studies, measurements are made amongst cohorts of different age-groups, or subjects are asked to recall retrospectively data from the past. If we wanted to measure changes in average muscle strength, for example, we might make measurements in 20-year-olds, 40-year-olds, 60-year-olds and 80-year-olds and show a progressive diminution of strength with age. However, a limitation of this method is the influence of secular changes. For example, we know that 20-year-olds are now taller, heavier and therefore perhaps stronger than 20-year-olds at the beginning of the century. Similarly, cross-sectional studies of intelligence cannot separate influences due to 'ageing' from those due to change in education and training. A cross-sectional study of retirement would also be unable to detect changes which were the cause rather than the consequence of retirement.

An alternative approach is to use a longitudinal study, in which the same individuals are assessed at intervals over time. Thus we can show that women do lose a little height as they age, due to shrinkage of the backbone, but not nearly as much as we might have predicted had we measured and compared 80- and 20-year-olds. However, longitudinal studies are difficult to carry out. By definition we would need a lifetime to follow people throughout their lives, so we can only follow people over a limited period of time. Longitudinal studies also suffer because the tools of research, especially of biomedical research, become outmoded over time. They suffer from the impact of important historical events, like wars, which may affect the behaviour of lots of people but which could not be described as ageing changes. Selective survival is also an important factor to consider in longitudinal studies. For example, if people scoring higher than average on IQ tests live longer this will give a faulty impression of the relationship between advanced age and intelligence. A combination of cross-sectional and longitudinal studies, referred to as a cross-sequential design, in which cohorts of different ages are simultaneously followed up over time appears to give the best chance of sorting out the relative influence of social, historical and intrinsic factors.

In biology, longitudinal studies are more easily undertaken in short-lived laboratory animals such as rodents. For this reason as well as others including economy, availability and the possibility of restricting genetic and environmental sources of variation, much biological research on ageing has used animals or even cultures of cells or tissues. There is, of course, a danger in extrapolating findings from such experiments to humans. However, research in 'model' biological systems may elucidate the basic nature and mechanism of the ageing process, and give rise to hypotheses which may be tested in humans.

UNDERSTANDING HUMAN AGEING

In this chapter we have been concerned with delineating the various approaches taken by different disciplines to the study of human ageing. We have shown how these different approaches consider the subject of dementia, highlighting the complementary nature of the different scientific enterprises. The emphasis of this book is on social gerontology and in subsequent chapters a number of theories introduced here will be discussed further.

3

BIOLOGICAL AGEING

Roger Briggs

In the previous chapter, we discussed biological theories of ageing in the context of living organisms in general (including humans) and within the framework of biological concepts of evolution and natural selection. We shall now turn to the effects of ageing on humans in particular. Although some of the material may seem fairly complex to non-biologists, it is necessary to realise that biology and physiology cannot be ignored in understanding behavioural changes with age, just as clinicians cannot do their elderly patients justice without some grasp of psychological and sociological concepts.

AGEING AND THE POPULATION

In primitive societies, or non-industrialised societies even now, death-rates are high around the time of birth and in childhood, and subsequently the risk of death remains relatively constant throughout life. A survival curve for such a population is represented in Figure 3.1.

Such a survival curve is known as a 'wild-type' because it is found in natural animal populations as well as in human populations living under severe conditions (for example, Europe in the middle ages, Mexico in 1930, some African countries now). It can be seen that most of the population survive for less than half the maximum lifespan, so that *average* age of death might be 30 to 40 years in such conditions, though a few individuals may live to about 100 years of age. Characteristically, these populations would have a 'pyramidal' structure, with large numbers of children and young people but comparatively few old people – perhaps 1 or 2 per cent of the population being over 65. The major concern for 'public health' in such countries is the prevention of infant and child mortality.

Modern, industrialised societies (or animals protected in an artificial environment such as a laboratory) have largely removed the problems of infant and child mortality, causing a 'rectangular' survival curve as shown in Figure 3.2.

As the survival curve of a population becomes increasingly rectangular, average lifespan approaches maximum lifespan; it should be noted that maximum lifespan is presumed to remain more or less constant.

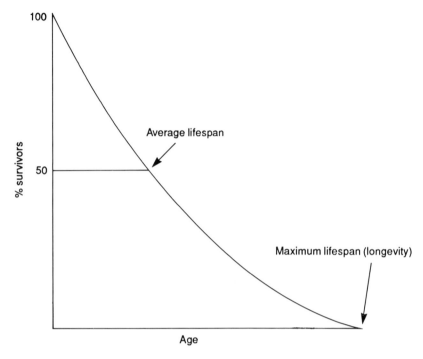

Figure 3.1   *Wild-type survival curve*

Thus, in 1900, only about a quarter of the population survived their 65th year, whereas now over two-thirds do so. This dramatic change has come about very quickly, and the major challenge to public health in industrialised societies is how to cope with the problems associated with a high proportion (15 to 25 per cent) of people over 65 in the population, many of whom will be in their 80s and 90s (see Chapter 1). It has optimistically been suggested, as medical and social interventions continue to promote a healthy middle age,

> that the average period of diminished physical vigour will decrease, that chronic disease will occupy a smaller proportion of the typical lifespan, and that the need for medical care in later life will decrease. (Fries, 1980, p. 130)

This view is appealing, particularly to health policy makers and fiscal planners, but it must be said that there is very little supporting evidence. In our present state of knowledge, it would be dangerous to ignore the potential for increasing levels of disability in our ageing population (Brody, 1985).

AGEING AND DISEASE

As discussed in Chapter 2, ageing is associated with a decline in physiological effectiveness which affects us all sooner or later and is an

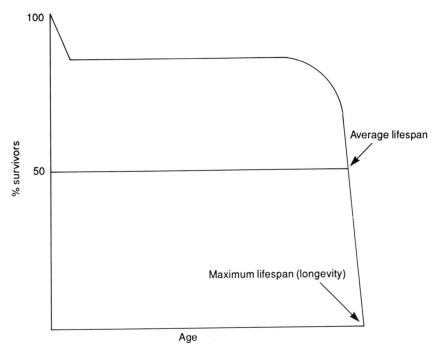

Figure 3.2 *Rectangular survival curve*

intrinsic part of growing old. Unlike the universal changes of senescence, *disease* is sporadic, a particular disease affecting only certain
members of the population. However, many diseases are *age-related*.
Thus strokes, which are uncommon before the age of 50, are becoming
increasingly prevalent with age and are the third most common cause of
death in Britain today. Another example of an interaction between
ageing and *accident* is that of fractured hip, a rare injury in young people
but one which affects one women in eight by the age of 85. As people
age, their bones become *thinner*, a senescent change which is more
pronounced in women. A fall which might cause a younger person no
serious injury may fracture the weakened hip of an old person.

This last example shows that the distinction between 'ageing' and
'disease' is somewhat arbitrary and artificial. An elderly lady may have
thinning bones, weaker muscles, a nervous system which is slower to
react, but look and feel quite fit – until she trips over at home. She may
then lie on the floor throughout a cold winter's night, unable to summon
help because her hip is broken. When admitted to hospital, she will be
diagnosed as having two 'medical conditions', a fractured hip and
hypothermia, but these have arisen because her ageing constitution has
been less able to withstand environmental stresses. The notion of
increasing 'vulnerability' with ageing provides a conceptual link
between the biological theories discussed in the previous chapter and

the more clinical approach adopted in this chapter. Decline in
physiological function may be of little consequence to an older person
until they cross some threshold so that they are no longer able to
carry out necessary activities, and are then perceived to suffer from
'disease' or 'disability'. A disadvantage of the traditional 'medical model'
can be that ageing is seen as inevitable and unworthy of attention,
whereas disease or disability should be responded to actively and
sympathetically.

Not only are old people at risk of particular age-related diseases, they
may also suffer from a combination of several diseases and senescent
changes. In addition to the multiple disabilities caused by the diseases
themselves, complications may arise due to the complexity of drug
treatment prescribed.

It is important to note that 'good health' is not synonymous with the
absence of disease. Only 10 per cent of those over 75 years admit to no
physical symptom; on average elderly people complain of over five
medical problems each. The 'top ten' for men and women aged 65 and
over are shown in Table 3.1.

However, the symptoms of many of these conditions are well
tolerated by the majority of elderly people, and do not interfere greatly
with their lives. Thus, in a survey of 1406 over-65-year-olds interviewed
in Manchester, Luker and Perkins (1987) found that 93 per cent believed
their health to be 'fair or good' and the number of those unable to
perform a range of activities of daily living was relatively small. Whilst it
is unjustified to 'see all older people as being frail, dependent and
diseased' (Freer, 1988), it is also a mistake to see 'the elderly' as a
homogeneous group. It is true that most 'young elderly' are fit and active,

Table 3.1 *Reported longstanding illness or disability of women and men aged 65 and over, 1986 (%)*

Women		Men	
Arthritis	18.5	Heart disease	11.5
Heart disease	10.5	Arthritis	7.5
High blood pressure	9.5	High blood pressure	7.5
Orthopaedic condition	3.5	Bronchitis	5.5
Back trouble	3.5	Orthopaedic condition	4.5
Sight	3.5	Sight	4.0
Stroke	3.0	Stroke	4.0
Bronchitis	3.0	Deafness	3.0
Diabetes	3.0	Back trouble	2.5
Gastric/intestinal	2.0	Diabetes	2.5
		Respiratory disease	2.5
N =	936	N =	697

Sources: The Health and Lifestyle Survey, 1986, Cox et al, 1987; Sidell, 1991 but it has long been known that the prevalence of chronic illness and disability rises rapidly with age. Thus, defining disability as inability to exist at home without help and dependence as a further degree of impairment of self-care, the prevalence of disability increases from 12 per cent at age 65–69 to over 80 per cent above the age of 85; dependence is found in only 2 per cent below 85 years, but in 25 per cent of those older (Akhtar et al, 1973).

The remainder of this chapter describes ageing changes and diseases which commonly affect old people. However, it must be remembered that each old person is more than just a collection of isolated tissues or organs, and that the particular combination of problems or disabilities will vary from one individual to another. Finally, it should be borne in mind that diseases do not affect all old people, and that whilst ageing is universal it affects different people at different rates.

Hearing

Deafness is a common accompaniment of ageing, though not inevitable. The gradual deterioration in hearing ability associated with ageing is known as *presbyacusis*, and results from wear and tear of the cells in the inner ear which respond to sound waves. Prolonged exposure to excessive noise earlier in life, for example a noisy working environment, may predispose to hearing loss in later life. Perhaps one-third of the population over 65 years suffers from a hearing impairment (see Table 3.2) which can have unfavourable social consequences.

The hearing loss of presbyacusis is usually greater for high frequency sounds than those of low frequency. Normal conversation consists of sounds over a wide spectrum of frequencies: consonants are generally of higher frequency than vowels. Thus, an old person has poor speech *discrimination* – he or she may know that someone is talking, but cannot discern what is said because some elements such as consonants are missing. Hearing loss is usually assessed clinically by means of an *audiogram*, in which the subject listens to pure tones, whose loudness can be varied, across a range of frequencies between 125 and 8000 Hertz. Normal speech generally ranges between 250 and 3000 Hertz. Poor

Table 3.2 *Difficulty with hearing among elderly people*

Age:	65–69	70–74	75–79	80–84	85+	All 65+
	%	%	%	%	%	%
Wears an aid	4	8	10	14	22	8
Does not wear an aid, but has difficulty	20	22	28	31	34	24
Does not wear an aid, has no difficulty	76	70	63	56	44	68

Source: Office of Population Censuses and Surveys (1982), Table 10.11

speech discrimination is exacerbated by high levels of background noise, such as are often found in institutions, and where the deaf person cannot see the speaker (consonants are relatively easy to lip read).

In addition to poor speech discrimination, presbyacusis commonly causes *loudness recruitment*: this means that sounds become disproportionately louder to the sufferer as they increase in intensity. There may be only a small increase in intensity between a sound that is loud enough for the person to hear and one that causes discomfort or pain. Many old people who find a normal, quiet speaking voice inaudible find shouting intolerable, and for the same reason cannot wear a hearing aid with comfort. Presbyacusis also causes impaired *sound localization*, making it difficult to tell where a sound is coming from.

When an old person complains of deafness, the first step is to make sure that their ears are not stuffed with wax. The diagnosis of presbyacusis is established by an audiogram, and if hearing loss is significant a hearing aid may be helpful. Many old people find a hearing aid difficult to use, and they need adequate training and encouragement, preferably from an after care service run by a hearing therapist. Although deafness is common, it is often neglected and may be associated with significant psychiatric problems such as depressive illness (Herbst and Humphrey, 1980). (See Chapter 5.)

Vision

Young people are able to focus on objects at different distances from the eye because the lens is elastic and its shape can be changed by small muscles from which it is suspended. By the age of about 50, the lens invariably becomes less elastic and focusing becomes difficult: vision for distant objects usually remains intact, but close vision (such as reading) becomes blurred. This is a usual feature of ageing known as *presbyopia*, and the majority of the population eventually requires glasses. Table 3.3 shows the prevalence of vision impairment among elderly people. Many old people just use spectacles for close vision; an alternative is bifocal lenses, in which the upper part of the spectacles is designed for distance

Table 3.3 *Difficulty with eyesight among elderly people*

Age:	65–69	70–74	75–79	80–84	85+	All 65+
	%	%	%	%	%	%
Wears glasses, still has difficulty	18	20	30	32	45	24
Wears glasses, then has no difficulty	78	77	68	65	51	73
Does not wear glasses	4	3	3	4	4	3

Source: Office of Population Censuses and Surveys (1982), Table 10.9

vision and the lower part for close vision, but bifocals may cause problems of their own due to the borderline between the two lenses.

The reason that the lens in the eye becomes less elastic with age is because it is constantly growing by the addition of new layers – rather like an onion. In some old people the centre of the lens is compressed, becomes hard and opaque: this opacity is known as a *cataract*. Initially the cataract may disperse light entering the eye so that vision is affected in bright light, which is why some old people need eyeshades or peaked caps. As the cataract enlarges and 'ripens', vision becomes obscured and only surgical removal can restore vision. After removal of the cataract, an artificial lens must be implanted in the eye or the patient must wear special glasses or a contact lens. Old people with diabetes are much more likely to be affected by cataract than their peers.

Light entering the eye is focused by the lens on specialised nerve cells in the retina. The eyeball between the lens and the retina is filled with fluid, which may develop small opacities known as 'floaters' since they appear to drift across the field of vision. Floaters are usually harmless, though occasionally they herald the sudden loss of vision due to retinal detachment. Raised pressure of the fluid in the eyeball is known as glaucoma, and becomes more common with age. Sometimes glaucoma can come on acutely, with pain and impaired vision in the eye, but more commonly the condition is chronic with insidious loss of peripheral vision: only at a late stage is central vision affected. The most important part of our visual field is the central part, since objects we see when looking straight ahead are focused on a specialised part of the retina, the 'macula'. The most common cause of intractable blindness in elderly people is *senile macular degeneration*, in which the specialised nerve cells deteriorate. Unfortunately, the scope for treatment is very limited except in the earliest stages, though magnifying aids are helpful.

Skin, muscle and bone

The most obvious change in skin is the familiar wrinkling. This is due to degeneration of the elastic tissues in the skin, and is more severe in people who have had extensive exposure to sunlight. With ageing, skin tends to lose its pigment, as does the hair. Irregular purple patches may develop, particularly on the backs of the hands, which occur spontaneously though the old person may often attribute them to 'bruising'. Sweat glands work less efficiently with ageing and the skin surface is rougher and drier: some old people complain of intolerable itching (*pruritus*).

Increasing age is also accompanied by a decline in muscle power. Part of this decline is due to an age-related loss of nerve fibres which supply muscles, leading to degeneration of the muscle cells. However, reduced physical activity also plays a part, particularly in those retiring from active work, and there is much current interest in the role of exercise in maintaining fitness in old people.

Bones become 'thinner' from middle age onwards, this bone loss being more marked in women after the menopause. Extreme thinning of the bones is known as *osteoporosis*, and makes fractures more likely after a fall (particularly broken wrists and hips), or bones in the spine may even collapse spontaneously causing episodes of severe back pain. Treatment of osteoporosis is not very satisfactory; continued physical activity and an adequate diet including a good supply of calcium may help to minimise bone loss. Fracture of the hip is now a very common injury among elderly people and is a terminal event in a significant number.

Arthritis affects many old people. The commonest form, *osteoarthritis*, is mainly due to wear-and-tear on large, weight-bearing joint such as the spine, hips and knees. *Rheumatoid arthritis* may develop for the first time in old people and usually affects smaller joints such as the hands, wrists and ankles. The mainstay of treatment for the pain and stiffness of arthritis is with drugs, but artificial joints can be implanted surgically if symptoms are severe.

Nutrition and digestion

Malnutrition affects a surprisingly small proportion of the elderly population – obesity due to overeating is a much more common problem. When malnutrition does arise, it is often in the context of significant mental impairment or physical illness rather than for purely 'social' reasons, though isolation and poverty play their part. Most old people have an adequate intake of food in terms of protein, carbo-hydrate and fat to service their reduced energy requirements. However, intakes of vitamins (such as Vitamin C) or 'trace' elements (such as zinc) are sometimes borderline or inadequate, particularly among frail elderly people living alone (Panel on Nutrition of the Elderly, 1972).

Old people often have poor teeth, since regular dental treatment is a comparatively recent development. Most British people aged 65 or more have no teeth of their own, and wear dentures which may be ill-fitting. Taste sensation and salivary flow tend to deteriorate with ageing, and all these oral problems may add to loss of enjoyment of eating in addition to any limitations of the 'social' quality of meals.

In general, the absorption of food from the intestine is not significantly affected by ageing. A few old people lose the cells in the stomach which are responsible for the absorption of Vitamin B12; this condition causes *pernicious anaemia*, which responds readily to regular injections of the vitamin. Ulcers in the stomach or duodenum, or lesions such as cancer of the lower bowel, may cause continued blood loss from the intestinal tract (known as occult bleeding since the amount passed in the stools is too little to be noticed by the patient). Stomach ulcers may cause pain, and bowel cancer may lead to a change in bowel habit, but often there are no specific abdominal symptoms and the only clue to intestinal disease is the finding of *iron-deficiency anaemia*. Identification of the various types of anaemia is by means of a blood test, which is often done for rather non-specific reasons such as a patient being tired or breathless, looking pale or losing weight. Although change in bowel habit may be a worrying symptom, *constipation* is often due to a general reduction in activity and mobility, coupled with a decreased dietary intake of roughage.

Kidneys and bladder

The function of the kidneys is to excrete waste products and excessive fluid in the urine. From the age of about 30 years, kidney function deteriorates so that by the age of 60–70 it is about half that found in young adults. Under normal circumstances this decline in kidney function does not cause any problems since there is a considerable 'reserve', but if an old person is stressed by illness or given drugs which are excreted by the kidney then the impaired, ageing kidney may be unable to cope.

Urine excreted by the kidney is held in the bladder until it is voided through the urethra. In women, the urethra is comparatively short and continence is partly maintained by muscles of the pelvic floor. These muscles tend to weaken after the menopause, particularly if there has been a history of difficult childbirth, so that the walls of the vagina sometimes *prolapse* and distort the urethra. Prolapse may cause *stress incontinence* in women with leakage of small amounts of urine when straining or coughing; treatment is aimed at supporting the walls of the vagina, either mechanically with an internal ring pessary or by surgery. In men, the urethra is surrounded by the prostate gland, which may become enlarged either by benign growth or due to cancer. An enlarged prostate causes difficulty in starting to pass urine with a poor stream of urine flow.

In both sexes, continence is maintained by the nervous system, which prevents contraction of the bladder muscle until it is desired to pass urine. These nervous pathways may be damaged by brain disease such as stroke or senile dementia, so that the patients are unable to control bladder function. Initially, such incontinence is often worse at night but ultimately patients may be quite unaware of their bladder, not even realising when they have been incontinent. Incontinence is a common and distressing condition, probably affecting some two million people in the United Kingdom to a greater or lesser extent. Patients often do not report incontinence to their general practitioner or nursing staff, presumably out of embarrassment. There are now several helpful books on the subject, including short, simple texts suitable for patients themselves such as that by Feneley and Blannin (1984).

Heart, lungs and circulation

The heart pumps blood through the lungs, where oxygen is taken up and carbon dioxide released, then around the body via the arteries before blood returns to the heart through veins. Ageing is accompanied by a variety of changes affecting all these elements of the circulation. Heart muscle degenerates with age, and the heart valves become less pliable. In some old people, the heart rhythm becomes abnormal, the heartbeat becoming too fast and irregular (in which case digitalis treatment may be needed) or too slow (in which case an artificial pacemaker may be required). For many old people, these changes in the heart do not cause any problem at rest, but limit the amount by which the heart can respond to exercise. Some elderly patients develop *heart failure*, when blood is not pumped effectively away from the heart so that blood returning from the venous system and lungs becomes dammed back. The ensuing lung congestion causes breathlessness, and impaired venous return leads to ankle swelling. Treatment is with diuretics ('water tablets'), which remove excessive fluid from the circulation to relieve congestion.

Ageing leads to reduced efficiency of the lungs, and weakness of the chest muscles also contributes to a loss of maximal breathing capacity on exercise. However, a normal old person should be able to walk steadily, even if they are unable to run. More severe breathlessness implies heart disease, or lung disease such as chronic bronchitis, rather than ageing alone. It is becoming increasingly apparent that old people can improve their ability to respond to physical stress by 'training', if not so dramatically as the young, and more emphasis is now being placed on the role of exercise in the maintenance of fitness among elderly people.

In industrialised societies, people's arteries tend to become 'furred up' over the years, a process known as *atherosclerosis*. Arterial disease is hastened by a number of factors, such as high blood pressure, excessive fat and salt intake, smoking and diabetes. Arteries may become so narrowed that blood flow to various organs is diminished, or an artery may even become completely blocked. Although the heart is full of blood, the muscle of the heart wall is so thick and works so hard that it needs a rich supply of blood from its own arteries, the coronary arteries. When blood flow to the heart muscle is limited, episodic chest pain may develop on exercise – *angina*. If a coronary artery becomes completely blocked (*coronary thrombosis*) an area of heart muscle may become irreversibly damaged, an event known as a *heart attack or myocardial infarction* which is a major cause of death in the western world. Atherosclerosis affects other arteries in addition to those supplying the heart; poor blood supply to the legs can result in pain on exercise, ulcers or even amputation, and blockage of arteries in the brain leads to stroke.

Hormones

In a large organism composed of many cells, tissues and organs, it is necessary for these different elements to 'communicate' with each other in order to coordinate the body's response to external stimuli and to maintain a stable internal environment. The latter function, maintenance of the internal environment, is crucial to the survival of complex organisms and is known as *homeostasis*. Examples of homeostatic mechanisms are the increase in heart rate in response to the increased oxygen demand of exercise, sweating in response to heat, or the regulation of the amounts of salt and water in the circulation. Many of the adverse consequences of ageing can be seen in terms of the breakdown of homeostasis, such as the development of *hypothermia* when an old person is unable to respond effectively to cold. 'Fast' signals from one part of the body to another are carried electrically by nerve cells; slower signals can be achieved by glands which liberate chemical messengers, known as *hormones*, carried to their target organ or tissue in the blood stream. Thus, in response to the increase level of sugar in the blood following a meal, a normal person secretes the hormone insulin from the pancreas gland, causing the sugar to be burnt up for energy production or stored. Defective production of insulin causes the condition known as *diabetes*, in which sugar cannot be utilised properly by the body and may cause damage to the eyes, kidneys and arteries. Diagnosis is made by detecting excessive amounts of sugar in the blood or urine, and treatment comprises restriction of sugar intake, tablets which help the body to deal with the excess sugar in the blood, or if necessary (mainly in younger patients) giving additional insulin by injection. Diabetes is common, affecting 1 or 2 per cent of the population over 65 years.

The *thyroid gland*, which is situated in the neck, may also become diseased in elderly people. Thyroid disease is often an example of *autoimmune* disease, in which the body attacks its own tissues as if they were foreign invaders such as bacteria. (Another example of an autoimmune disease mentioned previously is pernicious anaemia, in which the body attacks some of its own stomach cells. At one time, an 'autoimmune theory of ageing' was fashionable by which senescent changes were thought to be due to the body turning its defence mechanisms upon itself, but this theory has not stood the test of time.) Thyroid disease can manifest as an overactive gland, hyperthyroidism or *thyrotoxicosis*, when the patient tends to be irritable, losing weight, sweating and tremulous, or an underactive gland, hypothyroidism or *myxoedema*, causing a slow, lethargic patient tending to gain weight and with a dry coarse skin and croaky voice. Although these clinical pictures seem very distinctive in theory, in practice thyroid disease may be difficult to diagnose in elderly people. Both an underactive and an overactive gland may cause apathy and depressive symptoms. Thyroid disease is best detected by blood tests measuring the amount of circulating thyroid hormone; these tests are very worthwhile for sick elderly people, since both thyrotoxicosis and myxoedema are easy to treat.

In women, after the *menopause* the female hormone oestrogen is deficient. Apart from cessation of menstruation, other symptoms such as depression, anxiety and headache may have a biological basis in women between approximately 40 and 55 years. The soft tissues of the vulva and vagina lose substance, and reduced vaginal lubrication may make sexual intercourse difficult. Men may also experience a 'climacteric' period, based on a decline in the secretion of the male hormone testosterone, some 10 to 15 years later. Erections are less frequent and less well maintained, and the force of ejaculation is diminished. In both men and women, therefore, there are physiological changes in the secretion of sex hormones with ageing which may reduce the potential for intercourse and orgasm irrespective of any additional problems posed by disease. Many sexual difficulties in later life, however, are caused by psychological problems or restricted opportunity and reinforce the need for caring, loving relationships unhindered by ignorance, insensitive relatives or uninformed professionals (Weg, 1983b).

Brain and nervous system

The nervous system consists essentially of two parts, a 'peripheral nervous system' of nerves travelling to the limbs and organs, and a 'central nervous system' in the brain and spinal cord. Nerve cells are 'fixed' in that they do not undergo cell division once they have reached maturity and have to carry out their function for the remainder of the person's life. It is not surprising that the function of nerve cells deteriorates over lifespan; a nerve supplying a muscle in the foot is nearly a yard long, originating near the base of the spine. Nerve cells cannot get rid of some of their waste products, and with age accumulate substances such as the pigment *lipofuscin*. It has been proposed that some features of ageing are due to 'waste-product accumulation', though many believe that these substances do no harm to cells in themselves but simply bear witness to the passage of the years. Nerves transmit messages by a process similar to electrical conduction throughout most of their length, except where they meet the next nerve cell with which they communicate: here they release a chemical across a tiny gap (the 'synapse'), which interacts with the next nerve cell. Chemical transmission across the synapse is similar to the action of hormones, except that the whole process of nerve signalling is much quicker. With ageing, the transmission of nerve signals to muscles or the return of messages conveying touch, pain or temperature, slows down due to deterioration of the peripheral nervous system.

With regard to the central nervous system, function also tends to deteriorate with ageing in some areas of the brain such as those concerned with learning and memory. The psychological effects of 'normal' ageing will be considered in more detail in Chapter 4, and the remainder of this section is devoted to the effects of age-related disease on the brain.

The brain is organised such that particular brain regions subserve particular functions. Thus, a lesion affecting a discrete brain region will cause a specific pattern of disability. Atherosclerosis may cause impairment of the blood supply to a part of the brain, causing a sudden loss of function known as a *stroke* either because the artery supplying that part of the brain becomes blocked or because it bleeds into the brain substance. Usually, a stroke affecting the right side of the brain causes weakness and sensory disturbance on the left side of the body and a stroke in the left side ('dominant hemisphere') of the brain causes weakness in the right arm and leg which is often associated with difficulty in speaking. Stroke is common, affecting one or two people in every thousand each year and being the third commonest cause of death in Britain; the incidence of stroke rises dramatically with age, most of those affected being over 60. Of those who survive their first stroke, roughly one half regain functional independence, a quarter need some help with activities of daily living, and a quarter are dependent on help from a carer.

Some diseases affect areas of the brain not according to the pattern of blood supply but according to the function of that brain region or the chemical transmitter substance. The classical example is *Parkinson's disease*, affecting those nerve cells which release the transmitter dopamine. The reasons for this selective degeneration are unknown. *Senile dementia* affects perhaps 2 or 3 per cent of those aged over 65 years, rising to 20 per cent of those aged over 80. About one in five cases of senile dementia are due to diffuse atherosclerosis affecting the blood supply to the brain; the majority of cases of senile dementia are due to a degenerative condition known as Alzheimer's disease (see Chapter 2). The underlying cause of Alzheimer's disease is unknown, though there is a relatively selective degeneration of nerve cells in a brain region known as the hippocampus which is concerned with learning and memory. The clinical presentation of senile dementia is initially with gradual loss of memory for events over recent months or years, with increasing behavioural disturbance including insomnia, wandering and sometimes aggression, and finally the patient is virtually mute, incontinent and bedridden. The course of the disease is relentlessly downhill over five to ten years before death, progression being gradual in the case of Alzheimer's disease and by a series of stepwise deteriorations in the case of dementia due to a series of small strokes – 'multi-infarct dementia'. Some patients show combined features of degenerative (Alzheimer) dementia and atherosclerotic (multi-infarct) dementia.

The gradual onset of dementia over months or years must be distinguished from the sudden onset of an *acute confusional state*. The delirium of an acute confusional state supervenes over hours or days and the picture is often of a previously competent old person who rapidly becomes totally disorientated with a fluctuating level of arousal – one moment lying quiet, the next shouting and fighting. Acute confusional states are usually due to the effect of intercurrent illness such as infection or heart disease tipping the balance for an ageing brain working near the margin of its reserve. The investigation and treatment of an acute confusional state is a medical problem of some urgency, the outlook depending on the underlying illness (Briggs, 1985).

Depressive illness is the commonest mental disorder of old age, affecting some 10 to 15 per cent of people over 65 years at any one time. There is scope for argument as to how much depressive symptoms in late life are a response to life-events and losses such as bereavement, and how much 'depression' is an illness with a biological basis (Jacoby, 1981) (see also Chapter 5). Having said this, although minor depressive symptoms may be a common feature of old age, so too are 'psychotic' depressive illnesses with severe symptoms of withdrawal or delusions and an appreciable incidence of suicide. Such symptoms cause considerable distress which may be alleviated by treatment with drugs (or, in severe cases, electroconvulsive therapy), but not all cases make a good initial response and there is a significant relapse rate (Murphy, 1983). A full discussion of psychiatric illness among elderly people is beyond the scope of this chapter, but specialized psychogeriatric services have become increasingly important in Britain in the management of this large burden of misery.

CONCLUSION

This chapter has reviewed, very briefly, the effects of ageing and disease on the human body and its component parts. Most old people do not present with their symptoms falling neatly into a particular 'system': an elderly woman with 'falls' may have a combination of poor eyesight, arthritis and Parkinson's disease, whilst an old man with 'confusion and incontinence' may be suffering from a urinary tract infection, heart failure and senile dementia. Just as the 'medical' components of an old person's problems may be a complex mix of ageing and disease affecting bodily structure and function, so too will the psychological and social aspects of their situation require detailed evaluation. This summary can only give a superficial overview of the medical input to a multidisciplinary team. The rehabilitation of the sick old person requires the expert help of practitioners from many disciplines, each of whose skills and views on management are relevant and worthy of consideration.

Many of the conditions discussed above are due to the 'wearing out' of tissues and cells with ageing. However, as we saw in Chapter 2 some cells continue to reproduce by division throughout life, and this process of cell division is open to error. When 'faulty copies' of cells replicate without constraint, a malignant tumour may grow and possibly spread to sites remote from its origin. Several forms of malignant growth (cancer) are increasingly common with age such as cancer of the bowel, lung and certain forms of leukaemia, cancer of the breast in women and of the prostate in men.

Finally, although relatively minor consequences of ageing are virtually inescapable, such as impairment of vision and hearing, greying of the hair and wrinkling of the skin, not all is gloom. Although 20 per cent of the population over 80 suffer from mental impairment, this means that 80 per cent do not. Whilst there is no certain way of preventing the deleterious effects of ageing, there is much to be said for a good mixed diet and plenty of exercise.

FURTHER READING

Bennett, G.J. and Ebrahim, S, (1992) *The Essentials of Health Care of the Elderly*. Edward Arnold, London.

Kane, R.L., Grimley Evans, J. and MacFadyen, D (1990) *Improving the Health of Older People: A World View*. Oxford University Press, Oxford.

Squires, A. (1990) *Rehabilitation of the Elderly Patient*. Croom Helm, London.

Tout, K. (1989) *Ageing in Developing Countries*. Oxford University Press, Oxford.

4

PSYCHOLOGICAL AGEING

Peter Coleman

In Chapter 2 we have described the short but complex history of psychology as a systematic study of individual human behaviour and its contribution to the study of human ageing. This chapter focuses on the major findings from the psychology of human ageing: intelligence and ability, personality change and life-span perspective.

In the area of intelligence and ability a considerable amount of research has been carried out on age differences in performance. However, this approach has been criticised for paying almost exclusive attention to the general intellectual abilities that decline with age and neglecting those special expertises that characterise the individual person which do not. The second area of investigation is that of personality change. The research work here is more slender by comparison and has produced less in the way of substantive results in regard to generalisable changes with age. Little psychological research has been done on the emotional life of older people or on important specific topics such as sexuality. Nevertheless, general developmental theories of ageing are still being proposed and deserve serious consideration for the insights that they offer.

Much is currently expected of studies which seek to understand the behaviour of older people within the context of a life-span perspective, which is the third area of investigation considered. This approach takes into account formative life experiences and differences in social circumstances in explaining changes in behaviour with age. As age by itself does not appear to be a crucial marker of psychological change whether in intellectual functioning or personality, research ceases to be aimed at establishing general age changes and becomes more the creation of a 'differential gerontology' (Thomae, 1976), defining different patterns of ageing and the factors associated with them.

AGEING AND ABILITY

Studies of intelligence in later life

Within the study of the psychology of ageing, studies on intelligence and cognitive performance have predominated. In part this is because these are relatively easy topics to study in the laboratory. However, intelligence – which can be defined as a general ability to think, solve problems and learn new tasks – is a complex phenomenon that cannot only be studied in laboratory conditions. We also need to examine the exercise of intelligence in real life. Therefore, although there is much published research on the subject of intelligence and ageing, it needs to be examined critically and set in context.

Improvement and decline in ageing
The influence of a crude 'rise and fall' model of the life course has also biased the study of intelligence to look for negative rather than positive changes in later life. But psychological ageing is not necessarily negative. It is important to avoid the error of identifying it with biological ageing which by definition implies decline and deterioration. This inevitably affects psychological ageing, and much of the research on the psychology of mental ability has focused justifiably on such deleterious changes in function. But age also carries with it the benefits of additional experience. Wisdom has been seen as a characteristic of old age in most cultures. In many situations experience enables older people to make better judgements about life decisions than younger people.

In really advanced age the negative effects of biological ageing upon psychological functioning may be more evident than the benefits of experience, but for the greater part of the life course the gains are likely to be as evident as the losses. This of course will depend very much on which activities one considers. Athletic performance declines early on in adult life after the optimal levels of biological functioning are passed, but political activity often reaches its peak in later life. The prospects of further improvement are cut short by biological decline. As George Bernard Shaw lamented, 'if only we were allowed to live longer to properly benefit from life's experience. Youth is wasted on the young!'

Conceptualisations of intelligence reflect this dual aspect of human development (Cattell, 1971; Dittmann-Kohli and Baltes, 1990). The basic mechanisms of intelligence are developed in childhood and thereafter remain well set until subjected to attack with biological decline in later life. But more relevant to behaviour in adulthood are the particular kinds of intelligence or repertoires of ability that the individual develops. Such abilities are essentially pragmatic, related to the way individuals cope with their own life situation, and can only be appropriately studied in a naturalistic way in the settings in which they occur. A number of psychologists have recently begun to stress the importance of observations on human performance in natural contexts (see for example Neisser, 1982), but most of the literature on ageing and performance is based on laboratory experiments and thus neglects this broader perspective on human abilities. Restricted focus on the decline of the basic mechanisms in advanced old age provides a very incomplete and misleading view of the relationship between age and mental ability.

It is important to stress this point at the outset of a review of the literature on intelligence and ageing, as two different types of comparison are often confounded. The first is the comparison between 'younger' and 'older' adults and the second that between adults and very old people. Studies of the former kind may vary very much in the age groups they consider – 20-year-olds with 40-year-olds, for example, or 40-year-olds with 60-year-olds. It is important to pay attention to the crucial detail of who is being compared with whom. By and large 'older' people come out well from these comparisons. But studies of the second kind choose to focus on very old people, usually those over the age of 70 and often over the age of 80, whom they compare with 'younger' people. This 'elderly' group is the one in the age spectrum most likely to reveal defects in cognitive functioning when considered collectively (although not necessarily individually).

The influence of disease and biological ageing upon mental functioning in later life

Effects of disease

In the last thirty years a clearer picture has emerged about the destructive factors acting upon older people's mental abilities. The most evident of these are the diseases that are especially prevalent in later life. Diseases of the brain account for most cases of intellectual decline. It is now generally accepted that the mental deterioration of dementia, including memory failing and clouding of understanding, is associated with brain disease and is not typical of the fate of most old people. As a result the 'senility' stereotype of old age has begun to disappear and those afflicted with dementing illnesses are treated with more understanding. However, the more general relationship between health and mental functioning in later life is less widely understood (Coleman, 1983). For example, many studies of cognitive functioning in older people still neglect adequate control of the health status of their subjects and therefore are less likely to accurately estimate the influence of factors other than disease.

This neglect is the more surprising when one considers that it is already more than twenty-five years since a study by the National Institute of Mental Health in America (Birren et al, 1963) showed that the presence of even a mild degree of chronic disease has a noticeable effect on a wide variety of mental functions in old age. Negative associations between mental ability and pathology indicators were evident in people who had been selected for their ostensible good health. Subsequent studies have repeated these findings for particular bodily systems such as the cardiovascular system and for sensory deficits such as hearing loss (see Woods and Britton, 1985). Holland and Rabbitt (1991) provide a review of recent literature, including an analysis of their own research on the effects of diabetes on cognitive performance. This is research with practical implications, since it clear that the cognitive decrements resulting from poorly controlled non-insulin-dependent diabetes may themselves complicate adherence to medical regimens. Studies that neglect the health status of their subjects thus tend to overestimate the influence of chronological age on cognitive functioning. Effects which appear age-related may in reality be health-related.

Essentially the same point can be made in regard to the phenomenon of 'terminal decline', in which intellectual performance deteriorates in the period before death. This may not necessarily indicate that death is inevitable but that the person is seriously ill. As Siegler concludes in her review of the subject: 'any large change in the cognitive capacity of an older person should be treated with suspicion – it may be a terminal sign, or it may indicate a potentially treatable illness' (Siegler, 1980).

Effects of biological ageing
Nevertheless some changes in cognitive performance with age do appear to be independent of physical pathology (Salthouse, 1991). Studies which have attempted to control for health status have still found some age-related differences in performance. For example, in a large multidisciplinary Dutch study on people between the ages of 65 and 90, measures of perceptual problem-solving ability were found to be related independently to age as well as to a number of health indices (including sensory functioning, lung capacity, coordination and functioning of joints) and to education and past occupation (Coleman, 1983). Although one can often question whether the health indicators in particular studies have been sensitive enough, it does seem possible to make a distinction between those cognitive changes due to health and those due to age. Health-related changes seem to be much more global, affecting performance on all types of tests, whereas age-related changes generally seem more limited to non-verbal performance tasks and especially those requiring to be performed at speed.

The distinction between intellectual abilities to do with words and language (verbal skills) and those concerned with visual and spatial aptitude (non-verbal or performance skills) is reflected in the design of intelligence (IQ) tests. People can perform quite differently on the corresponding parts of such tests. The differential response to age in fact is one of the most striking demonstrations of the value of the distinction. Its discovery led Wechsler, who devised one of the original large tests of intelligence, to formulate the terms 'hold' and 'don't hold' tests (Wechsler, 1944). Many subsequent studies have confirmed his observation that vocabulary test scores and memory for words show very little change with age, whereas certain performance skills like copying symbols or completing visual puzzles show a small but significant decline in people over the age of 40 (see for example Hooper et al, 1984).

However, it now appears that the expression 'verbal' vs 'non-verbal' misses the essence of the distinction. More to the point is the distinction made by the American theorist Raymond Cattell between 'fluid' and 'crystallised' aspects of intelligence (Cattell, 1971). Fluid ability involves the immediate adaptive ability of the individual to perceive relationships between objects and events, to reason and to abstract. Crystallised ability on the other hand reflects the aggregated experience of the individual, the acquired familiarity with materials and relationships. Whereas fluid abilities are adversely affected by the biological ageing of the individual, crystallised abilities appear to remain more stable and may even continue to develop. This view explains the findings from some studies where certain 'verbal' tests, for example involving reasoning, show decline with age whereas tests of vocabulary do not (Savage et al, 1973; Hooper et al, 1984).

It is important to bear in mind that these effects are most noticeable in advanced old age. A number of studies have shown only minimal average changes in general intelligence up to the age of 70. A major study using the type of cross-sequential design referred to in Chapter 2, in which cohorts of different ages are followed up over time, was carried out by Schaie and his colleagues in Seattle in the United States. They began with a first study of this type in 1956, and repeated observations on the same people where possible in 1963 and 1970, as well as beginning second and third studies respectively at the same times. In the most recent account of this research Schaie (1990) emphasises that there is no uniform pattern of age-related changes across all intellectual abilities. Only a few measures showed average decrement in the decade of the 50s. Most showed it by the age of 75. However many individuals did not show decline even at the age of 80. A notable finding as well is the large size of cohort differences. Different generations can perform quite differently at equivalent ages. Variables found to be predictive of lack of decline include an absence of cardiovascular and other chronic disease, an intellectually stimulating environment and a flexible personality style at mid-life.

Cognitive decline therefore may not be inevitable. From both American and British studies it appears that a small but significant proportion of people growing old, maybe as many as 10 per cent, do not show any deteriorating change at all, except perhaps in extreme old age. This was an observation not only from the Seattle study but from an earlier longitudinal study carried out over twenty years at Duke University in the United States (Siegler and Botwinick, 1979). An early study of elderly people in Britain also identified a group of 'super-normals' who were noticeably free from physical and mental health problems, adjustment and social difficulties, and who also obtained higher IQ scores than their peers and indicated much less intellectual deterioration, as measured by the discrepancy between verbal IQ (more likely to be stable with age) and non-verbal IQ (less likely to be stable with age) (Savage et al, 1973). More recently, Rabbitt (1984b) has identified from his own cross-sectional study a group of 10–15 per cent of people in their eighth decade who performed on fluid intelligence tests at the same level as the best of those twenty years younger. Further research is needed to identify what underlies maintained good functioning of this order.

A persistent problem in making advances in this area is the lack of general models, beyond the fluid/crystallised distinction, of cognitive processes against which one could explain what is or is not changing with age. At this stage we can do little more than postulate associations between the slowing down that we observe in older people's reactions and the comparable age-related changes in measures of electrical activity (EEG frequency) of the brain. Both may reflect an adaptation to decreased efficiency of the brain with age. Brain cells, unlike most other cells in the body, but like the cells in some organs as the liver and kidney, do not regenerate. It is not surprising that decline occurs as some cells die and are not renewed. It should be noted that the brain changes associated with dementia are generally considered to be of a wholly different order to that of normal ageing. However, even this point is controversial as critics have pointed to the relatively poor association between observable brain pathology (on post-mortem investigations and on brain-scan measures) and recorded mental deterioration (Kitwood, 1989).

Experimental studies
The fundamental advances required to establish models of cognitive processes which also allow for changes with age will likely depend on experimental studies of these processes in action. However, as Salthouse (1991) points out in a detailed overview of the state of research in this field, experimentation itself needs to be based on more sophisticated theories about cognitive changes with age and detailed descriptions of the phenomena in question. Painstaking observational studies are required. British as well as American psychologists have made a notable contribution to analysing one of the basic features assumed to underly cognitive decline with age, namely speed of information processing, firstly through the pioneering work of Miles (1931) and Welford (1958), and more recently through the work of Rabbitt (1980). Much of this research has focused on analysis of the individual's speed of response to a signal, for example pressing a button when a light appears, at various levels of complexity, both regarding the possible signals and alternative responses required.

These studies themselves have obvious practical importance. Many of the tasks analysed are similar to those required of older workers on production lines. The early studies showed that having controlled for age changes in sensory acuity and speed of limb movement, increased delay with age in reaction time must be due to slowing in the central processing mechanism. Some experimenters quantify the decrement in response as some 20 per cent between the ages of 20 and 60. In older individuals a more severe decrement may exist. Physical health status is again an important explanatory factor. Raised blood pressure, cerebro-vascular and cardiovascular disorders and low levels of activity have all been related to slower reaction time (Birren et al, 1979).

More recent work has tried to find more ecologically 'natural' tasks on which to analyse differences in performance with age. It is recognised that older people may well use different strategies in tackling a task compared with younger people. For example, they may give greater relative importance to accuracy rather than speed, thus artificially raising their reaction times. Older people also seem less able to maintain readiness during the preparatory interval, between the warning signal and the stimulus, and if a fast rate of responding is required may be impaired because they are still involved in monitoring the previous response. With suitable encouragement and preparation their perfor-mance can be speeded up (Gottsdanker, 1982). What is required is more descriptive analysis of the way people actually do cope with growing failures in their own efficiency by devising ways of compensating for them (Rabbitt, 1982b). Such successful techniques could then be applied more generally.

What does disturb older people in particular is when other infor-mation competes for their attention (Stuart-Hamilton, 1991). In tasks in which they have to divide their attention (try to do two things at once) decline with age is very marked and is already evident in those over 30. Experiments carried out by Rabbitt (1985) lead him to conclude that older people find it difficult to ignore irrelevant information. This again is a finding with practical implications. Older people may be at a particular disadvantage in group conversation. It has even been suggested that the elderly car driver may be adversely affected by roadside advertising!

Learning and memory ability

Many older persons claim to be functioning to their own satisfaction, from a cognitive perspective (Pratt and Wood, 1984). However, the deterioration that they themselves seem to notice and complain about more than anything else is memory. Because of the association with early symptoms of dementia this is often a cause for worry. However, the memory in question is usually memory of a particular kind, namely the ability to remember bare data like names and numbers. When it comes to remembering factual information like what they have read or seen on TV or heard other people saying, older people's memories are usually no worse at all (Cohen and Faulkner, 1984). We need to be much more precise about the nature and extent of the greater difficulties older people have than younger people in memory ability.

Deficits with age

A more exact analysis of the increased problems older people incur is very much dependent on our general understanding of the processes underlying memory. It is important to stress at the outset that what is being considered is a relatively small increase in limitations. To be human is to be limited in one's capacity.

This is well illustrated by experiments of 'immediate memory', the memory mechanism which registers incoming information and keeps it for a few seconds while waiting for action, for example holding a telephone number in one's head while dialling. This kind of memory is limited in duration. To remember the number accurately beyond a few seconds it would be necessary to repeat it constantly to oneself or write it down or learn it (ie consign it to one's memory store proper). Immediate memory is strictly limited also in the amount of information it can hold. Seven or eight items seem to be the limit for most people. There are strategies for holding more in one's head but this involves 'chunking' information into larger units. Older people are little different in this regard, right up to the age of 60s. Even in their 60s and 70s people can still remember five or six items, so that the decline in later life is quite small (Craik, 1977).

Studies on longer-term memory in which, for example, people are asked to recall as many as possible words out of a list they have been given a few minutes earlier, show up clearer differences between older and younger people (Botwinick, 1984). Older people typically recall fewer, but appear less deficient when it comes to recognising the material with which they have been presented (eg Perlmutter and Mitchell, 1982). This suggests that the age difference is not so much in establishing memories in the first place but in 'retrieving' information from 'store'. Other studies suggest that the problem lies in the way memories are organised. Older people appear not to organise material that they are required to remember as well as younger people, for example, by grouping them into categories and so on. Techniques of presentation which encourage them to use such strategies appear to be beneficial (Twining, 1988).

More recent thinking has moved away from the idea of conceptualising memory deficits as reflecting an acquisition deficit or a storage deficit or a retrieval deficit. A simple hypothesis which underlies much contemporary research is that, as people grow older, they suffer a general decline in information-processing resources which reduces their accuracy at both recognition and recall (Craik and McDowd, 1987; Stuart-Hamilton, 1991). Difficulties occur for older subjects when they have to process novel information (a measure of fluid intelligence) and especially if at the same time they have to deal with other problems and distractions. The 'strength' of a memory is seen to depend on the strength of the processing carried out on it. Shallow encoding would be in terms of the item's physical characteristics; deep levels relate to the item's meaning. Elderly people seem to encode material more generally, and take in less of the specific, unique features of the item or its context

(Rabinowitz and Ackerman, 1982). This deficit is reflected both in acquisition, in what people take in of the item in the first place, and in retrieval, since retrieval cues are more limited. Again, it needs to be stressed that there are large individual differences in this respect among the elderly population, some showing performance on recognition tasks and active encoding strategies comparable to younger adults (Bowles and Poon, 1982; Zacks, 1982). But some elderly people seem to lack the necessary mental 'energy' to take in more than the most obvious features of their environment.

Recent studies have also tried to examine more natural situations. For example, Rabbitt (1981) has tried to analyse elderly people's performance in group conversations. Although they remembered what had been said, they had much more difficulty in remembering who said what and to whom. This makes it easy to understand why they could become ineffective in a group, failing to distinguish between different people's points of view, while maintaining one-to-one conversations perfectly well.

Although it is commonly thought that elderly people's memories for distant events are better than for more recent events there is no experimental evidence to support this generalisation. It is difficult to devise appropriate experiments to test remote memory, but tests of memory for events and faces from the past have shown people to have similar failings as with memory for more recent events and faces (Warrington and Sanders, 1971). Of course, in cases of dementia where the ability to remember new events is greatly affected, the contrast with memories for the distant past will appear great. But it is important to distinguish abnormal from normal ageing. For example, studies on memory deterioration in people with dementia show qualitative differences, affecting not only effortful but also automatic learning processes (Hasher and Zacks, 1979; Nebes, 1989). Normal age changes by contrast are generally small. Indeed, the literature on the subject indicates that older people's memories of past events, as well as of more recent events, are remarkably accurate (Botwinick and Storandt, 1980; Field and Honzik, 1981).

Persisting strengths with age
Many studies now have stressed the strengths that remain in elderly people's memory and learning and memory ability. Simple measures of learning show little or no decline into old age (Savage et al, 1973). Particularly if the material is fully learned initially, elderly people appear to retain information as well as younger people. They are at a disadvantage with speedy and novel (unexpected) forms of presentation, but in many situations they appear to learn as well as younger people.

Indeed, there are psychologists who argue that the differences observed in older people's test performance reflect sometimes not deficits but different ways of approaching tasks to that of younger people. For example, following a developmental model similar to that of Riegel (1973), referred to in Chapter 2, Schaie (1977–78) argues that adults develop from an acquisitive stage, through achieving, responsible and executive stages to a final, reintegrative stage. As existing intelligence tests relate only to the first two stages we fail to examine the qualitatively different ways of thinking of the latter part of the life course.

There are some studies that report evidence that people over the age of 60 can actually perform better than younger people at certain tasks. Typically, these are situations where people are required to remember personal, meaningful information as opposed to meaningless information. Older people do much worse at the latter than younger people but may do better at the former, probably because they attend to it better (Cohen and Faulkner, 1984). Other studies report that older people remember better than younger people the gist of a story that they have been read, again perhaps because they seem better able to focus on essentials (Labouvie-Vief and Blanchard-Fields, 1982).

Such findings seem to be at variance with those which report considerable muddle and forgetfulness on the part of elderly people in reporting back, for example, the content of a television news episode. However, it is worth repeating the point that we need to avoid confusing the comparisons drawn between younger and older people with those comparisons drawn between the adult population as a whole and very old people. The latter will be heterogeneous in ability, containing some people whose abilities are well preserved but also others who have been affected by both physical and mental decline. We must avoid seeing all people over a certain age, whether it be 40, 50, 60, 70 or more as a single group.

Certainly, we need more studies which report older people's abilities rather than disabilities. A very real problem in our society is that older people underestimate themselves. In one experiment in Toronto (quoted by Cohen and Faulkner, 1984) an experimenter asked old and young people to remember to telephone his laboratory at prearranged times over a period of weeks. The older members were expected because of poorer memory to do worse. In fact they did much better than the younger members, maintaining near perfect performance. What they were doing of course was relying on written reminders. They realised better than the younger people that they were liable to forget and as they were more concerned about remembering they remembered better. Younger people tend not to complain about their memories, although they may forget appointments quite as readily as older people!

Some of the most interesting studies on older people's learning are those that focus on real-life situations. For example, Harwood and Naylor in Australia (Harwood and Irvine, 1985; Naylor and Harwood, 1977) investigated a group of eighty volunteers aged 63 to 91 years in an exercise in which they were expected to learn German from scratch, a convenient choice for a naturalistic study of learning since learning to read a foreign language is not difficult to assess quantitatively. The learners were remarkably successful. After six months the majority of people had reached a level of skill in reading German which normally takes schoolchildren five years to achieve. A study by the same group on the learning of recorder playing was likewise very successful.

Experience and wisdom

Reference has already been made to a theoretical distinction between two different types of intelligence: 'fluid' intelligence which is the person's basic potential to acquire new ideas and to adapt to new situations, and 'crystallised' intelligence which reflects the person's cultural and environmental experience. The former is assessed mainly by non-verbal methods of IQ testing and is liable to decline with biological ageing. The latter is assessed mainly by verbal tests and is considered to remain stable with biological ageing, although like 'fluid' intelligence it can be affected by disease. However, more recently psychologists have begun to point out that 'crystallised' intelligence may not only remain stable with age but may also increase, and that current methods of approach to studying it are inadequate.

Researchers at the Max Planck Institute for Human Development and Education in Berlin, for instance, have argued that intelligence tests become more inadequate the longer people have lived and therefore acquired different experience from one another (Dittmann-Kohli and Baltes, 1990). Such tests are capable of measuring age decline but not age improvement. They do not do justice to the complex and socially valued activities that many people continue to develop over a long lifetime. To assess such development one would need tests attuned to the specialist activities of the people in question, whether politicians, writers, managers or therapists. There is considerable variation in the know-ledge and problem-solving skills required for the position in life different people hold, and they consequently come to vary considerably in the domains of expertise they possess. This expertise can be heightened by further challenges, it can decline through lack of use, but it remains as essential a part of the individual and the individual's adjustment to his or her life situation as the basic 'fluid' intelligence potential he or she is born with.

Older people with particular skills are likely still to impress in advanced age, if those skills are still required and maintained in use. The elder statesman – Harold Macmillan was a good example even in his 90s – can still write and deliver complex speeches. In some cases older people can make use of their experience to develop more efficient ways of doing a job. This may sometimes help counteract decline in speed of action with age. For example, it has been observed that older workers faced with difficulties on a production line can develop their own of altering the job to keep up the pace (Twining, 1988). It is a sign of increased recognition that the benefits of experience may outweigh the detriments of age that insurance policies of older car drivers are less cautious than they used to be. We can expect more such recognition of the abilities of older people as advanced age becomes less associated with decrepitude. The study of the influence of experience upon cognitive ageing is now a recognised research topic (Salthouse, 1987).

While expertise can distinguish a person, it can also be limiting. Indeed, some of the problems of old age may relate to overspecialisation, and inability to pursue new ways of thinking, feeling and behaviour which are required by present circumstances. Nevertheless, some people as they age succeed in acquiring a greater general expertise in dealing with life's concerns. This is the concept of wisdom, which is difficult to define but appears as a generalised form of intelligence in judging life situations that are both important and uncertain. Not all tasks of life require wisdom.

The philosophical and religious thought of many cultures associates old age with wisdom (Clayton and Birren, 1980). It is usually considered to depend on an extended period of experience, but it is not an inevitable product of a long life. Not all old people are wise. This was well recognised also by earlier writers. The Greek tragedian Sophocles for example, in his work *Oedipus at Colonus*, written in his own old age, explicitly contrasts the wisdom of the long-suffering Oedipus with that of his brother-in-law Creon who thinks he can persuade Oedipus to return to the city from which he was banished. Creon is 'old' too, but not 'wise'.

Attempts to study wisdom empirically are very recent and have begun by delineating key characteristics of wise judgements, including the situations to which they are applied (Holliday et al, 1986; Dittmann-Kohli and Baltes, 1990; Sternberg, 1990). They appear to rely on integration of knowledge and experience over a long period; they consist of problem definition and judgements of exceptional clarity. Their field of application comprises situations that involve important decisions that have long-term implications, and situations that are complex and perhaps also ambiguous in interpretation.

While having a personal concern for the issues he or she is judging or thinking about, the wise person will not let emotion distort his or her judgement. Crucially, therefore, wisdom does not only deal with cognition. Rather it involves the integration of cognitive, affective and reflective components of understanding and reasoning. Wise judgements are often characterised by the reconciliation of contradictory information and the recognition of factors that have been neglected. Sometimes it is the solution that is proposed which is complex, recognising alternative strategies and multiple goals. It is interesting that a number of recent authors have suggested a progress to higher levels of cognition in adulthood involving greater degrees of relativistic

, 1983; Kramer, 1983; Labouvie-Vief, 1985). Such
rlie the development of wisdom. Recent studies at
itute in Berlin indicate that older people are over-
those who make the 'wisest' judgements on
resented with (Baltes et al, 1992).

ental factors influencing cognitive

Intelligence does not develop or decay in a vacuum. Much greater consideration needs to be given to the environmental and social circumstances which hinder or promote the continued growth of established expertise or the development of new expertise, as well as to those which lead to atrophy of function and mental decline. As has been stressed before, old age is a particular time of inequality. This is evident in the incidence of disease, but it is also reflected in social circumstances. While many older people maintain respected roles and positions within society and within their families, many also find themselves in a marginal position.

A number of models of intellectual change with age have been proposed which take the environment into consideration. For example, Labouvie-Vief et al (1974) present an operant model in which intellectual behaviour among elderly people is seen as changing due to altered stimulus or reinforcement patterns. Lack of prompting and poor quality reinforcement lead to cognitive decline.

Probably the most well-known model of socially-induced decline in older people is the vicious cycle of 'social breakdown' described by the sociologists Kuypers and Bengtson (1973). According to this view elderly people are often actively induced into a role of social and intellectual incompetence. Role loss as a result of retirement and departure of children from the family house is accompanied by 'ambiguous normative guidance' and 'lack of a reference group'. In other words, there are no guidelines on how one should spend one's time and who one can look to as exemplars. Instead, older people become receptive to ageist attitudes. They begin to see themselves as incompetent, which leads to a slow diminishing of the skills they still have. A downward spiral is created in which failure in one aspect of daily life is used to justify and excuse failure in other areas.

Central to this model of social breakdown is the idea that individuals become willing actors in their own decline by adopting society's expectations of their own behaviour. For example, when people define themselves as 'old' they will, unconsciously, conform to external beliefs about old people. They will think, feel, sound and act older. What is required is the creation of strategies for avoiding self-categorisations in terms of negatively valued stereotypes. Investigators on the influence of social discourse have recently turned their attention to older people as well as to other negatively stereotyped groups (Coupland et al, 1991). They explore how certain images, models and assumptions about the nature of ageing lie behind everyday speech, and how the very language we use may restrict and inhibit older people, and even promote their decline (see also Chapter 13).

The role of social attitudes in older people's cognitive decline is as yet a little-explored subject, but will become more recognised as older people develop their own pressure groups to resist social stigmatisation as has already happened in the United States. The most telling empirical studies so far have been experiments in American homes for elderly people where attempts have been made to reverse this spiral of decline. Competent behaviour is often undermined by the attitudes and practices of staff working within institutions. Even minor interventions can change the situation dramatically, for instance giving people more control over what is happening to them and involving them more (Rodin, 1986). Improvements in mental alertness and increased involvement in activities as well as high adjustment levels have been reported from controlled studies where residents have been encouraged to take initiative for themselves (Langer, 1983). This is not an easy matter when people have long been used to having decisions made for them, but it is possible.

Consideration of mental function in old age therefore cannot be isolated from the broader study of adjustment in later life, issues such as motivation of interest, maintenance of morale and a sense of control over the environment in which one lives, which are the subjects of the next chapter. Disuse of functions and abilities leads to their decline, and this is true at any age. Much is now known about the psychological effect of such brain-washing treatments as isolation and sensory deprivation on younger people. Disorientation and confusion are common results. We are often slow to recognise that older people may be living in circumstances where, by any ordinary standards, they are extremely isolated and deprived of stimulation.

Rabbitt (1988) also concludes that it is necessary for cognitive psychologists of ageing to take account of social factors. He gives illustrations from his own studies, citing for example how cognitively intact but institutionalised people showed patterns of recall similar to neurologically impaired individuals but dissimilar to community-resident volunteers, in that they remember relatively more from their early years and less from the recent past. He looks for an explanation in the circumstances of their lives.

> The institutionalised, but cognitively alert, elderly do not have to plan the routine lives which they share with all their immediate acquaintances. In this static, communal environment rehearsal of everyday minutiae makes poor conversation. When the theatre of the mind becomes the only show in town archival memories begin to be actively explored for scripts. Remote memories

are increasingly rehearsed for recreation and the pattern of memory accessibility across the life-cycle is changed. (Rabbitt, 1988, p. 503)

AGEING AND PERSONALITY

Intellectual functioning comprises only one part of human behaviour. Psychologists reserve the term 'personality' to refer to the many other characteristics which can distinguish individuals one from another in the types of behaviour they display. The question has long been posed whether individuals as they age display distinct differences in social and emotional behaviour as well as in their mental capacities (see for example Burrow, 1986), but it was not systematically researched until the latter half of this century.

Many reviews of the research findings indicate considerable stability in personality with ageing (eg Woods and Britton, 1985; Stuart-Hamilton, 1991). However, the use of personality inventories does indicate a shift on the introversion–extroversion dimension towards introversion. This is apparent from British as well as American studies which have asked people of varying ages to fill in questionnaires (Schaie and Marquette, 1972; Savage et al, 1977). This suggests that as people grow older they become somewhat more preoccupied with their own inner selves, their own thoughts and feelings, and less with the outside world. Recent studies comparing coping strategies in younger and older people also indicate that older people use proportionately more passive, intrapersonal, emotion-focused forms of coping (for example, distancing, acceptance of responsibility and positive reappraisal) as opposed to active, interpersonal, problem-focused forms of coping (for example, confrontive coping, seeking of social support, planful problem solving) (Folkman et al, 1987).

Gender differences have been highlighted by some studies. Results on the Eysenck Personality Inventory show higher initial 'extraversion' levels in young males than young females, but a more rapid decline with age in males, so that by their 60s males are more introverted than females (Eysenck, 1987). Use of the same measure also indicates a decline in 'neuroticism' for both sexes with age, which accords with the previously reported findings that older people are calmer in their reactions. But in all age groups women score appreciably higher on this scale than men.

Age and gender differences in personality and attitudes are evident too from responses to projective tests, where subjects are asked to describe or react to stimuli they are presented with, such as pictures of individuals and groups in unclearly defined situations. Men become less and women more assertive with age (Gutmann, 1987). Some psychologists question the validity of these techniques, principally because of the lack of agreement with other measures (eg Savage et al, 1973).

However, as Gutmann (1987) points out, measures of inner fantasy are not measures of current behaviour. Correlations with objective data may be revealed only over time. It is also worth pointing out that questionnaire measures of personality are essentially measures of self-concept, how the person views him- or herself, and are open to conscious and unconscious bias.

The individual in fact may perceive a greater measure of stability in his or her behaviour than is evident to an outside observer. This could be because the reference group is also changing in the same direction. As the personality questionnaire studies also suggest, relative to people of the same age (and gender) a person will appear more constant. For example, even though he becomes more introverted with age, the more extraverted man remains more extraverted than most of his acquaintances (Kogan, 1990). It is interesting that a rare longitudinal study of observers' ratings of personality over a time span of more than fifty years does indicate systematic changes in personality, even over the period from 'young' (65–74 years) to 'old' (75–84 years) old age. The older people were rated significantly more open-minded, cheerful and accepting, which the authors interpret in terms of Erikson's theory of 'integrity' as the last task of life (Field and Millsap, 1991).

Others, adopting a more phenomenological approach to personality change in adulthood, have also shown that adults do have a subjective sense of change as well as stability in themselves as they age. For example, Ryff and Heincke (1983) present data which also supports Erikson's notion of 'integrity' as the goal of later life. Old persons rated themselves higher on this dimension (ie accepting the limitations of the life cycle and viewing their lives as inevitable, appropriate and meaningful) than they recalled being in the past. Young adults and middle-aged individuals also anticipated scoring higher on 'integrity' in old age than they saw themselves in the present. It is interesting that similarly consistent findings did not emerge in regard to 'interiority' (ie the extent to which people associated ageing with turning inwards). Ryff and Heincke conclude that there is a lack of consensus in American society regarding the inevitability or desirability of the process of turning inward in the later years.

There is then a range of views on the subject of personality change with age. At the one extreme considerable stability is indicated by studies such as those of McCrae and Costa (1990) which have followed samples of adults males over many years using detailed and standardised personality inventories. At the other extreme Gutmann argues for fundamental developmental changes in later life also on the basis of many years' collection of projective and other material in various cultures in different parts of the world (Gutmann, 1987). To understand these differences we need to pay close attention to the purposes and methods of the studies in question.

Disengagement theory

The best starting point for considering research on personality change with age is provided by the so-called 'disengagement theory'. This was formulated following the first major study of ageing carried out in Kansas City in the late 1950s by a team from the University of Chicago (Cumming and Henry, 1961). The main authors were sociologists and, as discussed in Chapter 2, the theory is generally regarded as a sociological theory of older people's place in society, but the research team also contained a number of psychologists who have become subsequently major contributors to the study of ageing. As a general sociological theory, in which ageing was seen as a normal and necessary process of disengagement whereby the individual withdrew from the major roles of life whilst society concomitantly ceased to depend on the individual for the performance of those roles, disengagement theory aroused immediate controversy. Opposing theories were established and research activity for more than ten years was dominated by the attempt to prove which was the most valid perspective.

It is important to bear in mind that the original theory of disengagement itself was set up consciously as a reaction to what the authors regarded as the underlying 'theory' of ageing current in American society at the time, namely that ageing was intrinsically deteriorative and that successful ageing consisted in being as much like a middle-aged person as possible. The suggestion was that 'personality should ideally be immutable, that the valued outgoingness of middle-aged Americans should persist throughout life' (Cumming and Henry, 1961).

Cumming and Henry and their collaborators challenged this view of ageing. Their data dealing with 279 people between the ages of 50 and 90 years indicated older people to have lower levels both of social activity and psychological involvement in the outer world, but they did not interpret these findings negatively, rather as indicating a different standard of behaviour for older people. Far from being pathological, social disengagement in later life, they argued, was universal, inevitable and healthy. Crucially, so they interpreted their data, it did not lead to any loss of morale, well-being or satisfaction with life. There is a harmony between the individual and society. Society does not offer new roles and the individual does not seek them either. Society thus prepares itself for the older person's eventual demise, while the individual turns inward on himself becoming more self-centred and reflective.

As we saw in Chapter 2, objections to the theory have been considerable. It was pointed out that social disengagement is not universal. When it did occur it was not related to age as such but to various losses and stresses connected with age, such as bereavement, retirement or ill-health. Most importantly, some studies indicated that those who did not disengage but remained active and socially integrated had a greater degree of life satisfaction than those who did disengage.

Certainly it is easy to imagine how 'disengagement' from one's surroundings can be the result not of any inherent personality change but of failings, for instance in sensory acuity and cognitive capacity. Uncertain situations, where it is not clear how one should behave, make even younger people agitated and lead to avoidance reactions. A good example of this phenomenon is older people with failing hearing who avoid conversations with others because they find them too difficult to cope with. It is not because they really want to withdraw. Such self-inflicted isolation is well documented as is its association with depression (Gilhome-Herbst, 1983).

However, disengagement theory has been widely criticised for encouraging certain negative aspects of social policy and attitudes towards older people (eg Estes et al, 1982). It provided a scientific rationale for the new twentieth-century practice of retirement from the labour force. It justified the rocking-chair lifestyle, and placement of housing schemes for older people on the periphery of towns and cities, away in the peace and quiet. It could even be seen to excuse custodial forms of treatment in institutional care. It was a peculiarly dangerous form of theory because of its potential of becoming a self-fulfilling prophecy. If we expect and demand less of people because they are old, they are likely to conform to this expectation.

It is also true that, just as with the studies on intelligence referred to earlier, the disengagement theory research suffered from the limitations of its cross-sectional design. Differences between age groups could more properly be interpreted as differences between generations. When the activities of older people are studied longitudinally, as with the later follow-up studies of the Kansas City Study of Adult Life, the activity patterns typically reported involve considerable continuity with previous styles of life.

The subject is more complex because continuity of lifestyle is easier for certain work roles than for others. The relative importance of leisure interests and family life also has to be taken into account. Some people may look forward to, while others dread, the opportunities provided by retirement. Gender differences in life experiences and opportunities also have to be taken into account. But it is worth stressing that the British literature including the large-scale studies of Hunt (1978) and Abrams (1978, 1980a) have demonstrated that people continue active participation in all aspects of living well into old age. Ill-health is the indicator for withdrawal from activity, not through a person's choice, but through reduced energy.

Nevertheless, although many of the criticisms voiced about disengagement theory are well made, in particular the non-interventionist policies on ageing it appeared to condone, some of the insights that emerged in the course of the research and that gave rise to the theory still remain of considerable interest. For example, it was recognised that society allows old people a degree of 'permitted deviance'. They are granted a kind of licence for eccentricity, which permits them oddities and idiosyncrasies of behaviour which would not be tolerated from younger people. For some old people this is a genuine liberation. Perhaps for the first time in their lives they feel able to express themselves freely. Disengagement thus means not only a decrease in social responsibilities but the development of self-expression that is in Cumming and Henry's (1961) words 'egocentric, cheerful and blunt'.[1]

Arguments suggesting intrinsic personality change with age

More importantly, additional data collected by the Chicago psychologists involved in this same research project came to constitute the empirical basis for the construction of a developmental psychology of ageing (Neugarten, 1988). The observed shift in coping styles is one example (Gutmann, 1964). On projective tests older men in particular reacted as if they were less oriented towards coping with stress by producing changes in the stressful situation itself, and more oriented towards accommodating themselves to the environment. As a result adjustment appeared to be increasingly achieved through changes in perceptions of the self in relationship to the environment.

One reason for thinking that some at least of these changes are intrinsic to the individual is that they are evident already in people in mid-life, from the age of 40 onwards, before the physical and social losses associated with ageing are usually felt (Neugarten, 1964). Earlier psychodynamic theorists, notably Jung who like Erikson was referred to in Chapter 2, also stressed the importance of inner changes occurring at mid-life reflecting the different goals of the second part of life. This increased focus on the self can lead to heightened self-awareness and help facilitate expression of creative impulses. At the same time, depression can result from the individuals' confrontation with aspects of themselves about which they feel shame. These positive and negative outcomes are of course also central to Erikson's description of the last task of life as the achievement of 'integrity' versus 'despair'.

In advanced old age, however, a narrowing of psychic focus to the self may be more an adaptation to the biological processes of ageing in that 'it ensures survival by utilising remaining energy to meet one's essential needs' (Newton et al, 1986). Disengagement from external interests and other personality changes, such as preference for simple and familiar situations, may be ways of preserving energy for more urgent tasks. The priority of maintaining a coherent sense of one's self in later life, particularly in stressful situations such as relocation, is the theme of much current writing on ageing. For example Tobin (1991) stresses the

---

[1] In this consideration of disengagement theory the author would like to acknowledge his debt to an unpublished manuscript by the late Alastair Weir.

importance of being able to make the past vivid, to transform reality in desired ways, and to be assertive in defence of one's own interests. Certainly it is a common observation that older people may neglect superfluous details of everyday life, but will attend carefully to information that is most personally relevant to them. For example, an elderly person with a hearing deficit may miss much of what is going on around but become surprisingly attentive when his or her children talk in hushed terms about placement in residential care.

Development in later life?

We have as yet few conceptions of psychological development in later life which are at the same time well grounded in empirical evidence. But this does not mean that the views of theorists as Jung and Erikson are not to be taken seriously. However, British psychologists have always been suspicious of including adult life under the rubric of developmental psychology. The British Society of Developmental Psychology is explicitly devoted to child development, and the result has been an unfortunate neglect of adult development. The basis to this exclusion, however, seems to be a rather restricted epigenetic concept of development, derived from biology, where development is understood to proceed along a certain path towards a specific end point, and for the pattern to be universal in the species.

Certainly it has become more difficult to imagine that psychological development in adulthood is determined in epigenetic ways. It is the social environment that determines which developments are feasible. Erikson himself, particularly in his more recent writings, acknowledges this point. His earlier accounts express in places what appears, to late twentieth-century eyes, a rather over-optimistic view of the influence that social environments have on human development. Moreover, in the last twenty years the rate of change in society has quickened. As a result it is conceivable that patterns of development observed in one generation may not apply to the next. In this case research into human development would become primarily of historical interest. To quote two contemporary Californian psychologists: 'it is now of importance for longitudinal researchers to begin to explore the possibility that societal upheavals and responses to them in the "generation of the sixties" may have disrupted such normative or presumed stage sequences, and that as this generation grows older may well continue to do so' (Fiske and Chiriboga, 1985, p. 185).

The implication for a notion like 'integrity' is clear. There can be no guarantee that society is organised so as to encourage older people to develop the qualities subsumed under this term. Successful ageing depends on the satisfactory resolution of issues raised earlier in life, but this internal development is itself dependent on the opportunities and encouragement provided in the person's present environment. The crucial spur to growth and resolution may be lacking. Clayton, in her analysis of the theory's applicability, comes to the conclusion that 'many people simply do not complete the life cycle. They die uncommitted, unresolved and frustrated, never having arrived at the stage where they could fully integrate and utilise their accumulated years of experience and knowledge' (Clayton, 1975). Erikson admits the same possibility:

> each new development must wait for the inner and outer conditions which make its full unfolding possible and necessary . . . the fate of old age clearly reflects the way in which ingrown habituations and social mores can inactivate an individual's potential, even as they isolate and incarcerate him – actually and symbolically – from the beginning to the end of life. (Erikson, 1982)

It is therefore possible to argue that some 'developments' in later life are not apparent because our present society itself inhibits them. One would expect moreover that recognition and interpretation of signs of development would also be impoverished in such a society. These considerations make the approach of an anthropologist who is well acquainted with a number of different cultures particularly relevant to the study of ageing. Indeed, it seems significant that the psychologists who have had the most constructive things to say about ageing have also had a wide knowledge of other cultures. This applies to Carl Jung who travelled widely and had an almost encyclopaedic knowledge of the symbols used in different cultures, and to a lesser extent to Erik Erikson. It also applies to David Gutmann, who both studied with Erikson and worked in the original Chicago research team in Kansas City.

Gutmann has subsequently worked widely in other cultures, notably in the Middle East and Central America, and on this basis in his most recent writings sets out a well-argued view of psychological development in later life (Gutmann, 1980, 1987). He claims that in modern western society we both miss the evident strengths that older people do display, such as the capacity to adjust to loss, and do not allow them to exploit their full potential. Development is easier to observe in more traditional societies because these societies provide the necessary circumstances for old age to flourish, namely a 'coherent culture with well defined traditions' (Gutmann, 1980, p. 493). Just as a maternal figure is vital to development in infancy, and a peer group is crucial to the formation of identity in adolescence, so a well-rooted culture is a necessary requirement for later life to achieve its real potential.

In traditional societies, Gutmann claims, older people come to take on new roles as 'emeritus parents' – thus echoing Erikson's developmental task of 'generativity'. While women become more assertive and powerful within the realm of the extended family, older men appear to 'disengage' from the world of pragmatic action, but in order to become tenders of the values of their cultures. Their detachment from ordinary affairs frees them to make this advance so that they represent the abstract but vital elements underlying their culture. They do this by engaging closely in the moral values and religious practices which underlie their cultures. In doing so they gain new meaning in their own eyes and in the eyes of others. 'Old men help to provide young men with the powerful meanings that they require in exchange for giving up the temptations of barbarism and random procreation in favor of civility and fatherhood' (Gutmann, 1987, p. 233).

Although comparable possibilities do exist for older people in western society – one of Gutmann's favourite examples is the courage of the old lawyers who, more than their younger colleagues, were determined to prosecute President Nixon because he had offended against the fundamental ideals of the American constitution – the bases of western civilisation have been diluted in the rapid social changes of the last two hundred years and more. Increased pathological behaviour shown by older people, regression into self-absorption and self-pity, are for Gutmann the signs of loss of stability in a culture. Lack of shared meanings and values is shown in the decline in respect for and consequent degeneration of the older members of society. They have lost their vital role in renewing and strengthening the basis of their culture. Degeneration of these older members is the first sign of the decay of a culture. But it is followed by degeneration of the younger members of society as they lose the security and guiding presence that the older members represent.

This then is Gutmann's thesis. A shifting, changing society poses a threat to the realisation of integrity in old age. A coherent culture with well-defined traditions is the necessary context for the development of characteristics such as wisdom and self-transcendence which give old age its special meaning.

One does not necessarily have to agree with this argument and its radical implications, of counter-revolution in favour of tradition, to acknowledge some of the important insights that it contains, such as the loss of traditional roles that older people have incurred in modern societies and the difficulties for them of adjusting to a fast-changing society. It is clear that technological innovation and the development of information systems have made cultural transmission much less of a role for older people. But much more significant because of its threat to a sense of continuity is value change within a society.

This perspective should also sensitise us to the potential problems which people who migrate to societies with very different cultures may encounter. Anthropological research suggests that people retain the values of their previous culture if they have already reached adulthood at the time of migration. The subsequent adoption of new values by their children can be a source of disharmony (Francis, 1984; see also Chapter 5).

It is also important that Gutmann counters the damaging conse-quences of pitying the old by pointing out that older people by dint of experience have often acquired a much greater strength in coping with loss. But his indisputable contribution is to point to the need for a much broader cross-cultural perspective in the study of the psychology of ageing. We cannot pretend that we know what the potentials of older people are if we restrict our consideration to modern western societies.

Psychology inhabits an area of study situated between biology and sociology. Both the physical body and society provide limits to what is psychologically possible. Unlike biological constraints, social constraints vary considerably. Moreover societies also can change and develop in response to individual strivings. A psychology which is based on only one culture is always in danger of making over-restrictive and unnecessary assumptions. This is as true in the field of personality development as of cognitive ability. For example Alexander et al (1991) challenge common interpretations of Erikson's concept of 'generativity' provided by, for example, Kotre (1984). They point out that a concern with 'generativity' in the sense of leaving some of oneself in tangible forms to the next generation is in itself the consequence of the individualism of western culture where the survival of the self is all important. In other societies, where thinking is more in terms of community, death requires an affirmation of cultural continuity and the role the individual has fulfilled in life. Individual survival is not the primary concern. Another example is provided by the embarrassment and sometimes downright hostility shown towards the sexuality of older people in British and other western societies. Yet Winn and Newton (1982), on the basis of their study of the subject in 106 countries, conclude that it is mainly in western culture that sexuality in old age is considered so unusual.

Alternative viewpoints on behaviour in old age

It is apparent that even within the field of psychology there are many occasions where different interpretations are possible for an older person's behaviour. Thus, deterioration in cognitive performance can be seen to reflect intrinsic psychological changes, the product of biological ageing, but it can also be the result of living in circumstances which are themselves incapacitating. Likewise, social withdrawal can be interpreted as 'natural' disengagement, or the result of a depressive illness, or of the lack of stimulus to further growth. It requires careful observation and comparison of similar cases in different circumstances to reach justifiable conclusions about the merit of such conflicting views. Before we have such studies available it is better to keep an open mind on the subject of psychological change with ageing.

Take, for example, the subject of 'cautiousness'. It is commonly stated that people become increasingly cautious with age (Botwinick, 1984). Certainly older people appear more likely to 'play safe' than younger people, and this may reflect in part an adaptive response to ageing. Risk taking is less likely to be profitable when one does not have extra energy in reserve to call on.

But other factors are also implicated. Tests of cautiousness overlap considerably with tests of intellectual ability, and age differences may reflect the same generational differences in education. The same observation applies to reported increases with age in 'rigidity', a stereotyped response to situations (Chown, 1962). Intellectual factors can force people into dealing inadequately with complex situations whatever their other characteristics may be. This illustrates the artificiality of attempting to divide intelligence from personality.

On the positive side, the longer people live the more chance they have to develop expertise in the areas of life in which they have 'specialised'. This in itself will tend to guarantee a greater certainty of response in those areas. Regular as opposed to random responses may therefore indicate not cautiousness *per se* but expertise as the product of experience.

Added experience may also have quite a different result. There is a striking passage in the writings of the Swiss author Max Frisch (1975) which refers to the relationship between age and 'not-knowing'. Despite growth and knowledge, it is the awareness of what one does not know which increases with age, he argues, a theme which Socrates also stressed. So it may be that when ageing people become cautious, it is no longer that they no longer trust themselves, but rather that the number of things they question has become greater. They can no longer be so certain in their reactions as they were (Munnichs, 1987). It should be evident by now that 'cautiousness' itself may mean quite different things both to the actor and to an observer. It is best, therefore, to avoid hasty generalisations about its meaning.

AGEING IN A LIFE-SPAN PERSPECTIVE

In Chapter 2 it was suggested that the study of the psychology of ageing is best placed within the study of the whole lifespan. Erikson's theory of life stages is one of the forerunners of an approach to the human life course which conceptualises it in its entirety and looks for connections between earlier life experiences and later behaviour and attitudes. Life-span developmental psychology is at last sufficiently well established in Britain to have produced its own textbook (Sugarman, 1986). Applications to the study of ageing are as yet limited but are growing (eg Munnichs et al, 1985). It should be pointed out, however, that there are those who argue that such an enterprise is too ambitious and prefer a more limited focus on the processes of ageing itself (eg Bromley, 1990).

Research on development during adulthood

One of the most publicised studies on adult development is the work at Harvard University on the structure of adult life conducted by Daniel

Levinson (Levinson et al, 1978; Sheehy, 1976). As a result of in-depth interviewing of forty men in different occupational groups a normative theory of the life structure was proposed which consisted of a series of alternating stable (structure-building) and transitional (structure-changing) phases.

Thus, the early adult transition (17–22 years), in which the individual distances himself from the pre-adult role within the family of origin, leads into a structure-building phase (22–28 years), in which choices are made for an occupation and also a life partner. A transitional phase follows (28–33 years) in which the first life structure may be changed, then another stable 'settling down' phase (33–40 years). The mid-life transition (40–45 years) heralds a wish to be more oneself and more self-generating in one's actions, and its successful resolution leads into another stable period (45–50 years), before yet another transition around the age of 50. Beyond the age of 50 Levinson's data fade but his expectation is that there will be a continuing sequence of structure-building and structure-changing periods.

Although there are many stimulating ideas in Levinson's theory, for example the importance of formulating a 'dream' when young of how one's life could be, and the role of a 'mentor' in sustaining one's belief in oneself and in one's dream, and also his discussion of the components of the period of mid-life individuation (which have close parallels to the ideas of both Jung and Erikson), the generalisations he makes are open to criticism. His basic work was carried out on a group of subjects which was small and restricted to men (Levinson is currently directing a study on a similar group of women born between 1935 and 1947). At best, his account describes the life course of Americans growing up in the middle of the twentieth century, but we must be wary of generalising too far. Moreover, much of the theory rests on retrospective descriptions of an individual's life course which though of interest in their own right are not a substitute for proper longitudinal study. Memory itself is susceptible to many influences (Neisser, 1982).

One can expect in the coming years more substantial longitudinal studies on adult life which will test the applicability of models such as Levinson's. It is important that data on ageing – and childhood – are included in their design. This is the requirement of a life-span perspective. But it has to be admitted that this will only be possible in academic climates where teamwork is emphasised and working for long-term results is promoted.

Differential ageing

Anthropological studies such as Gutmann's suggest that ageing may be quite a different experience in a culture which offers new roles to older people. But even within one culture, circumstances of life can vary widely. Almost all data, physiological as well as psychological, show increased variability with ageing (Palmore, 1974; Rodin, 1986). If we conceive of development as at least partly the result of learning then this is not surprising. The longer one lives the longer one's learning history will be.

When one takes into account as well the influence of changes in patterns of upbringing and social habits over time and the vital role these play in determining the characteristics of ageing people, the search for generalisations in the psychology of ageing comes to appear over-ambitious. Perhaps the most we can hope for is to determine 'patterns' of ageing and to define their associates and determinants.

This type of thinking was already reflected in the studies that flowed from the disengagement research. During the 'disengagement' versus 'activity' theories controversy (see also Chapter 2) both sides pointed to the fact that their respective patterns of behaviour could be associated with high levels of well-being. They could also be associated with low levels. Further differentiation therefore was required.

An important early study using the same Kansas City data attempted to define patterns of good and poor adjustment in old age in terms of the attitudes individuals expressed (Reichard et al, 1962). Despite the predominance of older women over older men this study only considered the latter. There were three well-adjusted groups: the 'mature', who took a constructive, considered and flexible view of life; the 'rocking-chair' type, who were relaxed, dependent on others and essentially rather disengaged; and the 'armoured', who strove to stay active and at work, avoiding retirement and especially being dependent. The two poorly-adjusted groups were the 'angry', who blamed others for their misfortunes, resented their wives and had a great fear of death, and the 'self-haters', who blamed themselves for their troubles, were depressed and welcomed the prospect of death. A somewhat more sophisticated typology was published a few years later on further re-analysis of the data (Neugarten et al, 1968).

Although crude in their groupings these accounts were a considerable advance in thinking about psychological ageing. Subsequent studies in the United States have resulted in further groupings of styles of ageing. Some of these are based on the major areas of interest and investment in life which an individual displays, such as work or family (Williams and Wirths, 1965; Maas and Kuypers, 1974). Indeed, some of the most useful studies on personality in old age are those which have shown how important it is to take into reckoning a person's lifestyle: for instance, in explaining why people react differently to changes and losses such as retirement, bereavement and living alone, or a move to a residential home.

Any research finding about old people usually has to be qualified by a reference to lifestyle. For example, one American study demonstrated the advantages to be found in grouped housing for elderly people in allowing for more contact with people of similar ages and interests. But it was careful to point out that this did not apply to those with a lifestyle exclusively oriented to family, or those who could be classified as inveterate 'outsiders' (Carp, 1966, 1968).

The most substantial contributions in recent years have come from publication of the results of large-scale longitudinal studies, notably the Bonn study in West Germany (Thomae, 1976, 1983; Lehr and Thomae, 1987) and the Berkeley and Duke studies in the USA (Munnichs et al, 1985; Busse, 1985; Siegler, 1983). The major impression from these studies is the considerable stability in people's behaviour over time spans of up to ten years and more (Palmore, 1970; Maddox and Douglass, 1974; Thomae, 1976). Individuals continue to enjoy the same interests and activities, and display the same attitudes that characterised them earlier. Differences between individuals relate little to age, and much more to factors such as social class, education, health and environmental stimulation.

Some systematic changes in patterns of coping with changing circumstances are observable (Olbrich, 1985; see also Chapter 5). But clearly distinguishable patterns of ageing have not yet emerged. The variety of patterns of consistency and change are too great. Major influences are evident but these are compensated for or reinforced by a host of other factors. The numbers involved in the studies are too small to allow for statistical analysis of the interaction across the wide range of variables involved. In the Bonn study in particular, systematic classification has eluded the researchers, and led some to wonder whether more detailed investigation of individual cases over time may not be a more profitable means of proceeding (Thomae, 1976).

Moreover, it is probably misleading to search for 'types' of individuals ageing in different ways as in the earlier American typologies, since this gives too much weight to the assumed existence of underlying stable traits of personality. A more reasonable working assumption is that patterns of ageing should be defined in multidisciplinary terms including, therefore, biological and social as well as psychological processes.

AGEING AND NEW BEGINNINGS

Although it is undoubtedly mistaken to think that old age must necessarily be a time of change, it is also possible to exaggerate the degree of stability in the last period of life. One needs to bear in mind that later life not only presents threats but also offers opportunities to develop abilities and capacities that have been inhibited earlier in life. This is the perspective on the second part of life emphasised not only by Jung but also by Gutmann, Levinson and others. In the pursuit of 'wholeness' individuals may cultivate potentials in areas that they have neglected in the first half.

The often sudden changes in societal roles and family relationships that follow in later life may provide further occasions for the emergence of other aspects of the self. For example, older men who have been preoccupied with production and competition during the achievement, career-oriented period of adulthood may be confronted with previously repressed needs to nurture and desires for intimacy. Women, by contrast, may become more aware of previously submerged strivings to be assertive and to live out their own needs. These developments pose problems as well. Adults who cannot negotiate the necessary changes in their marriages and other areas of life may be vulnerable to developing emotional problems (Gutmann et al, 1982). Certainly, there is a growing awareness of the need for marital therapy as well as retirement preparation for older people.

These issues are also reflected in general literature. For example, Vita Sackville West's *All Passions Spent* (1931) illustrates well the emergence of a new independence and of artistic interests in a recently widowed older woman. These facets of her character have lain dormant since her marriage, and her children are disturbed by their appearance. She is led to reflect on the different course her life could have taken and to empathise with the current dilemmas of her granddaughter.

Whether ageing means change or stability, its study can only benefit from being placed within the context of the study of the whole lifespan. Childhood and old age are part of the same story. The handlings of issues early in life have major repercussions for later development. This is the major insight of Freud and later psychodynamic theorists. It could now be a primary question of investigation for life-span psychology. But there is an unfortunate trend for psychologists of ageing to neglect child psychology. Gerontologists should in fact pay much more attention to concepts current in child development – concepts such as attachment, competence and commitment – which can be studied over the whole lifespan (Maas, 1985). For example, attachment theory has been applied recently to the study of dementia (Miesen, 1992). The study of childhood too can only benefit from this broader life-span perspective.

CONCLUSION

Most early research work on the psychology of ageing concentrated on the subject of intelligence. As a result we have a rather unbalanced picture of the changes that occur with age. This is the more so because investigations on intelligence have examined the decline in basic mechanisms, but have paid little attention to the continued development of particular areas of expertise which enable individuals to excel in many fields of life, such as politics and art, late in life.

Cognitive decline is not usually marked before the age of 70 and is primarily determined by processes of physical disease. Decline due to biological ageing *per se* is more limited and mainly affects tasks which have to be performed at speed. Social and environmental factors also play an important part in encouraging or discouraging older people to maintain high levels of mental functioning. As a result there is considerable variation in capacity among people of an advanced age.

Stability in outer attitudes and interests appears to characterise most people as they grow old. There does, however, appear to be a shift towards an increasing focus on inner thoughts and feelings, already evident in mid-life, consistent with the ideas of developmental theorists such as Jung and Erikson. A culture's expectations of older people's roles within society have a vital place in encouraging or inhibiting personality change in later life.

Psychological change with age is best studied in a life-span and multidisciplinary context, thus taking account of formative experiences earlier in life as well as present biological and social circumstances. The complexity of the issues involved requires that we make careful observations, in context, of the individual's behaviour and attitudes, paying full attention to their meaning for the individual. Generalisations based on superficial recordings of behaviour are unlikely to improve our understanding of the process of ageing.

5

ADJUSTMENT IN LATER LIFE

Peter Coleman

ADJUSTMENT AND AGEING

Is old age a difficult period of life?

Adjustment, adaptation and the various expressions that are used to refer to the individual's experience of well-being, morale, life satisfaction, depression and so forth, are some of the most commonly used terms in social and psychological studies of ageing. Such is the frequency of their use in British and American gerontology that a naive observer would be likely to conclude that ageing was a particularly problematic period of life. The same impression is conveyed in other ways as well. For example, the very first British government discussion document on policy for older people, issued in 1978, was entitled *A Happier Old Age* (DHSS, 1978). That in itself suggests that old age is often not a happy period of life, certainly not as happy as younger periods of life.

Moreover, there is also evidence from British epidemiological surveys that there is a high prevalence of depression among older people, affecting one in seven of all people over the age of 65. This is not only true of Britain. Similarly high rates of depression have been recorded in the USA and in other countries (Gurland and Toner, 1982). It is then not so surprising that the study of ageing has adjustment as one of its main foci of interest.

Above all old age is associated with the experience of loss. As Lieberman and Tobin observe in one of the most notable recent books on the subject of adjustment to ageing:

> The psychology of old age is often synonymous with the study of crises that alter the elderly's social world and psychological milieu. Retirement, economic changes, widowhood, alterations in family constellation, numerous signals that the body and mind are not functioning as well as they previously did, frank physical illness, and the increasing sense of personal finitude have all been considered within a stress perspective. These conditions have become the bench marks of the last decade or two of life; they are the filters through which investigators examine what it means to grow old, as well as what is necessary to age successfully. (Lieberman and Tobin, 1983, p. 3)

Yet it is worth stopping to reflect whether this emphasis is justified. Might this negative orientation not just be another of the ways in which we unjustly stigmatise old age? Do we give sufficient weight to the positive elements in later life? Certainly there is something to this criticism. Policy makers do tend to look at old age with blinkers which make them recognise sickness, poverty and mental deterioration, but not the pleasures and achievements. Depressive symptoms are prevalent among older people, but epidemiological studies suggest that severe depression is more common among younger groups in the population (Henderson, 1989).

It has to be acknowledged, too, that older people display much higher rates of expressed satisfaction with their lives than younger people. The national survey The Elderly at Home (Hunt, 1978) pointed out that the over-60s age group in Britain had a greater degree of expressed life satisfaction than any other age group with all aspects of life, apart from health. The same findings have emerged from American studies (Larson, 1978; Palmore and Kivett, 1977). Expressed self-esteem, contrary to expectations, also remains high in late life (Dittmann-Kohli, 1990; Baltes and Baltes, 1990; Coleman et al, 1993a). These findings seem paradoxical when set against the evidence on high rates of depression. They may reflect the particular stoical characteristics of the recent generations of older people. Or they may represent genuine developmental changes towards greater self-acceptance and resilience in the face of difficulties. But they certainly suggest that we should consider more carefully the preconceptions that we may have about old age as a difficult and tragic time of life.

Every change that occurs in the life course requires adjustment. Taking up an adult role, beginning work, marriage and childbirth require particularly major adjustments, often in close proximity to each other early on in adult life. If old age has a special character in this regard it is the likelihood of *unwanted* changes occurring, sometimes also in close proximity and often unprepared for: loss of work role, loss of spouse, decreased income and increased physical frailty.

Loss is a common element in many old people's lives. Indeed, from this perspective the rates of depression observed in later life are not remarkably high but remarkably low. Older people cope well with loss. But too often gerontologists 'miss the particular resilience that the aged can show in the face of death. They forget that many older individuals are like combat veterans, who have seen "a thousand fall"' (Gutmann, 1980, p. 490). Often indeed it seems that depression occurs when the losses of old age reawaken earlier losses that have never been properly healed.

The capacity to adjust to life's changes does not appear to be diminished in later life but is rather enhanced. This appears from the observations of psychiatrists that older patients can be maintained in the community with less frequent contact with the therapist than younger people require (Gutmann, 1980), but also from more general studies on life satisfaction and living circumstances (Abrams, 1978), and specific topics such as adjustment to bereavement (Bowling and Cartwright, 1982; Lund, 1989) and to kidney dialysis (Auer, 1987). They show how well many older people do adjust to loss. But this is often not the message that is read from them. The focus tends to be on the minority who show signs of maladjustment.

Methods of investigation

The American sociologist Rosow (1977) has suggested that the emphasis on adjustment and well-being in the study of ageing reflects the applied orientation which also has been characteristic of gerontological litera-ture, less interested in understanding the experience of ageing in its own right, more in the product and the conditions which seem to maximise 'welfare'. This applied bias has been very evident in British research on ageing which has developed considerable sophistication in evaluating types of service provision (see, for example, Goldberg and Connelly, 1982; Bond and Bond, 1987; Sinclair et al, 1990), to the neglect perhaps of more fundamental theoretical issues. Fortunately there are now signs of a greater interest in the study of normal ageing.

Rosow's view helps explain why measures of 'well-being' have become so popular, measures which allow the efficacy of services to be evaluated. They were first developed in the course of American sociological studies on older people in the 1950s, and there are now a variety in common use. The most well known in Britain are the Chicago Life Satisfaction Index (Neugarten et al, 1961) and the Philadelphia Geriatric Center Morale Scale (Lawton, 1975), both of which have been slightly altered to suit British linguistic usage (Luker, 1982; Challis and Knapp, 1980). They contain items like: 'As I grow older, things seem better than I thought they would be'; 'My life could be happier than it is now'; 'As you get older do you feel less useful?'; 'Are you satisfied with your life today?'.

Although convenient for research purposes, there are many problems with such measures which have been well articulated in an article by Gubrium and Lynott (1983). They observe that the methods used force a frame of reference onto the respondent, for example on past/present comparisons, and do not allow for further qualification of the meaning of questions and answers. As anyone knows who has administered such a questionnaire, the comments people make while answering are often more revealing than whether they say yes or no. The measures are also excessively individualistic in that the resulting scores are attributed solely to the individual, rather than to the measurement occasion and the particular themes raised in the individual's mind by the questions.

Of course, this is perfectly understandable since the aim is to provide standardised scores with which individuals can be compared and, for example, the impact of different living circumstances of different types of service delivery can be contrasted (Wenger, 1992). But these measures have limited value and have been of relatively little use in understanding ageing or adjustment. We do, therefore, need to question why in a field so underdeveloped as ageing we have so much research of this nature and so little which asks individuals to describe their actual experience or observes their actual behaviour. Older people's emotional life, in particular, has been given little detailed consideration. However, the need for research on ageing and the emotions is now recognised and a recent advanced text devotes a chapter to the subject (Bromley, 1990).

Is adjustment always desirable?

One final query that needs to be placed against the study of 'adjustment' is the dangerous assumption that adjustment is always desirable. The notion of individual adjustment implies a harmony between an inner state and outer condition. A perfectly adjusted organism would be silent, wrote Freud. But some conditions are intolerable and deserve protest rather than acquiescence. Dylan Thomas urged his father to 'rage, rage against the dying of the light'. His own perception of his father's situation may have been faulty, but why should there not be 'angry old men' as there are 'angry young men'? The writer Graham Greene gave himself this title in an interview at the age of 82 (*The Spectator*, June 1986, pp. 9–12).

SPECIAL ASPECTS OF ADJUSTMENT IN LATER LIFE

Theories of ageing

We have little systematic knowledge about how people manage the latter parts of their lives. What we do possess are certain 'pictures' or 'images', positive and negative, about how people cope with problems in this period (see Chapter 2). Stereotyped views, for example stoic acceptance of hardship on the one hand and crippling loneliness and depression on the other, play a large part in people's thinking about being old. These images affect our own everyday and working attitudes, perhaps more than we imagine, and it is good to try and bring them out into the open and examine them. As has already been mentioned in Chapter 1 there is a growing number of popular books which address the subject of attitudes to ageing and propose more positive ones to those commonly expressed.

In both the physical and social sciences, 'theories' also provide a way of thinking about the world and about human behaviour and society which satisfy the need for a model which fits our experience of reality (see Chapter 2). The study of ageing has as yet generated little theory of its own, and even less has percolated through to influence ordinary attitudes. One exception is the theory of 'disengagement', which is an interesting example both of the power and danger of theories (see Chapters 2 and 4).

Experience with the negative implications for social policy of a theory such as disengagement made gerontologists wary of embracing too eagerly any generalisation about how older people do or should behave. Indeed, American sociologists such as Rosow (1974) and Rose (1965b) have argued that an essential point to be recognised about old age in late twentieth-century western society is that there are no societal or cultural expectations about how old people should behave and live. Therefore, if there are goals or values for which they are to live they must be created by the old themselves. Although this might seem a rather depressing conclusion, it can also be seen as a liberating one. The old person is free to follow whichever path he or she chooses. This is not to deny the influence of social or physical constraints due to low income or disability for example, or the influence of events earlier in life upon the individual's attitudes and motivations, but it is to assert the uniqueness of each individual's situation and decision-making.

But lack of theory and lack of norms can be as detrimental as overemphasis on a particular theory or way of life in old age. People require some framework in which to understand their experience of life, including growing older and interpreting older people's behaviour. Absence of constructive ideas breeds the kinds of stereotypes and prejudices about the deterioration, self-absorption and rigidity of old age which are certainly as damaging as disengagement theory has been. Gutmann has recently offered a vigorous challenge to atheoretical views on ageing. He criticises in particular any confounding of the study of development

> with the study of 'whatever works' or 'whatever feels good' to the isolated individual . . . Such 'humanism' ends by making the older person particularly vulnerable to the general, cultural phobia against aging. When spokesmen for the unique and imperial self consider aging from their favored perspective, of idiosyncratic individualism, the second half of life appears as a wasteland. (Gutmann, 1987, p. 19)

Writing from the more general context of life-span developmental psychology Gergen (1980) also argues for the importance of theories.

> Theory offers a means of dissecting the flux; through theory the rough and tumble of passing experience is rendered orderly. Theory furnishes an essential inventory of what there is and ideally satisfies the individual's quest for why the units of the inventory are related as they are. In this way, theory furnishes a satisfying sense of understanding, along with terms enabling the individual to communicate this understanding to others. (Gergen, 1980, p. 50)

Moreover, Gergen stresses that there is a continual need for new theories to counter the myopia induced by established accounts of reality. A theory can outlive its usefulness, and instead of drawing our attention to phenomena we had not noticed before, become a hindrance to developing new insight.

It is striking how researchers and students learning about ageing turn to the handful of writers who do present an ideal model for growing old. In particular, the writings of Erikson whose contributions as a precursor of life-span developmental psychology have already been referred to in Chapter 2, have attracted considerable attention from those working with older people. This is not because he wrote much about ageing in itself, but because he saw ageing as an integral part of the lifespan. He also powerfully conveyed the idea that in order to understand a person in old age it is necessary to see him or her in the context of a whole life history with the problems both successfully and unsuccessfully resolved from earlier periods of life.

This is a challenge, above all to professions working with older people and Erikson's writing can be illuminating and provide new horizons precisely in those settings where work with older people often seems dull, as in long-stay hospitals. Archer, for example, provides a telling account of how she came to find added meaning in working with mentally infirm older people on British psychogeriatric wards, through a consideration of each of Erikson's stages of development (Archer, 1982). It allowed her to recognise each person's individuality, to acknowledge the achievements and struggles different people displayed in maintaining a sense of 'trust' or 'industry' or 'identity', and striving for 'intimacy', 'generativity' and 'integrity'. The insights she gained enabled her to continue responding to the people she cared for as persons and not only as patients.

More recently Kivnick has developed a method for assessing what she describes as 'life strengths' in elderly clients in long-term care which are based on updated versions of Erikson's eight concepts (Kivnick, 1991). The assessment encourages care staff to see that these strengths have been built up in unique ways over a long life. Kivnick argues that if they consider people's functional needs together with these abilities, they are less likely to exaggerate their disabilities and miss chances for enhancing the quality of their lives.

Erik Erikson's concept of integrity

The notion of 'integrity', the last stage of life, is only sketchily worked out in Erikson's early writing. Subsequent accounts have given more substance to it (Peck, 1968; Erikson et al, 1986). Essential characteristics of a state of integrity seem to include: first an acceptance of one's life and the way it has been lived; secondly the abandonment of a self-centred view of life and the movement to a transcendent interest in humankind; thirdly an acceptance and loss of fear of death.

Such an ideal model of ageing has been criticised for being too idealistic. As mentioned in Chapters 2 and 4, the nature of modern society itself may make it more difficult for someone to achieve such positive qualities. Certainly, since in Erikson's account the possibility of successful resolution of each stage seems to depend on success at previous stages, the probability of failure increases exponentially throughout the life stages. Others, however, would argue with such a strict interpretation of the stage theory and suggest that there are, even in late old age, alternative roads to the state of integrity that Erikson describes (eg Sherman, 1981).

It would be foolish to pretend that Erikson offers a worked out theory of adjustment in later life. His value is that he points to key elements that have to be taken into account in any consideration of adjustment to ageing. He raises the special issues of adjustment which older people must face.

Judgements on the value of one's own past life do become inevitable in old age as new opportunities diminish. It may appear too late to start again or to make amends for wrongs done. The lack of a sense of fulfilment can be crucial to adjustment in later life, as indicated by the author Somerset Maugham: 'what makes old age hard to bear is not a failing of one's faculties mental and physical, but the burden of one's memory' (Maugham, 1959). Reminiscence has long been regarded as a characteristic behaviour of old people, but its purposes and functions were disparaged at the time that Erikson formulated his account of the lifespan. Yet he stressed that 'acceptance of one's one and only life cycle' was a key element in later-life integrity.

People should be generally concerned with what will happen to their society after they die. Ill health and the other stresses of later life may lead to self-absorption with one's own problems unless interest in the world outside can be maintained. Yet if society is to be so different from the one one has known, if it appears likely to overthrow or indeed already has overthrown the values that were so important in guiding one's own life, it can be harder to die. It needs courage and imagination to see through the different manifestations of human interests and activities and to perceive an underlying constancy. Erikson refers to

> the comradeship with the ordering ways of distant times and different pursuits . . . Although aware of the relativity of all the various life styles which have given meaning to human striving, the possessor of integrity is ready to defend the dignity of his own style against all physical and economic threats. (Erikson, 1965, p. 260)

It is not to deny that there are differences. It is to be confident enough about one's own life to defend the course it has taken, yet be able at the same time to tolerate other ways as well. Self-acceptance and acceptance of others go hand in hand.

Death itself must be central to the interests of the study of old age. Yet much gerontological writing almost gives the impression that death is an avoidable rather than inevitable conclusion to old age. But those who are old know well enough that their life is nearing an end. As those researchers who have investigated attitudes to death readily acknowledge, older people do not generally share the same hesitancy and reluctance to discuss death. They talk about it openly and in personal terms (eg Lieberman and Tobin, 1983). Coming to terms with one's 'finitude' is a key feature of adjustment to old age and one which Erikson clearly signalled. In fact, he brings his account of the life cycle full circle with the closing statement: 'it seems possible to further paraphrase the relation of adult integrity and infantile trust by saying that healthy children will not fear life if their elders have integrity enough not to fear death' (Erikson, 1965, p. 261).

Each of these three aspects of adjustment to ageing will now be considered in detail: the role of reminiscence, attitudes to present society, and death and dying. Although not peculiar to old age, together they give an idea of some of the general features of adjustment that characterise the last stage of life. Adjustment to the particular physical and social stresses and difficulties occurring in old age – which will be considered later in this chapter – is best studied against the background of the individual's understanding of the meaning of life and death.

Attitudes to past life and to reminiscence

Ideas on the role of reminiscence

The role that reminiscence can have in older people's lives has only recently been affirmed. Although recognised by Aristotle as an important feature of old age, its treatment has often been unsympathetic. Even fairly recent textbooks have stressed an association with mental deterioration rather than any positive role it might have in old-age adjustment. The formulators of 'disengagement theory' (Cumming and Henry, 1961) saw increased reminiscence as one manifestation of the process of ageing, which they understood as involving growing interiority and withdrawal from concerns with the outside world. Since their intent was to put forward disengagement as a normative process of adaptation to old age and death, reminiscence appeared in a more positive light. But the subsequent backlash against the thinking typified by disengagement theory – and in particular the research which demonstrated that the greater part of the withdrawal from involvement with the outside world shown by elderly individuals was forced upon them rather than initiated by them – tended to confirm the original negative connotations given to reminiscence.

Serious consideration first began to be given to the value of reminiscence following the publication of an article by the American psychiatrist Robert Butler: 'The life review: an interpretation of reminiscence in the aged' (Butler, 1963). Quoting his own clinical experience as well as a wide range of literary authorities, Butler made out a case for viewing reminiscence as a normal activity in old age, and the life review indeed as a process that people may have to undergo if they are to come to terms with their lives as they have lived them. Although he made but slight reference to Erikson's account, Butler's 'life review' can be considered a means by which a person achieves 'integrity'. Indeed, both Butler (1963) and Erikson (1978) cite Ingmar Bergman's film *Wild Strawberries*, in which an elderly egocentric professor achieves more sensitivity in helping those around him as a result of a process of life review, beginning with disturbing dreams but continuing with conscious recollections.

Butler's article was followed by a number of other important contributions to the understanding of reminiscence. For example, McMahon and Rhudick (1964) published a study of veterans of the Spanish/American War. They were struck by how well adjusted this particular group of men was, and also by the extent of reminiscing they displayed. Reminiscence, therefore, did not appear to be a negative sign, but on the contrary seemed closely related to freedom from depression. They observed that the reminiscence of these men tended to be of a story-telling nature, meant to be entertaining and/or instructive, and McMahon and Rhudick related this to anthropological studies on the role of old people in primitive societies in preserving and handing on traditions. They also noted that the 'reminiscers' tended to exaggerate the value of the past in comparison with the present, claiming 'to have seen the best'. They suggested that reminiscence could play a significant role in the face of the losses of role and function in old age, in preserving self-respect by investing in the image of oneself as one has been, and stressing its importance.

Both these perspectives on reminiscence suggest the importance to the individual of the achievement in old age of a positive view of past life. Those who feel they have lived their lives as they would have liked will be happier in the present as well. This is the concept of 'sense of fulfilment'. But the two strands of thought are also quite distinct and it is worth drawing attention to the differences.

Butler implied that the mental process of reviewing one's life is a universal experience in older persons. Often as a result of this life review, negative experiences can be better understood, lessons are drawn from them and the person gains in the process. He or she feels more 'whole', develops a sense of peace, even of wisdom. But there is also the possibility of a negative outcome, a continuing obsession with certain events and actions, the lack of any 'solution' to them, and persisting feelings of guilt and depression. It should be noted that a number of other therapists have also emphasised the importance of reflecting upon one's accumulated personal history as a task to be accomplished prior to death (for example, Frankl, 1963; Blum and Tross, 1980).

However, it is not so much the 'life review' theory which lies behind recent trends to promote 'reminiscence therapy' with groups of older people, especially those living in institutions (Help the Aged, 1981). Rather it is 'identity maintenance' theory which claims that a greater identification with past lives and past achievements is helpful to older people in situations of deprivation and loss. The discrepancy between how one would like to live one's life and how one is actually leading it is minimised by stressing the value of the life that has already been lived, and that this in itself justifies a sense of self-worth. In addition, reminiscence therapy can also be seen as a tool, a ready means of promoting interest and engagement, provoking the traditional role of the older person as a 'story-teller', a preserver of memories.

Evidence on the adaptive value of reminscence
The first empirical studies which followed up the work of Butler and of McMahon and Rhudick and investigated whether reminiscence was related to individual adjustment, produced disappointing results. Taken together, as many studies found no evidence for the adaptive value of reminiscence as found positive evidence (Merriam, 1980; Thornton and Brotchie, 1987). These results led to reflection on the varying functions of talking and thinking about the past. It was realised that reminiscence may mean different things to individuals in different situations. For example, a frail disabled elderly person may learn to appreciate thinking back on past memories in a way as yet inconceivable to a younger, active person. Whether people stand to gain from reminiscence will depend on their past histories as well as their present needs. More detailed analysis of individual cases seemed to be called for, using diverse samples of older people.

Coleman (1986) carried out a longitudinal study on fifty older people living in sheltered housing over a period of up to fifteen years, interviewing them in detail about their attitudes to past life and to reminiscence, paying particular attention to any changes in attitudes. The most striking finding was the stability of people's attitudes. The largest group were those who valued their memories of the past and thought reminiscence to be helpful in adjustment. But also numerous were those who saw no point in reminiscence and preferred other modes of adjustment. This group of people seemed as well adjusted as the first group. The least well-adjusted groups were those who reminisced but were troubled by memories of regret and hardship which they could not avoid, and those who avoided reminiscence because it made them depressed to think of the contrast between the past and the present. These differences helped explain why neither the presence nor absence of reminiscence is likely in itself to be associated with morale. Both reminiscence and non-reminiscence can be expressed positively and negatively. Reminiscence can be an encouraging or comforting activity, but it can also be a worrying and disturbing process. Similarly, not reminiscing can be purposeful because there are better things to do. But it can also be avoidance of memories of a past that overshadow the present, and that heighten the experience of loss. This study illustrates a general point, that in understanding human adjustment we may do better to study people in their own terms rather than as large groups in which we neglect vital differences between individuals.

Recent studies have brought further clarification to the subject. More precisely executed studies of group intervention using reminiscence, such as Fielden's study within a British sheltered housing scheme (Fielden, 1990), have shown the potential benefits of such initiatives, also for the community's sense of cohesion. From her review of the literature Haight has demonstrated that many of the earlier studies involving one-to-one reminiscence were insubstantial interventions, often amounting to little more than one session (Haight, 1991). Her own studies in the United States of structured 'life review' over six weekly sessions have produced encouraging results (Haight, 1988). But life review may not be appropriate for everyone. Lieberman and Tobin (1983) have stressed the functional importance of the reminiscence which they observed in elderly people being admitted to homes for the elderly in the Chicago area. Its character, however, was not that of seeking new understanding or reconciliation, rather the creation of an image of the past that would enable the person to withstand the stresses of relocation and institutional life.

A differential approach to reminiscence has been taken further in recent work by Wong and Watt (1991) which showed that only certain types, 'integrative' and 'instrumental', reminiscence were associated with high morale. 'Obsessive' reminiscence was characteristic of less well-adjusted people. Disappointingly no association was found with 'transmissive' reminiscence but, as the authors point out, this could be because the interview setting was not an appropriate forum for transmitting personal wisdom or cultural heritage. It is important to appreciate that reminiscence is not only a private activity. Renewed emphasis has been given to its social and cultural function in giving witness to a continuing public world (Moody, 1984). It has even been suggested that older people's heightened ability and readiness to recall the distant past may have an evolutionary function in informing society of events beyond most people's experience (Mergler and Goldstein, 1983). Certainly, as also McMahon and Rhudick (1964) observed in their early study, psychological health is best achieved when social and personal functions coincide in the same behaviour. In the last twenty years there has been a recovery of respect for the role of story-teller and a growing appreciation of the social function of autobiography. A recent review of these perspectives is provided by Coleman (1993).

Attitudes to the present and to modern society

A more general loss older people face which has only begun to be given much attention is the global change in the nature of the society in which they live. Although a common perspective on ageing is on change experienced by the person, in many ways older people display great continuity between their past and present in their basic activities, interests and values. Stability of attitudes is the finding of most longitudinal studies that have followed people in later life over a number of years. Indeed, it is often the outer world that has changed most. Speaking from the context of research on cognitive functioning, Rabbitt has compared older people recently to time travellers.

> . . . people now aged eighty are time travellers, exiled to a foreign country which they now share with current twenty year olds. These groups have been fed, housed, and educated very differently, have received, or failed to receive, different medical treatment for different conditions, have been taught to prize different skills and attitudes, and have been shaped by dramatically different experiences. (Rabbitt, 1984a, p. 14)

It is worth reflecting on the social changes that British people have witnessed in the twentieth century. Besides the First and Second World Wars and the dissolution of the British Empire following the last war, they have also seen dramatic political and economic change: the post-war nationalisation of industries and creation of the welfare state (and the reversal of these policies in the 1980s through the privatisation of many public services), the development of new technology and reduction in working hours, the development of a multi-cultural society with the immigration into Britain of people from its former colonies. Perhaps even more important have been the changes in culture and values, the rise of the so-called 'permissive society', the decline in church attendance and the growth of television and the media. Value changes can be disturbing to people brought up with very different values. Seabrook has identified such problems from his own interviews with older people.

> . . . Many of the old grew up in the world where they had to be disciplined, frugal, stoical, self-denying, poor; and what this taught them, often in bitterness and pain, appears to be of no use to their children and grandchildren, who have been shaped for different purposes by changed circumstances . . . (Seabrook, 1980, p. 118)

In a study in Southampton on older people's attitudes, McCulloch has adopted the concept of 'moral siege' to describe a set of attitudes characteristic of a large number of the people he interviewed living in sheltered housing accommodation. Such people actively compared the past with the present, emphasising differences between the generations rather than similarities, and giving a high moral estimation to old people and a low one to the young. Strongly associated too was a tendency to attribute changes in society to the upheavals of the First and Second World Wars. It appears that many of these people felt obliged to condemn modern society. Accepting the values of modern society is tantamount to denying meaning to their own lives as they have led them (Coleman and McCulloch, 1990). Similar observations have been made by Jerrome from her study of the functioning of older people's organisations (Jerrome, 1988).

Such work helps make much more understandable what is often seen as a fault of older people. We saw in Chapter 1 how older people are often seen to be criticising the young and present-day society. It would perhaps help if we were more sensitive to the very understandable reasons why they do so criticise.

At the same time we must be careful not to exaggerate the extent to which the experience of old age is different nowadays than it was in previous generations. It has probably always been a challenge to older people to adjust to the changes they experienced in their own lifetime. There is an interesting comment made by the writer of the book of Ecclesiastes in the Old Testament: 'Never ask why the old times were better than ours: a fool's question' (Ecclesiastes, 7.10).

Nevertheless, a fast-changing society poses particular problems. It is harder to die in a society that is so different from the one that one was brought up in, a point brought out by George Orwell in a passage written nearly fifty years ago:

> . . . it's also true that people then had something that we haven't got now. What? It was simply that they didn't think of the future as something to be terrified of. It isn't that life was softer then than now. Actually, it was harsher . . . and yet what was it that people had in those days? A feeling of security, even when they weren't secure. More exactly, it was a feeling of continuity. All of them knew they'd got to die . . . but what they didn't know was that the order of things could change . . . it's easy enough to die if the things you care about are going to survive . . . individually they were finished but their way of life would continue . . . (Orwell, 1939, p. 106)

The attitude of 'moral siege', therefore, is a way of coping with social change which enables individuals to remain satisfied with their own past lives. It is not entirely satisfactory, however, because the old person will always experience some social pressure to adopt more modern values. There are others indeed who are confused by change and are left in a no man's land between their own past values and beliefs and the values of a new world, an unhappy state which McCulloch calls 'questioning' (Coleman and McCulloch, 1990). In this study 'questioning' was represented by an association between the failure to understand modern society and a questioning of personal religious beliefs, in particular, belief in a beneficent god. Also associated was a low level of thought about the past, which would suggest that such people found difficulty in finding solace in reminiscing. Still others managed to transcend the differences between past and present, and achieved a sense of continuity or even of progress with which they could identify their own lives. But such a state of harmony with a changing world does not appear easy to achieve.

Death and dying

Attitudes to finitude
A number of authors have kept death in perspective in theorising about

adjustment in old age. Disengagement theory was explicitly formulated as a functional theory of ageing, in which older people prepare society for their eventual demise by disengaging first. Both Erikson and Butler saw the key task that they identified in old age, developing integrity and life reviewing, as being triggered by awareness of the end of life. Likewise Munnichs has continued to stress that the growing awareness and acceptance of death are major developmental tasks of adulthood and a crucial part of the dynamic of ageing (Munnichs, 1992). And yet, since his early study of the subject (Munnichs, 1966) older people's attitudes to death, to the awareness that their life is coming to an end, have received comparatively little attention in their own right.

The most well-known work on the psychology of adjustment to death is the pioneer study by Kubler-Ross (1969) in which she describes five stages in the process of psychological preparation for death observed in terminally-ill patients. This kind of process is not age-specific and books on death and dying make little or no reference to old age. Yet, as already observed in Chapter 1, in modern western societies it is predominantly elderly people who die. This is one of the major demographic changes affecting older people this century. Perhaps for this very reason the focus of studies on adjustment to death has been with younger people who have not been brought up to expect death early in life. Death is thought to be less of a problem for the old.

Studies which have compared attitudes to death of older people with those of other age groups have consistently shown that the former think and talk more about death (Kalish and Reynolds, 1976; Cameron et al, 1973). The few researchers who have investigated the subject have commented on how readily older people speak about death (Munnichs, 1966; Lieberman and Tobin, 1983; Schneider, 1987). Most refer to it calmly and without anxiety. Studies which have focused on fear of death have found as expected less fear expressed in the older groups (Bengtson et al, 1977; Kalish and Reynolds, 1976).

Kalish (1985) makes a link between Kubler-Ross's observations and those of the disengagement theory writers. Her final stage of dying, 'acceptance', is described as pertaining to a dying person who is well advanced in reducing attachments to people, groups, material possessions and ideas. The dying person's sense of loss diminishes as attachments diminish in importance. Kalish argues that, to the extent that an elderly person has already begun a process of disengagement from worldly concerns, the additional detachments involved in the coming of death will be easier to bear, than for a young person whose disengagement has only begun in response to the dying process itself.

This view accords with common observations and also has the merit of helping explain why some older people remain fearful. Keith has developed a useful typology of four 'life–death' attitudes: 'positivists', people who have achieved the goals they have set themselves in life, and who 'reflect positively on both their present activities and death as an aspect of the future'; 'negativists', people who show the qualities of Eriksonian despair, disgusted with their lives but unable to start again; 'activists', people who have achieved much but fear death as an end to achievement and opportunity; 'pacifists', people who see death as a respite from the disappointments of life (Keith, 1979). The continued 'activity' in old age shown by the third group may be a defence mechanism which, although effective in maintaining well-being, does not prepare the individual for death. However, recent research does not support the view that acceptance of death ought to enhance feelings of well-being. High death acceptance appears to be associated with low personal well-being (Reker et al, 1987). Individuals who are satisfied with their present lives and who remain very engaged with situations around them are most likely to want to go on living and to be anxious about giving life up.

As far as religion is concerned, a general finding has been that religious belief reduces fear of death. However, this general statement must probably be qualified to take account of differing degrees and types of religious commitment. Kalish and Reynolds (1976) found that strong religious believers were rated lowest on death anxiety, but those with confused religious beliefs were rated higher than agnostics or atheists. Kalish and Reynolds also found that old people differ from other age groups in the opinions they expressed about preparation for their own death. They asked people to imagine that they had been told that they would die within thirty days, and to report what changes they thought they would make in their lives as a result. Old people were more likely to say that they would not change their lifestyle, but that they would concentrate on the inner life. They were less worried by the idea that experience and opportunity would end and that they would no longer be able to care for others. Some of those who have followed the psychoanalytic theories of Jung have stressed that the unconscious 'believes' in a life after death, and that from middle age onwards, but especially as death approaches, dreams prepare us for the hereafter, pointing to imbalances in our attitudes which need to be corrected, a concept similar to that of the life review (von Franz, 1986).

Taken together, the literature available on the subject does not support a fearful idea of death in old age. In Kastenbaum's study of the meaning of death, older people most often personified death as 'gentle, well-meaning' (Kastenbaum and Alsenberg, 1976). Yet the research to date has been dominated by American studies and we need to integrate observations from quite different cultures. British literature on the subject in particular is still very sparse. Death is very much a part of life and attitudes to it will most likely be responsive to changes in other areas, in evaluation of past life and in changing patterns of value and religious belief within society as already noted. Clinical observations suggest that some older people may have severe problems with anticipatory grieving of their own demise and separation from those that they love.

Impending death

A separate issue is the experience of impending death itself. But again comparatively little research has been done. The various stage theories of the dying process that have been proposed, including that of Kubler-Ross (1969), have not yet been subjected to the substantial empirical evaluation required, so we do not know whether it is important that people follow a particular psychological path to death. Individual differences are no doubt very important. A significant British study was a detailed investigation of sixty terminally-ill cancer patients by Hinton (1975). The results suggested that those whose mood and acceptance of death were highest were those who had previously shown high coping skills, high life satisfaction and good marital relationships. This indicates that a life-span approach is also important to the subject of dying.

Age differences in dying behaviour would not be surprising since the circumstances of elderly people's deaths are likely to be different from those of younger people. They are most likely to die from chronic disease that develops over a period of time, to be of frailer physical and mental condition. They are therefore more likely than younger people to be confused or comatose during the period leading up to their deaths. Death is regarded as less tragic. But because communication can become difficult or impossible, greater stress may be placed on the dying person and the relatives. The phenomenon of 'terminal drop' in which some degree of cognitive deterioration occurs prior to death has been observed in a number of studies (eg Riegel and Riegel, 1972; Savage et al, 1973). More recent studies suggest a wider area of change reflected in the person's 'sense of decreased adequacy, a sense of ego-disintegration that manifests itself in lessened cognitive abilities as well as a lessened potential for maintaining a stable and consistent self' (Lieberman and Tobin, 1983, p. 231). People cope by withdrawing from the environment around them, by emotional constriction, by simplification and also by a turning away from their inner life. A passive stance suits a world that is no longer experienced as controllable.

It is important to stress that these strategies are generally successful. Eruption of anxiety and unmanageable fears are not normal, as indicated by a recent Dutch study involving careful observations in nursing-home institutions (Bruning and Hesselink, 1986). It is when issues not related to death impinge upon the elderly person, and force him or her to come to terms with life again, that anxieties are more usually aroused. The circumstances of death are important and deserve much more public consideration. Unfortunately, we live in a society in which the discussion of death continues to be largely taboo. (Chapter 7 of this volume gives further detailed consideration of a range of issues relating to death and dying.)

COPING WITH STRESS

Stress and ageing

Coping with stress in old age is an area of investigation with two distinct traditions of research, that of research by psychiatrists into the symptoms, prevalence, causation and prognosis of affective disorders, especially depressive illness, which has been particularly well represented in Britain, and research within the social sciences linked to theories of stress appraisal and coping which has flourished more in the United States (Markides and Cooper, 1989) and the continent of Europe (Thomae, 1986). There is obviously a connection between the two types of research. But few constructive links have yet been made between them, which is a pity.

Variations in reactions to stress
It is clear from all kinds of investigation that there is considerable variation in the way people adapt to changing life events and circumstances. Although there is a clear connection between such stress and the onset of depressive illness, 'only relatively few old people develop depressions in the wake of the kind of life experience to which practically all their peers are sooner or later exposed' (Post and Shulman, 1985, p. 125). To explain such observations connections have been made with research on lifestyles, thus categorising the event differently according to its importance for the individual's total pattern of activities. For example, people who are exclusively dedicated to their work roles will experience forced retirement from this role quite differently from those whose work roles are only a subsidiary part of their lives' activities.

Connections are also tentatively being made with observations on earlier periods of life. Experiences of attachment and loss in childhood may determine to a considerable extent experiences of loss in later life (Bowlby, 1980). Furthermore, there has been an awakening of interest in a more phenomenological approach to understanding experience in old age. It is what events *mean* to people that counts, not necessarily how they appear to an outside observer. We know well enough how apparently similar events can be experienced differently by different people. To understand their significance we have to try to interpret the individual's experience (Sherman, 1981).

Types of stressful experience
There is a danger in talking of stressful life events as if they formed an easily definable category. The most commonly used concept to describe the experience of ageing is 'loss'. This is seen as a common denominator in many experiences in later life: loss of home and possessions in moving to residential care; loss of relationships, of spouse, of friends and neighbours; loss of memory in the early stages of dementia where

there is still insight into what is going on. It is easy indeed to see loss as the only form of stressful life event in old age. In fact, this is not the case. There are other types of external factors which can contribute to the development of depression.

Hanley and Baikie (1984) provide a useful breakdown of stress factors in terms of four categories: 'loss', 'attack', 'restraint' and 'threat'. 'Loss' is defined as the removal of external circumstances which people have relied on to satisfy their needs. Bereavement of spouse would be a clear example. 'Attack' on the other hand is an external force which produces discomfort. This could be an illness or the hostile reaction of others. 'Restraint' is constituted by external restrictions on activities which have been necessary for the satisfaction of needs. Immobility and being obliged to stay indoors, or not being allowed to go to work, could be examples of 'restraint'. Finally, 'threat' is defined as any event which warns of possible future loss, attack or restraint. These distinctions can be useful in helping to understand the relative difficulty of adjusting to different life events. For example, a physical illness such as a heart attack, although it is not strictly speaking a 'loss' can be linked to all three other categories. It attacks the individual, restrains him or her and forebodes loss of life in the future. It is strongly linked to depression.

It should also be noted that it is not only major threatening life events such as illness and bereavement which are related to the onset of depression. Minor events which are annoying and persistent also bring about depressive reactions in some people. Basically, this is what the Americans call – and the British are learning to call – 'hassle'. 'Daily hassles' are defined by the American stress researcher Lazarus as 'irritating, frustrating, distressing demands and troubled relationships that plague us day in and day out' (Lazarus and DeLongis, 1983, p. 247). These kind of continually annoying difficulties in everyday life, for example in dealings with the neighbours, in doing the shopping or even crossing a busy road, seem to put as excessive demands on some individuals' ability to cope as do threatening life events, and remain a source of damaging stress. Indeed, there is evidence that among older people daily hassles are more strongly related to psychological distress than major life events (Holahan et al, 1984).

Depression and demoralisation

Although there appear to be two separate research traditions on old age adjustment, one focusing on the phenomenon of 'depressive illness', the other more broadly based, both groups of researchers have inevitably strayed into each other's territory. Social scientists speak loosely about 'depression' in older people and psychiatrists have now started referring to 'demoralisation' and 'senile dysphoria' as distinct from clinical depression (Post and Shulman, 1985). There are important issues of definition to be clarified.

Symptoms of clinical depression

Though persistent feelings of misery, hopelessness and inertia are the most characteristic symptoms of depressive illness, these are usually accompanied by vegetative symptoms, loss of appetite, weight loss and sleeplessness. The individual usually withdraws into himself, but may also appear very anxious and agitated.

There is evidence from both clinical experience and research (Gurland, 1976) that older people who become depressed show more hypochondriacal symptoms than young depressed people. Concern about health and bodily states may indeed be the most persistent symptom and is difficult to handle because of the close link between depression and physical illness. It is easy to reinforce depressed older people's concern about their health. However, it is often not concern about matters that are wrong with them that preoccupies their thoughts but typical health 'bogies', cancer for example (in Britain, especially of the bowels).

It is also said that older people rarely come to the doctor saying they are depressed. Often this is because they think something else is the matter with them. It may also reflect relatively unsophisticated thinking about psychiatric illness. This is likely to change in the future as older people gain greater expectations about their lives, and awareness that depressive illness can be treated very successfully in old age becomes more widespread (eg Godber et al, 1987).

Epidemiological studies of 'depressions'

There have been a large number of recent studies on the prevalence of depressive states among older people. Results have differed according to the types of measurement instrument used (Kay et al, 1985; Bond, 1987). Using a sophisticated instrument comprising a semi-structured interview, Gurland and colleagues reported a prevalence among 800 elderly people living in the community in New York of 22 per cent as possibly depressed, but only 13 per cent with depressions which, if known to mental health personnel, might have triggered action from them (Gurland et al, 1980). In a study in London of 396 patients aged over 65 years in GP practices 17 per cent were diagnosed as depressed (Copeland et al, 1986).

It should be noted that not only do definitions of depression vary between psychiatric and ordinary usage, also psychiatrists vary in their usage between countries. For example, British psychiatrists favour a wider definition of depression than their American counterparts. In fact, Copeland and colleagues tried to apply American criteria to their London data and came up with a 13 per cent rather than a 17 per cent prevalence of depression, ie exactly comparable to the New York figures. Gurland himself in his review of various studies states that 'the rates of clinically significant depressions are in the region of 10–15% of the general elderly population; 2–3% would fit the criteria for major affective disorder or manic-depressive disorder' (Gurland and Toner, 1982, p. 229). Although these are clearly not insignificant figures they are also not abnormally high. Indeed, comparative studies indicate higher rates of depression in other age groups (Henderson, 1989).

Demoralisation

Many more older people are troubled by depressing thoughts and feelings than actually develop full-blown levels of clinical depression. Gurland and Toner (1982) estimate that the rates of demoralisation are at least double that of clinical depression. It is probably misleading, however, to view demoralisation in the same way as clinical depression. Mood, for example, is a continuum between high and low, and most individuals experience both extremes over relatively short periods of time.

It is also necessary to differentiate among various aspects of subjective well-being in old age. It was mentioned at the beginning of this chapter that a plethora of questionnaires measuring what are variously called 'life satisfaction', 'morale' and 'adjustment' has been formulated in the last thirty years. It can be very confusing for a researcher trying to decide what is the best method for use in a particular project. The problem is also a conceptual one, because the terms are not always used in consistent ways. 'Morale', in particular, is given a variety of meanings by different authors. Some proposals to standardise usage have been made (eg George, 1981) but a consensus in this respect is far from being achieved. Different questionnaires show both large areas of overlap as well as unique features. Some, for example, do not include questions on satisfaction with past life. Others neglect attitudes to health, or direct questions on self-esteem. There seems to be no nucleus of essential concepts at the core of subjective well-being. Assessment includes a variety of criteria including attitudes to health, old age, one's environment, one's life as a whole, as well as feeling of loneliness, depression and anxiety and feelings of uselessness.

The most detailed attempt to differentiate aspects of subjective well-being has been made by Lawton who administered a large number of questionnaires for different scales to 285 American subjects. His initial analysis produced thirteen different dimensions. On a second-order analysis these divided into two broad groups. The first had 'negative affects', as a core indicator and loaded heavily also on 'self-esteem', 'subjective health', 'psycho-physiological symptoms' and 'congruence between desired and attained goals in life'. The second had 'positive effects' as a core indicator and loaded also on 'residential satisfaction', 'perceived quality of time use' and 'satisfaction with friends'. Interestingly, simple expressions of 'happiness' loaded equally highly on both factors. Lawton argued plausibly that the first set represents 'interior well-being' and the second 'exterior well-being' (Lawton, 1984).

Certainly, this distinction between psychological or inner well-being and perceived quality of life seems intuitively reasonable. Discrepancy between them also does quite often occur in the way older people speak about their lives. For example, one can think of many elderly people who are depressed within themselves, yet are quite uncomplaining about external factors and express satisfaction about their environment. They say that they are 'happy with' their circumstances in life, but do not 'feel happy'. This distinction explains the apparent paradox mentioned at the beginning of this chapter, that older people display relatively high rates of depression but express themselves the most satisfied with the circumstances of their lives.

Determinants of depression and demoralisation

Coping and stress over the lifespan

Research in the area of stress and adaptation has outgrown its early over-simplistic phase of ranking and counting objective life events and circumstances as measures of severity of stress. It is necessary to take into account people's appraisal of stress, not only its objective severity, in explaining whether their mood changes or not (eg Lehr, 1982). People employ various methods of coping with different degrees of success in stress reduction (eg Folkman and Lazarus, 1988), and the frequencies of use of these coping responses may change over the course of life. Thus one cannot expect much from studies which simply investigate associations between objective life circumstances and morale in old age. Lohmann (1980) has concluded that forty years of research on the influence of five prime variables on life satisfaction in older people – marital status, retirement, health, social activity, and housing and the physical environment – has 'not resulted in any clear-cut answers with regard to the causes or correlates of satisfaction' (Lohmann, 1980, p. 35). In Larson's (1978) review of the gerontological literature, only health – and that self-reported – consistently correlated as high as 0.40 with measures of subjective well-being.

To make further advance in understanding why some individuals cope better than others we need to examine closely how they experience what happens to them, and the internal (ie intrapsychic) as well as external coping resources they have available. As mentioned already in Chapter 4, there is evidence from American studies that the use of intrapsychic methods, involving the control of emotions, become more common with age and problem-focused approaches decline. It has of course also to be borne in mind that sources of stress tend to change with age. Thus, Folkman et al (1987) reported that younger adults experienced significantly more hassles in the domains of finances, work, home maintenance, personal life, and family and friends than did their older counterparts. Older men and women reported proportionately more having to do with environmental and social issues, home maintenance and health. Nevertheless, the age differences in styles of coping did remain even with individual areas, which tends to support a developmental interpretation of change in coping methods with age. The findings of other American studies, however, indicate a large measure of consistency in styles of coping with age (Costa and McCrae, 1989).

One of the most substantial studies into the styles of coping shown by older people has been the Bonn longitudinal study (Thomae, 1976, 1983, 1986), which is still unfortunately little known in Britain. This has investigated stresses in the areas of health, family, housing and income, among a sample of 222 older people of 55 years and over followed up over periods of twenty years and employing in-depth interviews. The investigators developed the concept of 'hierarchies of coping responses' with which to describe their observations over time (Thomae, 1986). Considerable consistencies have been demonstrated but also changes. 'Hope for change' and 'active resistance' diminish whereas 'revision of expectancies' and 'asking for help' increase. However, differences between areas of stress in the coping methods employed remained significant. For example, 'asking for help' did not increase in regard to problems of income, perhaps because older people, of this generation at least, found it too demeaning a solution to their problems. The investigators also found a significant decline both in 'depressive reactions' and in the number of 'resistance' responses to health stresses in their female group (who had initially scored more highly than the male group on both indices) in the course of ageing. They postulate a process of learning on the part of these women to cope more effectively with health problems (Rott and Thomae, 1991). Subsequent studies in Germany have developed further this approach to the study of coping (eg Kruse, 1989).

The American stress researcher, Lazarus, argues that researchers investigating stress and coping in old age should do more than carry out sophisticated assessments, taking account of individual differences in appraisal of stress and methods of coping. They should also recognise that any particular encounter with stress is part of the individual's 'lifelong drama', and the commitments, values, fears and hopes shown throughout that life have to be taken into account in understanding the individual's reactions (Lazarus and DeLongis, 1983). Clearly, major determinants of later-life adjustment do lie in experiences earlier in life. For example, it has been suggested that a non-normative crisis such as the death of a child can inhibit the bereaved family's ability to cope with subsequent losses (Callahan et al, 1983). We are beginning now to gain evidence on this subject from the earliest longitudinal studies of child development which began in California in the early 1930s. The then parents of young children were interviewed and data on them at that time has now been compared with data collected forty years later when the survey parents were about 70 (Mussen, 1985). Analysis shows consistent patterns of relationship between later-life satisfaction and earlier traits reflecting a relaxed, emotionally stable personality. Good health when young also seems to be an important predictor. So too is marital adjustment, although later-life adjustment is based on more than simple continuity of a compatible marriage.

Inconsistencies in development have also been revealed by longitudinal study. A different study on the same sample of people revealed that mothers in two lifestyle clusters who reported the highest life satisfaction in old age were not happy with their family roles as young adults, but in mid-life and later years became happily involved in occupations or social organisations. 'By contrast, among the least satisfied in old age are another cluster of mothers who were completely and very contentedly engaged as wives and mothers all through their early and middle adult years. Their lives were completely family-centred, but in old age they seem bereft' (Maas, 1985, p. 171). Longitudinal studies thus provide important lessons for thinking in a life-span way about one's own commitments and interests.

Stress and clinical depression
In recent years we have learned a good deal more about the origins of depression, biologically, psychologically and socially. Although we appear to be a long way from a generally acceptable theory of depression, attempts at integrating information from different types of scientific research are being made (eg Willner, 1985). The role of stress in the aetiology of depression has emerged with greater clarity. It is no longer possible to view psychosocial factors only as precipitating factors of a depressive illness which would have occurred eventually without them. The most influential studies in the UK have been those carried out by Brown and colleagues among younger women living in the London area. Employing a more sophisticated assessment of stress which involved an analysis of the subjective implications and emotions aroused by the life events, they demonstrated that events with severe long-term threatening implications – eg bereavement, news of a shattering nature – were major causes of depression (Brown and Harris, 1978).

The same methods have been employed by Murphy in a study of older people in East London. She examined 150 depressed people over the age of 65 consecutively admitted into an Area Psychiatric Service as out-patients, day-patients or hospital in-patients. As well as these she found 19 cases of depression among the people in the community while selecting 168 controlled subjects. In comparison with the controlled subjects the depressed older people had experienced in the preceding year significantly more severe life events, major social difficulties, and poor physical health. In only 15 per cent of cases some independent and severe precipitating causes of depression could not be discovered (Murphy, 1982). As in a number of other studies on depression in older people, physical health problems appeared to play the major role in its onset. Because of the wide range of conditions involved Murphy argues that they have their impact through their meaning – of loss, attack, restraint and threat – for the individual rather than through a direct organic effect via biological mechanisms.

In some studies, however, other forms of stressful life events, notably bereavement, have appeared more significant. For example, Linn et al (1980) found that deaths of friends and relatives as well as personal arguments were more frequent antecedents to non-clinical depression than illness or financial problems. In a national survey of recently widowed elderly persons in the UK, one half still described themselves as depressed some five months after the death of their spouse (Bowling and Cartwright, 1982). Apart from medication received by 37 per cent of them, very little professional assistance had been given. Understanding of bereavement in Britain has been greatly influenced by the pioneering work of Parkes, much of which is summarised in his book (Parkes, 1986).

Another way of looking at the impact of stress is to consider the additive effect of a number of stresses. Data from Murphy's study indicate that as the types or numbers of stress present increase so does the risk of developing depression. For her community subjects the risk of developing depression was 25 per cent following one severe event, 44 per cent when a severe event occurred in the context of a marked personal health difficulty, and 50 per cent when a severe event was combined with a major social difficulty. Of those subjects with all three risk factors, 80 per cent developed depression (Murphy, 1982).

All of the losses and other problems that occur with age deserve recognition in their own right. However, some are less noticeable than others and deserve closer examination. One of the most neglected problems associated with ageing is hearing loss. In a detailed study in London using audio-metric techniques Gilhome-Herbst (1983) found well over two-thirds of her sample of over 70-year-olds to be impaired. A much smaller proportion admitted to difficulty, but this would appear to be due in part to the stigma associated with being labelled deaf. Remarkably, it seems to be the one disability that is laughed at and found annoying by others. One only has to contrast common reactions to blindness to realise the degree of stigma. It therefore is not surprising that people are reluctant to admit to hearing impairment, and prefer to hide their problem by withdrawing from society – by 'disengaging' in fact. Gilhome-Herbst found people with hearing impairment to go out less and to have fewer friends than people without impairment. In such circumstances – where, for example, three-quarters of those who admitted to hearing problems said they would not admit it to anyone else – the high incidence of depression is not surprising (Gilhome-Herbst, 1983). Much work needs to be put into public education in this field.

Evidence on factors protecting against depression

None of what has been said so far on the relationship between stress and depression might seem surprising. The striking point is the individual variation in reaction. Many people – perhaps even the majority of people – manage to cope well with severe social losses, adverse life events and poor health, and retain or regain their balance within a short time, while others become chronically depressed. Of course, a certain degree of stress and daily hassle is to be expected in life. It is therefore essential to find ways earlier on in life of managing difficulties. While most people manage to cope, there are some who can be disturbed by what would appear to others quite minor events. The question inevitably arises why is it that some people appear better protected against depression. This is obviously a very practical area of research because if we understood better how people are normally protected against developing depression, we would have a better idea of how to intervene more effectively with those who are vulnerable.

Both Brown's and Murphy's research already mentioned demonstrate the importance of having a confidant – someone in whom one can 'confide' and speak to about one's problems and concerns. The role of a confidant – as a buffer in life's difficulties – was first stressed in the gerontological literature many years ago (Lowenthal and Haven, 1968). The issue was tackled as a central one by Brown who showed that young women who lacked a close confiding relationship with a husband or some other person appeared to be highly vulnerable to developing depression in the face of adversity. Murphy followed up the same theme in her comparable research with older people (Murphy, 1982). It was those elderly people who reported a lack of confiding relationships who were most vulnerable to depression when they encountered poor health and adverse life events.

Although the knowledge of the value of the confidant is important, it would be even better to understand what it is about a confiding relationship that protects against depression. There are a number of possibilities. For example, is it the value of having someone to whom one can speak out one's problems that is crucial, or has it more to do with the behaviour and attitude of the confidant him or herself? Furthermore, it has to be borne in mind that some people still become depressed even though they appear to have a close confiding relationship and others do not become depressed even though they face great difficulties alone.

Certainly, the value of having a confidant does not lie in any quantitative aspect of human interaction. In Murphy's study those who reported seeing a confidant only once every two to three weeks, often a child or sibling who lived at some distance, were as protected against depression as those who had intimate relationships. The key to the support gained did seem to be the feeling of reciprocal warmth, trust and – perhaps above all – a sense of being valued. There was someone who understood. Brown, too, in his study stressed the importance of factors in relationships which had an effect on the self-esteem of the young women he studied (Brown and Harris, 1978; Murphy, 1982). A greater understanding of the nature and development of social support networks is likely to become a major field of study within the social sciences (see for example Pilisuk and Parks, 1986). One contemporary view on adjustment that has received much support emphasises the importance of a view of oneself as a good person, both lovable and respected. But one cannot gain such a perception of oneself without reference to the external world. We are dependent on others, especially those closest to us, those in whom we can confide. There are extreme variants on both sides. Some people's self-esteem is more vulnerable than others, perhaps as a result of childhood experiences. Some people, on the contrary, appear to have almost an inviolable sense of their own worth. Research, again with younger women, has confirmed that the former are liable to become depressed even without major stressful life experiences and despite the presence of a confidant, whereas the latter appear to survive severe stress and with relatively low social support (Parry, 1986). The former tend to attribute responsibility to themselves for negative outcomes, and to others for positive outcomes, while the latter do the opposite.

As a result of their recent research, Brown and colleagues have suggested that low self-esteem is the final common pathway of factors causing vulnerability to depression (Brown et al, 1986). They make a distinction between core support and resource support, the former provided by individuals who are especially close to the person in question, the latter provided by others with whom the respondent feels less close. The former are likely to involve long-standing relationships with a high degree of reciprocity. The latter may not and as a result individuals may actually experience a loss of self-esteem if they seek support from this type of relationship. Studies on older people also suggest that effective social support helps to reduce the deleterious effect of stress upon depression primarily by boosting self-esteem (Krause, 1987). Thus, we are led once more to recognise the importance of subjective experience in understanding human adjustment. It is with a review of contemporary approaches to this subject that the chapter continues.

ADJUSTMENT AND INDIVIDUAL MEANING

The role of subjective variables in human experience

Advances in our understanding of individual differences in coping responses will come from research in a variety of fields, biological, psychological and social. In the social sciences investigation into relationships between early life and later-life experience have only just begun and will hopefully provide many rich insights in the years to come. Also crucial to further progress are improvements in our methods of collecting and analysing data on subjective experience.

Wherever one turns in the field of ageing, one is struck not by any commonality of reaction as the stereotypes about ageing people would have us believe, but by the diversity of personality and responses to similar life situations and events. On examination, these differences very often relate to differences in perception. Take, for example, two older women both living in residential care homes. Both are visited once a month by their only daughter who lives 20 miles away. For one this is a source of strength and joy, but the other is saddened, by what on a standard questionnaire ('How often are you visited by members of your family?') would appear the same circumstances. The reason for this difference lies in the interpretation. The first woman is buoyed by the thought that her daughter, in the midst of her busy life, finds the time to visit her mother regularly. The other interprets the frequency of visits to mean that her child does not love her enough, not as much as other daughters love their parents. She might even go further and interpret her child's actions as a judgement on how good a parent she has been, with depressing consequences.

The approach of phenomenology
The 'phenomenological' tradition of research in psychology requires that we take the individual's point of view and try to discover the meaning he or she gives to experience. If the theories (described in Chapter 4) which emphasise the salience of 'inner life' in middle and old age are correct, and development becomes more concerned with self-knowledge and self-awareness than external achievement, then a phenomenological approach may be particularly appropriate to the study of ageing. Neugarten, for one, emphasises the need for research employing self-reports:

> In general, in studying the relations between personality, adaptation, and major life transition, psychologists will probably gain enormously by focusing more attention on the issues that are of major concern to the individual – what the person selects as important in his past and his present, what he hopes to do in the future, what he predicts will occur, what strategies he elects and what meanings he attaches to time, life and death. In short, psychologists would do well to make greater use of the person as the reporting and predicting agent, and by gathering systematic and repeated self-reports along with other types of data, to combine the phenomenological with the 'objective perspectives'. (Neugarten, 1977, pp. 639–640)

Thus, rather than following the positivist tradition of looking for causal or mechanistic explanations of 'observed' behaviour, the researcher is encouraged to seek a fuller description and understanding of behaviour and consciousness by elaborating the meaning that it has for the individual. Typically, this method of research requires an involved interviewer rather than a detached 'scientist'. It also requires 'open-

ended' procedures employing spontaneous reports and personal narra-
tives. However, the recognition of the danger of biasing one's accounts
towards the experience of the most articulate and expressive of people
has led some researchers to prefer a more structured approach to
interviewing. In such interviews a greater number of standard probes
are used, despite the inevitable loss of naturalness. Of course, there are
some experiences which are difficult for most people to put into words.
They may require the skills of a great writer or someone who has spent
time pondering their meaning. In such circumstances the formulations
of others can be used as probes. Phenomenological research would
therefore seem to benefit from a variety of methods, some emphasising
the recording of natural personal descriptions as they occur in context,
others following a more guided form of questioning. For a well-
informed review of phenomenological methods in relation to the study
of adult development, see Ryff (1984).

Anthropological approaches
Recent anthropological studies on adjustment to ageing have also
served to illustrate the greater interpretative power achieved by the
attempt to see things 'from the inside'. Thus, Hazan (1980), in his study
of a Jewish day centre in north-east London, discovered that the centre
offered a radically different way of coping with life, which was
acceptable to most attenders. Certain norms of behaviour and interpretations of events were enforced. Most features of the individual's
past were eliminated, except those to do with shared experiences (eg
anti-Fascist demonstrations in the 1930s) which did not single out
individuals. The role of luck and chance in events was emphasised.
Thus, any relationship was denied between investment in children or
good health and the return on such behaviour. Talk of death was also
taboo, even any public display of grief and mourning. The centre thus
became an alternative reality, a timeless and changeless sanctuary.
Hazan describes how this reality was 'defended', against those who
contravened the norms, through joking, ostracism and other means.
People who could not conform eventually left the centre.

It is important to stress that it was Hazan's patient, attentive and
sensitive approach to relationships and interactions within the home
that allowed him to come to these penetrating and rather shocking
conclusions. It is highly unlikely that the same results could be achieved
by more superficial methods of research.

A further good example of the importance for personal adjustment of
the interpretation people make of their life situation is provided by the
work of another anthropologist. Francis (1984) looked at two communities of Eastern European Jewish origin, one in Cornell, USA and one in
Leeds, England. In both cases the children provided relatively similar
services for their aged parents. They assisted in illness, gave financial
help, telephoned and visited regularly, and demonstrated concern. But

the differences in attitude to these same children could hardly have been greater. Francis sums it up in this way:

> Cornell parents seem uncertain and ambivalent. They want to be with their children, yet they are uncomfortable when they are, they feel that their children are too busy for them, too involved with business or their own families. Leeds informants, in contrast, seem genuinely to do things on their own, out of a sense of independence rather than a fear that they might be a burden. Cornell informants want to receive such support. . . (Francis, 1984, p. 75)

Of the many explanations she offers for these differences, the most convincing involves the life histories of the people concerned. The Cornell elderly informants were mainly Russian-born Jews who emigrated to America in their teens, but failed to adopt new modes of intergenerational relationships. The Leeds elderly informants by con- trast were English-born and had a similar understanding of family ties to that of their children.

The area of gerontological work with some of the best recorded material on the impact of subjective interpretation is in the study of the influence of health on morale. Although there is an association between subjectively perceived health and objectively (medically) determined health, morale and health-related activities are much more closely related to subjective health than to objective health (eg Maddox and Douglass, 1973; Palmore and Luikart, 1972; Olbrich and Thomae, 1978). The point was illustrated in research in the Netherlands on older people who applied for places in residential care homes. Those who were refused admission on the grounds that they were not disabled enough were found on analysis to have felt if anything worse about their health than those who were accepted. Presumably, this explained in part why they wanted to enter care (Coleman, 1983). Also from the same research it was evident that although indices of disability and pathology were higher in the older members of the sample, subjective estimates of health were not associated with age. This was despite the fact that there was in general an association between objective and subjective indicators.

The most natural explanation has to do with expectations. People may expect to be somewhat disabled as they grow older and become unable to do all the things they used to. In fact, they will adapt better to infirmity in old age if they do have such expectations. On the other hand, if they remain fit and healthy, they will feel fortunate. Perception of salience of an issue (for example, as a result of mass-media coverage of rising crime rates) and expectations (for example, of poorer health with advanced age) are important subjective factors in later-life adjustment. It is important that older people are given the opportunity to discuss the matters that concern them. Lack of contact with others can intensify anxieties and inhibit activities. For example, people may not feel able to go out because of exaggerated fears of being mugged or false notions of what is good for their health. In discussion with others they are more likely to achieve realistic attitudes to life.

Experience of the self

Central to the analysis of subjective experience are individuals' perceptions and feelings about their own self and their place in relationship to others. Self-perception is in a very real sense fundamental because so many perceptions relate directly or indirectly to the self, from the woman who interprets her daughter's visits as a judgement on her own value, to the contribution of health and vigour to a person's self-concept, and even the position of being old in a society where crimes appear to be increasingly perpetrated on older people. The American gerontologist Schwartz has called self-esteem – the affective component of the self-concept, what people feel about themselves – 'the linch pin of quality of life in old age' (Schwartz, 1975). This conveys the centrality of self-perceptions.

Maintaining self-esteem

We have seen that the notion of 'vulnerable self-esteem' is a helpful one in understanding why some people appear to become depressed more easily than others. But virtually all people are vulnerable to a degree. We rely on sources in the world around us, in our contacts with others, our roles and activities, to maintain our sense of who we are. The challenge often in advanced old age is to maintain a strong sense of self-identity when so many of these contacts, roles and activities are lost. Maintaining a sense of continuity of self and of self-esteem can become an overriding motivation, representing the psychological survival of the person.

In their study of old people moving into residential care homes in the USA, Lieberman and Tobin (1983) point to the analogies between maintenance of sense of self and of physical survival. It can be a desperate matter. Many people find it difficult to acknowledge change. For example, changing appearance can be hard for a woman to bear who has always prided herself on her appearance. The same applies to a man who has always emphasised his physical strength which he now sees declining. Evidence of change, whether from mirrors, photographs, individual comparisons, is resisted. Sometimes extreme strategies are used to maintain the old sense of self, which can appear strange and illogical to observers. Often these involve myths – which exaggerate and dramatise certain personal qualities – myths of being in control of circumstances when really one is not, myths of self-constancy which deny change, and the blurring of the boundaries between past and present. People may reiterate behaviour which points to their own importance, for example writing to one's MP to complain about ordinary daily hassles!

Tobin (1991) has elaborated further on the behaviours people may use to maintain the self in advanced old age, including making the past vivid and distortion of both past and present. Sometimes these behaviours can appear bizarre even disturbing, as when an elderly resident refers to a picture taken fifty years ago as if it was a picture of him or her today. To an older person living in drastically changed circumstances it may be important to see identities as persistent. He or she is not the frail, impaired person that you see but the sum of a long series of life experiences and events, of which the last may be of relatively little importance. Sometimes the distortion of past or present reality will become too extreme and diminish the possibility of successful adaptation, but generally a great deal of bending of reality is acceptable, and indeed in certain difficult circumstances may seem almost essential to survival.

For most older people, however, the experience of ageing does not require such extreme manoeuvres. As already noted older people generally maintain a high level of self-esteem and this is often achieved by gradual adjustment of expectations and greater self-acceptance (Dittmann-Kohli, 1990). From research conducted with people living in their own homes and in residential homes in Southampton, it is evident that most can readily point to sources for a positive view of themselves, in their relationships with their family or other people, in their activities, interests and social responsibilities, and in their continuing ability to manage their lives and see meaning within them (Coleman, 1984b). From longitudinal study it was evident that expressed sources of self-esteem remained relatively stable over a period as long as thirteen years. Mention of interests and free time pursuits, however, did increase as the average age of the sample passed 80 years. The most resilient self-esteem over this period of time appeared to be that based on a broad interest in other people, not only family members (Coleman et al, 1993a). The ability to adapt to changing circumstances and to find new sources of self-esteem also appears to be important, a point emphasised by theorists on successful ageing (Baltes and Baltes, 1990).

Sense of control

One important form of self-perception is the perception of being in control of events. It is clear from recent studies that this is both a crucial component of adjustment to life in an institutional setting and that it can be influenced (Langer, 1983; Rodin, 1986). Loss of perceived control is damaging both to morale and eventually to physical health. A number of experiments have shown that it is possible for people to regain a greater sense of personal responsibility. For example, in one investigation in a residential-home setting (Langer, 1983) a group of residents was addressed with speeches from the home administrator which emphasised their responsibility for their own lives. A control group received speeches from the same person which emphasised rather the staff's responsibility for them. Of the latter group, 71 per cent were rated as becoming more debilitated over a period of time as short as three weeks. In contrast with this group, 93 per cent of the people who were encouraged to make decisions for themselves, given decisions to make, and given responsibility for something outside of themselves actually showed overall improvement. Based on their own judgements and by the judgements of the nurses with whom they interacted on a daily basis, they became more active and felt happier. Perhaps more important was the judged improvement in their mental alertness and increased behavioural involvement in many different kinds of activities.

What is particularly striking about these studies is the demonstration

> that the belief that one can affect outcomes relevant to one's own life is of paramount importance to psychological and perhaps even physical health. Interestingly, this has been shown to be true regardless of whether or not such belief in fact reflects the reality of control. (Langer, 1983, p. 280)

They emphasise the gains to be expected from shifting people from a passive state of 'mindlessness' to an active state of 'mindfulness' (Langer, 1989), reversing the process of social breakdown referred to in Chapter 4 (Kuypers and Bengtson, 1973).

Perception of meaning

Self-evaluation and self-worth

Self-esteem is a broad concept which is worth differentiating further. Sometimes self-esteem is used to mean simply the ascription of positive qualities to oneself, implicitly by comparison with others or at least by reference to some standard that indicates that one is intelligent, beautiful and so forth. But there is more to self-esteem than this. The Swedish psychologist Freden makes a distinction between 'self-evaluation', which is self-esteem in this sense of 'measuring up to', and 'self-worth', which is less involved in measurement and assessment and more concerned with the perception of absolute value. People have self-worth if they value themselves and see their life as meaningful (Freden, 1982).

This distinction is important for the study of old-age adjustment. For we may be mistaken to overemphasise the self-evaluation component of self-esteem, as in feelings of being useful and capable for example, and neglecting the cultivation of perceptions and feelings of self-worth, such as perceiving and feeling there is meaning to one's life, having a sense of purpose, and having hope. These are different matters from self-evaluatory ascriptions but are no less important. I remember well a man I interviewed some years back, in his late 80s, living in sheltered housing, very frail and totally dependent on others for his survival. Someone got him up in the morning, someone brought him his meals and others helped him throughout the day. He answered my questions on self-esteem calmly. Yes, he said, he felt useless, but in his condition and at his age he was entitled to feel useless, he did not struggle with the thought at all, he accepted it with equanimity. It was quite a revealing experience to me, because of the way he said what he did, he took away the negative connotation from the term 'useless' as it applied to his situation. What was more important was that he still saw meaning in his life.

Meaning is not an abstruse issue. It is a very interesting question whether people find meaning in their lives and how they do it (Antonovsky, 1979). Some find it in the course of their ordinary everyday pursuits, whereas others do not. Some lose it with their partner, with their job or with their health. In old age the issue of meaning often becomes more acute because previously given meanings disappear, contained for example in the tasks that society requires of one in growing up, working, raising a family, and so on. It is probably no accident that many great writers have chosen old age as their theme when it comes to raising issues of the meaning of existence. Loss of meaning is the ultimate loss, the feeling of emptiness and disgust conveyed by Shakespeare's Macbeth when he hears that his wife has committed suicide and as he begins to realise the collapse of his ambitions: 'A tale told by an idiot . . . full of sound and fury . . . signifying nothing.' Researchers have recently begun to address the question of how older people find and continue to hold on to acceptable meanings in their lives, also in situations where their abilities and resources may be seriously impaired (see for example Nies and Munnichs, 1986; Kaufman, 1987; Reker and Wong, 1988; Thompson, 1992).

As meanings are constructed and continue over a period of time, negative and positive reactions are to a certain extent predictable. For example, a recent Dutch longitudinal study has highlighted attitudes to dependency as the major predictor of changes in self-esteem in older people being relocated to institutional settings. Those who previously had negative feelings about being taken care of by others suffered the most damage to their sense of self once they had moved (Mertens and Wimmers, 1987). A similar association between negative attitudes to ageing and depression ten years later emerged in a British longitudinal study (Coleman et al, 1993b).

Religion, values and psychophilosophy
Religion is one of the great providers of meaning to life, and it is a great shame that the mutual antipathies between many psychologists and religious ministers have meant that we have very little understanding of the role of religion in human development generally. Fortunately that situation is now changing (see for example Leech, 1977; Bergin, 1983). From recent research it is clear that religious faith and sentiment play an important part in older Americans' lives. For example, religious thinking constitutes one of the most prominent and successful ways older people

control their emotional responses in difficult situations (Koenig, 1992, 1993). Although religious attitudes to life appear to be less common in Britain than in America, it is surprising that their study has been so neglected by gerontologists (see Coleman, 1990).

A religious faith is not the only provider of meaning in people's lives. Many philosophies do the same, whether the stoicism of the classical world or the existentialism of the twentieth century. The American writer on counselling older people, Sherman, has pointed to the special importance in old age of what he calls 'psychophilosophy', ie a philosophy which has the power to change a person's psychology, their way of feeling as well as thinking about themselves (Sherman, 1981). He argues that older people need a way of thinking and feeling that allows them to be compassionate with themselves, and indeed, in the last analysis to transcend concern with themselves. This is a lifetime's task, of course, but one which culminates in later life. We should provide opportunities for older people to talk and discuss issues relating to their perception of life, its values and meanings, and the things which concern them. It is an advantage if they have the opportunity to clarify their thoughts and feelings together with people who have the same concerns.

A fundamental issue for the present generation of older people is that often they are caught between two sets of values, which is one of the problems they may need to clarify for themselves. The so-called 'functional worth ethic' has been dominant for most of their lives, and works against them in later life when lack of occupation seems akin to idleness. But now we are approaching a period in human history where leisure time pursuits, voluntary community work and creative expression are becoming more important and paid work less. Older people, therefore, should feel entitled to make good use of the free time they have available. They should be able – if they have the resources – to fully partake in this new pattern of life.

Meaning and case-study analysis
The study of meaning, of what makes life worth living, is less susceptible to recognised forms of scientific investigation than other areas of enquiry. This is part of the reason for its neglect. If what we are concerned with is people's own understanding of their situation, standard tests and questionnaires on which individuals can be scored and generalisations made are less applicable. Such perceptions are by their very nature complex. More detailed acquaintance and investigation of the individual subject is required, which places particular observations of a person's attitudes in the context of his or her daily life. The person in context becomes the focus of investigation. Within personality psychology there is a resurgence of interest in the study of the individual case, focusing on particular episodes in a person's life as well

as considering the life as a whole in the construction of a psychobiography (McAdams, 1990; Runyan, 1984).

Bromley has argued in favour of the development of systematic case-study methods, particularly in the field of the study of adjustment. He demonstrates that judicial and natural-history methods are capable of dealing rationally with empirical data and are respectable scientific procedures (Bromley, 1978, 1986).

> The essential feature of a psychological case study is that it focuses upon the 'person in a situation'; it does not attempt to study the personality as a whole (an impossibility) but to study this or that specific problem of personal adjustment. The case study method, in other words, is a way of solving problems – human problems. (Bromley, 1978, p. 35)

If data were collected systematically a body of 'case law' could be built up based on comparisons and contrasts between individual cases. Such 'case law' already exists, mostly informally and unsystematically, in many areas of professional work such as psychogeriatrics. It is a pity that not more advantage is made of opportunities for more systematic studies. We must not, of course, only look at examples of maladjustment in later life. A proper consideration of examples of well-adjusted older people could in the long run be of much greater benefit in indicating the conditions conducive to optimal living in later life.

UNDERSTANDING ADJUSTMENT IN LATER LIFE

This chapter began by pointing out that the focus on adjustment to old age in so many studies of ageing may conceal an ageist bias. It is only more recently that investigators have pointed out just how well older people do cope with life. In fact, theorists who have seen old age positively provide the most useful models of adjustment. Thus, Erikson's ideal of 'integrity' as the goal of life was drawn on to focus interest on the special tasks that confront people in advanced age: coming to terms with life as it has been lived, making sense of a changing society, and facing the reality of death.

Stress in old age has been the object of study of psychiatrists as well as social scientists. The former have highlighted the depressing effects of poor physical health in particular and the importance of the presence of a confidant. Social science research has demonstrated age differences both in frequency of types of stress encountered and styles of coping employed. However, individual differences remain large and improved understanding of the ways people cope with difficulties requires intensive study, preferably both multidisciplinary and longitudinal.

Above all, we need to understand better the way in which individuals interpret experience. This requires the introduction of different research methods to the standard scientific paradigms, for example approaching social situations in a more holistic anthropological way, employing phenomenological means of data collection, and carrying out detailed case-study analyses of individual adjustment. Successful ageing seems to involve not only maintenance of self-esteem, but also perception of continuing meaning in life. Detailed investigation of the latter has only just begun.

6

ENVIRONMENT AND BEHAVIOUR: A HEALTH PSYCHOLOGY PERSPECTIVE

Jeffrey Garland

Defining 'behaviour' as a function of personality interacting with a range of environmental situations, and encompassing what people do, say, think and feel, this chapter develops a perspective from health psychology, reviewing the main environmental issues which appear to be important for the psychological well-being of older people and their carers.

Our concern here is with factors both external (physical surroundings and the reactions of others), and internal (personality characteristics and health status), interacting in the process of appraisal of and response to environmental stimuli.

As already outlined in Chapters 2 and 4 a promising context for understanding human ageing is provided by life-span development theory (Sugarman, 1986). As Bromley (1986) explains in his presentation of case-study methods of research, professionals in health and social care are prime examples of investigators who need to consider both current events and life history in their accounts of the behaviour of individual clients

Inevitably, the practice of health psychology in relation to the needs of older people and their carers is grounded most firmly in the study of processes of abnormal ageing and failure to cope with normal ageing. Understanding and management of disturbed behaviour in older people would benefit from a more balanced perspective (Garland, 1991). We need more and better information concerning normal individuals and carers coping relatively well with the demands of later life (see also Chapter 5).

Theory and technology for understanding and influencing the behaviour of older people and carers is developing rapidly, though not always in a reflective way. Complicating factors include: heterogeneity of population; conflicting aims; a history of piecemeal and uncoordinated research; narrowness of approach by specialists neglecting approaches of proven benefit to younger people; and lack of resources for early detection of potential crises.

This chapter attempts to illustrate the major contribution of environment to psychological well-being. The clinical significance of stress as a mismatch between environmental demands and an individual's perceived ability to cope is examined, and scope for increasing knowledge of the ways in which older people shape their own environments is recognised.

Requirements for institutional living and the establishment of guidelines for residential care practice are outlined. Key issues concerning the management of psychological problems of individuals and of the systems which contain them are discussed, with examples. Finally, some difficulties in measuring quality of life and in assessing change in psychological functioning of older people are explored, with suggestions for their partial resolution.

It is argued that understanding of enviroment and behaviour is advancing unevenly. There are encouraging signs of recent progress in identifying and fostering coping skills (Jones and Miesen, 1992), but much remains to be done in bringing social and health care perspectives closer to each other through shared setting of priorities and mutual engagement in research, teaching and practice.

THE ROLE OF THE ENVIRONMENT

'Environment' is a complex term embracing internal and external factors, and with physical, psychological and social features. Effects of the environment cannot be understood in isolation from characteristics of the older person, and of interaction between the individual's predisposition to respond, environmental stimuli, the person's response and its consequences for that individual. Understandably, faced with such complexity, theories of human ecology strive to simplify, although at the risk of sometimes verging on caricature.

With ageing there is a loss of adaptability, as homeostatic mechanisms underpinning adaptive responding to environmental challenges lose sensitivity and accuracy. The ultimate manifestation of such change is of course death, as a result of demands that can be met no longer. Reduced tolerance may interact with increased pressure: for example, as the general standard of home insulation and heating for older people is poorer than that enjoyed by younger adults, risk of exposure of the most frail to hypothermia is increased (Wilcock et al, 1982).

Those individuals most impaired by ageing can be expected to show increased 'environmental docility' (Lawton, 1982), with greater dependence on external environmental cues to trigger responses, and reduced likelihood of purposeful 'spontaneous' internally cued responses. As an individual's competence decreases, the proportion of behaviour apparently directly attributable to external influence appears to increase.

Three models of environmental influences on older people are reviewed by Scheidt and Windley (1985). The first of these, the adaptation theory proposed by Lawton and Nahemow (1973) assumes that the individual constantly works to maintain a steady state between two factors: awareness of environmental press (challenge from stimuli that activate behaviour), and consciousness of competence (the sum of physical and psychological coping resources). It is proposed that a relatively close match is optimal for maintaining adaptive behaviour.

This resembles the congruence model of Kahana (1982), which relates environmental press and individual needs, and views adaptive behaviour as a balancing mechanism by which a person can regulate external stimulation or review priority of needs to achieve or maintain optimal congruence. It is suggested that complete congruence can have a negative impact, and that the more competent older person can be expected to seek out environmental challenge, stretching adaptive capacity.

Taking account of older people's increased vulnerability to environmental risk, Schooler (1982) adopts a cognitive theory of stress and coping influenced by Lazarus et al (1974). The individual is assumed to scan environmental challenges (primary appraisal), and when threat is perceived, to review choice of reactions to remove potential harm (secondary appraisal). This perspective has allowed, for example, evaluation of whether the presence of a social support network has a positive effect on primary or secondary appraisal.

The global concept 'environment' needs to be broken down into component factors if it is to be understood more clearly. Scheidt and Windley list the following ten factors:

1. sensory stimulation;
2. comfort, with adequate temperature and lighting, compensating for increased sensitivity to glare, and for slowness in dark/light adaptation;
3. aesthetic attractiveness for the occupant;
4. privacy and security, supporting maintenance of self-esteem, with a feeling of attachment and belonging;
5. clearness and consistency of lay-out, with relatively stable organisation and structure;
6. flexibility if remodelling is required to suit the older person's needs;
7. a feeling of control by the occupier, so that the territory is free from trespass;
8. opportunity for social contacts as required;
9. accessibility for the occupier, so that any part of the surroundings can be reached as needed; and
10. whether the density of population is variable, rather than consistently empty or always crowded.

It should be noted that detailed evidence on which to assess the relative significance of such a range of factors is scarce. For example, Zeisel et al (1977) reported the opinions of a group of eight experts (psychologists, sociologists, architects and interior designers), who advised on the design of accommodation for older people. They were asked to rate the importance of each of 123 design features, on the basis of availability of research evidence. Only eight features were known by at least three experts to be the subject of systematic data to support a judgement, and only 32 were known by at least two experts to have such evidence.

Nearly all the research into environmental influences on the behaviour of older people has focused on institutional settings. In Britain, findings point to the importance of the size of the setting and the desire of many older residents for having a room of their own (Wyvern Partnership, 1977; Willcocks et al, 1987).

However, as Rowles (1980) and Lawton (1980) explain, an older person's own home and locality, territory which is familiar and secure, is wherever possible the most desirable of all prosthetic environments in facilitating adaptation. Discussing 'the meaning of place in old age', Howell (1983) affirms the importance of designed environments for the shaping and maintenance of personal identity and social relationships.

Such considerations can be expected to prompt sustained growth in the investigation of older people within their domestic and community settings. A notable example is offered by Sixsmith (1986a), who has investigated the 'amalgam of subjective feelings and physical opportunities and constraints' that appears to represent meanings and experiences of home for a group of people over 65 living in their own homes, either rented or owned, in two working-class areas of Newcastle upon Tyne. And Ford and Sinclair (1987, p. 5) point out that their in-depth interviews with older women across a range of community settings offer a balanced perspective, 'a counter-balance to the problem-centred stance, an approach that draws out a more holistic picture of their lives by focusing on the routine daily round, the everyday taken-for-granted, and which charts the fears, achievement, problems and pleasures of being an older woman'. (For further discussion of domestic settings see Chapter 9.)

EFFECTS OF STRESS ON INDIVIDUAL FUNCTIONING

The role of accumulated consequences of acute and chronic stress over the lifespan for health problems in later life is an extremely complex issue which is largely unresolved. A generally accepted model (Lazarus, 1966; Lazarus et al, 1974), is that 'stress' represents demands from within or without that tax or exceed available resources of the individual or social system. Key components in stress reaction include both psychological mechanisms (cognitive appraisal of the significance of stress stimuli, preferred coping strategies, and repertoire of behavioural responses) and physiological mechanisms (internal stimuli and body changes, emotional states, and physiological responses). Feedback loops connect these components and their elements, and there are pronounced individual differences in the expression of response to stress.

For example, Mr Burns, an 83-year-old patient in a community hospital who will remain unfit to return home, refuses to agree to apply for a place in an old people's home. He is obdurate, becomes increasingly difficult to nurse, and is referred to a health psychologist for assessment. Mr Burns explains that he feels 'bothered' and 'distressed' by his situation. He views the local home as 'a place where they sit around in bunches waiting to die'. He construes the repeated requests by carers for him to sign his application papers as tantamount to the proverbial invitation 'dilly, dilly, come and be killed'.

During such sessions he feels tightness in his chest, difficulty in breathing, and increased awareness of his arthritic stiffness, as though he is becoming 'just like a corpse'. These physical sensations feed back into a state which he labels as 'panic', and he shouts at the carers because 'I just want them to clear out and leave me alone.' In emotional arousal, he frequently finds himself thinking of a grandson who, he claims, owes him several thousand pounds. Mr Burns considers that while he is in hospital he is 'free' to pursue (or at least to feel that he could pursue) his claim against the young man. Once in the home, he argues, he would become a powerless 'inmate' and the grandson would be confirmed as 'having won'.

He acknowledges that he alternately bullies his carers ('because I can't abide being so helpless'), and cajoles them ('because I know I need them for every blessed thing'). He contrasts his working life as a lime burner ('16 hours a day, 7 days a week') with his present existence ('not being able to do a damn thing'), and recognises that being demanding with carers and rehearsing endless details of projected litigation is his way of coping with the stress of prolonged inactivity.

Not all stress is necessarily experienced as negative. Studies of younger adults frequently divide 'stress' in terms of 'normal' stress, produced by disturbing events or changes, either positive or negative, which evoke emergency reactions; 'distress', chronic normal stress associated with prolonged frustration and conflict, often accompanied by a feeling of helplessnes, and capable if unduly extended of depressing the immune system and increasing liability to infection and illness; and 'eustress', in which an individual feels positively challenged to energetic achievement (Selye, 1976).

Such distinctions are not usually made in studies of older people. It may indeed be the case that with ageing stress tends to be experienced in a less differentiated way, and hence individuals have a less flexible range of responses and, with lower adaptive capacity, are more likely to respond in a disorganised way. For example, disturbed bowel function-ing, with cycles of chronic constipation, or diarrhoea, can be linked with

prolonged stress, and preoccupation with bowel functioning characterises many older people receiving treatment for chronic stress.

Stress and caring

Stress is also experienced by family and friends of disturbed older
people (Gilhooly, 1987; Light and Lebowitz, 1990), and the appraisal of
such burden (summed objective problems) and strain (overall subjective
awareness of being overloaded), is well developed (Gilleard, 1984). The
rapidly developing body of investigation into carer support should assist
in understanding the gross discrepancies between burden and strain
that are sometimes reported.

The model of family-oriented community care for older people who
are suffering from dementia proposed by Gilleard is influential in
practice, and his analysis of the situation of both sufferer and carer is
worth quoting:

> Dementia is fundamentally the erosion of self, whose management requires
> an increasingly supervisory and supportive agency to take responsibility for
> the dementing person's behaviour as their intending and adaptive self fades.
> The difficulties and limitations of family carers that are evinced in this process
> are sufficiently stressful for the majority of carers to require some form of
> professional intervention, but one based upon developing a shared commit-
> ment to the supervisory and supportive aspects of caring at a rate which
> permits the principal carer to maintain their caring role as they have the desire
> and resources to do so. (Gilleard, 1984, pp. 119–20)

The most noxious product of stress is abuse of old people by carers or
of carers by old people. Definition of what constitutes physical or
psychological 'abuse' remains a vexed question, as Pritchard (1992)
recognises in her handbook for professionals. There are no easy
answers. For example, it may be observed, as Gilleard points out, that
emphasis on community care first and foremost may involve colluding
with ongoing 'care' that is vestigial or ill-conceived, bordering on abuse.

One example from the experience of a health psychologist involved a
referral from a home-care assistant, of a client couple (Garland, 1991).
The assistant sought advice because she was becoming increasingly
concerned that the home-care package was wrongly addressed. The
devoted, but frail and increasingly forgetful, wife was the principal carer
for her physically disabled husband. She had developed a detailed care
routine. This began each morning with giving him a blanket bath. On
the carer's more harassed mornings, which were not infrequent, this
could seem interminable for the long-suffering husband, as she tended
to forget where she had got to, and 'went back to the top to start again,
just to be on the safe side'. The care assistant had gently remonstrated
with her but had been told bluntly that the wife had learned this way of
caring during her nursing experience, and 'if you know so much, take
him into hospital and they'll do it properly there'.

The extent to which home-care practice, excellent in principle though it is, colludes with such borderline procedures appears to be relatively undocumented, and this topic merits research.

OLDER PEOPLE SHAPING THEIR ENVIRONMENT

In considering environmental influences on behaviour, it is important to recognise a principle of reciprocity. Older people are not necessarily passive recipients of influence, but can shape the responses of the relatively young who have set out to influence *them*. This fascinating phenomenon of reverse behaviour change ('the biter bit'), in which carers find their own activity being altered by a resistant target, was described by Rebok and Hoyer in 1977, but has not yet received the attention it deserves.

A related consideration, also neglected, is that even apparently maladaptive acts in late life can represent attempts to maintain relatively intact functioning, or at least a semblance of it, by a disturbed older person trying to make sense of a confusing world (Garland, 1992).

For example, a new resident at an old people's home scandalises staff. Asked how he is settling in, he replies: 'It's not too bad – down here on the pig farm!' This is interpreted as unequivocal evidence of 'confusion' until examination from a psychological perspective ascertains that as a teenager he had worked unhappily on the family pig farm at his father's insistence, until the business went bankrupt, releasing him to do what he really wanted, but leaving him with a continuing tendency to label any situation in which he felt under duress as 'just like the pig farm'.

Five basic coping styles have been outlined by Kahana and Kahana (1983), based on longitudinal study of old people in institutional care. They list these as: instrumental (to recognise a problem and deal with it directly); intrapsychic (to avoid conflict by changing one's attitude); affective (to release tension by expressing feelings); escapist (to turn to alternative activities); and resigned helplessness. As they illustrate, a resident in an old people's home finding a lack of privacy stressful, may: attempt to establish 'private' territory; come to accept 'it doesn't really matter'; express resentment of the situation; keep on the move to avoid contact; or just give up trying.

OLDER PEOPLE DETERMINING THEIR HEALTH

While much has been made of the malign influence of 'ageism' (see Chapter 13) on public and professional attitudes, we should recognise that older people can be 'ageist' too in their health beliefs and behaviour. The origins of these health attitudes need to be carefully considered. An increasingly cost-conscious National Health Service in Britain is directing more attention towards health promotion, with older people as a priority target. This prospect is stimulating professionals' interest in influencing health-related behaviour.

Johnson (1986) forecasts that this interest will be spurred on by the demands from within the retired population of a rising number of people who will have experienced relative prosperity, support of the welfare state, and the rise of consumerism. A new and more aggressive climate of expectation can be expected to replace the polite acquiescence and minimal expectations to which researchers are currently accustomed (Johnson, 1986, p. 24).

Commenting that surprisingly few studies of health beliefs deal with older people, in spite of their visibility as a high demand group, Ford (1986) points out that the low explanatory power of a health beliefs model in predicting illness behaviour is hardly surprising in view of the complex structure of such behaviour. He suggests:

> The decision to seek medical aid is only one possible outcome in a complex process of assessment and decision-making which is shaped by culture, attitudes, folk medical knowledge, personal biography, influence from social networks, present goals and perceptions of the costs and benefits of entering the 'sick role', as well as by the inherent ambiguity of most symptoms themselves. (Ford, 1986, p. 130)

Although the literature is limited, Ford comments, a few stereotypes can be challenged effectively. For example, old people in general are not heavy users of the health service, but this impression has been given because there is intensive use (by a relatively small proportion). We are only just beginning to learn more about the diversity of health beliefs amongst older age groups and the influence of cohort, gender and ethnicity (see Blaxter, 1990; Sidell, 1993).

Reviewing the use of medicines by older people, Anderson and Cartwright (1986) find that general practitioners tend to lack knowledge about medicines (both prescribed and otherwise) being taken by their older patients. They acknowledge that, until regular review and audit of medicines is universal, not all compliance by patients can be regarded as necessary compliance. These authors see:

> wide scope for research in this field, documenting first who uses what medicines when, and including the use of non-prescribed medicines, and secondly considering the role of some factors, other than the demographic, as influences upon the use of medicines, particularly, perhaps, the meaning and significance of medicine use from the patient's perspective. There is a need to establish the frequency of drug problems in the elderly and to identify the medicines with which these problems are associated: from study of side effects and difficulties in using medicines, to identification of medicines which are not used when they could be helpful, and of other medicines which continue to be used when they are no longer helpful and may be hazardous. (Anderson and Cartwright, 1986, p. 195)

ENVIRONMENTAL REQUIREMENTS FOR INSTITUTIONAL LIVING

Ideally, residential care would cater for individual needs, and promote residents' sense of being in control of their lives, remaining as independent as possible, and being approached as individual persons rather than under the collective label of 'the residents'.

In practice it is inevitable that residential living enforces a degree of conformity, in that an individual's rights and responsibilities have to be weighed against those of the group, and the process of balancing these can involve restrictions on liberty. Finding the right balance between individual and organisational needs can be difficult and Norman's *Rights and Risk* (1980) has been particularly influential in shaping the attitudes of staff towards encouraging relative independence for residents, while recognising that this can entail risk for the more physically frail.

However, as Atherton (1989) suggests, the requirements of institutional living are in practice governed by working myths, 'the set of assumptions that appear to be held by participants in the work of a residential establishment about what they are doing which influence their day-to-day practice' (p. 101). Such myths tend to be based on commonsense theories. They are not necessarily accurate, they are likely to be woven into an institutional fabric of story-telling on the lines of 'this is the way things happen here', with many elements being the product of deeply held 'gut feelings' which can be difficult to express.

If, as Atherton argues, the organisation's need to sustain its working myths is a powerful antagonist lurking in ambush on the battleground between individual and organisational need, researchers and practitioners alike would do well to reconnoitre this sector more thoroughly. These conflicts may be explored in greater detail with regard to the physical and social environments and the characteristics of residents.

Willcocks et al (1987) discuss the relationship between the physical environment and resident and staff behaviour by examining a number of aspects of residential life: privacy, autonomy, negotiability, safety and community integration. Here we consider three examples where physical and social factors interrelate (for more detailed discussion see Gibbs and Sinclair, 1992; Peace, 1993a).

Physical environment

Physical and social factors interrelate frequently. For example, following Sommer and Ross (1958) many papers on environmental issues have underlined the value of changing chair arrangements from round-the-walls rows to clusters in order to promote social interaction. Perhaps because of its intuitive appeal this manipulation probably has been applied more widely than any other in this field. Research emphasis has also moved on to the position of the person in the chair and the extent to which a well-designed chair is a prosthetic aid; and improved standards have been developed on the basis of studies such as that of Finlay et al (1983).

The relationship between resident autonomy and safety is another major issue in residential care, particularly for those residents deemed to be at risk because of their likely disorientation should they 'wander' out of the care setting. The physical environment may be used to maintain such residents through various means, including: locked doors, double-handled doors, and photo-electric circuit with bell or buzzer. Other forms of containment rely on the actions of staff which can be seen as positive or negative. For example: dressing residents in night clothes by day for ease of recognition should they leave; physical restraint, for example in a geriatric chair locked in by a tray; a 'chemical straitjacket' of medication; behaviour modification programmes; activity, exercise and structured day design which features areas of protected space where residents may move in safety; and confident, positive staff attitudes, perceiving in place of 'wandering', understandable and tolerable mobility.

Finally, the residential care setting need not exclude the outside world. Rowles (1981) points out that an important source of stimulation for residents comes through the provision of viewing areas looking out onto foyers, courtyards or entrances, to watch the parade of life. However, requirements of keeping building costs down and of maintaining residents' safety can conflict with the need to offer a rewarding environment, and compromise is needed, since an undue emphasis on custodial care interferes with expression of residents' individual needs (Willcocks et al, 1987).

Social environment

The social environment of institutional settings is commonly equated with regime, an all-embracing term which encompasses the level of structure and rigidity which may characterise the routines and the relationships between staff and residents (Willcocks et al, 1987, p. 12).

Attempts to conceptualise and measure different care environments suffer from the fact that studies are undertaken for different purposes, focus on different features and assess them in different ways. However, notable research has been carried out in North America by Moos who has developed a number of indicators to measure social environment. Lemke and Moos (1986) report on eight of these: comfort, security, staffing levels, staff richness, services, autonomy, control and rapport. These are only modestly correlated, suggesting that the social environment is multi-dimensional and that staffing levels are relatively independent of the other indices. Pincus (Pincus and Wood, 1970) also has developed assessment of social environments, through residents' descriptions of such characteristics as physical features, the kinds of rules, regulations, and programmes, and staff behaviour with residents.

Goldberg and Connelly (1982) in their review of British literature on social care, found little consensus on this topic, but offer a list of positive aspects:

1. flexibility of management practices;
2. individualisation and autonomy for residents;
3. opportunities for privacy;
4. opportunities for social stimulation;
5. communication and interaction with the outside world;
6. social interaction between staff and residents (in addition to instrumental communication);
7. maximum delegation of decision-making to care staff and to residents;
8. good communication channels between staff;
9. a minimum degree of specialization of rules and tasks among staff (Goldberg and Connelly, 1982, pp. 272–273).

In addition other attempts to look at correlates of quality highlight the importance of the leadership offered by the head of home, especially within the independent sector (Gibbs and Sinclair, 1992; Peace, 1993a).

What the research does show is that variation exists 'between' and 'within' settings with regard to aspects of residential life (Booth, 1985). One way of reducing institutional pressures is through the development of group living schemes, breaking down a home of, say, 40 or 50 places into living units of between 8 and 10 residents. Each unit has its own living space, group tasks and domestic activities, maintaining normal living as far as possible. Rothwell, Britton and Woods (1983) found residents in group living more engaged (in constructive activity) and happier, and noted that staff attitudes and expectations became much more positive.

Among those to advocate group living units have been Lipman and Slater (1977), suggesting that such units need to be shielded from care staff by physical barriers (stairs, lobby areas), to reduce excessive staff contact which could erode residents' independence. However, Booth and Phillips (1987), in a comparative study of outcomes of care for residents in traditional regimes and in group living, find only modest differences, not all of which favour the latter, and conclude that group living arrangements have been 'oversold' and promise more than they can deliver. The debate continues.

Resident characteristics

Willcocks et al distinguish the 'resident mix' as a distinctive factor affecting well-being. They define it as 'the characteristics of all the elderly people using the homes either as permanent residents, short-stay residents, or day-attenders, for example their age–sex distribution, and levels of physical and mental impairment' (1987, p. 12).

In the arguments for segregation versus integration of more severely impaired residents, useful facts are in remarkably short supply. For example, it has been estimated that a proportion of 30 per cent of 'confused' residents in any integrated home could be a critical mass, triggering breakdown, and de facto segregation (Evans et al, 1981). However, such a formula would be of little value in prediction for individual cases without specifications for assessing 'confusion' in residents and stability in homes. In an unstable home unused to dealing with mental frailty, even one eccentric resident could be deemed too much (Garland, 1991).

Establishing guidelines for practice

Guidelines for residential care such as *Home Life* (Centre for Policy on Ageing, 1984), the report of the independent review *Residential Care: A Positive Choice* (National Institute for Social Work, 1988), and formulations of good practice in services for people with dementia such as that produced by the King Edward's Hospital Fund for London (King's Fund Centre, 1986), are invaluable aids for structuring thinking on environmental requirements.

Home Life: A Code of Practice for Residential Care is a report of a working party sponsored by the Department of Health and Social Security and convened by the Centre for Policy on Ageing under the chairmanship of Lady Avebury. Although not a mandatory code it forms an important part of the documentation used in the regulation of care settings (see Registered Homes Act, 1984). A wide range of client groups including older people are featured, and among 218 recommendations are five based on research findings (Goldberg and Connelly, 1982), referring specifically to old people: the right of elderly residents to autonomy and choice should always be recognised; the layout, decor and furnishing of the home should be designed to minimise confusion; staff should be trained to understand the needs of mentally and physically frail old people; community support and treatment services should be consulted in the care of mentally ill older people; and physical restraint and control by sedation should not be used.

The King's Fund project paper *Living Well into Old Age* sets out principles of good practice for services for older people with psychiatric disorders, with particular attention to dementia, and relating to support services in the community as well as institutional settings. As the paper recognises, the principles underpinning our existing services are very muddled. They are based on a mixture of government statements, the traditions of the past and day-to-day solutions to problems drawn up by staff. Much of the policy is unwritten (King's Fund Centre, 1986, p. 7).

Five key principles are spelt out: people with dementia have the same human value as anyone else irrespective of their degree of disability or dependence; people with dementia have the same varied human needs as anyone else; people with dementia have the same rights as other citizens; every person with dementia is an individual; people with dementia have the right to forms of support which do not exploit family and friends. In each case the paper proceeds to examine what this means for the individual; the implications for frontline staff and services; how to establish the effectiveness of a service in relation to the principles; and implications for managers and planners in the strategic tasks of service development.

How may such guidelines be translated into practice? Barrowclough and Fleming (1986) suggest goal planning is the key for meeting residents' needs, based on the principles spelt out by Houts and Scott (1976):

1. involve the resident from the beginning;
2. use the resident's strengths to set goals which help with her individual needs;
3. set reasonable goals;
4. spell out the steps necessary to reach each goal; and
5. state clearly what the resident will do, what the staff will do and when you hope to reach each goal.

As Houts and Scott comment, such principles seem obvious, but are often forgotten because residents tend to be seen as passive recipients of care and professional carers are apt to focus on 'problems' which take up so much of their attention that goal-setting is relatively neglected.

During the 1980s many training packs were developed which attempted to promote informed practice in residential settings. Notable examples include: *In Our Care* (Crosbie and Traynor, 1985); 'Over the hill and far away' (Murphy, 1986); *Images of Residential Life* (CESSA, 1986), and *Working with Older People* (The Open University, 1990). In recent years the *Caring in Homes Initiative* set up to pursue some of the recommendations of the Wagner Report has also tackled important areas such as: information needs; community integration; staff training and quality assurance (DoH, 1992b).

MEASURING QUALITY OF LIFE

This multi-dimensional concept involves both relatively objective variables such as health and socio-economic status, and relatively subjective ones such as life satisfaction and self-esteem. Davies and Knapp (1981) review the status of both kinds of assessment in care of older people.

In recognition of the complexity of successfully identifying a global index of quality of life, researchers are seeking improved definition and measurement of component variables, as Fillenbaum (1984) demon-strates. However, as Booth (1985) comments, not only do many of the instruments which purport to measure subjective well-being need further development, but the effects of apathy and undue compliance undermine older people's reporting.

Attempts to take a more objective approach, by measuring outcomes such as morbidity or dependency which may be held to indirectly indicate subjective well-being have run into difficulty because of the complexity of diagnosis and behaviour rating, and the elastic nature of the concept of 'dependency'. Walker (1982b) reminds us that this is used in at least four different ways: life-cycle dependency, physical and psychological dependency, political dependency, and economic and financial dependency (see also Chapter 11). Woods and Britton (1985) view measuring quality of life in residential care as an increasingly sophisticated process, involving not just discussions with staff, but also gathering of residents' views, careful observation of day-to-day happen-ings, and analysis of discrepancies between values enshrined in official policy and those expressed in actual procedures. Such a multimethod approach is supported by Kellaher et al (1990, p. 115) who point out that 'it is no longer seen as sufficient to measure gross "satisfaction" levels amongst older people as users of services'. They demonstrate how evaluative research gains from triangulation, combining and contrasting data, perspectives, theory or method, to obtain a clearer understanding of what happens in delivery and effectiveness of services.

While a high level of engagement of residents in activity that is apparently purposeful has been said to characterise a good-quality residential setting (Jenkins et al, 1977), Woods and Britton would seek to understand the meaning of activity for each resident, and see little to choose between enforced inactivity and enforced activity. They con-clude that because methodologies for assessing engagement vary considerably, for the great majority of studies direct comparisons cannot be made. One common factor emerges: 'Doing nothing appears to be the norm, whether in terms of proportion of total time, or of observations, or of residents present' (Woods and Britton, 1985, p. 260). They report that the average older person in residential care, 'has less than eight minutes per hour social contact, mostly with other residents. Contact with nursing staff will be largely related to physical care' (Woods and Britton, 1985, p. 263).

However, quality of life may be enhanced, even in such unpromising settings. Baltes and Baltes (1986) offer useful perspectives on increasing older people's feelings of being in control of what happens to them, through, for example, encouraging residents to exercise choice in events of daily life. A well-planned example of a project which put increased self-determination into practice is reported by Dixon (1991). As already stressed in Chapter 5, maintaining a sense of control over one's own life appears to be an important feature of adjustment to ageing.

As Willcocks et al (1987) make clear, advocacy of 'normalisation' as a philosophy of care is required.

> The aim would be to devise a form of care that old people and their carers might choose on the basis of the particular balance of security and freedoms that can be achieved in a residential setting. This involves three sets of assumptions: first, that responsible authorities will have a view to the heterogeneity of the population they are serving and develop, accordingly, services that are different in kind but equivalent in status for different needs and different aspirations; second, that sufficient information will be provided to clients in a manner that enables them to negotiate the optimum package of care for their personal requirements after weighing up the 'gains' and 'losses' inherent in the various options; and third, that old people will be encouraged and assisted to work their way through this gains and losses equation so that they are in a position to exercise real consumer choice (Willcocks et al, 1987, p. 144).

DISTURBED BEHAVIOUR OR DISTURBED ENVIRONMENT?

Referrals to a health psychologist concerning 'disturbed', 'difficult' or 'challenging' behaviour of older people receiving health care occur under a variety of headings: absence of purposeful behaviour; 'aggression'; anxiety; 'attention seeking'; 'confusion'; death and dying; depression; incontinence; pain complaining; passivity; sexuality (disinhibited); sleep dissatisfaction; and 'wandering' (Garland, 1992).

A detailed discussion of these will not be offered here, but it must be noted that health care settings can be disturbing in their own right offering overwhelming environmental challenges, and that health care professionals in tending to locate the source of the problem in the 'disturbed' older person can lose sight of disturbing environmental factors that need be alleviated.

Psychological approaches have been used extensively as environmental interventions with older people who have a dementing process and their carers (Jones and Miesen, 1992). Some of the approaches used are briefly outlined below.

Reality orientation (RO), which is used more generally in residential care than in the community, is described by Holden and Woods (1988). The term covers a range of environmental features designed to orient intellectually impaired older people verbally and behaviourally, so they can be made aware of what is happening around them, and use this information in their daily lives. Informal or 24-hour RO is used throughout the day in staff–resident interactions, and patients are encouraged to use memory aids, signs, and notices for orientation. The advantages of such cues are demonstrated by Hanley (1981). In so-called 'classroom RO' small groups of about four to six residents engage in supervised structured activities and discussion with cues, prompts, reinforcement of approximations to improved orientation, and with-drawal of attention from confused behaviour.

Reality orientation prescribes distinct staff attitudes to be adopted for different types of patient: active friendliness for the apathetic; passive friendliness for the frightened or suspicious; matter-of-fact for the manipulative or maladjusted; kind and firm for the depressed; and no-demand (other than to stay, not to harm others and to take medication) for the angry.

Many researchers have pointed out that RO's main recommendation could be that it is a philosophy of care which gives staff encouragement to communicate with patients and a rationale for doing so. In view of the aversive nature of many demented patients (Bromley, 1978), such an incentive is particularly important.

Recently, other approaches to interacting with demented people have been recommended, including 'reminiscence', which makes use of the fact that a confused person's more remote memories can appear to be relatively well preserved (Norris, 1987), and 'validation therapy' which encourages the worker to recognise the validity of the emotions the older person is expressing (Feil, 1992).

Cognitive-behavioural approaches have also been widely used in health care settings (Garland, 1992). A key concept is that much of our thinking and our overt behaviour operates on our environment to produce consequences which shape our subsequent thinking and behaviour. If an activity is followed by consequences that we value, these are reinforcers (making it more likely that the activity will be repeated). Consequences that we do not value, do not act as reinforcers and may make the activity less likely to recur. Activity also is shaped by its antecedents – environmental cues or triggers that may themselves be modified in order to modify the subsequent activity.

ABC analysis – a thorough review of antecedents, behaviour and consequences – is an invaluable tool in working with older people in any setting where they are the focus of concern and where a wider, systemic view needs to be taken if intervention is to address the real issues in a given situation. The understanding and management of continence is a good example here (Smith and Smith, 1987).

MEASURING CHANGE

Ideally, the effectiveness of any attempt to increase well-being of an older person through enhancing their environment needs to be demonstrated by a reliable and valid assessment procedure which samples behaviour either directly or by reasonable inference. Yet as we have seen measuring 'quality of life' is not a simple task.

A wide range of tests, techniques and systems of interview and observation has been applied with this population, and many of these have been devised for use with older people and standardised for them. There is no lack of painstaking effort to develop measures of change which are sensitive to altered functioning, and which possess a substantial degree of ecological validity in that they are credible for older people who recognise them as tapping aspects of behaviour acknowledged as relevant for their daily living (Kendrick, 1982; Rabbitt, 1982a).

Nevertheless, there are substantial difficulties in the interpretation of such measures. Older people can have a variety of health problems appearing in a fluctuating way to affect results; they can be exposed to a variety of ongoing treatments to deal with these, so it may be well-nigh impossible to determine the effectiveness of a particular environmental change in influencing behaviour; barriers to communication tend to be experienced more frequently; and the 'old' old are not well served, there being relatively few procedures with well-developed norms sufficiently extended to take account of age-related performance after 80.

CONCLUSIONS

While the topic of environment and behaviour is indeed a vast one, and has suffered as much as any area of psychology from the discipline's historic tendency to engage in piecemeal and uncoordinated research, targets for improved theory and practice can be singled out as:

1. increased understanding of older people's experience of everyday environments;
2. more comprehensive analysis of the role of coping styles and health care beliefs in determining psychological adjustment;
3. development of more flexible multivariate approaches to assessing behaviour and environments; and
4. more effective means of intervening in service systems and support networks to promote 'social role valorisation' so that the rights and responsibilities of older people and their carers are respected not only in theory but also in practice.

SUMMARY

While models (based largely on the study of residential care), for understanding the interaction between behaviour and environment are in place, a more thorough understanding of the influence of environmental factors is still needed.

Progress is being made in establishing how older people shape their surroundings and view their health maintenance needs. Research into staff and resident perception of institutional living has identified positive options, and has encouraged the development of guidelines for practice, including staff training and goal planning.

Health psychology has contributed to improved understanding of environmental influences on 'disturbed' behaviour.

Reality orientation, cognitive therapy, anxiety management, systemic intervention, groupwork and behaviour management offering a 'menu' for individualised care are among psychological interventions available to those working with older people whose behaviour is disturbed.

While 'quality of life' is difficult to evaluate, interest is being maintained in developing normalisation and enhancing experience of residential care by, for example, encouraging residents to exercise greater choice. Awareness of need for more sensitive measurement of change and of interactions within systems is increasing.

FURTHER READING

Garland, J. (1991) *Making Residential Care Feel Like Home. Enhancing the Quality of Life for Older People*. Winslow Press, Bicester,

Woods, R.T. and Britton, P.G. (1985) *Clinical Psychology with the Elderly*. Croom Helm, London.

7

DEATH, DYING AND BEREAVEMENT

Moyra Sidell[1]

In western societies most people can reasonably expect to live out their span, and a bit more, and death has become associated very much with old age. We tend to operate with notions of 'timely' and 'untimely' deaths. The death of an 15-year-old evokes epithets such as 'tragic' 'wasteful' or 'premature', whereas the death of an 85-year-old is likely to attract phrases such as 'had a good innings', 'died in the fullness of time' 'lived to a ripe old age' (Hockey, 1990, p. 37). Death has become increasingly unfamiliar to younger people who, in spite of seeing a myriad of media images of death, are unlikely to be touched by the death of someone close until they reach middle age.

Most deaths in Britain occur at older ages – 79 per cent in 1986 were of people aged 65 and over, and 55 per cent were of people over 75 years old (Seale, 1993, p. 46). This contrasts with a life expectancy in England in the Middle Ages of 33 years and 41 years in the nineteenth century. Combined with the fact that only one in four people die at home this means that death is simply outside most people's practical experience. Indeed western societies have been characterised as 'death denying' and death named the last 'taboo' (Ariès, 1981; Gorer, 1965). Others disagree and the claim has generated a great deal of debate and counter-argument (Walter, 1993). There remains, however, a strong case for asserting that our society is wary of death, people are uneasy and embarrassed in the face of death, find it hard to approach dying and bereaved people and often go to great lengths to avoid them. Death is marginalised and the categories 'living' and 'dying' are kept rigidly separate (Hockey, 1990). This has profound implications for older people and for older people who are terminally ill or who are bereaved.

This chapter will begin with a discussion of societal attitudes to ageing and death before going on to explore individual older people's attitudes to the prospect of losing their own life and the lives of those they love and have loved. As Britain is a multi-cultural society, the impact of religious and cultural beliefs and practices on the way that older people

[1] In writing this chapter the author would like to acknowledge the assistance of Donna Dickenson, Jeanne Katz, Malcolm Johnson and Alyson Peberdy, members of the Open University course team for K260, Death and Dying.

approach death will be explored. The subject of euthanasia and the 'living will' is one which has received a lot of attention in recent years with arguments for and against legislation. Current thinking on the subject and the possible effects any legislation might have on the experience of older people will be assessed. All of these issues will be addressed in the context of the care available to older people who are dying and finally in the way that older people experience bereavement.

SOCIETAL ATTITUDES TO AGEING AND DYING

It was Geoffrey Gorer in his *Death, Grief and Mourning*, written in 1965, who claimed that death was a 'taboo' subject in our society leading to avoidance, repression and denial of the fact of death. He claimed that alongside this avoidance of natural forms of death our mass media was obsessed with violent death. Gorer's thesis has been developed further by the French historian Phillipe Ariès whose extensive research into attitudes towards death in western Christian cultures over the last thousand years indicates that in the twentieth century death has come to be characterised by silence, denial and dishonesty. He argued that death became progressively concealed: first by talk about illness (with the implication of cure) and disgust at the 'dirtiness' of death; second, by locating dying people in hospitals away from public view; and finally by the regulation and organisation of death by doctors for whom death is a failure (K260 Course, Open University, 1993, Workbook 1, p. 303).

Two British sociologists have recently engaged with this issue, David Armstrong and Tony Walter. Armstrong (1987) believes that there is not so much a silence about death but a new way of speaking about it and a preoccupation with the dead body. This is largely a legal and medical phenomenon and very much connected to the introduction of a legal requirement that deaths should be certified. The cause of death must be given and it is significant that on the occasion of a death it is the doctor who is first summoned. Death is defined as a medical event: the power to declare that death has occurred and to say what has caused it lies in the hands of the medical profession. We take for granted the notion that deaths are certified in terms of a physical cause, death is a physical event. We use the term 'social death' to describe someone who is unconscious and physically functioning, perhaps with the aid of medical technology, but not socially functioning. This term is also used to describe severe forms of dementia. In other times and in other cultures death is attributed to the will of God or to emotional or moral causes. In western culture death is not so much denied as medicalised.

Walter (1993) argues that the last twenty years has seen a proliferation of literature on the subject of death and dying. Whilst accepting that the death denial thesis resonates with the experience of dying and bereaved people, Walter believes that it is an over-simplification and suggests various revisions. He argues that it is not modern society as a whole which is death denying but certain occupational groups within it. He includes in these groups the medical profession, for whom death represents failure, and mass media personnel whose work is so bound up with youth and glamour that death becomes an embarrassment (Walter, 1993, p. 38–9). These two groups influence the images we receive about death and dying and the medical care available.

Walter also questions the belief that death denial is only a modern phenomenon. He refers to the work of Ernest Becker who believed that denial of death is not so much a modern condition as it is the human condition. In Becker's view the fear of death is, and always has been, universal and potentially overwhelming. People are caught in an existential paradox too painful to contemplate.

> Man [sic] is literally split in two: he has an awareness of his own splendid uniqueness in that he sticks out of nature with a towering majesty and yet he goes back into the ground a few feet in order blindly and dumbly to rot and disappear forever. It is a terrifying dilemma. (Becker, 1973, p. 28)

Becker sees no rational way to cope with this overwhelming fear. Walter suggests that modern society deals with death by elevating 'youth, education, and progress' (Walter, 1993, p. 41). Such a move is clearly bad news for older people, death is not so much a forbidden topic but a hidden one, making the impact of death less on society (Blauner, 1966). Others have argued that both death and older people have been marginalised precisely because of the association of death with old age. Society is unable to cope with either. Older people are segregated in order to make their dying unobtrusive (Berdes, 1978). Yet others have used much stronger language. Michael Kearl (1989), writing from an American perspective, claims that older people have become 'the social shock absorbers of death and contemporary death lepers' (p. 93). 'They are disengaged from many of their social roles to minimise the disruptions caused by their deaths' (p. 95). This puts an interesting slant on Cumming and Henry's disengagement theory which is discussed fully in Chapter 2. Kearl argues that older people are disengaged involuntarily in order for the rest of society to avoid facing up to its own mortality. For Cumming and Henry older people voluntarily disengage. Disengagement is therefore both functional for society and consistent with the wishes of older people. Society and older people themselves are then prepared for death. Disengagement theory has many critics (see Chapter 2, p. 32). Activity theory (Havighurst, 1963), in direct contrast to disengagement theory, claims that many older people remain active members of society until they die.

These overarching theories about 'the elderly' do not do justice to the great diversity of experience to be found amongst older people nor the influence of gender, class or ethnicity. But real concerns about the position of older people in our society remain. Ageism and ageist attitudes have been well documented and there are some indications of gerontophobia in response to the demographic changes in the age distribution of western society. Whether this is wholly or even in part related to anxieties about death remains at the level of speculation. But gerontologists have been at pains to dissociate ageing and death in order to counter these negative connotations. Indeed, the first edition of this volume did not contain a chapter on death and dying. Between 1967 and 1980 only forty out of the 2600 articles printed in the *Gerontologist* and the *Journal of Gerontology* dealt with aspects of death and dying. Does this amount to a collusion with a death-denying society? Or is it an attempt to dissociate death from old age, to concentrate on life for, as Simone de Beauvoir claims:

> The truth of the matter is that the idea of death's coming closer is mistaken. Death is neither near nor far: it is not. Over all living beings, whatever their age, there hangs an inescapable exterior fate: in no case is there a set moment at which this fate will strike. . . It is not correct to speak of a relationship with death: the fact is that the old man [sic], like all other men, has a relationship with life and with nothing else. (1972, p. 492)

There is a real dilemma. If death is denied then people will be without adequate guidance on how to support dying and bereaved people. This was the concern of Norbert Elias who wrote a moving account of *The Loneliness of the Dying*. In it he writes of: 'our inability to give dying people the help and affection they are most in need of when parting from other human beings, just because another's death is a reminder of our own' (Elias, 1985, p. 10). Elias was concerned about the institutionalisation and medicalisation of death and dying. He believed that we cope with our anxieties about death by turning it into a medical condition and institutionalising those about to die whilst at the same time providing only limited financial support to these institutions.

Death in contemporary western society has then had a 'bad press', dehumanised and characterised by 'repression, isolation, medicalisation and bureaucratisation' (Prior, 1989, p. 5). This is perhaps something of an overstatement. It does not represent the variety of experience in relation to death and dying and it tells us little about the attitudes and beliefs of the large numbers of people from different ethnic and religious groups who live and fully participate in this society. Neither does it give credit to the work of the the hospice movement over the last thirty years, which has sought to relieve the pain and suffering of dying people both physically and emotionally. The AIDS epidemic has also focused the attention of many people on the needs of dying people. Although proportionately few older people die in hospices, and AIDS is a disease of relative youth, the lessons learnt about how to improve the quality of life for dying people apply to dying people of all ages. Still, there remains disquiet about the way in which many older people die (Hanvey, 1989). What do we know about how older people themselves perceive death and how they approach the prospect of losing their own lives?

INDIVIDUAL OLDER PEOPLE'S PERSPECTIVE ON DEATH AND DYING

In Chapter 5 Peter Coleman reviewed the literature on adjustment to death and dying and awareness of finitude in older people. The evidence he reviews (Munnichs, 1966, 1992; Kalish and Reynolds, 1976; Cameron et al, 1973; Lieberman and Tobin, 1983; Schneider, 1987), suggests that older people 'think and talk about death' more than other age groups, they 'speak about it calmly and without anxiety' and in general 'death is thought to be less of a problem for the old'. Much of this evidence is in tune with disengagement theory and Kubler-Ross's final stage of preparedness for death, acceptance. Elisabeth Kubler-Ross (1970) has made an intensive study of the attitudes of dying people to death. Her work has become very influential in understanding people's reactions to their own impending death. She identified four other stages: first denial (no, it can't happen to me), then anger when the initial shock wears off (it's not fair, why me?), bargaining is the middle stage, attempting to make some sort of deal either with God or fate for an extension of life, depression usually follows when it becomes clear that there will not be a recovery and the person is overwhelmed with sadness. The fifth, and final stage, acceptance, represents the end of the struggle, the person is letting go and the depression lifts although acceptance is not necessarily a happy state; it may be almost void of feelings. Although it was not Kubler-Ross's intention that her model should tell people how they ought to feel, it has in fact sometimes been used or understood in that way, with the expectation that a dying person needs to make 'progress' through the stages and not 'get stuck' in a particular response such as denial or anger, even when that is a response typical of his or her personality. The emotional responses of people to the prospect of their own death may not proceed in accordance with Kubler-Ross's model and they may experience feelings other than those she identifies. But it is the final stage of acceptance which is perhaps the most contentious. Do dying people invariably reach that stage and should they be encouraged to do so? The Welsh poet Dylan Thomas urges rage and anger at the prospect of death in his famous lines:

> Do not go gently into that good night,
> Old age should burn and rave at close of day;
> Rage, rage against the dying of the light.

From the evidence reviewed by Coleman in Chapter 5, it would seem that most older people do not do as Dylan Thomas would have them do and, on the contrary, seemed to have reached some stage of acceptance. But do we need to be cautious about taking such a comfortable picture of the relationship of older people to their own and their loved ones' death? Coleman also refers to clinical observation which suggests that some older people do experience anxiety at the prospect of losing their own lives.

The most obvious problem is that of acknowledging diversity in older people's attitudes. Do men and women approach death in the same way and what is the influence of religious and cultural beliefs? What do individual older people say? What qualitative evidence is available to answer such questions as: do older people think and talk about death a great deal? Do they accept death with equanimity, with relief or with anxiety?

Awareness of finitude

As Coleman noted, the British evidence is sparse but the subject of death and dying is sometimes aired in biographical studies of older people. Thompson et al (1990) asked their respondents: 'Do you ever think about dying?' and contrary to the evidence surveyed by Coleman they found that typical responses were: 'Not really. . .', 'I don't think much about it', 'Don't give it a thought'. Such statements do not necessarily represent denial of death but could indicate a greater familiarity with death. In a study of the health experiences of older women which I conducted (Sidell, 1991), I found myself reticent about bringing up the subject of death and resorted euphemistically to questions such as 'How do you view the future?' Most of the older women showed no such reticence and raised the subject spontaneously with such matter-of-fact statements as: 'Well I know I'm nearer death, you are nearer death when you get older.' Many found that they could not ignore death because of the loss of their contempories:

> There's a woman I used to play with when I was a kid. Now she was 83 or 4 I think. She was buried yesterday. Another woman along here, she was 79 I think, she was another pal. Now she died in May.

Others found that Christmas time brought thoughts of death to the fore, as one woman told me when she went down her Christmas card list '[I] do my book at Christmas and it's crossing out such a lot.'

One study which gives us a rich source of insight into the attitudes of older people to death and dying is that carried out by Rory Williams (1990) amongst older Aberdonians, looking specifically at attitudes to death and illness. He stresses not only the diversity of attitudes found but the inherent contradictions not just between people but within individuals. He cautions against 'supposing that individuals exemplify one coherent pattern of thought' and reminds us that 'contradiction is as frequent as coherence'. He does, however, pick out trains of thought and identifies certain recurring themes.

Many of his respondents showed an awareness of the nearness of death. This was based to some extent on the Biblical 'span', but mostly it was in relation to the death of people with whom they identified. This defined a new stage of life as this couple explained:

Wife: Practically a' wir [our] folk are deid. The amount o' folk that's died since
we came to the town, it's been terrible.
Husband: Och, well, I suppose it's just the fact we're getting older wirselves,
and wir friends are getting older, and that's that. Coming tae that stage.
Wife: Just tae that stage, as you say.

(quoted in Williams, 1990, p. 65)

Williams reflects on this notion of 'a time to die' drawing out two
important ramifications, that people 'ought to die only when old' and
that 'they ought to die before they were too old'.

This acceptance that there is a natural time to die was definitely a
moral expectation: the old should go before the young and make way for
them. Williams identifies another way of contemplating the expectation
of death – that was a notion of individual destiny or 'your time'. This
was not age related but it was accompanied by a need to be prepared for
death. This inner readiness was spiritual as well as practical as
illustrated in the following conversation:

Wife: Well of course we should always be prepared, this is the thing – we
should always be. There's another question.
Husband: It all depends. Preparation spiritually – but then you need
preparation for your family too. Another thing that should be done
beforehand is all your will and affairs all sorted out beforehand – but how
many people do that?
Wife: There's always a reticence in dealing with that. They think that it's a
foreboding, that it hastens it on, but it doesn't. A cousin of Hamish's lost
his mother and his sister within a very short time and sadly he went himself
within a couple of years, the same trouble. But I always remember what he
said: when he was left alone he said he was going to prepare, have
everything in order, prepare for going and continue living. And he did so,
and forgot about it; did all his preparations, forgot about it and then went
on living.

(quoted in Williams, 1990, p. 96–7)

Although theoretically 'your time' could come at any age, an
awareness of the statistical probability that death occurs in old age
meant that the moral imperative to be prepared lay mostly on older
people. This resonates with Erikson's stages of life theory of personality
development which is discussed in Chapter 2. In the last stage of life the
task is to achieve 'ego integrity', to have found meaning in one's life as it
comes to its end. Perceiving one's life as meaningless leads to despair
and a sense of failure because 'the time is now short, too short for the
attempt to start another life and to try out alternate roads to integrity'
(Erikson, 1963, pp. 268–9). Butler (1963) found from his clinical
observations that many older people engage in reminiscence. This life-
review process, which is discussed in Chapter 5, represents an attempt
to make sense of one's life as death approaches, to survey and try to
reintegrate past conflicts: 'Such reorganisation of past experience may
provide a more valid picture, giving new and significant meanings to
one's life; it may also prepare one for death, mitigating one's fears'
(Butler, 1963, p. 68).

The perspectives of Erikson and Butler have been very influential in understanding the processes of ageing and dying and critics have mainly focused on claims of universality (Marshall, 1980). An awareness of finitude and the acceptance of death does not necessarily indicate that the process is free from fear and anxiety or that it enhances personal well-being as Coleman noted in Chapter 5. A 74-year-old woman quoted in *Ourselves Growing Older* (Shapiro, 1989) indicated that fears can lurk behind the intellectual acceptance of death. She said: 'Intellectually, I'm very glib about it, but in my gut I can't accept that one day I won't be here' (quoted in Shapiro, 1989, p. 555). Although many of my interviewees seemed to accept the inevitability of death with equanimity others, whilst not exactly 'raging against the dying of the light', were nevertheless not too happy about it such as an 84-year-old woman who said:

> I love life, that's why I'm so worried about it [death], I don't want – you see in my bones we cling to it. We cling on, who wants to die? I love life, I don't want to go, I want to go on, but I'd like to be more happy.

She could be described as one of the 'activists' described by Keith (1979) and discussed in Chapter 5, who were so actively engaged with life that they were loath to part with it. Keith's 'positivists' on the other hand were those who felt that their lives had been satisfying and fulfilled and were 'ready' to die. When they reviewed their lives they found meaning and order as did this woman: 'I have lived life fully and enjoyed it greatly, which makes it easier to consider bowing out than if you feel that you have missed out on a lot' (Shapiro, 1989, p. 556). Some people even find an acceptance of death can give a new dimension to life:

> I feel a greater awareness of a mystery and beauty in life since I have accepted death as a personal eventuality for me. I don't remember exactly when that awareness came. Before then, I had thought of death 'out there', and now I know that one day it will be a reality for me. Eventually I am going to die. In a way, that has released me for more vivid living. (A 78-year-old woman, quoted in Shapiro, 1989, p. 555)

Awareness of death can evoke different emotions in different older people and we need to remember Williams's warning that it can evoke contradictory emotions within one individual older person. Nor are a person's attitudes and feelings necessarily consistent; events and circumstances can bring about different reactions. However, in reviewing the literature Marshall maintains that there 'is the general tendency for the fear of death to diminish with increasing age' (1980, p. 78).

While fear of death is expressed by only a minority of older people, fears of dying and the manner of their actual death are frequently mentioned. Typical of many in my own study was one 70-year-old woman who said:

> I'm much more afraid of what's going to happen to me between now and the day I die. That's the thing I've got to worry about. After I'm dead somebody else will worry about it . . . No, I think the deepseated anxiety is, am I going

to become incontinent, dotty, not able to communicate, and a burden? Those
are the things that really worry me. If I could die with a bit of dignity and not
having taken up too much of other people's time, I would be happy. If I had
some guarantee of that I would be fine.

This sentiment was echoed by some of the respondents in Williams's
and Thompson et al's studies. Williams identified notions of 'good' and
'bad' deaths. Good deaths were one of two types. There were either
those who, like Keats wanted to 'cease upon the midnight with no pain'
– a quick, easy, tranquil death, or those who wanted to be cared for by
friends and family, reunited with loved ones, to experience a proper
leave-taking. This latter type of death was thought to be better for those
left behind. Bad deaths were described as prolonged when the
emotional and physical resources of kin became stretched to a point
where the dying person is a 'burden', a 'nuisance' or has no dignity, or
where he or she is either suffering and in pain or in an unaware state,
described as a 'vegetable'. This relates very much to the idea that there is
a right time to die – being too old or taking too long to die were equally
bad. These attitudes were tested by Williams in relation to controlling
the time of death and we will elaborate on them later in this chapter in a
discussion of euthanasia.

Unfortunately Williams does not address the issue of gender in his
otherwise very thoughtful analysis. Do men and women approach
death differently? In the absence of any reliable empirical evidence
Nicky James has tried to tease out what these differences might be
(James, 1993) She points out that through the lifespan men and women
have different relationships to death, both in terms of their experience
and in terms of their different role expectations. Men are statistically
more likely to die at younger ages than women. Between the ages of 15
and 44 years much of this difference is accounted for by deaths from
AIDS, accidents, injury and poisoning. James characterises male deaths
as external due to 'outside' causes, a proportion of which will be death
by violence. This suggests that boys take more risks than girls and this is
encouraged in the roles ascribed to males and females (Kastenbaum,
1977). Archer (1989) has suggested that much of this is a residue from
the need to prepare for a combat role. James goes on to suggest that
women's relationship to death is more internal and is based on women's
reproductive capacity and the nurturing roles ascribed to them. The
integral nature of life and death and the tenuous boundaries between
them means that women's psyche is intimately bound up with both life
and death which can be interpreted and understood 'inside' them. With
the breaking down to some extent of gendered roles this analysis may
not hold true for future generations. But our present cohort of older
people have certainly experienced the effects of a gendered division of
paid and domestic work and the reality of men going to war.
Unfortunately, the question we do not have the answer to is whether
death is more or less fearful and threatening if perceived of as 'outside'

rather than 'inside'. This is a very difficult question to answer because of a range of intervening variables, perhaps the most important of which is the beliefs that people hold.

CULTURAL AND RELIGIOUS BELIEFS

Attitudes to death and dying, notions of good and bad deaths, and fears of death and dying are influenced by religious and cultural beliefs and practices. Belief in an afterlife does seem to take the 'sting' out of death for many older people with the hope of being reunited with loved ones. Those in my study who had a religious faith did derive comfort from it. And one of the respondents in Thompson et al's study who expressed a fear of death associated this with a lack of faith: 'I'm frightened of it. I worry about it, 'cos I don't think I've got any faith, you see. I mean, you know, to me death is that, that's the end of it' (quoted in Thompson et al, 1990, p. 135).

Jung sees a belief in an afterlife as the only hope of coping with fears about death and positively prescribes this in order to make the second half of life bearable:

> As a physician I am convinced that it is hygienic – if I may use the word – to discover in death a goal towards which one can strive; and that shrinking away from it is something unhealthy and abnormal which robs the second half of life of its purpose. I therefore consider the religious teaching of a life hereafter consonant with the standpoint of psychic hygiene. (Jung, 1972, p. 129)

Freud took the opposite view. Belief in an afterlife, or ideas of immortality, are just as much a denial of death as is an unwillingness to think and talk about death. Humanists believe that if death is seen as an end rather than a transition then it is life and its quality which becomes the important issue. Humanists therefore put great emphasis on the importance of human linkages and interactions. Death can only be described as 'good' if it comes at the end of a long and satisfying life and then there is nothing to be feared in nothingness.

Many people have a sense of immortality but do not subscribe to a definite religious belief in an afterlife. Lifton and Olson (1974) suggest that there are five basic forms of a sense of immortality which can be held separately or in various combinations: biological, creative, natural, experiential and theological.

The biological form means living on through one's offspring. Creative immortality is a sense that we continue through works of teaching, painting, writing and research. Natural immortality lies in the continuity of matter, a sense of constant recycling of plants and animals. The concept of experiential immortality is more obscure. It lies in transcending ordinary life and time through music, art, dance, athletics or love, experiencing a form of other-worldly ecstasy. Theological immortality is the belief in an afterlife based on religious conviction.

According to two sample surveys, one conducted in five counties in England and the other in Nottinghamshire, about half the population of England hold a belief in some form of immortality, about a quarter definitely do not and the other quarter are keeping their options open (Davies, 1991). Of the believers in Davies's studies 25 per cent believed in bodily resurrection and 10 per cent in reincarnation. Although belief in an afterlife is likely to be influenced by religious tradition many people hold some notion of immortality without subscribing to a particular religion. In an Italian study it was found that whilst 80 per cent of the respondents were practising Roman Catholics only 37 per cent believed in an afterlife (Toscani et al, 1991).

Most of the world's major religions hold some belief in an afterlife but these beliefs are always open to interpretation. There is a general feeling that by providing a framework for death and dying certain cultures ensure that support for dying people is available through kin or wider community networks but we have very little evidence on whether this is in fact the case. In a multi-cultural society we need to know something about the various religious traditions on which people's attitudes to death and dying are based if we are to be able to understand, communicate with and support dying and bereaved people.

Christianity, still the dominant religion in British society, is ambiguous about the precise nature of life after death and beliefs have changed over time. Of course there are different versions of Christianity. Literal meanings of heaven and hell are held less firmly now than in the past and are subject to a great deal of debate within the churches. The Christian understanding of death originated in a Jewish context but eternal life can be found through the death and resurrection of Jesus. As death approaches some Christians may wish for prayers and anointing with oil by a minister or priest and when death is imminent a priest or minister might be called in. Many Christians may wish to receive communion which will include some form of repentance and forgiveness and prayers of commendation may also be said. Christians can be buried or cremated.

British people who are practising Muslims will hold attitudes to and expectations of death and dying based on the teachings of the Qur'an. Death belongs to God and God determines its time and circumstances. Death must be accepted because it is the will of God. Life is a time of probation and at the final judgement a person will be faced with all their words and deeds. The dying person and the dead body should be treated in certain ways because it is to be restored on the Day of Judgement. As death approaches other Muslims from the family and local community gather round the dying person to make their peace with the dying person and to join in prayer and recite verses of the Qur'an. If possible the dying person should face towards Mecca. At the point of death the Declaration of Faith (*Shahada*) is said. After death the body should be kept covered and ritually washed by another Muslim of the same sex. Non-Muslims should not touch the body and health workers must use disposable gloves if this is necessary. Post-mortems are disliked and Muslims are always buried.

Christianity and Islam are connected by a common source, the Jewish scriptures. However, the continuation of the Jewish people and the importance of this world remain very central to the Jewish faith. A major theme within the Jewish understanding of death is the affirmation of affinity. For this reason a Jewish person should not be left alone as they die. A Rabbi may be called in to join in prayer and facilitate the recitation of the Confession on a death bed and Jews present should recite psalms and when death occurs, the Declaration of Faith or *Shema*. As with Muslims post-mortems are disliked and non-Jewish people should handle the body as little as possible. The Jewish burial society will perform the ritual wash. Orthodox Jews are always buried but some less observant Jews are cremated.

Although Christian, Muslim and Jewish faiths have different interpretations of resurrection, they do not believe in reincarnation. Elements of this belief can be traced to Buddhism, and the Hindu and Sikh religions. Buddhism, which has many different forms, has no real sense of heaven or hell but a strong belief that the dead are not wholly extinguished. Death is not extinction because there is continuity and consequence. Life is very much a preparation for death and for that reason the state of mind in which one dies is important to the kind of rebirth that will follow. A dying person needs peace and quiet to allow for meditation and the ideal is to die in a fully conscious and calm state of mind. A monk or religious teacher should be invited to chant passages from the scriptures to encourage this state of mind. There are no special requirements relating to the care of the body and Buddhists can be buried or cremated.

It is Hinduism which has the strongest sense of reincarnation. The true aim of life is to free the self to be with the god Krishna. It takes many 'lives' to free the self and unfreed selves are reborn repeatedly until they reach this state of godliness. A soul may be reborn as a human or animal depending on its moral state. The family should be present at a death and read from the Hindu holy books. A dying Hindu should be given Ganges water and the sacred Tulsi leaf in the mouth. A person should die with the name of God being recited. Failure to perform these rituals is thought to be bad for the dead as well as the remaining family.

Sikhs also believe in reincarnation and indeed Sikhism grew out of Hinduism and is in many ways similar except that Sikhism aspires to egalitarianism and renounces the Hindu caste system. Sikhs are required to prepare for death and live their lives in constant readiness for death. Ideally, Sikhs should die surrounded by family and friends who recite from the Sikh holy book and they should die with the name of God being recited and holy Amrit water in the mouth. Sikhs wear the five Ks at all times. These are symbols of their faith and should not be removed after death. Hindus and Sikhs are always cremated.

Many of these religious customs and practices have been adapted to suit life in Britain and we should always bear in mind that there is likely to be a degree of flexibility in the way that people apply and interpret their religious principles. But it is useful to have some understanding of these different customs, especially when we come to discuss the actual care of dying people later in this chapter.

It is the case that the greater part of the population of Britain does not belong to any religious group. We are a secular society although many people use the rituals of the established church to mark the major transitions of life, birth, marriage and death. We are not allowed simply to bury someone in the back garden or under a favourite tree and until recently there have been few models on how to bury someone without resorting to a religious framework. The British Humanist Society, mindful of the expressed wish of many people not to be involved with any religious tradition, have published a guide on how to conduct a funeral, *Funerals without God* (Willson, 1989). This is in line with Humanist philosophy of life and death and the belief in the importance of human linkages and relationships. Death is the end and if we live on at all it is in the memory of those we have known. A Humanist funeral is, then, a celebration of the life of the dead person and an act of remembrance. In their guide they suggest a structure for the funeral which includes the use of various media, music, poetry, readings and accounts of the dead person's life. They suggest that people before their death might like to design their own funeral or at least discuss it with friends and relatives. Such funerals can be extremely moving occasions because they are so personal. Openly remembering the dead person also allows for more overt forms of grieving.

The subject of euthanasia, to which we now will turn, is one which is influenced a great deal by religious belief.

EUTHANASIA AND LIVING WILLS

Euthanasia is an issue on which many religions take a firm stand. Jewish teaching emphasises the sanctity of human life and includes an obligation to heal the sick and prolong human life although this does not imply the prolonging of dying (Katz, 1993). Jewish Law specifically states: 'A patient on his death bed is considered a living person in every respect . . . and it is forbidden to cause him to die quickly' (*Yoreh De'Ah*, a compendium of law, 339:1, quoted in Katz, 1993, p. 200).

Hindus and Sikhs believe that life should never be ended artificially. A Punjabi doctor quoted in Firth (1993) said: 'I can't dream of a Hindu considering euthanasia' and 'I can't imagine a Hindu signing something like a living will' (Firth, 1993, p. 30).

The Muslim belief that death is entirely in the hands of God prohibits human intervention in controlling the time of death. However, a Muslim doctor may want to distinguish between active euthanasia, which would be abhorrent, and recognising the inevitability of God's will which might allow doctors not to continue resuscitation over and over (Karimjee, 1993). A Muslim family might well pray actively to God for the dying person's suffering to end.

In the case of Buddhism it is the motive more than the action which is important:

> Behind every act is the motivation that is the energy of the act, and the first consideration should always be compassion. Suicide or euthanasia as acts inspired by compassionate motivation are certainly different in their Karmic [roughly, moral] consequences than those inspired by anger or greed. (Ngakpa Chogyan Ogyen Togden, 1989/90, 9)

Catholicism is also concerned with the intention of an act. The *doctrine of double effect* allows a pain reliever or sedative to be administered which *may* conceivably cause the death of a terminally ill person so long as the intention was to relieve pain.

Whilst it is always important to be aware of the beliefs and value systems inherent in the different religious traditions it is equally important to remember that these are not necessarily fixed for all time nor that every adherent accepts every belief. This is particularly true in the case of such a complex issue as euthanasia.

The word 'euthanasia' is derived from the Greek word meaning 'good death' and has been popularly referred to as 'mercy killing'. It is at best an attempt to prevent unnecessary pain and suffering in someone who is hopelessly ill, or to assure a dignified death to someone who is hopelessly non-functioning.

The terms 'active' and 'passive' euthanasia are used to make the distinction between taking concrete action to end a life, like giving a lethal injection, and omitting to do everything which could be done. Euthanasia is not a clear-cut issue, especially now there exist techniques to prolong life artificially and so impede natural death. The boundaries between 'active killing' and 'allowing to die' are therefore sometimes difficult to define. The ruling, in March 1993, to allow Tony Bland to die, gave withdrawal of treatment only limited legal backing, insisting that each case must still be decided on its merits. Another important distinction to be made is that between voluntary and involuntary euthanasia. In the case of voluntary euthanasia the stated wish of the person either actively or passively to end their life is required, whereas with involuntary euthanasia the consent of the individual is not required and would not be possible to obtain, as in cases of comatose patients.

One of the central themes in the debates on euthanasia is the potential it offers for dying people to exert some control in the manner of their death. Voluntary euthanasia promises more control to the dying person, involuntary euthanasia gives control to the medical representative or the relatives. However, the question is whether euthanasia actually puts more control in the hands of doctors (Ten Havey,1992). A more patient-centred way forward now being examined by the Law Commission, and more likely to become legislation than euthanasia is the use of 'advance directives' or 'living wills'. The aim is to take away any ambiguity surrounding the wishes of people who, for whatever reason, are unable to express them. The advance directive therefore represents an attempt to give control in advance of death and prevent the need for involuntary action. Like the making of an ordinary will it should ideally be made when a person is fit and well, but in practice it would be generally used by people who are terminally ill but still in full possession of their faculties. It is important to remember that it can be revoked by the individual at any time. Currently, advance directives relate in the main to medical decisions, but it would be interesting to explore other wishes that might concern people about the end of their lives, such as the quality and style of care. For instance, a preference for place of death could be made or to make provision for religious or cultural rituals to be performed such as those discussed above. Thus choice and control could be extended beyond medical decisions.

There are many legal and ethical issues to be resolved before 'living wills' are made legal documents. These issues are labyrinthine and could not be done justice to here. Briefly, the situation at the time of writing is that euthanasia is not legal anywhere. Countries, however, differ in the degree to which 'a blind eye' is turned to infringements of the law, and the severity in the way these infringements are dealt with. In Britain euthanasia remains an offence under Section 2 of the Suicide Act (1961), with a maximum sentence of 14 years. The situation in Britain and America is similar. In neither country is euthanasia formally legal, but in both countries professional persons are less likely to be convicted of the crime than lay people. Indeed, before the conviction of the Winchester rheumatologist Dr Cox in 1992, no British doctor had ever been found guilty. The Criminal Law Revision Committee has twice recommended changing the law, in 1973 and 1976, but this recommendation was not taken up. There is a widely held misconception that euthanasia is legal in the Netherlands but this is not so. However, what is considered unofficial policy in Britain is accepted public policy in the Netherlands. Physicians who 'assist 'death at the request of the patient will not be punished if the situation fulfils certain criteria based on the following guidelines:

1. The dying person's request is explicit and repeated, leaving no doubt in the doctor's mind about the patient's desire to die.
2. The mental or physical suffering of the dying person is beyond palliation or relief.
3. The dying person's request is well informed and freely made, with no backtracking.

4. The doctor must consult another physician and, if he or she chooses, may also discuss the request with nurses, clergy and others.
5. There is no other treatment option, or the dying person has rejected the remaining options.

                    (K260 Course, Open University, 1993, Workbook 2).

Opponents of euthanasia point out that older people are most vulnerable to abuses of euthanasia. It is thought that if euthanasia becomes acceptable practice this could easily lead to indirect or involuntary forms of euthanasia such as the rationing of scarce resources on the basis of age. Decisions not to resuscitate patients are already made in some hospitals purely on grounds of age and for many years kidney transplant and dialysis programmes operated arbitrary age barriers as low as 45 years. Around the time of the second attempt by the Law Revision Committee to liberalise the law on euthanasia, the European Federation for the Welfare of Older People expressed the fear that:

> at some indefinable point in the future, national legislation may provide for or permit practices whose object is to put an end to the lives of old people allegedly incurable or incapable of improvement, who have become a burden on society. (European CARITAS, 1976, p. 51)

Older people suffering from dementia are thought to be most at risk. The term 'social death' is commonly used to describe severe dementia sufferers with the implication that little or none of life's quality remains and that their situation is one which is worse than death. Many older people fear this state and openly express the wish not to be kept alive in such circumstances. It is also a very distressing condition for relatives to observe. One of the dangers inherent in more liberal use of euthanasia lies in the fact that accurate diagnosis of dementia is still difficult to achieve. Acute forms of confusion which mimic dementia are reversible and so proving the incurablity of dementia is difficult and could be dangerous if euthanasia were to become common practice. There have already been cases in the US in which patients with early Alzheimer's disease have obtained 'mercy killing' from the notorious Dr Jack Kevorkian who was under threat of prosecution at the time of writing. If poor quality of life is a criterion for euthanasia, one commentator asks, shouldn't we also practice mercy killing on handicapped newborns? Why is that any less abhorrent (Baumrin, 1991)? The fact that it is abhorrent should make us think twice before we accept a distinction between those who are 'merely alive' and those who 'have a life to live' (Rachels, 1986).

Another anxiety is that the widespread practice of euthanasia will erode the collective will to extend and explore techniques of palliative care and symptom control. It is precisely these techniques which, the opponents of euthanasia argue, can bring dignity to dying people and relieve their suffering and pain, thus minimising the need for euthanasia.

Opponents of euthanasia also believe that even though legislation is only considered in relation to voluntary euthanasia the pressures on older people will be great to seek such action in an attempt to relieve relatives or society of the burden of caring for them.

The Institute of Medical Ethics (IME, 1990) looked at the objections to 'assisted death'. They countered arguments that older people would feel under pressure to ask for euthanasia so as not to become a burden to others by expressing the view that doctors would be able to discern any undue pressure and discuss this openly with the person and those concerned. Robert Twycross, a hospice physician, writing in *The Lancet* (1990) accused the IME of naiveté on this issue, stating that he has felt the need for the protection which existing law gives to refuse to assist death in order to cope with unscrupulous relatives.

The IME also dismiss the anxiety that the practice of euthanasia would reduce the pressure for research into better methods of symptom control and the provision of resources for palliative care. They maintain that past attempts to bring in legislation to legalise voluntary euthanasia has acted as a catalyst in improving the techniques of symptom control, making the demand for euthanasia much smaller. Failure to relieve the suffering of terminal care evidenced by the demand for euthanasia would increase the demand for more research into terminal care. Again Robert Twycross is sceptical of this argument. He points to the realities of economic pressures on terminal care institutions saying: 'The temptation to move from voluntary assisted deaths to involuntary assisted death would be too great for some of us to resist, myself included, as patients clamour for admission to non-existent beds for symptom relief or respite' (Twycross, 1990, p. 797).

The IME's most powerful argument points to the fact that the present system of tacit agreement to overlook the illegal actions of those doctors who are willing to assist death provides no real safeguards for doctors nor equal access to such a service for those terminally ill people who genuinely desire it. And they stress that the impetus to legalise voluntary euthanasia comes from a humane desire to relieve suffering and is not the product of closet eugenicism.

Interestingly public opinion seems to support calls for the legalisation of euthanasia. Public opinion has been consistent, at about 75 per cent pro-euthanasia, for the past twenty to thirty years. But there is little evidence which relates specifically to older people. One study under-taken in the late 1970s in America (Kalish and Reynolds, 1976) found that 40 per cent of their respondents over the age of 60 thought that people should be allowed to die if that was their wish. More recently, Williams's study of older Aberdonians provides us with some qualitative data on older people's views on the subject. When asked for their preferences in the event of predicted death only a minority chose to 'be helped on'. But when 'arrested' or prolonged deaths were discussed most expressed a preference for being helped on. They also made it clear that they thought that it was the doctor's responsibility, some even felt that it was best left to the doctor's own judgement without seeking the patient's or relatives' consent. These responses were to questions about hypothetical situations. When asked about specific situations of which they had experience and which involved people they knew well, they displayed much more ambivalence at the idea of 'finishing it' or 'getting it over with'. As with other attitudes to death and dying contradiction was more in evidence than consistency.

Marshall (1980) drawing on his research in a retirement village in America identified five situations in which his respondents felt death would be preferable to life. Death was preferable to: (1) inactivity, (2) to the loss of the ability to be useful, (3) to becoming a burden, (4) to the loss of mental faculties and (5) to living with progressively deteriorating physical health and concomitant physical discomfort.

It is mainly an anxiety about the manner of dying which lies at the heart of the debates about euthanasia. Older people do worry about being a burden to others and about dying a lonely and painful death. What reassurance can be found from current practices in caring for dying people?

CARING FOR DYING PEOPLE

Those who characterise western society as 'death denying' see the medicalisation of death as partly responsible for that state of affairs. Death has come to be defined mainly as a medical event. It is the doctor who is called in to certify death and to say what has caused the death. Death is conceived of as the consequence of disease and an event with a physical causation. Within this medical framework the tendency is to fight against it and resist it, the atmosphere is one of combat rather amelioration, the emphasis is on saving life rather than on the quality of dying.

The modern hospice movement has developed out of a dissatisfaction with this limited medical framework. The hospice approach does not turn its back on the benefits to be had from scientific medicine but takes a broader concept of caring for dying people. Dame Cicely Saunders, one of the hospice movement's most famous exponents, explains: 'In the the hospice movement we continue to be concerned both with the sophisticated science of our treatments and with the art of our caring, bringing competence alongside compassion' (Saunders, 1981, p. 4). The emphasis is to redress the balance in medicine between caring and curing, to focus medical intervention on the relief of symptoms and to pay attention to the emotional, psychological and spiritual well-being of the dying person and close relatives and friends. Hospice care can therefore be equated with whole-person care.

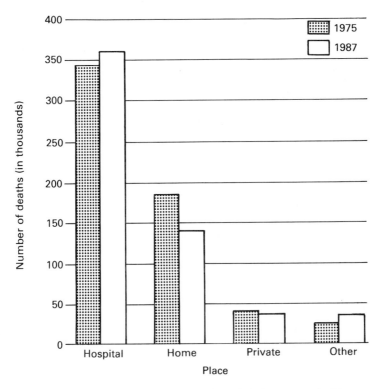

Figure 7.1 *Place of death, all causes, England and Wales 1975 and 1987.*
Source: Hospital In-patient Enquiry, cited in Griffen, 1991

The principles of hospice-type care now reach beyond the hospices and into home and hospital care. Palliative care is now a specialism within medicine. But there is little room for complacency. The care of dying and bereaved people is still only an optional extra in some medical schools and not part of a trainee doctor's core curriculum. Similarly, in nurse training the care of dying people is an optional post-basic training course. Yet about 60 per cent of deaths in Britain take place in hospitals (Victor, 1993) and in Seale's survey of deaths in 1987 only 6.9 per cent of the sample received the benefit of hospice care (Seale, 1991). Hospice care has developed primarily in the voluntary sector and availability remains patchy and geographically uneven. Its focus has been mainly on cancers. For these reasons, the vast majority of older people do not benefit from hospice care.

Most older people die in hospitals, nursing homes or residential homes for older people (Figure 7.1). Some die 'at home' but this is dependent on the availability of support. Older women make up a disproportionately large number of those who live alone and without support they would need to be able to die in their own home. Most of them will have nursed their husbands to their deaths, grieved alone and then face the prospect of dying alone. As Seale put it, 'the elderly widow living on her own may be as important an image to bear in our minds as the terminally ill cancer patient' (Seale, 1993, p. 53).

Dying in hospital

Good practice in the care of dying people is not the sole prerogative of hospice care, nor is hospice care without its critics, but generally it has had a better press than the terminal care given in hospitals. Hedley Taylor points out that much of what is considered good practice in hospice care is also accepted theoretically as good practice in hospitals. Hospital staff do claim that recent advances in nursing and medicine have been made in moving from a disease model to a 'whole person' model of treatment and that nowhere is this more widespread than in the care of terminally ill people (Taylor, 1983a). Moreover, the principles of pain relief and symptom control are more widely appreciated and many hospitals have symptom control teams. But there remains a nagging and persistent feeling of disquiet that the care of dying people in hospital is not as good as it might be. Much of that disquiet is concerned with the amount of personal attention and emotional support available for dying people. Busy hospital wards do not lend themselves to the calm, attentive, unhurried support that dying people may need. In the still predominantly curative atmosphere of a hospital, death may be seen as a failure from which hospital staff may tend to withdraw. Hospitals are inevitably unfamiliar places to the dying person and their relatives and friends and the routines and sheer lack of space may make it difficult for relatives and friends to give emotional support to the dying person. Carrying out some of the cultural customs described above also becomes very difficult on a busy hospital ward.

Hospital staff are aware of shortcomings in the way dying is often handled in hospitals. In one survey 50 per cent of junior doctors and nurses were unhappy about the lack of adequate training in terminal care and most of the nurses felt that hospital wards were unsuited to the needs of dying people (Wilkes, 1984).

Dying at home

Most people would prefer to die at home (Townsend et al, 1990) on familiar territory and surrounded by loved ones. Sadly, this is not easy to achieve. As we mentioned earlier, older people and most older women live alone. Even if they live with a spouse the demands of terminal care often prove too much for another possibly frail and older person to give. Christina Victor (1993) points out that the most vulnerable group are older people who live alone and who depend on a range of different relatives and friends. Ideally they need a good deal of support from the official agencies. In fact only 38 per cent received such official care (Seale, 1990). As with other forms of community care informal carers bear the brunt of the terminal care. Seale reports that in his study a half of these informal carers would have liked more formal help and 45 per cent reported that their own health suffered. As well as the chronic problems of funding for community care services Victor points out that community care for dying people is difficult to coordinate because it is provided by a wide range of organisations, health social services, and voluntary medical and social agencies, leading to a fragmentation of responsibility.

Dying at home without proper back-up services can be less than the ideal that most people seek. The late David Widgery, an East End of London GP, reminds us that old age reflects all the class disadvantages of the life that preceded it and graphically describes the deaths of some of his poorest and most socially isolated patients: 'These are the bodies keeled over in the toilet or stiff in a stale bedroom, blue and contorted in the time they have lain undiscovered' (Widgery, 1991, p. 134). Compared to such circumstances a busy hospital ward with all its shortcomings might seem a more secure place to die.

Many of the religious and cultural practices described above are concerned with supporting the dying person through their last days. Not only kin but the local community will offer help and spend time comforting the dying person. A young Muslim woman who lived in a Pakistani community in Bradford was interviewed for a course on Death and Dying recently developed at the Open University. She described the death of her father. The family refused to allow him to go to hospital and nursed him at home. Her uncle took charge and wider kin and the whole community provided help and support. But she had mixed feelings about what was a very public death. She resented the lack of privacy for herself and her mother but valued the help given. She was unable to get close to her father when he actually died because of the crush of people around him. For those who might seek a quiet peaceful death this would not be the ideal. We cannot always assume that cultural rituals will guarantee a high quality of dying. Nor can we assume that those who do subscribe to a religious or cultural tradition will be taken care of by their family and friends. Many of these traditions have been eroded in Britain and older people from ethnic minorities may well need help from the official agencies. Ebrahim (1992) believes that in relation to ethnic minority communities the host community holds a 'myth' of the extended family that 'they look after their own'. This 'myth' effectively enables the host community to ignore the needs of those from ethnic minority communities who live alone. Approximately a third of all Afro-Caribbean and one in twenty Asian elders living in Birmingham were found to be living alone (Blakemore, 1982, 1983a).

Dying in 'homes'

Many older people, and particularly older women, die in residential homes and nursing homes. Between a quarter and a third of residents are likely to die each year (Clough, 1981, p. 134). Here again there are indications that the care given to dying people is in many ways unsatisfactory. Despite the frequency of deaths, research and training relating to residential care tends to focus on maintenance and rehabilitation (Peace, 1988). There is a great deal of emphasis on quality of life but very little attention paid to the quality of dying. For instance the Review of Residential Care chaired by Lady Wagner in 1988 barely makes mention of the issue of death and dying. The few studies that have explored the quality of dying in residential homes indicate that there is a good deal of denial of death. Dying people are moved away from the main living areas of the home and in some homes people just disappear after their death and a new resident is allocated the empty bed. Discussion of a recent death is discouraged and no collective mourning or remembrance takes place (Hanvey, 1989; Hockey, 1990).

Sheila Peace draws our attention to the difference in the quality of care available for dying people in institutional environments for older people compared to that provided by the hospice movement:

> Nowhere is this more clearly demonstrated than in the contrast that exists between the highly respected personalised care provided by the hospice movement. . . and the negative image which still surrounds the residential home, the nursing home, the geriatric ward. (Peace, 1988, p. 231)

There are some examples of good practice in terminal care in residential homes. For instance Franks (1990) quotes an officer in charge of a home in south London who describes the care in her home:

> When a member of a group dies, other members will have been told of the progress of the illness and the treatment given. Some residents who have formed a close relationship with the sick person are invited to his or her bedroom. They are encouraged to sit and hold hands. And when this person has died, they are invited into the room. Sometimes they don't wish to be reminded of death, and then we leave them alone. (Franks, 1990)

This contrasts sharply with Jenny Hockey's ethnographic account of dying in a residential home. She suggests that residential homes are primarily dying spaces concerned 'with the slow process of deterioration' (p. 92). She maintains that the attempt to create a 'homely here and now' atmosphere demands that the categories 'life' and 'death' be kept separate lest one should intrude upon the other. The task of 'keeping them going' is the overt preoccupation of the staff. The task of 'supervising the process of dying and the event of death' (p. 116) becomes more covert and is carried out in the sickbay and mortuary, separated from the 'living' spaces. This runs counter to the philosophy of terminal care developed by the hospice movement which attempts to 'reintegrate the two categories of experience, "life" and "death", thereby highlighting the processual rather than the oppositional nature of their relationship' (Hockey, 1990, p. 155). These sentiments are echoed by Seale but he queries the status of 'dying' which is only recognised in the presence of a terminal illness such as cancer. Anselm Strauss introduced the concept of 'dying trajectories' in understanding the organisation of terminal care. Any dying trajectory has two main elements, it has *duration* taking place over time and it has *shape*, like a graph, and can move slowly or rapidly downward, it can vacillate or reach a long plateau before plunging downward and so on. Within these two elements of duration and shape Strauss identified certain 'critical junctures' which relate to the organisation of terminal care. These are:

> 1, The patient is defined as dying; 2, Staff and family then make preparations for his [sic] death, as he may himself if he knows he is dying; 3, At some point, there seems 'nothing more to do' to prevent death; 4, The final descent may take weeks, or days, or merely hours, ending in 5, the 'last hours', 6, the death watch and 7, death itself. (Strauss, 1971, p. 13)

In the case of many older people junctures 1 to 3 are likely to be very blurred and consequently hard to define. If we are to adapt the principles of hospice care to the care of older people dying from a range of conditions we need to take a much more long-term approach to the care of frail older people who may suffer from chronic illness. Symptom relief in its broadest sense is particularly appropriate as is the emphasis on a person-centred approach. Hospice-type care should no longer be confined to those who are medically predicted to have only a short time to live (Seale, 1993). Good hospice care also involves family and friends in the care of the dying person. Their needs are taken into account, particularly after the death, and bereavement support is usually available if they want it. This is particularly important for older spouses who may have been through a long and stressful period of caring only to find they have to face their grief alone.

BEREAVEMENT

Older people are likely to have encountered many losses as they age. Does this make it more or less difficult for older people to face bereavement in later life? Are losses cumulative in their effect or do people learn to deal with them better the more they have to encounter?

How we cope with bereavement in adult life is said by some theorists (Klein; 1940, Bowlby, 1969), to depend on our ability as infants to cope with the 'separation anxiety' induced by the inevitable separation from the breast, in both a physical and metaphorical sense. On our success in creating an inner life to deal with this anxiety as infants depends our future ability to deal with losses that hurt. Other theorists following Freud (Parkes, 1986; Worden, 1982) focus on the need to test reality when facing major losses, to learn to accept the reality that the lost loved object is no longer there. This is necessary in order to release the energy invested in that attachment and re-invest it in new attachments. From these theoretical bases some pervasive and quite prescriptive models have been developed which have a lot in common with the Kubler-Ross stages model of attitudes to the loss of one's own life.

In so far as these models resonate with people's own feelings and experience they have the virtue of reassuring people that their painful and seemingly irrational behaviour is shared by others, that they are 'normal' and their behaviour is predictable. By the same token they also define others, whose behaviour and feelings do not fit into the model, as 'abnormal' and sometimes 'pathological'. They therefore seek to mould individuals into a set pattern. That individuals vary in their reaction to loss is clear to anyone who encounters bereaved people. Can we discern patterns and what are the effects, if any, of age?

Parkes, a long-time advocate of the stages model of grief, has rooted his theoretical position in a great deal of empirical research, mainly concerned with the effects of the death of a spouse. His work has focused on widows and widowers and, although it is not always possible to differentiate the evidence on the basis of age, it does provide a rich source of data on the physical and psychological effects of grief (Parkes, 1986). The pattern which was clearest to Parkes was that bereaved spouses experienced an initial stage of shock and numbness. This gave way to denial of the death when the widow or widower still felt the presence of the dead person sometimes actually seeing them or hearing their voice. These feelings could be very disturbing to people because at some level they sensed they were irrational and fears of madness were not uncommon. When the widow or widower finally realises that the husband or wife does not exist in any earthly sense great anguish is felt, reality is painful and often quite disabling. Gradually the pain eases and the person is able to focus on other things and rebuild his or her life. This final stage of reintegration and reorganisation was often interpreted as meaning the beginning of a new relationship but the relationship is not necessarily with another person but with a new life in which the lost loved person does not figure. Only then can it be truly said that the person had resolved their grief. The estimated time it took to arrive at this stage of resolution has varied from one to four years. Parkes himself has, over the years, relaxed his position on this sequential stages model, feeling that not everyone necessarily should experience all the stages and certainly not within a set timescale (Parkes, 1986). Nevertheless this model has percolated into popular literature in a highly prescriptive way. It also guides much bereavement counselling although there are attempts such as the 'grief wheel' model to work with much more flexibility and recognise that the stages are not necessarily sequential (Grief Education Institute, 1986).

The stages model could be said to be more appropriate to reactions to sudden and unexpected deaths where shock and disbelief would seem inevitable. Many bereavements experienced by older people come after a long period of illness and have been anticipated. The question of whether such 'anticipatory grief' relieves the pain of the eventual grief has been the subject of much debate in the bereavement literature (Lindemann, 1944; Kutscher, 1969; Fulton and Gottesman, 1980). It seems safe to say that grief which has been forewarned is less painful than grief which is sudden and unexpected (Glick et al, 1974; Parkes, 1975). Feelings of relief at the end of a loved one's suffering can bring consolation. Proper leave-taking and the satisfaction that one had done everything in one's power to ease the dying process can also bring comfort. But there is evidence that a long and protracted period of terminal illness can cause a great many problems for the subsequent bereavement period (Gerber et al, 1975). The sheer exhaustion of caring over a long time can take its toll on the mental and physical health of the carer (Bass and Bowman, 1990). Very often older people cannot maintain the physical demands of caring for a dying person and have to allow their spouse to be taken into hospital to die. This sense of failure can 'play on the mind' for many years after the death. There may be many instances when the carer felt they should have done more and consequently feelings of guilt can complicate their grief (Parkes, 1986). Bowling and Cartwright (1982) in their study of older widowed people found that some of their respondents reproached themselves and wished they had done things differently. Some wished they had spent more time with the dead person, others that they had sought medical help sooner, some wished they had talked more about the impending death.

Being present at the time of death is very important to bereaved spouses. Of the widows in Bowling and Cartwright's study who had not been able to be present at the death well over half deeply regretted it. This, Bowling and Cartwright believe, could adversely affect their adjustment to their bereavement.

In the stages model of grief if the final stage of reintegration and reorganisation is not reached the grief is thought to be unresolved. The metaphor of a lesion is much used to describe grief, resolution of grief is akin to a healing wound. By implication a wound that does not heal becomes poisonous and festers, 'pathology' sets in. But increasingly a third outcome to bereavement is being acknowledged where the wound does not heal but neither does it fester. It remains an unhealed wound. This has become known as 'enduring grief' and has been particularly recognised in the grief of parents who lose a child. Although they resume a normal life, possibly have other children, they never stop grieving for that child. Their grief does not poison their lives but neither does it diminish greatly. When interviewing older women I found that many of them had also never stopped grieving for their dead spouses ten or fifteen years after the death yet they led active and full lives (Sidell, 1991).

Another form of grief which I found amongst the women I interviewed was what can only be called 're-kindled grief'. What became clear when listening to these women who had lost their spouses many

years ago and who had ostensibly 'accepted' the loss, was that the sense
of loss of a partner could be re-awakened and actually felt again if and
when their circumstances deteriorated. It is not difficult to appreciate
that if children and even grandchildren are grown up and are perhaps
geographically inaccessible, if infirmity renders one housebound then
that is the very time when one would most benefit from a close and
special partner. Clearly the quality of the actual partnership is
important, but in its absence it is the absence which is painful.

It would be foolish to ignore the fact that many marriages and
relationships are extremely unhappy and that the death of one of the
partners may release the other from a great deal of aggravation. Not
everyone is sorely missed. But even if the relationship had been
thoroughly bad there are other losses to contend with, loss of social
status, income and security all have to be dealt with. But it has been
found that grief when there was a good deal of ambivalence about the
relationship that is lost can be quite complicated because there is the
guilt of actually feeling relief that someone has died (Raphael, 1983 and
Littlewood, 1992).

Grief can be disabling and bereavement is always high on any list of
potentially threatening 'life events'. Parkes's studies on bereavement
provide an excellent review of the evidence of links between bereavement and mental and physical illness. He explores what he calls 'the
broken heart' syndrome (Parkes, 1986, Chapter 2) and asks whether
people can actually die from grief. Mortality data indicate that widows
and widowers have higher mortality rates than people of the same age
who are married, but this is complicated because of remarriage and it is
suggested that the fittest are likely to remarry. However, Parkes shows
that the mortality rate for widowers in the first six months after the
death of their spouse was 40 per cent higher than the expected rate for
men of the same age who were married. The evidence for widows is
conflicting, a study by Mellstromm et al (1982) found a significant increase
in the death rate amongst widows in the first three months after the
death of their spouses but not after that.

Parkes is satisfied that for men bereavement is linked to subsequent
deaths from diseases of the cardio-vascular system, but he is careful not
to make direct causal links, instead he uses terms such as 'exacerbate' or
'precipitate' such conditions. What we know about the body's reaction
to shock – raised pulse and blood pressure, palpitations, sweating and
acute anxiety – make this a plausible theory.

Loneliness is one of the most serious problems identified by most
older widowed people. About half of the widows in both Lopata's (1973)
and Bowling and Cartwright's study (1982) found loneliness to be a
major problem for them. Depression also has been linked to bereavement in a number of studies (Brown and Harris, 1978; Dohrenwend and
Dohrenwend, 1974; Parkes and Weiss, 1983). Although these studies are
not age-specific, those focusing on older people have found that

bereavement is a factor in depression in older people (Murphy, 1982). An American study which compared younger and older widows (Sanders, 1988), found that younger widows suffer more in the short term but that older widows have more long-term problems. This same study also points out that low socio-economic status makes bereavement more difficult. Sanders cites a study of a group of older working-class widows which found that a reduced financial state led to reduced social participation resulting in greater loneliness and anxiety. Another study went so far as to conclude that 'the negative impact sometimes attributed to widowhood derives not from widowhood status, but rather from socio-economic status' (Harvey and Bahr, 1974, p. 106). Older widows are one of the most impoverished groups in our society. Widowhood, especially for women, represents many losses, not only the loss of financial status. Dorothy Jerrome in Chapter 10 mentions companionship, a partner in a world which is couple oriented and the loss of a sexual partner. Four out of ten of the widows in Helen Lopata's (1979) study claimed to have a less active social life than before their spouses' deaths. Another problem identified by Lopata was the need to adopt new roles and this was particularly difficult for older widowed people for whom gendered role divisions had been fairly rigid before the death.

However, widowhood is not an entirely negative experience for women and, as noted earlier, they seem to fare better than widowed men. The gender composition of the widowed state has certain positive aspects for women, although only if they are still mobile and relatively fit. Because widowhood is almost the norm for older women they form a recognisable group, role models abound and there is no shortage of other widows to identify with. They can go on holiday together, join clubs together and even dance together. Widowers on the other hand are a much more isolated type. They do not have a 'pool' of men in the same situation as themselves, but they do have greater opportunities to remarry, which many do, and it is the widower without a partner who seems most at risk. The impact of gender and socio-economic status are clearly important to the way grief is experienced but there are other independent variables.

As with attitudes to death in general an important independent variable is the impact of religion and culture. Many bereaved people take comfort in the belief that they will somehow meet their loved ones again. A high proportion of the widowed in Bowling and Cartwright's study (1982) said they held a religious belief. They were all Christians and between a third and two-thirds of them felt that this had helped them to adjust to their bereavement. However, no difference was found on the adjustment scale used by Bowling and Cartwright between those who felt that their belief had helped them and those who had no such belief, nor was there any difference in reported loneliness between these groups. Much of the debate about the effect of religious and cultural traditions focuses on the effect of mourning rituals on the experience of grief. There is a general assumption following Gorer (1965) that the apparent lack of ritual in contemporary western societies makes grieving more difficult. Mourning rituals do provide a socially acceptable framework for grief, they allow people permission to weep openly and they provide milestones during the period of mourning to allow the bereaved a time to adapt gradually to the changes in their lives. But above all they ensure social support for the bereaved which should help prevent the loneliness and isolation felt by so many bereaved people. We have no research information to show whether the private grief of people whose culture or religion provides a set pattern of mourning is any different from the grief of those whose culture lacks such rituals. We are left with the difficult question, does the experience of sorrow match the expression of sorrow? Certainly in a cultural atmosphere which finds the expression of sorrow hard to deal with, those experiencing such sorrow will feel isolated and alone.

Another factor in bereavement which is thought to exacerbate grief is the experience of multiple losses, either at the same time, as in an accident, or over a short period of time. Older people frequently find themselves in the latter position. We have so far concentrated on the death of a spouse but other deaths may be equally, if not more distressing for older people, especially if they happen in close proximity. The deaths of siblings, friends and contemporaries are, as well as reminders of one's own finitude, often a loss of links with the past or the loss of a valued confidant or companion. Female friendship in later life is often a lifeline for many older women (Jerrome, 1993) and there is evidence that loss and grief when it happens in such circumstances is not acknowledged. The term 'hidden grief' has been used to describe those who are not recognised as legitimate mourners where the emphasis is on familial ties. Sklar and Hartley (1990) identified this as a problem particularly for gay men and women but also for adolescents and older adults, especially widows whose attachment to other older widows is extremely close and supportive.

Older people also lose adult children and grandchildren and their grief can be compounded by feelings of guilt that they are outliving their offspring. Compassionate Friends, an organisation which provides support to those who lose a child, point out in their literature that grandparents' needs are often not acknowledged. Grandparents can, in effect, suffer a double loss because their own offspring, the parent of the dead child, may withdraw affection and distance themselves.

Compassionate Friends is one of many organisations, mostly run by voluntary but trained counsellors who offer help to bereaved people. CRUSE is perhaps the best known and has a national network. Originally set up to support widows, CRUSE now offers help to anyone bereaved and it runs many group therapy sessions. It has been reported that only a small percentage of those seeking help are very old (Pincus,

1976). The reasons are not known. Maybe older people have few expectations of receiving help, maybe they are unaware of what is available or of how to negotiate help. Maybe they do not feel the need for help or maybe they have all the support they need. In the absence of any reliable data on the subject we can only assume that any of these probabilities are possible.

CONCLUSIONS

For a variety of reasons the subject of ageing and death and dying has received relatively little attention. Because death is the outcome of the dying career there are certain peculiar difficulties attached to researching the subject. As Marshall points out 'there are no graduates' (1980, p. 126). Although the greater prevalence of resuscitation techniques has led to a growing number of claims of 'near-death experiences' these have been explained by the raised levels of carbon dioxide in the brains of people who lose consciousness (Ivan and Melrose, 1986). For most of us death remains a mystery. Some of us fear it, others accept it. On the whole older people seem more inclined to accept it, perhaps because as the poet Philip Larkin observed: 'Death is no different whined at than withstood.'

The process of dying, on the other hand, is different. We can help to relieve pain and suffering whether this is physical or emotional. While we may find it hard to conceive of the process as ever being 'good' clearly the manner of some people's dying is better than others. Striving to improve the quality of dying will mostly benefit older people and so it is an issue with which gerontology should engage both in terms of research and service provision for the dying and bereaved.

8

THE SOCIOLOGY OF RETIREMENT

Chris Phillipson

Retirement has, over the past thirty years, been a major focus for research and debate in social gerontology. Its significance has been acknowledged in a variety of ways: as a mechanism for assisting the individual's withdrawal from social life (Cumming and Henry, 1961); as an institution helping to redistribute work from older to younger people (Graebner, 1980; Phillipson, 1982; Laczko and Phillipson, 1991); as part of the movement to a 'leisured society' (Hochschild, 1973); and, from a critical perspective, as a contributory element in the creation of dependency in old age (Walker, 1981; Townsend, 1986; Phillipson 1991a).

These differing interpretations complicate any assessment or discussion about the nature of retirement. An additional element is that our understanding of this institution is closely tied to and affected by dominant cultural values. Thus, in a culture which values work, retirement is seen as a 'problem' and a source of tension for the individual. Moreover, we all know – or claim to know – people who have suffered stress after compulsory retirement. Worse still, we can point to cases of people who have died in the ensuing months or years: proof, it would seem, of the harmful consequences which loss of a lifetime's work brings. Reflecting this pessimism, very few social scientists appear ready to defend the present retirement system. As Peter Stearns (a historian) writes:

> A cultural history of gerontological literature would note that its authors are often work enthusiasts themselves who find it difficult to imagine a satisfactory life divorced from employment. This is not to say that their judgement is wrong, however, and in individual cases empirical results on the problems posed by retirement have been impressive. There is a tendency, however, to assume a capacity for continued work that is not in turn empirically tested, rather reversing, but not necessarily improving upon, the exaggerated sense of elderly decay that dominated the literature of the nineteenth century. (King and Stearns, 1981, p. 595)

As a generalisation, it might be argued that there is a powerful mythology which affects our thinking about retirement. The purpose of this chapter is to analyse, from a critical perspective, the present status of this important institution. The chapter will assess, from a sociological perspective, the impact of retirement upon both individuals and groups.

The analysis presented will highlight the contradictory feelings often expressed about leaving work and the variety of meanings attached to retirement. Finally, in a concluding section, the future of retirement will be assessed along with some key issues for social policy.

RETIREMENT AND OLD AGE IN HISTORY

Historical perspectives on old age have begun to challenge orthodox views about the position of older people in past society.[1] In particular, there has been a questioning of the view that industrialisation and urbanisation necessarily weakened the status of elderly people, in comparison to their position in rural and peasant communities. In pre-industrial society, for those elderly people without property, growing old could be a desperate and humiliating experience (Hufton, 1974; Thomas, 1976). According to Thomas:

> for most manual workers old age meant, first, a move to lighter (and lower-paid) work, then a decline to abject dependence. Every contemporary list of paupers contains a proportion described as 'ancient and decrepit', 'aged and past work', 'old and her work done'. For miners, tailors, and metalworkers, this stage could come very quickly. Almshouses did not take those capable of working, yet the minimum age of admission was sometimes as low as forty. For literary commentators fifty was usually the point when old age began: 'at fifty', said Bishop Babington, 'we go down the hill again and every day grow weaker and weaker'. When old age pensions were first proposed, by Defoe in the 1690s, and by Dowdeswell in 1772, fifty was the age at which they were to be payable. On this point Burke agreed with Paine: from the age of fifty a workman's decline became 'every year more sensible'. (Thomas, 1976, p. 240)

With only limited accommodation available in almshouses and with retirement pensions virtually non-existent before the nineteenth century, there was a genuine fear of old age amongst working people. Most, as Thomas (1976) observes, had little choice but to struggle on as best they could:

> At Norwich in 1570 there were octogenarian women still spinning, while in 1679 Oliver Heywood was pleased to hear that a man of ninety-four and his wife of 104 had been seen carding in front of their house. Ralph Thoresby cited the equally inspiring example of Lawrence Benson of Leeds, who one afternoon reaped half an acre of wheat, ground it at the mill, made a cake with the floor, and ate it for his supper, all at the age of ninety-one. (Thomas, 1976, p. 240)

The research by Thomas and other historians has also been helpful in

---

[1] In Britain, some of the most influential work has been produced by the Cambridge Group for the History of Population and Social Structure, led by Laslett (see, for example, Laslett, 1977 and the special issue of *Ageing and Society* on History and Ageing, Vol. 4 (4), 1984). For important American research see Achenbaum (1978), Graebner (1980) and Haber (1983). Thomas's (1976) study of young and old in early modern England remains one of the most exciting examples of historical scholarship on old age. A valuable collection of essays has also been edited by Margaret Pelling and Richard Smith (1991), under the title *Life, Death and the Elderly*.

explaining some of the contradictions and doubts expressed about retirement. Modern retirement policy is a product of the late nineteenth century as large private companies and branches of the civil service adopted pension policies. Subsequently, at key periods in the twentieth century (usually in periods of economic slump or through the impetus of war), pension coverage has been extended to cover virtually all sections of the population (Hannah, 1986).

Behind this development in social policy can be traced some important industrial, economic and political influences. Thus, as a number of studies have shown, retirement and the spread of pensions was stimulated by demands for greater efficiency and productivity in the workplace (Graebner, 1980; Phillipson, 1982; Thane, 1978). For factory workers, retirement may also have been hastened by workmen's compensation legislation, introduced in 1897. This required employers to insure against accidents at work and may have increased their tendency to lay off older and possibly accident-prone employees. According to Thane: 'Employers both introduced occupational pensions and pressed for a state scheme as this would let them lay-off older workers with clear consciences' (Thane, 1978, p. 236)

Fischer (1977) suggests that the growth of the factory system accelerated the process of retirement, with the development of assembly-line production hastening the displacement of older workers. However, as Quadagno (1982) and others note, the issue is not simply one of technological change creating the right climate for the emergence of retirement. First, older people probably entered the new industries at a slower rate than younger workers. The reverse side of this is that they tended to be clustered in industries subject to economic decline. Secondly, retirement has to be seen in more global terms. For industrial capitalism, according to Graebner (1980), retirement provided a means of challenging security of tenure or jobs for life. It was a reaction against the persistence of personal modes of behaviour and provided a mechanism for discharging loyal workers. As an added bonus, it also assisted the stabilisation of corporate hierarchies, creating a permanent flow of employees and guaranteeing promotion through the ranks. Thirdly, as Graebner (1980) and Phillipson (1982) suggest, retirement has played an important role in periods of mass unemployment. The idea of older workers being surplus to labour requirements has been crucial to the development of pensions both in Britain (the 1925 pensions legislation) and America (the Social Security Act of 1935). Similarly, the growth of unemployment in the 1970s and 1980s stimulated early retirement policies in a number of countries (Laczko and Phillipson, 1991).

An additional perspective introduced by historians concerns the differential impact of retirement on working-class and middle-class life. Stearns argues that retirement created considerable difficulties for working-class people:

First, of course, inadequate material preparation, so that retirement was a time of immense physical hardship. But second, the lack of any active concept of what retirement should be: it represented stopping something, work, but did it represent starting or continuing anything of interest? Without pretending to fathom the fate of retirees as a whole, for even in old age, and perhaps particularly then, individuals' variations are immense, we can suggest that a rapidly changing behaviour pattern found no correspondence in public policy or collective activities. (Stearns, 1977, pp. 65–6)

Despite these difficulties, retirement has, in the twentieth century, become a mass experience. In Britain in 1881 73 per cent of the male population 65 and over were in paid employment; by 1951 this had fallen to 31 per cent; and by 1991 the figure had shrunk to below 10 per cent (Laczko and Phillipson, 1991). But this revolution in work patterns has created much uncertainty. In the late 1940s and early 1950s there was widespread concern about the burden of an ageing society and, in particular, the economic threat imposed by increased numbers of retired people (Political and Economic Planning, 1948; Royal Commission on Population, 1949). Similar views have been expressed in the 1980s and early 1990s, with politicians and some academics suggesting that the increasing cost of pensions will create tensions between generations (Johnson, Conrad and Thomson, 1989). Such views have had a significant impact both on the attitudes of older workers and on the conduct of research on retirement.

ATTITUDES TO RETIREMENT

Historians and sociologists have argued that the 'triumph of retirement' only took place after the Second World War (Graebner, 1980; Phillipson, 1982; Freter et al, 1987). In the period from 1950 to 1980, retirement grew in three particular ways: first, in terms of the proportion of people reaching retirement age; secondly, in terms of the decreasing significance of paid work after retirement; thirdly, as regards the number of people who receive state and occupational pensions.[2]

Yet the idea of triumph suggests that retirement was viewed as a positive development both in policy terms and amongst middle-aged people. Both these suggestions have, however, been contested in the literature. In policy terms, as has already been noted, retirement was viewed with some hostility in a climate of post-war austerity and manpower shortages (Morgan, 1984; Phillipson, 1982; Blaikie and MacNicol, 1989). At the same time, and especially in Britain (in part because of economic problems immediately after the war), there was particular emphasis on loss of work representing a 'crisis' for the individual.

---

[2] The number of state pensions paid in Britain grew from 2.5 million in 1936 to 8.9 million in 1979. In the same period, the number of occupational pensions paid grew from 0.2 to 3.7 million (Hannah, 1986).

In the 1950s, retirement was seen as causing 'problems' less because of its financial implications, rather more because of its social and psychological impact, for example, the loss of work-based friendships and the reduction in status and self-esteem. This perspective was explored in a range of studies undertaken in Britain, America and elsewhere and was supported by perspectives drawn from structural functionalism (see Chapter 2); the main theoretical orientation used in sociological studies, at least up until the 1960s.[3]

The view of retirement representing a social and individual problem was a powerful theme in early gerontological writings. Stieglitz, for example, one of the founders of gerontology argued, in his handbook on old age, published in Great Britain in 1949, that:

> Abrupt and obligatory retirement even if anticipated and accepted intellectually, almost invariably induces severe emotional stress. Its consequences are often drastic. There is an old saying among clinicians that to order the retirement of a businessman is tantamount to signing his death certificate within the year. (Stieglitz, 1949, p. 251)

In similar vein, Gumpert (1950), in a study entitled *You Are Younger Than You Think*, suggested that:

> Most physicians agree that the essence of any treatment of the aged is to keep them at work. Idleness is the greatest enemy of the aged and presents them with their ticket to death. Financial premiums on retirement, which become automatically effective at a certain date, confer none of the blessings of real security and are not only socially unsound but detrimental to the health of the individual. (Gumpert, 1950, p. 128; see also Wermal and Gelbaum, 1945; Todd, 1946)

RETIREMENT AND HEALTH

These general statements were reinforced by numerous socio-medical studies, of varying quality, which appeared to show: first, that retirement *was* detrimental to health; and, secondly, that it was actively disliked by *most* retirees. This was the view of pioneer geriatricians such as Sheldon (in his study in the 1940s of older people in Wolverhampton) and sociologists such as Townsend (in his research in the 1950s on family life in Bethnal Green).

The connection between retirement and poor health was explored in numerous medical studies in the 1950s (see, in particular, those by Anderson and Cowan, 1956; Batchelor and Napier, 1953; Logan, 1953; Johnson, 1958). The sociological studies were fewer but followed the same theme in equating retirement with a deterioration in mental well-being (see, for example, Townsend, 1955; Tunstall, 1966).[4]

---

[3] For a more detailed analysis see Fennell, Phillipson and Evers (1988, Ch. 3).
[4] Comprehensive reviews of the health effects of retirement are provided by Minkler (1981) and McGoldrick (1989).

Some of the negative findings can be attributed to methodological problems in much of the above research. For example, medical research tended to include those who had a physical or mental health problem *before* retirement. This raises the question of whether ill health might not have been a cause rather than a consequence of leaving work (see below). But leaving this point aside, we should also note those studies in the 1950s and 1960s which gave a different interpretation to the experience of retirement. Some examples here are Richardson's (1956) work in Scotland in the 1950s; Emerson's (1959) research on the transition to retirement, also in the 1950s; national surveys (for example by the Ministry of Pensions and National Insurance, 1954); studies on the future of work and leisure (see, especially, Le Gros Clark, 1966); research in the field of industrial and occupational psychology (Welford, 1958, 1976) and finally the longitudinal research by Crawford in the 1960s, of couples facing the transition to retirement (Crawford, 1971, 1972a).

These different research projects were significant in that they indicated a more complex view of the reasons which people gave for leaving work and the impact retirement had on their lives. Early research, for example, tended to assume that compulsory retirement forced people to leave work against their will and, moreover, that most retirees were only too willing to return to paid employment. In contrast, both the small-scale study by Richardson (1956) and the national survey by the Ministry of Pensions and National Insurance (1954) suggested that ill health was a major factor people gave for leaving (or wanting to leave) work and an important reason as well in preventing many from returning to a paid occupation. Similar findings were reported in America in this period (see Corson and McConnell, 1956) and in British research some twenty years later (Parker, 1980).

The work of the various research units on ageing, at the Universities of London, Bristol and Liverpool, highlighted the difficulties facing older workers in the labour market. These included: occupational downgrading and loss of pay (Heron and Chown, 1967); the pressure of assembly-line work (Brown, 1957); and inadequate retirement preparation (Heron, 1962, 1963; see also Phillipson and Strang, 1983).

Some of the research also questioned views which necessarily linked retirement with a period of anxiety and disorientation (Townsend, 1955). Emerson (1959), for example, in a study of 125 65-year-olds, whilst confirming that retirement had some initial impact in increasing tensions and anxieties, found that psychological problems were usually resolved after the transitional period. Moreover, his research suggested that even during the first year of leaving work, retirement *per se* had little effect on physical or mental health. The findings in Richardson's study of 244 men came to a similar conclusion:

The extremes of complete contentment and bitter dissatisfaction with retirement were easily discerned but the majority of statements revealed mixed feelings; attitude to retirement was the product of a number of variables – state of health, the meaning of former jobs, length of retirement, use made of retirement, the relationship with family and wider social groups – all of these in varying degrees and diverse ways affected the replies. (Richardson, 1956, p. 385)

Some ten years later, Crawford's research on the way couples anticipated retirement, the rituals associated with it and its effect on lifestyles and relationships, confirmed the influence of the variables identified by Richardson. Moreover, her research, although indicating that some couples did indeed perceive retirement in crisis terms, found no evidence that this was expressed in the form of psychosomatic illnesses (Crawford, 1972b).

The challenge to the view of retirement as necessarily creating problems and tensions was also apparent in American social gerontology (see, especially, the work of Streib and his colleagues at Cornell University).[5] In line with this, it is interesting to find the following argument in Cumming and Henry's controversial study of the process of disengagement (see Chapters 2 and 4):

> If health care and economic independence are guaranteed, those few retired men who cannot reintegrate with a membership group and cannot shift their skills are probably the only true 'problem' group among old people in society. Generally speaking, our findings support those [who argue] that retirement in itself does not appear to be a problem for most men; it is the lack of horizontal ties and of a suitable way of relating, which retirement may carry with it, that seem to make trouble. (Cumming and Henry, 1961, pp. 153–4)

SOCIOLOGICAL ISSUES IN THE CONSTRUCTION OF RETIREMENT

As the number of research studies increased, so there was a shift towards viewing retirement as less problematic for men and, correspondingly, more difficult for some groups of women (see below). At the same time, this empirical observation was reinforced by (and in some cases arose out of) new theoretical arguments about the nature of retirement. In the 1940s and 1950s, the dominance of role theory led to a virtual consensus in gerontology that loss of a primary role such as work deprived the individual – men especially – of status and identity (Cavan et al, 1949; Parsons, 1942; Tibbitts, 1954). This argument was modified with the arrival of the disengagement hypothesis, although the assumption that retirement was entirely non-problematic for women remained (Cumming and Henry, 1961).

By the 1970s, other theoretical models were beginning to challenge the assumptions of role theory and the discredited disengagement hypothesis (Hochschild, 1975). For example, the political economy perspective

[5] The Cornell research is summarised in Streib and Schneider (1971).

(see also Chapter 2) focused on the way in which retirement was shaped by the social structure and by the social and economic factors which affect the individual's place in that structure (Stone and Minkler, 1984; Minkler and Estes 1991; Phillipson, 1991a). This approach emphasised the impact of class, gender and race in influencing the experience of retirement. In short, retirement came to be seen as 'socially constructed', varying according to lifelong social status and prevailing state policies and ideologies (Phillipson and Walker, 1986).

This theoretical argument, along with others, was important in shifting the focus of investigation from one of asking how individuals have adjusted to retirement, to examining the socio-political factors which influence and control retirement outcomes (Estes, 1979, 1986; Phillipson, 1991a).

As well as the contribution from social gerontological theory, two additional factors have played an important role in terms of influencing debates about adjustment to retirement. First, during the 1970s and 1980s there were important methodological debates about the conduct of research and the interpretation of survey findings. For example, there was growing appreciation of the limitations of cross-sectional studies and concern with the restricted nature of many samples, especially as regards the under-representation of women and some minority ethnic groups. In Britain, the majority of retirement studies have employed a cross-sectional design (see, for example, Parker, 1980). With this method, however, as noted in Chapter 2, it is virtually impossible to distinguish between the causes and consequences of retirement. Thus, as noted earlier, many studies in the 1950s and 1960s reported increased rates of sickness as a consequence of retiring from work. Unfortunately, on closer inspection of the design of these studies, it is impossible to say whether this sickness is caused by the poor health which people bring into retirement or whether it is an outcome of leaving work (Minkler, 1981). One solution to this problem is the longitudinal design which follows people's lives prospectively from an earlier point in the life cycle. These designs are, however, expensive as well as taking a long time to complete. Fortunately, the findings from American surveys of this kind are now available and they have added considerably to our own understanding of the retirement period (see, for example, Palmore et al, 1985).

There is, however, a second issue to be considered in studies of retirement. When people are asked about their attitudes towards leaving work, it is important to remember that their replies are framed within a social and political context. In the 1950s, when people were urged to remain at work and when retired people were seen as a 'burden', it is hardly surprising to find negative views expressed about retirement. In the early 1990s, when there was pressure on people to leave work (to create jobs for the young), different views may be expressed. People certainly have views about retirement but these are subject (as with any individual or group) to manipulation within a given social and political climate. Moreover, this is particularly likely given a historical context in which retirement has been a relatively weak and unpopular institution (Blaikie and MacNicol, 1989).

We must be careful, therefore, in interpreting research findings in the field of retirement studies: is sufficient account taken of the limitations of particular research designs? Do these designs acknowledge the effect of social and cultural forces in marginalising retirement? These points need to be borne in mind when reading the next section of this chapter which reviews research in the 1970s and 1980s on the experience of retirement.

THE EXPERIENCE OF RETIREMENT

We suggested at the beginning of this chapter that retirement has often been seen as disruptive and disturbing to the individual. How far does contemporary research show this to be the case? What are the attitudes and views of retired people themselves?

In the years or months leading to retirement important changes and developments may be experienced. The loss of a job in middle age can cause great hardship and distress, with an extended period of unemployment and consequent loss of income (Walker, Noble and Westergaard, 1985; Itzin and Phillipson, 1993). For those remaining at work, there may be social pressures arising from redundancy or early retirement programmes, technological changes in the workplace, and adjustments due to the impact of health problems (Dex and Phillipson, 1986). A minority may feel and express concern about their future retirement. Parker's (1980) British survey found 35 per cent of women workers under pension age were expecting that they would find it difficult to settle down when they retired; the figure for men was 27 per cent. Both groups anticipated similar types of problems, financial difficulties being uppermost. Overall in Parker's survey, two-fifths of older workers were looking forward to retirement, one in eight were definitely unhappy about the prospect, and the rest had mixed feelings.

Studies have shown that the availability and size of (occupational) pensions influence individuals' retirement decision in Britain and in the US; most of the studies have been done in the US (see, for example, Shaw, 1984) but one British econometric study has been done on Parker's OPCS data (Zabalza et al, 1980). The availability of an occupational pension is related to whether a job is full- or part-time. Since many women are in part-time jobs, or have spent some proportion of their working life in part-time work, their eligibility for occupational pensions will be more restricted in comparison with men (OPCS, 1991). The lack of an occupational pension is likely to act as a disincentive for women to retire, and certainly to retire early (Dex and Phillipson, 1986; Groves, 1993).

Early retirement may also create difficulties. Here, we must distinguish between on the one hand, a minority of people who choose to retire early (because they have sufficient income) and who usually report satisfaction with the decision (McGoldrick and Cooper, 1989). On the other hand, there are a much larger number of workers who retire early because of health problems (Bone et al, 1992). This group appear more likely to report uncertainty about the future and to experience problems of adjustment (Cribier, 1981; Parker, 1980).

Early retirement may lead to some tensions, even where resources are relatively secure and there are no health problems. Bytheway (1986), in a study of Welsh steelworkers, found dissatisfaction being expressed with men feeling that their skills were being wasted. Walker, Noble and Westergaard's (1985) research on the impact of redundancy amongst steelworkers in Sheffield, found those who had taken the early retirement option to be evenly divided between those relieved to be leaving work and those expressing regret.

Guillemard (1986) relates the problem of the early retired to ambiguities in their social position. She sees such people as neither really unemployed nor actually retired. Very few accept the label 'senior citizen'; yet society has no category or role in between that of worker or pensioner.

Guillemard (1986), along with Walker (1982a), highlights the way in which, during a period of economic recession, old age is being redefined to incorporate people from middle age onwards (see also, Kohli et al, 1991). The similarity between this argument and the historical perspective outlined earlier is clear: retirement – as an economic and social policy – is an area over which very few individuals (particularly women or those from the working class) have direct control. People cannot, in most cases, choose their retirement; nor can they (unless they have a scarce skill) carry out the option of remaining at work. It is for these reasons that many researchers continue to view retirement in negative terms. Townsend (1986), for example, argues that:

> Those reaching retirement age do not welcome retirement as warmly as they thought they would or others suppose. Many who have retired deeply regret their inactivity or loss of status, and as time goes on many regret the restrictions on their activities imposed by a greatly reduced income. The satisfaction often expressed by many retired people turns out on closer examination to be more an assertion of hope, or what they think is expected of them, than a true representation of what they feel. As in most human situations of change, there are profound reservations and regrets as well as advantages or at least mild compensations. (Townsend, 1986, p. 25)

This argument finds a reflection in research findings which shows a substantial minority of male and female pre-retirees who have no idea about what to do in their retirement. This was indicated in Crawford's research in Bristol in the 1960s; it also received some confirmation in Phillipson and Strang's (1983) study of pre-retirement education. In this research in an interview two weeks before their pre-retirement course, nearly 40 per cent of those interviewed (n = 217) professed not to have a clear idea of what to do with their retirement; a similar percentage expressed doubts about their ability to keep occupied. The same study also confirmed earlier British and American research by Heron (1963) and Kerckhoff (1964) regarding the lack of planning for retirement. On the specific question of financial planning, Ritchie and Barrowclough's survey (1983) found that one-quarter of men and one-third of women aged 50 plus had given no thought to the income they would have once retired.

However, if the lead-up to retirement appears stressful, it is less clear that the same can be said for retirement itself.[6] Indeed, the general conclusions from research points in a more optimistic direction. Atchley, for example, conducted a series of studies in America throughout the 1960s and 1970s, all of which pointed to the impact of reduced income and the change in lifestyle associated with it as the major factor in producing negative retirement attitudes. From his research Atchley found little evidence for those with moderate incomes and above actually 'missing work' to any great extent. From a sociological perspective he put forward the view that:

> Each person generally has several roles that he stakes his identity on. Work may be at or near the top, but not necessarily so. There simply is not the kind of homogeneous consensus of the value of work that would keep it at the top for everyone. In fact, the many systems of competing values in a complex society ensure that there will be a wide variety of self-values. Thus, the probability that retirement will lead to a complete identity breakdown is light, and there may be just as many people who rely on leisure pursuits for self-respect as there are who rely on work, particularly among those with unsatisfying jobs. (Atchley, 1971, p. 16)

Palmore et al's (1985, p. 167) analysis of a number of American longitudinal data sets concluded that:

1. Retirement at the normal age has little or no adverse effect on health for the average retiree. Some have health declines, but these are balanced by those who enjoy health improvement.
2. Retirement at the normal age has few substantial effects on activities, except for the obvious reduction in work and some compensating increase in solitary activities.
3. Retirement at the normal age has little or no effect on most attitudes for the average retiree. Some become more dissatisfied, but these are balanced by those who become more satisfied.

Cribier's French study confirmed both a 'marked increase in the

---

[6] For reviews of research, dating from the 1950s to the 1980s, on the topic of adjustment to retirement, see Nadelson (1969), Friedmann and Orbach (1974), George (1980) and Braithwaite and Gibson (1987). For a sociological interpretation of retirement, Maddox's (1966) essay, 'Retirement as a social event', is outstanding.

proportion of people who view retirement as a desirable goal, and early retirement as particularly desirable' (Cribier, 1981, p. 66). The retirees in Parker's (1980) British study, whilst more cautious in their views, had still, in the majority of cases, 'settled down' some twelve months after leaving work (see also, Phillipson and Strang, 1983; Long, 1987).

Beyond these general findings, however, some qualifications must be expressed. What research also tells us is that biographies and work histories remain important in influencing retirement outcomes (Long, 1987; Thompson et al, 1990). We can see this in very obvious ways: people in retirement are survivors and this in itself is class determined (if you are in social class five you are two and a half times more likely to die before reaching retirement than if in social class one). Working-class people are also more likely to enter retirement with a chronic health problem and, in consequence, to have some limitation placed on their retirement activities (Shephard, 1978; Townsend et al, 1987; Bone et al, 1992).

Research also points to other consequences of given class and occupational positions. Guillemard's French study suggested that social withdrawal was a typical mode of response for working-class retirees, because their exploited position presented them with few resources to consume and convert into meaningful leisure (see also Phillipson, 1987).

Such relationships have also been indicated in the American longitudinal research. Parnes and Less (1983), for example, found that amongst white men, both family income and occupational level had independent effects on the amount of time spent on leisure activity in retirement. They concluded from this that:

> the kind of work that men do influences leisure activities not only through the income that it generates, but also by conditioning or reflecting their interests. If participation in leisure activities contributes to satisfaction, one might therefore expect men who had retired from high level jobs to manifest above average satisfaction with retirement even when such factors as income and health are held constant. (Parnes and Less, 1983, pp. 90–1; see also Simpson and McKinney, 1966)

WOMEN IN RETIREMENT

Another area of differentiation concerns the question of women in retirement. Women's experience of retirement is affected both by their position in the labour market and ideologies regarding their role as carers (Bernard and Meade, 1993). In the case of the former, there has been a substantial growth in the number of women employees. Women's participation rates display, in fact, a bimodal pattern, with the first peak occurring between the ages of 20–24 and the second at 45–50 (Dex, 1985; Department of Employment, 1992a).

Early research argued that entering retirement was less stressful for women, partly because work had been a less important element in their lives, and partly because of the maintenance of the role of housewife (Donahue et al, 1960; Tibbitts, 1954). However, Dex (1985) suggests that the later research literature indicates strong similarities in the attitudes of men and women towards work. Women, she notes, have been found to be more economistic or instrumental than was thought to be the case (and men less so), and both experience variations through the life course in orientations to work. Martin and Roberts's (1984) analysis of the *Women and Employment* survey found that the majority of working women had a high financial dependence upon working and enjoyed working.

Loss of work may, therefore, have profound implications for women. At the same time, the type of work carried out by women workers also raises difficulties for their retirement. Various researchers point to the clustering of women in low-paid jobs with limited or non-existent pensions (O'Rand and Henretta, 1982; Stone and Minkler, 1984; Davies and Ward, 1992; Groves, 1993). The majority of women who work are located in low-status, low-paid, sex-segregated work (Abdela, 1991). In 1990 in the UK women still earned less than three-quarters of male earnings, and there has been little change in the earnings gap between 1975 when women's earnings were 72.1 per cent of men's (the year the Sex Discrimination Act came into effect) and 1990 when women's were 76.9 per cent of men's, based on average gross hourly earnings. When weekly earnings are considered, there is a gap of more than a third between male and female full-time earnings (Department of Employment, 1991).

Gender differences in adjustment to retirement have been reported by a number of researchers. Szinovacz (1982) provided one of the first reviews of this issue (see also, Szinovacz, 1991 for an additional summary). Jacobson's (1974) British study in the early 1970s found women less likely than men to be positively oriented to retirement. Streib and Schneider (1971) found women to be more apprehensive than men about the effects of retirement. Atchley (1976) found women taking longer than men to adapt to the retirement transition, a finding confirmed in Fox's (1976) research on the adaptation of women workers to retirement.

Szinovacz (1991) notes that the discontinuous nature of women's work histories means that many women view their mid-life as a special challenge and opportunity and may view the later phase of their work career in a different way to that of men. They are also less likely than men to have achieved their career goals at the time their spouses wish to retire or employers' retirement incentives encourage their husbands' retirement.

More detailed explorations on women's retirement still await detailed theoretical and empirical study. Research on women's experience of retirement is still limited in both quantity and quality. Palmore et al's (1985) description of their longitudinal research is typical of the gender bias in this area, admitting that: 'The theoretical models and variables used in [our] analysis were largely orientated toward retirement among men. As a consequence, major factors that explain individual differences in retirement among women were not included' (Palmore et al, 1985, p. 170). However, research has also been deficient in its failure to acknowledge the important role of the sexual division of labour in affecting women's retirement experience (Stone and Minkler, 1984). The unequal nature of social care has been highlighted in research summarised in Arber and Ginn (1991) and Dalley (1993). Retirement may, in some cases, be caused by an increase in responsibilities in the area of informal care – either for a sick husband, relative or both (Parker, 1980; Bone et al, 1992). Alternatively, the retirement experience may itself be structured around a range of caring activities.

The nature of women's experience has, however, changed in ways which have yet to be documented in respect of British research. For example, the increases in labour force participation of middle-aged women imply that retirement is becoming a 'couple experience'. This raises important questions regarding how partners time their retirement in relation to each other, the problems which may arise from differential timing patterns, and how couples adapt during the transition process from dual-earner to dual-retired couple (Szinovacz, Ekerdt and Vinick, 1992).

A more general issue concerns the need to shift the nature of the debate on retirement away from a male-oriented model of work and family life (Bernard and Meade, 1993). The characteristic feature of this model has been to emphasise the segregation between these two spheres. However, family obligations may play an important role in influencing the timing of retirement and in shaping the retirement experience itself. Moreover, pre-retirement marital and family roles may be crucial in determining the social world of older women and their partners.

The experience of retirement: continuity or discontinuity?

What conclusions can we draw from the extensive literature on retirement in the 1970s and 1980s? Perhaps the most important theme concerns the relationship between retirement and other phases in the life course. Here we have seen an important shift from the 1960s, where retirement was seen as entailing a dislocation 'whose effects would be common to everyone' (Stone and Minkler, 1984, p. 226). The impact of twenty years of research has been to focus, instead, on variations in the experience of retirement, here reflecting lifelong inequalities and differences produced by class, gender and ethnicity.

The implication of this argument is that retirement is shaped at least as much by continuities as discontinuities in life experiences. Indeed, as has been argued elsewhere, the transition to retirement is not a movement from an old to a completely new life (as the disengagement and role theories would suggest); rather it is the final resolution of the advantages and disadvantages attached to given class, gender and ethnic locations. A resolution in the sense that once the advantages arising from a particular position are consolidated they are likely to be sustained even into very old age. Similarly, where there are disadvantages, retirement and old age may simply add to the individual's sense of powerlessness and loss of control (Phillipson, 1987).

Such arguments still leave many problems unresolved. For example, taking the above orientation, the case for classifying retired men by their previous occupation or social class might be emphasised. This, it might be argued, would be the surest indicator of the material advantages or disadvantages of the older person. But continuity in terms of class, whilst often accurate (along with gender) as an objective indicator of resources, may be less satisfactory as a subjective indicator of attitudes. Retired people may, in fact, feel that their class location is contradictory. Separated from the routine of wage labour, they may respond and have their attitudes shaped by different priorities and circumstances. At the same time, they tend not to form a common interest group in old age. The reasons for this have been analysed by Alan Walker as follows:

> as an analysis of the political economy of old age shows, elderly people are just as deeply divided along class and other structural lines as younger adults. While both functionalist and pluralist analyses suggest a common interest among elderly people, with age acting as a leveller of class and status differentials, a political economy perspective shows that the social construction of old age is a function of two separate sets of relations. On the one hand, older people carry into retirement inequalities created and legitimated at an earlier phase of the life cycle, particularly though not exclusively through the labour market. On the other hand, the process of retirement imposes a reduced social and economic status on a large proportion of older people in comparison with younger economically active adults. Social gerontology and especially political gerontology has put too much emphasis on the latter and too little on the former. (Walker, 1986a, pp. 37–8)

A future task for research is to explore how these conflicting pressures influence behaviour in retirement. As this indicates, we have moved considerably beyond a view which sees the individual adjusting to retirement in isolation from his or her own life history and the wider social structure. Both are now taken to be crucial variables in understanding behaviour and attitudes. The next few years should see a clarification of how the contradictory forces affecting older people influence both patterns of adjustment and the shape of retirement as a social institution.

THE FUTURE OF RETIREMENT

The question that remains to be asked is whether the 1990s and beyond will see the final triumph of retirement as a social and economic institution. In some respects, of course, this has already happened. In the 1970s and 1980s older people withdrew from the labour force in increasing numbers and at earlier ages. The key factors which consolidated the drift of older workers from employment were: (1) the decline in semi- and unskilled jobs; (2) the entry or re-entry into the labour market of women workers; (3) the growth – through occupational pension schemes – of financial provision for early retirement on the grounds of ill health; and (4) the growing number (albeit a minority) who choose early retirement as a positive and valued alternative to full-time work.

Table 8.1 examines the changes in the position of older men during the 1970s and 1980s. This confirms the steep fall in economic activity for men aged 60–64, especially in the 1970s and early 1980s. By the early 1990s, only around 50 per cent of men aged 60–64 could be counted as economically active.

The trends amongst older women are more complex to assess because of inadequacies in manpower statistics: in particular, the failure of many women to register as unemployed or the omission of part-time workers (the majority of whom are women) from some labour statistics (Dex and Phillipson, 1986). The official statistics (see Table 8.2) for the 1970s and 1980s indicate a marked decline in the percentage of women aged 60 plus who are defined as economically active. In contrast, the rates for women aged 55–59 fluctuate at between 51 per cent and 55 per cent

Table 8.1   *Male economic activity rates in Britain, 1971–2001*

| Age | Percentage of each age group economically active | | | | | | | | | | |
| | Estimates | | | | | | | | | | |
	1971	1981	1982	1983	1984	1985	1986	1987	1988	1989	1990
Men											
45–54	95.7	94.8	94.0	93.1	92.6	92.4	91.8	91.0	91.3	91.7	91.5
55–59	93.0	89.4	86.8	84.1	82.1	82.2	81.1	79.4	80.3	79.8	81.0
60–64	82.9	69.3	64.3	59.4	56.7	55.4	53.8	55.2	54.9	54.6	54.4
65–69	30.4	16.3	14.8	13.5	13.6	14.4	13.2	13.3	12.2	14.6	14.4
70+	10.9	6.5	5.9	5.3	5.5	5.2	4.7	4.6	5.4	5.5	5.2
	Projections										
	1991	1992	1993	1994	1995	1996	1997	1998	1999	2000	2001
Men											
45–54	91.0	91.2	91.1	91.0	91.0	90.9	90.9	90.8	90.7	90.7	90.6
55–59	80.3	80.4	80.4	80.4	80.4	80.4	80.4	80.4	80.4	80.4	80.4
60–64	54.1	53.4	52.8	52.3	51.9	51.5	51.3	51.0	50.9	50.7	50.6
65–69	15.1	14.4	14.0	13.6	13.4	13.2	13.0	12.9	12.8	12.7	12.7
70+	4.7	4.2	4.0	3.9	3.8	3.6	3.5	3.4	3.3	3.2	3.1

Source: Department of Employment, *Employment Gazette*, 100 (4), 1992b

Table 8.2 *Female economic activity rates in Britain, 1971–2001*

Age	Percentage of each age group economically active										
	Estimates										
	1971	1981	1982	1983	1984	1985	1986	1987	1988	1989	1990
Women											
45–54	62.0	68.0	68.1	68.1	69.2	69.5	70.5	70.8	70.5	72.2	72.8
55–59	50.9	53.4	52.0	50.6	51.1	52.1	51.8	53.0	52.7	54.3	54.9
60–64	28.8	23.3	21.9	20.5	21.3	18.9	19.1	19.2	19.9	22.9	22.7
65+	6.3	3.7	3.5	3.2	3.0	3.0	2.7	2.7	2.8	3.4	3.3
	Projections										
	1991	1992	1993	1994	1995	1996	1997	1998	1999	2000	2001
Women											
45–54	72.7	72.5	72.7	72.9	73.1	73.2	73.4	73.5	73.5	73.6	73.6
55–59	54.5	54.9	54.9	54.9	54.9	54.9	54.9	54.9	54.9	54.9	54.9
60–64	24.1	23.8	23.8	23.9	24.0	24.3	24.5	24.9	25.2	23.6	26.0
65+	3.1	3.0	3.0	2.9	2.9	2.9	2.8	2.8	2.8	2.8	2.8

Source: Department of Employment, *Employment Gazette*, 100 (4), 1992.

throughout this period and for women aged 45–54 there is a gradual rise in economic activity.

Taking both men and women, the evidence suggests that the marginalisation of older employees gathered pace in the 1970s. This arose through: first, their concentration, in many cases, in contracting industries; secondly, the operation of particular schemes to promote worker redeployment (eg the Redundancy Payments Act) or replacement (the Job Release Scheme); thirdly, the pressure of mass unemployment; fourthly, changing attitudes amongst government, business, trades unions and older people themselves, in respect of the older workers' right to employment in relation to other, younger age groups (Bytheway, 1986).

In general terms, it is also clear that a different type of retirement began to emerge in the 1980s in comparison to that which existed in the 1970s. More especially, there is the growing importance of early exit from paid work together with the emergence of a range of different pathways which people take from full-time work to full-time retirement, a trend affecting virtually all industrialised countries (Kohli et al, 1991). Retirement (defined in terms of entry into a public old-age pension scheme) and withdrawal or 'exit' from the workforce, no longer coincide for increasing numbers of workers. Thus it is misleading to view the fall in male participation rates simply as part of a trend toward earlier retirement. Retirement, as it is traditionally defined, is seen to come at a predictable point, accompanied (for men at least) by a pension provided by the state. In contrast, the retirement which emerged in many industrialised countries from the 1970s, did not come at the traditional stage in the life course. Moreover, many of those generally considered to be retired do not receive a public pension and may not even consider themselves retired (Laczko and Phillipson, 1991).

In the case of the retirement transition, the template of previous generations – long work, short retirement – is being dissolved (Schuller, 1989). For many (mostly male) workers, the predictability of continuous employment is being replaced by insecurity in middle and later life – an experience shared with the majority of women workers (Groves, 1993; Itzin and Phillipson, 1993). Older workers increasingly find themselves on the margins of the labour market but with a number of years ahead of them before they reach the comparative safety of retirement. The retirement transition has also come to be organised on a more flexible basis with a range of pathways (eg unemployment, long-term sick, redundancy) which people follow before they either describe themselves, or are defined within the social security system, as 'wholly retired' (Kohli et al, 1991).

These developments have substantially altered approaches to understanding adjustment to retirement. Up to the 1970s, research in this area tended to be based on assumptions about continuity in work patterns, the exception being early retirement because of ill health. The context here was one of full employment and a view that most workers wished to remain at work up to and even beyond state pensionable age. Adjustment was interpreted in terms of how people coped with either mandatory retirement or the problems associated with poor health in the period around retirement. However, this model is no longer adequate for understanding the issue of retirement adjustment. There are now numerous pathways which people take from mid-life through to retirement – all of these producing different types of adjustment and change within the retirement period. The research agenda here is for a range of new studies which assess responses to different forms of detachment from the workforce. These include:

- forced early retirement (Bytheway, 1986);
- voluntary early retirement pathways (McGoldrick and Cooper, 1989)
- redundancy pathways (Walker, 1989);
- disability/ long-term sick pathways (Laczko and Phillipson, 1991);
- informal care pathways (Dalley, 1993);
- unemployment pathways (Laczko and Phillipson, 1991);
- discouraged worker pathways (Laczko, 1987);
- the state retirement pathway (Laczko and Phillipson, 1991).

The complexity of the process of withdrawal from work suggests an underlying fragmentation in the retirement experience itself. In this sense, the institution of retirement has moved from a position of relative stability in the 1950s and 1960s (albeit within the context of impoverishment for most retirees) to considerable instability in the 1990s (with enduring poverty for some and affluence for a minority). This development will produce increased stratification within retirement, with social divisions based upon unequal access to occupational pensions and considerable variation in the amount and quality of the pension received by different groups (see Chapter 12). This fact, together with the likely emphasis of governments on the 'burden of old age', will place major constraints on the development of retirement as a social institution. Undoubtedly, there will be many retired people (from the middle classes especially), who will develop a leisure-oriented lifestyle, built around the expanding consumer market aimed at the over-50s: specialist holiday companies; second homes; retirement communities (most notably in America but variations on this theme in Britain as well); and private sheltered housing schemes (an area of rapid expansion in Britain in the 1980s).

These are the trends for those privileged to continue their middle-aged lifestyle into retirement. But to set against this is the fact that in the 1990s pensioners are still the second largest group in poverty, with 30 per cent of those in poverty consisting of older people (Oppenheim, 1993). With reduced opportunities for paid work, dependence on social security benefits has increased. In 1991 retired households were dependent on social security benefits for an average of 41 per cent of their household income (the remainder coming from savings, occupational pensions and small earnings), in contrast to 11 per cent of all households.

These material realities will continue to cloud the future of retirement. But of equal importance to the lives of older and retired workers will be social and political attitudes towards retirement itself. Here, the evidence suggests the start of a new phase, in the 1990s, in the development of policies towards older workers. In the decade from 1979 to 1989, there was active government support for early retirement. For a brief period in the early 1990s, this trend was reversed in the context of a debate about the 'burden' of retirement and what was seen to be a problem of labour shortages arising from too few younger people entering the labour market (National Economic Development Council, 1989).

An additional factor of concern has been the difference in the state pension age between men and women. This issue was raised by the European Court of Justice ruling in the Barber *v* Guardian Royal Exchange case that pensions are part of pay and that discrimination on the basis of sex is unlawful. For some time it seemed apparent that the most likely response by government to this ruling was to propose an equalisation of state pension ages at 65 (the dominant view from the Treasury in the late 1980s and early 1990s). However, the political fall-out from raising the pension age of women could make this an undesirable option. An additional factor is that sustaining a pensionable age of 65 is increasingly difficult in the context of unemployment levels of at least three million (1 in 10 of the workforce) and with only a minority of men actually working up to 65. The alternative option of equalising pension ages at 60 may increasingly be seen as more realistic, this having the merit of removing large numbers of the long-term unemployed from the dole queue as well as being cheaper than supporting those in need through income support.

At present (in 1993) the outcome of the debate about retirement ages is still uncertain, although the persistence of high levels of unemployment may be the determining factor in settling the debate one way or the other. However, it is almost certainly the case that one effect of the policy upheavals has been to consolidate the high level of financial and social insecurity experienced by many older workers in the 1980s. On the one hand, few governments in the future are likely to want to increase the attractiveness of retirement: the economic 'costs' will be viewed as too substantial and burdensome. On the other hand, very few initiatives are being developed – in Britain at least – to give older people greater security in the labour market (Itzin and Phillipson, 1993). In fact, although older people are still clearly targeted as a reserve of labour, it is married women who are seen as the key group for meeting shortages in labour supply (women are likely to take the bulk of the new jobs which may be created through the 1990s). Older people are more likely to be used for low-paid jobs, particularly in the new service industries (Itzin and Phillipson, 1993).

But an increase in part-time working may not greatly reduce the degree of insecurity experienced by older workers. They may still face above-average unemployment; at the same time, financial support from the state may become more limited and targeted at particular groups. In short, in Britain at least, the social institution of retirement, whilst continuing to develop in new and important ways, will still to be regarded with some ambivalence at the level of the state. In consequence, the tension between the aspirations of retired people and the legitimacy accorded them in the 1990s will remain a crucial issue for researchers to address.

9

LIVING ARRANGEMENTS OF ELDERLY PEOPLE

John Bond

One of the most influential factors on all our lives is the environment in which we live. For older people this may be particularly so since they may spend more time in their own home than many other groups in society. In this chapter we will look at both the geographical location of older people, especially the phenomenon known colloquially as 'Costa Geriatrica', and the type of living accommodation experienced by older people. Although only about 5 per cent of people aged 65 or over are resident in an institution of some kind we will give relatively more space than this to the experiences of older people living in institutions.

There have probably been a number of favoured locations to which older people have retired in the past although these were probably restricted to a wealthy group of people. However, with the increasing numbers of relatively well-off retired people these favoured locations have become more popular. In addition, the depopulation of rural areas by younger people, particularly in the hundred years prior to 1950, has resulted in an ageing rural population. These trends, although significant, should not mask the fact that the majority of older people do not move away from their life-long associations with a particular community.

Most older people live in normal housing. Yet generally in everyday life we associate old age with specialist housing. It has been estimated that just under 400,000 people lived in sheltered housing in 1981 (Butler et al, 1983) and some 650,000 in 1991 (Fletcher, 1991). Thus, when considering housing for elderly people we will be reviewing not only the specialist housing needs of older people but the role of the general housing stock in the living arrangements of older people.

The variety of housing accommodation available to elderly people is matched by the variety of institutional care used by very frail elderly people. Elderly people are resident in NHS hospitals, local authority, private and voluntary residential homes and in NHS, private and voluntary nursing homes. Although only a small number of older people live in institutions at any one time a significant proportion will experience institutional living at some time during their later life, particularly those people who attain at least 80 years of age.

Residential location

The geographical distribution of elderly people in Britain in 1991 can be contrasted with that of 1921. In 1921 the pattern was characterised by above average concentrations of elderly people in an axial belt across the centre of the country from the south-west to Norfolk, and two additional clusters of concentration in mid-Wales and Sussex. The axial belt reaching from the north-west through the Midlands to London and the home counties supported below average proportions of elderly people (Allon-Smith, 1982). Table 9.1 shows that by 1991 the Regions with the highest proportions of elderly people were the South West, East Anglia and Wales, while the West Midlands, East Midlands and Scotland had the lowest. Analysis of the populations of the counties indicates a more varied pattern.

Table 9.2 ranks the top fifteen and the bottom fifteen county districts according to pensionable population in Britain in 1991. The counties with the highest proportions of elderly population were found along the south coast (except for Hampshire), in non-industrial Wales, East Anglia, Lancashire, North Yorkshire, and the Borders and Tayside in Scotland. The counties with the lowest proportion of elderly people included most of Midland England, the northern and western home counties, Cleveland and West Central Scotland. The metropolitan counties were just below average in the proportion of elderly people resident. The distribution of these county districts is shown in Figure 9.1.

These simple statistical data, which show the high concentrations of

Table 9.1 *Regional distribution of pensionable population in Britain, 1991*

	Pensionable population (000s)	Percentage of total population
South West	1000	21.7
Wales	570	20.1
East Anglia	403	19.9
North	575	19.0
Yorkshire and Humberside	914	18.9
North West	1161	18.6
East Midlands	727	18.4
Scotland	910	18.2
West Midlands	932	18.1
South East	3097	18.0
Great Britain	10264	18.7

Source: Office of Population Censuses and Surveys (1992) National Monitor CEN 91 CM 56 December 1992

Table 9.2 *County districts with the largest and smallest proportions of the pensionable population in Britain, 1991*

Rank	Areas with highest and lowest proportion of elderly people	Percentage of total population
1	Christchurch, Dorset	34.6
2	Rother, E. Sussex	34.1
3	Eastbourne, E. Sussex	32.0
4	East Devon	31.5
5	Arun, W. Sussex	31.1
6	Tendring, Essex	30.4
7	West Somerset	30.0
8	Worthing, W. Sussex	30.0
9	South Wight	29.8
10	Colwyn, Clwyd	27.9
11	Torbay, Devon	27.9
12	Bournemouth, Dorset	27.9
13	Thanet, Kent	27.7
14	North Norfolk	27.6
15	East Dorset	27.6
445	Gordon, Grampian	14.0
446	Haringey, London	13.8
447	Huntingdon, Cambs	13.8
448	Basingstoke, Hants	13.6
449	Luton, Bedfordshire	13.4
450	Rushmoor, Hants	13.2
451	West Lothian	13.1
452	Surrey Heath	13.0
453	Bracknell, Berkshire	12.9
454	Redditch, Hereford and Worcs	12.9
455	Hart, Hampshire	12.6
456	Wokingham, Berks	12.0
457	Cumbernauld and Kilsyth	11.7
458	Milton Keynes, Bucks	11.7
459	Tamworth, Staffs	11.7

Source: Warnes and Ford, 1993

elderly people in particular areas, are often seen as supporting the predominant societal view that old age is a problem. Concentrations of some other social groups are usually viewed as social problems. Thus we are regularly confronted with the 'problems' associated with concentrations of people from ethnic minorities or unemployed people. To national and local planners such variations make the task of planning more difficult and challenging. Similar difficulties will be faced by planners concerned with the estimation of services for elderly people or school and other education services, for example, in areas where there exists a relatively high or low population of these groups. The underlying problem may be society's inability to respond to these kind of data irrespective of social group, in terms of a more equitable distribution of resources to match the needs of a local community.

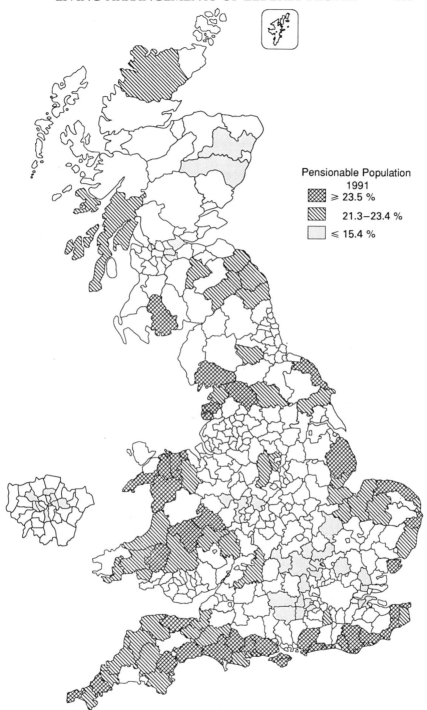

Figure 9.1   *The percentage of pensioners in county districts of Great Britain, 1991: two highest deciles and the lowest decile*
Source: Warnes and Ford, 1993

Meeting the needs of a population with a high proportion of older people is not a short-term challenge. Unlike other age groups, there is little evidence of pronounced fluctuations in the numbers or the proportion of elderly people living in an area. Allon-Smith (1982) has shown that the post-war patterns of residential location of elderly people reflect historical patterns which may have been evident for over fifty years. His detailed examination of retirement areas reveals that not only favoured regions and counties but also individual retirement areas within counties were marked out as early as 1921. Like many contemporary social patterns the development of retirement areas is not a post-war phenomenon.

The meaning of home

Both Peace (1988, 1993b) and Sixsmith (1986b, 1990) emphasise the importance of the meaning of home to people in later life. Home has been characterised as an essentially private place which is the centre of domesticity, a place of intimacy and sometimes a place of solitude. It is often linked to the idea of family (Willcocks et al, 1987; Peace, 1988, 1993b). From a study of older, employed and unemployed people Sixsmith (1990) identifies three themes which underlie the meanings that older people generally associate with home and which are central to an understanding of home and residential experience in later life.

The first theme is one of the home providing the major focus in life. As people age they become more oriented towards home; it is seen as a refuge and becomes increasingly important as other social roles in later life are relinquished. The second theme highlights the need of elderly people to remain independent of others; they appear more concerned with the instrumental aspects of home. The third theme reflects the attachment that older people have for their homes. The importance of 'memories' is significant, with past associations affecting the present experience of home.

Of course, how older individuals perceive home will be influenced by their life careers and how others in society have allowed men and women, and people from different social minorities to relate to 'home'. There will exist a diversity of such experiences and therefore a diversity of perceptions of home.

One influence on people's perceptions of home will be their experience of the communities in which they have lived throughout their lives. Here the idea of community is used in the sense of a distinct territory (Bell and Newby, 1971). Following retirement most elderly people continue to live in the community in which they have lived during their working lives. Retirement migration is still a minority activity which has been estimated to affect about 10 per cent of elderly people (Law and Warnes, 1982).

Migration in later life

In reviewing patterns of residential location of elderly people much attention has focused on migration between areas of the country (Warnes, 1992a, 1992b) and recently this has extended to migration between countries (Warnes, 1991a). However, a distinction should be made between trends which reflect natural changes in the population structure and in the migration of different groups in society.

Urban sociology, the study of patterns of urban life, provides a useful framework in which to consider the way that changes in the population structure in a locality affects the lifestyles of older people. Urban life is distinctively patterned. Specific districts of our cities, towns and counties have acquired their own distinctive characteristics and social styles. Although clearly identified by early sociographers it was the Chicago School of sociologists who set about systematically document-ing changes in social life caused by population change and developing models which have general application. Burgess (1925) proposed a simple ecological model derived from his knowledge of Chicago, which described cities as having a series of concentric zones of distinctive social and physical characteristics (see Figure 9.2). Such a model provides a classic example of an ideal type used by Max Weber to make explicit the

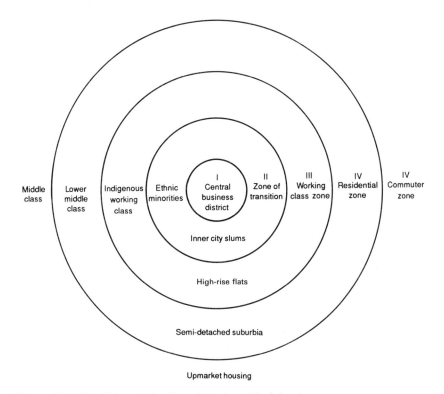

Figure 9.2   *The Chicago School's ecological model of the city*

procedure by which social scientists formulate general abstract concepts. They are hypothetical constructs formed by emphasising aspects of behaviour and institutions which are observable (Gerth and Mills, 1948). Thus geographical features like major rivers, hills and transport systems disrupt the simplicity of the model which has been used by Young and Willmott (1973) in their analysis of family life in London and by Rex and Moore (1967) in their study of race relations in Birmingham.

Central to the ecological model is the idea that through the social Darwinian concepts of competition and invasion and succession, small 'natural areas' form a mosaic of segregated social worlds reinforced by physical environments. Individuals are selected for different areas according to their ability to control resources and in particular physical and social space. Those in the most dominant positions control the most valuable part of the city: the central business district (zone I). Next to this is the zone of transition (zone II) which is characterised in modern British cities by the decaying inner city areas containing high proportions of Asian and Black families living in overcrowded multi-occupied large Victorian houses vacated by the middle classes after the Second World War. The economically and upwardly mobile families within the zone of transition migrate outwards through zone III where semi- and unskilled workers live in the smaller Victorian houses vacated by the lower-middle classes or in post-war council flats. Zone IV is characterised by the predominance of skilled workers living in their semi-detached houses, both owner-occupiers and council tenants. Zone V (the commuter zone) which nowadays with the development of modern transportation systems may include a large rural area around towns and cities, is characterised by the middle classes seeking space and privacy. The demand for cheap land and space, coupled with the inevitable decay of older properties, creates a pattern of central decline and peripheral expansion, which continues until the core is renewed or until they run out of money in the 'core', such as has happened in the London docklands and on the River Tyne in Newcastle.

The complexity of the British housing market and rapid changes in the structure of modern urban areas accentuated by continuing high levels of unemployment and the collapse of the industrial substructure in many British towns and cities in the last decade makes the original model less appropriate. Contemporary urban sociologists while accepting the descriptive value of the model reject the substantial ecological framework upon which it is based (Robson, 1975; Pahl et al, 1983).

Elderly people come from all social groups and classes in society. Residential location will be to a greater part determined by their position in the urban structure prior to old age. Thus, the older members of ethnic minorities will tend to remain close to their relatives and kin in the zone of transition or in areas to which they migrated earlier in their lives. A lack of resources as well as family and kinship ties will prevent the migration of many ethnic elderly people. A lack of resources will also be prohibitive to many working-class and lower middle-class elderly people (Mutchler and Burr, 1991). Thus, we might predict that migration in later life is a predominantly middle-class activity (Law and Warnes, 1982; Grundy, 1987; Warnes, 1991b).

The characteristics of migrants in later life

Migration in later life is increasing in France and the United States (Cribier, 1975; Barsby and Cox, 1975; Graff and Wiseman, 1978) as well as in Britain (Law and Warnes, 1975, 1980), although a fall in migration rates between 1970–71 and 1980–81 in the retirement age groups has been reported (Grundy, 1987). It is estimated that at present about 10 per cent of retired people move 40 km away from their previous residential location (Law and Warnes, 1980). Although migration in the retirement age groups has tended to be within national boundaries the freedom of movement between people within the European Community has seen a significant increase in later-life migration from the richer northern countries of Europe to the poorer Mediterranean countries (Warnes, 1991a).

The majority of moves within and between countries take place around retirement age. Karn (1977), in her study about retirement to the seaside, found that just under half moved in the year of their retirement and Law and Warnes (1980) found that about two-thirds moved within two years of retirement. This is of course a period in the later stage of the life cycle when people are most healthy and have the resources to undertake such moves. When they are older their incomes decline and their health deteriorates (Townsend, 1986) and this tends to restrict mobility. However, the majority of older people do not desire to move or are unable to move.

A number of factors have been suggested as influencing migration. First, individuals must have the ability to move. Thus, migrants in later life tend to be from the middle or upper income groups and from the professional social classes. Usually this means that they are owner-occupiers who are able to realise capital assets in order to make the move. Local authority or private tenants are unlikely to have the necessary resources, even if they desire to migrate. Local authority tenants also have an additional obstacle to migration because of the difficulty of exchanging tenancies.

Second, potential migrants must have the desire to move. Karn (1977) found that people moved because they were attracted to the area of their new home, were dissatisfied with their old home or moved to be nearer families and friends. Similarly, Law and Warnes (1973) found that the proximity of friends and relatives and the attractiveness of the new area were important influences on migrants' decisions to move. However, they did not find that dissatisfaction with their former residence or area of residence was a major influence for many of the people studied.

Third, social networks play an important role in the decision to migrate, not only in influencing people to move to an area but in influencing people to stay put in the family home. Law and Warnes (1980) report that people who were experienced migrants during their working lives were more likely to move in retirement while those living close to their children, as measured by frequency of contact, were more likely to stay put.

The French and British experience of migration in later life supports the view that older people who are relatively affluent will increasingly seek retirement homes away from the major urban conurbations. This pattern will be influenced by the increasing experience of lifetime migration; greater home ownership; earlier retirement and the more widespread location of a smaller number of children. Experience from the United States suggests that the majority of moves in later life will be relatively local (less than 40 km) (Golant, 1977). However, the majority of older people are likely to stay put partly because of the lack of the necessary resources.

THE HOMES OF ELDERLY PEOPLE

In Britain over 95 per cent of people over 60 years live in private households (OPCS, 1993b), although as people age they are likely to experience living in some kind of institution. Of older people living in private households about 5 per cent will live in some form of sheltered accommodation with a warden (Butler et al, 1983).

Since the introduction of the welfare state there has been a rapid increase in owner-occupation and until 1979 an equally rapid increase in local authority housing at the expense of the privately rented sector (Boleat, 1986), although there are substantial regional variations. These trends have been reflected in the experiences of older people (Hunt, 1978; OPCS, 1982, 1989; Smythe and Browne, 1992). Just under two-fifths of elderly people who live alone and just over half of elderly couples are home-owners (see Table 9.3). Most of these older people own their homes outright, and this proportion is increasing, both as younger generations with higher levels of ownership reach retirement, and as growing numbers of local authority tenants, particularly the older ones, buy their own council houses. Leather and Wheeler (1988) have estimated that the number of elderly owner-occupiers will increase by about one-third from 2.8 million in 1985 to 3.7 million households by 2001.

Around 6 per cent of the population now live in privately rented accommodation. However, older people, particularly those aged 70 or over, elderly women and those who live alone, are more likely to rent accommodation privately (Smythe and Browne, 1992). Older people

Table 9.3 *Tenure and type of housing of older people's homes in Britain, 1980, 1985*

	One adult 60 or over		Elderly couples		Other elderly households		Households with no elderly people	
	1980	1985	1980	1985	1980	1985	1980	1985
Tenure:	%	%	%	%	%	%	%	%
Owner-occupied	37	41	54	59	52	58	56	65
Local authority	47	47	36	33	38	34	33	27
Private rented	15	12	10	8	9	8	11	9
N = 100%	1502	1336	1214	980	744	521	8109	7108
	1980	1985	1980	1985	1980	1985	1980	1985
Type of housing:	%	%	%	%	%	%	%	%
House or bungalow	64	62	84	82	88	86	82	82
Ground or first-floor flat	30	28	12	14	10	9	13	11
Other flat	6	10	4	4	2	5	6	7
N = 100%	1502	1332	1214	979	744	511	8109	7068

The header above spans "Elderly person households" over the first three pairs of columns.

Sources: Office of Population Censuses and Surveys (1982), Table 10.4 and (1989), Table 12.4

living alone are also more likely to live in purpose-built flats or maisonettes (see Table 9.3).

Elderly people are more likely to live in older housing (see Table 9.4), which is likely to be in poorer condition, lacking in amenities and with sub-standard heating. Privately rented accommodation is particularly subject to these deficiencies (DoE, 1988). Elderly owner-occupiers are also increasingly likely to be living in older housing stock than younger householders (DoE, 1988) and they are also likely to experience poorer housing conditions.

One method of estimating general housing conditions is the general state of properties. The 1986 English House Condition Survey (DoE, 1988) found that households in unsatisfactory housing were likely to be headed by an elderly person. People aged 75 or over were more likely than other groups to have homes which were unfit or lacked basic amenities. Although they made up only 10 per cent of households they occupied almost one-third of dwellings lacking amenities and 16 per cent of unfit dwellings. The survey found that many older people were not motivated to undertake repairs. The growing repair problem for elderly owner-occupiers is likely to increase as a growing number of older people own their homes unless financial support and counselling is provided to this group of owner-occupiers (Rose, 1982; Smith, 1989).

For many years the importance of adequate heating in elderly-person households has been a neglected area of social policy, but with the

Table 9.4   *Age of accommodation and amenities of older people's homes in Britain, 1980, 1985*

	One adult 60 or over		Elderly couples		Other elderly households		Households with no elderly people	
Age of	1980	1985	1980	1985	1980	1985	1980	1985
accommodation:	%	%	%	%	%	%	%	%
Pre-1919	28	22	24	19	29	27	23	23
1919–1944	27	27	30	27	35	29	24	23
1945–1964	23	24	29	29	25	25	27	24
1965 or later	23	27	17	25	11	18	26	30
N = 100%	1486	1303	1216	968	747	520	8089	7128
	1980	1985	1980	1985	1980	1985	1980	1985
Amenities:	%	%	%	%	%	%	%	%
Lacking own indoor WC	8	3	5	1	6	2	3	1
Lacking bath or shower	4	3	3	1	3	2	1	0
Lacking central heating	55	41	49	32	54	38	39	28
N = 100%	1500	1342	1220	985	750	522	8200	7142

(Columns grouped under heading: Elderly person households)

Sources: Office of Population Censuses and Surveys (1982), Table 10.4 and (1989), Table 12.4

increasing concern about hypothermia (Wicks, 1978) and the effect of poor housing conditions on people's health (Byrne et al, 1986) concern about heating is firmly on the policy agenda. Only about half of the elderly-person households surveyed in the 1980 and 1985 *General Household Surveys* (OPCS 1982, 1988) had central heating (see Table 9.4) compared to about two-thirds of younger-person households. In addition, Hunt (1978) showed from her survey of elderly people living in the community in England that a small but significant proportion of respondents were not warm enough in bed (8 per cent), in their own living room (8 per cent) or the kitchen (12 per cent). Many of those who reported being cold blamed it on inadequate heating facilities often arising from financial stringency.

Developments in housing policy for elderly people

Inadequate housing conditions are particularly problematic for older people who are impaired, handicapped or disabled. A lack of adequate housing has been blamed for the unnecessary admission of frail elderly people into residential care (Townsend, 1962; Townsend and Wedderburn, 1965; Neill et al, 1988; Phillips, 1992). The development of special housing for elderly people was seen as the most appropriate solution.

With the emphasis on providing support in the community successive governments in the 1960s and 1970s encouraged local authorities to build warden-controlled sheltered housing and for many years this policy continued to be an attractive way of maintaining very frail elderly people in their own homes.

Studies of sheltered housing have questioned whether it is the most appropriate policy. Butler et al (1983) concluded that sheltered housing created an elite whose housing needs were not different from those of the elderly population as a whole. Not surprisingly successive studies have shown that actual and potential tenants of sheltered housing are strongly in favour of them (M. Abrams, 1978; Rose, 1978; Goldberg and Connelly, 1982; Wirz, 1982; Butler et al, 1983; Butler and Tinker, 1983; Thompson and West, 1984; Fleiss, 1985; Clapham and Munro, 1988; Oldman, 1990), as is evident from the long waiting lists. However, a number of writers have continued to doubt the philosophy of such schemes. The most frequently cited disadvantages refer to the desirability of old people moving (Lawton and Yaffe, 1970); the desirability of segregating old people from the rest of the population (Bytheway and James, 1978; Butler and Tinker, 1983); the expense of providing a resident warden and the appropriateness of tenants' disabilities (Goldberg and Connelly, 1982); the over-provision of services (Robson, 1980); and the appropriateness of the warden's role (Boldy, 1976). Despite these concerns sheltered housing still remains the panacea for the housing problems of elderly people (Thompson and West, 1984).

A growing concern with the perceived demographic implication of continuing expansion in the provision of sheltered housing has led to alternative policies being promoted. Since 1979 central government policy has severely curtailed local authority expenditure on both ordinary council housing and specialist housing for elderly people (Kilroy, 1982; Murie, 1983; Wheeler, 1986). This reduction in the provision of public-sector housing has been matched by a marked increase in the provision of sheltered housing funded by the private and voluntary sectors (Sharp, 1988; Williams, 1990). It has been estimated that the private sector provided some 50,000 units by the end of 1989 (Mackintosh et al, 1990). However, the effects of the recession on the housing market at the beginning of the 1990s has had serious implications for the continuing development of private sheltered housing. Not only are private-sector providers of specialist housing for elderly people having to reappraise the market opportunities but it is clear that prospective purchasers are becoming more discerning in their approach to privately owned retirement housing.

Housing associations are increasingly involved in managing housing schemes for elderly people constructed by both private and public funding. In 1991 there were over 700 housing associations involved in sheltered housing provision managing over 150,000 units (Fletcher, 1991).

One policy response to the severe reduction in public expenditure on housing during the 1980s and 1990s has been the idea of 'staying put'. This policy aims at helping elderly people remain in their own homes more satisfactorily (Wheeler, 1982). 'Staying put', which presents a flexible approach to addressing the housing needs of elderly people, has come about through the activities of voluntary organisations, building societies and local authorities, rather than central government. Tinker (1984) reviews a number of these innovatory services provided by local authorities as alternatives to both residential care and sheltered housing. From the evidence presented it would appear that the majority of elderly people living in the innovatory schemes studied were satisfied with the service provided and desired to remain in their own homes. An important element of this study, given the emphasis of central government on value for money and public expenditure reduction, was an estimation of the relative costs of different schemes. There was a wide variation in the basic costs of the innovatory schemes and the associated statutory services elderly people received. Overall the services' costs, including income and housing costs, were lower for the 'staying put' schemes than for residential homes or sheltered housing. However, if the cost of informal care was added, as a cost attributable to people in their own homes, both for sheltered houses and the 'staying put' schemes, overall costs might rise above the costs of residential care.

As part of the 'staying put' philosophy policy makers and financial institutions have encouraged the use of home equity by elderly people. A small number of elderly owner-occupiers have used home equity transfer schemes to release cash income from the equity stored in their homes. Only 50,000 of the 2.5 million home owners over the age of 70 have taken up mortgage annuity schemes or home income plans (Leather, 1990). Thus the equity withdrawn under existing schemes is minimal and is likely to remain so due to lack of demand and inflexibility in the supply of existing schemes (Mullings and Hamnett, 1992). The unwillingness of older owner-occupiers to use their equity for home improvements also reflects the inability of most older people to afford the interest charges on loans based on equity. It also reflects consumer resistance to borrowing because equity release schemes consume accumulated wealth which older people wish to pass on to their families (Mackintosh et al, 1990).

Household structure

Demographic, economic and social factors have all combined to change the pattern of living arrangements of elderly people. Table 9.5 illustrates the dramatic nature of these changes, highlighting the decline in the proportion of elderly people living with others. Among a number of factors which have influenced this decline are the reduction in the average number of children and their earlier and more frequent

Table 9.5   *Household structure of elderly people in Britain, 1945–1989*

	1945[1] %	1962 %	1976 %	1980 %	1985 %	1989 %
Living alone	10	22	30	34	36	36
Living with spouse only	30	33	44	45	45	46
Living with others	60	44	27	22	19	18

[1] These data are not nationally representative. See Dale et al (1987) for details.
Sources: Dale et al (1987), Table 1; Department of Health (1992a), Table 4

Table 9.6   *Household structure of elderly people by age*

	Under 75 %	75 or over %	Total %
Lone elderly woman	22	38	27
Lone elderly man	6	9	7
Living with spouse only	52	28	45
Living with other elderly people only	4	6	4
Living with younger people	17	19	18
Total	100	100	100
(Base number)	*3170*	*1383*	*4553*

Sources: Office of Population Censuses and Surveys (1982), Table 10.2; Dale et al (1987), Table 2

marriage for the current cohort of elderly people, greater geographical mobility, the increase in employment opportunities for women over the last twenty years and the improvement in the availability of housing for younger families since the war. The opportunity to express a general preference to live alone has been enabled by increasing personal resources, particularly among middle-class people. Data from the 1980 *General Household Survey* (OPCS, 1982) show that the majority of elderly people live with a spouse, or after widowhood, alone (see Table 9.6). The greater longevity of women than men means that they are more likely to be widowed and therefore live alone.

In their analysis of the 1980 *General Household Survey* (OPCS, 1982) Dale et al (1987) show that about 95 per cent of elderly people retain their own households, only a small minority moving into households of younger generations. This analysis found that adult sons are more likely to remain in the parental home than adult daughters, except where the elderly person is moderately or severely disabled. Elderly people are more likely to join their daughters' households than those of their sons. Among widowed elderly people, their greater age was shown to be more important in determining their household structure than either their level of disability or gender. Figure 9.3 summarises Dale et al's analysis showing the household structure of elderly people in 1980 and the likely directions of change.

NON-ELDERLY HOUSEHOLDS | ELDERLY HOUSEHOLDS
(non-elderly is HOH) | (elderly is HOH)

Figure 9.3   *Flow diagram to illustrate the household structure of elderly people showing the likely direction of change at different stages of the life cycle in later life*
Source: Dale et al (1987), Figure 1
Note: These data are based on the *General Household Survey 1980* (OPCS, 1982) and some simplifications and approximations have been necessary.
(N = 4553)

It is difficult to obtain a clear picture of the household structure of elderly people from ethnic minorities because of the paucity of data about elderly people from different ethnic communities. Local studies suggest that the household structure of elderly people in ethnic groups from outside Asia are similar to the general population. Older people from Asian communities are more likely to live with others (Bhalla and Blakemore, 1981).

INSTITUTIONAL LIVING

Throughout history a small proportion of all age groups have lived in an institution of some kind. At the 1991 Census in Britain some 468,342 persons of pensionable age were usually resident in a non-private household excluding persons in places of detention or defence establishments (OPCS, 1993b). In addition, some 161,565 were present on census night but were not usually resident. Thus, at any one time, between 4 and 5 per cent of people of pensionable age are living either temporarily or permanently in an institution. Within Europe the proportion of elderly people living in institutions ranges from 10 per cent in the Netherlands to less than one per cent in Poland (Wall, 1989).

Institutional living is something we are all likely to experience in our lives. As mental or physical frailty increases, so an elderly person is increasingly likely to experience institutional living. At the 1991 Census, 9.7 per cent of people aged 75 or over and 23.7 per cent of people aged 85 or over were resident in an institution on census night (OPCS, 1993b). This contrasts with the Netherlands where three times the proportion of people aged 75 or over live in nursing homes or so-called 'caring homes' (Coleman, 1984a).

Since 1948 the care of frail elderly people has been provided by their families and by the private, statutory and voluntary sectors. Families continue to provide the majority of care (Parker, 1990) but where family care has not been available frail elderly people have always been cared for in a variety of institutions (Thomson, 1983). Long-term institutional care for elderly people currently includes local authority, private and voluntary residential homes, NHS and private nursing homes, and geriatric and psychiatric NHS hospital wards.

The United Kingdom was one of the first industrialised countries to provide a specialist service for the medical care of elderly people (Brocklehurst, 1975; Hall, 1988). However, throughout the UK this service takes on a variety of forms (Williamson, 1979). In general, all departments of geriatric medicine set out to provide a service for a defined population and provide a comprehensive range of facilities including the long-term care of elderly people. However, the type of person cared for varies from those who are acutely ill to those who are chronically ill. As a result of the NHS and Community Care Act (1990) the provision of long-term care places in NHS hospitals has declined (Age Concern, 1991) (see Figure 9.4).

Under the terms of the 1948 National Assistance Act local authorities were required to provide residential care for frail people. During the 1960s and 1970s there was a change in the condition of local authority old people's homes, and more residential homes are now purpose-built for the care of disabled people. With the increasing numbers of mentally impaired elderly people entering residential homes some authorities developed separate facilities for the elderly mentally infirm, in the form of either separate units within existing homes or separate homes (Willcocks et al, 1987).

The main impact on long-term care in the UK since the election of a

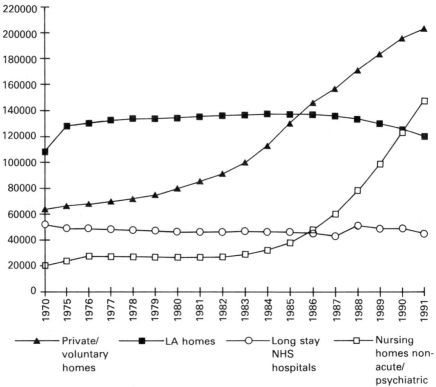

Figure 9.4 *Long-term care places in UK, 1970–1991*
Source: Lang (1992), Table 4.2

Conservative government in 1979 has been the encouragement of the independent sector and the dramatic expansion in the provision of private residential homes from about 25,000 residents in 1979 to 120,000 residents in 1990 (Department of Health, 1992a). In some areas, particularly in the coastal retirement areas, throughout this century, there has always been a substantial private sector. Up to 1979 almost all residents of private residential and nursing homes were self-financed. Following changes in the 1979 supplementary benefit regulations, residents in private nursing and rest homes became eligible for supplementary benefit. Until 1983 there were varying interpretations of the Act so that local DHSS officers set different levels of benefit. Variations in the provision of private homes between areas of the country reflected differences in benefit payments. Health and local authorities also responded in different ways to the availability of private homes and thus in some areas there has been more encouragement to develop private residential facilities for elderly people. In addition, consumer demand for private homes has been greater in some areas than others. Thus, across the country there exist considerable variations in the provision of places in the private sector, but generally with a higher provision in the south than the north of the country (Larder et al, 1986).

There has been a similar development in the provision of private nursing homes although their expansion has not been quite so dramatic (see Figure 9.4). In contrast, although the DHSS promoted the concept of NHS nursing homes (DHSS, 1983b; Secretaries of State for Health et al, 1989) few have been established and only one of the original three experimental NHS nursing homes remains operating within the NHS (Bond, 1992a).

An alternative to nursing-home and residential care currently being explored by some housing associations is the development of very sheltered housing with extra care services being provided to frail tenants rather than transferring them to institutional care (Tinker, 1989; Fletcher, 1991).

With the implementation of the NHS and Community Care Act (1990) further changes will occur in the structure of long-term institutional care. From April 1993 local authorities became responsible for the purchasing of long-term residential care on behalf of frail elderly people from the public and independent sectors. The introduction of controls on funding for residential care in 1993 will reduce the increase in provision by the private sector. In the longer term we might expect that the control of the supply of residential and nursing-home care by limiting the amount of money available to spend on institutional care will lead to only extremely frail people being cared for in institutions (Bond, 1992a) except where individuals and families have private means. It is very difficult to predict, however, whether this scenario will evolve. At present, for every person exhibiting extreme frailty living an institution, there are at least three living in private households including sheltered housing facilities (Townsend and Wedderburn, 1965; Bond and Carstairs, 1982). Into the twenty-first century we can expect to continue to find a substantial number of extremely frail elderly people living outside institutional care.

Characteristics of institutional living

A number of studies have highlighted the similarity of the characteristics of frail elderly people who live in these different types of institutions (Townsend and Wedderburn, 1965; Wilkin et al, 1978; Gilleard et al, 1980; Bond and Carstairs, 1982; Wade et al, 1983; Atkinson et al, 1986; Lowrey and Briggs, 1988; Bond et al, 1989a). The findings from these studies show the overlap in clientele. For example, Atkinson et al (1986) found that although there were similarities in demographic and behavioural characteristics, it was the NHS hospitals and nursing homes which contained the highest proportion of severely frail persons and the private residential homes which contained the lowest proportions. However, there were important differences between health authorities surveyed, particularly in terms of the behavioural characteristics of residents in the private homes. In addition, there is considerable overlap between the characteristics of elderly people living in private households, sheltered housing and in institutions (Townsend and Wedderburn, 1965; Bond and Carstairs, 1982).

Many institutions in the United Kingdom, existing for the care of elderly people, exhibit a number of the characteristics of what Goffman (1961) termed 'the total institution'. Goffman's description of the total institution as an abstract concept has dominated much of our thinking in the last thirty years to such an extent that we are all likely to be guilty of accepting the inevitability of the characteristics described. The essential feature of the total institution as described by Goffman is that, unlike life outside, there is no separation between the three central spheres of modern life: work, leisure and family. All aspects of life are conducted within the boundaries of the institution and under the control of a single authority. Each phase of daily activities is shared with a large number of other people, all of whom are treated alike and are required to do the same things together. These activities normally follow a strict routine imposed from above by a system of explicit formal rulings and a body of officials. The routine of daily activities comprises a single rational plan which has been designed to fulfil the official aims of the institution.

The extreme nature of Goffman's description, which he also applied to prisons and monasteries as well as psychiatric hospitals, might be questioned by many workers providing care to elderly people in residential settings on the grounds that many of these characteristics are not exhibited in their institution. Yet the consistency of findings from studies of residential and hospital care for elderly people and chronically sick and disabled people supports the value of Goffman's analysis, which shows how institutionalised ageism and the disadvantaged position of elderly people in society can be reinforced in an institutional setting during later life.

Townsend's (1962) study of residential care in England and Wales remains, after over thirty years, the best description of the ubiquity of the total institution. His case studies of residents in old workhouses, which provided the mainstay of local authority residential services for elderly and disabled people, vividly describe the isolation of residents from the outside world, the lack of individual privacy and independence, the routinisation of activities, and the separation of residents from staff.

Although many of the physical conditions described by Townsend no longer exist with the development of purpose-built homes for elderly people the legacy of the workhouse often continues within the organisational culture of residential settings. Miller and Gwynne (1972), Booth (1985) and Willcocks et al (1987) in their studies of residential homes and Baker (1978), Evers (1981), Clark and Bowling (1989) and S. Bond and J. Bond (1994) in their studies of hospital wards for elderly people have identified the continuing existence of many of the characteristics of the total institution described by Goffman. As Booth concludes, differences between residential homes should 'be seen as a veneer that decorates the massive uniformity of institutional life. . . Underneath lies the same crushing panoply of controls over the lives and doings of residents. Changing the wrapper does not alter the contents' (Booth, 1985, p. 206).

As a result of these and other studies there have been various efforts to overcome the effects of institutionalisation through the process of normalisation: the principle that people living in institutions should be able to follow a lifestyle similar to the patterns they would experience living in private households (Wolfensberger, 1972).

Attempts at providing a normal environment for frail people in institutions have been constrained by the historical legacies of institutions and the ubiquitous scarcity of resources. Townsend's early studies of residential care poignantly highlight the legacy of the Victorian workhouse. Many of the public-sector institutions currently used for the care of frail elderly people by local authorities and local health authorities were originally workhouses (Longmate, 1974). Most will have been modernised and upgraded, but the physical memory of the workhouse continues to dominate local communities and remind residents and the local population of the social heritage of these buildings. In addition, many health authorities have inherited large isolation hospitals used before the discovery of antibiotics for the care of TB patients and other patients with infectious diseases. In a study of institutional facilities for the long-term care of elderly people in six health authorities Bond et al (1989a) found that in each study area there was at least one former workhouse and one former isolation hospital and only one health authority had a hospital ward which had been purpose-built for the care of long-stay elderly patients. With the current policy of closing psychiatric hospitals and the continuing scarcity of resources for health authority managers it is increasingly likely that these facilities might also become appropriated for the institutional care of elderly people.

It is not only the former uses and locations of facilities which have hindered the development of policies of normalisation but also the institutional attitudes of staff and residents alike. The preservation of individuals' dignities and the provision of privacy has been difficult to achieve. In the health service the acute model of care dominates the training of all health care workers so that the hierarchical structure socialises staff to think and work in ways which contradict normalisation and reinforces the social environment of the total institution (Bond, S. and Bond, J. 1994). Within local authority homes the presence of a large number of untrained workers who remain in the same setting for a number of years makes innovation difficult. Although staff are highly motivated there have been few examples of good continuing in-service training which would have enabled the principles of normalisation to be widely implemented. There has also been a paucity of social work literature about the care of elderly people (Willcocks et al, 1987).

There has been little research into the quality of care provided in private and voluntary homes in Britain (Sinclair et al, 1990). Those who promote private care argue that it cannot be worse than that provided in the public sector and that a mixture of public and private provision promotes a more efficient and equitable system (Judge et al, 1983). Others have expressed concern based on the American and Australian experience that some proprietors of private homes might seek to exploit vulnerable elderly people (Mendelson, 1974). Weaver et al (1985) highlight the difficulties faced by British proprietors in pursuing the dual goals of profit and care. Willcocks et al (1987) suggest that even the development of an advisory code of practice (Centre for Policy on Ageing, 1984) and the introduction of new legislation introduced in the Registered Homes Act of 1984 will not necessarily ensure good practice. History will tell whether 'arm's length inspection' (Department of Health, 1991) has any appreciable affect on the quality of institutional care in the UK.

LIVING ARRANGEMENTS AND COMMUNITY CARE

It has long been recognised that the provision of appropriate living arrangements for elderly people who are mentally or physically frail is fundamental to successful independent living at home in the community. Yet the provision of appropriate living arrangements and the organisation of health and welfare services has been confused in the policies of successive governments. In particular, the housing policies of the Department of Environment, the health and community care policies of the Department of Health, the income support and housing benefit policies of the Department of Social Security and the financial controls and strategies imposed by the Treasury have been in conflict and have been detrimental to older people. At the local level competing priorities between health authorities and local authorities about which services to purchase for the local population and the effects of 'cost shunting' (the process whereby different budget holders avoid purchasing care for an individual whose needs may be met by either health or welfare services) have been detrimental to successful partnership in the care of elderly people. Few local authorities have heeded Townsend and Wedderburn's (1965) conclusion that the provision of appropriate housing is the keystone to successful community care. It is the housing associations, with their concept of taking care into people's purpose-built housing, which most closely reflect this idea (Fletcher, 1991).

Continuing change in health and welfare services, particularly in relation to the financial organisation of housing services, health services, residential care and social support services, will continue to have a major impact on elderly people in future years. The NHS and Community Care Act (1990) is a significant response to the increasing acceptance by sections of society of the policy values of the anti-collectivists. Anti-collectivism emphasises the distribution of health and welfare resources through the free market with a minimal role for the state. Thus throughout the 1980s and early 1990s the UK experienced an increasing number of New Right anti-collectivist policies including a reduction in public housing and the promotion of private housing, the privatisation of long-term care, increasing selectivity in the provision of income support to pensioners and other vulnerable groups in society and the promotion of community care in the community and by the community. Popular support for such policies is a response to the moral panic encouraged by the politicians and some policy makers who interpret the ageing of the population in terms of a demographic time-bomb.

Long-term care for mentally or physically frail elderly people and younger people with physical disabilities or psychiatric, chronic or terminal illnesses were always lower in government priorities than acute health services or education. Through implicit privatisation the UK government has attempted to shift the financial and social costs of supporting disadvantaged people away from the State and onto individuals and their families. Implicit privatisation is the keystone to community care policies into the twenty-first century. What do we understand by the notion of community care?

The concept of *community care* is hazardous to use because of the variety of meanings attached to it. For example, it has been defined as the 'provision of help, support and protection to others by lay members of societies acting in everyday domestic and occupational settings' (P. Abrams, 1978, p. 78). In contrast, it has traditionally been used in government policy to refer to care which occurs outside institutional settings, and most recently applied to elderly people, people with a mental illness or with learning disabilities (Walker, 1982c). This confusion is perhaps best understood by Bayley's (1973) distinction between *care in the community* and *care by the community*. Care in the community refers to the trend of replacing large and often geographi-cally remote institutional facilities with smaller units of residential provision which would, if possible, be familiar to individual residents. This was replaced by the notion that 'community care' referred to the fact that carers or caregivers resided in the community, incorporating the notion of the *community* actually doing the caring. Nowadays, the concept of community care by the community dominates the *assumptive world* of policy makers and service providers. (The term *assumptive world* is used to describe our image or our perception of the environment in which we live [Young, 1977].) Following a number of implicit official

statements about the nature of community care in the UK an explicit
policy was published for the World Congress on Ageing in 1982:

> The primary sources of support and care for elderly people are informal and
> voluntary. These spring from ties of kinship, friendship and neighbourhood,
> and they are irreplaceable. It is the task of the public authorities to sustain and
> where necessary to develop this vast grass-roots network, but the responsi-
> bility is one for the community as a whole. Care in the community must
> increasingly mean care by the community. (DHSS, 1982, p. 1)

An examination of the reality of community care reveals that the
provision of support and care falls not on the community at large but
upon the family. Within the family it is the women who provide the bulk
of care (Land, 1978; Finch and Groves, 1980; Walker, 1982c; Charlesworth, Wilkin and Durie, 1984; Ungerson, 1987; Finch, 1989; Qureshi
and Walker, 1989; Finch and Mason, 1990; Graham, 1991). This
observation has been expressed in terms of the double equation: 'in
practice community care equals care by the family, and in practice care
by the family equals care by women' (Finch and Groves, 1980, p. 494).
Even where community care is outside the family, such as in
neighbourhood care, it is women again who provide the majority of
support (Abrams et al, 1989).

In the UK there are an estimated six million informal caregivers
looking after frail elderly people, people with learning difficulties and
people who have a mental illness (Green, 1988). It is estimated that four
million informal caregivers are looking after people with significant
disabilities (Martin et al, 1988a).

Much of the caregiving literature has focused on family relationships
and gender issues. There is little data about class (Arber and Ginn, 1992)
or ethnic differences (Cameron et al, 1989). Informal caregivers are
found at all ages, including children. Most predominantly, however,
male caregivers tend to be of retirement age and, where spouses are the
principal caregivers of older people they tend, naturally, to be old
themselves (Bond, 1992b).

Government policies for community care lay the responsibility for
providing support to informal caregivers on the local authority in
collaboration with health service provider units, housing associations
and other independent providers of housing, residential, health and
social support services. Local social service departments are expected to
coordinate packages of care for individuals based on their and informal
supporters' needs, which will include the purchase of housing and
residential services. The budget for the provision of community care,
unlike the social security budget, is finite and a reduction in the number
of elderly people living in residential and nursing homes is expected
(Secretaries of State for Health et al, 1989) while some commentators
predict an increase in bedblocking within NHS hospitals (Bond, 1992a).

THE LIVING ARRANGEMENTS OF ELDERLY AND FRAIL ELDERLY PEOPLE

Old age has for many years been seen as a social problem (MacIntyre, 1977) and this perspective has helped perpetuate ageism. As a result, in any discussion of living arrangements there has usually been more emphasis on the needs of frail elderly people than on elderly people in general. The majority of older people are not mentally or physically frail, although it has been estimated that of those aged 85 or over one in five might suffer from moderate or severe dementia (Jorm, 1990; Kay, 1991) and three in five a limiting longstanding illness (Department of Health, 1992a). In other words, four in five of those aged 85 or over are not mentally frail and two in five are not physically frail.

In this chapter we have indicated that the living arrangements of older people are strongly influenced by their structural position in society at earlier stages of the life cycle. Owner-occupiers tend to remain owner-occupiers, council tenants tend to remain council tenants, and private tenants tend to remain private tenants, but some transitions in tenure do occur as a result of bereavement or the onset of frailty. Thus, the political economy perspective outlined in Chapter 2 has shown that our lives in later life are strongly marked out by our access to resources and social goods throughout our lives. Housing tenure remains one of the most sensitive indicators of an individual's access to resources, although as we have seen in this chapter many elderly people lack the resources to keep their own property in good repair. However, as owner-occupiers become older and more frail, they have a disposable asset for the securing of a smaller or more appropriate dwelling than council or private tenants. In the event of requiring institutional care owner-occupiers could also use these resources to fund institutional care of their choice. However, as we keep emphasising, most elderly people are not likely to require long-term institutional care and the majority remain in their own homes for much of their old age.

Admission to institutional care is often regarded as an inevitable consequence of frailty in later life. However, frailty alone is not a good predictor of institutional care. Townsend (1965) in an earlier analysis of reasons for admission to an institution found that family composition, structure and organisation strongly influenced admission to a residential home. Functional capacity, homelessness, and lack of economic resources were found to be less influential. More recent studies have indicated the importance of the availability of family and social support (Isaacs et al, 1972; Berkeley, 1976; Farrow et al, 1976; Bond and Carstairs, 1982; Graham and Livesley, 1983; Booth, 1985; Wenger, 1991). In a study to evaluate continuing-care accommodation for elderly people Bond et al (1989b) have found that nursing staff give lack of social support as a common reason for old people remaining in NHS hospitals and nursing homes.

Townsend (1986) has argued persuasively that many people living in institutions, particularly local authority residential homes, could be readily cared for in the community if an adequate level of resources, particularly special housing, were made available for services for elderly people. From a political economy perspective he argues that this unnecessary institutionalisation is due to the wider functions that residential homes undertake for society. While accommodating only a tiny percentage of the elderly population they symbolise the dependence of elderly people and legitimate their lack of access to equality of status. This conclusion is supported by the evidence that many residents have the capacities to live in private households and the evidence of social restrictions and authoritarian styles of management in many homes.

We have described the considerable data that support the view that the current living arrangements for many elderly people are inappropriate and that new social policies must be conceived which remove long-term institutionalisation. Townsend (1986) argues that the three kinds of public-sector institutional provision should be merged. Residential homes should be abolished and the small minority of NHS long-stay geriatric and psychogeriatric patients should be cared for in NHS nursing homes. Sheltered housing provided in the public sector and day-care provision should be expanded to care for the substantial minority of less severely incapacitated elderly people. This radical solution takes little account of the current explosion in the supply and demand of private residential and nursing homes or the realities of the difficulties of establishing an egalitarian method of allocating sheltered housing.

Tinker (1987) has advocated a more flexible approach to the use of housing for frail elderly people, arguing that since most elderly people wish to remain in their own homes a variety of options should be made available. These include ordinary housing, living with a family, granny annexes, sheltered housing with a warden, extra care housing, continuing-care communities and residential care. Willcocks et al (1987) have proposed that the residential flatlet should replace the traditional residential home. Such a proposal would combine the advantages of independent living with the security and support essential for a frail population by attempting to capture the essence of what an old person would call home. The Department of Health set up three experimental NHS nursing homes in an attempt to provide a more homelike environment for severely frail elderly people (DHSS, 1983b) which have been evaluated (Bond et al, 1989c). A number of local authorities and local health authorities are also experimenting with different forms of care for very frail elderly people. Some housing associations also manage specialist housing into which health and support services are put as the frailty of tenants increases (Fletcher, 1991). However, experience of similar developments for the care of people with learning difficulties suggest that attempts to abolish all institutions may be unsuccessful even with the necessary political will. Small residential units, including flatlets, built for use by people with learning disabilities have suggested limited gains when compared with conventional institutions (Renshaw et al, 1988). Similarly, the building of modern residential homes with the exclusive provision of single rooms has not changed the fundamental nature of residential care for elderly people. Changes in physical design may be a necessary but not sufficient condition for independent living. Without changes in social attitudes towards elderly people, their living arrangements are unlikely to meet their needs or their desires.

10

INTIMATE RELATIONSHIPS

Dorothy Jerrome

Intimate relationships are characterised by emotional intensity, self-disclosure and a high degree of personal involvement. In the psychological literature on ageing, intimacy tends to be discussed in connection with mental health. We need to 'exist in the thought and affection of another' to be emotionally secure, well adjusted and have high morale. The importance of an intimate, confiding relationship has been noted in studies of depression in earlier years (Brown and Harris, 1978) and in studies of the ability to cope with age-related losses in later years (Lowenthal and Haven, 1968).

In sociological accounts of ageing, intimate relationships are seen as synonymous with primary group ties (Creech and Babchuk, 1985). Small group size, frequency of interaction and a long history of association are conditions in which primary relations develop. Primary relationships are informal, personal and subject to negotiation. They meet a number of needs: for personal support, for sociability, for physical and emotional intimacy, and for stimulation.

In our society value is attached to caring, to sociability and to social success. Loneliness is a stigma. The capacity to make, maintain or replace intimate relationships is important. In the literature of social gerontology it is commonly assumed that sources of intimacy become attenuated through the lifespan, to the detriment of the ageing individual's health, capacity for social involvement, and general well-being.

THE FAMILY: IDEALS AND REALITIES

An obvious starting point for a discussion of intimate relationships, given the pattern of emotional investments of most people in British society, is the family. Viewed from a structuralist sociological perspective (see Chapter 2), the family has a crucial role in social reproduction – the transmission of values and existing social arrangements from one generation to the next. It is the main institutional setting for childhood, and is one of the two realms of experience which give form and meaning to adult life (the other is work). In modern industrial society and in our own welfare state the family is a most useful institution. Its members, particularly the adult female ones, are the primary caregivers for dependants – generally speaking, the very old and the very young. It generally meets people's needs for intimacy and companionship. It is the main unit of consumption in a consumer-oriented society. It is the supplier of a reserve labour force (unemployed women) and it services those active in the work force. It produces future workers and generally educates the young in the ways of their particular communities.

This range of functions explains the official and popular concern shown periodically for the well-being of the family, and the regularity of state intervention. 'As a general election approaches, the family is once again unwrapped, patched up and worshipped to assure the electorate that politicians are in favour of all things good' (*New Society*, 14 October 1982, p. 67).

It has been suggested that concern with the family is growing. On the one hand, changing family patterns have become visible since the 1970s, with the increase in rates of divorce and single-parent families, illegitimacy, and cohabitation before marriage, suggesting to some that the family is under threat. On the other hand, there has been evidence that the demands on families are growing. The changing age structure of the population (see Chapter 1) has meant a growth in the number of very elderly people who make disproportionate demands on health and personal social services and for whom the family has traditionally been the major source of support. At the same time there have been constraints on public expenditure, with social welfare expenditure figuring prominently in the cuts. A further factor causing concern has been the increasing evidence about family poverty, which was redis-covered in the 1960s, largely through the efforts of the Child Poverty Action Group.

There is strong ideological emphasis on the family. One is expected to be a member of a couple, and a family, and exclusion from either type of relationship is viewed as a misfortune, if not a personal failing. The couple- and family-orientation of social life and the value attached to sociability make the family – or lack of it – a main reference point in the ageing process. Ageing needs to be understood in the context of the family.

Three contrasting views are discernible in recent public discussions about the family. Which view one adopts depends on fundamental values about society and the place of the family within it. We can call them the traditionalist, socialist and feminist perspectives following Craven, Rimmer and Wicks (1982). Within these perspectives the family is seen as an agent for stability or change, conservation or social progress, depending on one's ideological position.

The traditionalists, viewing the family as the key unit in society, will often

view change and signs of family breakdown with suspicion. Feminists and
other radicals will view the traditional family with suspicion, regarding it as
an oppressive unit, a barrier to individual experience and fulfilment and
radical advance. They will focus attention on what happens within the family
and the distribution therein of income, responsibility, work and power.
Socialists and others on the left, while working for changes within the family,
will also seek more state support for families with responsibility for children
and other dependents (Craven, Rimmer and Wicks, 1982, pp. 23–4)

In all three, a critical area for debate is the way in which the
dependency needs of older and younger family members are met.
Within the traditionalist perspective the emphasis is on duties and
obligations rather than on individual rights. The duty to care for elderly
dependent relatives would take precedence over the rights of other
members, especially the right of younger female relatives to work.
Within feminist thought, women are oppressed by the pattern of gender
roles and responsibilities in the traditional family. Domestic labour
performed mainly by women is idealised as care, love and protection. It
includes caring for the old and sick, at little cost to the state. Within the
socialist perspective, the highest values of family life – caring, non-
competitiveness, cooperation and the non-contingent love of others –
are threatened by hardship and poverty.

Conflicting views and objectives produce conflicting social policies.
Over a period of time we might expect to find social policies designed in
terms of one perspective to be imposed on a family shaped by a different
pattern of intervention. Political intervention in family life clearly
reflects an ideological position. Politicians, policy makers, churchmen
and other public figures pronounce on the family on the basis of a
commitment to a particular set of values. These values – 'community',
'authority', 'equality', 'individual freedom' – have powerful prescriptive
force which blinds people to objective facts about family life. Assumptions are made, evidence is used selectively and ideologically 'sound'
material is adopted uncritically in support of a particular viewpoint. The
supposed inadequacies of the contemporary family are commonly
placed in historical perspective to strengthen the case for intervention.
Reference is made to earlier times when social arrangements were more
satisfactory: children respected their parents, relationships were more
caring, and so on.

For a different account of family life we can usefully turn to the
literature of social science. Social scientists are not primarily concerned
to change existing social arrangements, though their interest in
particular social phenomena often arises from a personal concern with
social problems. We have to remember that they, like politicians, are
inclined to make apparently objective statements based on a set of
implicit values. But ideally their value premises are consciously held and
articulated.

THE FAMILY AND SOCIAL CHANGE

Social scientists have tended to share the concern of policy makers with the fate of the family as an institution. Indeed, much of the sociological literature in the 1940s and 1950s considered the possibility that the process of industrialisation had undermined the family, stripped it of its functions and reduced it to a small, isolated, highly specialised unit which only met its adult members' needs for intimacy and provided role models and socialisation for its younger members. This transformation was seen as part of a larger social trend involving community relations in general (Fischer, 1977). In terms of the quality of family life, the shift was thought to be from the large, multifunctional extended family to the small and inward-looking 'nuclear' family consisting of parents and their dependent biological offspring, highly mobile in response to the demands of the industrialising society, putting their own interests above those of more distant relatives and in particular neglecting the hitherto sacrosanct heads of a respected older generation. The 'classical myth of western nostalgia' (Fletcher, 1962) has since been repudiated. Writers of the 1960s, in the course of investigating the decline-of-community thesis, found the extended family alive and well, particularly in long-established working-class areas like East London (Willmott and Young, 1962; Tunstall, 1966). Others declared that it survived in modified form; family ties were activated in time of need (Rosser and Harris, 1965).

Historians added a new dimension with a suggestion which challenged the assumption of the before-and-after school of thought: the extended, multifunctional family unit had indeed never been typical in pre-industrial English society (Laslett, 1977; Anderson, 1971). It was only in the new industrial areas, cramped and impoverished, that the family members had created networks of mutual support and co-residence. This refutation of the classical myth has come fairly recently to social gerontology. As late as the mid-1970s social gerontologists were still seeking to demonstrate the strength of ties in the extended family and the persistence of this particular structure, albeit in modified form, 'even in today's industrialised, urbanised, migratory world' (Troll and Smith, 1976). In gerontology during the 1960s and early 1970s, much intellectual energy was spent in opposing the widespread assumption of the death of the extended family. The belief that older people are alienated from their families was widespread in the media, in research and among older people themselves. In America, the work of many social scientists helped to counteract what Shanas called the myth of family neglect (Shanas, 1979).

They showed that there was little evidence to support the belief in alienation. Their findings were that a significant proportion of old people and their children lived in close physical proximity; that they interacted frequently; and that families were still important to the care of old people. This optimistic view has been most recently supported by data from the longitudinal study at the University of California. The facts of family life which emerge from the study contradict popular notions of decline and also the pessimistic views advanced by some academics. Despite evidence of structural change created by changes in marital status over the last fifteen years in almost all the families in the study, intergenerational bonds are close and viable. If anything, there is now more solidarity and interaction than when the study began, with almost 60 per cent of the youngest generation reporting an improvement in relationships (Bengtson, 1986).

However, changes of a dramatic nature *have* taken place over the last hundred years. These need to be taken into account in understanding the family experiences of people born in different decades, bringing with them expectations shared with others in the same cohort. Much of the contemporary American literature employs a static, ahistorical approach which conveys nothing of the meaning of dependency or the expectations of autonomy and involvement brought to the situation by elderly people whose own experiences of family life span many decades of change in family structure and processes. The result of ignoring the historical dimension and hence the perception of older people themselves, is a curiously one-sided analysis which does not tell us much about the realities of family life in old age.

To understand relationships in the later-life family – those families who are beyond the child-rearing years and have begun to launch their children (Brubaker, 1983) – we have to see them in the context of various changes which have affected the family in Britain over the last hundred years. Five areas of change can be identified.

Demographic In the last hundred years we have seen falling rates of fertility and mortality, a reduction in family size, age at marriage and the number of children born to each family. These trends – particularly the falling age of marriage – have produced a narrowing of the distance between the generations, and a change in age distribution within the family.

Technological The structure of employment has changed, with increasing numbers of women joining the work force. A general increase in mid-life options has had implications for women's family roles.

Legal New legislation regulating marriage, divorce, homosexuality and children's rights has affected the structure and composition of the family. It has increased the proportion of families which are divided, reconstituted and otherwise unconventional in structure.

Ideological Within social policy there has been a growing emphasis over the last fifteen years on community care, legitimated by a conservative model of the family, as opposed to care within institutions. In popular culture, changing ideologies of marriage and parenthood have introduced new value conflicts into family life.

Economic Rising levels of affluence and the introduction of state welfare provision have allowed the operation of choice in family relationships. Ties between elderly parents and their adult children are increasingly governed by sentiment rather than obligation.

Changes in the structure of the family

Increasing depth and top-heaviness

Over the last eighty years the time span between the generations has been reduced. An increase of vertical ties and narrowing of lateral ties has produced a family shaped like an inverted triangle, top heavy. It is now possible to belong to a five-generation family, or six if you are a black woman in Los Angeles (Burton and Bengtson, 1985). You can have grandparents and grandchildren simultaneously. For the first time in history, adults can have more parents than children.

There are two dimensions to consider here: the vertical structure, involving an increase in depth as the generations are multiplied; and the breadth of the family system, a reflection of the numbers of children born in each generation. The notion of increased depth has recently been put into perspective. Talk of numerous five-generation families, it is argued, has been based largely on speculation (Rossi and Rossi, 1990). In the Rossis' New England sample, less than 1 per cent belonged to such families. The majority still lived in three-generation families. In terms of the structure – pyramid, inverted triangle – the position is ambiguous. It seems that the decline in fertility which has narrowed the range of siblings in successive generations will continue to produce a lineage which is 'skinny' though not necessarily Bengtson's 'beanpole'. What *is* unambiguous is the increased length of the parent–child relationship now typically fifty to sixty years.

Despite the Rossis' caution, there are still grounds for conceptualising the family as top-heavy. The condition of top-heaviness is well illustrated by the scene from the children's film, *Charlie and the Chocolate Factory*, based on the book by Roald Dahl, in which the young widow, who is Charlie's mother, tends to Charlie's four grandparents as they pass their lives at opposite ends of the same large bed. An excess of parents over children is a condition exacerbated in British society by divorce and remarriage, as illustrated by the following case study:

Judy is a mature student of 52, married to Michael, a retired airline pilot, whose earlier marriage to Jean had broken up. Jean had also remarried. Michael and Jean had had two children. One of them, Christopher, had married a girl called Nicki whose parents had also divorced and remarried. At the young people's wedding there were four parents and four step-parents. The marriage of Nicki and Chris got into difficulties. Under the strain of two children (now 8 and 6) it broke up. Nicki went home to her mother, Jane and her step-father, Peter. Jane was somewhat put out at the arrival of her daughter and grandchildren and called upon her daughter's ex-father-in-law Michael to shoulder the

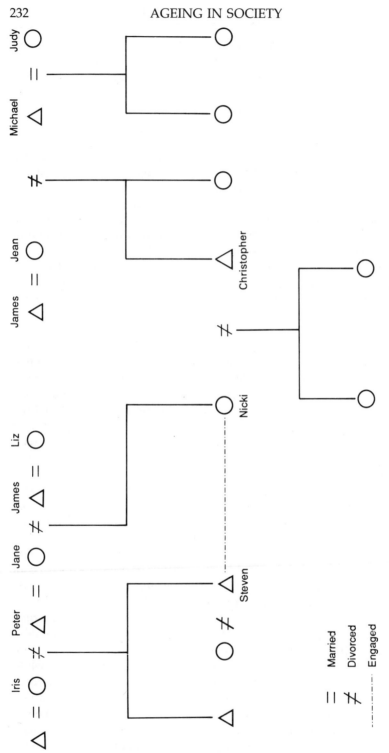

Figure 10.1   *Case study of a 'top-heavy' family*

financial burden of the grandchildren's school fees. Feeling that the grandchildren now belonged more to their mother's side than to his, he refused to do so, claiming that his 'own' grandchildren (ie through his second marriage) would have more right to his resources. Chris's mother Jean was not going to help either. She had never really liked Nicki and had moved away from the area

A solution to the problem emerged in the form of Steven. Steven is Nicki's step-brother, the son of Jane's second husband Peter by his first marriage. Steven had also been married before but had no children. The young people – Steven and Nicki – were not passionately in love but in the circumstances 'everyone' (ie the many parents and step-parents) agreed that their relationship was a good idea. Jane was pleased because her step-son Steven would take care of her daughter, and take responsibility for her daughter's children by marrying their mother. Nicki's step-father would become her father-in-law. Steven's step-mother would become his mother-in-law. (See Figure 10.1.)

Structural complications
The kinship complications introduced here by divided and reblended families replace earlier complications caused by family size. In the earlier, larger families with more children born to a single set of parents, a single generation – in the sense of position in the family line – might span several cohorts, or time periods. One cohort might include two generations. Modern blended or reconstituted families have these complications too. There is the step-mother who is close in age to her step-children, and half-siblings frequently span two cohorts. We often tend to forget that generational position does not tell us much about either age or cohort, and vice versa (Hagestad, 1985).

The group of people described in the above case study, linked by birth and marriage, is untypical in several respects. Its members are wealthy, and relationships between the formerly married are more cordial than is the case following many divorces. But in terms of the structure of relationships it might be more typical than we think. Divorce is now a major social trend in Britain. Between 1971 and 1982 the number of annual divorces granted in England and Wales doubled, one of the highest divorce rates in Europe (Family Policy Studies Centre, 1984b). One in three new marriages is now expected to end in divorce. It is thus increasingly likely that elderly people will be members of families disrupted by divorce (Timaeus, 1986).

There is also a growing minority of retired people who are themselves divorced. In 1981, 1.6 per cent of elderly men were divorced and this is expected to rise to 3.6 per cent by 2019. For women the proportions are higher: 2.2 per cent in 1981 rising to 7.2 per cent (Henwood and Wicks, 1985). In America it is estimated that by 2005 over half of those reaching retirement age will have been divorced at least once. In Britain, as in America, remarriage is also more frequent, at all stages of the lifespan.

Currently one in every three marriages involves remarriage for one partner. The remarriage rate is higher for men than women at all ages, leading to an increased likelihood of women being alone in future years.

Divorce and remarriage have several implications for the family lives of older people. The multiplication of parents has been mentioned already. If the rate of birth does not keep up with the rate of divorce and remarriage, on whom will the burden of care for the many elderly parents and step-parents fall? How far will the eight parents at the wedding of Nicki and Chris look to them for support in old age? Another issue is the loss of relationships, both linear (to grandchildren and children-in-law) and collateral (to favourite sisters-in-law for instance) in divorce. Both of these problems – that of roles and responsibilities in reconstituted families and behaviour in families divided by divorce – reflect the confusion which exists about the rights and obligations of individual members in the modern family.

Normative confusion
The majority white kinship system in Britain has always had relatively few prescriptions for behaviour compared with traditional kinship societies. Priorities are undefined (Rosow, 1975). Roles and responsibilities in the new multigenerational family, and the new reblended family, are vague and undefined. It has been argued that with the introduction of state benefits and rising levels of affluence, obligation has given way to sentiment as a basis for family relationships (Eversley, 1982; Cheal, 1988). Whether or not obligations are recognised is a matter for personal discretion and people are highly selective in the process (Hoyt and Babchuk, 1983). There is scope for this in any case in a bilateral kinship system such as this. In the illustration given earlier, Michael, for his own convenience, defined his grandchildren by his first marriage as belonging less to him than to their maternal grandmother; as more distant from him than the grandchildren of his second marriage. In biological terms their relationships were identical.

In the novel situation of remarriage and the top-heavy family, prescriptions for behaviour are lacking. Some caring roles, such as those involving children, are expected in adulthood and have been learnt from older family members. By contrast, caring for an elderly relative is not generally expected, and no role models are available. Today the caregiver is herself likely to be ageing and possibly unequal to the task of caring. If she is younger, she is likely to be involved in paid employment and forced to make choices with no normative guidelines. In either case the role of caregiver to a very frail old person is not a natural developmental stage of life for the adult child (Brody, 1979).

Historically, society has relied primarily on the family to meet the 'normal' dependency needs of the main dependent population group: children (see Chapter 11). Faced with the emergence of a new population group with substantial needs – ie elderly people – society has continued to rely on the family. But what constitutes 'healthy' family functioning and 'normal' behaviour has yet to be decided. In the absence of established cultural patterns and prescriptions for behaviour, there is often anxiety, resentment and guilt when people find themselves having to give help. On the other side, too, there may be resentment at having to ask for help which might have been offered. However, the evidence is that people do not ask often (Michaud, 1986). There may be guilt at imposing on a busy daughter-in-law; and frustration at one's helplessness in a culture which values independence and mastery of the environment (Clark, 1972).

Several events or crises in the career of the ageing family threaten its well-being (Kuypers and Bengtson, 1983). These include: the independence of adult children; the retirement from a job; serious illness and death or divorce, which radically alter the structure of the domestic group. The difficulty in handling these events is caused by what Kuypers and Bengtson call the historical baggage carried in each case. Each family inherits a legacy of ways of managing conflict and dealing with issues like autonomy.

In all families these crises create conflicts of loyalty, for the general assumption is that as families age the intensity of family involvement will diminish: that primary loyalties will transfer from parents and the family of origin to spouse and children in the new family, and that parents care for children, not the other way round. Children faced with the likelihood of a reversal of these expectations resist it. They tend to minimise the importance of impending change in the situation of an older member, denying its implications.

The main problem for the older family, in trying to function competently, is 'in coming to terms with change against a background of powerful forces promoting continuity' (Kuypers and Bengtson, 1983, p. 211). Family traditions and identities, norms and values transmitted from one generation to the next, and the culturally defined age–status positions of mother and child promote continuity. The need to accept and handle impending change is not helped by the negative cultural stereotypes of ageing, and the withdrawal of social and institutional support which tends to accompany ageing in our society.

For the participants in the intimate dramas of family life, all trying to achieve personal continuity in the face of change, issues like family traditions and 'our way of doing things' can become the focus of intense emotion and personal conflict. Children's departures from family tradition can be a source of acute frustration for elderly parents. Equally frustrating is the lack of easy access to younger kin and shortage of conversation time with them. Daughters are often inaccessible on account of their physical distance and involvement in the labour force. Grandchildren may be inaccessible too.

Grandparenthood

Grandparenthood in the dominant culture is contingent on the actions of children, who produce the grandchildren and control access to them. The American system of grandparenthood and presumably the British, too, is distinguished by several factors. First, there is a structural separation between two generations, which results in more autonomy and privacy in the conjugal family and more remote status for the grandparents. Second, the system is not regulated by explicit rights and obligations. The grandparent–grandchild dyad, like others in the family, is voluntary and rests on personal initiative. Third, the dominant value system encourages independence and personal freedom. In any conflict of interest the conjugal family would tend to have priority over the interests of the grandparents and others in the extended family (Johnson, 1985; Cherlin and Furstenberg, 1985).

The change in timing of life events described earlier – earlier marriage, earlier and more closely spaced children – have made grandparenthood a more youthful role and given it a new cultural image. The strongest feature of modern grandparenting is its diversity. Talking of role expectations, Hagestad has pointed out that 'in a society where grandparents range in age from 30 to 110, and grandchildren range from newborn to retirees, we should not be surprised to find a variety of grandparenting styles and few behavioural expectations regarding grandparenting' (Hagestad, 1985, p. 36).

Now that long life is the rule rather than the exception, and marriage more popular than ever (the propensity to marry has gradually increased to the point where marriage is now an almost universal experience in western society – in America 95 per cent of the over-65s have been married at least once) and infertility reduced by modern reproductive technology, more people become grandparents than ever before. In Britain too, the proportion of older people without descendants has declined and is likely to shrink even more rapidly as the century wears on (Timaeus, 1986). It is estimated that three-quarters of Americans over the age of 65 are grandparents (Shanas, 1979, 1980; Rossi and Rossi, 1990). The corresponding figure for Britons is 60 per cent (Abrams, 1980b). A growing number of women may be for a time both grandmothers and granddaughters, a situation which is historically unique (Hareven, 1977).

The ambiguities surrounding normal grandparenting roles are exacerbated by divorce and remarriage. There are no models for behaviour with ex-daughters-in-law or step-grandchildren. Custody of children in divorce still used to go to the mother in the majority of cases and, despite changes in legislation conducive to alternative arrangements, it is still the mother who retains closest contact. This means that paternal grandparents are more likely to have problems with access to their grandchildren. The most vulnerable relationship is that between a grandfather and his son's son (Hagestad,1985). Women, it seems, are more likely to retain some contact with the divorced daughter-in-law as 'the mother of my grandchildren', and often as a friend.

The frustration of grandparents denied access has led to the formation of pressure and support groups such as The Grandparents' Federation. Fortunately their legal position has become much more secure under the recent 1989 Children Act. The act gives any relative or person important to the child the right to apply to the court as a suitable caretaker in a case of divorce.

Students of grandparenthood see it as vitally important in a time of rapid social change. The grandparent generation provides continuity with the past. Within the family, grandparents have an interpretive function. They reconstruct the family autobiography connecting its past to its present in a way that gives hope for the future. This might be particularly important in families marked by discontinuity, as in immigrant groups. Ethnic minority grandparents also differ in the degree of influence and authority they exert within the family (Jerrome, 1993, forthcoming a).

Grandparents are seen as stabilisers. In their wisdom and diplomacy they carefully manage interaction between the generations and minimise conflicts of value. Certain subjects are avoided as topics of conversation. Families are skilled at avoiding potentially disruptive scenes, creating safe areas, demilitarised zones in the interests of family harmony (Hagestad, 1987). Despite the widespread notion that the older generation, strangers in a world they have not made, have little to offer the young in terms of knowledge and skills, they might have valuable life experience which can uniquely benefit their grandchildren (Jerrome, forthcoming a).

ISSUES IN INTERGENERATIONAL RELATIONS

In spite of the growing interest in grandparenthood in the USA we still tend in Britain to think of intergenerational family ties in terms of ageing parents and adult children. Within that parent–child dyad, we think first of the kinds of exchanges which go on – of help in domestic and personal tasks in return for childminding, for instance – and the amount of affection or sense of obligation which accompanies them. In British gerontology our thinking is limited to these two dimensions, largely as a reflection of the preoccupation with dependency in later life. This preoccupation can, in turn, be related to anxiety over demographic trends (Hagestad, 1987).

But there are other dimensions, as the study of grandparents reminds us. Treas and Bengtson (1987) offer a conceptual framework for the analysis of intergenerational relations in terms of six variables: family structure (household composition, geographical proximity), association or patterns of contact (the amount and type of interaction between family members), affect (feelings of warmth and liking, perceptions of closeness), consensus or similarity (the extent of agreement or disagreement in attitudes and outlook), norms (perceptions of what should go on between the generations, parental and filial responsibility) and exchange or power (the balance of resources held by each generation, the degree of exchange or support between them). Thinking in these terms we will ask how much interaction takes place between the generations, how far these are ties of affection and intimacy, and the extent of similarity in outlook between old and young. Other dimensions are dealt with elsewhere (see, for instance, Jerrome, forthcoming a).

Contact and closeness

Enough research has been conducted in Britain over the last fifteen years for us to be able to refer with some certainty to the availability to old people of kin, the amount of contact with them, levels of satisfaction with the relationships, and the role played by relatives in older people's lives. Urban and regional, gender and class differences have been explored in a number of major studies (Hunt, 1978; M. Abrams, 1978; Wenger, 1984) and attention has been drawn to the influence of other variables such as ethnic origin.

   In terms of availability we know that, contrary to popular assumptions, two-thirds of retired people with children have at least one of them living within a few miles. Proximity increases with age and with widowhood. However, a significant number of older people have never married or had children. In 1981, among people aged 65 or over, the never-married amounted to 8 per cent of men and 11.2 per cent of women (although we have seen that these percentages are likely to decrease). A study in 1978 found that 30 per cent of those aged 75 and over had never had children and 7.5 per cent had outlived them (Abrams, 1980b). There are, indeed, some people who are outside the family system altogether. According to Hunt (1978) 5 per cent of people of retirement age have no living relatives outside the household and a further 5 per cent have lost contact with their relatives. But the vast majority of elderly people – 97 per cent – do have relatives they describe as 'close'. Female relatives tend to be closer than male relatives (Cicirelli, 1983). The unattached in Wenger's sample include a concentration of women living alone. People with children tend to be closer to them than to any other relatives, and parents report being closer to daughters than to sons – the former are more often described as 'favourite' children (Aldous, Klaus and Klein, 1985; Jerrome forthcoming a). Siblings, and after them a sibling's children are important, particularly for the never-married or childless widowed person (Allen, 1989).

A similar picture emerges in relation to social contact. Older people with adult children, particularly daughters, see them regularly. 'Family work' – the work of keeping in touch, providing services, keeping up with individual developments and disseminating family information, tends to be undertaken by women. Women are described as family monitors, kin keepers, the linchpins of family life (see Jerrome, 1993, for a summary of this literature).

In general, the amount of contact between elderly people and their relatives again contradicts the widely held view of isolation and neglect. They both visit regularly and are visited, the latter more frequently than the former, especially among the oldest age groups. More than 70 per cent of elderly people see a relative at least once a week. Almost half see one (especially the spouse) every day of their lives. Frequency of contacts diminishes from 65 to 86 years after which it increases again with more than half of very elderly people being in daily contact. The sharpest drop in daily contact is between 65 and 70 as aged parents die and remaining children leave home. The pattern is similar in rural and urban areas, though in the former, retirement migrants are a group with significantly less contact with relatives. Christmas Day, a time which epitomises the loneliness of old age, in the media at least, is invariably spent in the company of relatives or, if single, with friends. Only one in ten of Wenger's sample spent the day alone, often by choice, though the proportion rose sharply in the oldest groups. Four times as many over-80-year-olds spent Christmas Day alone and lonely. They were likely to be single or widowed, and living alone.

The majority of people were satisfied with the amount of contact they had with children, though more people were unsatisfied in urban areas – two-fifths – than in rural. Even more – a quarter – would have liked to see more of their grandchildren. Significantly, old people most likely to agree with the statement 'children don't care about their parents except for what they can get out of them' are persons who have no children.

Obviously, these generalisations based on statistical evidence obscure a wide range in types of family interaction. Relations in later-life families vary enormously, from those where family contact is vital, to those where it matters little, by mutual consent. In the former it is a time- and energy-consuming activity, a rewarding series of transactions among people who spend as much time with their families as they can and prefer being with them to doing anything else (a family-centred lifestyle, in Taylor and Ford's [1983] analysis). The opposite situation corresponds to the image of grandparenting offered by Kornhaber (1985), in which the older generations pursue solitary, work-oriented or narcissistic lifestyles. It might, as some have suggested, be a bitter acknowledge-ment of their children's lack of interest which makes some elderly parents report satisfaction with little contact. Issues like this, which have been debated in the American literature for many years, underline the inadequacy of research designs which ignore the subjective experience of ageing in the family. Rates of face-to-face contact do not tell us much about the quality of relationships and their personal significance. Physical distance might not itself preclude close and meaningful ties, a fact recognised in the concept of intimacy-at-a-distance. This has been described as a euphemism; others argue, pessimistically, that what really exists is pseudo-intimacy, a state of concern based on a sense of obligation on account of children's earlier dependence. Family solidarity no longer exists but elderly people cannot bear to admit their marginality in their children's lives (Blau, 1973).

The picture this conjures up is rather gloomy, and possibly exaggerates the sense of ties that bind but do not satisfy. However, recent research supports the idea of an imbalance in the perceptions of parents and children. Parents consistently describe the relationship in more positive terms than their children do (Bengtson, 1987). An explanation for this asymmetry might be that elderly parents have invested more in the relationship, have more to lose if it fails and less time to put things right. The potential for divergence in thinking about family roles and obligations is greatest in ethnic minorities, given the exposure of the second generation to values very different from those of their immigrant parents (Jerrome, 1991, 1993, forthcoming a).

Roles

Methodological problems of the same order exist in the study of the roles played by relatives in the lives of elderly people. We know from the literature that younger relatives provide help of various kinds and that they are approached before people in other categories such as friends and neighbours, particularly when the crisis requires a long-term support (Litwak and Szelenyi, 1969). For intimate personal tasks female relatives are called upon, for normative constraints of modesty and propriety suggest that outside the marital relationship, it is quite inappropriate for adult men to tend adult women whatever the relationship (Wenger, 1987a). Some constraint exists on daughters tending fathers and sons tending mothers, but children in these categories will be chosen in the absence of a carer in the appropriate category. This means that daughters are the main carers, since far more elderly mothers require care. The mother–daughter relationship is, in any case, one of our culture's two significant dyads (the other is the husband–wife dyad), the basis of significant mutual exchanges throughout the younger woman's lifetime.

This is a rather different way of looking at the female caring role from the usual one in which women care because caring is unpaid, unrewarding work. It emphasises the importance of seeing caring as one more (perhaps the ultimate) act in a series based on reciprocity. Wenger

(1987b) argues that the principle of reciprocity is fundamental in the caring role. Wenger points out that, contrary to popular belief, moving in with children does not appear to be triggered by the need for care. It is, indeed, difficult to make a long-term case for the dependency of any one member of the family on another. Taking a life-span approach helps us to appreciate the personal significance of family transactions and reminds us of something we often forget: that the act of caring means caring about as well as caring for (Wenger, 1987c). This approach also puts the concept of filial maturity – the coming to terms with a parent's dependence – into perspective. It is not to deny, however, that very occasionally caring for takes place in the absence of caring about. We are reminded by a growing literature on the abuse of elderly people by their families that negative feelings may dominate a care relationship with harmful consequences (Eastman, 1982).

But what of the attitudes and experience of parents themselves? It is easy to slip into the one-sided and one-dimensional view of the old parent–adult child relationship, in which care is the single item in the transaction, moving in one direction only. Parenthood continues to be important as parents grow older, though for some it becomes a vestigial activity. Parents and their grown-up children encounter each other as equals, on 'the level playing field of adulthood'. They must face each other without recourse to roles and 'come to terms with fidelity and treachery, love and contempt, the strong and weak moral qualities of the people they have all become' (Eisenhandler, 1992, p. 244). Whether they continue to need and to influence one another's development – a topic which now occupies the attention of gerontologists on both sides of the Atlantic – depends to a large extent on whether they like each other and get on (see Rossi and Rossi, 1990; Moss and Moss, 1992; Jerrome forthcoming b, for a review of the issues).

The personal significance of family ties varies through the lifespan. In some respects it might be greater for the younger person than the older. Some young men discover an interest in genealogy when they become fathers; young women with only distant ties or none at all report that the arrival of their own children brings an acute sense of being without relatives (Jerrome forthcoming b). They need them for practical reasons, for advice and guidance, but also for a sense of social and historical location. Older women do not need their children to provide them with this sense of being in the flow of time; departed relatives are more significant in meeting that need.

The evidence reviewed so far indicates solidarity on two of the fronts identified at the outset. In terms of interaction and sentiment there is little sign of a generation gap but, given the methodological and conceptual problems involved, this cannot be said with certainty. Even in terms of attitudes and expectations it would appear that the generation gap is largely illusory, a figment of popular imagination.

Consensus

Over the lifetime of elderly people the traditional values governing sexual morality, duty, the importance of work, patriotism and authority have been challenged. There have been broad changes in the definition of family roles. Ideologies of marriage and parenthood have changed in ways older people often find unacceptable. In the United States, sociologists have been concerned for several decades with the apparent gap in attitudes, though it was the radical student generation of the 1960s which sparked their interest. In family research the attitudes of the three generations have been compared across a range of issues, embracing politics, religion and gender. The main divergence of views appears to be in the area of gender roles (Glass et al, 1986).

Women's roles have changed over the century. The demographic trends mentioned earlier – earlier marriage and fewer children – have lengthened the period of adult life not devoted to active parenthood. This has paved the way for another trend: the entry of married women into the labour market. The rise in women's participation in the labour force is, like the ageing society, a worldwide phenomenon. In Britain it is a product of technological changes creating employment opportunities in three areas: public administration; education, health and social services; and in the distribution of goods and personal services, itself a consequence of rising income and consumption (Eversley, 1982). Women have entered the work force in increasing numbers since the Second World War, albeit in areas of low-paid, part-time work. Even the mothers of young children are more likely to be in employment than they were forty years ago. Today, 35 per cent of mothers with dependent children are in part-time work and 14 per cent work full-time.

Hand in hand with these trends in women's roles has been a shift in the dominant ideology of motherhood. In the period after the Second World War, when the current generation of young-old people were having their children, the philosophy of child-centredness reached a peak (Rapoport and Rapoport, 1977). Parents of the 1940s and 1950s, themselves products of a much stricter and more repressive era, were beginning to treat children with a new sensitivity and respect, though still establishing firm guidelines for behaviour (Newson and Newson, 1965). The mothers of the 1940s were likely to see motherhood as a full-time job and as their main occupation in life. The needs of their children were of paramount importance. Today, children are less likely to be the pivot on which family life turns. It is recognised that parents have developmental needs too, and that a woman's need for fulfilment (as well as the family's need for an adequate income) might be met by paid employment. At the same time the trend to respect children's autonomy has developed. Modern parents, particularly in middle-class families, are more likely to negotiate with their children than dictate to them.

Older people often disagree strongly with current childrearing methods with their emphasis on autonomy at the expense of conformity and success (Rossi and Rossi, 1990). They object to a supposed lack of constraint, an abundance of television, too much spending money, tolerance of answering back and sexual permissiveness in adolescence. But the ambiguous role of grandparents, as we have seen, offers little scope for intervention.

In conversation with their peers in the privacy of their clubs older people deplore these practices. Invidious distinctions are drawn between themselves and younger people. The affluence and selfishness of sons and daughters, the food fads of visiting grandchildren are popular topics of conversation. In gatherings at pensioners' clubs old people express their feelings of being apart from younger people. Their belief in the cultural and moral superiority of their own generation is confirmed in conversation, song and prayer (Jerrome, 1992).

PEER RELATIONSHIPS

Peers are vitally important in the ageing process (a lengthy discussion can be found in Jerrome, 1992). Members of the same cohort have much in common. They provide continuity with the past, and socialisation to a variety of roles at a time of life when normative prescriptions are vague, social supports have been withdrawn, and cultural stereotypes are negative. Peer-grouping may be a product of identification with elderly peers and voluntary association with them, as in the case of working-class women in Britain (Harris, 1983). It is sometimes, however, a product of necessity rather than choice, in the face of abandonment by younger people. For elderly Jews in East London and in California a sense of rejection by their younger kin produces powerful ties with each other (Hazan, 1980; Myerhoff, 1978).

It is the community of interest among old people in relation to the young that is striking in meetings of the elderly peer group. At the club, among friends, elderly people are in good company. Pensioners' clubs in Britain are largely societies of widows (Harris, 1983; Jerrome, 1986). The typical member is an elderly working-class widow living alone. These women (and a few men) provide each other with moral and practical support, with companionship and with help in navigating socially uncharted waters. Through conversation with friends the elderly mother, mother-in-law or grandmother is able to achieve a balance of dependence and independence within the family. The confused old woman whose son seems to be taking over her affairs is advised to go to the citizens' advice bureau to find out about her legal rights; friends commiserate with the mother whose adult daughter takes her help for granted. Discussions about family problems help to put them into perspective and provide an outlet for strain and tension

(Jerrome, 1984; Johnson and Ariès, 1983; Jones, 1980). Elderly parents renegotiate their roles through exchanges with other older parents, as well as with their adult children (Francis, 1981).

For married women as for single, recounting and comparing the intimate details of family life with friends is helpful, satisfying and role supportive. This is the case even when marriages are longstanding and stable. Married women are more likely than their husbands to have a confidant outside the marriage. When asked who their confidants are, elderly men are likely to say their wives; elderly women are just as likely to name an adult child or same-sex friend (Lowenthal and Haven, 1968). The marital relationship in later life is potentially the greatest source of affection and companionship, given the dominant ideology of companionate marriage. Like the mother–daughter relationship, it is a significant dyad. Although in America only 3 per cent of all marriages attain the golden wedding anniversary (on account of rates of divorce and age at widowhood) it is in many cases the lengthiest and most meaningful peer relationship.

Marriage

Hess and Soldo, comparing married people with those without partners, describe married couples as living longer, staying healthier and feeling better, though in each case the relative advantage to men is greater than to women (Hess and Soldo, 1985). In our society, men are likely to be married until they die, and women to become widows. The majority of couples who stay married can expect to live alone together in the community for a significant period, from the departure of the youngest child until the death or, much rarer, the institutionalisation, of one partner. (See Chapter 9.) We would expect the quality of this relationship to have an important bearing on morale and life satisfaction, which is, indeed, the case. People who are happy with their marriages tend to be satisfied with life in general. However, it appears that intervening variables such as health or poverty might be responsible for this. Studies of marital satisfaction see it varying through the lifespan (Ade-Ridder and Brubaker, 1983), though the shape of the curve – the position of peaks and troughs, highs and lows – varies from study to study. Three patterns emerge. In the first, marital satisfaction increases again in the later stages, after a drop in the childrearing phase, but it never attains the high level of the initial, pre-child phase. The second pattern is a gradual decline in satisfaction, a phenomenon described by some writers as disenchantment, as romance, love and companionship become eroded by separate tasks and development. The third pattern of findings suggests that the quality of the marriage in the middle years remains unchanged after retirement.

The major difficulty with studies of marital satisfaction through the lifespan is methodological. Most are cross-sectional in design, involving a selection of couples, at different stages of development. Differences in satisfaction are possibly a product of differing expectations, given changing attitudes to marriage and gender roles. Another factor which makes interpretation of these findings difficult is the marital status itself of the older couple. These are couples who, by definition, have remained married when others in their cohort will have experienced separation and divorce. The findings could, therefore, be interpreted to suggest that those people whose marriages have survived thirty years enjoy a high level of satisfaction. An alternative explanation might be, however, that such couples have remained married because their expectations have been scaled down to fit existing possibilities. The longer the relationship, the more salient it is to self-identity and the harder to disengage from or admit failure (Hess and Soldo, 1985). Evidence of long-term marriages – golden-wedding couples – does suggest though, a special quality of intimacy and satisfaction (Brubaker, 1985). But to relate present experiences to earlier phases of a marriage requires a research design which charts the development of particular marriages over time.

Looking at the later-life couple it is clear that the way in which the crisis of retirement, ill health and other changes are accommodated depends on the pattern of coping built up over the years, and the degree of mutuality in the relationship. The same is true, according to the American literature, of the eventual division of labour achieved within the household. Couples vary from the traditional arrangement with gender-specific tasks to that in which roles are interchangeable or tasks undertaken jointly. However, not all the arrangements negotiated by elderly husband and wife are equally acceptable to both spouses. In a theoretical essay, Hess and Soldo (1985) offer four possibilities, two of them based on a consensus of view about appropriate conjugal roles, the others involving a husband frustrated by his wife's unwillingness to let him join in her activities, and a wife angered by her husband's refusal to do so.

Marital arrangements are obviously determined to some extent by the health and physical capacity of the partners. The health status of both parties is a major determinant of satisfaction (Mackinnon, Mackinnon and Franken, 1989). If they have always done things together, the impairment of one partner can lead to guilt, or a sense of exclusion, or of holding the mate back (Longino and Mancini, 1990). Performing intimate personal tasks in addition to all the household maintenance tasks might eventually fall to one partner. When one of the partners needs care the spouse is the first person to supply it. This is so even in the case of frail elderly wives or husbands with adult children near at hand. Interestingly, in Wenger's small, intensive sample of very elderly people, the men commented on the physical strain of nursing, lifting and keeping house, while women found the social and emotional needs of caring most difficult. This finding adds to the evidence of gender differences in sources of emotional support. Similarly, the fact that men find widowhood more stressful seems to confirm the suggestion that old men rely primarily on their wives to meet expressive and instrumental needs while elderly wives turn for emotional support to people outside the marriage (Lipman and Longino, 1981). Women expect to outlive their husbands, and the common stereotype of the caring wife helps them to accept the caring role. Men expect to predecease their wives rather than care for them. But researchers have been struck by the unquestionable devotion with which both wives and husbands accept the caring role for their spouse.

This devotion is the product of half a lifetime's affection and mutuality. Marriage creates a world of shared meaning and experience from which it is difficult to disengage. As Comfort puts it when talking of bereavement in later life, the elderly married couple resemble two beams propped together; if one is removed, the other falls down. A satisfactory marriage in our society provides a number of benefits such as material support and caregiving. Perhaps the most obvious, though, is stable companionship. The permanent presence of the spouse, which might evoke negative as much as positive affect, is nonetheless vital in creating a secure and predictable environment. The couple in George Simenon's novel, *The Cat* (1976), live in a state of habituated conflict but when one dies the other cannot survive. This may not be typical of long-term marriages though as Cuber and Haroff (1963) have pointed out, the majority of stable and apparently happy marriages are far from the vital and fulfilling ideal fostered by our romantic ideology. Nevertheless, many long-term relationships will be important sources of affection, approval and sexual gratification.

Sexuality

Studies of sexuality in later life, like those of marital satisfaction, are beset by methodological problems. The topic is a sensitive one, particularly for generations unaccustomed to self-disclosure about such matters. But there is a growing literature including some useful cross-cultural material (Weg, 1983a).

Contrary to popular assumption, old people are sexual beings. Sexual interest and activity are sustained throughout life, though the volume of activity might diminish, and sexual expression take different forms. As with other aspects of marriage, the rate of sexual activity in married couples is largely determined by earlier patterns. In some cases it ceases altogether, but this is often the culmination of an unsatisfactory relationship. It may be the wife who feels with the arrival of menopause that she can legitimately cease to engage in an unrewarding activity. More often, the husband is responsible for the termination of sexual activity, through ill health or impotence induced by temporary disability or fear of failure. Social attitudes and expectations seem to play an important part in sexual performance for men and women (Hendricks and Hendricks, 1977). The views of one's partner in particular are vital in restoring (or taking away) self-confidence and a belief in one's sexual attractiveness. From an earlier interest in rates of intercourse and comparison between youthful and older performance (the youthful being considered the norm) writers have gone on to consider psycho-sexual issues. Some note the importance of sexual expression for self-esteem, self-acceptance, and general well-being at all ages but particularly later on when other sources of support might be reduced (Burnside, 1975). Thus, sexual expression affirms the older woman's sense of herself as feminine, a sense undermined by the media and popular stereotypes (Huyck, 1977). For the older woman without a sexual partner this confirmation is missing, and Huyck, noting the importance of orgasmic sexual expression goes on to stress the acceptability of self-pleasuring (masturbation) and homosexual contact in the absence of a heterosexual relationship.

However, there is a danger of exaggerating the importance of sexual contact in old age and so creating another area of deprivation. If the spotlight on some old people's sexual behaviour is unnecessarily bright, for others it is too dim. The attention given to the needs of homosexual men and women in later life is sparse. However, there are indications that in their case too the stereotypes of a lonely and bitter old age is misleading (Jerrome, 1991, 1993).

Widowhood

Many older women regard marriage as the only legitimate context for sexual activity, and the loss of the husband signals the end of an active sexual life and all that that involves. This loss is compounded by others: companionship; material support; a partner in a world which is couple-oriented; someone to negotiate on her behalf in a male-dominated society where women often do not acquire the skills necessary to promote their own interests; in short, all the advantages conferred by marriage. There are, of course, compensations in the form of personal freedom, the ability to develop personal resources, the opportunity to build up peer relationships outside marriage, especially when friends are women widowed themselves. But not all widows are equipped to exploit these advantages. For widowers the potential loss is even greater, as we have seen. But given the tendency for men to marry younger women, and women's greater life expectancy, there are far fewer widowers than widows.

The ageing society described in earlier chapters contains increasing numbers of older women, a large proportion of them without partners. A significant proportion are widowed, rising to approximately two-thirds of those over 80. Increasing numbers of divorced women also swell the ranks of unattached elderly people. Some widows remarry but the majority do not. The remarriage rate is higher for men than women at all ages, leading to the increased likelihood of women being alone in future years.

Responses to widowhood vary. Most new widows and widowers experience pain: pain over being deserted, of losing a love object or at least a significant other, of grief and loneliness (Lopata, 1980). Their suffering is compounded by the difficulty others have in handling death and accepting the needs of the bereaved for essential grief work. The degree of initial disorganisation depends partly on the extent to which the spouses were involved in each other's lives. Beyond that, the personal and interpersonal resources of the survivor come into play (Lopata, 1980). For women the new independence is made bearable by their early training in the denial of dependency needs (Clark and Anderson, 1967). Some widowed people remain desolate. Others adopt a variety of strategies, ranging from mummification – the preservation of the deceased spouse's possessions and physical space within the house as it was – to remarriage; from deliberate self-isolation to the intensification of existing ties or the establishment of new ones; from a determination to remain in the past to the vigorous development of a new lifestyle. This new lifestyle does not generally include aspirations to remarry. In Lopata's study, over 75 per cent of older widows said they would not want to remarry, for a number of reasons. They included losing their independence and taking on the role of wife again; a shortage of men of the appropriate age; having to care for another sick man; unhappiness in the first marriage; fear of fortune hunters; the possibility of conflict between a new husband and adult children; and idealisation of the former husband.

To these one might add the problems of proceeding from acquaintanceship to marriage in a society where courtship is geared to youth. Relations with members of the opposite sex are problematic. Both men and women report being sexually propositioned. Widowers seem frightened by the abundance of female attention, though widows, even when they feel sexually deprived, frequently react to overtures with anger.

Remarriage

Despite social constraints, however, the remarriage rate is increasing partly as a result of the increase in numbers of older people, and partly for normative reasons, in particular the growing acceptability of new sexual liaisons in old age. Although the amount and nature of one's need for intimacy varies across the life course and between men and women there is no reason to suppose that it disappears with old age.

In the literature on primary relationships the assumption has sometimes been made of 'functional interchangeability' within the primary group. In the hierarchical compensatory model of relationships, referred to by Dono et al (1979), same-sex friendships and kinship networks might offer adequate outlets for intimate attachments in later life following the loss of the partner. Indeed, evidence of renewed ties with siblings, adult children and friends through co-residence or intensified social contact and service-exchange following bereavement might be taken to support that thesis. But evidence presented by Hochschild (1973), Litwak and Szelenyi (1969) and Dono et al (1979) indicates that the different primary group ties are not interchangeable with respect to the satisfaction of personal needs. This, the task-specific model of relationships, helps us to account for the dating patterns of older Americans described by Bulcroft and Bulcroft (1985).

The literature on primary groups and support networks tends to assume emotional and physical dependency in old age. But dependency is only one need met by close ties. Intimate relationships meet a number of needs, and involve a number of interpersonal exchanges. They have a variety of functions: personal support of a practical nature, such as in ill health, poverty and adverse circumstances; sociability, companionship and entertainment; intimacy, both emotional and physical, which provides validation of the self, a sense of self-worth and of having personal history; and challenge, in which the stimulation of intimate involvement lends purpose to existence, and gives life added meaning.

Different relationships meet different needs. The first, personal support, is largely a function of close kinship, particularly spouse and adult children. The spouse or other sexual partner is the primary source of intimacy, too. Emotional intimacy, sociability and challenge are provided by other members of the peer group – by siblings and same-sex friends. In the rest of the chapter we examine these two remaining peer relationships – with siblings and friends.

Siblings

Some brothers and sisters, like some spouses, meet all one's personal needs (apart from sexual gratification) and the loss of such siblings can be devastating. It has been suggested that elderly siblings grow more accepting and approving of one another as they age, though this closeness rests less on contact than on memories of a shared past (Scott, 1990). Abrams (1980b) suggests that siblings get closer in later life with the loss of friends and need for physical security. But although 69 per cent of people over 75 in his 1978 study had living siblings, face-to-face contact was comparatively rare. Only one-third of the group saw each other as often as once a month. Presumably other ways of making contact become important with increasing frailty.

In a study of women's friendship in 1980, several women who declared themselves close to no-one and seemed, indeed, to have no intense same-sex relationships turned out to be very close to siblings, cousins and in some cases nieces. They described them as best friends and it was clear that the intensity was a product of the recent past. The relationships had been cultivated both as expedient, given the likelihood (as they saw it) of failing powers, and as emotionally rewarding (Jerrome, 1981). Other studies report the same closeness and absence of rivalry between siblings, though it is not clear whether this is a product of mellowing or simply diminished contact. It could also reflect a positive value attached to 'family', or vulnerability when one is confined at close quarters with a sibling caretaker. In such cases a *modus vivendi* is rapidly reached, though ambivalence is apparent in public. Some recent work indicates, in fact, that sibling rivalry is carried into later life, exacerbated by parental preference and rejection (Moss and Moss, 1989; Jerrome, 1991, 1993 for summary).

In terms of practical support, siblings are 'standing ready' (Cicirelli, 1985), third in line after spouses and adult children. More is known about elderly sisters than elderly brothers, possibly because there are more of them. Old women provide their brothers with security and draw their sisters into social activities and networks. Sisters tend to be closer than brothers, though the intensity of childhood relationships is not normally achieved after marriage unless they are co-resident. Sisters are especially important for never-married women. For the childless widow, too, sisters can often move into first place as potential caretakers, companions and co-habitees.

Friendship

From Abrams's survey of retired people in 1978 it emerged that good friends and neighbours are thought to be more important than family for a satisfying life. Other writers have confirmed the importance of friendships (Wenger, 1987b). Friends, especially longstanding ones, provide continuity (Francis, 1984). Belonging to the same cohort, they have similar values based on common life experiences. Operating within a shared frame of reference they can help each other with age-related transitions in a way younger relatives cannot (Rosow, 1975; Jerrome, 1981, 1984). The process of socialisation within the peer group can be witnessed in the formal setting of clubs and associations and adult education classes, and in informal friend relationships. At the psycho-social level, friends provide confirmation of existence as a person worth knowing.

Friendship has received little attention in gerontology and in the social sciences generally (Chown, 1981). Its private, informal and ephemeral nature makes it both difficult and unattractive as a subject for study. But interest has been growing, partly in an attempt to assess the significance of the different components of primary groups – kin, friends and neighbours. Friendships are distinguished by their basis in free choice and mutual attraction (Dono et al, 1979; Heinemann, 1985; Allan, 1986). Friendship needs change through the lifespan, and there are striking gender differences (Hess, 1979; Pleck, 1975; Seiden and Bart, 1975). Men's friendships tend to be sociable rather than intimate, and focused on shared activity. Women's friendships are characterised by emotional intensity and self-disclosure. Conversation is, indeed, one of the main activities of female friendship, from early childhood onwards. Letter-writing may take over as the sole means of communication of elderly friends who cannot meet. Gender differences persist into old age, with women's relationships continuing to be more extensive and meaningful.

Some writers suggest that women's capacity to involve themselves in intense relationships and their greater openness and responsiveness to others, may make them more vulnerable in old age. Huyck (1977) and Bernard (1976) argue that this capacity may involve considerable stress as the people in whom they have invested die or in other ways become inaccessible. Contrary to this view, the evidence that women retain a capacity for making new relationships throughout life prompts the view that they are slightly better off (Heinemann, 1985; Jerrome, 1981; Bankoff, 1981). Men are less likely to replace lost friends and, relying on their wives for intimacy, experience great disruption after widowhood.

Several writers have commented on class and educational influences on the meaning and expression of friendship (Lopata, 1979) and indeed on the shape of social networks generally (Taylor and Ford, 1983). Middle-class men and women tend to have extensive and active extra-familial ties through membership of age-mixed associations, voluntary work and other aspects of public life. Friendship dyads and groups are sustained through shared activities and reciprocal visits (Jerrome, 1981, 1984, 1986). Working-class men, similarly, have a tradition of group membership. Working-class women's closest ties tend to be with female kin though following retirement or bereavement there is a tendency to join age-specific clubs (Harris, 1983; M. Abrams, 1978; Jerrome, 1992). Old people's clubs are attractive to working-class people for reasons already given. Attendance is an activity of friendship and for the few who attend (less than 13 per cent of the over-75s, with wide regional variations according to M. Abrams, 1978), club-going is the main social activity. It is in the clubs that the expressive orientation of old age is most evident: the commitment to being rather than doing; and rituals of social acceptance and approval (Jerrome, 1992; Creech and Babchuk, 1985). But the club is also a forum for competitive strivings in a status-conscious society. Status attributes in this community of working-class widows include the achievements of children and grandchildren, and their demonstrations of concern.

In fact, family ties have first priority. Family commitments are a legitimate cause for absence, despite the serious obligations involved in club membership. Despite vigorous participation and the obvious enjoyment of club activities, membership is acknowledged to be a fall-back position: a solution to loneliness and inactivity, better than staying at home.

THE BALANCE OF ATTACHMENTS

Research suggests that embeddedness in a social network is vital for general well-being. The image of the convoy has been used in longitudinal studies to suggest the movement through time of a person flanked by supportive relationships (Abrams, 1980b). The convoy concept helps us understand responses to current loss and change in terms of earlier life experiences. Involvement in a social network has emerged as the single most powerful predictor of survival (Berkman and Syme, 1979), its absence a predictor of early death (Abrams, not dated). Within the network, the presence of one or more confidant relationships has been seen to protect older people from loneliness and the damaging psychological effects of various age-related losses.

Certain social groups are more vulnerable to loneliness than others. In respect of elderly people we tend to think of widows, childless people and the never-married and those who live alone, as at risk. In fact, the never-married tend to be less vulnerable. One explanation for this is that they have well-developed strategies for establishing and maintaining social contacts (Gubrium, 1975; Jerrome, 1981). Another is that since loneliness is most often a reaction against relationship deficits, single women are less vulnerable because they are emotionally more independent (Essex and Nam, 1987).

Studies of loneliness in old age suggest that the most lonely are as likely to be married as unattached (Wenger, 1984). Married women have fewer social ties outside marriage than men or unattached women (Altergott, 1985). Acute loneliness can be a feature of the lives of women who have concentrated most of their emotional resources in marriage and find themselves in widowhood with neither friends nor the social skills to make them (Jerrome, 1983). Loneliness for married women revolves around the quality of the marital relationship; for the formerly married it is the time since the ending of the marriage and the quality of the closest friendships that are critical. For the never-married, health is the most important factor (Essex and Nam, 1987).

Another group of elderly people whose loneliness tends to surprise us are those living with adult children. Unfortunately, women from older generations were encouraged to see family roles as their main source of fulfilment. But people who have concentrated on family relationships at the expense of others are more vulnerable to loss in old age. In emotional terms, today's sensible behaviour might be tomorrow's risk factor.

It is generally assumed that family relations influence the well-being of older family members for the better. But despite our cultural bias towards family life there is surprisingly little explicit evidence that older people without supportive families are at a psychological disadvantage. The evidence, indeed, warns us against the view 'that more family is necessarily better, or that closer is happier' (Bengtson and Kuypers, 1985, p. 26).

We should not go so far as to deny the importance of kinship, however. If we ask about the effect of being without any relatives at all we find indications of loneliness and a sense of deprivation which is hardly surprising given prevailing values and social arrangements. The ideological emphasis on the family means stigma and lost privileges for those outside the couple and family framework (Jerrome, forthcoming b).

In terms of practical support being alone is to be disadvantaged, for families tend to be called upon before friends and neighbours (Litwak and Szelenyi, 1969); they feel they have a right to intervene and that neighbours should keep their distance, and having made a commitment to help they find it harder to withdraw (Wenger, 1986). This reflects the idea of family ties as primordial, and non-contingent, expressed in the popular saying 'Blood is thicker than water'. Against this is the view which stresses the growing basis of family ties in sentiment, and the discretionary element in the recognition of kinship obligations.

In structural terms there are, today, two typical situations in old age. One is to be almost totally alone; the other is to be at the pinnacle of a three- or four-generation family. Variations are caused by sexual orientation, family stability and ethnic group membership. It is much harder to generalise about the meaning of family ties or the shape of the family network. Family members negotiate over the inclusion or exclusion of particular units. Irregular units such as widows tend to be 'unhooked' by their in-laws. The death of the 'kin-keeper' might precipitate the break-up of the family. In some families there is a reservoir of barely differentiated female kin – daughter, sister's daughter, daughter's daughter, sister – existing to support the old person. This is a condition well-illustrated by M. Forster's novel *Have the Men Had Enough?* A relationship between a childless person and her sibling can be inherited by the nieces and nephews (Troll and Smith, 1976; Wenger, 1984). Each family constellation has unique elements.

As far as the general spread of attachments is concerned, some generalisation is possible. Wenger (1987a) has identified six types of network, on a continuum from family-oriented to detached. In the family-oriented network the old person lives near kin on whom she is dependent, other ties being unimportant. Next there is the fully integrated network in which the old person, long-term resident in the area and with a local family, has an active network even if housebound. The third type, described as community-integrated is more likely among middle-class or single people, among migrants and among the rich. The family is local, but uninvolved. As a variation on this another type of community-integrated network exists in which the family is geographically distant, though supportive. Ties are, again, stronger with community than family. Fifth is the attenuated network in which kin are again distant and supportive. But the retired married couples, often migrants, in this category have little local contact. Finally, there is the detached network characterised by very few ties of any kind, and dependence on public services. This type accounts for very few indeed of Wenger's sample of old people in rural Wales.

The eventual pattern of ties is a product of a host of factors ranging from health and income to values and expectations. Whatever the situation, we should accede to the older person the major part in determining the balance of attachments.

SUMMARY

A major premise of this chapter has been that family relationships, particularly between the generations, are problematic in view of changes in the culture, technology and demographic composition of British society that have transformed the family in the lifetime of the present generation of old people. The task of older people, and indeed of the whole family, is to come to terms with these changes. Family members must learn new ways of relating to each other in what is essentially a normative vacuum. The establishment of appropriate ways of behaving in the modern family, and socialisation to new family roles, is achieved through discussion and monitoring within the family itself and with members of the peer group. The role of elderly peers as helpers in the process of adjustment is generally underestimated.

11

DEPENDENCY AND INTERDEPENDENCY

Malcolm Johnson

Dependency is one of the words closely associated in the public mind with old age. The image of older people becoming like children – dependent on able-bodied adults – and the loss of mental faculties, are other stereotypes which have wide currency. Even my own children, long schooled in the rejection of ageism, like to remind me of the epigram 'Old professors never die, they only lose their faculties.'

In this chapter it is my objective to examine the validity of these distilled, negative notions of old age. To do this it will be necessary to give some consideration to what the two key words of the title mean (Bytheway and Johnson, 1990; Scrutton 1990). With greater conceptual clarity, it will be necessary to examine research literature to see how far the realities of later life reflect the images and beliefs. In asking the question 'What is done to assist elderly people?', an attempt will be made to analyse current policy and practice.

Before proceeding to the analysis, it is worth pausing to listen to the voice of the commentators of life, on the subject of old age. Poets have acted as the mouthpiece of inarticulate society for thousands of years. What do they tell us about ageing and old age?

In compiling an anthology of poems of ageing Barbara Gray and I found ourselves deeply depressed by classical and 'high' poetry (Gray and Johnson, forthcoming). From Shakespeare onwards, and particularly amongst the nineteenth-century romantic English Poets, old age brings out a melancholy for lost youth. Its corollary is a revulsion from old age. The very language of their writings has helped to shape Victorian and hence contemporary usage.

Longfellow writes 'O give me back the days when loose and free to my blind passion were the curb and rein . . . In an old man though can'st not wake desire . . .?' His heirs in this century offer equally bleak images. The cheerful face of Betjeman becomes a gargoyle when he looks at old age. His poem 'Late Flowering Lust' is a grotesque mourning of the loss of carefree independence and youthful beauty. In the middle of the poem he writes more moderately: 'I cling to you inflamed with fear, as now you cling to me, I feel how frail you are my dear and wonder what will be!' And his contemporary Philip Larkin,

never a romantic, brings a similar deathly pallor in his 'The Old Fools':
'What do they think has happened, the old fools, to make them like this?
Do they somehow suppose it's more grown up when your mouth hangs
open and drools . . .'.

Not all of poetry is ageist and revolted by age. Many writers adopt a
more hopeful posture, but usually based on a celebration of life in
general rather than the fruits of longevity. A few adopt a fulsomely
positive view. Robert Browning's lines 'Grow old along with me, the
best is yet to be' are rightly famous. So too are Jenny Joseph's
contemporary words of defiant warning in her poem which begins
'When I am an old woman, I shall wear purple' and goes on to say 'I
shall go out in slippers in the rain, and pick the flowers in other people's
gardens, and learn to spit.'

Another modern poet, Adrian Mitchell, sums up the theme of this
chapter. In his 'Old Age Report' he condemns the way society rewards
retired people with poverty and symbolic gestures. He rails against a
retirement which is a soulless ghetto at the end of the line of life. Here is
a sample:

> When a man's too ill or old to work
> We punish him
> Half his income is taken away
> Or all of it vanishes and he gets pocket money.
> We should reward these tough old humans for surviving
> Not with a manager's soggy handshake
> Or a medal shaped like an alarm clock –
> No, make them a bit rich.
> Give the freedom they always heard about
> When the bloody chips were down
> And the blitz or the desert
> Swallowed up their friends.

What Mitchell observes are the twin dependency-creating agencies of
illness and inadequate income, which much research has shown are
intimately linked together. Those who enter retirement after a lifetime of
professional work and with a solid income face the prospect of a much
more comfortable, varied and trouble-free time than a former bus
conductor, mill worker or coalminer. Life experience is a significant
indicator of the quality of life in old age. Money cannot (usually) buy
good health, but it can buy freedom from many of the limitations which
accompany retirement in most countries of the developed world. In this
respect it is also a device which can be used to avoid some of the
dependencies which come with old age.

WHAT IS DEPENDENCY?

The implication of the term is that there is a minority of people who lead
independent lives and another minority who do not and those in the

latter group are in need of help. But is this a realistic set of assumptions? Who is independent in modern society? Whose lifestyle would remain unchanged if those who support them withdrew?

The Dutch psychologist Munnichs has highlighted the fallacy of the strict dichotomy between dependence and independence. He writes:

> Dependency is always placed in contradiction to independency as if they exclude each other. In the opinion of many Western policy makers these concepts are even used to denote the object of policy aims and the means by which existing measures are tested. When these measures promote independency it is all right, if not, dependency is the root of the problem and then measures need to be changed. (Munnichs, 1976, p. 4)

Clark (1972) has distinguished a range of socio-psychological and individual-psychological forms of dependency which immediately take us into a much more analytic frame of mind. She has identified (i) dependency of crisis (the loss of spouse or similar trauma), (ii) neurotic dependency (where individuals develop a pathological reliance on others), (iii) development or transitional dependency (arising from puberty, menopause, retirement, etc.), as afflictions which arise out of individuals. In further elaboration Clark even begins to rank these conditions, nominating neurotic dependency as the worst form because

> . . . it persists throughout life as a dominant technique of adjustment and especially in stressful situations. The dependency is expressed in such attributes as self-effacement, dread of loneliness, ingratiation and indecision. (Clark, 1972)

The psychological conditions to which Clark draws attention would certainly reduce any individual's ability to manage their personal lives well. But so, too, would many other influences. Being grossly overweight or drinking too much alcohol would also inhibit social performance; so too would the absence of educational qualifications or the inability to form worthwhile relationships. All of the elements would act as inhibitions to the achievement of personal potential. They can be seen as limits to our progress. Equally they can be viewed as handicaps or disabilities for these terms are often used loosely as synonyms for dependency. Yet there is a curious circumscription of the usage of these words, which confines their general application to particular categories of people. Wheelchair users who cannot do their own washing and ironing are 'handicapped' and 'dependent', but middle-aged bank managers who cannot do their own laundry are considered to be neither. Women who cannot change electrical fuses and men who cannot cook are fundamentally dependent on others, but the term is never used.

From these everyday examples it is evident that we live in an interdependent world. There is no-one who in any proper sense is independent. In simpler societies than ours, individuals and families may be largely self-sufficient in food, clothing and shelter. Apart from hermits and recluses who choose to lie outside of them, there is interdependence for all who exist in human societies. Indeed, the very notion of society, as a social system in which human beings live in community with each other, presupposes an agreed system of social rules and conventions which regulate our behaviour and recognise the different contributions of others to the common good. These fundamental principles of social life require certain components to be present. Salient amongst these are mutual trust, a workable system of social exchange (of goods and services) and a willingness to involve every member of society in a way that provides them with recognised social roles and consequent livelihood.

In complex societies the extent of interdependence is greatly increased. We are all totally dependent on many strangers (who produce food, power, clothing, etc.) as well as on those with whom we live, work and have other personal relations. These forms of universal dependence are acknowledged, but not encompassed in the usage of the word. The logic for this appears to be that we are all contributors as well as receivers and thus equal partners in a social contract. It is those who for some reason are unable to contribute, or are disbarred from contributing in economically recognised ways, who are prone to being labelled dependent. Thus, it is children, unemployed people, those who have physical and mental handicaps, the retired and the old, who fall into the category.

Inclusion in the groupings of dependent people involves a process of *social* definition. Yet public and private reactions to those who have special need of the support of others to maintain their existence, tends to be on an *individual* basis. Whilst there is some recognition that illness is 'not their own fault', there remains a strong tendency to treat people who are handicapped in the performance of routine activities as personally responsible for their plight. Such victimisation is not peculiar to any particular group of people, but is most strongly expressed in cases where incompetence can be observed, but the causes cannot. People with hearing impairments, and those with mental health problems are, in general, subject to less sympathetic and more controlling actions by others, than wheelchair users or frail elderly people (Herbst, 1976, 1991).

David Wilkin (1990) has helpfully refined these ideas in the process of applying them to the task of measuring dependency. He expresses reservations about the central use of helplessness and powerlessness as important dimensions, and dismisses them as too restrictive to be at the core of any definition or measure. Instead he argues that 'The key component is the reference to a social relationship' and goes on to offer his own definition 'A state in which an individual *is reliant* upon other(s) for assistance in meeting *recognised needs*.' The analysis which led him to these conclusions was then applied to currently accepted causes and features of dependence. These were set alongside a summary list of

CAUSES OF DEPENDENCY	CATEGORIES OF NEED								
	Orientation	Activities of daily living	Mobility	Occupation	Social integration	Economic	Emotional	Environmental	Other
Life-cycle dependency									
Dependency of crisis (excluding disablement)									
Dependency resulting from disablement									
Dependency as a personality trait (Neurotic dependency)									
Socially/culturally defined dependency									

Figure 11.1 *Classification matrix – dependency*
Source: Wilkin (1990)

recognised needs and presented in the form of a matrix (Figure 11.1), with the intention of illustrating the complexity of dependency situations.

It is clear then that interdependency is a real phenomenon which is an integral component of citizenship. A special subset of this interdependency has been isolated and identified as dependency in modern societies. It is applied in the following circumstances:

1. Where individuals, congenitally or by acquisition, are incapable, temporarily or permanently, of performing a range of actions which are assumed to be within the competence of full citizens of a given society.
2. In particular, where there is an inability to carry out essential tasks related to personal maintenance, physical mobility, sensory functioning, mental stability, and communication (verbal or written).
3. Where society by its laws, conventions, buildings and social institutions places individuals in a dependent role or situation, e.g. children, those who are unemployed, sick, financially insolvent or otherwise deemed incompetent to live an independent and unsupervised life.

The interaction of personal factors and social mechanisms varies according to the characteristics of the person and the nature of the disability. For example, Cypriot or Pakistani women who come to Britain as non-English-speaking people are dependent and limited in their social participation in a similar way to a prelingually deaf person (Blakemore, 1983b, 1993). An unemployed person shares the same dependence on government agencies and the same restriction in consumer behaviour as an elderly person on income support.

It will be necessary to look in more detail at the processes and circumstances which create dependent situations. However, it remains an inescapable fact that a significant minority of the population falls into this category. Millions of people in Britain can only function as human beings if others wash them, launder their clothes, clean their homes, cook their food, transport them, etc. Elderly people constitute the largest group within this pool. As evidenced by the OPCS survey, (Martin et al, 1988a) the majority of people with hearing or visual impairments, mental health problems and mobility restriction are beyond the retirement ages. It is inevitable, therefore, that gerontologists have long been interested in the causes, consequences and relief of dependency.

We have already encountered a set of definitional problems which need to be clarified if the notion of dependency is to be useful. More importantly, if ways are to be found of reducing dependency, it is essential that causation is understood. So, before examining the more practical problems which arise, some attention can usefully be given to a selection of key concepts which underpin both discourse and policy.

Reciprocity and altruism

It is in the nature of dependency relationships that a person in profound need of help is given assistance, by one or more other people. They may do this as part of their paid occupation and are therefore rewarded for the service they provide. But it is now well established that the overwhelming bulk of what is called caring is done by relatives, friends and neighbours (OPCS, 1992; Arber and Ginn, 1991; McGlone, 1992; Finch and Mason, 1992). For them the help is given without direct payment. It is a gift. It may be a gift in return for gifts received in the past (children returning parental care) or in expectation of some return in the future (perhaps an inheritance). Equally, there may be no expectation of a reciprocal gift from the dependent person. The giver may give in the belief that if and when he or she needs help someone will be to hand. Or the aid may be provided with no expectation or hope of reward or exchange benefit – altruistic giving.

Since Mauss in his classic essay *The Gift* (1925) and the anthropologist Malinowski in his study of the Trobriand islanders (1922), formulated general propositions about the nature of social exchange, there has been much debate about its role in modern societies. These early studies postulated a set of powerfully stated social obligations to give to others both known and unknown. Accompanying sanctions reinforced the system which ensured that there was a proper balance of reciprocity both direct and indirect. Not only is courtesy returned by courtesy and favours by favours between people who know each other, but gifts are given to strangers in the expectation that yet other strangers will give to them.

Blau (1964) writing forty years later supported the notion of generalised exchange relationships, but drew attention to the highly developed sense of expected and observable reward which was generated by market transactions. Economic relations are fundamentally reciprocal exchanges, where all the parties involved are both givers and receivers. They involve trust – those who provide goods must trust that promises of payment will be honoured. Blau also observed another distinct set of social exchanges characterised by unseeking generosity. In his important book *The Gift Relationship* (1970), Titmuss explored this quality of altruism through a study of blood donors. He believed that two forms of value have taken a grip of contemporary society – those of the market place and those of bureaucracy where every action demanded a matching, measured and inflexible response. His socialist conviction led him to conclude that a third and more moral force was essential to act as a counterbalance; that of gift values.

As a challenge to the rising view that altruism had no place in industrial societies, Titmuss set out to demonstrate that it was alive and well in such systems as blood donorship. Moreover, he argued that social exchanges which made people ask not 'Who is my neighbour?' but 'Who is my stranger?' were normally superior to market exchanges and should be fostered by governments. Subsequent empirical studies have provided less optimistic conclusions. The economist Hirsch (1977) came to the view that the trend was for individuals to choose actions which were most likely to be to their personal benefit. Abrams's research on informal care and neighbouring was also broadly consistent with this view (Bulmer, 1986). He found that much neighbouring activity was short-lived and highly instrumental. The mobile middle classes were seen to engage in neighbourly activities as a way of gaining access to local social systems.

In Britain it is estimated that over six million people (OPCS, 1992) are the primary, unpaid carers of dependent – mostly elderly – people. In addition, unmeasured millions provide regular assistance to the older population. The motives and pressures which generate that help are still imperfectly understood. Yet governments in the western world are engaged in what is known as the interweaving of statutory services with informal care. Experiments like those in Thanet (Davies and Knapp, 1987) and North Wales (Wenger, 1984) consciously manipulated the willingness to give assistance by modest payments to family and other carers. They showed that financial inducements and sensitive organis-ation can increase the quantity, quality and cost-effectiveness of care. But it could prove to be a further set of involvements to make informal care yet another saleable commodity.

It is frequently assumed that older people are the beneficiaries of giving relationships. For people who are very old, sick or frail, there is certainly a marked shift in the balance, which would justify this view. However, as I show in detail later in this chapter, only about one in three of the retired population is placed in this 'dependent' situation. Such people may require round-the-clock attention which is very demanding indeed. But in considering their transfer into the receiver group, some countervailing factors need to be taken into account.

Intergenerational giving
People who have lived to become old and sick have by definition lived through all the earlier stages of life in which they have been contributors to the social good – as workers, parents, friends, neighbours, supporters of their own elderly relatives and contributors to wartime effort. They have usually given to the stock of social benefits more than they have received. It is by design that we ask the younger and more able-bodied to provide for their contemporaries who have neither of these characteristics, in return for similar aid when they too are in need. Old age is the classic example of the giver receiving back reciprocal gifts, presented and received over time.

Old age pensions are the most obvious example. To receive assistance in old age is an earned right, based upon an age-old social contract. When politicians and commentators speak of the 'burden of the aged', they exhibit a lack of moral responsibility, a willingness to disregard time-honoured arrangements or membership of that self-serving group which wants the well-to-do middle aged to further maximise their privileges and benefits. In the United States this last set of motives has given rise to a movement which calls itself Americans for Generational Equity (AGE).

To argue that reciprocity between generations and over time is a necessary arrangement is not to say that any particular pattern or level of support is equally right. As the numbers of elders in need of help grow, it will be necessary to constantly reassess what is equitable and deliverable. AGE and bodies like it have a part in that debate. What would be regrettable and damaging is the substitution of accountancy and rationing solutions for ones based on the historical contributions of one generation to the welfare of its successors and its reasonable expectations of reciprocity in the later stages of life. It should be remembered that the state assumed responsibility at the turn of the century for the support of elderly people, when other arrangements failed (Gunn, 1986).

The debate about intergenerational equity has become more vigorous during the past five years, drawing in economists, historians, philosophers and lawyers. They have extended the discussion in three principal ways. The historians have enabled comparisons to be made over time which allow us to see how generous societies were in earlier time periods (Thomson, 1984). Philosophers have attempted to clarify what is meant by (a) the generational contract and (b) the nature of obligation (Laslett and Fishkin, 1992; Callahan, 1987; Daniels, 1988) and economic analysis has led to claims that the costs of supporting the growing population of retired people cannot be sustained under current conditions (Johnson et al, 1989).

As the discussion is still actively in process it is not possible to identify any outcome. But the existing consensual view of the intergenerational contract established in the welfare states of northern Europe in the early post-Second World War period is no longer unchallenged, even in those countries (Johnson, 1993). The reality of an upward trend in dependency and the demand for health and human services has produced strong attacks on the nature and extent of public and private support to the old and even on the existence of an obligation at all (Epstein, 1992).

Gift giving in old age
Another erroneous assumption is that retired people, because they are out of the remunerated work force, no longer make contributions to society. Once stated, this proposition becomes self-evidently inaccurate. The linkage between 'work' and social value is an unreliable one. Whilst the main weight of family.caring falls on women aged 45–59 (Allen, 1983; Arber and Ginn, 1991), Enid Levin and her colleagues (1988) found that the average age of the supporters of confused old people was 61 and 30 per cent were over 70. This trend for the 'young old' to care for the 'old old' is projected to increase. At the same time this group is known to provide financial and social support to their children and grandchildren. More specifically, as more women become economically active the caring tasks they leave unfulfilled fall to the older generation.

The General Household Survey report *Informal Carers* (OPCS, 1988) reports that there are over 6 million carers in Britain, with 1.7 million caring for someone in their own home. Of these 3.9 million are women and 2.9 million, men (OPCS, 1992). Whilst there is no doubt that women are the principal contributors to 'informal' care, it is worth noting that so many men are involved. Indeed, in the over-65 age group, men carers outnumber women carers.

There is also an observable rise in the involvement of the 'young old' in voluntary bodies, self-help groups and community activities. Within the older population itself there is a great deal of mutual aid. Keith (1977) describes this graphically in *Old People, New Lives*. Her research in a new retirement community provides documentary accounts.

> Friends and neighbours check on each other daily; curtains not open by mid morning are a cue for a visit to make sure nothing is wrong. Meals are prepared, shopping done, and laundry washed and ironed for one blind resident. (Keith, 1977, p. 186)

Reciprocity and receiving
The next part of the paragraph in Keith's book continues as follows:

A look inside Merrill Court refrigerators also reveals an exchange network of food specialities. Except for the most extreme cases, such as the blind person, the exchanges are reciprocal. Of course, in a less tangible way, the blind man did offer a great deal in return to his caretakers. They enjoyed being the givers and carers, and they missed him bitterly when he died. (Keith, 1977, p. 86)

Gift receiving need not be an ungracious act of taking what is offered. Qureshi's (1986) study of carers in Sheffield indicates the wide variety of relationships which can exist. Some have always been one-sided. Others are based on mutual regard and long experience of mutual help. The following selection of quotations represents the range:

I think she helps me more than I help her at the moment. (Daughter)

Anytime I needed her she'd come at the drop of a hat, so I feel I owe it back, see, if she needs it. It works both ways doesn't it? (Daughter)

She's never been a mother as mothers should be. She was out every day of her life and she didn't want anyone . . . to upset her routine (Son-in-law)

He's never lifted a finger for anyone in his family (Daughter)

Wright's (1986) study of lone family carers confined itself to the debilitating effects of the caring task. It would be wrong to give the impression that the full-time care of sick elderly people is anything other than immensely demanding and exhausting. But it should be equally improper to presume that it is always unrewarding. The gift relationship which Titmuss drew to our attention is an integral and durable part of intergenerational relations even when one of the parties did most of his or her giving in the past. The grateful and the thoughtful receiver is still a giver.

Finch and Mason's (1992) major empirical study of family obligations in care giving concludes:

However our main point is not so much that these experiences of giving and receiving help within families were common experience (though many of them were), but that they were treated as unremarkable experiences by many people who talked to us. They were seen as a characteristic part of family life. (p. 163)

LABELLING AND DEVIANCES

To carry the label 'dependent' is to carry the burden of being a deviant – someone who no longer enjoys a place in the mainstream of society and whose behaviour is 'abnormal'. Others who share this status suffer a range of indignities and punishments which reinforce the deviance. Being excluded from social recognition and having no role in social relations is hurtful and damaging. Perhaps more importantly, it carries with it a set of attitudes, sanctions and prohibitions which have the effect of dehumanising the individual and engenders depression and reduction of self-esteem.

Social scientists have written extensively about the impact of labelling and the cluster of consequences which customarily accompany it. The literature encompasses criminals (Matza, 1969), drug users (Becker, 1963), those who are deemed mentally ill (Scheff, 1974; Skultans, 1979) and anyone – especially elderly people – who becomes reliant on the services of others for their everyday existence.

What characterises those who are subject to the labelling process is that the attribution of deviance results in negative stereotyping. Old age remains a deviant state in a society which celebrates youth and has not yet accustomed itself to the demographic revolution (Laslett, 1989). But it is the disabilities that accompany old age which attract the penalties. It is a response to perceptions of the abnormal, to the threatening and the unexpected. Such reactions are socially conditioned categories of action, rather than reflections on the individual.

Becker summarised the construction of deviance when he wrote:

> Deviance is not a quality of the act the person commits but rather a consequence of the application by others of rules and sanctions to 'an offender'. The deviant is one to whom the label has been successfully applied; deviant behaviour that people so label. (Becker, 1963, p. 9)

The existence of differences between older people and those of younger generations are well known, but exaggerated. There are, for example, no medical conditions exclusive to 'old age', so in that sense they are sick in common with all ages. It is the association – often misinformed or simply wrong – between ageing and decline which provides the foundation for stereotypical treatment. Sadly, elderly people themselves and those who seek to represent their welfare frequently provide fuel for such misconceptions, Repetition of 'Oh dear; it's my age . . .' by elderly people or 'What can you expect at your age?' by doctors only add to the conspiracy of ignorance against truth in the matter of ageing. Even organisations which set out to promote the well-being of elderly people and know the scientific evidence will amplify the negative features of later life in order to raise funds or make political points.

This 'structural ageism', which Scrutton (1990) feels has such damaging consequences, especially for very old people, remains stubbornly persistent, despite the increasing reports of abuse and discrimination (Eastman, 1985).

It would not be proper, however, to make too much of the notion of old age as deviance, for it has too many flaws to be a worthwhile theory. What is valuable about the analysis of old age as a labelling phenomenon, is that it draws attention to the negative circumstance which the visible maladies attract (Martin, 1990).

MEASURING DEPENDENCY

With the definitional problems which remain unsolved, it is inevitable that statistical information about the nature and extent of dependency-creating disability and illness is subject to the same uncertainties. On the one hand there are many research studies and population surveys which allow quantitative description of the retired population. On the other hand much dispute exists about what these data mean. Before looking at the incidence of these conditions, we will look briefly at the technical definitions of dependency used by demographers, planners and economists, who see old people as an economic 'burden'.

Dependency ratios

Economic analyses of population structure and change are preoccupied with the relative sizes of the economically active (ie in paid employment) segment of the population and those who are designated as dependent (all those not in paid employment, including children and retired people). The United Nations publication *The World Ageing Situation: Strategies and Policies* (1985) summarises the position well.

> As the proportion of the population of working age increases, total dependency ratios (defined for the purposes of the present report as the number of young people, aged 0–14, plus the ageing, aged 60 and over, divided by the population of working age, aged 15–59) concurrently become lower. The total dependency ratio is often used as an indicator of economic potential, the principal argument being that a low dependency ratio implies relatively more workers and the need to divert fewer resources to dependent populations. (United Nations, 1985, p. 46)

As the total dependency ratio includes young and old the two can be separated and their independent impact assessed and compared. Falkingham (1987) has studied the UK figures which are used to measure the cost to the economy. She points out that as dependency is defined by age, the 'gerontic' (old age) ratio will inevitably rise as the population ages. It has increased during this century from 12 old people (60/65+) per 100 in the working age ranges to 34 in 1981 and this figure is projected to reach 38 by 2021. During the same period, the child dependency (neontic) ratio (aged 0–19) has fallen from 83 to 54. Projections indicate it will fall further by 2021, to 48. Figure 11.2 presents these trends graphically.

It is widely assumed that this shift in the balance of population is in itself bad and likely to damage the economy. As older people consume higher proportions of the national budget for health, social services and social security this has a somewhat self-evident aspect. Data such as that produced by Clark and Spengler (1980) serve to encourage that view. For the USA, they estimate that the *per capita* costs for elderly persons are approximately three times those incurred by youth. Comparable figures for the developing world indicate that economic progress brings increased 'dependency' costs. In Africa and East Asia, the costs of elderly people are only 1.5 times higher than for young people (United Nations, 1985). More recent studies (Johnson and Falkingham, 1988) confirm these patterns.

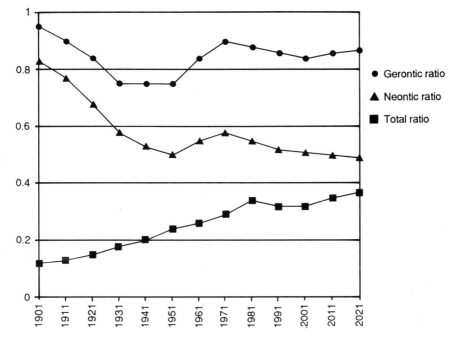

Figure 11.2 *Dependency ratios, Great Britain, 1901–2021*
Source: Falkingham (1987)

The assumptions about relative costs and their damaging economic effects have come under attack from two separate quarters. First, from those who have adopted a political economy view of ageing which sees old age as a period of dependency created by modern society (see Chapter 2). The other reaction comes from the ranks of demographers, economists and historians, who have looked more closely at the real (as opposed to assumed) economic worth as well as the costs of old age. Falkingham (1987) argues it is not necessarily the case that a change in the age structure will lead to a greater dependency cost. Demographic factors alone do not determine the ratio of workers to non-workers. In addition, shifts in labour-force participation involving many more women make dependency assumptions based on age and gender very suspect (Arber and Ginn, 1991).

Thane (1987) sets out to quell the panic, first by drawing attention to the stability of the total dependency ratio throughout the twentieth century and the fact that this is scheduled to continue into the next. Within this framework she envisages a fall in *per capita* health and social services costs, as the increased healthiness of younger cohorts is transmitted into old age. This is a case also promoted by Bosanquet (1978) and more recently using American data by Pifer and Bronte (1987). In a similar essay on the implications of greater activity in old age, Johnson (1982) associated these arguments with evidence of considerable increases in the income and wealth of a portion of the elderly cohorts of the next century, who will constitute not an economic burden but a much sought-after market.

In some ways more fundamental than these technical arguments is an ethical point about what counts as economically and socially worthwhile activity. Calculations are based on all income-generating activity which is recorded in the public domain. But is all of it worthy to count in the calculus of human welfare? Is the making and selling of hard drugs, pornography or 'stink bombs' to count equally with the production of wholesome food and nursing skill? And what about the work which is done and valued but not paid for (like informal care and domestic labour)? Not only are the dependency ratio calculations simplistic and inaccurate, they embody a set of values which leave much to be desired.

DISABILITY AND DEPENDENCE

The universal association of disability, both physical and mental, with increasing age is also present in the UK. There is some evidence to support Fries and Crapo's (1981) claim that morbidity is being compressed into the later years of life, but there is no denying that incapacity increases significantly beyond the age of 70. Distinctions between those with different levels of impairment are therefore of importance, for both the self-perceptions and the reality experienced by most elderly people is that they are fit and able to lead their own lives (Johnson, 1972; OPCS, 1991a)

No national register of disability or disabled persons in Britain exists, despite the intentions set down in the Chronically Sick and Disabled Persons Act 1971. As a consequence there is no census-based inventory from which reliable data can be drawn. Instead we must look to a range of sample surveys and estimates shaped from a range of sources. Wicks and Henwood (1988) calculated that 1.1 million people over the age of 65 are severely disabled constituting one in eight of the total age group. A further two million were estimated by Walker and Phillipson (1986) to be moderately disabled.

As the result of a series of major surveys conducted by the Office of Population Censuses and Surveys (OPCS) during the late 1980s we now have access to a more reliable data set. The studies, which are reported in two main publications (Martin et al, 1988a, 1988b), draw on a large sample of the general population (100,000 addresses) including private households and 'communal establishments'. So they included people in hospitals, residential and nursing homes, where the most frail elderly persons would be found. As part of the studies, those whom we deemed to be disabled were assessed on a range of dimensions to identify the nature and degree of disablement. This allowed researchers to classify respondents on a scale of severity, from 1 (the lowest) to 10 (the

Table 11.1   *Estimates of disabled adults in Great Britain, 1988*

| | Numbers (000s) | | | Rate per 1000 | |
	Private households	Communal establishments	Total	Private households	Total
60–69	1298	36	1334	236	240
70–79	1589	98	1687	395	240
80+	1037	217	1254	674	714
All ages	5780	422	6202	135	142

Source: Martin et al (1988a), Tables 3.3 and 3.4 as reproduced in Victor (1991, p. 64)

Table 11.2   *Estimates of disabled adults by severity in Great Britain 1988*
(000s)

| Severity category | Private households | | | Total all ages | Communal establishments | | | Total all ages |
	60–69	70–79	80+		65–69	70–79	80+	
10	15	23	39	102	7	24	58	108
9	57	68	93	285	7	18	45	80
8	59	92	87	338	5	12	30	58
7	78	115	123	447	3	9	22	39
6	85	149	107	511	2	9	18	34
5	146	176	132	679	2	6	15	29
4	152	179	105	676	3	8	12	27
3	173	212	109	732	2	6	8	19
2	225	263	105	824	2	5	6	16
1	308	310	138	1186	3	3	3	13
Total	1298	1589	1037	5780	36	98	217	422

Source: Martin et al (1988a), Table 3.3, as reproduced in Victor (1991, p. 65)

highest). For example, someone in category 1 may have a hearing impairment in one ear; in category 6 have had a stroke or heart condition which limits mobility and severely restricts self-care; whilst category 10 would include people who were totally dependent on others as a result of advanced dementia, immobility or multiple chronic illness.

In Table 11.1 we can see the simple distribution of those over 60 who were judged to be disabled, by age groups and location. Of the 6.2 million disabled adults in Britain 4.27 million (69 per cent) are over the age of 60 – all but 7 per cent of them living in private households. Predictably the proportion of those living in communal settings rises with age; so that 17 per cent of people over the age of 80 live in institutions.

A closer examination of the distribution of disabilities in terms of severity (Table 11.2) shows that the smallest numbers are in the most severe category and that those within it rise steeply with advancing old age. Indeed there is an almost linear relarionship between age and severity with the largest numbers being 'younger' and mildly disabled and those profoundly restricted being smaller in number and more likely in older age groups.

As Christina Victor (1991) points out in her commentary on these findings, there are obvious problems in using the kind of scale adopted in the OPCS studies. The criteria used are not universally agreed ones and if they were modified to match other studies would produce very different patterns. She writes:

> For example there were 1,186,000 adults in private households classified in severity category 1 compared to 102,000 in severity category 10. Changing the definition of disability so that severity category 1 was excluded would reduce the number of disabled people in the total population from 6,202,000 to 5,004,000 (a reduction of 1,198000)! (Victor, 1991, p. 65)

A further anomaly is that 'older people are over-represented in the more severe disability groups: those aged 60+ constitute 75 per cent of the most severe disability group but only 64 per cent of the least severe category'.

These methodological points are important in alerting us to the uncertainties in national data about long-term illness, though there is every reason to be confident that the general patterns are correct. The same problems beset information about mental illnesses, but are amplified by the greater difficulty in clinical diagnosis. Nonetheless it is possible to say that two-thirds of all mentally and physically handicapped people are over 65. Over a third of those 65+ (rising to half of the over-80s) are estimated to have hearing impairment (Coni et al, 1992). Again there are no wholly reliable figures for the numbers of people with significant visual handicap; but it is known that three-quarters of the 100,000 people registered as blind are over 65. These conditions, along with other physical disabilities, mental frailty, incontinence and the limitations of poor housing, represent the range of handicap for older people.

Bond and Carstairs (1982) in their survey of elderly people in Scotland identified heart conditions (15 per cent), arthritis and related conditions affecting the back (10–15 per cent), joints (15–35 per cent) and sight defects (2–21 per cent) as the most widely reported illnesses which restrict functional capacity. These in turn have consequences for the performance of activities of daily living (ADLs) where bending and stooping are ingredients in the process. The ability to cope with everyday tasks of personal hygiene and domestic tasks in the home is critical to the maintenance of an independent existence. These Activities of Daily Living (ADLs) have received much attention in social surveys and together they provide a picture of about half of the older population coping without assistance. As for the rest there is again a steep rise with age.

In McGlone's commentary on the statistics, shown in Table 11.3 he concludes that 'there is still only a minority of elderly people who are

Table 11.3 *Inability to undertake mobility, self-care and domestic tasks in the population 65+, 1985*

	Age					
	65–69	70–74	75–79	80–84	85+	All 65+
Walk out of doors	5	7	14	24	47	13
Getting up and down stairs and steps	4	5	10	17	31	9
Getting around the house (on the level)	1	1	2	3	6	2
Getting to the toilet	1	1	2	2	7	2
Getting in and out of bed	1	1	3	2	7	2
Cut toenails	16	24	34	48	65	29
Bathing, showering, washing all over	4	5	10	16	31	9
Brushing hair (females), shaving (males)	1	1	1	3	7	2
Washing face and hands	0	1	1	1	2	1
Feeding	0	1	0	1	2	1
Household shopping	7	10	16	29	56	16
Wash paintwork	8	13	24	34	62	20
Clean windows inside	9	13	21	34	63	19
Clean and sweep floors	5	7	13	20	45	12
Job involving climbing	17	25	36	52	76	31
Wash clothing by hand	4	5	9	12	32	8
Open screw-top jars	7	7	11	15	29	10
Cook a main meal	4	4	9	13	29	8
Use a frying pan	2	2	5	8	19	5
Make a cup of tea	1	1	3	3	8	2
N	1062	1025	788	395	240	3510

Source: Office of Population Censuses and Surveys (1988), Tables 12.14, 12.31, 12.33 and 12.37 (from Victor, 1991, p. 71)

unable to cope. Only 16% are unable to do their own shopping, 12% cannot sweep or clean floors and 10%, cannot open screw tops' (McGlone, 1992). Similarly, a very small percentage have problems with self-care except for toenail cutting. Despite these small proportions the numbers involved can be large. For example there are an estimated 1.4 million people over 65 who cannot do their own shopping. Overall, at least 15% of the elderly population are likely to be dependent on others for the performance of some tasks they would previously have performed independently. This latter group is highly likely to contain the 1 in 250 over-65s who suffer strokes, and frequently the 7 per cent of males and 18 per cent of females over 70 whom Vetter (1981) reports as suffering from regular urinary incontinence.

Mental health problems are prevalent at all ages, but there is a cumulative effect which manifests itself in higher levels within post-retirement populations. It is usual to separate organic syndromes (those with a physical cause) from affective disorders. Distinctions between the two are very difficult to sustain with the result that both practical diagnosis and research leave large areas of doubt. Within the organic syndromes, dementia in its various forms and that of the Alzheimer's type in particular are both very disabling and relatively common in later life, according to current research. Unfortunately, it is virtually impossible to be sure of a diagnosis of Alzheimer's in a living patient. Moreover, as those with this condition are at high risk of institutional-isation, community studies suffer from a number of well-known deficiencies both of sampling and methodology. Nonetheless, it is commonly accepted as Brayne and Ames (1988) report that dementia occurs in about 5 per cent of the population aged over 65 and up to 20 per cent of those over 80. 'The rate of new cases is about one per cent per annum in the over 65s, rising with increasing age.'

Of the functional mental illnesses for which no definite organic cause is yet established (which includes symptoms such as delusions and hallucinations), depression is the most prevalent. It is the commonest psychiatric condition encountered in epidemiological studies and routine medical practice alike. Depression is the epidemic condition of old age. Again, because of the problems of definition as well as study methodology, research findings vary. Brayne and Ames's tabulation of the most important British studies (Table 11.4) depicts a range from 6 per cent to 26 per cent of over-65s which is at least an order of magnitude greater than the much discussed forms of dementia.

Table 11.4 *Depression in UK community samples*

Study	Location and age	n	Instrument	Findings
Kay et al 1964	Newcastle 65+	505	Psychiatrist interview	26% affective illness and neurosis (inc. 1.3% endogenous affective illness)
Parsons 1965	Swansea 65+	228	Psychiatrist inverview	0.9% endogenous depression (lifetime prevalence ED 6%)
Hare and Shaw 1965	London 65+	211	Interview	11% depressive symptoms
Gurland et al 1983	London 63+	396	Interview (CARE)	12.4% pervasive depression (inc. 1.3% manic depressive illness)
Maule et al 1984	Edinburgh 62+	487	Psychiatrist interview	5.1% depression
Copeland et al 1987	Liverpool 65+	1070	Interview (GMSA/AGECAT)	11.3% depression (inc. 3.0% depressive psychosis)
Morgan et al 1987	Nottingham 65+	1042	Interview (SAD)	9.8% depression (4.9% met stricter clinical crtieria)

Source: Brayne and Ames (1988), p. 20

It is essential to restate that the majority of elderly people in the UK lead lives as independent of the assistance of others as people in younger age groups. Media reports and even governmental statements about the 'burden of dependency' serve only to reinforce unwarranted images.

CARING SERVICES

It has already been established that family and informal carers provide the major part of the support given to dependent people. Nonetheless, the system of statutory and voluntary services – both health and personal social services – is an indispensable professional complement. Historically they have grown up in five unrelated organisational patterns (i) local health authorities which provide hospital treatment, containing specialist geriatric provision, (ii) primary health care providing general practitioner home nursing and health visitor services, (iii) local authority social services departments offering a range of residential, day and domiciliary forms of care, (iv) voluntary bodies, some of which offer residential accommodation and other community services including meals on wheels and day centres, and (v) private-sector residential and nursing homes. To this range we must now add a variety of NHS and social services Trusts which have taken over provision of some parts of the services previously supplied by health authorities and local government.

At the time of writing there is considerable change in process, so the exact form of services to older people in the mid-1990s cannot be confidently predicted. Following the full implementation of the NHS and Community Care Act on 1 April 1993, local social services departments have become principally contractors or purchasers of services rather than direct providers as in the past. In their document *The Community Revolution.' Personal Social Services and Community Care* (1992) the Audit Commission write:

> The delivery of care and support to adults in the community will undergo a fundamental change in the 1990s . . . local social services authorities will move from being suppliers of a range of services to adopting the Lead Agency role. From April 1993 they will be required to assess the needs of individual people, arrange with them individually tailored services to meet these needs as appropriate . . . secondly . . . the core element of social security income support for nursing and residential home care, currently available to people through a means test, will be paid instead to local social services authorities. At present this form of income support is paid to some 200,000 people . . . potential new claimants will need to approach social services for support.

This is not the place for a detailed account of the likely shape of the new services except to say that the balance of service provision will move significantly to a mixed economy of 'independent' agencies and away from public bodies (local government and the NHS). Of particular relevance to elderly people will be the large-scale transfer of local authority (LA) old people's homes and homes for those with learning disabilities and mental health problems to either the private sector or to independent (not-for-profit) Trusts.

The changes will be an accelerated version of those which have taken place since 1975 in the long-term care sector. At that stage there were 95,000 beds in LA old people's homes with only 18,750 in private residential homes. There was a small voluntary sector. At the same time there were 25,000 beds in private nursing homes. Today there are 328,000 beds in private long-term care (including nursing homes and other hospitals) and 140,000 in the public sector (Laing, 1990; Mitchell, 1993). There are about 69,000 beds in private nursing homes.

Laing's tabulation of the bed distributions and capital values in Table 11.5 provides an indication of the scale of what is now a major care 'industry'.

The expansion has been driven largely by the dramatic growth in the numbers of very old dependent people (and in part by the failure of other support systems). John Bond's graphic Figure (Figure 9.4, p. 216) shows that, to date, the public provider has borne the major task of supporting the largest proportion of very confused residents

Long-stay care in geriatric hospitals or wards of general hospitals has become far less common than in early 1980s and before, when old people were often described as 'bed blockers'. Extension of private provision has provided a ready discharge route for the chronically sick patient, leaving beds free for more acute care and rehabilitation. Despite this change hospital geriatrics remains a low-status and medically under-regarded service. Evans (1981) has reported that whereas consultants in general medicine had an average of 30 beds in their care, geriatricians had about 180, plus commitments to outpatients, day hospitals and domiciliary visits. Even against these odds the length of hospital stay by elderly people has declined since 1970. Victor (1987) reports that the mean length of stay for males aged 65–74 in 1974 was eighteen days, but had fallen to thirteen days by 1983 and continues to fall year on year. John Bond in Chapter 9 also examines these issues from a historical and policy viewpoint.

For those who are sick at home or discharged from hospital a variety of domiciliary services are supplied by the NHS and by local authority social services departments. Supplemented by home-based voluntary services, these inputs build upon family and other informal care. Linkages between hospital and community services have been notoriously poor and the system's ability to coordinate services so that an elderly person returning home from hospital care gets home help, home nursing or meals on wheels at the point of discharge is very limited. The Continuing Care Project's survey (Amos, 1980) showed that fourteen days after discharge about half of all elderly patients could not cope with domestic tasks or personal care, of whom more than a quarter had no one to help them. Of these two categories together, 84 per cent either

Table 11.5 *Market value of care of elderly, chronically ill and physically
disabled people, UK, annualised at March 1992*

(A) INSTITUTIONAL PROVISION	Places	£ million
Private nursing homes	152800	2225
Private residential homes	162400	1572
TOTAL PRIVATE CARE HOMES	315200	3797
Voluntary nursing homes	13700	200
Voluntary residential homes	46900	430
TOTAL VOLUNTARY CARE HOMES	60600	630
NHS long-stay geriatric	41300	942
NHS elderly mentally ill	24300	554
NHS younger disabled	5400	123
Local authority Part III	103800	1090
TOTAL PUBLIC SECTOR	174800	2709
TOTAL INSTITUTIONAL	550600	7136
(B) NON-RESIDENTIAL CARE		
Private home care	–	422
Private aids and adaptations	–	146
PRIVATE NON-RESIDENTIAL	–	568
NHS district nursing	–	891
NHS day care	–	67
NHS chiropody	–	79
Local authority home care	–	815
Local authority day care	–	130
Local authority meals on wheels	–	90
Local authority other services	–	452
PUBLIC NON-RESIDENTIAL	–	2524
TOTAL NON-RESIDENTIAL	–	3092
GRAND TOTAL	–	10228
[INFORMAL CARE*]	–	[39100]

*Calculated following a method originally used by the Family Policy Studies Centre (1989),
valuing each hour of informal care at £7.00 per hour (based on local authority pay rates).

Source: Laing, 1993

had a caring person who could not cope, or had no caring person at all.
By twenty-eight days after discharge 39 per cent of the principal caring
persons were themselves found to be frail and at risk. Home visits from
general practitioners (family doctors) are also delayed. The same survey
showed that 63 per cent of patients had not received a call by fourteen
days after discharge.

An increasingly impressive range of services exists for elderly people

Table 11.6 *Domiciliary services for elderly people*

Service	Provider
Primary health care teams	NHS
Clubs	Local authority/voluntary
Day centres	Local authority/voluntary
Meals on wheels	Local authority/voluntary
Luncheon clubs	Local authority/voluntary
Health visitors	NHS
Domiciliary physiotherapy	NHS
District nursing	NHS
Nursing auxiliaries	NHS
Aids for daily living/house adaptation	Local authority
Nail cutting services	Voluntary
Library service for housebound	Local authority/voluntary
Night sitting	Local authority/voluntary/private
Sheltered housing	Local authority/voluntary/private/Trusts
Incontinence laundry	Local authority/NHS/Trusts
Community psychiatric nurse	NHS
Social worker	Local authority/voluntary/private
Respite care	Local authority/NHS/Trusts
Geriatric day hospital	NHS/private
Good neighbour scheme	Voluntary
Community rehabilitation	NHS/Trusts
Care managers	Local authority/NHS
Community physiotherapists	Local authority/NHS
Home care organisers	Local authority/private

Note: From 1993 onwards almost any of these services could be supplied by the different Trusts which have taken over NHS or local authority responsibilities.

But the identification of what individual 'clients' need will be determined by care managers (some of whom will be social workers, but may also be nurses, health visitors or other categories of staff). They will arrange 'packages' of care from different suppliers and be responsible for coordinating and monitoring those services.

at home, but there is great geographical diversity in the extent and availability of them. Table 11.6 summarises the domiciliary services available for elderly people in the United Kingdom. However, there are considerable variations in quantity and quality of these services across the country.

Up-to-date and reliable data on the delivery of these services are difficult to find; but Health and Personal Social Services Statistics 1985 (DHSS, 1985e) reported findings for a one-year period in 1982. It was found that of these aged 65 or over, 605,462 received NHS chiropody services and 765,754 received the services of a home help. Such global figures tell only of relative magnitude and nothing of the effectiveness, match with needs, regularity or duration. In general, research evidence indicates a shortfall of provision on all these principal services, inadequacies in design to meet the needs of consumers and failure to coordinate care packages for individuals (Johnson et al, 1981; Midwinter, 1987; Means, 1984; Clarke, 1984; Allen, Hogg and Peace, 1992).

STRUCTURED DEPENDENCY

Reference has already been made to the proposition that dependency amongst elderly people is amplified, if not created, by the manner in which modern societies are structured and organised (see Chapter 2). Such notions are not new, for it has been evident for some time that mandatory retirement which removes older people from the work force also reduces their income and social esteem. Similarly, it is well documented that the shortage of support services and the regimes in residential-care establishments have created a reliance on others. Yet it was only in Townsend's article in *Ageing and Society* (1981) that the concept of structured dependency was articulated. He draws upon his own extensive research, especially of residential care (Townsend, 1957) to argue that the present degree of dependency experienced by old people is unnecessary. He writes:

> I am arguing, then, that society creates the framework of institutions and rules within which the general problems of the elderly emerge and are indeed manufactured. Decisions are being taken every day in the management of the economy and in the maintenance and development of social institutions which govern the position which elderly people occupy in national life, and these also contribute powerfully to the public consciousness of different meanings of ageing and old age. (Townsend, 1981, p. 9)

The argument proceeds through a series of claims about the ways in which retired people are excluded from socially valued activities and status. Governments find it convenient to reduce unemployment figures by enforced retirement, whilst new technology makes their skills redundant or undervalued. Townsend adds:

> Less consideration tends to be given to sickness and disability at older than younger ages and, indeed, retirement is cavalierly associated with failing health and incapacity. Thus, the combined effects of industrial, economic and educational reorganisation are leading to more rigid stratification of the population by age. (Townsend, 1981, p. 11)

This influential paper rapidly gave rise to a body of writings in the political economy of ageing. Prior to its publication the American gerontologist Estes (1979) had produced her book *The Aging Enterprise* which gave a critical edge to previous writings about old age and the state, by entering into a class analysis. Concurrently Walker (1980, 1981) was producing material which developed the same themes by examination of income and wealth in later life. His contention was:

> . . . that poverty in old age is primarily a function of low economic and social status prior to retirement and the depressed social status of the retired, and secondarily, of the relatively low level of state benefits. (Walker, 1981, p. 73; see also Chapter 12)

Gaullier (1982) analysing post-war policies for retired people in France asserts that the government converted the positive aspects of the Third Age movement to create a new social ghetto. A similar process was described by Kohli et al (1983) based on their studies of prematurely retired tobacco workers in Germany. By the mid-1980s volumes of collected papers began to emerge (Guillemard, 1983; Minkler and Estes, 1984) to supplement monographs like Phillipson's (1982) which located the modern formula of retirement as a repressed social category in the development of western capitalism.

For half a decade the Townsend thesis had such a self-evident quality to it that no serious challenge was offered. But in very recent times a number of criticisms have appeared. Johnson complains that the economic position of elderly people has been extensively examined by social policy analysts, but virtually ignored by economists. In beginning to correct the imbalance he contends that:

> theories of 'structured dependency' rest on the explicit or implicit argument that elderly people have experienced a constriction of economic liberty because of . . . the development of welfare and employment policies . . . [but] much of the detailed research that has made use of the concept of structured dependency has focused on the relatively small and exceptional group of elderly people living in institutions, for whom the concept of dependency seems more immediately relevant. (Johnson, 1987, p. i)

Moreover, he suggests that the existence of old age pensions has given both a security of income and a range of choice which sometimes exceeds what is available to younger people in employment.

Dant (1988) takes issue even with the strongest part of the case as it relates to people in residential care. He points out that 'some may even prefer the "hotel" qualities of residential life, of not being bothered with cleaning and cooking' (p. 174). Townsend is further taken to task by claims that 'He seems to regard both elderly people and all other people in society who do not have a functional role in the running of the state as "cultural dopes" devoid of autonomy and self-determination' (p.174). In a more oblique way Wilkin (1987) also offers a critical refinement, by returning our attention to the detailed assessment of disability as a dependency-creating attribute. More sophisticated measures which place physical and mental impairments in the context of relationships and environment will produce the capacity to release elderly people from excessive dependence on others. His call for more focus on 'dependency relationships' draws discussion back to individuals and their settings rather than the macro-economic structure.

The structured dependency debate has a long way to go before it is concluded. What it has provided so far is a strongly presented alternative to the view that elderly people are not only the victims of old age, they are the unconscious perpetrators of its deprivations. Similarly, it has stimulated a more constructive view of the definitions, causes and measurements of dependency. Whatever the outcome, it is inevitable that the political economy view of old age will have established itself as a permanent and proper vantage point for viewing problems in a more politically comprehensive way.

CONCLUSION

The seemingly simple notion of the dependency older people have on other people has proved to be both conceptually complex and methodologically difficult to measure. Earlier attempts to encapsulate the everyday requirements of people who have lost capacities to maintain themselves, by the use of check lists and rating scales now appear inadequate – if still widely used. Exclusive attention to the shortcomings of the person in being able to carry out 'activities of everyday living' is demonstrably incomplete, even if the measures are valid. If dependency is to gain a useful meaning – rather than being another negative label – it must be considered within both the local and national context. Much more attention is now being given to the specific identification of conditions which inhibit independent functioning and their matching with tested and effective social, medical and financial support. Developments of this sort which individualise assessment and responses to it, whilst removing the individualisation of the causes of pathology, appear to be fruitful lines of progress.

12

POVERTY AND INEQUALITY
IN OLD AGE

Alan Walker

The purpose of this chapter is to analyse the distribution of income and wealth both among older people and between older people and younger age groups. It does so, first, by outlining the financial status of pensioners in contemporary Britain; secondly, the sources of income in old age are discussed, with particular reference to the main source of income: the state retirement pension; and, thirdly, the causes of poverty and inequality in old age are examined. (For accounts of the development of the approach to the analysis of poverty and inequality in old age adopted here see Walker, 1980, 1981.)

FINANCIAL STATUS OF OLDER PEOPLE

Poverty and low incomes

The observation that poverty and deprivation are concentrated on a significant proportion of older people has been a recurring theme of research on ageing in all industrial societies. In Britain, pensioners were the largest group in the population living in poverty from the late nineteenth century when such statistics were first collected systematically (Booth, 1892, 1894) until the early 1980s when unemployed people and their families took over this unfortunate position. Research has confirmed, over and over again, the deep-seated nature of poverty in old age (see, for example, Cole and Utting, 1962; Townsend and Wedderburn, 1965; Townsend, 1979). A report from the then Ministry of Pensions and National Insurance (1966) was particularly important in establishing officially the acceptance by government of both widespread poverty among older people and also the large proportion eligible for but not drawing social assistance (then called supplementary benefit and now income support). The Royal Commission on the Distribution of Income and Wealth (1978, p. 234) reported that one in every three older person's families had incomes on or below the poverty line in 1975 and that nearly three in every four lived in or on the margins of poverty.

Today, despite the significant political commitment given to pensions in the 1970s – culminating in the introduction of the New Pension

Scheme in 1975 and the series of pledges to up-rate pensions in line with earnings or prices, whichever was the greater – which resulted in some improvements in the relative position of older people in the income distribution (see below), and the gradual decline in the proportion of pensioners with relatively low incomes during the 1980s, poverty is still the principal financial problem faced by this group. This is one extreme aspect of the inequalities in income and other resources between the majority of those under and those over retirement age.

While just over one in five (21 per cent) of all persons in Great Britain are over pension age they comprise nearly three out of ten of those living on incomes on or below the income support level, the official, or socially agreed, standard of poverty. As Table 12.1 shows, the risk of experiencing poverty is nearly three times greater for adults over retirement age than it is for adults below retirement age. The most recent information on poverty made available by the government is for 1985 (DHSS, 1988). However the House of Commons Social Security Committee has commissioned and published analyses covering later years. The latest data show that, in 1989, just under one-third of pensioners were living on incomes at or below the poverty line compared with less than one-fifth (17 per cent) of those under pension age. In all nearly three out of five older people, 5.5 million people, live in or on the margins of poverty (ie within incomes of up to 140 per cent of the appropriate income support rates) compared with less than one-quarter of those under pension age (House of Commons Social Security Committee, 1993).

Not only does poverty affect a substantial proportion of older people but, when it does, it is likely to be an enduring experience. Thus, older people predominate among both claimants of income support and long-term claimants. The national survey of supplementary benefit claimants, carried out by the Policy Studies Institute in 1982, found a large proportion of long-term claimants among pensioners. Also, pensioners were much more likely than other claimants to have been living on unsupplemented social security pensions *before* claiming supplementary benefit, that is, below the poverty line (Berthoud, 1984, p. A5). Thus, as Table 12.1 shows, there are over one million people living on incomes *below* the income support poverty line. For several reasons, but primarily because of the stigma associated with claiming (Townsend, 1979; Walker, 1986b) over one million pensioners who are eligible for income support or housing benefit do not claim it. So the take-up rate of income support among pensioners is 67 per cent compared with 83 per cent for those under pension age (Central Statistical Office, 1988).

In addition to the problem of poverty, older people are likely to experience low incomes compared with younger adults, particularly those in paid employment. The independent national survey of household resources and standards of living, conducted by Townsend

Table 12.1   *Numbers and percentages of people of different ages living in or on the margins of poverty in Britain, 1975–1989*

Family income in relation to supplementary benefit/income support standard	Thousands						
	1975	1977	1981	1983	1985	1987	1989
Adults over pension age							
Below	740	2760	1120	1080	960	1220	1280
Receiving SB/IS	1930	1970	1960	1880	1880	˙1860	1740
On margins	2870	2860	2810	2750	2730	2390	2470
All on low income	5540	5590	5890	5710	5570	5520	5490
Per cent of all pensionsers	66.3	65.4	66.8	63.7	61.3	58.0	57.1
Adults under pension age							
Below	690	760	1130	1310	1080	1820	2250
Receiving SB/IS	970	1170	1720	2620	3190	3810	2890
On margins	2170	2240	2600	2860	2050	1770	1640
All on low income	3830	4170	5540	6790	6320	7400	6780
Per cent of adults	12.6	13.7	17.3	21.1	19.6	21.9	19.8
All under pension age							
Below	1100	1140	1690	1700	1460	2510	3070
Receiving SB/IS	1780	2150	2880	4250	5080	5890	4890
On margins	4120	4110	4540	4720	3320	3070	2720
All on low income	7000	7400	9110	10670	9860	11470	10680
Per cent of all adults and children	15.8	16.7	20.4	23.8	21.9	24.8	22.9

Sources: DHSS (1983a), Tables 1–6: DHSS (1988), Tables 1–6; House of Commons Social Security Committee (1993)

(1979) found a striking difference in the proportion of older people and younger adults living in poverty and on low incomes:

> Twenty per cent, compared with seven per cent, were living in poverty; another 44 per cent, compared with 19 per cent, were living on the margins of poverty. At the other end of the income scale, more than twice as many of the non-elderly than of the elderly were living comfortably above the (supplementary benefit) standard . . . Although the elderly comprised one third of those in poverty, and nearly one third on the margins of poverty. (Townsend, 1979, p. 788)

Expenditure provides an alternative to income as a measure of living standards. A study carried out by the DHSS, using the data from the 1975 Family Expenditure Survey, showed that the expenditure of pensioner households was about one-quarter of the median for households not receiving supplementary benefit (SB), as income support was then called. In fact, the total expenditure of pensioner households living on supplementary benefit was less than half that of pensioner households not receiving SB but designated as poor (ie in the bottom quintile of the income distribution) (Baldwin and Cooke, 1984, p. 44). Some two-thirds of the budgets of pensioner households receiving supplementary benefit are consumed by food, fuel and clothing.

This suggests that at 1992/93 benefit levels a single pensioner would spend about £38.09 out of the income support allowance and pensioner (60–79) premium of £57.15 on these items, leaving £19.06 per week to be spent on so-called 'non-essentials'. By comparison median income level households spend less than half of their budget, which is nearly four times as large, on 'essential' items (Baldwin and Cooke, 1984, p. 45). Moreover, some older people have lower expectations and aspirations than younger adults and, therefore, are more likely to choose to go without or consume less than they need of basic necessities. The Breadline Britain survey found that 73 per cent of pensioners on low incomes 'chose' to go without at least one necessity compared with 57 per cent of non-pensioners, while 24 per cent of the former 'chose' to go without three or more necessities compared with 9 per cent of the latter (Mack and Lansley, 1985, p. 97).

A special analysis of data from the 1982 Family Expenditure Survey, by the DHSS Economic Advisers' Office, found that despite improvement in the general financial position of pensioners over the last 30 years, many pensioners still had relatively low incomes. On the one hand, few older people were among the very well off: only one in ten had an income above the average for working families. On the other hand, few of those in paid employment had incomes as low as most pensioners; only a fifth of working families had incomes below the average pensioner income (DHSS, 1984).

The high incidence of poverty and low incomes among older people is reflected in other measures of deprivation. For example, they (especially those living alone) are less likely than non-pensioners to own certain consumer durables, such as television sets and refrigerators; they are less likely to eat fresh meat most days a week; they are less likely to have a summer holiday and to take part in social activities requiring money (Townsend, 1979). Pensioners are disproportionately more likely to experience poor housing conditions: although they comprise only 10 per cent out of all households, those with a head aged 75 or more occupied nearly one in three dwellings lacking amenities and 16 per cent of those classified in the 1986 English House Condition Survey as being unfit (Kirk and Leather, 1991). Some 19 per cent of lone older people were in houses in poor conditon compared with 14 per cent of households consisting of more than one older person. In 1986 some 800,000 households headed by someone aged 60 or more were living in housing costing £1,000 or more per annum in repairs.

Poor housing conditions tend to be concentrated in the private rented sector (42 per cent in poor condition in 1986 compared with 13 per cent of owner-occupied dwellings and 11 per cent of those owned by local authorities). However, some 43 per cent of owner-occupied households headed by a retired person had repair costs of £1,000 or more with 10 per cent having costs greater than £5,000. These owner-occupiers are likely to be living on low incomes: two-thirds of older households in the owner-occupied sector with repair costs of £1,000 or more in 1986 had an annual income below £3,000 (see also Chapter 9).

Official underestimation of poverty in old age

A considerable body of data could be adduced to show further that there is a significant difference between the incomes and other resources and expenditure of pensioners and non-pensioners and that a very large group of older people live in poverty or on its margins (Walker, 1980). Moreover, the problem of poverty in old age is not peculiar to Britain, it is endemic among both western and eastern advanced industrial societies as well as Third World countries (Hendricks and Hendricks, 1977; Maeda, 1978; Neysmith and Edwardh, 1984). Yet in recent years the argument has been gaining ground in official circles, and some academic ones, that poverty in old age is no longer a serious problem. The ministerial foreword to the Green Paper on elderly people issued by the last Labour government implied that the problem had been solved (DHSS, 1978). It was not mentioned at all in the White Paper issued by the Conservative government (DHSS, 1981). This official forbearance turned to antagonism in the mid-1980s when the government and some independent commentators began to question openly the extent of the financial needs among older people and, either directly or by impli-cation, the level of social security expenditure on them. The four reviews of social security initiated in 1983 by the Secretary of State for Social Services – particularly the Inquiry into the Provision for Retirement – were the forums in which the arguments against further increases in pensions were most trenchantly expressed (DHSS, 1985a). There is not space here to examine the reasons for this sea-change in official attitudes (see Walker, 1986c) which has resulted in reductions in state pensions. However, these cuts have been legitimated by the argument that pensioners are relatively well off – which has led to the proposition that Britain may actually be overproviding for old age – and, therefore, it is important to assess the factors underlying this apparent paradox.

Official reports and some independent social scientists in the mid-1980s started to point to relative improvements in the position of older people in the income distribution. The most influential of these commentaries was prepared by the DHSS Economic Advisers' Office as a background paper to the Inquiry into Provision for Retirement (DHSS, 1984). This showed that between 1951 and 1984/5 pensioners' share of total disposable income (total income from earnings, savings, invest-ment, pensions and other social security benefits) increased from 7 per cent to 15 per cent (DHSS, 1984). The reasons given for this improvement include both the growth in numbers of pensioners and their rising incomes. While the former is relatively straightforward the improvement in the disposable income of pensioners relative to non-pensioners rests on two factors. On the one hand, there has been a slowing down in the growth of real disposable income among those below pension age, caused mainly by the reduction of the numbers in full-time employment and, on the other, the value of the basic pensions has risen in relation to average earnings (see below).

This official analysis of rising incomes among pensioners was supported by other independent assessments. For example, one examination of changes in the distribution of income over the life cycle showed that whereas 45 per cent of married pensioners were in the bottom quintile of net income in 1971, this had fallen to 28 per cent in 1982. For single pensioners the proportions were 43 per cent in 1971 and 22 per cent in 1982 (Bradshaw and O'Higgins, 1984). However, while analyses such as this correctly highlight recent improvements in the relative incomes of pensioners, they have mistakenly been translated into the myth that all older people are now affluent, a myth that has legitimated policy proposals which redistribute income from older people to other groups in poverty. Three factors should be considered.

First, the relative 'improvement' in the value of the basic NI pension was modest and only short-lived: from 17.5 per cent of gross average weekly earnings of male employees for a single pensioner in 1973 to 19.8 per cent in 1983 (back in 1948 it had been 19 per cent of gross male earnings and had peaked at 21 per cent in 1977). However, by 1992 the value of the NI pension had fallen to 15.9 per cent of gross male earnings. For a married couple the proportions are 31 per cent in 1948, 28 per cent in 1973, 31.6 per cent in 1983 and 25.4 per cent in 1992 (DHSS, 1986; Twigger, 1992). The rapid decline in the relative value of the NI pension from the mid-1980s was due to the decoupling of increases in pensions from average earnings, in 1980, and the rapid rise in earnings in the late 1980s. (The value of occupational pensions, which rose rapidly along with earnings in the late 1980s, should also be taken into account but nearly half of pensioners do not receive such income – see below.)

Second, the validity of any assessment of relative poverty depends on the group with which comparisons are made. The previous discussion of poverty and low incomes in old age rested on a comparison between pensioners and non-pensioners, particularly those in employment. This was the relative framework implicitly accepted by Parliament, in 1977, when it linked pensions' up-ratings to earnings (or prices, whichever rose faster) and so gave pensioners a share in rising national prosperity. This link was broken in 1980 and subsequent comparisons have not been between older people and those in employment, but between older people and other groups in poverty. So a major plank in the official case against increasing pensions relative to earnings, as well as against the State Earnings Related Pension, has been the recent relative improvement in the incomes of pensioners in comparison with other groups living in poverty (DHSS, 1985a). Incidentally, this argument also entails the denial of the relative nature of poverty, so that policy makers have chosen to concentrate their attention on the relative position of various poor groups rather than looking at the relationship between poverty and affluence.

While state pensions have not increased significantly in value compared with average earnings, they have increased against other social security benefits, particularly unemployment benefit. In 1972/3 unemployment benefit and retirement pension were paid at the same rates (and had been for most of the period since 1948); by 1984/5 the latter was worth 26 per cent more than the former, as it is in 1992/3. However, this increase had as much to do with cuts in the value of the unemployment benefits during the 1980s as rises in the value of pensions and, therefore, it is partly artificial. Moreover, the decoupling of pensions from earnings had an immediate impact on the relative value of the retirement pension, which fell from a high of 132 per cent of the level of the unemployment benefit in 1981 to 126 per cent in 1984 (DHSS, 1985b). Thus, the 'advantageous' position of pensioners among the poor has been manufactured, to some extent, by government policies largely outside of the pensions field: the creation of mass unemployment, the abolition of earnings-related supplement, cuts in unemployment benefit, failure to maintain the value of child benefit and encouragement of low wages (Walker and Walker, 1987). The outcome of these policies is that there has been an increase in people, particularly single people below pension age and families with children, falling into the bottom fifth of the income distribution and, because unemployment benefit is set at a lower rate than the pension, the average income of the lowest income group has declined as their numbers have swollen. This change is reflected in the composition of the lowest quintile group of the income distribution: in 1971 pensioners comprised 52 per cent of the lowest fifth, single people of working age 19 per cent, and working-age couples with children 17 per cent. By 1985 the picture had changed considerably: pensioners made up 27 per cent of the bottom quintile, single adults under pension age 34 per cent and couples with children 22 per cent (Central Statistical Office, 1988). As the Central Statistical Office notes, this shift 'does not necessarily indicate an improvement in the living standards for pensioners', but the increase in unemployment (Central Statistical Office, 1988, p. 96).

Figures compiled by the House of Commons Social Security Committee lend support for this explanation and suggest that some of the gains made by older people in comparision with families may be a temporary function of recession. The impact of the changes to the Social Security system in 1988, coupled with a fall in unemployment, was that the proportion of the poorest tenth of the income distribution made up by couples with children fell (from 50 per cent in 1987 to 40 per cent in 1988) while the proportion consisting of pensioners rose (from 17 per cent to 23 per cent). Taking income *after* deducting housing costs there was a rise of more than one million in the numbers of pensioners living on incomes below half of the average between 1987 and 1988 (2.4 million or 26 per cent to 3.5 million or 38 per cent).

The answer, of course, would be to reverse recent policies and improve the incomes of the unemployed and families with children. However, the reviews of social security in the 1980s did not propose any improvement in the social security status of the unemployed. The Green Paper (DHSS, 1985a) and the ensuing White Paper (DHSS, 1985d) and Social Security Act, 1986, did propose increases in benefits for families with children (some of whom have unemployed heads), but because of the nil-cost constraint imposed on this reform of social security, older people were viewed as the source of finance for these improvements. Thus, when the changes in the Social Security Act, 1986, were introduced in April 1988, it was officially estimated that some 2.1 million pensioners would be worse off as a result (DHSS, 1985c).

Third, as was shown earlier, the majority of older people still live in or on the margins of poverty – in terms of both the official poverty line and average living standards – in spite of recent improvements in the value of pensions. In so far as older people have shifted, or, more correctly, have been shunted, out of the bottom fifth of the income distribution they have been moved predominantly into the adjacent quintile. Thus, although there was a decline in the proportion of the bottom quintile made up of older people, between the mid-1970s and mid-1980s, this was not matched by an increase in the proportion of the top quintile who were older people (only 4.8 per cent in 1974 and 1985) (Falkingham and Victor, 1991, p. 11).

Inequalities between older people

Like all good myths, the myth of affluence in old age has some basis in reality. While there has only been a slight relative improvement in the incomes of the majority of pensioners, for some the increase has been substantial – giving rise to the so-called WOOPIE, or well-off older person. The 'two-nations' in old age, forewarned by Titmuss (1963) thirty years ago are now firmly entrenched at the extremes of the income distribution, with a third group making up the bulk of low-income pensioners. Differences based on class, age, gender, race and marital status are reflected in income inequalities and, at the extremes are younger (60–74) middle-class males and married couples, and older (75+) women and working-class families.

The dynamics of the rapid changes under way in the relative position of these two groups of pensioners may be illustrated by official data. Between 1978 and 1988 the average total net income of pensioners rose by over 33 per cent but the increase for those in the bottom fifth of the income distribution was 14 per cent compared with 52 per cent for those in the top fifth. Underlying this increasing inequality is the differential rate of increases in the various components of pensioners' incomes.

Between 1979 and 1988 social security rose by only 14 per cent in real terms, compared with 99 per cent for occupational pensions and 110 per cent for savings income. A significant part of the explanation for this varying rate of increase is the policy descision to de-index the basic pension from earnings, while many occupational pensions schemes remain tied to earnings.

Inequalities in old age are primarily a function of access to resources over the earlier stages of the life cycle. Occupational status in earlier life determines salary or wage levels and, therefore, the opportunities to save and invest in property and other possessions. Access to occupational pensions also rests on employment status. In addition to inequalities based on occupational class, certain groups, such as women, ethnic minorities, people with disabilities and older workers, experience discrimination in the labour market and are, therefore, less likely to gain access to secure well-paid employment. These groups are likely to be particualrly reliant on public policy to determine their income levels. Finally, retirement itself superimposes reduced social status and lowered incomes on pensioners and resources tend to diminish the longer an individual survives in retirement. Hence the tendency for very elderly people to have the lowest incomes.

Townsend (1979) found that a markedly larger proportion of manual than non-manual pensioners were living in poverty or on its margins. Higher proportions lacked basic consumer durables and were less likely than non-manual groups to own their homes outright. In addition, there were significant inequalities in income between older women and men and a close relationship between diminishing resources and advancing age. For example, the proportion of women aged 65–69 with incomes on or below the poverty line was 63 per cent compared with 48 per cent of men in the same age group. The percentage of women aged 80 and over living in poverty was nearly double that of women aged 60–64: 86 per cent and 46 per cent respectively (Townsend, 1979).

The incidence of poverty among older women, particularly lone women, is significantly higher than among men (Walker, 1987, 1992; see also Arber and Ginn, 1991; Groves, 1993). If the data in Table 12.1 are reanalysed according to the gender of the older person we find that more than one in three older women (35 per cent) were living on incomes on or below the poverty line, as defined by SB levels, compared with 23 per cent of older men. Just under half of lone older women compared with just under two-fifths of single older men had incomes on or below the poverty line (Walker, 1992). Since a much higher proportion of women than men survive into advanced old age they increasingly dominate the poverty profile of successively older age groups. The explanation for this is not simply that there are more women in older age groups, older lone women, especially widows, are more likely than lone men and married couples to have to rely on social assistance (DHSS, 1984).

Further evidence of the disadvantaged positio
relation to men can be gained from information
income. Older women in the bottom fifth of th
have slightly lower incomes than men in the sar
men in the top fifth have much higher incomes t
1988 the spread of disposable income for lone wo
per week to £81 per week compared with £82 to
men. Average disposable income varied from £15'
couples, to £86 for lone men and £76 for lone w........

The important combined influence of class, gender and age in determining the structure of inequality was confirmed by a survey of older people living in private households in Aberdeen. None of the sample of younger (60–74) middle-class men had a household income of less than £30 per week and more than half had incomes over £60; whereas more than three-fifths of older (75+) working-class women had incomes of less than £30 per week and none had more than £60 (Taylor and Ford, 1983). The authors of this study concluded that: 'most personal resources do diminish with age, men tend to have more than women and those from middle-class backgrounds tend to have more than those from working-class backgrounds' (Taylor and Ford, 1983, p. 200).

In comparison with information on social class, gender and disability there is very little concerning the impact of 'race' on income inequalities in old age in the UK. However, what infomation there is suggests that black older people are more likely than their white counterparts to experience material deprivation and that this is particularly the case for black women (Norman, 1985; Blakemore, 1989).

Wealth and other assets

Poverty and inequality are not solely dependent on the incomes available to individuals and families. The position of different groups of older people in the class structure depends on their command over other resources such as savings, interest on capital, housing, employment benefits and social services. There is, usually, a close association between income and assets, particularly readily realisable ones and inequalities in wealth between older people of different classes has the effect of widening inequalities based on incomes.

A recent review of asset ownership among pensioners has shown that asset holdings are linked to income. Those with above average incomes prior to retirement have a higher than average chance of owning outright their own home, having built up significant savings and having accrued rights to occupational and other pensions. Furthermore, the greater the pre-retirement income, the larger is likely to be the value of these assets.

lies with above-average incomes after retirement (derived from an pational pension) have a high probability of owning their own home and o of having a significant block of savings. Again, in general, the greater the income, the larger the assets. Moreover, those with satisfactory incomes tend to retain or increase their savings, while low income pensioners tend to run down the limited stock of savings with which they may have entered retirement. (McKay, 1992, pp. 64–5)

Inequalities in savings were found in the 1980 Aberdeen survey. Only 4 per cent of younger middle-class men, the groups with the highest income, had savings of less than £2,500 whereas 42 per cent of the poorest group, older working-class women, had savings under £2,500 (Taylor and Ford, 1983). Not surprisingly, those with the lowest savings anticipated most difficulty in obtaining emergency cash and those with the most savings anticipated least difficulty.

These disparities in the ownership of assets are exaggerated when the lifelong social status of older people is taken into account. Thus, in Townsend's (1979) survey a quarter of older people from non-manual occupations whose fathers had also held non-manual occupations, had net assets of £10,000 or more, with one-half holding £5,000 or more, compared with zero per cent and 2 per cent of those who, like their fathers had held semi-skilled or unskilled jobs. If the annuity value of assets (ie potential income) was added to net disposable incomes two-thirds of the non-manual compared with only 6 per cent of the semi-skilled/unskilled group had resources of three or more times the SB poverty line.

The most significant physical asset is owner-occupied housing. Although poor older people are more likely than poor younger adults to own their own homes, the average home ownership for pensioners is well below that for younger age groups: 50 per cent compared with 73 per cent among those aged 30–44 and 65 per cent among those aged 45–59 (Central Statistical Office, 1988). There has been a substantial increase in home ownership among younger age groups over the last ten years whereas the proportion of older owner-occupiers has remained virtually static. The main factor here is that most of the local authority tenants who bought their houses under the 'right to buy' scheme have been under 60. Pensioners are much more likely than younger adults to own older houses which lack one or more basic amenities (see Chapter 9).

The most important income-generating asset held by many older people is an occupational pension. But, while just over half of all pensioners receive income from occupational pensions, the average amount for those in the bottom fifth of the income distribution, in 1988, was £7.10 per week compared with £96.80 per week for those in the top fifth. Also it may be that the incomes of older owner-occupiers will be increasingly augmented by schemes intended to annuitise some of the capital value of their home. This further emphasises existing inequalities in income and wealth between different groups of older people, but what little evidence there is on this issue suggests that such schemes are unlikely to have a substantial impact on the transfer of housing equity (Mullings and Hamnett, 1992).

Poverty and inequality in international context

Is Britain unique in having a high incidence of poverty in old age? Are the incomes of pensioners and non-pensioners more or less equal in Britain compared with other countries? Answers to questions such as this have been notoriously difficult to find, largely because of the lack of reliability in comparing published statistics from different countries. However, this situation is gradually being improved: a special study of the economic position of families in various age groups in seven western industrial countries was conducted in 1980 and, since this was based on common methodology, it provides some reliable answers (Hedström and Ringen, 1987). Also the EC Observatory of Ageing and Older People is beginning to yield reliable comparative information. The seven countries surveyed in the 1980 survey are shown in Table 12.2 along with some of the main results.

As the Table shows, income differences (adjusted for family size) between elderly people and average income levels are greatest in the UK and least pronounced in Canada, Israel and the USA. Thus, the income of the UK's 65–74 and 75 and over age groups, at 76 per cent and 67 per

Table 12.2   *National differences in disposable income, inequality and poverty*

	Income, inequality and poverty according to age								
	Disposable income in relation to national mean[a]			Inequality[b]			Poverty rates[c]		
Country	65–74	75+	All Ages	65–74	75+	All Ages	65–74	75+	All Ages
Canada	0.94	0.81	1.00	0.309	0.291	0.299	11.2	12.1	12.1
W. Germany	0.84	0.77	1.00	0.298	0.340	0.355	12.2	15.2	7.2
Israel	0.92	0.96	1.00	0.360	0.429	0.333	22.6	27.1	14.5
Norway	1.01	0.79	1.00	0.250	0.229	0.243	2.7	7.3	4.8
Sweden	0.96	0.78	1.00	0.143	0.126	0.205	0.0	0.0	5.0
UK	0.76	0.67	1.00	0.266	0.240	0.273	16.2	22.0	8.8
USA	0.99	0.84	1.00	0.342	0.355	0.326	17.8	25.5	16.9
Mean	0.92	0.80	–	0.281	0.287	0.291	11.9	15.6	9.9
SD	0.08	0.08	–	0.067	0.092	0.050	7.5	9.2	4.4

Notes:
[a] Disposable income (adjusted for family size) as a proportion of the national mean for the total population.
[b] Gini coefficients for distribution of adjusted disposable income within age groups and for total population.
[c] Poverty rate defined as percentage of persons in families with adjusted disposable income below half of the median for all families in the population.
Source: Hedström and Ringen (1987), Tables 4, 5 and 6.

cent respectively of the national mean, compares with an average for the
other six nations of 94 per cent and 82 per cent. Moreover, since this
study was carried out in 1980 the position of older people in Britain is
likely to have worsened in relation to average incomes, primarily as a
result of the de-indexation of pensions from earnings. Income is more
equally distributed among older people in the UK than in the USA,
Israel and West Germany, but less so than in Sweden and Norway. The
extent of relative poverty is greater in the 65–74 and 75 and over age
groups in UK compared with Sweden, Norway, West Germany and
Canada, but less than in Israel and the USA. However, there are
different explanations for the roughly similar poverty rates in the UK
and USA: in the former case the high poverty rate among older people
derives from the low level of income of older people as a whole, whereas
in the case of the latter a similar poverty rate is due mainly to the
unequal distribution of income among this group.

Overall, the Nordic, collectivist welfare states appear to achieve lower
levels of inequality and poverty – both between different groups of older
people and between pensioners and the rest of society – than the
residual welfare state and dominant private sector in the USA, with the
liberal mixed economies such as West Germany and Canada in between.
Unfortunately, Britain appears to be in the worst position: it has a
longstanding infrastructure of welfare state provision for older people
but it has not managed to protect them from poverty as well as other
welfare states. As the authors of this comparative study conclude 'with
the exception of Britain, the standard of living of elderly families is not
far behind the national average' (Hedström and Ringen, 1987, p. 238).

Support for this conclusion is provided by the latest report from the
EC Observatory on Ageing and Older People. When comparisons are
made between EC countries in terms of the replacement ratios of
pensions (pensions as a proportion of previous earnings) the UK has the
joint poorest record with Ireland. When poverty rates are compared, the
UK hovers just above the southern European states at the bottom of the
EC league, whereas coutries such as Denmark, Luxembourg and
Germany have single figure poverty rates among their older citizens
(Walker, Guillemard and Alber, 1993). It is to an explanation of the
relatively low incomes of British pensioners that the second half of this
chapter is devoted.

SOURCES OF INCOME IN OLD AGE

A description of the main sources of the income of Britain's older people
is the first step in explaining the continuance of poverty in old age and
the existence of marked inequalities in income and wealth between older
people.

There have been important changes in the sources of older people's

Table 12.3 *Comparison of the sources of pensioners' income and total UK household income (percentages)*

Income	Pensioners' income 1988	Total household income 1988
Wages and salaries[a]	8	70
Investment and rent	18	8
Private pensions, annuities	23	8
Social security and other transfers[b]	51	15
Total	100	100

Notes:
[a] includes self-employment.
[b] other = mainly supplementary benefit and housing benefit.
Sources: Central Statistical Office (1992) pp. 90, 93

income over the last thirty years. In 1951 the proportion of total gross income derived from earnings was more than three times the current level (27 per cent), while the proportion received from occupational pensions was 15 per cent. The contribution of social security was two-thirds of the current level (42 per cent of total income) largely due to the significant role of earnings (DHSS, 1984). These gross income figures hide major inequalities between different groups of pensioners.

Employment

The main distinguishing feature of the incomes of older people, compared with younger adults, is the low proportion deriving from wages and salaries. Low labour-force participation is the primary source of inequality between pensioners and non-pensioners and, in turn, it proves an important source of inequality between older people. Those who continue working after retirement age are less likely than the retired to experience poverty. Thus, there is a close relationship between employment and income level in old age. This can be illustrated among both single-person and two-person elderly households. Taking single-person households first, among men aged 65–73, 30 per cent of those in work had net weekly incomes under £30 compared with 82 per cent of the retired; for women aged 60–73 the figures were 53 per cent and 85 per cent. In two-person households, among men aged 65–73, 3 per cent of those in work had net weekly incomes of less than £30 compared with 26 per cent of the retired; the figures for women aged 60–73 were 5 per cent and 28 per cent respectively (Parker, 1980).

     Labour-force participation among older people is dependent on a large number of factors, including socio-economic status, health, pension rules, attitudes of employers and custom, the most important of which are discussed later. Although the proportion over retirement age in full- or part-time employment is small – 7 per cent of men aged 65 and over and 6 per cent of women aged 60 and over – there are marked differences based on age and marital status. Young senior citizens, married men and single women are more likely to be employed than older senior citizens, single men and married women.

Retirement pension

The national insurance (NI) retirement pension still provides the largest proportion of total pensioners' income, but its significance for different groups varies according to the extent of their access to other income. The NI pension is the main source of income in single-person pensioner households with gross weekly incomes of less than £80 (in 1982). In fact, the lower the incomes of this group, the greater the proportion provided by the retirement pension: one-half for those with incomes between £50 and £80 and seven-tenths for those on incomes under £50. The proportions of incomes contributed by occupational pensions were 18 per cent and 5 per cent respectively (Central Statistical Office, 1985). Among single-pensioner households with weekly incomes of £80 or more only a quarter was derived from the retirement pension and well over two-fifths from occupational pensions. For two-person households the proportion of income derived from the NI pension nearly halves between those with incomes under £80 and those with £80 or more per week (71 per cent compared with 37 per cent), while the proportion received from occupational pensions increases by nearly five times (7.5 per cent compared with 35 per cent).

For the majority of pensioners in Britain the amount of the state retirement pension has an important influence on their living standards and the level of their incomes compared with younger adults. For low-income older people the retirement pension, together with supplementation by income support, effectively determines whether or not, they will live in poverty, a point returned to later.

Occupational pensions

Access to private welfare in the form of occupational pensions is of fundamental importance in determining the inequalities in income between different groups of older people outlined earlier and marks the main boundary between the two main economic nations among Britain's pensioners. There are two sources of inequality based on occupational pensions. On the one hand, there is unequal access to occupational and other private pensions, based primarily on socio-economic group and employment status and, on the other, there is inequality between generations of older people arising from changes in pension conditions and levels.

The coverage of occupational pensions increased from 2.6 million employees in the 1930s to a peak of 12.2 million in 1967, since then it has declined slightly and stabilised at around 11 million (Government

Actuary, 1991). However, in 1983 some 10 million employees were excluded from such pensions schemes because there was no scheme provided by their employer (six million), the scheme did not cover part-time or manual employees (three million) or because they were too young or their service with the employer was too short (one million). Women working part-time are particularly prone to exclusion from occupational pension schemes (Government Actuary, 1986). The majority of those excluded from their employer's scheme are manual employees. Thus, in 1983, 71 per cent of full-time non-manual employees were members of an occupational pension scheme, compared with 54 per cent of manual employees (OPCS, 1984a). The contrast was greatest between professional employees (83 per cent membership) and unskilled employees (48 per cent). Moreover, if they do have access to a pension scheme it is likely to be on less favourable terms than non-manual employees and the final pension paid is much lower. Thus, occupational pensions are an important mechanism for preserving in retirement income and status differentials forged in employment (as noted above the average occupational pension for someone in the lowest fifth of the income distribution was £7.10 in 1988 compared with £96.80 for someone in the top fifth). Of course, occupational pensions are of little or no benefit to those, such as the long-term unemployed, people with disabilities and single parents, who have been excluded from the labour market.

Turning to the second form of inequality arising from occupational pensions; as successive cohorts of older people have become eligible for pensions on more favourable terms, previous generations of beneficiaries have become relatively worse off by comparison. Thus, in 1988, some 51 per cent of all pensioners were in receipt of an occupational pension and the median sum was £27.20 per week. This compares with only 33 per cent of single women aged 75 and over being in receipt of an occupational pension and an average of £18.40 (House of Commons, 1991).

Income packages in different countries
Is the mix of different sources of income received by pensioners, shown in Table 12.3, typical of other western industrial societies? Compared with the other countries listed in Table 12.2 the proportion of 65–74-year-old pensioners' income derived from earnings in Britain was lower than every country except Sweden, which has encouraged widespread early retirement (Laczko and Walker, 1985). The proportion of income from social security and other transfers was much lower, in 1980, than in Sweden and West Germany and greater than in the USA and Israel. The proportion of total income provided by occupational pensions in Britain was much larger than in Sweden and Norway, but roughly similar to the position in the other countries, except Israel. The percentage of pensioner income derived from capital income was

highest in Canada, USA and Israel and lowest in West Germany and Norway, followed by Sweden and UK. Again, there is a clear division in the constituents of pensioner income packages between the Nordic welfare states, with their heavy reliance on transfer income, and the more mixed economies of North America and Israel, which have a greater dependence on other sources of income, particularly capital and earnings. In between, West Germany's pensioner income package is closer to the former, while Britain's is closer to the latter (Hedström and Ringen, 1987). These differences are particularly profound in the case of those aged 75 and over who are more likely than younger pensioners to be economically dependent. The fact that the Nordic welfare states have the lowest poverty rates among older people and inequalities between them and other groups has already been reported.

THE SOCIAL CREATION OF POVERTY IN OLD AGE

The observation that older people are one of the largest groups among the poor has sometimes resulted in the mistaken conclusion that old age is a cause of poverty. In fact, poverty in old age may be seen as one form – usually the most extreme one – of multi-faceted dependent status that many older people occupy (Walker, 1980, 1981, 1983). The inadequacies of explanations of this economic dependency couched in individual terms such as 'disengagement', 'frailty' or 'failing abilities' has been exposed previously (see Walker, 1981, and Chapters 2 and 11 in this volume). Rather than being old age itself, it is various social policies which have combined to create, enhance or maintain economic dependency and poverty in old age. Thus, poverty in old age is primarily a function of low economic and social status *prior* to retirement and the depressed social status of the retired and secondly, of the relatively low level of state benefits. The main elements of this structurally created dependency may be outlined (see also Chapters 2 and 11). Policies in the fields of employment and social security have been particularly influential in the production of poverty in old age.

Retirement policies

The growth of retirement and, subsequently, early retirement, has ensured that an increasing proportion of older workers have been excluded from the labour force over the course of this century. This social process of exclusion has denied older people access to earnings and other economic, social and psychological benefits of the workplace. This major social change has progressed rapidly and continues to do so. Between 1931 and 1971 the proportion of men aged 65 and over who were retired increased from under one-half to more than three-quarters and by 1992 the figure was around 92 per cent. Thus, in a relatively short space of time, 'old age' has come to be socially defined as beginning at retirement age and, whether by institutional rule or customary practice, the age at which older workers have to leave the labour force (Parker, 1980) (see also Chapter 8).

The operation of this social process of exclusion has been closely related to the organisation of production and the demand for labour. Accounts of the emergence of retirement and early retirement suggest that older people have, in fact, been used as a reserve army of labour, to be tapped when labour is in short supply, and to be shed when demand falls (Phillipson, 1982; Graebner, 1980; Walker, 1985). It is not that retirement has grown alongside industrialisation – large numbers of older people were economically active in all industrial societies during the first half of this century – but that changes in industrial processes and in the organisation of employment, particularly the employment of women, have been developed and managed in ways intended to exclude older workers. Work processes have been reorganised, the division of labour has increased and the labour process has been rationalised (Braverman, 1974). Various factors have combined to mean that older workers were the most likely to be affected by these changes. For example, the influential scientific management school of thought in the USA argued that efficiency in the labour process depended on the removal of those with low levels of marginal productivity, which was crudely related to age; the historical tendency of capital to reduce its necessary labour to the minimum; the process of technological innovation and the high birth rate of the early 1960s all provided some impetus for the displacement of older workers and, where necessary, their replacement with younger ones (Walker, 1983). Finally, the advent of the large-scale unemployment in the 1930s was crucial in the institutionalisation of retirement, and its return in the early 1980s has resulted in the growth of early retirement.

These main factors in the twentieth-century development of British society have combined to reduce the demand for older workers. At the same time, on the supply side, as retirement and early retirement have been encouraged by employers and the state they have been accepted as customary and have become part of trade union bargaining for improved labour conditions. Moreover, many of the changes in production processes, such as the spread of assembly-line production, have reduced the attachment of workers to employment and, together with the failure of employers and the state to improve the working conditions of many, have contributed to a desire to leave work.

This indicates that, like the experience of employment, attitudes towards retirement and the experience of retirement itself are socially divided. There are those, mainly salaried workers, who are able to choose whether to leave work at the retirement age or to leave prematurely or perhaps to work on. The proportion of self-employed people working beyond retirement age is double that of those employed by others (Walker, 1983). Then there are those, predominantly manual

workers, who are effectively coerced into retirement, and sometimes
early retirement, by poor working conditions, ill-health, redundancy,
unemployment and age discrimination (Palmore, 1978; Olsen and
Hansen, 1981; Walker, 1985; Taylor and Walker, 1992). Thus, for large
numbers of older workers, poverty is created prior to retirement. In fact,
sickness and unemployment account for nearly two-thirds of men and
one-quarter of women who retire prematurely (Parker, 1980). A study of
'voluntary' early retirers found that two important factors were health
and dissatisfaction with their job (McGoldrick and Cooper, 1980). So, for
a significant proportion of older workers the retirement age is effectively
lowered by unemployment, sickness or injury. As with unemployment
itself, semi-skilled and unskilled workers are over-represented among
the early retired (Parker, 1980). The policy of disengaging older workers
prematurely from the labour force was formalised for a decade in Britain
from 1977 by the introduction of the Job Release Scheme (abolished in
1989), which was 'designed to create vacancies for unemployed people
by encouraging older workers to leave their jobs' (Department of
Employment, 1980). Similar policies have been introduced in other
countries, including France and Sweden (Laczko and Walker, 1985;
Kohli et al, 1991).

Pension policies

The corollary to this social process of exclusion from the labour force is
that older people are heavily dependent on the state for financial
support – around 90 per cent of them receive some form of social
security benefit and three-fifths of them derive at least three-quarters of
their income from state transfers. Older people are, in effect, trapped in
poverty by their reliance on state benefits, which have already been
shown to be inadequate.

   The implicit rationale, or social policy, underlying the income
differential between those in employment and those dependent on state
benefits is the assumption that social benefits are intended to maintain
monetary incentives and the work, or rather employment ethic. Thus,
paradoxically, even those older people who have worked for a full term
are not entitled to non-dependent status, nor freedom from reliance on
minimum subsistence income support unless it has been earned
through contributions paid to a private or occupational pension while in
employment. We have seen that retirement has a differential impact on
older people – depending primarily on prior socio-economic status and
the access it grants to resources which might be carried into retirement –
but, in addition, because of the social limitation on the level of state
pensions and other benefits for those outside the labour force,
retirement imposes a lowered social status on the vast majority of
pensioners in relation to younger adults in the labour market (Walker,

1980). Hence the substantial inequalities both among older people and between them and the rest of society, which we outlined earlier.

Present pension policies have their foundations in the Beveridge Report. Beveridge built on the insurance principles established by the National Insurance Act, 1911, and the Widows, Orphans and Old Age Contributory Pensions Act, 1925, rather than the non-contributory, means-tested model provided by the 1908 Old Age Pensions Act or another more radical alternative. This meant that pensions were not regarded as a right but were contingent on the establishment of eligibility through the labour market, or 'work-testing' (Shragge, 1984). Moreover, pensions and other social security benefits were to provide only the minimum subsistence floor specifically in order to encourage additional private welfare provision (Beveridge, 1942). These fundamental principles, which have guided the construction and subsequent operation of the post-war welfare state, are enshrined in the following passage:

> Social security must be achieved by co-operation between the State and the individual. The State should offer security for service and contribution. The State in organising security should not stifle incentive, opportunity, responsibility; in establishing a national minimum it should leave room and encouragement for voluntary action by each individual to provide more than the minimum for himself and his family. (Beveridge, 1942, pp. 6–7)

As well as the contribution condition a second important constraint was proposed by Beveridge and institutionalised by the introduction of the National Insurance pension in 1948; the 'retirement condition'. Those who have built up a right to the state pension by virtue of their contributions are only awarded their pension following formal retirement from employment (Beveridge, 1942). The retirement condition institutionalised the dependency relationship between older people, the state and the labour market. It encouraged an end to labour-force participation and established an arbitrary age as the customary retirement age. Ironically, Beveridge had hoped that the retirement condition would encourage workers to defer retirement:

> Making receipt of pension conditional on retirement is not intended to encourage or hasten retirement. On the contrary, the conditions governing pension should be such as to encourage every person who can go on working after reaching pensionable age, to go on working and to postpone retirement and the claiming of pension. (Beveridge, 1942, p. 96)

But in practice, it resulted in the adoption of the pension ages as the retirement ages. Together with the high marginal rates of taxation levied on pensioners who took up employment by the notorious earnings rule (abolished in 1989), it militated against the continuation of work. Since 1981, the social security system has been used to further encourage the disengagement of older men from the labour market by awarding them the long-term rate of supplementary benefit (now the income support pensioner premium) to those over the age of 60 who are unemployed. Originally, this was conditional on them not registering as unemployed.

The social security system is also one of the main mechanisms through which women's dependence on men is enforced both prior to and after retirement. Most women still receive pensions as dependents on their husbands' contributions and, regardless of their age, have to wait until he reaches 65. Although the Social Security Act, 1980, contained some improvements in the status of women, these were only a tentative first step towards 'similar treatment' for women and men rather than equal treatment. Furthermore, until equality between men and women is established in the labour market it is unlikely to be realised in a social security system which is geared to the labour market. Older married women are less likely than men to receive a NI retirement pension in their own right and are overwhelmingly less likely to receive a pension from a former employer. As we have seen, older women are much more likely than men to live in poverty.

Subsistence principle in the state pension policy
The financing of state pensions and particularly the size of the Exchequer contribution has been the overriding political issue in post-war pensions policy. It was dominant too in the preparation of the Beveridge report. Many of the assumptions that Beveridge brought to his study of social insurance were based not on considerations of social welfare 'but on the prejudices of official economic opinion' and 'the notions of financial soundness which prevailed in Treasury circles' (Kincaid, 1973). Beveridge and the Treasury officials who scrutinised his proposals had intended that retirement pensions and other social security benefits should be self-financing according to actuarially sound insurance principles. This was to be achieved and a reserve fund established by phasing in the scheme over twenty-one years. However, the public pressure for retirement pensions was enormous and the 1946 National Insurance Act allowed the claiming of full benefits from the outset of the scheme (Shragge, 1984). Thus, rather than being based on the insurance principle, the NI pension has always been a 'pay-as-you-go' scheme in which those in employment support those drawing pensions. The immediate post-war period also saw a sharp diminution in the Exchequer contribution to social security, from 24 per cent of total receipts in 1950 to 12 per cent in 1953 (George, 1968). But it was to rise subsequently in the 1950s as the Beveridge principle of financing pensions began to collapse and the national insurance fund went into deficit.

The response of the government to the rising costs of pensions in the early years of the scheme and worries about the projected increases in the numbers of pensioners was to set up the Phillips Committee in July 1953, 'to review the economic and financial problems involved in providing for old age, having regard to the prospective increase in the numbers of aged' (Phillips Committee, 1954, p. 1). Like the subsequent Inquiry into Provision for Retirement 1983–85, set up thirty years later as part of the general social security review (DHSS, 1985a), the Phillips Committee was primarily concerned with the long-term growth in demand for and cost of pensions and the capacity of the working population to finance the scheme. The Committee's report reaffirmed the importance of individual contributions as a measure of 'social discipline' and, among other things, recommended an increase in retirement age to 68 for men and 63 for women. In addition, while not challenging the operation of the 1946 Act, the Committee proposed a limitation on the Exchequer contribution, support for the development of occupational pensions and restriction of the Beveridge principle (if not the practice) that NI pensions should provide a subsistence minimum: 'A contributions scheme cannot be expected to provide a rate of pension which would enable everybody, whatever his circumstances, to live without other means, such a pension rate would be an extravagant use of national resources' (Phillips Committee, 1954, p. 81).

Once older people had worked a full course and fulfilled 'the obligation of service' they were to receive 'an adequate income to maintain them' (Beveridge, 1942, p. 92). In fact, this has never been the case. Partly because of the Treasury principle of 'financial soundness' accepted by Beveridge the NI pension was set at a level of bare subsistence rather than adequate maintenance. Beveridge drew on the work of Booth (1889) and Rowntree (1901) and, in turn, nutritionalists, such as Atwater in the United States, on whose work Rowntree's calculations of food needs were based. Furthermore, Beveridge allowed only 75 per cent of the scientific food value necessary for 'physical efficiency' for old-age pensioners, plus 10 per cent for special food needs. The amounts required for clothing and housing were also set lower than those of a person of working age (Shragge, 1984).

Thus, the definition of need in old age adopted by Beveridge and followed by the 1945 Labour government and all subsequent governments was an extremely conservative, not to say a mean, one. Despite longstanding and widespread criticism of the pseudo-scientific basis of the calculations that Beveridge used for his assessment of food and other needs – not least that they bore little resemblance to what people actually spend their money on – they have influenced the levels of pensions and other social security benefits ever since. Not surprisingly, therefore, the single person's NI pension hovered at around only one-fifth of average gross earnings over the whole of the post-war period until the mid-1980s when its value began to be eroded drastically.

Further evidence may be adduced to show that the level of the state pension is low in both historical and comparative terms. When pensions are compared with the incomes of non-older people, post-war pensions are demonstrably lower than the relative values of pensions in the mid-nineteenth century, which were equivalent to two-thirds or more of the incomes of non-older working-class adults. Thus, in Thomson's words: 'In terms of pensions, an aged pensioner of mid-nineteenth century Britain was far more favoured under the 'harsh' New Poor Law than has been any twentieth century pensioner of the state' (1984, p. 453).

Furthermore, the basic pension is considerably lower relative to earnings than those provided by most other EC countries. This helps to explain Britain's relatively poor provision for pensioners, shown in Table 12.2, and suggests that the proposition that the country cannot afford higher pensions is a political rather than an economic judgement.

This review of employment and pension policies indicates that the economic dependency of older people – and therefore their poverty and low incomes – has been socially engineered in order to facilitate the removal of older workers from the labour force. As a matter of social and economic policy state pensions have been set at a bare subsistence level. In the interests of narrow financial efficiency and increased profitability mass superannuation has been managed through retirement, early retirement and unemployment among older people. Age-restrictive social policies have been used by the state both to exclude older workers from the labour force and to legitimate that exclusion through retirement. This socially reconstructed relationship between age and the labour market has not only been the primary cause of poverty in old age, but has also formed the basis for the spread of a more general dependency among elderly people as well as ageism in many aspects of public policy and wider social attitudes.

CONCLUSION

The concentration of poverty and deprivation in old age has persisted despite social recognition for over a century and more than thirty years of welfare state provision. The recurrent issue of pension reform has always been dominated by concern with a narrow conception of cost: direct Exchequer expenditure. The fact that the needs of older people have rarely been central to discussions of pensions reform is a major failing of post-war social policy. Part of the problem is that pension policies themselves have been employed to regulate the economy and labour force rather than to meet need. The main lesson from successive pension reforms is that unless there is a fundamental restructuring of the relationship between age and the labour market, on the one hand, and the incomes of pensioners and those in employment, on the other, poverty will persist into the next century and beyond. Resources have been available to overcome poverty in old age for at least the last fifty years but the political will has not.

FURTHER READING

Hannah, L. (1986) *Inventing Retirement: The Development of Occupational Pensions in Britain*. CUP, Cambridge.

Phillipson, C. and Walker, A. (eds) (1986) *Ageing and Social Policy*. Gower, London.

Shragge, E. (1984) *Pensions Policy in Britain*. Routledge and Kegan Paul, London.

Walker, A. (1980) 'The social creation of poverty and dependency in old age'. Journal of Social Policy, **9**, 49–75.

Walker, A., Guillemard, A.-M. and Alber, J. (1993) *Older People in Europe: Social and Economic Policies*, EC Commission, Brussels.

13

IMAGES OF AGEING

Mike Featherstone and Mike Hepworth

In this chapter we will discuss the significance of images of ageing and old age for the understanding of the position of elderly people in British society. When we speak about images we are primarily concerned with the wide array of public images which includes paintings, drawings, sculptures, photographs, advertisements, films, television productions, novels and plays. Our emphasis, therefore, is on ways of seeing, defining and describing ageing, which are, and have been, in public circulation and not on the private and unspoken thoughts of individuals.

One of the main concerns of this chapter is to highlight the considerable tension that can be generated between public images and the personal perceptions of elderly people. This tension is also to be found echoed in a more widespread tension existing in society between images and social realities. There is the danger that we still mistake images for reality and use images as concrete evidence of the actual social relationships and activities which occur in everyday life. At the same time, images and reality clearly interrelate, and images, representations and classificatory schemes are clearly in operation at the everyday level. Therefore, we have to be careful how we treat evidence drawn from images. We have to ask questions about what images can tell us about the actual everyday practices which occurred at the time they were created, as well as the subsequent impact images may have had in creating an enduring tradition which is handed down to us and acts as a significant reference point in our daily lives. It is not sufficient to say, for example, that our contemporary images of ageing are drawn from Ancient Judaism (the reverence for the old white-bearded biblical prophet) and Ancient Greece (the idealisation of youthful grace and beauty) – images which are clearly contradictory and the source of a persistent ambivalence towards ageing within western culture (Minois, 1989; Covey, 1991).

Rather than accept images of ageing and old age as accurate descriptions, of the attitudes and behaviour of elderly people, we need to look at the way in which these public images are actually used by men and women as they go about their daily lives. We have to raise such questions as 'How are images used by different gender categories, ethnic groups and social classes?', 'Do different gender categories, ethnic groups and social classes operate with different images?', 'Which groups create, circulate and have an interest in the widespread adoption of new images?', 'How do images as power resources relate to other power resources used by groups at different phases in history?', 'How does our self-image relate to the dominant cultural image: that is to say, the image which others apply to us as we age?' It is, of course, beyond the scope of this chapter to provide other than rudimentary answers to such questions and we are very conscious of the fragmentary evidence and the preliminary nature of research into the imagery of ageing in Britain. We do, however, seek to outline the basis for a sociological perspective on public images of ageing and would argue that any attempt to understand the position of elderly people in Britain today has to take into account the complex role they play in everyday social life.

In order to understand the nature and effectiveness of the images of ageing which operate in contemporary British society we will adopt a broad historical viewpoint. We compare the images of the pre-industrial period, which for convenience we label 'traditional images', with those which emerged out of the processes of industrialisation and modernis- ation in the nineteenth century which we have called 'modern images'. In the concluding section we sketch out some of the tensions between current images of ageing, tensions which we consider will become significant in the future. However, we begin by making a number of points about the general role of images in everyday life and in particular about images of the ageing body.

IMAGES IN EVERYDAY LIFE

Images and the human body

Human beings share with other living species an embodied existence involving birth, growth, maturation and death. Yet, when compared with other animal species, they have a biologically determined dissociation from the bodily or physiological mechanisms. In common with other animal species, human beings possess the biological equipment for both unlearned and learned behaviour but in the case of humans the balance between unlearned and learned behaviour is more strongly tipped towards the latter, and indeed their very survival depends on their capacity to communicate with learned forms of knowledge. To speak of human beings as symbol-producing or knowledge-producing beings, therefore, is to emphasise their natural disposition to learn, to produce signs and signals, and develop language to communicate with each other (Elias, 1978, 1987). Yet in emphasising the symbolic dimension we should not forget the human body, for in most forms of oral communication the co-presence of the other speaker or listener acts as a guide to the clarification of meaning through the capacity to observe bodily signals and facial expressions.

Images, both verbal and non-verbal, are a particular type of symbolic medium which we use in interpersonal communication. The images of ageing which circulate in a society normally draw upon the many representations of the body to be found in the public media. The general tangibility and mimetic quality of such representations, and the associated mental pictures we carry around with us, clearly have an immediacy and facticity which make us think that they are real and self-evident, and make it possible for us to ignore the fact that such representations are only able to function within a symbolic order. We make sense of the range of public images available to us in terms of the language-based interpretive schemes and classificatory systems which operate within a given cultural context. In different cultural contexts, or in the social life of other groups, the same representations of the body may be given a very different meaning. For example, the wrinkle which appears on the face of a Chinese grandmother and is apparently greeted with joy by granddaughters is a sign of higher status. This may become redefined in other cultural contexts as a sign of bodily and moral decay, a sign of impending low status. In his study of seventeenth-century Dutch culture Schama (1988) argues that artists of the period incorporated a special moral emphasis in their representations of the wrinkles of later life. Their art, he writes, 'explored an entire geography of the ancient face, but as always in Dutch culture, it was a moral topography'. In genre painting in particular, there were 'wrinkles of vice and wrinkles of virtue.' (p. 430). Likewise, feminists today are trying to alter the morally loaded symbolic framework within which the woman's body has been traditionally represented so that we may perceive it as other than a sex-object. Whilst images of human bodies often appear self-evident in their meaning (a good example is that of the representation of the naked body or 'nude'), their virtual facticity and tangibility depends upon the use of particular sets of everyday practical knowledge and classificatory schemes which direct us towards a specific meaning.

While images function to invoke a particular meaning in relation to the context in which they are used, they are also symbolically charged to to give expression to appropriate emotions and feeling tones. As Schama's reference to 'wrinkles of vice and wrinkles of virtue' clearly indicates, images are often constructed in sets of polarities (black and white; vice and virtue; heaven and hell; God and the devil, etc.). When we think of images of ageing bodies, it is evident that in our culture images of youth are positively charged with connotations of beauty, energy, grace, moral fortitude and optimism, whereas images of old age become negatively charged with ugliness, idleness, degeneration and moral failure. These symbolic polarities are never final and fixed, but change historically as groups struggle to define and reconstruct images to suit their own particular purposes and advantages. Recent scholarship has, for example, drawn attention to the ways in which relationships between white and coloured people have for several centuries been influenced by negative racist stereotypes. Nederveen Pieterse's recent study *White on Black: Images of Africa and Blacks in Western Popular Culture* (1992) examines racial stereotypes of Blacks in Europe and the United States to show how whites constructed images of Africa and Blacks which served to maintain the belief in the superiority of white over black. Books such as this are symptomatic of a shift in the public perception of racial and ethnic differences. They highlight and deconstruct the history of taken-for-granted stereotypes of biological and moral inferiority as reflected in the negatively charged images of 'Uncle Tom', 'Sambo', 'Golliwog' and, in both ageist and racist stereotypes 'Uncle Remus' and 'Uncle Ben', which are representations of the passive, obliging and tirelessly genial negro servant who never challenges the existing order. The highly successful film *Driving Miss Daisy*, which revolves around the relationship between a rich elderly widow and her ageing negro chauffeur, is an interesting variation on this theme. Nederveen Pieterse's book, therefore, is evidence of the ongoing struggle to analyse and challenge negative images of ethnicity and develop alternative more positive images which allow for cultural difference and mutual respect.

In challenging racial stereotypes Nederveen Pieterse also shows that we live in a world in which everyday classificatory schemes and images are taken-for-granted forms of knowledge. These classificatory schemes (black/white; young/old) function as guides to help us know how to act and feel. Such conceptual frameworks and images also dictate our sense of the appropriate use of the body, the style of presentation, demeanour, bearing, stance and way of sitting, as well as the appropriate taste and distaste for certain types of food, sport or exercise. Under certain circumstances particular body images may not only function as points of reference for the classification of other people, but actually become embodied or incorporated within a presentation of self as individuals seek to mimic a particular body image or ideal. The generationally bounded nature of the body images adopted in ways of talking, gesturing, sitting, walking, looking, etc., as well as in body shape and ways of dressing, are to a large extent formed by the time youth is reached and are in many instances never entirely lost as one moves through life. The datedness of a particular body image is particularly apparent in old people, who possess fewer resources and less motivation to modify their image in line with the ones which are currently enjoying popularity. Hence the very embodiment of a particular 'dated' body image can itself devalue the old person's social image independently of the perception of the actual physical effects of ageing manifest in such features as sagging flesh, wrinkling, greying hair or restricted movement, and further help to reinforce the negative stereotype.

Stereotypes in old age

In the literature of social gerontology public images of the ageing body are usually referred to as 'stereotypes'. In Barrow's textbook *Ageing, the Individual and Society* (1986), for example, there is a chapter on 'Stereotypes and Images' which, as is usual at the present time, draws particular attention to the perpetuation of negative stereotypes of ageing in the popular media. Similar arguments are advanced by Norman (1987) in her discussion paper on attitudes to ageing and elderly people. Terms such as 'senile', she notes, are openly derogatory but:

> still worse is the common use of 'geriatric' as a noun to describe a frail old person instead of its correct use as the branch of medial science concerned with old people and their illnesses. We do not call a woman who has just had a hysterectomy 'an obstetric' or a sick child 'a paediatric'. (Norman, 1987, p. 4)

The view that many of the images we use to describe ageing and elderly people are in fact negative stereotypes, is always accompanied by the warning that such stereotypes are damaging to our relationships with older people. They represent a form of symbolic stigmatisation which finds its way through to practical everyday action, thereby giving meaning (in this example a negative meaning) to the experience of growing old. In their path-breaking research into conversations between younger and older women in Wales, Coupland et al (Coupland et al 1991; Giles and Coupland, 1991) have shown how the range of topics and vocabularies open to younger and older people when they meet and talk actually reinforce ageist stereotypes. Young people, they point out, 'access as well as construct . . . negative identities for the old, as depressed and depressing, and as dull, grouchy and unreliable conversationalists . . . Talking to the old is perceived as a time-consuming duty and a necessary therapy, rather than as a relational development and broadening.' (Giles and Coupland, 1991, p. 163). Equally, older people themselves adopt an elderly vocabulary which focuses on the relative frailty of the body, the changing social scene and the passing of time because they feel that these are the topics of conversation which younger people expect them to choose. Ageing, therefore, is not reducible to biological processes of physical decline which take place in some vacuum sealed off from social life, but is shaped or constructed in terms of the symbolic imagery, both verbal and non-verbal, available to us at any given time. This is the reason social gerontologists are so concerned about the social and personal impli-cations of words such as 'wrinkly', 'crumbly', 'gaga', 'hag', 'crone', 'witch', 'biddy', 'fogey' and of course 'geriatric'. It is not true, they argue, that 'Words can never hurt us.'

The power of negative stereotypes of ageing to stigmatise is clearly grounded in the essentially symbolic nature of social life to which we have referred. The anxiety occasioned by such stereotypes is an acknowledgement of their central role in social life; we are highly dependent on stereotypes as a means of communication (Lippman, 1922). We do not, said Lippman, see first and then define but *define first and then see*. Stereotypes precede and shape our perceptions and are an inescapable consequence of living in a complex world in which a bewildering profusion of messages is generated. For Lippman, stereotypes are not inevitably negative, as the popular usage of the term often implies. They are simply a basic means of communication which help us to order potentially confusing experiences and impose some descriptive unity on them. The role of stereotypes is to make fast, firm and separate what is in reality fluid and changing (Dyer, 1979).

As reference points for human interaction, images of ageing are stereotypes which we use to locate and identify a wide diversity of individual persons in terms of socially prescribed age categories. In earlier chapters it has been emphasised that ageing is a highly individual process. Although the general patterns of physical change shared by all members of the human species are often plainly visible (for example, in the exposed surfaces of the face and body) the specific ways in which individuals, and members of particular social groups, age are determined by their social situation and a host of other factors. This is one reason why the study of ageing is usually described as 'interdisciplinary' (Gilmore et al, 1981). Such stereotypes have enormous convenience value since they help to simplify what is otherwise complex and often confusing, both to academics involved in the study of ageing and to everyone in their dealings with other people. The problem is, of course, that they do not do full justice to any particular individual who is labelled as 'ageing' or 'old' with reference to his or her observable appearance and behaviour. Thus, in Fairhurst's study of the ageing process as described by a number of elderly interviewees in Manchester, one man summed up the situation as follows:

> I think you'll find that you reach a stage where you don't grow any older inside. Outside you do but you're perpetually 28 or something or whatever it may be – wherever you stop. (Fairhurst, 1982)

In her introduction to her book about the lives of older women Hemmings writes:

> In my experience, younger women with an awareness of ageism tend to speak of all of us over about 45 as older women. However, women of 80 have daughters of 60, and granddaughters in their 40s. Lumping us all together in one generation means we all lose out. (Hemmings, 1985, pp. 2–3)

The perpetual tension between social categories based on generalisations about ageing and the actual personal experience of ageing in its diversity is of constant concern, and increasingly so, for those who work with older people. In recognition of this tension some writers find it convenient to describe the ageing process as a mask or disguise which, like some trick of the make-up artist's craft, conceals, layer after layer, the timeless human personality beneath. When asked to describe at the age of 79 what it felt like to be old, the celebrated author J.B. Priestley replied:

> It is as though walking down Shaftesbury Avenue as a fairly young man, I was suddenly kidnapped, rushed into a theatre and made to don the grey hair, the wrinkles and the other attributes of age, then wheeled on stage. Behind the appearance of age I am the same person, with the same thoughts, as when I was younger. (Puner, 1978, p. 7)

Priestley's reference to the 'appearance of age' reminds us of the primary role of physical appearance in the social construction of age categories; an importance which receives confirmation from psychologists researching the influence of appearance on human relationships (Wells, 1983; Hatfield and Sprecher, 1986; Pennington, 1986). As we shall see later, the predominant concern with physical appearance and especially the 'appearance of age' is very much a preoccupation of modern times although it can be shown to have deep roots in the past.

In his study of the human face, Liggett asserts that amongst the most interesting of its characteristics are:

> those produced simply by the passage of time itself. Many of the changes brought about by age such as greying of hair and wrinkling of skin, are easy enough to see . . . With loss of elasticity there comes an increasing tendency for the skin to crease under the influence of the muscles, usually in the same place, forming wrinkles and coarse folds or *rugae*, which can neither be prevented nor removed, except perhaps by surgery. Unlike some of the other marks of age, such as greying hair, they defy all attempts at concealment. As the Spanish proverb has it, 'the hair deceives, the wrinkles undeceive.' (Liggett, 1974, pp. 23–4)

As Liggett's observations indicate, it is not the wrinkles as such which are significant but their intrusive visibility which makes it very difficult for people to conceal the fact that they have lived for quite a long time or that they *appear* to have lived for quite a long time. As a consequence the wrinkling of the face may come to be seen as a gradual masking of the individual's sense of 'true' personal identity which is increasingly concealed and more difficult to express as time passes. The physical transformation of the face may thus lead to an experience of dissociation between inner selfhood and outward physical appearance. In her trenchant account of the effects of ageing in the United States, MacDonald describes the effects of wrinkling and other outwardly visible changes associated with ageing as a process of transformation whereby women in particular become socially invisible. On the personal level, she writes 'I lived with the never-knowing when people would turn away from me . . . because they have identified me as old' (MacDonald, with Rich, 1984, p. 5). When she was out with her younger friend Rich, the latter noticed significant differences in social interaction:

> It is I who receive the eye contact; questions are less often addressed to her.

When we go to a hardware store and Barbara asks about something, the man behind the counter looks at me when he responds. (MacDonald, with Rich, 1984, p. 11)

The body, which is of course easier to conceal from public gaze, also reveals ineradicable evidence of what we often describe as 'the march of time'. The bodily changes we associate with the passing of time have a long and not infrequently disenchanted history. Until very recently there does not appear to have been a period in western culture when the sight of the naked ageing body has given much pleasure. In for example her study of *The Nude Male*, Walters (1978) traces the shame of the ageing body back to the ancient Greeks. Their images of the body do not include any association between bodily decrepitude and beauty:

> Homer's Priam, foreseeing the fall of Troy exclaims that the most pitiful sight of all is the body of an old man who is 'dead and down, and the dogs mutilate the grey head and the grey beard and the parts that are secret'. The fall of a young warrior is less sad, for 'though dead, still all that shows about him is beautiful', and he will be remembered so. (Walters, 1978, p. 45)

In the history of art 'the naked body has been given memorable shapes' in order to 'communicate certain ideas or states of feeling' (Clark, 1960, p. 335). In these representations of either men or women, age is not generally an object of great respect. Rarely, writes Clark, is the aged body 'grandly portrayed'. When artists have created pictorial images of the ageing body which are close to reality they have usually been motivated by the desire to evoke pity, curiosity, repulsion, stoicism, or, only occasionally, as in the case of Rembrandt, dignity and nobility. It is scarcely surprising, therefore, that in Middleton's novel, *An After Dinner's Sleep*, when the elderly hero scrutinises his body after getting out of his bath he is relieved to discover he is not in too bad a shape:

> His body had not sagged into blubber; the hair on his chest, though grey, grew darker than that on his scalp. He turned his head, trunk to assess legs and buttocks, and not dissatisfied plugged in his razor. The mirror light wickedly etched wrinkes round his eyes, ruined his forehead, but his skin this morning at least looked healthy. He dragged on gardening clothes, and singing 'Prepare thyself, Zion', ran out to the kitchen, to a large mug of coffee and a folded *Guardian*, deciding that he was pleased with his life or himself. (Middleton, 1987, pp. 80–1)

The tragic belief that youth will fade and beauty is fleeting is not simply a reflection of the inevitable physical reality of the ageing process but is rooted in the symbolic equation between youth, beauty and goodness which is a 'core concept' of western culture. In her introduction to James Cotier's collection of photographs of naked older men and women Sarah Kent observes that there is a widespread assumption that the bodies of elderly men and women are 'almost too painful to look at'. This conventional expression of revulsion is a reflection of our awareness of our own mortality and 'the fact that one day one will also inhabit a ruin' (1992, p.1). In this collection Cotier sets out to provide an alternative perspective on the people in his photographs by providing an aesthetic framework within which the ageing body can be seen to have its own particular beauty and appeal.

Over a long period of time the outward and visible signs of ageing on face and body have acquired a meaning which, as we have noted earlier, is essentially ambivalent. On the one hand ageing in western culture, which is deeply rooted in Judaeo-Christian ideals, has never been entirely devalued. On the other hand, there is not much evidence, as far as the practical realities of life are concerned, that the process of growing old (with the exclusion of selectively honoured elderly individuals) has been generally regarded as a pleasurable and welcome experience. The example of the increasing quantity of research into the position of women and the social construction of gender forcibly reminds us that a stereotypically attractive physical appearance must be a youthful appearance if it is to continue as a source of power for those women who are fortunate enough to resemble the ideal (Lakoff and Scherr, 1984). Women's power, it is argued, is traditionally based almost entirely on physical beauty and, unlike the power of men which is built upon more enduring foundations such as wealth and occupation, it is bound to fade away. In general therefore it can be argued that the situation of ageing and older women is in certain respects less ambivalent than that of men (who don't of course live so long) because of their greater dependence on good looks. And indeed it is the case that images of ageing men in western art tend to be more positive than those of ageing women (Covey, 1991). This gender differential has been described by Sontag (1978) as 'the double standard of ageing'.

We shall return later to the important issue of the double standard of ageing; for the moment we wish only to underline the contribution of the particular symbolic meanings given to the changing human face and body by the images of ageing which occur with the greatest frequency on our society. In the course of their construction these images have helped to establish the distance often detected between the personal experience of ageing and the stereotype or age category which is so forcefully described as a mask or disguise (Featherstone and Hepworth, 1989; Hepworth, 1991).

But to describe the ageing process as a mask which conceals the enduring and more youthful self is not quite the same as saying that people attempt to disguise their age. The use of cosmetics to mask the physical signs of ageing has a long history and is, as Kathleen Woodward has shown in her analysis of the 'masquerade of youth', a recurrent theme in European literature (Woodward, 1991). Ageing as a disguise, in the sense we have used the term in this chapter, may be regarded as a tragic destiny or what Gonzalez-Crussi (1987) defines as 'the pangs of progressive bodily ruin', and it is one which contemporary images of ageing increasingly attempt to reconstruct and replace with a more positive vision. The ideal in the contemporary treatment of older people is to identify or rediscover the individual person who is perceived to be partially or totally concealed beneath the overlay of physical change brought on by that most modern enemy of the human race, chronological time.

The image of senility

Earlier we described the popular usage of the term 'geriatric' as a derogatory stereotype reflecting the deleterious effects on social competences which can accompany the process of physical ageing. The traditional image of 'senility' is a frightening vision of dribbling, drooling, incontinence, an absence of physical coordination and the inability to comport oneself or to communicate coherently. It is the image of one who is less than fully human (Goffman, 1968). It is, thus stereotyped, a nightmarish vision:

> Oh God, I know my mind is going. I cannot stem the tide of sleeplessness and sorrow. Keep me safe keep me safe. I beseech thee that I may not live long to be a burden to those I love so dearly. I have tried to see my way but I have failed all round. I know nothing, I understand nothing. I only know that I want to do right, and some time to meet the dear ones again whom I have loved so much. This is an agony far far worse than death yet I know I must cling to life however useless and broken it is. (Jalland and Hooper, 1986, p. 302)

In the terror of senility, public and private images of ageing have a poignant meeting place. We dread living on in a state of abject physical impairment which does not totally submerge a conscious awareness of our original selves and thus continuously reminds us of the powerless puppets we have ironically become. In this prevailing imagery, old age understood as senility is not so much a mask or disguise as an 'iron cage'. The self becomes imprisoned in a body which is no longer physically able to express its 'true' identity; the afflicted individual has lost his or her power of self-control: of being able to express the self-identity that he or she believes others have come to expect. This loss of the ability to live up to the expectations of others is described with great regret in Gathorne-Hardy's (1987) account of the last years of the author Gerald Brenan who died in Spain aged over 90 years. Brenan was a highly intelligent man whose independent and vital identity is described as being progressively masked by the restrictions and impediments of illness and deep old age. Towards the end he is treated by the servant girls:

> like an object, almost with contempt. He no longer gets up to eat but is spoon-fed in his chair. He asked for wine but was briskly forbidden it. After lunch they simply picked him up like a bundle of sticks and half-carried, half-dragged him out. . . Nicky said it was as though he *had* died and left behind that sad, tortured, mumbling husk. One could hardly have contrived a more terrible and lonely end if one had hated him and been able to dictate it. (Gathorne-Hardy, 1987, p. 22)

This fearful image of senility as the end result of the ageing process reflects a dread of any progressive decline in the ability to control the body through which we express our interdependent relationships with others. We become unable to disguise the fact that we are getting older, we are in the end incapable of resisting the age-related categories society has stored up for us one of which, as Hockey and James (1993) show is the tendency to 'infantilise' the dependent old. In their investigation of a hundred local authority residential homes, Willcocks et al (1987) show how the transition from one's own home to residential accommodation can swiftly undermine or remove completely the social and territorial props old people often utilise to maintain an independent identity. The very privacy of the British home ensures that elderly people can conceal to some extent their incapacities and limitations. Familiarity with the arrangement of the furniture and the general territory of the house can compensate an older man or woman for sensory loss and confers a power over his or her immediate environment which disappears very often with removal to a 'home'. In their own homes, where the majority of elderly people in Britain live until the end of their days, they are much more likely to be able to fulfil the expectation of an age-conscious society that 'older people should feel obliged to mask partial frailties for fear of being judged totally incapable of managing daily life' (Willcocks et al, 1987, pp. 7–8).

Reference to the social obligation of masking the frailties associated with ageing suggests that senility is itself a social construct. Any social arrangements which undermine the ability to express an independent self bring the person concerned progressively closer to the public image 'senile'. In this sense we are looking at a self-fulfilling prophecy. The research to which we have just referred shows how it is possible for what Bromley (1977) has memorably described as the 'aversive properties of the aged person' to become more apparent in the public setting of the residential local authority home where it is impossible to conceal one's weaknesses and avoid relentless if well-meaning scrutiny. Commenting on the factors which influence our impressions of elderly people Bromley observes that it is:

> common knowledge that for many younger people, the physical appearance and behaviour of some aged persons, especially deteriorated patients in departments of geriatric medicine, have 'aversive' properties. The effects of these characteristics may be aggravated by the unpleasant features of an institutional environment. Aged people, in other words, are often perceived as unpleasant or frightening, or at best, as pitiful. Fear, disgust, rejection and avoidance are not uncommon reactions. (Bromley, 1978, pp. 22–3)

The institutional environment, Bromley argues, constitutes a social setting where the effects of ageing on a person's expressive behaviour are accentuated and made more sharply reflexive. Their expressive weaknesses become much more apparent and, because such weaknesses make interaction more difficult, have the effect of masking the identity of the person who may be struggling to communicate 'normal' desires and feelings. Relevant to our concern with the role of images in understanding the ageing process is Bromley's suggestion that our first impressions of a person's expressive behaviour are important. These include:

1. a decline in spontaneity and response of posture, gesture, facial expression and eye contact which slow down interaction so that a younger person feels that communication is breaking down;
2. reduced ability to keep pace with the rapidity of the expressive behaviour of persons younger than themselves and difficulties in communicating when either misunderstand;
3. slower reactions which reduce sensitivity to social signs and which reflexively produce alterations in self-concept;
4. a reduction in mobility and sitting posture which in turn affects the range of expressive behaviours open to an older person, less control over his or her position and distance in interpersonal interaction.

The result of these limitations is that an older person becomes relatively isolated from normal interaction with inevitable consequences for the way he or she is perceived by those whose expressive skills are not impaired. Impaired social skills do not qualify a person for acceptance as a stereotypical 'normal'. An extra effort has to be made by all parties to the interaction to bring the normality of the problematic individual to light: to penetrate, as it were, the disguise. Those elderly patients who are seen to possess 'aversive properties' have lost the highly valued attributes of acceptable physical appearance, social skills, independence and expressive competence. As Bromley writes:

> In the crude cost-benefit terms of social exchange theory, the elderly patient may seem to have little or nothing to give in exchange for any services rendered by a younger person, and he is costly for the younger person to interact with. (Bromley, 1978, p. 26)

This situation is reproduced in its essentials in the film *No Surrender* where a party of grossly impaired elderly patients is taken into a Liverpool night-club to participate in a New Year's Eve celebration. The impact of this visit is such that several of the younger (though not much younger) visitors are provoked to aggressive or tearful resentment of the slovenly and repulsive behaviour of the patients. 'Is this the future?' asks one active and still physically combative man in late-middle life; whilst an elderly woman in a state of near collapse moans 'I don't want to end up like that', demanding that the patients be taken away and hidden from sight.

It should now be apparent that any attempt to define and describe ageing and old age will inevitably include symbolic evaluations of the appearance and behaviour we are trying to define. In his sociological analysis of Alzheimer's disease, Gubrium (1986) shows how the behavioural changes associated with senile dementia (confusion, forgetfulness, lapses of attention, speech impairment and other reductions in function, aggressiveness, unwelcome sexual behaviour, loss of bladder and bowel control) are very similar to those associated with 'normal ageing'. In other words, diagnostic techniques are not yet sufficiently precise to be absolutely certain that the cause of disturbing behaviour in many older people is a number of pathological changes in the brain resulting from an identifiable disease rather than the ultimately 'natural' or 'normal' and unavoidable process of growing old. According to Gubrium, the whole issue is complicated by the desire to see certain of the symptoms of ageing as the product of a curable disease. In other words, research into Alzheimer's disease is motivated by the desire to dissociate the ageing process entirely from any symptoms of physical and cognitive decline and to transform ageing into a totally positive physical process by eliminating what were previously seen as the signs of a natural decay. The transformation of images of decay into images of disease is one of the symbolic changes we make to remove ageing from the realm of nature and place it within the scope of medical science. The problems hitherto associated with ageing are thus no longer perceived as specific to the ageing process but are seen to be caused by identifiable diseases which, like any the other forms of illness occurring during earlier life, can be ultimately eliminated. The direction of scientific research in this instance reflects, says Gubrium, the predominant fear of ageing in American society.

Once again the prevailing image is that of the mask; the mask in this instance being Alzheimer's disease. Gubrium shows how caregivers are advised by experts on Alzheimer's disease to struggle to discover signs of the original loved one behind the mask of senile dementia. The symbolic meaning of the body and behaviour must be carefully interpreted and reconstructed to penetrate the disguise of disease which one day, with much more research, will be curable. In common with what are seen to be the more 'normal' processes of ageing which leave the individuals relatively unimpaired, Alzheimer's disease has its celebrities and exemplars. One of the most prominent of these is the late film star, Rita Hayworth, whose daughter Yasmin Khan became a key figure in the Alzheimer's movement in America. Gubrium quotes extensively from an article by Rosemary Santini and Katherine Barrett for the *Ladies' Home Journal*, January 1983, entitled 'The Tragedy of Rita Hayworth'. Their story of Rita Hayworth's decline is accompanied by 'before and after' photographs showing the nightmarish depredations of the disease on outward appearance and demeanour. In the 'after' photograph of the star she appears to be 'an elderly, dishevelled woman . . . glassy-eyed and pathetic'. Occasionally her daughter catches fleeting glimpses of her mother's former self: her eyes stare past her daughter. They are clouded and uncomprehending. ' "It's so hard to know what she's feeling, what's going on inside" Yasmin Khan says softly. "I don't know what she can understand but there are fleeting moments when I am sure she's at least somewhat aware"' (Gubrium, 1986, p. 136).

The image of the mask or disguise which is involuntarily assumed as we grow older takes us to the heart of the social construction of ageing which involves a tension or balance of power between the individual and society. Skinner writes:

> Someone has said that if you want to know what it feels like to be old, you should smear dirt on your glasses, stuff cotton in your ears, put on heavy shoes that are too big for you, and wear gloves; then try to spend the day in a normal way. (Skinner and Vaughan, 1983, p. 38)

This is a deliberate overstatement of the difficulties facing many people who are old but it does serve to highlight the struggle to avoid negative stereotyping and loss of independent identity with which we are confronted as we gradually get older.

Yet the images with which we struggle do not have a fixed shape or meaning; they can change over the years, and can be manipulated and modified within certain limits. We may be constrained by meaning but the meanings are much more flexible than we sometimes imagine. In the sections which follow we take a closer look at the prevailing meanings of ageing and old age as the available evidence suggests they have emerged in Britain.

Before we move on to our examination of the central characteristics of tradition and modern images of ageing, a final word of caution is in order. Until recently in Britain the images of ageing were white. Ethnicity was not an issue. Indeed, even in an ethnically plural society such as the United States, it is only during the last decade or so that social gerontologists have begun to 'accumulate a body of scientific generalisations concerning ethnicity as a mediator in problems of ageing' (Bengtson, 1979, p. 10). Bengtson further observes:

> Practitioners and policymakers have only recently begun to formulate programmes reflecting the service implications of ethnic contrasts among elderly Americans. Criticisms are raised frequently to the effect that both research and policy are insensitive, and therefore ultimately irrelevant, to current realities of ethnic differences amongst the aged. (Bengtson, 1979, p. 10)

Times are changing in Britain too, and there are clear signs that our images of ageing are gradually becoming enriched by accounts of the experience of ageing from differing ethnic backgrounds. Ethnicity is now an issue for social gerontologists in Britain as Bornat et al (1985) point out in their *Manifesto for Old Age*. Personal accounts of the experience of ageing include Asian women (Ford and Sinclair, 1987) and women who have settled in Britain from Jamaica, India and Nazi Germany (Hemmings, 1985). Ethnic identity, a sense of belonging to a distinctive cultural tradition, can function as a protective resource as individuals grow older and can be drawn upon to foster positive ageing.

Blakemore (1993) describes three models of adaptation to ageing which have been observed amongst minority ethnic communities in the UK. The first category, 'the self-reliant pioneer,' is a person who draws upon the strength of his or her ethnic background and traditions to develop positive solutions to the problem of identity by remaining within the boundaries of a common past shared with other members of the minority community. A good example of Blakemore's 'self-reliant pioneer' would be certain West Indian characters portrayed in the popular television programme *Desmond's*, a comedy series set in a South London barber's shop. Self-reliant pioneers retain the traditional ties of the ethnic group with its positive evaluation of cultural identity which includes a more active role for the elderly than may be found in the host society. Blakemore's second and third categories, 'the gradually adjusting migrant', and 'the passive victim', are less encircled by their own ethnic traditions. These are people who, as they grow older, make correspondingly larger concessions to expectations of ageing held by the host society. These expectations include adjustments to the demands of the wider host society which involve the abandonment of the more protective traditional ethnic cultural images of the elderly, and hence lay specific individuals and groups open to the double jeopardy of being black and old in modern western society.

TRADITIONAL IMAGES

Until comparatively recently there was a distinct tendency for images of ageing to be blurred by a nostalgically romantic view of Britain's past where the old were venerated for their skills and wisdom. The notion of the 'good old days' has distorted our perceptions not only of the treatment of elderly people in the past but also of our treatment and attitudes in contemporary society (Laslett, 1977). We have already seen that there is little evidence from the history of art that the naked ageing body has been portrayed as a desirable end. We can add to this reflection the general belief amongst historians that there was no 'golden age' of ageing (Quadagno, 1982). Those facial and bodily changes which gave an aged appearance have never been venerated in themselves; the main source of reverence of older people in pre-industrial Britain appears to have been wealth and power (Thomas, 1976; MacFarlane, 1986).

With diminished resources of physical strength, money and social influence the ageing process left many who survived into old age totally dependent on the goodwill and charity of family or neighbours. Although, as MacFarlane (1986) shows in his study of the period 1300 to 1840, there is strong evidence of the existence of ideals of charitable Christian duty towards elderly people, in practice men and women who had made little provision for an independent old age could find themselves neglected and even despised. The clear message to elderly individuals was: do not lose control of your resources. Thomas (1976) also notes that the ongoing process of social change tended not to improve relationships between younger and older generations:

> old age could never in itself command respect. If some of the elderly retained authority, it was because of the material resources at their disposal. 'Old people commonly are despised' said Richard Steele, adding the significant qualification 'especially when they are not supported with good estates'. The old man sitting at the fireplace was disregarded, but if he 'hath estate of his own to maintain himself and to pleasure his children, oh, then . . . his age is honoured, his person is reverenced, his counsel is sought, his voice is obeyed'. (Thomas, 1976, pp. 247–8)

What is clear, then, is that despite the images of authoritative and respected old age in pre-industrial Britain, a society where in *theory* elderly people enjoyed power and control over younger people, the stigmatisation of old age was in *practice* a familiar feature of everyday life. To quote again from Thomas:

> 'For any to have their understanding good, their memories and sense tolerable, their conversation acceptable, their relations kind and respectful . . . this' thought John Shower in 1698, 'is a rare case and happens seldom to old people.' The verbal prosecution of the elderly is explicit in proverbial lore about old trots and old shrews: there was no fool like an old fool and nothing worse than an 'old woman'. Schoolmasters constantly forbade their charges to mock the elderly, but the effect of such prohibitions must have been diminished by the presence in Tudor textbooks of such sentences for translation as 'this dotard waseth a child again'. (Thomas, 1976, pp. 245–6)

The concept of senility as the ultimate disqualification from full social acceptability in modern society has thus deep roots in Britain's cultural history. Its images can be detected long before the emergence of geriatric medicine in the closing years of the nineteenth century.

Indeed, as Haynes (1963) has shown in her study of images of ageing in classical Rome:

> old age was felt to be a burdensome stage rather than a blessing in a man's life, for it brought not only the loss of health but also, very often, a weakening of a man's mental powers. (Haynes, 1963, pp. 34–5)

The men whose names have been handed down to us through the ages as exemplars of a serene and pleasurable old age:

> lived a comfortable life in their villas, which overflowed with costly books, statues, and pictures, were attended by a staff of servants, and visited daily by a number of cheerful friends. They spent the days of their old age much in the same manner the upper class old men live today in Palm Springs, St Moritz, or at the French Riviera. (Haynes, 1963, p. 35)

Images of what we might now call 'successful ageing' as recorded in Cicero's classic *De Senectute* (44BC) are based, according to Haynes's analysis, on the lives of exceptionally advantaged people. This argument, when added to the findings of historians of pre-industrial

Britain, leads us towards the generally accepted view that prior to the process of modernisation, which accelerated rapidly in the last century, ageing and its end result, old age, were defined in comparatively simple terms. Old people were those who, regardless of chronological age, had become helpless and dependent and thus appropriate objects of charity. The broken-down labourer could therefore be old at 40 and a woman of this age worn out by the physical hazards of constant childbearing could present all the outward appearance of what we nowadays describe as 'premature ageing' (Shorter, 1983).

Prior to the 'modernisation of the life cycle' (Gruman, 1978), elderly people are those who have become powerless and dependent. The belief that industrial society has destroyed the respect traditionally accorded to elderly people in more closely-knit rural society does not, as far as Britain is concerned, gain a great deal of support from historical researchers. Nor does the image of the 'golden age of senescence' (Haber, 1983) command much support from historians of ageing in the United States where the issue of the respect given to elderly people in the past, simply because they were old, is hotly contested (Fischer, 1978; Stone, 1977; Achenbaum, 1978a; Graebner, 1980; Haber, 1983) (see also Chapter 1). Without becoming entangled in the subtleties of historical periodisation, it seems fair to summarise the situation in the words of Haber.

> at best attitudes towards senescence have always been ambivalent and . . . for the elderly who had lost status and power, the future was bleak. Grey hair, wrinkles and increasing infirmities did indeed become signs of ridicule. Despite biblical prescriptions that called for respect for the old, one did not gladly pass into this stage of existence. (Haber, 1983, p. 7)

Behind the lack of reverence for frail and dependent elderly people, which is the most noteworthy feature of traditional images of ageing recorded by historians, can be detected an ambivalence towards ageing and death (Kastenbaum, 1974). Death in pre-industrial Britain was much more familiar and taken for granted than it is in modern society where there is a tendency towards hospitalisation and concealment from public gaze (Ariès, 1981; Elias, 1985). At the same time, people with the necessary knowledge and resources have always struggled to avoid an untimely end. This tendency became particularly evident in the eighteenth century when confidence in medical science as a source of 'defences again death' (McManners, 1985) began to grow. In France there was, amongst educated people, an increasing optimism about medical progress reflected in 'increased concern with problems of health, a growing reluctance to accept illness fatalistically, and an intensified shrinking in face of pain' (McManners, 1985, p. 47). In Britain too the interest in health followed a similar pathway where it merged with the quest for youth and beauty. Eighteenth-century Britain was not:

> an era which revered grey hairs. Ageing Georgians did not try to impersonate

long-bearded patriarchs: wigs and cosmetics, used even by men, were to keep an appearance of youth. The outlook of the Age of Reason led Harry Fox to bring up his son to believe that 'the young are always right, the old are always wrong'. (Porter, 1982, p. 166)

The prevailing images of ageing in pre-industrial society do not suggest a tradition of interest in growing old or an optimistic prospect of old age. The growing eighteenth-century preoccupation with health, linked with a concern to prolong life, looks towards a youthful vision of life rather than its prolongation. The preferred choice has always been between youth and death and not youth followed by senility and decrepitude (Gruman, 1966; Kastenbaum, 1974). From this perspective distinctions of increasing subtlety are made between images of ageing and embellishments are added to the framework of traditional imagery we have inherited from the past. Within the broadly negative stereotype of ageing, therefore, a number of significant variations can be found; variations which in turn reflect changing moral evaluations of the ageing process.

In her analysis of children's stories, songs and games in nineteenth-century England Tamke (1978) describes three 'predominant models of the elderly':

1. wise and moral old people who are basically passive and do not take an active part in life. This is the quality most approved in the children's didactic literature. The dominant image is passivity and passionlessness: 'white-haired, slightly plump, and smiling' figures who behave affably towards the young and present themselves as self-supporting models of moral conduct;

2. old people whose behaviour does not conform to the above age category and who do not, as we say, 'act their age'. These are the men, and much more frequently women, who behave out of character by attempting (usually pathetically) to disguise their ageing appearance and by refusing to act out the roles which are stereotypically prescribed for them in literature. They are the women who have been described at least since the eighteenth century as 'mutton dressed as lamb'; and then men who usually appear as ageing dandies or beaux: caricatures of their former selves;

3. the group who are described by Tamke as the 'simply old'. These people are neither good nor bad: they are those who have been previously described as 'senile' or 'geriatric'. This category is 'rarely treated kindly: because they are old they are laughed at, their physical impairments are the subject of jests, and they are denied the rewards which are given to the young. They are punished simply because they are old'. (Tamke, 1978, p. 64)

This threefold distinction between the 'good old', the 'bad old' and those who are simply 'past it' is one which has roots deep in history. It is not, as Tamke points out, that these images reflect the total reality of growing old in Victorian England, where ageing 'most often entailed economic misery'. They demonstrate values and beliefs about ageing which are also found in the adult literature of the period and which in turn have strong links with the past. In his report of research into attitudes towards ageing amongst a small sample of men and women in Aberdeen, Williams (1986) locates the positive and negative attitudes towards ageing that he discovered in a broader European tradition dating from pre-industrial times. This long history is noteworthy on two accounts. First, the distinction that is made between a 'green old age'; and 'the last stage of withering'. Second, between 'the honoured and despised old, the honoured retaining their faculties through wealth and moral effort, and the despised losing theirs through poverty and moral weakness' (Williams, 1986, p. 4).

These traditional images of ageing which we have attempted to summarise in this section make, we suggest, a valuable contribution to our understanding of ageing in our own society at the present time for three reasons. First, they show how age-related images, or stereotypes of ageing men and women, contain prescriptions for what we nowadays call 'successful' (positive) as distinct from 'unsuccessful' (negative) ageing. Second, in the shape of positive and negative stereotypes they provide us with some idea of the gap which may well exist between the private and personal experience of ageing and the public images in circulation. This gap makes it possible to see old age as a mask or disguise which conceals the 'real' or enduring self. Third, a comparison of the images of the past with those of our own time gives us a clearer idea of the flexibility of images which we noted in our opening observations on the role of symbols in social life. We can see that although the images with which we are most familiar are rooted in our history, they are also subject to change and can indeed be moulded and and reconstructed in the attempt to change attitudes to ageing and old age in contemporary society.

It is to the effects of modernisation on the images we have defined as 'traditional' that we now turn in the next section of this chapter.

MODERN IMAGES

When we look at historical photographs, etchings, prints and paintings of people who are old we see the 'same grey hairs and deeply lined faces' (Achenbaum, 1978b, p. 9) with which we are familiar today. But, as Achenbaum indicates in his history of ageing in America since 1790, there are important differences in our perceptions of these images. We can summarise these with reference to the social changes which have reshaped our images of ageing in modern times.

Since the latter half of the nineteenth century there have emerged more elaborate programmes for defining the various stages of the ageing process (Haber, 1983) and categorising elderly men and women on an administrative basis (Cain, 1974; Roebuck, 1978; Roebuck and Slaughter, 1979; Graebner, 1980). There has also been the emergence of an enhanced awareness of the stigma of ageing or 'ageism' (Phillipson, 1982; Itzin, 1986). Taken together, these two developments are the products of modernisation which, although it is difficult to periodise with complete precision (Cowgill and Holmes, 1972; Achenbaum, 1978a; Gruman, 1978; Dowd, 1980), have fostered age consciousness on a scale which did not exist in the pre-industrial world.

The central values of modernity which are particularly relevant to our understanding of changes in the imagery of ageing are derived from an increasing celebration of the contribution of youthful energy and vigour to the positively evaluated processes of social change. Processes of industrialisation and technological innovation which provide the dynamic thrust of modernisation, it is argued, render the skills and knowledge of the older generation redundant. As a consequence old people become devalued and irrelevant to the productive process (Dowd, 1980). It is this perspective on social change since the mid-nineteenth century which has persuaded some commentators that elderly people were much more valued in the pre-industrial world (Fischer, 1978). As a result of modernisation, individuals become increasingly age-conscious because the stereotypical age categories handed down from traditional society are expanded and developed by experts such as medical scientists, psychologists, economists, management consultants, social administrators and others. The activities of these experts over the years, in the climate of urgent industrial and technological change, has gradually produced a shift in the imagery of ageing, which has percolated through into the wider society. This shift in the prevailing imagery of ageing in Britain follows developments elsewhere (particularly in the United States) and is a *gradual* process involving the social *reconstruction* of traditional images of ageing so that they will correspond to the demands of a more sophisticated world. The break with the past has never been complete, however, nor has the modernisation of ageing developed uniformly throughout the western world (Achenbaum, 1978a). Images of ageing in France, for example, differ in certain interesting ways from those found in Britain and elsewhere in the western world (Stearns, 1977; Zeldin, 1983).

It is also generally agreed that as far as changing images of ageing are concerned, the most significant developments have occurred since the First World War (Achenbaum, 1978b) which was followed by a rapid spurt in the expansion of a culture of mass consumption. Although the images of ageing with which we are now much more familiar began to appear in medical and other books of advice on how to age gracefully from the mid-nineteenth century in Britain and elsewhere (Haber, 1983; Featherstone and Hepworth, 1985a, 1985b), it was really during the inter-war years that the influence of consumer culture first began to make itself felt. A reconstructed public imagery of ageing reflected changes in the political economy of the western world which placed a greater premium on the value of a younger or more youthful work force. The introduction of new production methods and the effects of economic depression forced many workers to become unemployed and in this context of unsettling social ferment, the idea of retirement as an appropriate stage of life for ageing workers took a hold of the public imagination (Graebner, 1980; Phillipson, 1982). The concept of the old age pension had already been accepted and both on humanitarian grounds and grounds of expediency, retirement came to be seem as a 'natural' resting place, even a reward, for men in their 60s. During the inter-war years, too, women (many of whom were dependent on a male wage-earner) began to be treated as a distinct category who were increasingly seen as requiring special treatment (Roebuck and Slaughter, 1979).

Against this background, the images of retirement as a 'normal' consequence of reaching the age of 65 for men and 60 for women gradually emerged and added an extra layer to the traditional belief that as we get older we become more useless and should therefore gradually 'disengage' from active life. The difference between traditional and modern images of old age as uselessness – the precursor of 'second childhood' or infantilism – is that in pre-industrial Britain desuetude was the consequence of a physical inability to work whereas in modern Britain, as elsewhere in advanced societies, it is determined by a bureaucratic decision based on fashionable stereotypes of ageing which have little to do with the actual capacity of many individuals to carry out productive activity (Cain, 1974). Such bureaucratic features of social policy towards older people, linked with the emergence of 'geriatric' medicine and gerontology during this century (Armstrong, 1983; Haber, 1983), have played an important part in the development of the age-consciousness which is evident at all 'stages' of the contemporary everyday life 'course' (Cohen, 1987).

We noted earlier that images of ageing are often ambivalent. On the one hand they express concern for the old and frail whilst on the other they reveal anxiety and even fear. This combination is especially evident in modern images where the balance between these ingredients varies in a number of interesting ways. To illustrate this more clearly we shall examine the increasing sensitivity about the effects of ageing on the face, the body, and thus on general physical appearance which is reflected in the following typical observations:

> I was in my sixties but my body and mind were still youthful – yet my face looked wrinkled, sagging, and old. I wanted a youthful face to match my limber body . . . I now face the day with an eager new sense of joy. People say I seem much more vivacious . . . I used to be just as bright, but my wrinkles covered up the sparkle.

> I am 67 but I feel vital – anywhere from 45 to 55, but I resent being bound by

the arbitrary measurement of time . . . I have an appetite for life. (Hepworth and Featherstone, 1982, p. 3)

An examination of the main trends in images of ageing since the inter-war years shows that personal statements such as these are now possible because of six developments linked with the cultural and socio-economic changes we discussed earlier. First, advances in medical science have made us more aware of our bodies and the effects of the passage of time on the visible outer surfaces. We are becoming much more conscious, too, of the relationship between the internal state of our bodies and our external appearance (Glassner, 1989). Second, the increase in life expectancy (see Chapter 1) means that in general we live on into our 60s and 70s and are therefore more likely to die from diseases associated with old age. This probability has led to an upsurge in demand for medical treatments which will cure or control the diseases of age and a popular enthusiasm for techniques of prolonging active life and rejuvenation. Third is the impact of consumerism as a method of promoting mass-produced goods in terms of their capacity to enhance one's 'lifestyle'. This development has important implications for the social construction of ageing because these promotion techniques rely very heavily on an image of the consumer as a person with the youthful energy to carry on renewing his or her purchases; in effect to carry on consuming. The stylisation of consumer durables changes so rapidly nowadays that one can very quickly become out of date. Fourth, there is the expansion of the mass media which reproduce, stereotype, and circulate images at a faster pace and to a wider audience than ever before. It is now possible to close your eyes and ears to images with which you do not identify but it is not possible to ignore the pervasive presence of images as such. Fifth, the influence of feminism and the Women's Movement, especially since the 1960s, is changing attitudes towards masculinity, femininity and consciousness of the body. One aim of the Women's Movement has been to challenge the social acceptability of the 'adolescent ideal' of female beauty in which women strive to maintain a youthful appearance and 'girlishness' well into later life. Six, it is increasingly apparent that our society is multi-cultural and incorporates a diverse range of ethnic identities, each of which has its own set of images of ageing. As Blakemore (1993) observes there exists a variety of ethnic cultural resources to challenge the dominant western stereotype of old age as inevitable disengagement and decline. In effect, traditional and ethnic differences have not all given way to the modernisation process associated with consumer culture: Caribbean and Asian ethnic communities in Britain have been able to mobilise public opinion against racial discrimination and develop stronger counter-identities. This increasing consciousness and assertion of the 'right to be different' has made both academics, professional workers and the public in general more aware of the cultural complexities of the ageing process and it can be argued that this is a part of a more general process in which minorities of various types (homosexual, regional, disabled as well as ethnic) have sought to assert their citizenship rights.

It is, perhaps, unnecessary to add that these processes do not work on our awareness of ageing as separate and distinct conscious forces. These social influences merge together – sometimes subconsciously – so that the images we use in our conversations, our relationships with elderly people, and our subjective attitudes towards ourselves as *we* grow older, include a mixture of folklore, medical knowledge, media images and the like. These images act as *reference points* to give structure and meaning to our everyday lives and not as rigid programmes we are condemned to act out mindlessly.

To provide a more detailed illustration of the way these tendencies reveal themselves in modern images of ageing we now turn to two significant examples taken from our research into cultural aspects of ageing in contemporary Britain. First, the social construction of middle age or, as it is now generally described, 'mid-life'; and second, changing images of retirement (Featherstone and Hepworth, 1984).

Social construction of middle age

So pervasive is the strand of ambivalence running through the western imagery of ageing that it is impossible to ignore the widespread fear of what Henry (1972) poignantly described as 'deep ageing' and 'human obsolescence' which permeates handbooks and other texts on ageing. Almost without exception, the popular literature, conveys a sense of urgency, that time is running out. One of the most socially significant aspects of the social reconstruction of middle age, therefore, is the attempt to establish an ever-increasing distance between the 'middle years' (currently ranging from the mid-30s through to the late 60s) and deep or 'geriatric' old age and death. This distance is hopefully achieved through the redefinition of 'middle age' as 'mid-life' which is increasingly portrayed from the 1920s onwards as an extendible phase of vigorous and self-fulfilling life (Hepworth and Featherstone, 1982).

This gradual shift in the public imagery of middle age involves a transformation of the traditional into the modern. In the traditional stereotype of middle age the physical changes associated with the process of growing older – putting on weight, baldness, reduced energy, impaired vision and hearing, sexual lassitude – tend to be represented as the 'normal' consequences of living for a certain number of years. In seaside postcards of the years preceding the Second World War, for example, men in middle age are usually shown as balding, paunchy, and with dangerously flushed faces. The women who have reached a similar time of life have pot bellies and protuberant backsides which bulge through bathing costumes and everyday dress. In this image the body unambiguously betrays the 'stage' in life one has reached.

At the same time there are detectable signs of class variations in body shape and comportment and their influence on the ageing process (Schwartz, 1986). We have already noted the age-consciousness of socially-advantaged men and women in eighteenth-century Britain and France. The available evidence strongly suggests that this sensitivity showed no signs of waning through the nineteenth century. From the 1850s onwards medical men were urging that 'natural' ageing was influenced by factors such as diet, work, way of life ('lifestyle' as we now call it), childbearing and sexual activity. In particular, the attack which gained impetus under the influence of consumerism in the 1920s, on the idea that men and women should inevitably put on weight in middle age, began to receive major publicity among the literate classes. Members of fashionable society flocked to the seaside, watched their diets, swallowed pills, sweated in Turkish baths and invented taxing physical activities partly to ensure they aged in a socially acceptable way. The belief, derived from the physiognomic school of the eighteenth century (Finkelstein, 1991), that the body is a visible record of an individual's inner moral value had not diminished.

The traditional stereotype of middle age as 'natural' and inevitable was gradually being undermined by select groups of people and specific interests well before consumerism got fully under way. But it was during the 1920s and 1930s that *mass* interest in the connections between graceful ageing, health and physical and moral attractiveness became possible and began to exert a heightened influence in the social reconstruction of middle age. Thus, in the 1922 edition of *Old Age Deferred*, Lorand typically agreed it was not yet possible to create a young man out of an old one but it was:

> quite within the bounds of possibility, as we shall endeavour to demonstrate herein, to prolong our term of youthfulness by ten or twenty years. In other words we need no longer grow old at forty or fifty . . . All this can be brought about by the observance of certain hygienic measures, and by improving the functions of a certain few of the glandular structures of the body. (Hepworth and Featherstone, 1982, p. 67)

The signs of ageing on face and physique were increasingly portrayed as visible evidence of an unwise and socially unacceptable way of life, particularly when they became noticeable during middle age. The ageing process should be deferred as long as possible: a youthful appearance was the ideal and 'premature ageing' the dreaded enemy.

An increasing faith in the ability to discriminate in terms of outward appearance between those who aged 'honourably' and those who aged 'dishonourably', as Williams (1986) puts it, became one of the corner-stones of what we have described as the 'new middle age' (Featherstone and Hepworth, 1982). The accelerating impact of consumerism during the inter-war years sharpened awareness of the central role of the body in social life and the influence of imagery on the evaluation of individuals in a world of appearances (Featherstone, 1982). Throughout this period, too, middle age was steadily presented as a time of opportunity for 'taking stock' and self-development. 'At a certain age', wrote Knopf (1932) in typical fashion, 'people have to realise that tomorrow will never come'; they must therefore abandon regret for the past and begin to live in the light of the urgent knowledge that time is running out: the 'terror of the closing door' (Knopf, 1932, p. 226). The speeded-up pace of life demanded a faster reaction to life events and the capacity to continue in personal 'growth'. These pressures were seen to affect the lives of both men and women though their responses might be considered to vary according to the dictates of gender and their way of life.

Changes in the imagery of middle age reappeared to even greater public acclaim in the Britain of the 1970s where concern over the problems of mid-life showed no signs of waning. In her study of the portrayals of ageing women in American popular film, Stoddard (1983) writes that from the 1960s film images 'became more and more sympathetic' whilst by the early 1970s middle age was represented as a crisis period for men as well as women, 'measured more in terms of self-fulfilment than . . . traditional social expectations' (Stoddard, 1983, p. 121). The same picture applies to Britain in the images of mid-life (filmed or otherwise) which have been in circulation over the last decade and a half (Hepworth, 1987). But buried not too far beneath the enthusiastic celebration of potential self-fulfilment in mid-life lies the anxiety over the proximity of dependent deep old age that a youth-oriented modern society can do little to dispel. For still the hope is held out that an active and vigorously extended mid-life ('positive ageing') will push the deleterious consequences of physical decline well into the background and increase the power of those who age gracefully to maintain control over their lives.

Images of retirement

Against the backcloth of the social changes outlined above, retirement has come to be portrayed as a period of refurbishment. From its first appearance in Britain in 1972, the retirement and leisure magazine *Choice* (originally entitled *Retirement Choice* and the first in what is now an expanding range of popular retirement magazines) set out to dismantle the traditional image of retirement. In the second issue Lord Raglan, the president of the Pre-retirement Association, advanced the following message: because society has arbitrarily contrived the age of retirement and its conditions, society 'should play its full part in providing pre-retirement education to help people adjust to a new way of life, at what after all is a time in life when change is proverbially difficult'. There was a crying need for a 'dramatic change in attitudes to the whole question of retirement' (Raglan, 1972). The new magazine, then, set itself the task of confronting and dismantling the traditional image of retirement which associated the end of full-time employment with passive old age. Retirement should become a positive 'stage' in life. The section on women's fashion was especially interesting during those early days on account of its militant posture towards what was called the 'dull uniform' of retirement. In an article, 'Strictly Between Women – Yes, You Can Wear These Clothes', readers were told to adopt a modern outlook. The days were gone when they could skimp on make-up and wear something old and comfortable around the house; 'Now, when your husband is going to be home most of the time, is the moment to make him sit up and take notice of your elegant new image' (*Retirement Choice*, 1972, pp. 18–19).

In February 1973, a continuing sense of grievance was expressed over the outworn public stereotype of retirement which had a tendency, it was argued, to trap retired men and women behind a kind of metaphorical fence. 'Isn't it about time', the editor demanded, 'that the news got around that nowadays people stay younger and are not old in the same way that people were old in time of yore?' The processes of growing old were 'inevitable enough without officialdom giving them a shove along with an outdated vocabulary'. On the inside pages of this issue was a reference to Newport and Monmouthshire Regional Council which had issued a brochure including a lively sketch of an old man with a red nose and fringe of white hair leaping a GPO pillarbox: 'Don't be a Mouldy Oldy. Be a Lively Sixty Five!'

Between October and November 1974, the powers of the commercialised popular media were drawn upon in order to increase the impact of the magazine and attract a wider readership. The format was changed dramatically and almost out of all recognition. The title was changed from *Retirement Choice* to *Pre-Retirement Choice* (with the emphasis in bold print on the word *Choice*). The covers became glossy, featuring for the first time close-ups of celebrities from politics, show business and the media – all of whom were ageing gracefully and some of whom expressed no intention of retiring. The accent was now on preparation for retirement planning for, by implication, a new generation of men and women in mid-life, who could not be expected to be attracted by images of retirement and old age but who might reasonably be expected to have a long-term interest in leisure planning. The avowed intention was to expand the concept of pre-retirement to include a younger readership of 'people looking ahead to retirement'. 'We shall', the publishers announced, 'be covering a wide range of topics of special interest to men and women who *know* that sooner or later they have to *fashion their lives afresh*' (*Pre-Retirement Choice*, 1974).

Between May and June 1975, the word *Pre-Retirement* was dropped from the cover leaving the title of the updated magazine as simply *Choice*. In 1978 there was a merger with the Over 50s Club and *Choice*

s to present retirement as an extended leisure lifestyle within
\y infirmities that old age may bring can be managed with
, ..id skill.

These changes in the image of retirement as reflected in *Choice* have
clear and close connections with the social reconstruction of middle age
we previously outlined. In order to expand the readership and
communicate their message more widely the exponents of a positive
conception of retirement found it necessary to draw upon the
techniques of consumer culture. In order to transform the private
vocabulary of retirement it was imperative to transform the public
imagery so that it reflected the changing aspirations of new generations
of retirees who see themselves and feel themselves to be far distanced
from the passive and less than exhilarating traditional image of middle
life as the threshold of a disengaged old age.

IMAGES OF THE FUTURE

In conclusion, we believe it is important to ask the question: 'What are
the implications of our survey of images of ageing in Britain for the
future?' There are four possible future scenarios we would like to
identify. First, the long-term interest of the human species in longevity
and rejuvenation – increasing both the length and the quality of life –
shows little sign of abating. The possibility of developing technologies
which will slow down the processes of biological ageing, or even, as we
noted in our references to the imagery of Alzheimer's disease, eliminate
them entirely, clearly forms the basis for a speculative postmodern
imagery of ageing in the future. An imagery which symbolically
represents an end to the problems currently associated with ageing and
old age. We can predict (as is the case with regard to existing techniques
of cellular therapy) that the ability to purchase and utilise the new
expertise will be confined to the most powerful and privileged groups in
society who will use it to reinforce existing social inequalities and status
distinctions.

Second, it is clear that in a society such as ours in which consumerism
and material values are regarded as absolutely central, images of
youthful beauty and energy will continue to dominate the media. The
emphasis upon flexibility, adaptability and self-expression long associated with youth is now being extended for forthcoming generations
into old age. Here we can refer to the whole paraphernalia of consumer
cultural artefacts and services: jogging, exercise routines, cosmetics,
health foods and fashionable leisure-wear are now marketed to elderly
people to sustain health, youthful energy and the spirit of self-
improvement deep into old age. The consequences for the relationships
between the generations are momentous.

Third, the basis for a negative imagery of old age will persist because of the general insensitivity and disgust often expressed towards those who lose control over their bodily functions and expressive capacities. The disturbing image of old age as a dirty secret, of decrepit sub-human beings on the edge of death, who can only be physically and mentally shut away, will be difficult to displace from centre-stage.

Equally, however, alongside our heightened sensitivity and disgust for the aversive properties of old age, we should also note the emergence of a counter-tendency towards a more humanitarian and tolerant attitude towards minority groups such as elderly people. Over the last hundred years we have seen a shift in the balance of power between men and women, dominant groups and ethnic minorities, children and parents and younger and older people. Groups such as women, children and elderly people, which previously had relatively little power, have made some gains. There has also been a general diminishing of contrasts within society through an awareness of the chains of interdependencies that bind all human beings together. This increases the capacity to identify and empathise with outsiders and minority groups. Pressure groups and social movements such as the Gray Panthers are thus able to raise questions about the rights of elderly people in a more open cultural climate for minority group rights, whatever the particular sympathies and economic policies governments may choose to follow.

Of course, the realisation of this fourth scenario for old age will be difficult in the face of the third one. There are great difficulties in the way of constructing a positive image of deep old age which will help us detach ourselves from the negative emotional response of aversion and disgust. In all probability the future tendency will be to feature images which present old age as an active continuing phase of consumerism. Here the emphasis will be on old age not as settled, routine relaxation, but as a phase of continuous physical, mental and sexual renewal. One of the heroes of ageing in this context is Ronald Reagan, who in his 70s increased his chest measurement by over 2 inches through body building. Within consumer culture there will be little attention given to the problems of how to live in a post-active old age. There is still the tendency to hide away the hideous and disturbing. Few of us, for example, can face photographs of First World War facial injuries or massively disfiguring cancers which one finds in journals on plastic surgery, without a sense of disgust, embarrassment and helplessness at these seeming abominations of human nature. Deep old age offers a similar challenge to our capacity to balance out emotional involvement and detachment, to face and explore our emotional reactions in order to better understand the person who is conscious of being concealed behind the mask.

In this chapter we have highlighted some of the key tensions between imagery and reality, in later life. We have argued that it is a mistake to regard the history of ageing and old age as a unitary process and that distinctions must be made in terms of gender, class, power, wealth and ethnicity in the treatment of the elderly during different periods in the history of the west (Minois, 1989). Much research remains to be done and we are conscious of the need for systematic detailed research into images of ageing which examines the production, reception and day-to-day use of images by individuals from different class, racial and gender backgrounds. We wish therefore to end on a point which we have stressed throughout this chapter. Human society is a process and it is dangerous to assume that attitudes towards elderly people and images of old age which currently exist enjoyed the same currency in the past or necessarily will do so in the future. Hence, for all the talk about our youth-oriented society we should be aware that while the qualities associated with youthfulness have generally been valued in history, this valuation must be related to the balance of power between the generations, which undergoes periodic fluctuations (Featherstone, 1987). The large post-war 'baby boom' cohort which became the 1960s generation seemed to have gained a good deal of power for youth. Yet this generation is now in the process of entering middle age and in the early decades of the next century they will enter old age. They will take with them different values and command financial and other power resources on a very different scale from their parents. It is this generation which will play out the tensions between the current and future images and realities of old age. This generation will shift the balance of power a little towards elderly people, if not from some sense of altruism, then on the basis of realistic foreknowledge based on the strong possibility that they too will have to cope with the vicissitudes of old age one day and therefore have an interest in furthering the reconstruction of the images and realities of old age.

FURTHER READING

Hepworth, M. and Featherstone, M. (1982) *Surviving Middle Age*. Basil Blackwell, Oxford.
Featherstone, M. and Hepworth, M. (1989) Ageing and old age: reflections in the postmodern lifecourse. In: Bytheway, B., Keil, T., Allat, P. and Bryan Bryman, A. (eds) *Becoming and Being Old. Sociological Approaches to Later Life*. Sage Publications, London.
Hepworth, M. (1991) Positive ageing and the mask of age. *Journal of Educational Gerontology*, **6**, 2, 93–101.

14

AGEING INTO THE TWENTY-FIRST CENTURY

John Bond and Peter Coleman

Interest in the scientific study of human ageing is unlikely to diminish into the twenty-first century although emphases and foci might change. Throughout this book there has been an attempt to emphasise the normality of human ageing as a balance to the problem-oriented approach of many discussions about ageing. In Chapter 1 we noted that in the twentieth century there have been two dominant themes in social gerontology: demographic change and the role of attitudes. It is unlikely that these themes will disappear. However, we would expect other themes to become stronger. One thing is clear. Social gerontology as an academic discipline will increasingly become multidisciplinary, something which we hope this book has shown.

In this chapter we revisit some of the demographic data and consider some of the implications for the twenty-first century. Major determinants of future demographic patterns are changes in life expectancy and the effects of the physical and social environments, including the effects of medical science. The impact of future demographic patterns on social networks will be mediated by the economic and political structures in the twenty-first century. What will be the social policy response to these trends? This book has provided a rather ethnocentric view of human ageing and the answers to many such questions in the future will depend on social gerontology taking a wider comparative and historical perspective.

DEMOGRAPHIC CHANGES IN THE TWENTY-FIRST CENTURY

The prediction of the demographic structure of society in the twenty-first century is an inexact science. The size and structure of the present population and the distribution of the birth rate over time are important factors affecting the future size and structure of any population.

Birth rates are affected by the proportion of women of childbearing age. In the twentieth century this statistic has varied quite considerably as a result of a decline in mortality, particularly infant mortality, and fluctuations in the birth rate for earlier cohorts of woman of childbearing age. The two world wars each influenced the birth rate. Each war was followed by an increase in the birth rate and subsequent increases, for example, in the mid-1960s and mid-1980s, can be traced to the post-war cohort of female children reaching child-bearing age. Changes in the economic and social structure have mediated this cohort effect. Changes in family size, earlier marriage and many women delaying conception have led to a stabilising of the birth rate in European countries. However, ethnic minorities within countries often have different cultural expectations about childbirth which are reflected in their birth rate distribution. An important influence on the birth rate has been the wider use of birth control but again contraceptive practice is influenced by secular and social expectations within different cultural groups. In some countries political coercion has been applied to limit the birth rate, as in China, or to increase it, as in European Russia.

Once the size of any given birth cohort is known the prediction of the size and structure of the adult population is a relatively straightforward calculation. However, mortality and migration are important influences. In the twentieth century there was a marked improvement in the infant mortality rate such that the largest single cause of death up to the age of 40 was accidents. However, with the emergence of the Human Immunodeficiency Virus (HIV) epidemic it will be increasingly difficult to predict the future size of the adult population because, until the epidemiology of HIV is better understood, we have little idea about the prevalence of mortality from Acquired Immune Deficiency Syndrome (AIDS) into the twenty-first century. Similarly, changes in the smoking and dietary habits of men and women may have a significant effect on mortality in middle age. We just do not know what changes in lifestyle and the environment will occur in the twenty-first century which will influence mortality rates and the subsequent demographic structure of societies.

Migration does not have such an important effect between countries although changes in 1992 to the European Economic Community and the changes in Eastern Europe, particularly in the former Yugoslavia, may influence future cohorts of Europeans in ways which we cannot predict. Within countries migration has an important influence. In the late twentieth century, later-life migration between areas of a country has been estimated in Chapter 9 to be about 10 per cent of elderly people. However, as we have seen, a disproportionate number of elderly migrants move to a few relatively distinct areas. In the United Kingdom movement from urban environments to coastal and rural retirement centres has made the projection of population sizes very difficult for local planners.

However, these uncertainties should not prevent attempts to project the structure of future populations, since the planning of health, welfare and social security provision could not be undertaken without these

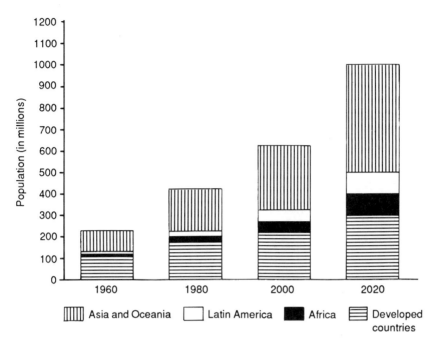

Figure 14.1 *Population aged 60 years or over, by major world regions, 1960–2020*
Source: World Health Organization (1989), Figure 1

data. In Chapter 1 we reported the marked increase in the population of elderly people in the twentieth century. Projections beyond thirty years ahead are not usually published.

In the first twenty years of the twenty-first century the number of people aged 60 or over throughout the world is expected to increase from some 600 million to over 1000 million (WHO, 1989) and as Figure 14.1 shows the increase in Third World countries is expected to be much more marked than in Europe and North America, due mainly to the significant improvement in infant mortality in the last thirty years. However, the effect of premature mortality from AIDS in Africa and Asia, where the incidence of AIDS-related deaths is reaching pandemic proportions, has not been included in the estimates. A whole generation of people currently aged 15–44 are affected by HIV infection, which implies a marked decline in the population of older people from 2020 onwards in the affected areas.

Estimates of the size of the elderly population for the United Kingdom indicate that within this broad age group there will be differential changes among age bands. Figure 14.2 shows the population projections for people aged 65 or over in the United Kingdom for the years 1989–2059. The most significant feature is the increase in the numbers of people of very advanced age. Although a substantial majority of these

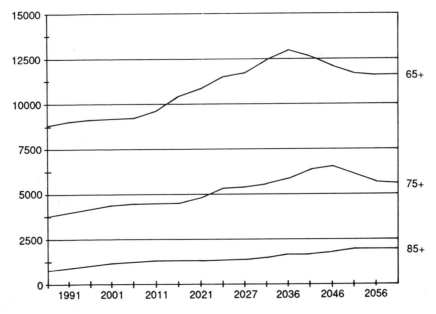

Figure 14.2   *Projected population of elderly people (in millions) in the UK, 1989–2059*
Source: Office of Population Censuses and Surveys (1991b)

will be women the projections for the future suggest that the current preponderance of women may slightly fall in the twenty-first century (Alderson, 1988).

INCREASING LIFE EXPECTANCY

Perhaps one of the most intriguing prospects in the twenty-first century is the possibility of increasing life expectancy. It is unlikely that medical science will play a major role, since as in the twentieth century it is likely to be the environment and lifestyles of individuals which have the greatest impact on longevity (McKeown, 1979). However, we would expect medical science to have an important role in increasing the quality of life of elderly people. The difficulty we face is in predicting what will be the hip replacement of the twenty-first century.

What evidence exists to suggest that life expectancy will increase during the next century? Current theories of human ageing predict that life expectancy is unlikely to increase much beyond present levels. Two explanations have been proposed (see Chapter 2). The first suggests that the limitation of lifespan is due to the cellular processes of senescence and the second suggests that there is increased societal risk of mortality from chronic disease.

Four types of evidence have been put forward to support the view

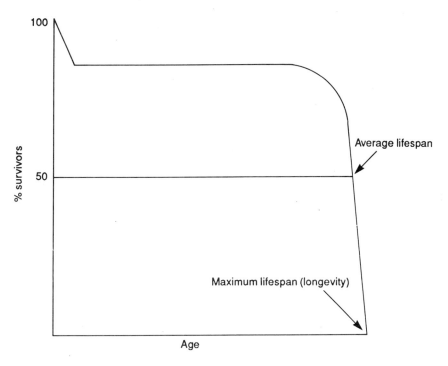

Figure 14.3   *Rectangular survival curve*

that senescence will soon limit life expectancy. First, historically, the maximum human lifespan has not been observed to change except in populations where age documentation is poor and literacy rates are low. Secondly, the risk of death seems to increase as an exponential function of age. Thirdly, standard actuarial computations indicate that the elimination of cancer and heart disease would increase average life expectancy only minimally. Finally, there is experimental evidence which suggests that certain human cells are internally programmed for only a limited number of reproductions (Manton, 1982).

   Within this school of thought there exist two different views on the expected changes in morbidity and mortality patterns. The optimistic view, illustrated by Fries and Crapo's rectangular curve (see Figure 14.3), sees the possibility of postponing the onset of chronic disease (Fries and Crapo, 1981). However, British and American data do not support this view (Isaacs et al, 1971; Manton, 1982). In contrast, the pessimistic view suggests that chronic illness and disability will increase as life expectancy is increased. Data from Northern Ireland on the prevalence of terminal dependency lends some support to this view (Stout and Crawford, 1988). However, an analysis of American data suggested that although more people were surviving to an advanced age there was little evidence to suggest that elderly people were more disabled than earlier cohorts (Manton, 1982).

Manton (1982) has also suggested that longitudinal ageing changes the age trajectory of mortality risks such that mortality reductions extend the productive lifespan of individuals, not by eliminating chronic disease, but by reducing its severity at any given age. The implication of these data for the twenty-first century is that the lifespan can be extended by controlling chronic diseases and there is increasing belief that the process of ageing may itself be controlled. The implication of this analysis is that medical science should increasingly turn its attention to identifying ways of preventing ill health and maintaining health in elderly people. If life expectancy is to increase in the next century individuals and society will need to control the consumption of tobacco and alcohol, improve diets, encourage healthier and more active lifestyles, and change the way societies are organised in order to eradicate environmental pollution.

PSYCHOLOGICAL CHANGE

As we have stressed before, biological decline is only one part of human ageing. Whether or not this seemingly programmed process can be manipulated, the prospects for enhancing psychological and social ageing remain vastly more significant. But our thinking on the subject remains confused. Birren and Schroots (1984) have pointed to the need for separate concepts to delineate the different processes referred to by the ambiguous term 'ageing'. As it is, the outdated metaphors and negative stereotypes that surround the concept are a hindrance to creative thinking about the possibilities for later life.

Three terms have been proposed to encompass biological, sociological and psychological ageing: 'senescence', the process of increasing probability of dying with age; 'eldering', the process of acquiring social roles and behaviours appropriate to older age groups; and 'geronting', the self-regulation we exercise over our lives as we age (Birren and Schroots, 1984). To have a proper perspective on ageing, we need to be able to envisage an overall model that allows some processes to decline, while others stay the same and indeed some may improve.

One of the major achievements of modern studies of ageing has been to demonstrate that most of the decline in psychological functioning with age is not an inevitable product of age. That might sound a rather dull conclusion, but society has still not caught up with its implications. An underlying fault is the failure to appreciate the significance of the enormous differences in the ways people age. Previous studies had tended to hide these discrepancies by the use of measures of average tendencies which consequently presented pictures of uniform decline.

Rowe and Kahn (1987) have highlighted a distinction between what they call 'usual' ageing and 'successful' ageing. In 'usual' ageing extrinsic factors heighten the effects of biological senescence, whereas in 'successful' ageing extrinsic factors play a neutral or positive role. They cite the examples already referred to in Chapters 2 and 4 which demonstrate the stability of cognitive performance for many individuals who have been followed throughout the latter part of their lives. Indeed, in studies where comparisons have been made between people of equal education, 'age effects' become insignificant. They also refer to the studies discussed in Chapter 5 which show the influence of autonomy (control) and social support (connectedness) on behaviour and subjective well-being, as well as on physiological indicators.

We can go further to postulate that much of the emotional disturbance and health deterioration observed in elderly people is due to the failures of modern society to satisfy such needs for autonomy and for relationships. We may have created the improved material conditions to allow people to live longer, but the psychological and social conditions in old age may be much inferior to those in traditional societies. In the future we can expect psychological research to go further along this path and focus more on the variables that can maintain or increase performance throughout life. Greater sophistication in concepts is required, for example in distinguishing autonomy-enhancing and autonomy-reducing modes of support. Such distinctions are commonplace in the study of child development but not yet in the study of ageing.

Not all psychological disturbance in later life, of course, can be attributed to the character of society. Individuals become locked into unsatisfactory situations, in their relationships with others and in the circumstances of their lives, which lead eventually to psychological decline and physical illness. Many would benefit by greater access to possibilities for counselling throughout life. At present, stereotypes about older people's inability to change their ways of thinking, feeling and acting, as well as practical considerations of availability of help and its financing, stand in the way.

But at least we can envisage gerontology growing into a more truly liberating subject, less concerned with charting decline and predicting outcomes, and more with outlining possibilities to enable people to make better choices about their lives. We can expect the present theoretical barrenness of thinking about age – illuminated by a few idealistic models of successful ageing, such as Erikson's (1950) concept of integrity – to be superseded by many other ways of thinking about ageing. Ageing itself will come to be seen as a creative enterprise.

Issues of maintaining and finding meaning, and the appreciation of the characteristic achievements of a long life, such as wisdom, will most likely play prominent roles in this venture (Reker and Wong, 1988). It is significant that the growth of ideas about possible ways of living open to older people has been accompanied by a greater readiness to accept the notion that old age itself has acquired certain special abilities in the process of evolution (Birren, 1988). It might appear paradoxical at first sight, but not on deeper consideration, that ideas on genetic determination and individual emancipation can go hand in hand.

We cannot judge where such developments will lead us. If we try to concretise a psychological future for old age we are likely to underestimate the impact of changing attitudes. Of all the current extrinsic factors operating in old age, public attitudes remain the most damaging. People's self-conceptions are so much moulded by the attitudes they perceive around them. Negative stereotypes die hard.

For example, Waldman and Avolio (1983) reviewed more than a dozen studies of adult performance in the work place and found little support for deterioration of performance with increasing age. Indeed, many objective measures of job performance showed improvement with age, especially for workers' performance in professional jobs. Nevertheless, supervisors rated older workers slightly worse than younger workers. Image has got in the way of reality.

We can justifiably hope that a more positive view of later life will have just as striking an effect in the contrary direction. Whereas at present a negative view of ageing itself contributes to the actual decline of many people in later life, so we can expect that images of continued potential will themselves facilitate the actualisation of much greater potential in later life.

SOCIAL CHANGE

Students of human ageing have difficulty in not considering the implications of ageing for themselves. A question we often consider is: 'What will social life be like when I'm older?' The pace of social change in the twentieth century has been phenomenal. What was life like before the computer, the motor car, universal piped water and electricity and all the other innovations of the twentieth century? Perhaps it is the science fiction writers of today who would make the better attempt at predicting the future for elderly people. If history tells us anything, the quality of life is unlikely to improve, unless 'the revolution of possibilities and hope' takes place (Maddox, 1985). Social change is likely to occur in a number of areas of elderly people's lives, but particularly in relation to work and leisure and in family and social networks.

Work and leisure

Working life has changed dramatically in the twentieth century. For many men the physical conditions of the work place have improved and the number of hours worked has declined. Particularly in recent decades there has been a movement away from heavy manufacturing jobs toward service jobs. The technological revolution has changed the face of work in innumerable ways. For the majority of women paid work has become a lifelong activity rather than something undertaken prior to marriage or motherhood. Increasingly women have entered the labour market in areas traditionally dominated by men. However, there is still a long way to go before equality in work is achieved.

Leisure time has expanded markedly in recent years and the range of activities available to elderly men and women has increased. A major revolution of the twentieth century was the development of television which has become the number one leisure activity for people of all ages (Smythe and Browne, 1992). People reaching the Third Age in the twenty-first century will have experienced these rapidly changing conditions and their expectations of leisure time activities will reflect these experiences. Whether they are able to participate in leisure activities will depend, as it does today, on the resources they have available.

The age of retirement in the latter part of the twentieth century has steadily declined for many older workers (see Chapter 8). However, it is not inevitable that this decline will continue. As we move into the twenty-first century we are all more likely to change careers and jobs more often than was the experience of our peers in earlier decades. Gone are the days when we are trained for a job for life. The next century may see an emerging pattern in which the statutory retirement age is formally abolished and individuals change jobs successively until they choose to retire. Employment patterns would need to change to accommodate these possibilities by allowing for job sharing on a greater scale and sabbaticals from work for other activities including family life and education. This optimistic view, of course, depends on the equality of opportunity for all and income support being available for those who choose to retire. It is difficult to see what will be the effect of the post-industrial revolution on retirement patterns. We can be sure of one thing. It will be different!

Family life and social networks

Marriage is more popular nowadays than it has ever been. Equally so is divorce (Haskey, 1988). These two social trends will have important implications for social networks in old age. Jerrome in Chapter 10 has already drawn attention to the changing balance of kin and friends in social networks. Historically children have experience of only one or two grandparents. In the future one child might have any number of parents, grandparents and great or even great-great-grandparents. In China where there is a single-child policy this has had detrimental effects in the form of overweight and spoilt children who are uncontrollable at school and at home.

Once the children of the twenty-first century reach adulthood they will still have the opportunity, not available to their peers in the earlier years of the twentieth century, of interacting with grandparents and great-grandparents. However, divorce has been shown to restrict access to grandchildren by grandparents (Hagestad et al, 1984). A significant change in the twenty-first century may therefore be further development in intergenerational relations.

Geographical mobility and changes in family size, however, imply a change in the balance of social networks. We have seen in Chapter 10 the increasing importance of peer networks on old age and how increasingly elderly people spend more time with friends than with kin. In the next century technological innovations may overcome some of the barriers to kin relationships created by geographical mobility.

Technological change

Technology has changed our lives, including the lives of elderly people, in the twentieth century more rapidly than in any other age. Never before has technological change intruded so much into the world of work, family life, leisure, health care, religion and education. As we move into the twenty-first century the pace of technological change is likely to increase and it will be difficult to predict its effects. We are able to predict, however, that people of all age groups will be affected.

Technological change has been reported to have undesirable outcomes: increased stress due to the faster pace of work, the increased obsolescence of older workers, the displacement of older workers, the reduction of face-to-face interaction, and the weakening of family and other social ties (Robinson et al, 1984). Some of the favourable outcomes of technological change have been identified as: the reduction in physical workload, the facilitating of communication, compensation for infirmities, and the increased safety of individuals living alone. Rapid technological advances now make it possible to address realistically some human problems which were unsolvable ten years earlier (Lesnoff-Caravaglia, 1988). Some recent practical applications of technological change which have facilitated independent living for elderly or frail people are portable telephones and personal alarm systems, alterations in lighting and heating controls and the introduction of escalators or lifts into people's homes.

Of increasing concern to gerontologists in the twenty-first century will be ways in which high and low technology can be further developed and utilised to prevent disease, assist health care organisations to deliver health care efficiently, and to foster independence among elderly people who are frail.

SOCIAL JEOPARDY

Norman (1985) has described the triple jeopardy of old age to refer to the position of elderly, black women in British society. All societies are stratified. Gender, ethnicity and age are three dimensions by which people are stratified. In our introduction we argued for not developing individual themes about the effects of gender and ethnicity on old age. We argued that because elderly people as a social group were heterogeneous it would be inappropriate to focus on gender or ethnicity issues. However, ageing in the twenty-first century will be strongly influenced by the pattern of social stratification.

Class   We use class in the Weberian sense that people can be divided into groups on the basis of their relationship to the economic structure of society (Gerth and Mills, 1948). Class is a much stronger predictor of lifestyle than age and we suggest that older people have much more in common with younger people of their own class than they do with elderly people from other classes. There is little evidence in Britain to suggest that the class divisions of modern society have changed in the twentieth century (Goldthorpe, 1980) and it is unlikely that there will be any change in the twenty-first century.

Gender   In Chapter 1 we reported that women have longer life expectancies than men. There are proportionately more women than men in each of the age bands over the age of 65 (see Chapter 1, Table 1.2). The implications of this for women in terms of living arrangements, social networks and poverty have been spelt out in previous chapters. Even though an optimistic view sees women as more economically independent in the twenty-first century this is unlikely to reduce the physical and emotional isolation of elderly women. Hagestad (1986) has suggested that rather than positive discrimination for women, who are the disadvantaged, we should positively discriminate in favour of men in order to redress the imbalance in the sexes. Life in the twenty-first century could be improved for women if we encouraged men to adopt healthier lifestyles in order to improve their life expectancy. Evidence, however, suggests that rather than men adopting the healthier lifestyles of women, women are adopting the unhealthy lifestyles of men. Of course, another solution would be to encourage men to marry older women and women to marry younger men.

Ethnicity   Being members of an ethnic minority implies not only that people belong to a minority culture but that they are disadvantaged by that membership. Whether you are black in Britain, Catholic in Northern Ireland, a guest worker in France or a refugee in Germany, ethnicity will play an important part in how you age. British social gerontology has seriously ignored the question of ethnicity in recent years (Fennell et al, 1988; Blakemore and Boneham, 1993). Not only is poverty disproportionately high among ethnic minorities but the response of the dominant culture has been excessively ethnocentric. In the twenty-first century the response to the ageing of ethnic minorities will need to be flexible and sensitive to the interests and needs of different minority groups.

POLITICAL CHANGE

Social change in the twenty-first century depends not only on technological advance but on political change. In Chapter 1 we highlighted two important themes of social gerontology, namely demography and attitudes. In the last two decades there has been a sustained attempt to reduce high public expenditure which, current political ideology argues, is inconsistent with the efficient operation of capitalism. Estes (1986) has argued that this ideology, in support of advanced industrial capitalism, uses the negative attitudes of society toward elderly people to justify the reduction in public expenditure and at the same time reinforces these negative attitudes by blaming demographic changes for increased public expenditure. We cannot place all the blame for negative attitudes at the door of advanced industrial capitalism because as we have seen negative attitudes toward elderly people have been an enduring feature of many societies.

Political action

One way that elderly people can protect themselves from such ideology is to develop their own group consciousness. However, as we have seen, elderly people are not a homogeneous group, they reflect the diversity of class and social and political interests of the whole of industrial society. It is therefore difficult to envisage how such a diverse group can organise themselves politically to work in their own common interests. Further, within the group of people defined as 'elderly' there are major inequalities between different cohorts. As Walker shows in Chapter 12 the 'young old', perhaps those recently retired, command more resources than those people defined as 'old old' who do not have occupational pensions and whose assets have withered away with inflation. Elderly people also have a relatively weak political base since much political activity originates through employment. Elderly people are difficult to organise politically because they do not generally meet as a group, as do for example, industrial workers, employers or students. Poor health and disability are also barriers to political participation and no formal organisation exists to represent the interests of elderly people within the major political parties. Finally, elderly people are often seen to be conservative by nature and therefore resistant to change. However, the political behaviour of those currently old may reflect experiences at earlier stages of the life cycle. The present cohort of elderly people may feel relatively advantaged, since it was this cohort which lived through two World Wars and an economic depression.

SOCIAL POLICY

If the position of older people in society relative to other groups is to improve then the twenty-first century will have to provide a very different environment for them. Obviously, the first change which will have an impact on the lives of all elderly people must be changes in attitudes. Featherstone and Hepworth in Chapter 13 were not very optimistic. There are some ways that we as individuals can change things. In our dealings with elderly people we can avoid a paternalistic approach by maximising their independence, autonomy, self-respect and dignity. We can interact with them in the way we would like younger people to interact with us when we are older by treating all people as individuals in their own right. We need to encourage elderly people themselves to think positively. However, major changes seem unlikely since, as the political economy of old age has shown, elderly people are not valued within capitalist society. Once people retire from the world of work they have less productive value and so their social status is reduced.

Education

One way in which attitudes might be improved is through education. Most professionals having contact with elderly people have had little or no specialist training for the care of elderly people. Those who have tend to be health professionals whose training has been dominated by the medical model, which focuses on the pathological aspects of ageing rather than normal ageing. Other workers involved with elderly people often tend to be untrained and low paid and have little professional commitment to the care of elderly people. Their attitudes will reflect those of society as portrayed by the media. In developing educational programmes for people involved with elderly people it will be important to examine the stereotypes of old age and to focus on the process of normal human ageing. Human ageing should be taught from a historical, cross-cultural and multidisciplinary perspective.

In the twenty-first century education will not be confined to the first twenty years of life but will increasingly become a life-long process. If we are to improve attitudes it will not be sufficient to educate professional workers and carers. It will be essential for normal human ageing to become a part of a variety of educational curricula starting in schools and colleges of education for the young and moving into all kinds of educational training programmes. Faced with the challenge of eight decades of life for the majority of twenty-first-century travellers young people and adults will need to be continually reminded that the quality of life in later years is a product of a lifetime.

Perhaps the most exciting prospect for elderly people currently reaching the Third Age is the increasing opportunity for education. Distant-learning facilities and the University of the Third Age now make it possible for elderly people to catch up on the missed opportunities of youth and read for a degree. Although this facility currently only reaches a small minority of relatively privileged individuals there is the beginning of a trend toward continuing education for elderly people (Laslett, 1989). More emphasis on developing the skills of all ability levels is required. The work of psychologists has been paramount in highlighting the importance of continuing mental activity in old age, since both physical and mental activity are essential ingredients of a good quality of life in later years.

Incomes and resources

In Chapter 12 Walker highlighted the relative deprivation of elderly people, particularly elderly women. He presented data which showed that about one-third of elderly people live at or below the poverty line in contrast to less than one-fifth of people under pension age and that nearly three out of five older people live in or on the margins of poverty (see p. 281). Clearly, if there is to be a significant improvement in the quality of life for elderly people into the twenty-first century governments will need to plan an equitable and effective social security system. For this goal to be achieved significant changes in retirement and pension policies will be required.

Retirement policies will need to be developed which allow elderly people both access to employment and genuine choice about retirement. However, this will be difficult to achieve in a system which does not have as its primary goal the provision of employment. Thus, the promotion of full employment will be the only effective way of providing real choice to elderly workers. It is difficult to see whether the post-industrial society of the twenty-first century will be equipped to provide full employment unless some of the assumptions of advanced industrial capitalism are modified in order to promote it. Health promotion in the work place and the prevention of occupational disease and disability will be essential if elderly workers are not to be forced to retire before they wish because of ill health or disability. A flexible retirement policy coupled with a minimum pension for both men and women at the age of 60 should provide the opportunity for elderly people to choose when precisely to retire (Walker and Laczko, 1982). Adequate minimum pensions should be provided through the public sector. Public expenditure on social security would need to be increased by a reallocation of public resources. However, current political ideology, which has encouraged the development of private pensions, militates against this happening in practice.

Housing

Poverty and inadequate incomes are often associated with housing deprivation among elderly people and often reflect housing provision in earlier life. But as we saw in Chapter 9, housing deprivation is also the result of paternalistic policies with few appropriate housing options available to elderly people.

Elderly people living in the twenty-first century have a right to enjoy housing which is comfortable and which suits their individual requirements. Future policy should be developed which increases real choices for elderly people and because the costs of home ownership are relatively high for elderly people, opportunities should be available throughout the life cycle to enable people to change tenure status. Policies are also necessary to secure the upkeep of owner-occupied property through home maintenance schemes. But in developing a housing policy for elderly people it is essential that trends toward segregated living arrangements or ghettos for elderly people should be avoided by planning for mixed housing types catering for all age groups and needs within a local community.

Institutionalised ageism and intergenerational relations

In Chapter 1 we emphasised the importance of social attitudes towards elderly people as the key to understanding the social context of later life. We suggested that the biological model of ageing has been used to justify common perceptions of later life: disability, senility, powerlessness and loneliness. In Chapter 13 Featherstone and Hepworth from a historical perspective highlight how negative attitudes towards later life are not only a feature of the twentieth century. The images of later life in pre-industrial and industrial society do not suggest a tradition of interest in growing old or an optimistic prospect for later life. They do, however, highlight the diversity of images held about later life and the discrepancy between our own experiences of individual elderly people and society's enduring stereotypes.

Our changing images of elderly people in the twentieth century although securely locked into history have been particularly influenced by modernity and the value systems of a modern consumer culture. We emphasise youthfulness and the energy of youth. The processes of modernisation and technological innovation render the skills and knowledge of older generations redundant. As a society we invest in youth, 'our future', rather than in the retraining and education of people in later life. Older workers are encouraged to take early retirement rather than investing in their retraining. As a result of this increased social change, we have all become increasingly age conscious. The stereotypical age categories handed down from pre-industrial and industrial society have been expanded by experts such as medical scientists, economists and management consultants, among others, to underpin the age-stratified society and reinforce ageism.

In most European countries people who are economically inactive are devalued and considered irrelevant to the production process. They are perceived as a burden since they are not part of the modern economy. Yet they remain an important part of the social economy. Not just as consumers, in which people in later life play a major part, but as

providers of social goods such as historical knowledge or companionship.

Ageism, the negative stereotyping of individuals on the basis of age,
is institutionalised in the UK and other European societies. Elderly
people are denied certain citizenship rights and have limited access to
social, political and economic power. Ageist attitudes are expressed in
the behaviour of personal social services and health service staff who
treat patients and clients as dependent children through invoking
cultural metaphors of childhood (Hazan, 1980; Hockey and James,
1990). Practices such as infantilisation at one level may be regarded as
being an unfortunate but inevitable response to human dependency. On
another level, however, the metaphoric strategies of ageism can be seen
as one means of creating and maintaining the powerful social divisions
between them, the aged and infirm, and us the younger and abler
members of society.

One way that institutionalised ageism has affected thinking is in
relation to the expectation of intergenerational conflict (Thane, 1988;
Johnson, Conrad and Thomson, 1989). In the United States this view
has been popularised by organizations such as Americans for Generational Equity (AGE) as the 'elderly emptying the coffers of the welfare
state and creating a tax burden beyond the means of the labor force to
support' (Katz, 1992, p. 203). Phillipson (1991b) has summarised the key
points in the British version of this view. Proponents argue that older
people in the UK have been active in designing a welfare state which
works largely for their own benefit. Younger people now perceive this to
be the case and are beginning to act as a generational group in opposing
inequities in welfare resources. Proponents suggest that the increasing
numbers of elderly people will generate instability within the system
and that the relative prosperity of elderly people in comparison with
younger households undermines their rights to extensive welfare
benefits.

Is intergenerational conflict likely in the twenty-first century? Critical
gerontologists and political economists provide counter arguments
which suggest that intergenerational conflict is not inevitable (Phillipson, 1991b; Katz, 1992). Elderly people form a heterogeneous group and
if they indeed have been acting with self-interest it would be a rare
example of an interest group forming an institution which actually
entails a drop in their economic and social status. There is little evidence
that older people are better off (see Chapter 12). The evidence suggests
that it is middle-aged people who are generally better off than either
'younger' or 'older' households.

Attitudes toward the welfare state remain as positive as ever and the
British Social Attitudes Survey (Cairncross, 1992) highlights the overwhelming support among all age groups for the policy of providing
health and welfare support to elderly people. Where elderly people have
the resources there is considerable evidence to suggest that the younger

generations are in receipt of financial assistance from older members of their families (Finch, 1989). As with elderly people, the younger generations are a heterogeneous group and there is little likelihood of them working together in political opposition to people from older generations.

The burden of ageing thesis is often promulgated by those whose objective is the reduction in the public provision of welfare. One way of estimating this 'burden' is to calculate the proportion of people who could be economically active to those who are 'retired' or still in 'education'. Thus with a shift in the distribution of the population there has been an increase in the proportion of the 'dependent' population. Phillipson (1991b) compares the ratio of United Kingdom National Insurance contributors to pensioners, and shows that the ratio declines fairly slowly into the next century. It is not for thirty or forty years that a significant decline is expected. Major economic, social and political changes may take place before then which will have a much greater influence on the balance of resources between the generations. Elderly people also provide important services for society that do not appear in the costs and benefits balance sheet of proponents of the 'burden' thesis.

Without political will and sustained social pressure it will be extremely difficult to eradicate institutionalised ageism. We will need more than just statutory legislation like the Race Relations Act before overcoming its effects. Importantly, society will need to provide more resources in the form of increased pensions, better access to high-quality housing and increased community and residential services. With competition from other public services for scarce resources the likelihood of making an impact on ageism at the macro level seems remote.

At the micro level, however, there are opportunities to have a substantial impact on ageism. Through education and example professionals and other care workers could change their attitudes and approach to elderly people. This change would not come about overnight and would need the sustained effort of all those on a day-to-day basis in our interactions with clients. Managers should take the lead in formal organisations and identify a target to rid the organisation of all features of ageism. A lot can be done without the use of financial resources.

TOWARDS THE TWENTY-FIRST CENTURY

The quality of life for elderly people in the next century will depend on a number of fundamental changes in the way that societies perceive and respond to human ageing. In this concluding chapter we have tried to identify the most crucial ones. Needless to say we have been selective in our choice. If we were to focus on just one theme it would be the theme of promoting positive attitudes. So much change could be realised if attitudes toward normal ageing and elderly people and elderly people's attitudes toward themselves were improved. However, it would be difficult to change attitudes without making some inroad into the policies advocated above.

This book is about widening the understanding of human ageing. In bringing together a number of authors of different disciplines we have identified a number of perspectives both theoretical and practical. These should be seen as complementary. However, this final chapter is somewhat speculative since we do not know what the future has on offer for us. Ecological changes may be of greater significance to all human societies in the twenty-first century than medical advances, psychological, political or social change. Those of us who are young enough will be able to see how correct we have been.

REFERENCES

Abdela, L. (1991) *Breaking Through the Glass Ceilings: A Practical Guide to Equality at Work for Women and Men*. METRA, Solihull.

Abrams, M. (1978) *Beyond Three-Score and Ten: A First Report on a Survey of the Elderly*. Age Concern Research Unit, Mitcham, Surrey.

Abrams, M. (1980a) *Beyond Three-Score and Ten: A Second Report on a Survey of the Elderly*. Age Concern Research Unit, Mitcham, Surrey.

Abrams, M. (1980b) Transitions in middle and later life. In: Johnson, M.J. (ed.) *Transitions in Middle and Later Life*. British Society for Gerontology, London.

Abrams, M. (not dated) *People in their Late Sixties: A Longitudinal Survey of Ageing. Survivors and Non-survivors, Part I*. Age Concern Research Unit, Mitcham, Surrey.

Abrams, P. (1978) *Community Care: Some Research Problems and Priorities*. Social Care Research, London, pp. 78–99.

Abrams, P.S., Abrams, R., Humphrey, R. and Snaith, R. (1989) *Neighbourhood Care and Social Policy*. HMSO, London.

Achenbaum, W.A. (1978a) Essay: old age and modernisation. *The Gerontologist*, **18**, 307–312.

Achenbaum, W.A. (1978b) *Old Age in the New Land: The American Experiences Since 1790*. Johns Hopkins University Press, Baltimore and London.

Ade-Ridder, L. and Brubaker, T. (1983) The quality of long-term marriage. In: Brubaker, T.H. (ed.) *Family Relationships in Later Life*. Sage, California, pp. 21–30.

Age Concern (1991) *Dis-continuing Care. Report of a Survey of District Health Authority Plans for Continuing Care of Elderly People*. Age Concern England, London.

Akhtar, A.J., Broe, G.A., Crombie, C., McLean, W.M.R., Andrews, G.R. and Caird, F.I. (1973) Disability and dependence in the elderly at home. *Age and Ageing*, **2**, 102–111.

Alderson, M. (1988) Demographic and health trends in the elderly. In: Wells, N. and Freer, C. (eds), *The Ageing Population. Burden or Challenge?* Macmillan, Basingstoke, pp. 87–102.

Aldous, J., Klaus, E. and Klein, D. (1985) The understanding heart: aging parents and their favourite children'. *Child Development*, **56**, 303–316.

Alexander, B.B., Rubinstein, R.L., Goodman, M. and Luborsky, M. (1991) Generativity in cultural context: the self, death and immortality as experienced by older American women. *Ageing and Society*, **11**, 417–442.

Allan, G. (1986) Friendship and care for elderly people. *Ageing and Society*, **6**, 1–12.

Allen, I. (1983) The elderly and their informal carers. In: DHSS (ed.) *Elderly People in the Community – Their Service Needs*. HMSO, London, pp. 70–92.

Allen, I., Hogg, D. and Peace, S. (1992) *Elderly People: Choice, Participation and Satisfaction*. Policy Studies Institute, London.

Allen, K. (1989) *Single Women/Family Ties*. Sage, Beverly Hills.

Allon-Smith, R.D. (1982) The evolving geography of the elderly in England. In: Warnes, A.M. (ed.) *Geographical Perspectives on the Elderly*. Wiley, London, pp. 35–52.

Altergott, K. (1985) Marriage, gender and social relations in later life. In: Peterson, W. and Quadagno, J. (eds) *Social Bonds in Later Life*. Sage, California, pp. 51–70.

Amos, G. (ed.) (1980) *Home from Hospital – To What?* Community Care Project, Birmingham.

Anderson, M. (1971) Family, household and the industrial revolution. In: Anderson, M. (ed.) *The Family*. Penguin, London, pp. 78–96.

Anderson, R. and Cartwright, A. (1986) The use of medicine by older people. In: Dean, K., Hickey, T. and Holstein, B.E. (eds) *Self-care and Health in Old Age. Health Behaviour. Implications for Policy and Practice.* Croom Helm, London, pp. 167–203.

Anderson, W.F. and Cowan, N. (1956) Work and retirement: influences on the health of older men. *The Lancet*, **ii**, 1344–1347.

Antonovsky, A. (1979) *Health, Stress and Coping.* Jossey-Bass, London.

Arber, S. and Ginn, J. (1991) *Gender and Later Life.* Sage, London.

Arber, S. and Ginn, J. (1992) Research Note. Class and caring: a forgotten dimension. *Sociology*, **26**, 4, 619–634.

Archer, J.L. (1982) Discovering a philosophy for working with the elderly mentally infirm. *Social Work Service* (Department of Health and Social Security), Summer 1982, 43–49.

Archer, J. (1989) Childhood gender roles: structure and development. *The Psychologist*, Sept. 1989, **9**, 367–370.

Ariès, P. (1981) *The Hour of Our Death.* Penguin, Harmondsworth.

Armstrong, D. (1983) *Political Anatomy of the Body: Medical Knowledge in Britain in the Twentieth Century.* Cambridge University Press, Cambridge.

Armstrong, D. (1987) Silence and truth in death and dying. *Social Science and Medicine*, **24**, 8.

Atchley, R. (1971) Retirement and leisure participation. *The Gerontologist*, **11**, 13–17.

Atchley, R. (1976) Selected social and psychological differences between men and women in later life. *Journal of Gerontology*, **31**, 204–211.

Atherton, J.S. (1989) *Interpreting Residential Life: Values to Practice.* Tavistock/Routledge, London.

Atkinson, A.B. and Rein, M. (eds) (1993) *Age, Work and Social Security.* Macmillan, London.

Atkinson, D.A., Bond, J. and Gregson, B.A. (1986) The dependency characteristics of older people in long-term institutional care. In: Phillipson, C., Bernard, M. and Strang, P. (eds) *Dependency and Interdependency in Old Age – Theoretical Perspectives and Policy Alternatives.* Croom Helm, London, pp. 257–269.

Audit Commission (1992) *The Community Revolution: Personal Social Services and Community Care.* HMSO, London.

Auer, J. (1987) Psychological aspects of elderly dialysis patients. In: Monkhouse, P. and Stevens, E. (eds) *Aspects of Renal Care 1.* Baillière Tindall, London.

Baars, J. (1991) The challenge of critical gerontology: the problem of social constitution. *Journal of Aging Studies*, **5**, 3, 219–243.

Baker, D.E. (1978) Attitudes of Nurses to the Care of the Elderly. Unpublished PhD Thesis, University of Manchester.

Baldwin, S. and Cooke, K. (1984) *How Much is Enough?* Family Policy Studies Centre, London.

Baltes, M.M. and Baltes, P.B. (eds) (1986) *The Psychology of Control and Aging.* Lawrence Erlbaum Associates, Hillsdale, NJ.

Baltes, P.B. and Baltes, M.M. (1990) Psychological perspectives on successful aging: the model of selective optimization with compensation. In: Baltes, P.B. and Baltes, M.M. (eds) *Successful Aging: Perspectives from the Behavioral Sciences.* Cambridge University Press, New York, pp. 1–34.

Baltes, P.B., Reese, H.W. and Lipsitt, L.P. (1980) Life-span developmental psychology. *Annual Review of Psychology*, **31**, 65–110.

Baltes, P.B., Reese, H.W. and Nesselroade, J. R. (1977) *Life-span Developmental Psychology: Introduction to Research Methods.* Wadsworth, Belmont, CA.

Baltes, P.B., Smith, J. and Staudinger, U.M. (1992) Wisdom and successful aging. In: Sonderegg, T.B. (ed.) Nebraska Symposium on Motivation, **39**, 123–167. University of Nebraska Press, Lincoln, Nebraska.

Bankoff, E. (1981) Effects of friendship support on the psychological well-being of widows. In: Lopata, H. and Maines, D. (eds) *Research in the Interweave of Social Roles: Friendship, Vol. 2.* JAI Press Inc., Greenwich, CT, pp. 109–139.

Barker, J. (1984) *Black and Asian Old People in Britain* Age Concern England, London.

Barrow, G.M. (1986) *Ageing, the Individual and Society*, 3rd edition. West Publishing Co., St Paul, NY.

Barrowclough, C. and Fleming, I. (1986) *Goal Planning with Elderly People. Making Plans to Meet Individual Needs. A Manual of Instruction*. Manchester University Press, Manchester.

Barsby, S.L. and Cox, D.R. (1975) *Interstate Migration of the Elderly*. Heath-Lexington, Toronto.

Bass, D.M. and Bowman, K.M. (1990) The transition from caregiving to bereavement: the relationship of care-related strain and adjustment to death. *The Gerontologist*, **30**, 1.

Batchelor, L.R.C. and Napier, M.B. (1953) Attempted suicide in old age. *British Medical Journal*, **2**, 1186–1190.

Baumrin, B. (1991) Putting them out on ice: curtailing care of the elderly. *Journal of Applied Philosophy* **8**, 2, 155–160.

Bayley, M. (1973) *Mental Handicap and Community Care: A Study of Mentally Handicapped People in Sheffield*. Routledge and Kegan Paul, London.

Becker, E. (1973) *The Denial of Death*. Free Press, New York.

Becker, H.S. (1963) *Outsiders. Studies in the Sociology of Deviance*. Free Press, New York.

Bell, C. and Newby, H. (1971) *Community Studies. An Introduction to the Sociology of the Local Community*. George Allen and Unwin, London.

Bengtson, V.L. (1979) Ethnicity and ageing: problems and issues in current social science inquiry. In: Gelfand, D.E. and Kutzik, A.J. (eds) *Ethnicity and Ageing Theory, Research and Policy*. Springer, New York, pp. 9–31.

Bengtson, V.L. (1986) Ageing, families and socio-cultural change. Unpublished paper presented to King's College Institute of Gerontology, London, March.

Bengtson, V.L. (1987) Parenting, grandparenting and intergenerational continuity. In: Lancaster, J. et al (eds) *Parenting Across the Lifespan*. Aldine de Gruyter, Berlin and New York, pp. 435–456.

Bengtson, V.L. and Kuypers, J. (1985) The family support cycle. In: Munnichs, J., Mussen, P., Olbrich, E. and Coleman, P. (eds) *Lifespan and Change in a Gerontological Perspective*. Academic Press, California, pp. 257–274.

Bengtson, V.L., Cuellar, J.B. and Ragan, P.K. (1977) Stratum contrasts and similarities in attitudes towards death. *Journal of Gerontology*, **32**, 76–88.

Berdes, C. (1978) *Social Services for the Aged Dying and Bereaved in International Perspective*. International Federation on Ageing, Washington, DC.

Berger, P.L. and Berger, B. (1976) *Sociology: A Biographical Approach*. Penguin, Harmondsworth.

Bergin, A.E. (1983) Religiosity and mental health: a critical re-evaluation and meta-analysis. *Professional Psychology: Research and Practice*, **14**, 170–184.

Berkeley, J.S. (1976) Reasons for referral to hospital. *Journal of the Royal College of General Practitioners*, **26**, 293–296.

Berkman, L.P. and Syme, S. (1979) Social network, host resistance and mortality. *American Journal of Epidemiology*, **100**, 186–204.

Bernard, J. (1976) Homosociality and female depression. *Journal of Social Issues*, **32**, 4, 213–238.

Bernard, M. and Meade, K. (1993) *Women Come of Age: Understanding the Lives of Older Women*. Edward Arnold, London.

Berthoud, R. (1984) *The Reform of Supplementary Benefit*, Working Papers. Policy Studies Institute, London.

Beveridge, Sir W. (1942) *Social Insurance and Allied Services*, Cmnd. 6404. HMSO, London.

Bhalla, A. and Blakemore, K. (1981) *Elders of the Ethnic Minority Groups*. AFFOR, Birmingham.

Birren, J.E. (1988) A contribution to the theory of the psychology of aging: as a counterpart of development. In: Birren, J.E. and Bengtson, V.L. (eds) *Emergent Theories of Ageing*. Springer, New York, pp. 153–176.

Birren, J.E. and Schroots, G.F. (1984) Steps to an ontogenetic psychology. *Academic Psychology Bulletin*, **6**, 177–190.

Birren, J.E., Butler, R.N., Greenhouse, S.W., Sokoloff, L. and Yarrow, M.R. (eds.) (1963) *Human Aging: A Biological and Behavioral Study*. Publication No. (HSM) 71–9051. US Government Printing Office, Washington, DC.

Birren, J.E., Woods, A.M. and Williams, M.V. (1979) Speed of behaviour as an indicator of age changes and the integrity of the nervous system. In: Hoffmeister, F. and Muller, C. (eds) *Brain Function in Old Age*. Springer-Verlag, Berlin.

Blaikie, A. (1990) The emerging political power of the elderly in Britain, 1908–1948. *Ageing in Society*, **10**, 1, 17–39.

Blaikie, A. and MacNicol, J. (1989) Ageing and social policy: a twentieth-century dilemma. In: Warnes, A. (ed.) *Human Ageing and Later Life: Multidisciplinary Perspectives*. Edward Arnold, London, pp. 69–82.

Blakemore, K. (1982) Health and illness among the elderly of minority ethnic groups living in Birmingham: some new findings. *Health Trends*, **14**, 69–72.

Blakemore, K. (1983a) Ethnicity, self-reported illness, and use of medical services by the elderly. *Postgraduate Medical Journal*, **59**, 668–70.

Blakemore, K. (1983b) Ageing in the inner city: a comparison of old blacks and whites. In: Jerrome, D. (ed.) *Ageing in Modern Society*. Croom Helm, London, pp. 81–103.

Blakemore, K. (1989) Does age matter? The case of old age in minority ethnic groups. In: Bytheway, B. et al (eds) *Becoming and Being Old*. Sage, London, pp. 158–175.

Blakemore, K. (1993) Ageing and ethnicity. In: Johnson, J. and Slater, R. (eds) *Ageing and Late Life*. Sage, London.

Blakemore, K. and Boneham, M. (1993) *Age, Race and Ethnicity in Britain*. Open University Press, Milton Keynes.

Blau, P. (1964) *Exchange and Power in Social Life*. Wiley, New York.

Blau, Z. (1973) *Old Age in a Changing Society*. Franklin Watts, New York.

Blauner, R. (1966) Death and social structure. *Psychiatry*, **29**, 378–394.

Blaxter, M. (1990) *Health and Lifestyles*. Routledge, London.

Blum, J.E. and Tross, S. (1980) Psychodynamic treatment of the elderly: a review of issues in theory and practice. In: Eisdorfer, C. (ed.) *Annual Review of Gerontology and Geriatrics*, **1**, 204–234.

Blumer, H. (1969) *Symbolic Interactionism: Perspective and Method*. Prentice Hall, Englewood Cliffs, NJ.

Boldy, D. (1976) A study of the wardens of grouped dwellings for the elderly. *Social and Economic Administration*, **10**, 59–67.

Boleat, M. (1986) *Housing in Britain*. The Building Societies Association, London.

Bond, J. (1987) Psychiatric illness in later life: a study of prevalence in a Scottish population. *International Journal of Geriatric Psychiatry*, **2**, 39–58.

Bond, J. (1992a) The future of long-term care. In: Young, R. and Higginson, I.J. (eds) *Long-term Care for Elderly People. Purchasing, Providing and Quality*. HMSO, London.

Bond, J. (1992b) The politics of caregiving: the professionalisation of informal support. *Ageing and Society*, **12**, 5–21.

Bond, J. and Bond, S. (1987) Developments in the provision and evaluation of long-term care for dependent old people. In: Fielding, P. (ed.) *Research in the Nursing Care of Elderly People*. Wiley, Chichester, pp. 47–85.

Bond, J. and Bond, S. (1994) *Sociology and Health Care. An Introduction for Nurses and other Health Care Professionals*, 2nd edition. Churchill Livingstone, Edinburgh.

Bond, J. and Carstairs, V. (1982) *Services for the Elderly: A Survey of the Characteristics and Needs of a Population of 5,000 Old People*, Scottish Health Service Studies No. 42. Scottish Home and Health Department, Edinburgh.

Bond, J., Atkinson, A., Gregson, B., Hughes, P. and Jeffries, L. (1989a) *Evaluation of Continuing–care Accommodation for Elderly People. Report No. 38. Vol. 4. The 1984 and 1987 Surveys of Continuing-care Institutions in Six Health Authorities*. Health Care Research Unit, University of Newcastle upon Tyne.

Bond, J., Gregson, B., Atkinson A. and Hally, M.R. (1989b) *Evaluation of Continuing-care Accommodation for Elderly People. Report No. 38. Vol. 2. The Randomised Controlled Trial of the*

Experimental NHS Nursing Homes and Conventional Continuing-care Wards in NHS Hospitals. Health Care Research Unit, University of Newcastle upon Tyne.

Bond, J., Bond, S., Donaldson, C., Gregson, B. and Atkinson, A. (1989c) *Evaluation of Continuing-care Accommodation for Elderly People. Report No. 38. Vol. 7. Overview of an Evaluation of Continuing-care Accommodation for Elderly People.* Health Care Research Unit, University of Newcastle upon Tyne.

Bond, S. and Bond, J. (1994) *Nursing Frail Elderly People.* Age Concern, London.

Bone, M., Gregory, J., Gill, B. and Lader, D. (1992) *Retirement and Retirement Plans.* HMSO, London.

Booth, C. (1889) *Life and Labour of the People in London.* Macmillan, London.

Booth, C. (1892) *Pauperism: A Picture; and the Endowment of Old Age; An Argument.* Macmillan, London.

Booth, C. (1894) *The Aged Poor: Condition.* Macmillan, London.

Booth, T. (1985) *Home Truths: Old People's Homes and the Outcome of Care.* Gower, Aldershot.

Booth, T. and Phillips, D. (1987) Group living in homes for the elderly. A comparative study of outcomes of care. *British Journal of Social Work,* **17,** 1–20.

Bornat, J., Phillipson, C. and Ward, S. (1985) *A Manifesto for Old Age.* Pluto Books, London.

Bosanquet, N. (1978) *A Future for Old Age.* Temple Smith/New Society, London.

Bottomore, T.B. and Rubel, M. (eds) (1965) *Karl Marx: Selected Writings in Sociology and Social Philosophy.* Penguin, Harmondsworth.

Botwinick, J. (1984) *Aging and Behavior: A Comprehensive Integration of Research Findings,* 2nd edition. Springer, New York.

Botwinick, J. and Storandt, M. (1980) Recall and recognition of old information in relation to age and sex. *Journal of Gerontology,* **35,** 70–76.

Bowlby, J. (1965) *Child Care and the Growth of Love,* 2nd edition. Penguin, Harmondsworth.

Bowlby, J. (1969) *Attachment and Loss Vol. 1: Attachment.* Hogarth, London.

Bowlby, J. (1973), *Attachment and Loss Vol. 2: Separation: Anxiety and Anger.* Hogarth, London.

Bowlby, J. (1980) *Attachment and Loss Vol. 3: Loss: Sadness and Depression.* Hogarth, London.

Bowles, N.L. and Poon, L.W. (1982) An analysis of the effect of aging on recognition memory. *Journal of Gerontology,* **37,** 212–219.

Bowling, A. and Cartwright, A. (1982) *Life After a Death: A Study of the Elderly Widowed.* Tavistock, London.

Bradshaw, J. and O'Higgins, M. (1984) *Equity, Income Equality and the Life Cycle: An Analysis for 1971, 1976 and 1982.* University of York, mimeo.

Braithwaite, V.A. and Gibson, D.M. (1987) Adjustment to retirement: what we know and what we need to know. *Ageing and Society,* **7,** 1–18.

Braverman, H. (1974) *Labour and Monopoly Capital: The Degradation of Work in the Twentieth Century.* Monthly Review Press, New York.

Brayne, C. and Ames, D. (1988) The epidemiology of mental disorder in old age. In: Gearing, B., Johnson, M.L. and Heller, T. (eds) *Mental Health Problems in Old Age.* Wiley, Chichester, pp. 10–26.

Briggs, R. (1985) Acute confusion. In: Lye, M. (ed.) *Acute Geriatric Medicine.* MTP Press, Lancaster, pp. 113–134.

Brink, T.L. (1979) *Geriatric Psychotherapy.* Human Sciences Press, New York.

Brocklehurst, J.C. (ed.) (1975) *Geriatric Care in Advanced Societies.* MTP Press, Lancaster.

Brocklehurst, J.C. (1978) Geriatric services and the day hospital. In: Brocklehurst, J.C. (ed.) *Text Book of Geriatric Medicine and Gerontology,* 2nd edition. Churchill Livingstone, Edinburgh, pp. 747–762.

Brody, E. (1979) Aged parents and aging children. In: Ragan, P.K. (ed.) *Aging Parents.* University of California Press, Berkeley, pp. 267–287.

Brody, J.A. (1985) Prospects for an ageing population. *Nature,* **315,** 463–466.

Bromley, D.B. (1977) Speculations in social and environmental gerontology. In: Carver, V. and Liddiard, P. (eds) *An Ageing Population: A Reader and Sourcebook.* Hodder and Stoughton/The Open University Press, Sevenoaks, pp. 50–57.

Bromley, D.B. (1978) Approaches to the study of personality changes in adult life and old age. In: Isaacs, A.D. and Post, F. (eds) *Studies in Geriatric Psychiatry*. Wiley, Chichester, pp. 17–40.

Bromley, D.B. (1986) *The Case-study Method in Psychology and Related Disciplines*. Wiley, Chichester.

Bromley, D.B. (1989) *Behavioural Gerontology*. Wiley, Chichester.

Bromley, D.B. (1990) *Behavioural Gerontology: Central Issues in the Psychology of Ageing*. Wiley, Chichester.

Brown, G.W. and Harris, T. (1978) *Social Origins of Depression: A Study of Psychiatric Disorder in Women*. Tavistock, London.

Brown, G.W., Andrews, B., Harris, T., Adler, Z. and Bridge, L. (1986) Social support, self-esteem and depression. *Psychological Medicine*, **16**, 813–831.

Brown, R.A. (1957) Age and 'paced' work. *Occupational Psychology*, **31**, 11–20.

Brubaker, T. (1983) *Family Relationships in Later Life*. Sage, California.

Brubaker, T. (1985) *Later Life Families*. Sage, California.

Bruning, H. and Hesselink, J.K. (1986) *Omgaan met Sterven*. Zorn, Leiden.

Bulcroft, K. and Bulcroft, R. (1985) Dating and courtship in later life. In: Peterson, W. and Quadagno, J. (eds) *Social Bonds in Later Life*. Sage, California, pp. 115–126.

Bulmer, M. (1986) *Neighbours: The Work of Philip Abrams*. Cambridge University Press, Cambridge.

Burgess, E.W. (1925) The growth of the city: an introduction to a research project. In: Park, R.E., Burgess, E.W. and McKenzie, R.D. (eds) *The City*. University of Chicago Press, Chicago, 1967, pp. 47–62.

Burnside, I. (1975) *Sexuality and Ageing*. Andrus Gerontology Centre, Los Angeles.

Burrow, J.A. (1986) *The Ages of Man: A Study in Medieval Writing and Thought*. Clarendon Press, Oxford.

Burton, L. and Bengtson, V. (1985) Black grandmothers. In: Bengtson, V. and Robertson, J. (eds) *Grandparenthood*. Sage, California, pp. 61–78.

Busse, E.W. (1985) Normal aging: the Duke longitudinal studies. In: Bergener, M., Ermini, M. and Staheline, H.B. (eds) *Thresholds in Aging*. Academic Press, New York, pp. 215–230.

Butler, A. and Tinker, A. (1983) Integration or segregation: housing in later life. In: *Elderly People in the Community: their Service Needs*. HMSO, London.

Butler, A., Oldman, C. and Greve, J. (1983) *Sheltered Housing for the Elderly*. George Allen and Unwin, London.

Butler, R.N. (1963) The Life Review: an interpretation of reminiscence in the aged. *Psychiatry*, **26**, 65–76.

Byrne, D.S., Harrisson, S.P., Keithley, J. and McCarthy, P. (1986) *Housing and Health. The Relationship between Housing Conditions and the Health of Council Tenants*. Gower, London.

Bytheway, W. (1986) Making way: the disengagement of older workers. In: Phillipson, C., Bernard, M. and Strang, P. (eds) *Dependency and Interdependency in Old Age: Theoretical Perspectives and Policy Alternatives*. Croom Helm, London, pp. 315–326.

Bytheway, W. and James, L. (1978) *The Allocation of Sheltered Housing*. University College, Swansea.

Bytheway, W.R. and Johnson, J. (1990) On defining ageism. *Critical Social Policy*, **29**.

Cain, L.D. (1974) The growing importance of legal age in determining the status of the elderly. *The Gerontologist*, **14**, 167–174.

Cairncross, F. (1992) The influence of the recession. In: Jowell, R., Brook, L., Prior, G. and Taylor, B. (eds) *British Social Attitudes. The 9th Report*. Dartmouth Publishing Co., Aldershot.

Callahan, D (1987) *Setting Limits: Medical Goals in An Ageing Society*, Simon and Schuster, New York.

Callahan, E.J., Brasted, W.S. and Granados, J.L. (1983) Fetal loss and sudden infant death: grieving and adjustment for families. In: Callahan, E.J. and McCluskey, K.A. (eds) *Life-*

span *Developmental Psychology: Non-normative Life Events*. Academic Press, New York, pp. 161–182.

Cameron, E., Evers, H., Badger, F and Atkin, K. (1989) Black old women, disability and health carers. In: Jefferys, M. (ed.) *Growing Old in the Twentieth Century*. London: Routledge and Kegan Paul.

Cameron, P., Stewart, L. and Biber, H. (1973) Consciousness of death across the life-span. *Journal of Gerontology*, **28**, 92–95.

Carp, F.M. (1966) *A Future for the Aged, Victoria Plaza and its Residents*. University of Texas Press, Austin.

Carp, F.M. (1968) Person–situation congruence in engagement. *The Gerontologist*, **8**, 184–188.

Carp, F.M. (1969) Senility or garden-variety maladjustment. *Journal of Gerontology*, **24**, 203–208.

Cattell, R. (1971) *Abilities: Their Structure, Growth and Action*. Houghton Mifflin, New York.

Cavan, R.S., Burgess, E.W., Havighurst, R.J. and Goldhammer, H. (1949) *Personal Adjustment in Old Age*. Science Research Associates, Chicago.

Central Statistical Office (1985) *Social Trends 15*. HMSO, London.

Central Statistical Office (1988) *Social Trends 18*. HMSO, London.

Central Statistical Office (1992) *Social Trends 22*. HMSO, London.

Centre for Environmental and Social Studies in Ageing (1986) *Images of Residential Life: A Training Pack for Residential Workers*. CESSA, Polytechnic of North London.

Centre for Environmental and Social Studies in Ageing (1992) *Inside Quality Assurance*. CESSA, University of North London.

Centre for Policy on Ageing (1984) *Home Life: A Code of Practice for Residential Care*. CPA, London.

Challis, D. and Knapp, M. (1980) *An Examination of the PGC Morale Scale in an English Context*, Discussion paper 168. University of Kent at Canterbury, Personal Social Services Research Unit.

Charlesworth, A., Wilkin, D. and Durie, A. (1984) *Carers and Services: A Comparison of Men and Women Caring for Dependent Elderly People*. Equal Opportunities Commission, Manchester.

Cheal, D. (1988) The ritualization of family ties. *American Behavioural Scientist*, **31**, 6, 632–43.

Cherlin, A. and Furstenberg, F. (1985) Styles and strategies of grandparenting. In: Bengtson, V. and Robertson, J. (eds) *Grandparenthood*. Sage, California, pp. 97–116.

Chown, S. (1962) Rigidity and age. In: Tibbitts, C. and Donahue, W. (eds) *Social and Psychological Aspects of Aging*. Columbia University Press, New York.

Chown, S. (1981) Friendship in old age. In: Duck, S. and Gilmour, R. (eds) *Personal Relationships*, Vol. 2. Academic Press, London, pp. 231–246.

Cicirelli, V. (1983) Adult children and their elderly parents. In: Brubaker, T. (ed.) *Family Relationships in Later Life*. Sage, Beverly Hills, pp. 31–46.

Cicirelli, V. (1985) The role of siblings as family caregivers. In: Sauer, W. and Coward, R. (eds) *Social Support Networks and Care of the Elderly*. Springer, New York, pp. 93–107.

Clapham, D. and Munro, M. (1988) *A Comparison of Sheltered Housing and Amenity Housing for Older People*. Scottish Office, Edinburgh.

Clark, K. (1960) *The Nude: A Study of Ideal Art*. John Murray, London.

Clark, M. (1972) Cultural values in later life. In Cowgill, D.O. and Holmes, L.D. (eds) *Aging and Modernisation*. Appleton-Century-Crofts, New York, pp. 263–274.

Clark, M. and Anderson, B. (1967) *Culture and Ageing*. C. Thomas, Illinois.

Clark, P. and Bowling, A. (1989) Observational study of quality of life in NHS nursing homes and a long-stay ward for the elderly. *Ageing and Society*, **9**, 123–148.

Clark, R. and Spengler, J. (1980) Dependency ratios: their use in economic analysis. In: Simon, J. and Devanzo, J. (eds) *Research in Population Economics, Vol II*. JAI Press, Greenwich, CT, pp. 63–76.

Clarke, L. (1984) *Domiciliary Services for the Elderly*. Croom Helm, London.

Clayton, V. (1975) Erikson's theory of human development as it applies to the aged: wisdom as contradictive cognition. *Human Development*, **18**, 119–128.

Clayton, V.P. and Birren, J.E. (1980) The development of wisdom across the life-span: a re-examination of an ancient topic. In: Baltes, P.B. and Brim, O.G. Jr. (eds) *Life-span Development and Behaviour*, Vol. 3. Academic Press, New York.

Clough, R. (1981) *Old Age Homes*. London: Allen and Unwin.

Cohen, G. (1987) *Social Change and the Life Course*. Tavistock, London and New York.

Cohen, G. and Faulkner, D. (1984) Memory in old age: 'good in parts'. *New Scientist*, 11 October, pp. 49–51.

Cole, D. with Utting, W. (1962) *The Economic Circumstances of Old People*. Codicote Press, Welwyn.

Cole, T. (1992) *Voices and Visions: Toward a Critical Gerontology*. Springer, New York.

Coleman, P.G. (1983) Cognitive functioning and health. In: Birren, J.E., Munnichs, J.M.A., Thomae, H. and Marois, M. (eds) *Ageing: A Challenge to Science and Society. Volume 3: Behavioural Sciences and Conclusions*. Oxford University Press, Oxford, pp. 57–67.

Coleman, P.G. (1984a) The Netherlands: poverty and disability in old age. In: Walker, R., Lawson, R. and Townsend, P. (eds) *Responses to Poverty: Lessons from Europe*. Heinemann, London, pp. 266–282.

Coleman, P.G. (1984b) Assessing self-esteem and its sources in elderly people. *Ageing and Society*, **4**, 117–135.

Coleman, P.G. (1986) *Ageing and Reminiscence Processes: Social and Clinical Implications*. Wiley, Chichester.

Coleman, P.G. (1990) Religion, ageing and adjustment questions for research. *Generations, Bulletin of the British Society of Gerontology*. **13**, 10–14.

Coleman, P.G. (1993) Reminiscence within the study of ageing: the social significance of story. In: Bornat, J. (ed.) *Reminiscence Reviewed*. Open University Press, Milton Keynes, pp. 8–20.

Coleman, P.G. and McCulloch, A.W. (1990) Societal change, values and social support: exploratory studies into adjustment in late life. *Journal of Aging Studies*, **4**, 321–332.

Coleman, P.G., Ivani-Chalian, C. and Robinson, M. (1993a) Self-esteem and its sources: stability and change in later life. *Ageing and Society*, **13**, 171–192.

Coleman, P.G., Aubin, A., Ivani-Chalian, C., Robinson, M. and Briggs, R. (1993b) Predictors of depressive symptoms and low self-esteem in a follow-up study of elderly people over ten years. *International Journal of Geriatric Psychiatry*, 8, 343–349.

Comfort, A. (1960) Discussion Session 1. Definition and universality of aging. In: L. Strehler (ed.) *The Biology of Aging*. American Institute of Biological Sciences, Washington, pp. 3–13.

Comfort, A. (1977) *A Good Age*. Mitchell Beazley, London.

Coni, N., Davidson, W. and Webster, S. (1992) *Ageing: The Facts*, 2nd edition. Oxford University Press, Oxford.

Copeland, J.R.M., Kelleher, M.J., Smith, A.M.R. and Devlin, P. (1986) The well, the mentally ill, the old and the old old: a community survey of elderly persons in London. *Ageing and Society*, **6**, 417–433.

Copeland, J.R.M., Dewey, M.E., Wood, N., Searle, R., Davidson, A. and McWilliam, C. (1987) Range of mental illness amongst the elderly in the community. Prevalence in Liverpool using the GMS–AGECAT package. *British Journal of Psychiatry*, **150**, 815–823.

Corson, J.H. and McConnell, J.W. (1956) *Economic Needs of Older People*. Twentieth Century Fund, New York.

Costa, P.T. and McCrae, R.R. (1989) Personality, stress and coping: some lessons from a decade of research. In: Markides, K.S. and Cooper, C.L. (eds) *Aging, Stress and Health*. Wiley, Chichester, pp. 269–285.

Cotier, J (1992) *Nudes in Budapest*. Aktok, London.

Coupland, N., Coupland, J. and Giles, H. (1991) *Language, Society and the Elderly: Discourse, Identity and Ageing*. Blackwell, Oxford.

Covey, H.C. (1991) *Images of Older People in Western Art and Society*. Praeger, New York.

Cowgill, D.O. and Holmes, L.D. (eds) (1972) *Aging and Modernization*. Appleton, New York.

Cox, B.D., Blaxter, M., Buckle, A.L.J. and Fenner, N.P. et al (1987) *The Health and Lifestyle Survey*. The Health Promotion Research Trust, London.

Craik, F.I.M. (1977) Age differences in human memory. In: Birren, J.E. and Schaie, K.W. (eds) *Handbook of the Psychology of Aging*. Van Nostrand Reinhold, New York, pp. 384–420.

Craik, F.I.M. and McDowd, J. (1987) Age differences in recall and recognition. *Journal of Experimental Psychology: Learning, Memory and Cognition*, **13**, 473–479.

Craven, E., Rimmer, L. and Wicks, M. (1982) *Family Issues and Public Policy*. Study Commission on the Family, London.

Crawford, M. (1971) Retirement and disengagement. *Human Relations*, **20**, 255–278.

Crawford, M. (1972a) Retirement and role playing. *Sociology*, **6**, 217–236.

Crawford, M. (1972b) Retirement as a psychological crisis. *Journal of Psychomatic Research*, **16**, 375–380.

Creech, J. and Babchuk, N. (1985) Affectivity and the interweave of social circles. In: Peterson, W. and Quadagno, J. (eds) *Social Bonds in Later Life*. Sage, California, pp. 129–142.

Cribier, F. (1975) Retirement migration in France. In: Prothera, R.M. and Koszinski, E. (eds) *People on the Move*. Methuen, London, pp. 360–373.

Cribier, F. (1981) Changing retirement patterns of the seventies: the example of a generation of Parisian salaried workers. *Ageing and Society*, **1**, 51–73.

Crosbie, I. and Traynor, J. (1985) *In Our Care: A Handbook of Workshop Activities for Those Caring for Older People*. Help the Aged Education Department, London.

Cuber, J. and Haroff, P. (1963) The more total view: relationships among men and women of the upper middle class. *Journal of Marriage and Family Living*, **25**, 140–145.

Cuff, E.C., Sharrock, W.W. and Francis, D.W. (1990) *Perspectives in Sociology*, 3rd edition. Unwin Hyman, London.

Cumming, E. and Henry, W. (1961) *Growing Old: The Process of Disengagement*. Basic Books, New York.

Dale, A., Evandrou, M. and Arber, S. (1987) The household structure of the elderly population in Britain. *Ageing and Society*, **7**, 37–56.

Dalley, G. (1993) 'Caring: a legitimate interest of older women'. In: Bernard, M. and Meade, K. *Women Come of Age*. Edward Arnold, London.

Daniels, N. (1988) *Am I My Parents' Keeper? An Essay on Justice Between the Young and the Old*. Oxford University Press, Oxford.

Datan, N., Rodeheaver, D. and Hughes, F. (1987) Adult development and aging. *Annual Review of Psychology*, **38**, 153–180.

Dant, T. (1988) Dependency and old age: theoretical accounts and practical understandings. *Ageing and Society*, **8**, 171–188.

Davies, B. and Knapp, M. (1981) *Old People's Homes and the Production of Welfare*. Routledge and Kegan Paul, London.

Davies, B. and Knapp, M. (1987) *Matching Resources to Community Needs*. Gower, Aldershot.

Davies, B. and Ward, S. (1992) *Women and Personal Pensions*, EOC Research Series. HMSO, London.

Davies, D. (1991) Cremation research project. *Pharos*, **57**, 1, 22–29.

de Beauvoir, S. (1972) *Old Age*. Penguin, Harmondsworth.

Department of Employment (1980) *Job Release Schemes*. Department of Employment, London.

Department of Employment (1991) *New Earnings Survey, 1991*. HMSO, London.

Department of Employment (1992a) Women and the labour market: results from the 1991 Labour Force Survey. *Employment Gazette*, September, 433–459.

Department of Employment (1992b) *Employment Gazette*, 100 (4).

Department of Environment (1988) *English House Condition Survey 1986*. HMSO, London.

Department of Health (1992a) *The Health of Elderly People. An Epidemiological Overview*. HMSO, London.

Department of Health (1992b) *Caring in Homes Initiative*. Department of Health and Department of Government, Brunel University, London.

DHSS (1978) *A Happier Old Age: A Discussion Document on Elderly People in Our Society*. HMSO, London.

DHSS (1981) *Growing Older*, Cmnd 8173. HMSO, London.

DHSS (1982) *Ageing in the United Kingdom*. DHSS, London.

DHSS (1983a) *Low Income Families – 1981*. DHSS, London.

DHSS (1983b) *The Experimental National Health Service Nursing Homes for Elderly People. An Outline*. DHSS, London.

DHSS (1984) *Population, Pension Costs and Pensioners' Incomes: Background Paper for the Inquiry into Provision for Retirement*. HMSO, London.

DHSS (1985a) *Reform of Social Security*, Cmnd 9517. HMSO, London.

DHSS (1985b) *Social Security Statistics 1984*. HMSO, London.

DHSS (1985c) *Reform of Social Security: Technical Annex*. HMSO, London.

DHSS (1985d) *Reform of Social Security: Programme for Action*, Cmnd 9691. HMSO, London.

DHSS (1985e) *Health and Personal Social Services Statistics*. HMSO, London.

DHSS (1986) *Low Income Families – 1983*. DHSS, London.

DHSS (1988) *Low Income Families*. DHSS, London.

Department of Health, Social Services Inspectorate (1991) *Inspection for Quality. Guidance on practice for inspection within Social Service Departments and Other Agencies*. HMSO, London.

DSS (Department of Social Security) (1989) *Social Security Statistics*. HMSO, London.

Dex, S. (1985) *The Sexual Divisions of Work*. Wheatsheaf Books, Brighton.

Dex, S. and Phillipson, C. (1986) Social policy and the older worker. In: Phillipson, C. and Walker, A. *Ageing and Social Policy*. Gower Books, London, pp. 45–60.

Dittmann-Kohli, F. (1990) The construction of meaning in old age: possibilities and constraints. *Ageing and Society*, **10**, 279–294.

Dittmann-Kohli, F. and Baltes, P.B. (1990) Toward a neofunctionalist conception of adult intellectual development: wisdom as a prototypical case of intellectual growth. In: Alexander, C. and Langer, E. (eds) *Beyond Formal Operations: Alternative Endpoints to Human Development*. Oxford University Press, New York.

Dixon, S.R. (1991) *Autonomy and Dependence in Residential Care. An Evaluation of a Project to Promote Self-Determination in a Home for Older People*, ACIOG Research Paper No.5. Age Concern England, London.

Dohrenwend, B.S. and Dohrenwend, B.P. (eds) (1974) *Stressful Life Events: Their Nature and Effects*. Wiley, New York.

Donahue, W., Orbach, H.L. and Pollak, O. (1960) Retirement: the emerging social pattern. In: Tibbitts, C. (ed.) *Handbook of Social Gerontology*. University of Chicago Press, Chicago.

Dono, J., Falbe, C., Kail, B., Litwak, E., Sherman, R. and Siegel, D. (1979) Primary groups in old age. *Research on Ageing*, **1**, 4, 403–433.

Dowd, J.J. (1980) *Stratification Among the Aged*. Brooks/Cole Publishing Co., Monterey, CA.

Durkheim, E. (1952) *Suicide. A Study in Sociology*. Routledge and Kegan Paul, London. (First published 1897.)

Dyer, R. (1979) The role of stereotypes. In: Cook, J. and Lewington, M. (eds) *Images of Alcoholism*. BFI, London.

Eastman, M. (1982) Granny battering: a hidden problem. *Community Care*, **413**, 12–13.

Eastman, M. (1985) *Old Age Abuse*. Age Concern, London.

Ebrahim, S. (1992) Health of elderly Asian women. In: George, J. and Ebrahim, S. (eds) *Health Care for Older Women*. Oxford University Press, Oxford, pp. 168–178.

Eisenhandler, S. (1992) Lifelong roles and cameo appearances. *Journal of Aging Studies*, **6**, 3, pp. 243–257.

Elias, N. (1978) *What is Sociology?* translated by S. Mennell. Hutchinson, London.

Elias, N. (1985) *The Loneliness of the Dying.* Basil Blackwell, Oxford.

Elias, N. (1987) On human beings and their emotions: a process sociological essay. *Theory, Culture & Society,* **4,** 287–316.

Emerson, A.R. (1959) The first year of retirement. *Occupational Psychology,* **33,** 197–208.

Epstein, R.A. (1992) Justice across the generations. In: Laslett, P. and Fishkin, J.S. (eds) *Justice Between Age Groups and Generations.* Yale University Press, New Haven, pp. 84–106.

Erikson, E.H. (1950) *Childhood and Society.* Norton, New York.

Erikson, E. (1963) *Childhood and Society* (2nd edn) Norton, New York.

Erikson, E.H. (1965) *Childhood and Society.* Penguin, Harmondsworth (first published, 1950).

Erikson, E.H. (1978) Reflections on Dr Borg's life cycle. In: Erikson, E.H. (ed.) *Adulthood.* Norton, New York.

Erikson, E.H. (1982) *The Life Cycle Completed: A Review.* Norton, New York.

Erikson, E.H., Erikson, J.M. and Kivnick, H.Q. (1986) *Vital Involvement in Old Age: The Experience of Old Age in Our Time.* Norton, New York.

Essex, M. and Nam, S. (1987) Marital status and loneliness among older women. *Journal of Marriage and the Family,* **49,** 1, pp. 93–106.

Estes, C. (1979) *The Aging Enterprise.* Jossey-Bass, San Francisco.

Estes, C. (1986) The politics of aging in America. *Ageing and Society,* **6,** 121–134. Reprinted in: Phillipson, C., Bernard, M. and Strang, P. (eds) *Dependency and Interdependency in Old Age – Theoretical Perspectives and Policy Alternatives.* Croom Helm, London, pp. 15–29.

Estes, C.L., Swan, J.S. and Gerard, L.E. (1982) Dominant and competing paradigms in gerontology. *Ageing and Society,* **2,** 151–164.

European CARITAS (1976) Working party on old people. Memorandum, European Federation for the Welfare of the Elderly, *Newsletter,* March 1976, 511.

Evans, G., Hughes, B. and Wilkin, D. with Jolley, D. (1981) *The Management of Mental and Physical Impairment in Non-specialist Residential Homes for the Elderly,* Research Report No. 4. Dept. of Psychiatry and Community Medicine, University of Manchester.

Evans, J.G. (1981) Hospital care of the elderly. In: Shegog, R. (ed.) *The Impending Crisis for Old Age.* Oxford University Press, Oxford, pp. 133–146.

Evers, H.K. (1981) The creation of patient careers in geriatric wards: aspects of policy and practice. *Social Science and Medicine,* **15A,** 581–588.

Eversley, D. (1982) Some new aspects of ageing in Britain. In: Hareven, T. and Adams, K. (eds) *Ageing: Life Course Transitions.* Tavistock, London, pp. 245–266.

Eysenck, H.J. (1987) Personality and ageing: an exploratory analysis. *Journal of Social Behavior and Personality,* **3,** 11–21.

Fairhurst, E. (1982) 'Growing old gracefully' as opposed to 'mutton dressed as lamb': the social construction of recognising older women. Paper presented to the British Sociological Association Annual Conference, University of Manchester.

Falkingham, J. (1987) *Britain's ageing population: the engine behind increased dependency?* Suntory Toyota International Centre for Economics and Related Disciplines, London School of Economics.

Falkingham, J. and Victor, C. (1991) *The Myth of the WOOPIE?* STICERD, Welfare State Programme Paper 55. London School of Economics, London.

Family Policy Studies Centre (1984a) *The Forgotten Army: Family Carers and Elderly People.* FPSC, London.

Family Policy Studies Centre (1984b) *The Family Today: Continuity and Change.* FPSC, London.

Farrow, S.C., Rablen, M.R. and Silver, C.P. (1976) Geriatric admissions in East London, 1962–1972. *Age and Ageing,* **5,** 49–55.

Featherstone, M. (1982) The body in consumer culture. *Theory, Culture & Society,* **1,** 18–33.

Featherstone, M. (1987) Leisure, symbolic power and the life course. In: Jary, D., Horne, S. and Tomlinson, A. (eds) *Sport, Leisure and Social Relations*. Routledge, London, pp. 113–138.

Featherstone, M. and Hepworth, M. (1982) Ageing and inequality: consumer culture and the new middle age. In: Robbins, D. (ed.) *Rethinking Social Inequality*. Gower, Aldershot, pp. 97–126.

Featherstone, M. and Hepworth, M. (1984) Changing images of retirement: an analysis of representations of ageing in the popular magazine *Retirement Choice*. In: Bromley, D.B. (ed.) *Gerontology: Social and Behavioural Perspectives*. Croom Helm/British Society of Gerontology, London, pp. 219–224.

Featherstone, M. and Hepworth, M. (1985a) The history of the male menopause 1848–1936. *Maturitas*, **7**, 249–257.

Featherstone, M. and Hepworth, M. (1985b) The male menopause: lifestyle and sexuality. *Maturitas*, **7**, 235–246.

Featherstone, M. and Hepworth, M. (1989) Ageing and old age: reflections on the postmodern lifecourse. In: Bytheway, B., Keil, T., Allat, P. and Bryman, A. (eds) *Becoming and Being Old: Sociological Approaches to Later Life*. Sage, London.

Feil, N. (1992) Validation therapy with late-onset dementia populations. In: Jones, G.M.M. and Miesen, B.M.L. (eds) *Care-giving in Dementia. Research and Applications*. Routledge, London, pp. 199–218.

Feneley, R.C.L. and Blannin, J.P. (1984) *Incontinence*. (Patient Handbook: 18). Churchill Livingstone, Edinburgh, London, Melbourne and New York.

Fennell, G., Phillipson, C. and Evers, H. (1988) *The Sociology of Old Age*. Open University Press, Milton Keynes.

Fenton, S. (1986) *Race, Health and Welfare. Afro-Caribbeans and South Asian People in Central Bristol*. Dept. of Sociology, University of Bristol.

Field, D. and Honzik, M.P. (1981) Personality and accuracy of retrospective reports of aging women. Paper presented at the International Congress of Gerontology, Hamburg, July.

Field, D. and Millsap, R.E. (1991) Personality in advanced old age: continuity or change. *Journal of Gerontology*, **46**, 299–308.

Fielden, M.A. (1990) Reminiscence as a therapeutic intervention with sheltered housing residents: a comparative study. *British Journal of Social Work*, **20**, 21–44.

Fillenbaum, G. (1984) *The Wellbeing of the Elderly: Approaches to Multidimensional Assessment*. World Health Organization offset publication no. 84, Geneva.

Finch, J. (1989) *Family Obligations and Social Change*. Polity Press, Cambridge.

Finch, J. and Groves, D. (1980) Community care and the family: a case for equal opportunities. *Journal of Social Policy*, **9**, 487–511.

Finch, J. and Mason, J. (1990) Filial obligations and kin support for elderly people. *Ageing and Society*, **10**, 151–175.

Finch, J. and Mason, J. (1992) *Negotiating Family Responsibilities*. Routledge, London.

Finkelstein, J. (1991) *The Fashioned Self*. Polity Press, London.

Finlay, D.E., Bayles, T.B., Rosen, C. and Milling, J. (1983) Effects of chair design, age and cognitive status on mobility. *Age and Ageing*, **12**, 329–331.

Finlinson, R. (1985) Chronic illness and care provision: a study of Alzheimer's disease. In: Peterson, W.A. and Quadagno, J. (eds) *Social Bonds in Later Life*. Sage, Beverly Hills, CA, pp. 325–347.

Firth, S. (1993) Approaches to death in Hindu and Sikh communities in Britain. In: Dickenson, D. and Johnson, M. (eds) *Death, Dying and Bereavement*. Sage, London.

Fischer, C.S. (1977) *Networks and Places*. Free Press, New York.

Fischer, D.H. (1978) *Growing Old in America*. Oxford University Press, New York.

Fiske, M. and Chiriboga, D. (1985) The interweaving of societal and personal change in adulthood. In: Munnichs, J.M.A., Mussen, P., Olbrich, E. and Coleman, P.G. (eds) *Life-span and Change in a Gerontological Perspective*. Academic Press, Orlando, CA, pp. 177–209.

Flavell, J.H. (1963) *The Developmental Psychology of Jean Piaget*. Van Nostrand Reinhold, New York.

Fleiss, A. (1985) *Home Ownership Alternatives for the Elderly*. HMSO, London.

Fletcher, P. (1991) *The Future of Sheltered Housing – Who Cares?* Policy report. National Federation of Housing Associations, London.

Fletcher, R. (1962) *The Family and Marriage*. Penguin, London.

Folkman, S. and Lazarus, R.S. (1988) Coping as a mediator of emotion. *Journal of Personality and Social Psychology*, **54**, 466–475.

Folkman, S., Lazarus, R.S., Pimley, S. and Novacek, J. (1987) Age differences in stress and coping processes. *Psychology and Aging*, **2**, 171–184.

Ford, G.G. (1986) Illness behaviour in the elderly. In: Dean, K., Hickey, T. and Holstein, B.E. (eds) *Self-care and Health in Old Age. Health Behaviour. Implications for Policy and Practice*. Croom Helm, London, pp. 130–166.

Ford, J. and Sinclair, R. (1987) *Sixty Years On: Women Talk About Old Age*. The Women's Press, London.

Forster, M. (1989) *Have the Men had Enough?* Penguin, London.

Foucault, M. (1973) *The Birth of the Clinic*. Tavistock, London.

Fox, J.A. (1976) Women, Work and Retirement. PhD Thesis, Duke University, Durham, USA.

Francis, D. (1981) Adaptive strategies of the elderly in England and Ohio. In: Fry, C. (ed.) *Dimensions: Ageing, Culture and Health*. J.P. Bergin, New York, pp. 85–107.

Francis, D. (1984) *Will You Still Need Me, Will You Still Feed Me, When I'm 84?* Indiana University Press, Bloomington.

Frankl, V.E. (1963) *Man's Search for Meaning: An Introduction to Logotherapy*. Pocket Books, New York.

Franks, H. (1990) 'The back-door approach to dying', *The Independent*, 6 February 1990.

von Franz, M. (1986) *On Dreams and Death: A Jungian Perspective*. Shambhala, Boston.

Freden, L. (1982) *Psychosocial Aspects of Depression: No Way Out?* Wiley, Chichester.

Freer, C. (1988) Old myths: frequent misconceptions about the elderly. In: Wells, N. and Freer, C. (eds) *The Ageing Population. Burden or Challenge*. Macmillan, Basingstoke.

Freter, H.J., Kohli, M. and Wolf, J. (1987) *Early Retirement and Work after Retirement – Implications for the Structure of the Work Society*. Freie Universität Berlin, Mimeo, Federal Republic of Germany.

Friedmann, E. and Orbach, H. (1974) Adjustment to retirement. In: Arieti, S. (ed.) *The Foundations of Psychiatry*, Vol. 1. Basic Books, New York, pp. 609–647.

Fries, J.F. (1980) Aging, natural death and the compression of morbidity. *New England Journal of Medicine*, **303**, 130–135.

Fries, J.F. and Crapo, L.M. (1981) *Vitality and Aging. Implications of the Rectangular Curve*. W.H. Freeman & Co., San Francisco.

Frisch, M. (1975) *Montauk*. Suhrkamp, Frankfurt.

Froggatt, A. (1988) Self–awareness in early dementia. In: Gearing, B., Johnson, M. and Heller, T. (eds) *Mental Health Problems in Old Age*. Wiley, Chichester, pp. 131–136.

Fulton, R. and Gottesman, D.J. (1980) Anticipatory grief: a psychosocial concept reconsidered. *British Journal of Psychiatry*, **137**, 45–54.

Garland, J. (1991) *Making Residential Care Feel Like Home. Enhancing the Quality of Life for Older People*. Winslow Press, Bicester.

Garland, J. (1992) Behaviour management. In: Evans, J.G. and Williams, T.F. (eds) *Oxford Textbook of Geriatric Medicine*. Oxford University Press, Oxford. pp. 646–652.

Gathorne-Hardy, J. (1987) The final chapter. *Observer Review*, 3 March, 21–22.

Gaullier, X. (1982) Economic crisis and old age: old age policies in France. *Ageing and Society*, **2**, 165–182.

George, L.K. (1980) *Role Transitions in Later Life*. Brooks/Cole, Monterey, CA.

George, L.K. (1981) Subjective well-being: conceptual and methodological issues. *Annual Review of Gerontology and Geriatrics*, **2**, 345–382.

George, V. (1968) *Social Security: Beveridge and After*. Routledge and Kegan Paul, London.

Gerber, L., Rusalem, R. and Hannon, N. (1975) Anticipatory grief and aged widows and widowers. *Journal of Gerontology*, **30**, pp. 225–229.

Gergen, K.J. (1980) The emerging crisis in life-span developmental theory. In: Baltes, P.B. and Brim. O.G. (eds) *Life-span Development and Behavior*, Vol. 3. Academic Press, New York, pp. 129–168.

Gerth, H.H. and Mills, C.W. (1948) *From Max Weber: Essays in Sociology*. Routledge and Kegan Paul, London.

Gibbs, I. and Sinclair, I. (1992) Residential care for elderly people: the correlates of quality. *Ageing and Society*, **12**, 4, pp. 463–482.

Giles, H. and Coupland, N. (1991) *Language: Contexts and Consequences*. Open University Press, Milton Keynes.

Gilhome-Herbst, K.R. (1983) Psychosocial consequences of disorders of hearing in the elderly. In: Hinchcliffe, R. *Medicine in Old Age: Hearing and Balance*. Churchill Livingstone, Edinburgh.

Gilhooly, M. (1987) Senile dementia and the family. In: Orford, J. (ed.) *Coping with Disorder in the Family*. Croom Helm, London, pp. 138–168.

Gilleard, C.J. (1984) *Living with Dementia: Community Care of the Elderly Mentally Infirm*. Croom Helm, London.

Gilleard, C.J., Pattie, A.H. and Dearman, G. (1980) Behavioural disabilities in psychogeriatric patients and residents of old people's homes. *Journal of Epidemiology and Community Health*, **34**, 106–110.

Gilmore, A.J.J., Svanborg, A., Marois, M., Beattie, Jr, W.M. and Piotrowski, J. (eds) (1981) *Ageing: A Challenge to Science and Society*. Oxford University Press, Oxford, New York, Toronto.

Glass, J., Bengtson, V. and Dunham, C. (1986) Attitude similarity in three generational families. *American Sociological Review*, **51**, 685–698.

Glassner, B. (1989) Fitness and the postmodern self. *Journal of Health and Social Behaviour*, **30**, June, 180–191.

Glick, L., Weiss, R., and Parkes, C.M. (1974) *The First Year of Bereavement*. Wiley, New York.

Godber, C., Rosenvinge, H., Wilkinson, D. and Smithies, J. (1987) Depression in old age: prognosis after E.C.T. *International Journal of Geriatric Psychiatry*, **2**, 19–24.

Goffman, E. (1961) *Asylums: Essays on the Social Situation of Mental Patients and Other Inmates*. Anchor, New York.

Goffman, E. (1968) *Stigma: Notes on the Management of Spoiled Identity*. Penguin, Harmondsworth.

Goffman, E. (1971) *The Presentation of Self in Everyday Life*. Penguin, Harmondsworth.

Golant, S.M. (1977) Spatial context of residential moves by elderly persons. *International Journal of Ageing and Human Development*, **8**, 279–289.

Goldberg, E.M. and Connelly, N. (1982) *The Effectiveness of Social Care for the Elderly: An Overview of Recent and Current Evaluative Research*. Heinemann, London.

Goldthorpe, J.H. (1980) *Social Mobility and Class Structure in Modern Britain*. Clarendon Press, Oxford.

Gonzalez-Crussi, F. (1987) *Three Forms of Sudden Death, and Other Reflections on the Grandeur and Misery of the Body*. Picador, London.

Gorer, G. (1965) *Death, Grief and Mourning*. Cresset, London.

Gottsdanker, R. (1982) Age and simple reaction time. *Journal of Gerontology*, **37**, 342–348.

Government Actuary (1986) *Occupational Pension Schemes 1983*. HMSO, London.

Government Actuary (1991) *Occupational Pension Schemes 1987*. HMSO, London.

Graebner, W. (1980) *A History of Retirement: The Meaning and Function of an American Institution, 1885–1978*. Yale University Press, New Haven and London.

Graff, T.O. and Wiseman, R.F. (1978) Changing concentrations of older Americans. *The Geographical Review*, **63**, 379–393.

Graham, H. (1991) The concept of caring in feminist research: the case of domestic service. *Sociology*, **25**, 61–78.

Graham, H. and Livesley, B. (1983) Can re-admission to a geriatric medical unit be prevented? *The Lancet*, **i**, 404–406.

Gray, B. and Johnson, M.L. (eds) (forthcoming) *Up the Long Track: Poems of Ageing*. Souvenir Press, London.

Green, H. (1988) *Informal Carers General Household Survey 1985*, OPCS, Series GHS no. 15 Supplement A. HMSO, London.

Grief Education Institute (1986) *Bereavement Support: Leadership Manual*. Grief Education Institute, Denver, Colorado.

Griffen, J. (1991) Dying with Dignity. Office of Health Economics, London.

Groves, D. (1993) Work, poverty and older women. In: Bernard, M. and Meade, K. (eds) *Women Come of Age*. Edward Arnold, London.

Gruman, G.J. (1966) A history of ideas about the prolongation of life: the evolution of prolongevity hypotheses to 1800. *Transactions of the American Philosophical Society*, **56**, 65–110.

Gruman, G.J. (1978) Cultural origins of present-day 'ageism': the modernisation of the life cycle. In: Spicker, S.F. (ed.) *Ageing and the Elderly: Humanistic Perspectives in Gerontology*. Humanistic Press, New York, pp. 359–387.

Grundy, E. (1987) Retirement migration and its consequences in England and Wales. *Ageing and Society*, **7**, 57–82.

Gubrium, J.F. (1975) Being single in old age. *Ageing and Human Development*, **6**, 29–41.

Gubrium, J.F. (1986) *Oldtimers and Alzheimer's: The Descriptive Organization of Senility*. JAI Press Inc., London.

Gubrium, J.F. and Lynott, R.J. (1983) Rethinking life satisfaction. *Human Organization*, **42**, 30–38.

Gubrium, J.F. and Lynott, R.J. (1985) Alzheimer's disease as biographical work. In: Peterson, W.A. and Quadagno, J. (eds) *Social Bonds in Later Life*. Sage, Beverly Hills, CA, pp. 349–367.

Gubrium, J.F. and Silverman, D. (1989) *The Politics of Field Research: Sociology Beyond Enlightenment*. Sage, London.

Guillemard, A.M. (ed.) (1983) *Old Age and the Welfare State*. Sage, London.

Guillemard, A.M. (1986) Social policy and ageing in France. In: Phillipson, C. and Walker, A. (eds) *Ageing and Social Policy: A Critical Assessment*. Gower Books, London, pp. 263–279..

Gumpert, M. (1950) *You Are Younger Than You Think*. Hammond, Hammond and Co. Ltd, London.

Gunn, P.A. (1986) Legislating filial piety: the Australian experience. *Ageing and Society*, **6**, 135–167.

Guralnik, J.M., Brock, D.B. and Brody, J.A. (1987) The changing demography of the elderly in the United States. In: Caird, F. and Evans, J.G. (eds) *Advanced Geriatric Medicine 6*. Wright, Bristol, pp. 3–20.

Gurland, B.J. (1976) The comparative frequency of depression in various adult age groups. *Journal of Gerontology*, **31**, 283–292.

Gurland, B.J. and Toner, J.A. (1982) Depression in the elderly: a review of recently published studies. *Annual Review of Gerontology and Geriatrics*, **3**, 228–265.

Gurland, B.J., Dean, L., Cross, P. and Golden, R. (1980) The epidemiology of depression and dementia in the elderly: the use of multiple indicators of these conditions. In: Cole, J.O. and Barrett, J.E. (eds) *Psychopathology in the Aged*. Raven Press, New York, pp. 37–60.

Gurland, B.J., Copeland, J., Kuriansky, J., Kelleher, M., Sharpe, L. et al (1983) *The Mind and Mood of Ageing. Mental Health Problems of the Community Elderly in New York and London*. Croom Helm, London.

Gutmann, D.L (1964) An exploration of ego configurations in middle and later life. In: Neugarten, B.L. (ed.) *Personality in Middle and Later Life*. Atherton Press, New York.

Gutmann, D.L. (1980) Psychoanalysis and aging: a developmental view. In: Greenspan, S.I. and Pollock, G.H. (eds) *The Course of Life: Psychoanalytic Contributions towards*

Understanding Personality Development. Volume III: Adulthood and the Aging Process. US Department of Health and Human Services, Washington DC, pp. 489–517.

Gutmann, D.L. (1987) *Reclaimed Powers: Towards a New Psychology of Men and Women in Later Life.* Basic Books, New York.

Gutmann, D.L., Griffin, B. and Grunes, J. (1982) Developmental contributions to the late-onset affective disorder. In: Brim, G.B. and Baltes, P.B. (eds) *Life-Span Development and Behaviour,* Vol. 4. Academic Press, New York.

Haber, C. (1983) *Beyond Sixty-Five: The Dilemma of Old Age in America's Past.* Cambridge University Press, Cambridge.

Hagestad, G. (1985) Continuity and connectedness. In: Bengtson, V. and Robertson, J. (eds) *Grandparenthood.* Sage, California, pp. 31–48.

Hagestad, G.O. (1986) Challenges and opportunities of an ageing society. In: Phillipson, C., Bernard, M. and Strang, P. (eds) *Dependency and Interdependency in Old Age – Theoretical Perspectives and Policy Alternatives.* Croom Helm, London, pp. 1–14.

Hagestad, G. (1987) Parent–child relationships in later life: trends and gaps in past research. In: Lancaster, J.B. et al (eds) *Parenting Across the Lifespan.* Aldine de Gruyter, New York, pp. 405–433.

Hagestad, G.O., Smyer, M.A. and Stierman, K.L. (1984) Parent–child relations in adulthood: the impact of divorce in middle age. In: Cohen, R., Weissman, S. and Cohler, B. (eds) *Parenthood: Psychodynamic Perspectives.* Guildford Press, New York.

Haight, B.K. (1988) The therapeutic role of a structured life review process in homebound elderly subjects. *Journal of Gerontology,* **43**, pp. 40–44.

Haight, B.K. (1991) Reminiscing: the state of the art as a basis for practice. *International Journal of Aging and Human Development,* **33**, 1–32.

Hall, M. (1988) Geriatric medicine today. In: Wells, N. and Freer, C. (eds) *The Ageing Population. Burden or Challenge?* Macmillan, London, pp. 65–86.

Hanley, I.G. (1981) The use of signposts and active training to modify ward disorientation in elderly patients. *Journal of Behaviour Therapy and Experimental Psychiatry,* **12**, 241–247.

Hanley, I. and Baikie, E. (1984) Understanding and treating depression in the elderly. In: Hanley, I. and Hodge, J. (eds) *Psychological Approaches to the Care of the Elderly.* Croom Helm, London, pp. 213–236.

Hannah, L. (1986) *Inventing Retirement.* Cambridge University Press, Cambridge.

Hanvey, C. (1989) Death in residence. In: Philpot, T. (ed.) *Last Things.* Reed Publishing/Community Care, London.

Hare, E.H. and Shaw, G.K. (1965) *Mental Health on a New Housing Estate,* Maudsley Monograph 12. Oxford University Press, London.

Hareven, T.K. (1977) Family time and historical time. *Daedalus,* **106**, 57–70.

Harris, C. (1983) Associational participation in old age. In: Jerrome, D. (ed.) *Ageing in Modern Society.* Croom Helm, London, pp. 14–24.

Harvey, C.D. and Bahr, H.M. (1974) Widowhood, morale and affiliation. *Journal of Marriage and the Family,* **36**, pp. 97–106.

Harwood, E. and Irvine, K.L. (1985) Psychological significance of the University of Queensland Longitudinal Study of Ageing: Retrospect and Perspective in the Twentieth Year. Paper given at the XIIIth International Congress of Gerontology, New York.

Hasher, L. and Zacks, R.T. (1979) Automatic and effortful processes in memory. *Journal of Experimental Psychology: General,* **108**, 356–388.

Haskey, J. (1988) Trends in marriage and divorce, cohort analyses of the proportion of marriages ending in divorce. *Population Trends,* **54**, 21–28.

Haskey, J. (1990) The ethnic minority population of Great Britain: estimates by ethnic group and country of birth. *Population Trends.* **60**, 35–38.

Haskey, J. (1991) Ethnic minority populations resident in private households – estimates. *Population Trends,* **63**, Spring, 22–35.

Hatfield, E. and Sprecher, S. (1986) *Mirror, Mirror: The Importance of Looks in Everyday Life.* State University of New York Press, New York.

Havighurst, R.J. (1963) Successful ageing. In: Williams, R.H., Tibbitts, C. and Donahue, W. (eds) *Processes of Ageing*, Volume 1. Atherton, New York, pp. 299–320.

Hayflick, L. and Moorhead, P.S. (1961) The serial cultivation of human diploid cell strains. *Experimental Cell Research*, **25**, 585–621.

Haynes, M.S. (1963) The supposedly golden age for the aged. *The Gerontologist*, **3**, 26–35.

Hazan, H. (1980) *The Limbo People: A Study of the Constitution of the Time Universe among the Aged*. Routledge and Kegan Paul, London.

Hedström, P. and Ringen, S. (1987) Age and income in contemporary society: a research note. *Journal of Social Policy*, **16**, 227–239.

Heinemann, G. (1985) Interdependence in informal support systems. In: Peterson, W. and Quadagno, J. (eds) *Social Bonds in Later Life*. Sage, California, pp. 165–186.

Help the Aged (1981) *Recall: A Handbook*. Help the Aged Education Department, London.

Hemmings, S. (1985) *A Wealth of Experience: The Lives of Older Women*. Pandora Press, London.

Henderson, A.S. (1989) Psychiatric epidemiology and the elderly. *International Journal of Geriatric Psychiatry*, **4**, 249–253.

Hendricks, J. and Hendricks, C.D. (1977) *Ageing in Mass Society*. Winthrop, Cambridge, MA.

Henry, J. (1972) *Culture Against Man*. Penguin, Harmondsworth.

Henwood, M. (1992) *Through a Glass Darkly: Community Care and Elderly People*, King's Fund Institute, Project Paper No. 14. King's Fund Centre, London.

Henwood, M.and Wicks, M. (1985) Community care family trends and social change. *The Quarterly Journal of Social Affairs*, **4**, 357–371.

Hepworth, M. (1987) The mid-life phase. In: Cohen, G. (ed.) *Social Change and the Life Course*. Tavistock, London and New York.

Hepworth, M. (1991) Positive ageing and the mask of age. *Journal of Educational Gerontology*, **6**, 2, 93–101.

Hepworth, M. and Featherstone, M. (1982) *Surviving Middle Age*. Basil Blackwell, Oxford.

Herbst, K. (1976) Communication problems of the elderly deaf. In: *Deafness in the Elderly*. Age Concern, London.

Herbst, K. (1991) Hearing. In: Redfern, S. (ed.) *Nursing Elderly People*. Churchill Livingstone, Edinburgh.

Herbst, K. and Humphrey, C. (1980) Hearing impairment and mental state in the elderly living at home. *British Medical Journal*, **281**, 903–905.

Heron, A. (1962) Preparation for retirement: a new phase in occupational development. *Occupational Psychology*, **37**, 1–9.

Heron, A. (1963) Retirement attitudes among industrial workers in the 6th decade of life. *Vita Humana*, **5**, 152–159.

Heron, A. and Chown, S.M. (1967) *Age and Function*. Churchill Press, London.

Hess, B. (1979) Sex roles, friendship and the life course. *Research on Ageing*, **1**, 494–515.

Hess, B. and Soldo, B. (1985) Husband and wife networks. In: Sauer, W. and Coward, R. (eds) *Social Support Networks and Care of the Elderly*. Springer, New York, pp. 67–92.

Hinton, J.M. (1975) The influence of previous personality on reactions to having terminal cancer. *Omega*, **6**, 95–111.

Hirsch, F. (1977) *Social Limits to Growth*. Routledge and Kegan Paul, London.

Hochschild, A. (1973) *The Unexpected Community*. Prentice-Hall, New York.

Hockey, J.L. (1990) *Experiences of Death: An Anthropological Account*. Edinburgh University Press, Edinburgh.

Hockey, J. and James, A. (1990) Metaphors of marginality: ageing, infantilisation and personhood. Paper presented at British Society of Gerontology Annual conference, Durham 21–23 September, 1990.

Hockey, J. and James, A. (1993) *Growing Up and Growing Old: Ageing and Dependency in the Life Course*. Sage, London.

Holahan, C.K., Holahan, C.J. and Belk, S. (1984) Adjustment in aging: the roles of life stress, hassles and self-efficacy. *Health Psychology*, **3**, 315–328.

Holden, U.P. and Woods, R.T. (1988) *Reality Orientation: Psychological Approaches to the 'Confused' Elderly*. Churchill Livingstone, Edinburgh.

Holland, C.A. and Rabbitt, P. (1991) The course and causes of cognitive change with advancing age. *Reviews in Clinical Gerontology*, **1**, 79–94.

Holliday, S.G., Burnaby, H.C. and Chandler, M.J. (1986) *Wisdom: Explorations in Adult Competence*. Karger, Basle.

Hollingshead, A.B. and Redlich, F.C. (1958) *Social Class and Mental Illness: A Community Study*. Wiley, New York.

Hooper, F.H., Hooper, J.O. and Colbert, K.K. (1984) *Personality and Memory Correlates of Intellectual Functioning: Young Adulthood to Old Age*. Karger, Basle.

House of Commons (1991) *Hansard*, 5 November, col. 89.

House of Commons Social Security Committee (1993) *Low Income Statistics: Low Income Families 1979–1989*, HC 359. HMSO, London.

Houts, P.S. and Scott, R.A. (1976) *Individualized Goal Planning in Nursing Care Facilities*. Department of Behavioural Science, Pennsylvania State University College of Medicine, Hershey, PA.

Howell, S.C. (1983) The meaning of place in old age. In: Rowles, G.D. and Ohta, R.J. (eds) *Aging and Milieu. Environmental Perspectives on Growing Old*. Academic Press, New York, pp. 97–107.

Hoyt, D and Babchuk, N (1983) Adult kinship networks: the selective formation of intimate ties with kin. *Social Forces*, **62**, 1, 84–101.

Hufton, O.H. (1974) *The Poor in Eighteenth Century France*. Oxford University Press, Oxford.

Hunt, A. (1978) *The Elderly at Home: A Study of People Aged Sixty-Five and Over Living in the Community in England in 1976*. OPCS, London.

Huppert, F. and Tym, E. (1986) Clinical and neuropsychological assessment of dementia. *British Medical Bulletin*, **42**, 1, 11–18.

Huyck, M. (1977) Sex and the older woman. In: Troll, L., Israel, J. and Israel, K. (eds) *Looking Ahead: A Woman's Guide to the Problems and Joys of Growing Older*. Prentice-Hall, New Jersey, pp. 43–58.

Institute of Medical Ethics Working Party on the Ethics of Prolonging Life and Assisting Death (1990) Assisted death. *The Lancet*, **336**, 610–613.

Isaacs, B., Gunn, J., McKechan, A., McMillan, I. and Neville, Y. (1971) The concept of predeath. *The Lancet*, **i**, 1115–1119.

Isaacs, B., Livingstone, M. and Neville, Y. (1972) *Survival of the Unfittest: A Study of Geriatric Patients in Glasgow*. Routledge and Kegan Paul, London.

Itzin, C. (1986) Ageism awareness training: a model for group work. In: Phillipson, C., Bernard, M. and Strang, P. (eds) *Dependency and Interdependency in Old Age: Theoretical Perspectives and Policy Alternatives*. Croom Helm, London, pp. 114–139.

Itzin, C. and Phillipson, C. (1993) *Age Barriers at Work*. Metropolitan Authorities Recruitment Association, Solihull.

Ivan, L. and Melrose, M. (1986) *The Way We Die*. Angel Press, Chichester.

Jacobson, D. (1974) Rejection of the retiree role: a study of female industrial workers in their 50s. *Human Relations*, **27**, 477–491.

Jacoby, R.J. (1981) Depression in the elderly. *British Journal of Hospital Medicine*, **25**, 40–47.

Jalland, P. and Hooper, J. (eds) (1986) *Women from Birth to Death. The Female Life Cycle in Britain, 1830–1914*. Harvester Press, Brighton.

James, N. (1993) Gender and attitudes to death and dying. In: *K260 Death and Dying*. Open University Course Workbook One, The Open University, Milton Keynes.

Jenkins, J., Felce, D., Lunt, B. and Powell, E. (1977) Increasing engagement in activity of residents in old people's homes by providing recreational materials. *Behaviour Research and Therapy*, **15**, 429–434.

Jerrome, D. (1981) The significance of friendship for women in later life. *Ageing and Society*, **1**, 175–197.

Jerrome, D. (1983) Lonely women in a friendship club. *British Journal of Guidance and Counselling*, **11**, 10–20.

Jerrome, D. (1984) Good company: the sociological implications of friendship. *Sociological Review*, **32**, 696–718.

Jerrome, D. (1986) Me Darby, you Joan. In: Phillipson, C., Bernard, M. and Strang, P. (eds) *Dependency and Interdependency in Old Age – Theoretical Perspectives and Policy Alternatives*. Croom Helm, London, pp. 348–358.

Jerrome, D. (1988) 'That's what it's all about': old people's organizations as a context for aging. *Journal of Aging Studies*, 2, 71–81.

Jerrome, D. (1991) Social bonds. *Reviews in Clinical Gerontology*, **1**, 3, 297–306.

Jerrome, D. (1992) *Good company: An Anthropological Study of Old People in Groups*. Edinburgh University Press, Edinburgh.

Jerrome, D. (1993) Relationships and sexuality. In: Bernard, M. and Meade, K. (eds) *Women Come of Age*. Edward Arnold, London.

Jerrome, D. (forthcoming a, 1994) Ties that bind. In: Walker, A. (ed.) *The New Generational Contract*, UCL Press, London.

Jerrome, D (forthcoming b, 1994) Time, change and continuity in family life. *Ageing and Society*, **14**, 1.

Johnson, C. (1985) Grandparenting options in divorcing families. In: Bengtson, V. and Robertson, J. (eds) *Grandparenthood*. Sage, California, pp. 81–96.

Johnson, D.E. (1958) A depressive retirement syndrome. *Geriatrics*, **13**, 314–319.

Johnson, F. and Ariès, E. (1983) The talk of women friends. *Women's Studies International Forum*, **6**, 353–361.

Johnson, M.L. (1972) Self-perception of need amongst the elderly: an analysis of illness behaviour. *Sociological Review*, **20**, 521–531.

Johnson, M.L. (1982) Implications of greater activity in later life. In: Fogarty, M. (ed.) *Retirement Policy – the Next Fifty Years*. Heinemann, London, pp. 138–156.

Johnson, M. (1986) Ageing as a labelling phenomenon. In: Dean, K., Hickey, T. and Holstein, B.E. (eds) *Self-care and Health in Old Age. Health Behaviour. Implications for Policy and Practice*. Croom Helm, London, pp. 12–34.

Johnson, M.L. (1993) Generational relations under review. In: Hobman, D. (ed.) *Intergenerational Solidarity: Fact or Fiction*? Age Concern Publications, London.

Johnson, M.L., di Gregorio, S. and Hughes, B. (1981) *Ageing, Needs and Nutrition*. Policy Studies Institute, London.

Johnson, P. (1987) *Structured Dependency of the Elderly: A Critical Note*. Centre for Economic Policy Research, London.

Johnson, P. and Falkingham, J. (1988) Intergenerational transfers and public expenditure on the elderly in modern Britian. *Ageing and Society*, **8**, 2, 129–146.

Johnson, P., Conrad, C. and Thomson, D. (1989) *Workers versus Pensioners*. Manchester University Press in association with The Centre for Economic Policy Research, Manchester.

Jones, D. (1980) Gossip. *Women's Studies International Forum*, **3**, 139–198.

Jones, G.M.M. and Miesen, B.M.L. (eds) (1992) *Care-giving in Dementia. Research and Applications*. Routledge, London.

Jorm, A.F. (1990) *The Epidemiology of Alzheimer's Disease and Related Disorders*. Chapman and Hall, London.

Judge, K., Knapp, M. and Smith, J. (1983) *The Comparative Costs of Public and Private Residential Homes for the Elderly*. DHSS Seminar Papers on Residential Research. DHSS, London.

Jung, C.G. (1972) The transcendent function. In: Read, H., Fordham, M., Adler, G. and McGuire, W. (eds) *The Structure and Dynamics of the Psyche, 2nd edition, Volume 8 of the Collected Works of C.G. Jung*. Routledge and Kegan Paul, London.

K260 Course, Open University (1993) *K260 Death and Dying*, School of Health, Welfare and Community Education. The Open University, Milton Keynes.

Kahana, B. and Kahana, E. (1983) Stress reactions. In: Lewinsohn, P.M. and Teri, L. (eds) *Clinical Geropsychology: New Directions in Assessment and Treatment*. Pergamon Press, New York, pp. 139–169.

Kahana, E. (1982) A congruence model of person–environment interaction. In: Lawton, M.P., Windley, P.G. and Byerts, T.O. (eds) *Aging and the Environment: Theoretical Approaches*. Springer, New York, pp. 97–121.

Kalish, R.A. (1985) The social context of death and dying. In: Binstock, R.H. and Shanas, E. (eds) *Handbook of Aging and the Social Sciences*. Van Nostrand Reinhold, New York, pp. 149–170.

Kalish, R.A. and Reynolds, D.K. (1976) *Death and Ethnicity: a Psychocultural Study*. University of Southern California Press, Los Angeles.

Karimjee, Z. (1993) Interview in *K260 Death and Dying*, Open University Course. The Open University, Milton Keynes.

Karn, V.A. (1977) *Retiring to the Seaside*. Routledge and Kegan Paul, London.

Kastenbaum, R. (1974) On death and dying. *Journal of Geriatric Psychiatry*, **7**, 94–107.

Kastenbaum, R. and Alsenberg, R. (1976) *The Psychology of Death*. Springer, New York.

Katz, J. (1993) Jewish perspectives on death. In: Dickenson, D. and Johnson, M. (eds) *Death, Dying and Bereavement*. Sage, London.

Katz, S. (1992) Alarmist demography: power, knowledge and the elderly population. *Journal of Aging Studies*, **6**, 2, 203–225.

Kaufman, S.R. (1987) *The Ageless Self: Sources of Meaning in Late Life*. University of Wisconsin Press, Madison.

Kay, D.W.K. (1991) Psychiatry of old age. The epidemiology of dementia: a review of recent work. *Reviews in Clinical Gerontology*, **1**: 55–66.

Kay, D.W., Beamish, P. and Roth, M. (1964) Old age mental disorders in Newcastle upon Tyne I. *British Journal of Psychiatry*, **110**, 146–158.

Kay, D.W.K., Henderson, A.S., Scott, R., Wilson, J., Rickwood, D.and Grayson, D.A. (1985) Dementia and depression among the elderly living in the Hobart community: the effect of the diagnostic criteria on the prevalence rates. *Psychological Medicine*, **15**, 771–788.

Kearl, M.C. (1989) *Endings: A Sociology of Death and Dying*. Oxford University Press, New York.

Keith, D.M. (1979) Life changes and perceptions of life and death among older men and women. *Journal of Gerontology*, **34**, 870–878.

Keith, J. (1977) *Old People, New Lives: Community Creation in a Resettlement Residence*. University of Chicago Press, Chicago.

Kellaher, L., Peace, S. and Willcocks, D. (1990) Triangulating data. In: Peace, S. (ed.) *Researching Social Gerontology*. Sage, London, pp. 115–128.

Kendrick, D.C. (1982) Why assess the aged? A clinical psychologist's view. *British Journal of Clinical Psychology*, **21**, 47–54.

Kerckhoff, A.C. (1964) Husband–wife expectations and reactions to retirement. *Journal of Gerontology*, **19**, 510–516.

Kilroy, B. (1982) Public expenditure on housing. In: Walker, A. (ed.) *Public Expenditure and Social Policy*. Heinemann, London, pp. 113–136.

Kincaid, J. (1973) *Poverty and Inequality in Britain*. Pelican, Harmondsworth.

King, G.B. and Stearns, P. (1981) The retirement experience as a policy factor. *Journal of Social History*, **14**, 589–625.

King's Fund Centre (1986) *Living Well into Old Age: Applying Principles of Good Practice to Services for People with Dementia*, Project Paper No. 63. King's Fund Centre, London.

Kirk, H. and Leather, P. (1991) *Age File: The Facts*. Anchor Housing Association, Oxford.

Kirkwood, T.B.L. (1977) Evolution of ageing. *Nature*, **270**, 301–304.

Kitchener, K.S. (1983) Cognition, metacognition, and epistemic cognition: a three-level model of cognitive processing. *Human Development*, **26**, 222–232.

Kitwood, T (1989) Brain, mind and dementia: with particular reference to Alzheimer's disease. *Ageing and Society*, **9**, 1–15.

Kitwood, T. (1990) The dialectics of dementia: with particular reference to Alzheimer's disease. *Ageing and Society*, **10**, 177–196.

Kitwood, T. and Bredin, K. (1992) Towards a theory of dementia care: personhood and well-being. *Ageing and Society*, **12**, 269–287.

Kivnick, H.Q. (1991) *Living with Care, Caring for Life: The Inventory of Life Strengths*. School of Social Work, University of Minnesota, Minneapolis.

Klein, M. (1940) Mourning and its relationship to manic depressive states. *International Journal of Psycho-analysis*, **21**, 125.

Knopf, O. (1932) *The Art of Being a Woman*. Rider and Co., London.

Koenig, H.G. (1992) *Successful Aging, Religion and Mental Health*. Haworth Press, New York.

Koenig, H.G. (1993) Religion and aging. *Reviews in Clinical Gerontology*, **3**, 195–203.

Kogan, N. (1990) Personality and aging. In: Birren, J.E. and Schaie, K.W. (eds) *Handbook of the Psychology of Aging*, 3rd edition. Academic Press, San Diego, pp. 330–346.

Kohli, M., Rein, M., Guillemard, A.-M. and Gunsteren, H. (1991) *Time For Retirement: Comparative Studies of Early Exit from the Labour Force*. Cambridge University Press, Cambridge.

Kohli, M., Rosenow, J. and Wolf, J. (1983) The social construction of ageing through work: economic structure and life world. *Ageing and Society*, **3**, 23–42.

Kornhaber, A. (1985) Grandparenthood and the new social contract. In: Bengtson, V. and Robertson, J. (eds) *Grandparenthood*. Sage, California, pp. 159–172.

Kotre, J. (1984) *Outliving the Self: Generativity and the Interpretation of Lives*. Johns Hopkins University, Baltimore.

Kramer, D.A. (1983) Post-formal operations? A need of further conceptualisation. *Human Development*, **25**, 91–105.

Krause, N. (1987) Life stress, social support and self-esteem in an elderly population. *Psychology and Ageing*, **2**, 349–356.

Kruse, A. (1989) Coping with chronic disease and elder abuse. In: Wolf, R.S. and Bergman, S. (eds) *Stress, Conflict and Abuse of the Elderly*. JDC-Brookdale Institute of Gerontology and Adult Human Development, Jerusalem.

Kubler-Ross, E. (1969) *On Death and Dying*. Macmillan, New York.

Kubler-Ross, E. (1970) *On Death and Dying*. London: Tavistock.

Kuhn, M. (1986) Prologue: social and political goals for an ageing population. In: Phillipson, C., Bernard, M. and Strang, P. (eds) *Dependency and Interdependency in Old Age: Theoretical Perspectives and Policy Alternatives*. Croom Helm, London.

Kutscher, A. (ed.) (1969) *Death and Bereavement*. Charles C. Thomas, Springfield.

Kuypers, J.A. and Bengtson, V.L. (1973) Social breakdown and competence. A model of normal ageing. *Human Development*, **16**, 181–201.

Kuypers, J.A. and Bengtson, V.L. (1983) Toward competence in the older family. In: Brubaker, T. (ed.) *Family Relationships in Later Life*. Sage, California, pp. 211–228.

Labouvie-Vief, G. (1985) Intelligence and cognition. In: Birren, J.E. and Schaie, K.W. (eds) *Handbook of the Psychology of Aging*, 2nd edition. Van Nostrand Reinhold, New York.

Labouvie-Vief, G. and Blanchard-Fields, F. (1982) Cognitive ageing and psychological growth. *Ageing and Society*, **2**, 183–209.

Labouvie-Vief, G., Hoyer, W.J., Baltes, M.M. and Baltes, P.B. (1974) Operant analysis of intellectual behaviour in old age. *Human Development*, **17**, 259–272.

Laczko, F. (1987) Older workers, unemployment and the discouraged worker effect. In: Di Gregorio, S. (ed.) *Social Gerontology: New Directions*. Croom Helm, London.

Laczko, F. and Phillipson, C. (1991) *Changing Work and Retirement*. Open University Press, Milton Keynes.

Laczko, F. and Walker, A. (1985) Excluding older workers from the labour force: early retirement policies in Britain, France and Sweden. In: Brenton, M. and Jones, C. (eds) *Year Book of Social Policy in Britain 1984*. Routledge and Kegan Paul, London, pp. 100–122.

Laing, W. (ed.) (1990) *Laing's Review of Private Health Care*. Laing and Buisson, London.

Laing, W. (ed.) (1992) *Laing's Review of Private Health Care.* Laing and Buisson, London.

Laing, W. (ed.) (1993) *Laing's Review of Private Health Care.* Laing and Buisson, London.

Lakoff, R.T. and Scherr, R.L. (1984) *Face Values: The Politics of Beauty.* Routledge and Kegan Paul, London.

Land, H. (1978) Who cares for the family? *Journal of Social Policy,* **7,** 257–284.

Langer, E.J. (1983) *The Psychology of Control.* Sage, Beverly Hills.

Langer, E.J. (1989) Minding matters: the consequences of mindlessness-mindfulness. *Advances in Experimental Social Psychology,* **22,** 137–175.

Larder, D., Day, P. and Klein, R. (1986) *Institutional Care for the Elderly: The Geographical Distribution of the Public/Private Mix in England,* Bath Social Policy Papers, No. 10. University of Bath, Bath.

Larson, R. (1978) Thirty years of research on the subjective well-being of older Americans. *Journal of Gerontology,* **33,** 109–125.

Laslett, P. (1976) Societal development and aging. In: Binstock, R.H. and Shanas, E. (eds) *Handbook of Aging and the Social Sciences.* Van Nostrand Reinhold, New York, pp. 87–116.

Laslett, P. (1977) The history of ageing and the aged. In: Laslett, P. (ed.) *Family Life and Illicit Love in Earlier Generations: Essays in Historical Sociology.* Cambridge University Press, Cambridge.

Laslett, P. (1989) *A Fresh Map of Life: The Emergence of the Third Age.* Weidenfeld and Nicolson, London.

Laslett, P. and Fishkin, J.S. (eds) (1992) *Justice Between the Age Groups and Generations.* Yale University Press, New Haven.

Law, C.M. and Warnes, A.M. (1973) The movement of retired people to seaside resorts: a study of Morecambe and Llandudno. *Town Planning Review,* **44,** 373–390.

Law, C.M. and Warnes, A.M. (1975) Life begins at sixty: the increase in regional retirement migration. *Town and Country Planning,* **43,** 531–534.

Law, C.M. and Warnes, A.M. (1980) The characteristics of retired migrants. In: Herbert, D.T. and Johnston, R.J. (eds) *Geography and the Urban Environment. Progress in Research and Applications,* Volume III. Wiley, London, pp. 175–222.

Law, C.M. and Warnes, A.M. (1982) The destination decision in retirement migration. In: Warnes, A.M. (ed.) *Geographical Perspectives on the Elderly.* Wiley, London, pp. 53–81.

Lawton, M.P. (1975) The Philadelphia Geriatric Center morale scale: a revision. *Journal of Gerontology,* **30,** 85–89.

Lawton, M.P. (1980) *Environment and Aging.* Brooks-Cole Publishing Co., Monterey, CA.

Lawton, M.P. (1982) Competence, environmental press and the adaptation of older people. In: Lawton, M.P., Windley, P.G. and Byerts, T.O. (eds) *Aging and the Environment: Theoretical Approaches.* Springer, New York, pp. 33–59.

Lawton, M.P. (1984) The varieties of well-being. In: Malatesta, C.Z. and Izard, C.E. (eds) *Emotion in Adult Development.* Sage, Beverly Hills, pp. 67–84.

Lawton, M.P. and Nahemow, L. (1973) Ecology and the aging process. In: Eisdorfer, C. and Lawton, M.P. (eds) *The Psychology of Adult Development and Aging.* American Psychological Association, Washington, pp. 619–674.

Lawton, M.P. and Yaffe, S. (1970) Mortality, morbidity and voluntary change of residence by older people. *Journal of the American Geriatric Society,* **20,** 821–831.

Lazarus, R. (1966) *Psychological Stress and the Coping Process.* McGraw-Hill, New York.

Lazarus, R.S. and DeLongis, A. (1983) Psychological stress and coping in aging. *American Psychologist,* **38,** 245–254.

Lazarus, R., Averill, J. and Opton, E. (1974) The psychology of coping: issues of research and assessment. In: Coelho, G., Hamburg, D. and Adams, J. *Coping and Adaptation.* Basic Books, New York, pp. 249–315.

Leather, P. (1990) The potential implications of home equity release in old age. *Housing Studies,* **5,** 1, 3–13.

Leather, P. and Wheeler, R. (1988) *Making Use of Home Equity in Old Age.* Building Societies Association, London.

Le Gros Clark, F. (1966) *Work, Age and Leisure.* Michael Joseph, London.

Leech, K. (1977) *Soul Friend: A Study of Spirituality*. Sheldon, London.

Lefebvre, H. (1968) *The Sociology of Marx*. Pantheon Books, New York.

Lehr, U.M. (1982) Depression und 'Lebensqualitaet' im Alter-Korrelate negativer und positiver Gestimmtheit. *Zeitschrift für Gerontologie*, **15**, 241–249.

Lehr, U. and Thomae, H. (eds) (1987) *Formen seelischen Alterns*. Ferdinand Enke Verlag, Stuttgart.

Lemke, S. and Moos, R.H. (1986) Quality of residential settings for elderly adults. *Journal of Gerontology*, **41**, 268–276.

Lesnoff-Caravaglia, G. (ed.) (1988) *Aging in a Technological Society*. Human Sciences Press, New York.

Levin, E., Sinclair, I. and Gorbach, P. (1988) *Families, Services and Confusion in Old Age*. Gower, Aldershot.

Levinson, D.J., Darrow, D.N., Klein, E.B., Levinson, M.H. and McKee, B. (1978) *The Seasons of a Man's Life*. Knopf, New York.

Lieberman, M.A. and Tobin, S.S. (1983) *The Experience of Old Age: Stress, Coping and Survival*. Basic Books, New York.

Lifton, R.J. and Olson, E. (1974) *Living and Dying*. Wildwood House, London.

Liggett, J. (1974) *The Human Face*. Constable, London.

Light, E. and Lebowitz, B.D. (1990) (eds) *Alzheimer's Disease Treatment and Family Stress. Directions for Research*. Hemisphere, New York.

Lindemann, E. (1944) The symptomatology and management of acute grief. *American Journal of Psychiatry*, **101**, 141–148.

Linn, M.W., Hunter, K. and Harris, R. (1980) Symptoms for depression and recent life events in the community elderly. *Journal of Clinical Psychology*, **36**, 675–682.

Linton, A. (1982) *Not Expecting Miracles*. Centreprise Trust Ltd, London.

Lipman, A. and Longino, C. (1981) Family support networks in two life-care communities. Paper presented at the XIIth International Congress of Gerontology, Hamburg.

Lipman, A. and Slater, R. (1977) Homes for old people. Toward a positive environment. *The Gerontologist*, **17**, 146–156.

Lippman, W. (1922) *Public Opinion*. Macmillan, New York.

Littlewood, J. (1992) *Aspects of Grief: Bereavement in Adult Life*. Routledge, London.

Litwak, E. and Szelenyi, I. (1969) Primary group structures and their functions: kin, neighbours and friends. *American Sociological Review*, **34**, 465–472.

Logan, W.P.D. (1953) Work and age: statistical considerations. *British Medical Journal*, **2**, 1190–1193.

Lohmann, N. (1980) Life satisfaction research in aging: implications for policy development. In: Datan, N. and Lohmann, N. (eds) *Transitions of Aging*. Academic Press, New York.

Long, J. (1987) Continuity as a basis for change: leisure and male retirement. *Leisure Studies*, **6**, 55–70.

Longino, J. and Mancini, J. (1990) Aging couples and the family system. In: Brubaker, T. (ed.) *Family Relationships in Later Life*, 2nd edition. Sage, Beverly Hills. pp. 29–47.

Longmate, N. (1974) *The Workhouse*. Temple Smith, London.

Lopata, H. (1973) *Widowhood in an American City*. Schenkman, Cambridge, Mass.

Lopata, H. (1979) *Women as Widows*. Elsevier North Holland, New York.

Lopata, H. (1980) The widowed family member. In: Datan, N. and Lohmann, N. (eds) *Transitions of Ageing*. Academic Press, New York, pp. 93–118.

Lorand, A. (1922) *Old Age Deferred: The Causes of Old Age and Its Postponement by Hygienic and Therapeutic Measures*. Davis, Philadelphia.

Lowenthal, M. and Haven, C. (1968) Interaction and adaptation: intimacy as a critical variable. *American Sociological Review*, **33**, 20–30. Reprinted in Neugarten, B.L. (ed.) *Middle Age and Aging*. University of Chicago Press, Chicago, pp. 390–400.

Lowrey, S. and Briggs, R. (1988) Boom in private rest homes in Southampton: impact on the elderly in residential care. *British Medical Journal*, **296**, 541–543.

Luker, K.A. (1982) *Evaluating Health Visiting Practice*. Royal College of Nursing, London.

Luker, K.A. and Perkins, E.S. (1987) The elderly at home: service needs and provision. *Journal of the Royal College of General Practitioners*, **37**, 248–250.

Lund, D.A. (ed.) (1989) *Older Bereaved Spouses: Research with Practical Applications.* Hemisphere, New York.

Maas, H.S. (1985) The development of adult development: recollections and reflections. In: Munnichs, J.M.A., Mussen, P., Olbrich, E. and Coleman, P.G. (eds) *Life-span and Change in a Gerontological Perspective.* Academic Press, Orlando, CA, pp. 161–175.

Maas, H.S. and Kuypers, J.A. (1974) *From Thirty to Seventy: A Forty-Year Longitudinal Study of Adult Life Styles and Personality.* Jossey-Bass, San Francisco.

MacDonald, B. with Rich, C. (1984) *Look Me in the Eye: Old Women, Ageing and Ageism.* The Women's Press, London; Spinsters Book Company, San Francisco.

MacFarlane, A. (1986) *Marriage and Love in England: Modes of Reproduction 1300–1840.* Basil Blackwell, Oxford.

MacIntyre, S. (1977) Old age as a social problem. In: Dingwall, R., Heath, C., Reid, M. and Stacey, M. (eds) *Health Care and Health Knowledge.* Croom Helm, London, pp. 41–63.

Mack, J. and Lansley, S. (1985) *Poor Britain.* Allen and Unwin, London.

Mackinnon, R., Mackinnon, C. and Franken, M. (1989) Family strengths in long-term marriages. In: Ade-Ridder, L. and Hennon, C.B. (eds) *Life Styles of the Elderly.* Human Sciences Press, New York, p. 49–59.

Mackintosh, S., Means, R. and Leather, P. (1990) *Housing in Later Life. The Housing Finance Implications of an Ageing Society.* School for Advanced Urban Studies, Bristol.

Maddox, G.L. (1966) Retirement as a social event. In: McKinney, J.C. and de Vyer, F.T. (eds) *Aging and Social Policy.* Appleton Century-Crofts, New York.

Maddox, G.L. (1985) Constructing the future of ageing. In: Coleman, M.T., Smith, B.K. and Warren, C. (eds) *Looking Forward: Texas and its Elderly.* Hogg Foundation for Mental Health, University of Texas, Austin.

Maddox, G.L. and Douglass, E.B. (1973) Self-assessment of health: a longitudinal study of elderly subjects. *Journal of Health and Social Behaviour*, **14**, 87–93.

Maddox, G.L. and Douglass, E.B. (1974) Aging and individual differences: a longitudinal analysis of social, psychological and physiological indicators. *Journal of Gerontology*, **29**, 555–563.

Maeda, D. (1978) Ageing in eastern society. In: Hobman, D. (ed.) *The Social Challenge of Ageing.* Croom Helm, London, pp. 55–70.

Malinowski, B. (1922) *Argonauts of the Western Pacific.* Routledge and Kegan Paul, London.

Manton, K.G. (1982) Changing concepts of morbidity and mortality in the elderly population. *Milbank Memorial Fund Quarterly/Health and Society*, **60**, 183–244.

Markides, K.S. (ed.) (1989) *Ageing and Health: Perspectives on Gender, Race, Ethnicity and Class.* Sage, Newbury Park, CA.

Markides, K. and Cooper, C. (eds) (1987) *Retirement in Industrialised Societies.* John Wiley, Chichester.

Markides, K.S. and Cooper, C.L. (eds) (1989) *Ageing, Stress and Health.* Wiley, Chichester.

Marshall, V.W. (1980) *Last Chapters: A Sociology of Aging and Dying* Wadsworth, CA.

Martin, B. (1990) The cultural construction of ageing: or how long can the summer wine really last? In: Bury, M. and MacNicol, J. (eds) *Aspects of Ageing.* Royal Holloway and Bedford New College, London.

Martin, J. and Roberts, C. (1984) *Women and Employment: A Lifetime Perspective.* HMSO, London.

Martin, J., Meltzer, H. and Elliot, D. (1988a) *The Prevalence of Disability Among Adults. OPCS Surveys of Disability in Great Britain, Report No. 1.* HMSO, London.

Martin, J., White, A. and Meltzer, H. (1988b) *Disabled Adults: Services, Transport and Employment (OPCS),* HMSO, London.

Matza, D. (1969) *Becoming Deviant.* Prentice-Hall, Englewood Cliffs.

Maugham, S. (1959) *Points of View.* (Cited by Butler, R.N. (1963) op. cit.)

Maule, M.M., Milne, J.S. and Williamson, J. (1984) Mental illness and physical health in older people. *Age and Ageing*, **13**, 349–356.

Mauss, M. (1925) *The Gift*. Cohen and West, 1966 (English translation).

Maynard-Smith, J. (1962) Review lectures on senescence. 1. The causes of ageing. *Proceedings of the Royal Society of London, Series B*, **157**, 115–127.

McAdams, D.P. (1990) *The Person: An Introduction to Personality Psychology*. Harcourt Brace Jovanich, San Diego.

McCrae, R.R. and Costa, P.T. (1990) *Personality in Adulthood*. Guildford Press, New York.

McGlone, F. (1992) *Disability and Dependency in Old Age: A 'Demographic and Social Audit*. Family Policy Studies Centre, London.

McGoldrick, A. (1989) Stress, early retirement and health. In: Markides, K. and Cooper, C. *Aging, Stress and Health*. John Wiley, Chichester, pp. 91–118.

McGoldrick, A. and Cooper, C. (1980) Voluntary early retirement: taking the decision. *Employment Gazette*, August, 859–864.

McGoldrick, A. and Cooper, C. (1989) *Early Retirement*. Gower, Aldershot.

McIntyre, S. (1977) Old age as a social problem. In: Dingwall, R., Heath, C., Reid, M. and Stacey, M. (eds) *Health Care and Health Knowledge*. Croom Helm, London, pp. 41–63.

McKay, S (1992) *Pensioners' Assets*. PSI, London.

McKeown, T. (1979) *The Role of Medicine. Dream, Mirage or Nemesis?* Basil Blackwell, Oxford.

McMahon, A.W. and Rhudick, P.J. (1964) Reminiscing: adaptational significance in the aged. *Archives of General Psychiatry*, **10**, 292–298.

McManners, J. (1985) *Death and the Enlightenment: Changing Attitudes to Death Amongst Christians and Unbelievers in Eighteenth Century France*. Oxford University Press, Oxford.

Mead, G.H. (1964) In: Strauss, A. (ed.) *On Social Psychology: Selected Papers*. The University of Chicago Press, Chicago.

Means, R. (1984) *Meals on Wheels*. School for Advanced Urban Studies, Bristol.

Mellstromm, D., Nillson, A., Oden, A., Rundgren, A. and Svanborg, A. (1982) Mortality among the widowed in Sweden. *Scandinavian Journal of Social Medicine*, **10**, 33–41.

Mendelson, M.A. (1974) *Tender Loving Greed: How the Incredibly Lucrative Nursing Home 'Industry' Is Exploiting America's Old People and Defrauding Us All*. Alfred A. Knopf, New York.

Mergler, N.L. and Goldstein, M.D. (1983) Why are there old people? Senescence as biological and cultural preparedness for the transmission of information. *Human Development*, **26**, 72–90.

Merriam, S. (1980) The concept and function of reminiscence: a review of the research. *The Gerontologist*, **20**, 604–609.

Mertens, F. and Wimmers, M. (1987) Life-style of older people: improvement or threat to their health. *Ageing and Society*, **7**, 329–343.

Merton, R. (1968) *Social Theory and Social Structure*. Free Press, New York.

Michaud, E. (1986) Old age in a rural English village. Unpublished paper presented at a workshop on The Anthropology of Client Groups, London.

Middleton, S. (1987) *An After Dinner's Sleep*. Methuen, London.

Midwinter, E. (1987) *Redefining Old Age*. Centre for Policy on Ageing, London.

Miesen, B. (1992) Attachment theory and dementia. In: Jones, G. and Miesen, B. (eds) *Care-giving in Dementia: Research and Applications*. Routledge, London, pp. 38–56.

Miles, W.R. (1931) Measures of certain human abilities throughout the life-span. *Proceedings of the National Academy of Science*, **17**, 627–633.

Miller, E.J. and Gwynne, G.V. (1972) *A Life Apart. A Pilot Study of Residential Institutions for the Physically Handicapped and the Young Chronic Sick*. Tavistock, London.

Mills, C.W. (1959) *The Sociological Imagination*. Penguin, Harmondsworth, 1970.

Mills, M.A. and Walker, J.M. (1993) Memory, mood and dementia: a case study. *Journal of Aging Studies*, **7** (forthcoming).

Ministry of Pensions and National Insurance Report (1954) *Reasons Given for Retiring or Continuing at Work*. HMSO, London.

Ministry of Pensions and National Insurance (1966) *Financial and Other Circumstances of Retirement Pensioners*. HMSO, London.

Minkler, M. (1981) Research on the health effects of retirement: an uncertain legacy. *Journal of Health and Social Behaviour*, **22**, 117–130.

Minkler, M. and Estes, C. (eds) (1984) *Readings in the Political Economy of Aging*. Baywood Publishing Co., Farmingdale, New York.

Minkler, M. and Estes, C. (eds) (1991) *Critical Perspectives on Aging: the Political and Moral Economy of Growing Old*. Baywood, New York.

Minois, G. (1989) *The History of Old Age*. Polity Press, London.

Mitchell, A. (1993) Community Care Act: Implementation, *This Caring Business*. 18 February.

Moody, H.R. (1984) Reminiscence and the recovery of the public world. In: Kaminsky, M. (ed.) *The Uses of Reminiscence: New Ways of Working with Older Adults*. Haworth Press, New York, pp. 157–166.

Morgan, K.O. (1984) *Labour in Power*. Oxford University Press, Oxford.

Morgan, K., Dallosso, H.M., Arie, T., Byrne, E.J., Jones, R. and Waite, J. (1987) Mental health and psychological well-being among the old and very old living at home. *British Journal of Psychiatry*, **150**, 801–807.

Morris, R.G. and Kopelman, M.D. (1986) The memory deficits in Alzheimer-type dementia: a review. *The Quarterly Journal of Experimental Psychology*, **38A**, 575–602.

Moss, S. and Moss, M. (1989) The impact of the death of an elderly sibling. *American Behavioural Scientist*, **33**, 1, 94–106.

Moss, M. and Moss, S. (1992) Themes in parent–child relationships when elderly parents move nearby. *Journal of Aging Studies*, **6**, 3, 259–71.

Mullings, B. and Hamnett, C. (1992) Equity release schemes and equity extraction by elderly households in Britain. *Ageing and Society*, **12**, 4, 413–442.

Munnichs, J.M.A. (1966) *Old Age and Finitude*. Karger, Basle.

Munnichs, J.M.A. (1976) Dependency, interdependency and autonomy: an introduction. In: Munnichs, J.M.A. and van den Heuval, W.J.A. (eds) *Dependency and Interdependency in Old Age*. Martinus Nijhoff, The Hague, pp. 3–8.

Munnichs, J.M.A. (1987) Ageing and meaning: some reflections. Paper given at an international workshop on Ageing and Meaning, University of Nijmegen.

Munnichs, J.M.A. (1992) Ageing: a kind of autobiography. *European Journal of Gerontology*, **2**.

Munnichs, J.M.A., Mussen, P., Olbrich, E. and Coleman, P.G. (eds) (1985) *Life-span and Change in a Gerontological Perspective*. Academic Press, Orlando, CA.

Murie, A. (1983) *Housing Inequality and Deprivation*. Heinemann, London.

Murphy, E. (1982) Social origins of depression in old age. *British Journal of Psychiatry*, **141**, 135–142.

Murphy, E. (1983) The prognosis of depression in old age. *British Journal of Psychiatry*, **142**, 111–119.

Murphy, G. (1986) 'Over the hill and far away': The production of a video-assisted training package. In: Hanley, I. and Gilhooly, M. (eds) *Psychological Therapies for the Elderly*. Croom Helm, London, pp. 151–162.

Murphy, J.W. (1988) Making sense of postmodern sociology. *British Journal of Sociology*, **39**, 600–614.

Mussen, P. (1985) Early adult antecedents of life satisfaction at age 0. In: Munnichs, J.M.A., Mussen, P., Olbrich, E. and Coleman, P.G. (eds) *Life-span and Change in a Gerontological Perspective*. Academic Press, CA, pp. 45–61.

Mutchler, J.E. and Burr, J.A. (1991) A longitudinal analysis of household and non-household living arrangements in later life. *Demography*, **28**, 3, 375–390.

Myerhoff, B. (1978) *Number our Days*. Simon and Schuster, New York.

Nadelson, T. (1969) A survey of the literature on the adjustment of the aged to retirement. *Journal of Geriatric Psychiatry*, **3**, 3–20.

National Economic Development Council (1989) *Defusing the Demographic Timebomb.* NEDO, London.

National Institute for Social Work (1988) *Residential Care. A Positive Choice*, Report of the Independent Review of Residential Care chaired by G. Wagner. HMSO, London.

Naylor, G.F.K. and Harwood, E. (1977) Das akademische Lernen bei alten Menschen. *Aktuelle Gerontologie*, **7**, 397–400.

Nebes, R.D. (1989) Semantic memory in Alzheimer's disease. *Psychological Bulletin*, **106**, 377–394.

Nederveen Pieterse, J. (1992) *Black on White: Images of Africa and Blacks in Western Popular Culture.* Yale University Press, New Haven and London.

Neill, J., Sinclair, I., Gorbach, P. and Williams, J. (1988) *A Need for Care? Elderly Applicants for Local Authority Homes.* Avebury, Aldershot.

Neisser, U. (1982) *Memory Observed: Remembering in Natural Contexts.* Freeman, San Francisco.

Neugarten, B.L. (ed.) (1964) *Personality in Middle and Later Life.* Atherton Press, New York.

Neugarten, B.L. (1977) Personality and aging. In: Birren, J.E. and Schaie, K.W. (eds) *Handbook of the Psychology of Aging.* Van Nostrand Reinhold, New York, pp. 626–649.

Neugarten, B.L. (1988) Personality and psychosocial patterns of aging. In: Bergener, M., Ermini, M. and Stahelin, H.B. (eds) *Crossroads in Aging.* Academic Press, London, pp. 205–218.

Neugarten, B.L., Havighurst, R.J. and Tobin, S.S. (1961) The measurement of life satisfaction. *Journal of Gerontology*, **16**, 134–143.

Neugarten, B.L., Havighurst, R.J. and Tobin, S.E. (1968) Personality and patterns of aging. In: Neugarten, B.L. (ed.) *Middle Age and Aging.* University of Chicago Press, Chicago, pp. 173–177.

New Society (1982) The Family Pack, editorial. *New Society*, **62**, 1039–1067.

Newson, J. and Newson, E. (1965) *Patterns of Infant Care.* Penguin, London.

Newton, N.A., Brauer, D., Gutmann, D.L. and Grunes, J. (1986) Psychodynamic therapy with the aged. A review. In: Brink, T.L. (ed.) *Clinical Gerontology.* Haworth Press, New York, pp. 205–229.

Neysmith, S.M. and Edwardh, J. (1984) Economic dependency in the 1980s: its impact on the Third World elderly. *Ageing and Society*, **4**, 21–44.

Ngakpa Chogyan Ogyen Todgen (1989/90) The torch of uncertainty: extracts from a question and answer session. *Raft, The Journal of the Buddhist Hospice Trust*, Winter, **2**, 9.

Nies, H. and Munnichs, J. (1986) *Sinngebung und Altern.* Deutsches Zentrum fur Altersfragen, Berlin.

Nijkamp, P., Pacolet, J., Spinnewyn, H., Vollering, A., Wilderom, C. and Winters, S. (1991) *Services for the Elderly in Europe.* HIVA, Leuven.

Norman, A. (1980) *Rights and Risk: A Discussion Document on Civil Liberty in Old Age.* National Corporation for the Care of Old People, London.

Norman, A. (1985) *Triple Jeopardy: Growing Old in a Second Homeland.* Centre for Policy on Ageing, London.

Norman, A. (1987) *Aspects of Ageism: A Discussion Paper.* Centre for Policy on Ageing, London.

Norris, A. (1987) *Reminiscence with Elderly People.* Winslow Press, London.

O'Rand, A.M. and Henretta, J.C. (1982) Midwife work history and the retirement income of older single and married women. In: Szinovacz, M. (ed.) *Women's Retirement: Policy Implications for Recent Research.* Sage, California, pp. 25–44.

Office of Population Censuses and Surveys (1982) *General Household Survey 1980.* HMSO, London.

Office of Population Censuses and Surveys (1984a) *General Household Survey 1983.* HMSO, London.

Office of Population Censuses and Surveys (1984b) *Population Projections, 1981–2021*, Series PP2, No.12. HMSO, London.

Office of Population Censuses and Surveys (1984c) *Census Guide No. 1*. HMSO, London.
Office of Population Censuses and Surveys (1984d) *General Household Survey 1982*. HMSO, London.
Office of Population Censuses and Surveys (1987) *General Household Survey 1985*. HMSO, London.
Office of Population Censuses and Surveys (1988) *General Household Survey 1985*. HMSO, London.
Office of Population Censuses and Surveys (1989) *General Household Survey 1986*. HMSO, London.
Office of Population Censuses and Surveys (1991a) *General Household Survey 1989*. HMSO, London.
Office of Population Censuses and Surveys (1991b) *Based National Population Projections*, Series PP2, No. 17, HMSO, London.
Office of Population Censuses and Surveys (1992) *General Household Survey: Carers in 1990*. HMSO, London.
Office of Population Censuses and Surveys (1993a) *Population Trends*, No. 71, Spring.
Office of Population Censuses and Surveys (1993b) *The 1991 Census Persons Aged 60 and Over, Great Britain*. HMSO, London.
Office of Population Censuses and Surveys and Registrar General Scotland (1983) *Census 1981. Persons of Pensionable Age. Great Britain*. HMSO, London and Edinburgh.
Olbrich, E. (1985) Coping and development in the later years: a process-oriented approach to personality and development. In: Munnichs, J.M.A., Mussen, P., Olbrich, E. and Coleman, P.G. (eds) *Life-span and Change in a Gerontological Perspective*. Academic Press, Orlando, pp. 133–155.
Olbrich, E. and Thomae, H. (1978) Empirical findings to a cognitive theory of aging. *International Journal of Behavioral Development*, **1**, 67–84.
Oldman, C. (1990) *Moving in Old Age: New Directions in Housing Policies*. HMSO, London.
Olsen, H. and Hansen, G. (1981) *Living Conditions of the Aged 1977*. National Institute of Social Research, Copenhagen.
Open University (1990) *Working with Older People. 564*, The School of Health, Welfare and Community Education. Open University, Milton Keynes.
Oppenheim, C. (1993) *Poverty: The Facts* (revised and updated). Child Poverty Action Group, London.
Orgel, L.E. (1970) The maintenance of the accuracy of protein synthesis and its relevance to ageing: a correction. *Proceedings of the National Academy of Science* (USA), **67**, 1476–1479.
Orwell, G. (1939) *Coming Up for Air*. Gollancz, London.

Pahl, R.E., Flynn, R. and Buck, N.H. (1983) *Structure and Processes of Urban Life*, 2nd edition. Longman, London.
Palmore, E.B. (ed.) (1970) *Normal Aging*. Duke University Press, Durham, North Carolina.
Palmore, E.B. (ed.) (1974) *Normal Aging II*. Duke University Press, Durham, North Carolina.
Palmore, E.B. (1978) Compulsory versus flexible retirement: issues and facts. In: Carver, V. and Liddeard, P. (eds) *An Ageing Population*. Hodder and Stoughton, Sevenoaks, pp. 87–93.
Palmore, E.B. and Kivett, V. (1977) Change in life satisfaction: a longitudinal study of persons aged 46–70. *Journal of Gerontology*, **32**, 311–316.
Palmore, E.B. and Luikart, C. (1972) Health and social factors related to life satisfaction. *Journal of Health and Social Behaviour*, **13**, 68–80.
Palmore, E.G., Burchett, B., Fillenbaum, G., George, L. and Wallman, L. (1985) *Retirement: Causes and Consequences*. Springer, New York.
Panel on Nutrition of the Elderly (1972) *A Nutrition Survey of the Elderly*. Department of Health and Social Security, Reports on Health and Social Subjects No. 3. HMSO, London.

Parker, G. (1990) *With Due Care and Attention: A Review of Research on Informal Care* (2nd edn). Family Policy Studies Centre, London.

Parker, S. (1980) *Older Workers and Retirement*. HMSO, London.

Parkes, C.M. (1975) Determinants of grief following bereavement. *Omega*, **6**, 4, 303–23.

Parkes, C.M. (1986) *Bereavement: Studies of Grief in Adult Life*, 2nd edition. Tavistock, London.

Parkes, C.M. and Weiss, R.S. (1983) *Recovery from Bereavement*. Basic Books, New York.

Parnes, H. and Less, L. (1983) *From Work to Retirement: The Experience of a National Sample of Men*. Center for Human Resource Research, mimeo, Ohio State University.

Parry, G. (1986) Paid employment, life events, social support and mental health in working-class mothers. *Journal of Health and Social Behavior*, **27**, 193–208.

Parsons, P.L. (1965) Mental health of Swansea's old folk. *British Journal of Preventive and Social Medicine*, **19**, 43–47.

Parsons, T. (1942) Age and sex in the social structure of the United States. *American Sociological Review*, **7**, 604–616.

Peace, S. (1988) Living environments for the elderly. 2: Promoting the 'right' institutional environment. In: Wells, N. and Freer, C. (eds) *The Ageing Population. Burden or Challenge?* Macmillan, Basingstoke.

Peace, S. (ed.) (1990) *Researching Social Gerontology: Concepts, Methods and Issues*. Sage, London.

Peace, S. (1993a) Quality of institutional life. *Reviews in Clinical Gerontology*, **3**: 187–193.

Peace, S. (1993b) The living environments of older women. In: Bernard, M. and Meade, K. (eds) *Women Come of Age: Understanding the Lives of Older Women*. Edward Arnold, London.

Peck, R.C. (1968) Psychological developments in the second half of life. In: Neugarten, B.L. (ed.) *Middle Age and Aging*. University of Chicago Press, Chicago, pp. 88–92.

Pelling, M. and Smith, R. (eds) (1991) *Life, Death and the Elderly*. Routledge, London.

Pennington, D.R. (1986) *Essential Social Psychology*. Edward Arnold, London.

Perlmutter, M. and Mitchell, D.B. (1982) The appearance and disappearance of age differences in adult memory. In: Craik, F.I.M. and Trehub, S. (eds) *Aging and Cognitive Processes*. Plenum Press, New York, pp. 127–144.

Phillips Committee (1954) *Report of the Committee on the Economic and Financial Problems of the Provision for Old Age*, Cmnd 993. HMSO, London.

Phillips, J. (1992) *Private Residential Care: The Admission Process and Reactions of the Public Sector*. Avebury, Aldershot.

Phillipson, C. (1982) *Capitalism and the Construction of Old Age*. Macmillan, London.

Phillipson, C. (1987) The transition to retirement. In: Cohen, G. (ed.) *Social Change and the Life Course*. Tavistock, London, pp. 156–183.

Phillipson, C. (1991a) The social construction of old age: perspectives from political economy. *Reviews in Clinical Gerontology*. **1**, 4, 403–410.

Phillipson, C. (1991b) Inter-generational relations: conflict or consensus in the 21st century? *Policy and Politics*, **19**, 1, 27–36.

Phillipson, C. and Strang, P. (1983) *Pre-retirement Education: A Longitudinal Evaluation*. Department of Adult Education, University of Keele, Stoke-on-Trent.

Phillipson, C. and Walker, A. (1986) *Ageing and Social Policy*. Gower, Aldershot.

Pifer, A. and Bronte, L. (eds) (1987) *Our Ageing Society*. W.W. Norton, New York.

Pilisuk, M. and Parks, S.H. (1986) *The Healing Web: Social Networks and Human Survival*. University Press of New England, Hanover, New Hampshire.

Pincus, A. and Wood, V. (1970) Methodological issues in measuring the environment in institutions for the aged and its impact on residents. *Ageing and Human Development*, **1**, 117–126.

Pincus, L. (1976) *Death and the Family*. Faber, London.

Pleck, J. (1975) Man to man: is brotherhood possible? In: Glazer-Malbin, N. (ed.) *Old Family, New Family*. Van Nostrand, New York, pp. 230–244.

Political and Economic Planning (1948) *Population Policy in Great Britain*. PEP, London.

Porter, R. (1982) *English Society in the Eighteenth Century*. Penguin, Harmondsworth.

Post, F. and Shulman, K. (1985) New views on old age affective disorders. In: Arie, T. (ed.) *Recent Advances in Psychogeriatrics*. Churchill Livingstone, Edinburgh, pp. 119–140.

Pratt, H.J. (1976) *The Politics of Old Age*. University of Chicago Press, Chicago.

Pratt, J.D. and Wood, L.E. (1984) Cognition and elderly people. *Ageing and Society*, **4**, 273–304.

Pre-Retirement Choice (1974) October.

Prior, L. (1989) *The Social Organisation of Death*. Macmillan, London.

Pritchard, J. (1992) *The Abuse of Elderly People. A Handbook for Professionals*. Jessica Kingsley, London.

Puner, M. (1978) *To the Good Long Life: What we Know About Growing Old*. Macmillan/The Open University, London.

Quadagno, J. (1982) *Ageing in Early Industrial Society: Work, Family and Social Policy in 19th Century England*. Academic Press, London.

Qureshi, H. (1986) Responses to dependency: reciprocity and power in family relations. In: Phillipson, C., Bernard, M. and Strang, P. (eds) *Dependency and Interdependency in Old Age – Theoretical Perspectives and Policy Alternatives*. Croom Helm, London, pp. 167–179.

Qureshi, H. and Walker, A. (1989) *The Caring Relationship. Elderly People and Their Families*. Macmillan, London.

Rabbitt, P.M.A. (1980) A fresh look at changes in reaction times in old age. In: Stein, D. (ed.) *The Psychobiology of Ageing: Problems and Perspectives*. Elsevier/North Holland, New York.

Rabbitt, P.M.A. (1981) Talking to the old. *New Society*, 22 January, 141–142.

Rabbitt, P.M.A. (1982a) How to assess the aged? An experimental psychologist's view. Some comments on Dr Kendrick's paper. *British Journal of Clinical Psychology*, **21**, 55–59.

Rabbitt, P.M.A. (1982b) How do old people know what to do next? In: Craik, F.I.M. and Trehub, S. (eds) *Aging and Cognitive Processes*. Plenum Press, New York, pp. 79–98.

Rabbitt, P.M.A. (1984a) Investigating the grey areas. *Times Higher Education Supplement*, 1 June, 14.

Rabbitt, P.M.A. (1984b) Memory impairment in the elderly. In: Bebbington, P.E. and Jacoby, R. (eds) *Psychiatric Disorders in the Elderly*. Mental Health Foundation, London, pp. 101–119.

Rabbitt, P.M.A. (1985) An age decrement in the ability to ignore irrelevant information. *Journal of Gerontology*, **20**, 233–238.

Rabbitt, P.M.A. (1988) Social psychology, neuroscience and cognitive psychology need each other; (and gerontology needs all three of them). *The Psychologist: Bulletin of the British Psychological Society*, **12**, 500–506.

Rabinowitz, J.C. and Ackerman, B.P. (1982) General encoding of episodic events by elderly adults. In: Craik, F.I.M. and Trehub, S. (eds) *Aging and Cognitive Processes*. Plenum Press, New York, pp. 145–154.

Rachels, J. (1986) *The End of life: Euthanasia and Morality*. Oxford University Press, Oxford.

Raglan, Lord (1972) *Retirement Choice*, **2**.

Raphael, B. (1983) *An Anatomy of Bereavement: A Handbook for the Caring Professionals*. Hutchinson, London.

Rapoport, R. and Rapoport, R. (1977) *Fathers, Mothers and Others*. Routledge and Kegan Paul, London.

Rebok, G.W. and Hoyer, W.J. (1977) The functional context of elderly behaviour. *The Gerontologist*, **17**, 27–34.

Registered Homes Act, 1984. HMSO, London.

Reichard, S., Livson, F. and Peterson, P.G. (1962) *Aging and Personality*. Wiley, New York.

Reker, G.T. and Wong, P.T.P. (1988) Aging as an individual process: toward a theory of personal meaning. In: Birren, J.E. and Bengtson, V.L. (eds) *Emergent Theories of Aging*. Springer, New York, pp. 214–246.

Reker, G.T., Peacock, E.J. and Wong, P.T.P. (1987) Meaning and purpose in life and well-being: a life-span perspective. *Journal of Gerontology*, **42**, 44–49.

Renshaw, J., Hampson, R., Thomason, C., Darton, R., Judge, K. and Knapp, M. (eds) (1988) *Care in the Community: The First Steps*. Gower, Aldershot.

Report of the Royal Commission on the Poor Laws (1834) *Report of the Royal Commission on the Poor Laws and Relief of Distress*. HMSO, London.

Retirement Choice (1972) November, **1**, 2.

Rex, J. and Moore, R. (1967) *Race, Community and Conflict*. Oxford University Press, Oxford.

Richardson, I.M. (1956) Retirement: A socio-medical study of 244 men. *Scottish Medical Journal*, **1**, 381–391.

Riegel, K.F. (1973) Dialectical operations: the final period of cognitive development. *Human Development*, **16**, 346–370.

Riegel, K.F. (1977) History of psychological gerontology. In: Birren, J.E. and Schaie, K.W. (eds) *Handbook of the Psychology of Aging*. Van Nostrand Reinhold, New York, pp. 70–102.

Riegel, K.F. and Riegel, R.M. (1972) Development, drop and death. *Developmental Psychology*, **6**, 306–319.

Riley, M.W., Johnson, M. and Foner, A. (1968) *Aging and Society: An Inventory of Research Findings*. Russel and Sage, New York.

Ritchie, J. and Barrowclough, R. (1983) *Paying for Equalisation*. EOC, Manchester.

Robinson, P.K., Livingston, J. and Birren, J. (eds) (1984) *Aging and Technological Advances*. Plenum, New York.

Robson, B.T. (1975) *Urban Social Areas*. Oxford University Press, Oxford.

Robson, P. (1980) *Profiles of the Elderly: 7, Their Housing, Vol. 5*. Age Concern, London.

Rodin, J. (1986) Aging and health: effects of the sense of control. *Science*, **233**, 1271–1276.

Roebuck, J. (1978) When does 'old age' begin? The evolution of the English definition. *Journal of Social History*, **12**, 416–428.

Roebuck, J. and Slaughter, J. (1979) Ladies and pensioners: stereotypes and public policy affecting old women in England, 1880–1940. *Journal of Social History*, **13**, 105–114.

Rose, A.M. (1965a) A current theoretical issue in social gerontology. In: Rose, A.M., Arnold, M. and Peterson, W.A. *Older People and their Social Worlds*. F.A. Davis, Philadelphia, pp. 359–366.

Rose, A.M. (1965b) The subculture theory of aging: a framework for research in social gerontology. In: Rose, A.M., Arnold, M. and Peterson, W.A. *Older People and their Social Worlds*. F.A. Davis, Philadelphia, pp. 3–16.

Rose, E. (1978) *Housing for the Aged*. Saxon House, Farnborough.

Rose, E. (1982) *Housing Needs and the Elderly*. Gower, Aldershot.

Rosow, I. (1974) *Socialization of the Aged*. Free Press, New York.

Rosow, I. (1975) *Socialization to Old Age*. University of California Press, Berkeley.

Rosow, I. (1977) Morale: concept and measurement. In: Nydegger, C.N. (ed.) *Measuring Morale: A Guide to Effective Measurement*. Gerontological Society, Washington DC.

Rosser, C. and Harris, C. (1965) *The Family in Social Change*. Routledge and Kegan Paul, London.

Rossi, A. and Rossi, P. (1990) *Of Human Bonding: Parent–Child Relations across the Life Course*, Aldine de Gruyter, New York.

Rossiter, C. and Wicks, M. (1982) *Crisis or Challenge? Family Care, Elderly People and Social Policy*. Study Commission on the Family, London.

Rothwell, N., Britton, P.G. and Woods, R.T. (1983) The effect of group living in a residential home for the elderly. *British Journal of Social Work*, **13**, 639–643.

Rott, C. and Thomae, H. (1991) Coping in longitudinal perspective: findings from the Bonn Longitudinal Study on Aging. *Journal of Cross-Cultural Gerontology*, **6**, 23–40.

Rowe, J.W. and Kahn, R.L. (1987) Human aging: usual and successful. *Science*, **237**, 143–149.

Rowles, G. (1980) Toward a geography of growing old. In: Buttimer, A. and Seamon, D. (eds) *The Human Experience of Space and Place*. Croom Helm, London, pp. 55–72.

Rowles, G. (1981) The surveillance zone as meaningful space for the aged. *The Gerontologist*, **21**, 304–311.

Rowntree, B.S. (1901) *Poverty: A Study of Town Life*. Macmillan, London.

Royal Commission on Population (1949) *Report*. HMSO, London.

Royal Commission on the Distribution of Income and Wealth (1978) *Lower Incomes*, Report No. 6. HMSO, London.

Rubin, S.G. and Davies, G.H. (1975) Bed blocking by elderly patients in general wards. *Age and Ageing*, **4**, 142–147.

Runyan, W.M. (1984) *Life Histories and Psychobiography: Explorations in Theory and Method*. Oxford University Press, New York.

Ryff, C.D. (1984) Personality development from the inside: the subjective experience of change in adulthood and aging. In: Baltes, P.B. and Brim, O.G. (eds) *Life-span Development and Behavior Vol. 6*. Academic Press, New York, pp. 243–279.

Ryff, C.D. and Heincke, S.G. (1983) Subjective organisation of personality in adulthood and aging. *Journal of Personality and Social Psychology*, **44**, 807–816.

Sackville-West, V. (1931) *All Passion Spent*. Hogarth Press, London.

Salthouse, T.A. (1987) The role of experience in cognitive aging. In: Schaie, K.W. and Eisdorfer, C. (eds) *Annual Review of Gerontology and Geriatrics*, **7**, 135–158.

Salthouse, T.A. (1991) *Theoretical Perspectives on Cognitive Aging*. Lawrence Erlbaum, Hillsdale.

Sanders, C.M. (1988) Risk factors in bereavement outcome. *Journal of Social Issues* **44**, 3, 97–100.

Saunders, C. (1981) (ed.) *Hospice: The Living Idea*. Edward Arnold, London.

Savage, R.D., Britton, P.G., Bolton, N. and Hall, E.H. (1973) *Intellectual Functioning in the Aged*. Methuen, London.

Savage, R.D., Gaber, L.B., Britton, P.G., Bolton, N. and Cooper, A. (1977) *Personality and Adjustment in the Aged*. Academic Press, London.

Schaie, K.W. (1977–78) Towards a stage theory of adult cognitive development. *Journal of Aging and Human Development*, **8**, 129–138.

Schaie, K.W. (1990) The optimization of cognitive functioning in old age: predictions based on cohort-sequential and longitudinal data. In: Baltes, P.B. and Baltes, M.M. (eds) *Successful Aging: Perspectives from the Behavioral Sciences*. Cambridge University Press, New York, pp. 94–117.

Schaie, K.W. and Marquette, B. (1972) Personality in maturity and old age. In: Dreges, R.M. (ed.) *Multivariate Personality Research: Contributions to the Understanding of Personality in Honour of Raymond B. Cattell*. Clautors, Louisiana.

Schama, S. (1988) *The Embarassment of Riches: An Interpretation of Dutch Culture in The Golden Age*. Fontana, London.

Scheff, T.J. (1964) The societal reaction to deviance: ascriptive elements in the psychiatric screening of mental patients in a Midwestern State. *Social Problems*, **11**, 401–413.

Scheff, T. (1974) The labelling theory of mental illness. *American Sociological Review*, **39**, 444–452.

Scheidt, R.J. and Windley, P.G. (1985) The ecology of aging. In: Birren, J.E. and Schaie, K.W. (eds) *Handbook of the Psychology of Aging*. Van Nostrand Reinhold, New York, pp. 245–258.

Schneider, W.F. (1987) Die psychische und soziale Situation von Hochbetagten. In: Lehr, U. and Thomae, H. (eds) *Formen seelischen Alterns, Ergebnisse und Eindrucke vom 8. Untersuchungsdurchgang*. Enke, Stuttgart, pp. 196–227.

Schooler, K.K. (1982) Response of the elderly to environment. A stress-theoretical perspective. In: Lawton, M.P., Windley, P.G. and Byerts, T.O. (eds) *Aging and the Environment: Theoretical Approaches*. Springer, New York, pp. 80–96.

Schuller, T. (1989) Working-ending: employment and ambiguity in later life. In: Bytheway, B., Keil, T., Allott, P. and Bryman, A. (eds) *Becoming and Being Old*. Sage, London.

Schutz, A. (1972) *The Phenomenology of the Social World*. Heinemann, London.

Schwartz, A.N. (1975) An observation on self-esteem as the linchpin of quality of life for the aged. *The Gerontologist*, **15**, 470–472.

Schwartz, H. (1986) *Never Satisfied: A Cultural History of Diets, Fantasies and Fat*. Free Press/ Collier Macmillan, New York and London.

Scott, J.P. (1990) Sibling interaction in later life. In: Brubaker, T. (ed.) *Family Relationships in Later Life*, 2nd edition. Sage, Beverly Hills, pp. 86–99.

Scrutton, S. (1990) Ageism. In: McEwan, E. (ed.) *Age: The Unrecognised Discrimination*. Age Concern Pulbications, London.

Seabrook, J. (1980) *The Way We Are*. Age Concern England, Mitcham, Surrey.

Seale, C. (1990) Caring for people who die: the experience of family and friends. *Ageing and Society*, **1**, 413–428.

Seale, C. (1991) Death from cancer and death from other causes: the relevance of the hospice appraoch. *Palliative Medicine*, **5**, 12, 12–19.

Seale, C. (1993) Demographic change and the care of the dying, 1969–1987. In: Dickenson, D. and Johnson, M. (eds) *Death, Dying and Bereavement*. Sage, London, pp. 45–54.

Secretaries of State for Health, Social Security, Wales and Scotland (1989) *Caring for People. Community Care in the Next Decade and Beyond*, CM849 (White Paper). HMSO, London.

Seiden, A. and Bart, P. (1975) Woman to woman. In: Glazer-Malbin, N. (ed.) *Old Family, New Family*. Van Nostrand, New York, pp. 189–228.

Selye, H. (1976) *The Stress of Life*. McGraw-Hill, New York.

Shanas, E. (1979) Social myth as hypothesis: the case of the family relationships of old people. *Gerontology*, **19**, 3–9.

Shanas, E. (1980) Older people and their families: the new pioneers. *Journal of Marriage and the Family*, **42**, 9–15.

Shanas, E., Townsend, P., Wedderburn, D., Friis, H., Milhoj, P. and Stehouwer, J. (1965) *Old People in Three Industrial Societies*. Routledge and Kegan Paul, London.

Shapiro, J. (1989) *Ourselves Growing Older: Women, Ageing with Knowledge and Power*. Fontana/Collins, London.

Sharp, A.D. (1988) The impact of ageing upon the attitudes and behaviour of elderly residents in McCarthy and Stone private sheltered housing. Unpublished PhD Thesis, University of Southampton.

Shaw, L.B. (1984) Retirement plans of middle-aged married women. *The Gerontologist*, **24**, 154–159.

Sheehy, G. (1976) *Passages: Predictable Crises of Adult Life*. Dutton, New York.

Sheldon, J.H. (1948) *The Social Medicine of Old Age*. Oxford University Press, Oxford.

Shephard, R.J. (1978) *Physical Activity and Ageing*. Croom Helm, London.

Sherman, E. (1981) *Counseling the Aging: an Integrative Approach*. Free Press, New York.

Shorter, E. (1983) *A History of Women's Bodies*. Allen Lane, London.

Shragge, E. (1984) *Pensions Policy in Britain*. Routledge and Kegan Paul, London.

Sidell, M. (1991) Gender differences in the health of older women. Research Report, Milton Keynes, Dept. of Health and Social Welfare, Open University.

Sidell, M. (1993) Health issues and the older woman. In: Bernard, M. and Meade, K. (eds) *Women Come of Age: Perspectives on the Lives of Older Women*. Edward Arnold, London, pp. 63–84.

Siegler, I.C. (1980) The psychology of adult development and aging. In: Busse, E.W. and Blazer, D.G. (eds) *Handbook of Geriatric Psychiatry*. Van Nostrand Reinhold, New York, pp. 169–221.

Siegler, I.C. (1983) Psychological aspects of the Duke longitudinal studies. In: Schaie, K.W. (ed.) *Longitudinal Studies of Adult Psychological Development*. The Guilford Press, New York.

Siegler, I.C. and Botwinick, J. (1979) A long-term longitudinal study of the intellectual ability of older adults – the matter of selective subject attrition. *Journal of Gerontology*, **34**, 242–248.

Simenon, G. (1976) *The Cat*. In: *Ninth Omnibus Edition*. Penguin, London.

Simpson, I.H. and McKinney, J.C. (1966) *Social Aspects of Ageing*. Duke University Press, Durham, North Carolina.

Sinclair, I., Parker, R., Leat, D. and Williams, J. (1990) *The Kaleidoscope of Care: A Review of Research on Welfare Provision for Elderly People*. HMSO, London.

Sixsmith, A.J. (1986a) Independence and home in later life. In: Phillipson, C., Bernard, M. and Strang, P. (eds) *Dependency and Interdependency in Old Age – Theoretical Perspectives and Policy Alternatives*. Croom Helm, London, pp. 338–347.

Sixsmith, A.J. (1986b) The meaning of home: an exploratory study of environmental experience. *Journal of Environmental Psychology*, **6**, 281–298.

Sixsmith, A.J. (1990) The meaning and experience of 'home' in later life. In: Bytheway, B., and Johnson, J. (eds) *Welfare and the Ageing Experience*. Avebury, Aldershot.

Skinner, B.F. and Vaughan, M.E. (1983) *Enjoy Old Age: A Programme of Self-management*. Hutchinson, London.

Sklar, R. and Hartley, S.F. (1990) Close friends as survivors: bereavement patterns in a 'hidden' population. *Omega*, **21**, 20, pp. 103–112.

Skultans, V. (1979) *English Madness: Ideas on Insanity 1580–1890*. Routledge and Kegan Paul, London.

Smith, H.W. (1975) *Strategies of Social Research. The Methodological Imagination*. Prentice-Hall, Englewood Cliffs, NJ.

Smith, K. (1989) *Housing Agencies for Elderly Home Owners*. SHAC, London.

Smith, P.B. and Smith, L.J. (1987) *Continence and Incontinence: Psychological Approaches to Development and Treatment*. Croom Helm, London.

Smythe, M. and Browne, F. (1992) *General Household Survey 1990*. HMSO, London.

Sommer, R. and Ross, H. (1958) Social interaction on a geriatric ward. *International Journal of Social Psychiatry*, **4**, 128–133.

Sontag, S. (1978) The double standard of ageing. In: Carver, V. and Liddiard, P. (eds) *An Ageing Population: A Reader and Sourcebook*. Hodder and Stoughton, The Open University Press, Sevenoaks, pp. 72–78.

Stearns, P. (1977) *Old Age in European Society: The Case of France*. Croom Helm, London.

Sternberg, R.J. (ed.) (1990) *Wisdom: Its Nature, Origins and Development*. Cambridge University Press, New York.

Stieglitz, E.J. (1949) *The Second Forty Years*. Staples Press, London.

Stoddard, K.M. (1983) *Saints and Shrews: Women and Ageing in American Popular Film*. Greenwood Press, London.

Stone, L. (1977) Walking over Grandma. *The New York Review of Books*, **24**, May 12, 26–29.

Stone, R. and Minkler, M. (1984) The socio-political context of women's retirement. In: Minkler, M. and Estes, C. (eds) *Political Economy of Aging*. Baywood Publishing Co., New York, pp. 225–238.

Stott, M. (1981) *Ageing for Beginners*. Basil Blackwell, Oxford.

Stout, R.W. and Crawford, V. (1988) Active-life expectancy and terminal dependency: trends in long-term geriatric care over 33 years. *The Lancet*, **i**, 281–283.

Strauss, A. (1971) *Anguish: The Case History of a Dying Trajectory*. Sociology Press, San Francisco, CA.

Strehler, B.L. (1962) *Time, Cells and Aging*. Academic Press, New York and London.

Streib, G.F and Schneider, C.J. (1971) *Retirement in American Society*. Cornell University Press, Ithaca.

Stuart-Hamilton, I. (1991) *The Psychology of Ageing: An Introduction*. Jessica Kingsley, London.

Sugarman, L. (1986) *Life-span Development. Concepts, Theories and Interventions*. Methuen, London.

Szasz, T.S. (1971) *The Manufacture of Madness*. Routledge and Kegan Paul, London.

Szinovacz, M. (ed.) (1982) *Women's Retirement*. Sage, London.

Szinovacz, M. (1991) Women and retirement. In: Hess, B. and Markson, E. (eds) *Growing Old in America*. Transaction Publishers, New York.

Szinovacz, M., Ekerdt, D. and Vinick, B. (eds) (1992) *Families and Retirement*. Sage, London.

Tamke, S.S. (1978) Human values and ageing: the perspective of the Victorian nursery. In: Spicker, S.F., Woodward, K.M. and Van Tassel, D.D. (eds) *Ageing and the Elderly: Humanistic Perspectives in Gerontology*. Humanities Press, Atlantic Islands, New Jersey, pp. 63–81.

Taylor, H. (1983a) *The Hospice Movement in Britain, its Role and Future*. Centre for Policy on Ageing, London.

Taylor, H. (1983b) The hospice concept and the National Health Service. In: Jerrome, D. (ed.) *Ageing in Modern Britain*. Croom Helm, London.

Taylor, P. and Walker, A. (1992) *Too Old At 50?* Campaign for Work, London.

Taylor, R. and Ford, G. (1983) Inequalities in old age. *Ageing and Society*, **3**, 183–208.

Ten Havey, H. (1992) Euthanasia in the Netherlands. In: Dickenson, D. and Johnson, M. (eds) *Death, Dying and Bereavement*. Sage, London, pp. 147–158.

Thane, P. (1978) The muddled history of retiring at 60 and 65. *New Society*, 3 August, 234–236.

Thane, P. (1985) Old age in Victorian Britain. *New Age*, **30**, 11–12.

Thane, P. (1987) *Economic Burden or Benefit? A Positive View of Old Age*. Centre for Economic Policy Research, London.

Thane, P. (1988) The growing burden of an ageing population. *Journal of Public Health*, **7**, 373–387.

Thomae, H. (ed.) (1976) *Patterns of aging: findings from the Bonn Longitudinal Study of Aging*. Karger, Basle.

Thomae, H. (1983) *Alternsstile and Altersschicksale*. Hans Huber, Bern.

Thomae, H. (1986) Response hierarchies related to different areas of life stress. In: Angleitner, A., Furnham, A. and Van Heck, G. (eds) *Personality Psychology in Europe Vol. 2*. Swets and Zeitlinger, Lisse, pp. 47–62.

Thomas, K. (1976) Age and authority in early modern England. *Proceedings of the British Academy*, **62**, 205–248.

Thompson, C. and West, P. (1984) The public appeal of sheltered housing. *Ageing and Society*, **4**, 305–326.

Thompson, P. (1992) 'I don't feel old': subjective ageing and the search for meaning in later life. *Ageing and Society*, **12**, 23–48.

Thompson, P., Itzin, C., and Abendstern, M. (1990) *I Don't Feel Old: The Experience of Later Life*. Oxford University Press, Oxford.

Thomson, D. (1983) Workhouse to nursing home: residential care of elderly people in England since 1840. *Ageing and Society*, **3**, 41–69.

Thomson, D. (1984) The decline of social welfare: falling state support for the elderly since early Victorian times. *Ageing and Society*, **4**, 4, 451–482.

Thornton, S. and Brotchie, J. (1987) Reminiscence: a critical review of the empirical literature. *British Journal of Clinical Psychology*, **26**, 93–111.

Tibbitts, C. (1954) Retirement problems in American society. *American Journal of Sociology*, **59**, 301–308.

Timaeus, I. (1986) Families and households of the elderly population. *Ageing and Society*, **6**, 271–293.

Tinker, A. (1984) *Staying at Home: Helping Elderly People*. HMSO, London.

Tinker, A. (1987) A review of the contribution of housing to policies for the frail elderly. *International Journal of Geriatric Psychiatry*, **2**, 3–17.

Tinker, A. (1989) *An Evaluation of Very Sheltered Housing*. HMSO, London.

Titmuss, R.M. (1963) *Essays on 'the Welfare State'*, 2nd edition. Allen and Unwin, London.

Titmuss, R.M. (1970) *The Gift Relationship: From Human Blood to Social Policy*. Allen and Unwin, London.

Tobin, S.S. (1991) *Personhood in Advanced Old Age: Implications for Practice*. Springer, New York.

Todd, A.T. (1946) *Medical Aspects of Growing Old*. John Wright and Sons Ltd, Bristol.

Toscani, F., Cantoni, L., Di Milo, G., Mori, M., Santosuosso, A. and Tamburini, M. (1991) Death and dying: perspectives and attitudes in Italy. *Palliative Medicine*, 5, 334–343.

Townsend, J., Frank, A., Fermont, D., Dyer, S., Karran, G., Walgrove, A. and Piper, M. (1990) Terminal cancer care and patients' preference for place of death. *British Medical Journal*, 301, 415–417.

Townsend, P. (1955) The anxieties of retirement. *Transactions of the Association of Industrial Medical Officers*, 5, 1.

Townsend, P. (1957) *The Family Life of Old People*. Routledge and Kegan Paul, London.

Townsend, P. (1962) *The Last Refuge – A Survey of Residential Institutions and Homes for the Aged in England and Wales*. Routledge and Kegan Paul, London.

Townsend, P. (1965) On the likelihood of admission to an institution. In: Shanas, E. and Streib, G.F. (eds) *Social Structure and the Family Generational Relations*. Prentice-Hall Inc., New York, pp. 163–187.

Townsend, P. (1979) *Poverty in the United Kingdom. A Survey of Household Resources and Standards of Living*. Penguin Books, Harmondsworth.

Townsend, P. (1981) The structured dependency of the elderly: creation of social policy in the twentieth century. *Ageing and Society*, 1, 5–28.

Townsend, P. (1986) Ageism and social policy. In: Phillipson, C. and Walker, A. (eds) *Ageing and Social Policy*. Gower, London, pp. 15–44.

Townsend, P. (1989) The social and economic hardship of elderly people in London: new evidence from a survey and a discussion of the influence of social policy upon current trends. *Generations*, 9, 10–30.

Townsend, P. and Wedderburn, D. (1965) *The Aged in the Welfare State*, Occasional Papers on Social Administration, No.14. Bell and Sons, London.

Townsend, P. with Corrigan, P. and Kowarzik, U. (1987) *Poverty and Labour in London*. Low Pay Unit, London.

Treas, J. and Bengtson, V. (1987) The family in later years. In: Sussman, M.B and Steinmetz S.K. (eds) *Handbook of Marriage and the Family*. Plenum Press, New York, pp. 625–48.

Troll, L. and Smith, J. (1976) Attachment through the lifespan. *Human Development*, 19, 156–170.

Tunstall, J. (1966) *Old and Alone*. Routledge and Kegan Paul, London.

Twigger, R. (1992) *The Pension and Pensioners' Incomes*, House of Commons Library, London.

Twining, C. (1988) *Helping Older People: A Psychological Approach*. Wiley, Chichester.

Twycross, R.G. (1990) Assisted death: a reply. *The Lancet*, 336, 29 September, pp. 796–798.

Ungerson, C. (1987) *Policy is Personal: Sex, Gender and Informal Care*. Tavistock, London.

United Nations (1985) *The World Ageing Situation: Strategies and Policies*. United Nations, New York.

Vetter, N. (1981) Urinary incontinence in the elderly at home. *The Lancet*, 1275–1277.

Victor, C.R. (1987) *Old Age in Modern Society*. Croom Helm, London.

Victor, C.R. (1991) *Health and Health Care in Later Life*. Open University Press, Buckingham.

Victor, C.R. (1993) Health policy and services for dying people and their carers. In: Dickenson, D. and Johnson, M. (eds) *Death, Dying and Bereavement*. Sage, London, pp. 55–63.

Wade, B., Sawyer, L. and Bell, J. (1983) *Dependency with Dignity*, Occasional Papers on Social Administration, No. 68. Bedford Square Press, London.

Waldman, D.S. and Avolio, B.S. (1983) *Enjoy Old Age*. Norton, New York.

Walker, A. (1980) The social creation of poverty and dependence in old age. *Journal of Social Policy*, 9, 49–75.

Walker, A. (1981) Towards a political economy of old age. *Ageing and Society*, 1, 73–94.

Walker, A. (1982a) The social consequences of early retirement. *Political Quarterly*, **53**, 61–72.

Walker, A. (1982b) Dependency and old age. *Social Policy and Administration*, **16**, 115–135.

Walker, A. (1982c) *Community Care. The Family, the State and Social Policy*. Basil Blackwell, Oxford.

Walker, A. (1983) Social policy and elderly people in Great Britain: the construction of dependent social and economic status in old age. In: Guillemard, A. (ed.) *Old Age and the Welfare State*. Sage, Beverly Hills, pp. 143–167.

Walker, A. (1985) Early retirement: release or refuge from the labour market? *The Quarterly Journal of Social Affairs*, **1**, 211–229.

Walker, A. (1986a) The politics of ageing in Britain. In: Phillipson, C., Bernard, M. and Strang, P. (eds) *Dependency and Interdependency in Later Life: Theoretical Perspectives and Policy Alternatives*. Croom Helm, London, pp. 30–45.

Walker, A. (1986b) The growth of poverty among the elderly population and the reasons for low take up of benefits. In: *Poverty and Older People*. Age Concern Scotland, Edinburgh, pp. 8–20.

Walker, A. (1986c) Pensions and the production of poverty in old age. In: Phillipson, C. and Walker, A. (eds) *Ageing and Social Policy*. Gower, London, pp. 184–216.

Walker, A. (1987) The poor relation: poverty among old women. In: Glendinning, C. and Millar, J. (eds) *Women and Poverty in Britain*. Wheatsheaf Books, Brighton, pp. 178–198.

Walker, A. (1989) The social division of early retirement. In: Jeffereys, M. (ed.) *Growing Old in the Twentieth Century*. Routledge, London.

Walker, A. (1992) The poor relation: poverty among old women. In: Glendinning, C. and Millar, J. (eds) *Women and Poverty in Britain*, 2nd edition. Wheatsheaf Books, Brighton, pp. 178–198.

Walker, A. and Laczko, F. (1982) Early retirement and flexible retirement. In: House of Commons Social Services Committee, *Age of Retirement*, HC 26–II, HMSO, London, pp. 211–229.

Walker, A. and Phillipson, C. (1986) Introduction. In: Phillipson, C. and Walker, A. (eds) *Ageing and Social Policy. A Critical Assessment*. Gower, Aldershot, pp. 1–12.

Walker, A. and Phillipson, C. (eds) (1986) *Ageing and Social Policy*. Gower, Aldershot.

Walker, A. and Walker, C. (1987) (eds) *The Growing Divide*. Child Poverty Action Group, London.

Walker, A., Guillemard, A.-M. and Alber, J. (1993) *Older People in Europe: Social and Economic Policies*. EC Commission, Brussels.

Walker, A., Noble, I. and Westergaard, J. (1985) From secure employment to labour market insecurity: the impact of redundancy on older workers in the steel industry. In: Roberts, B., Finnegan, R. and Gallie, D. (eds) *New Approaches to Economic Life*. Manchester University Press, Manchester, pp. 319–337.

Wall, R. (1984) Residential isolation of the elderly: a comparison over time. *Ageing and Society*, **4**, 4, 483–505.

Wall, R. (1989) The living arrangements of the elderly in Europe in the 1980s. In: Bytheway, B., Keil, T., Allatt, P. and Bryman, A. (eds) *Becoming and Being Old. Sociological Approaches to Later Life*. Sage, London.

Walter, T. (1993) Modern death: taboo or not taboo? In: Dickenson, D. and Johnson, M. (eds) *Death, Dying and Bereavement*. Sage, London, pp. 33–44.

Walters, M. (1978) *The Nude Male*. Paddington Press, New York and London.

Warnes, A.M. (1991a) Migration to and seasonal residence in Spain of northen European elderly people. *European Journal of Gerontology and Geriatrics*, **1**, 54–67.

Warnes, A.M. (1991b) The changing elderly population: aspects of diversity. *Reviews in Clinical Gerontology*, **1**, 185–194.

Warnes, A.M. (1992a) Age-related variation and temporal change in elderly migration. In: Rogers, A., Frey, W.H., Speure, A., Rees, P. and Warnes, A.M. (eds) *Elderly Migration and Population Redistribution*. Belhaven, London.

Warnes, A.M. (1992b) Temporal and spatial patterns of elderly migration. In: Stillwell, J.,

Rees, P. and Boden, P. (eds) *Migration Processes and Patterns. Vol. III Population redistribution in the 1980s*. Belhaven, London, pp. 28–55.

Warnes, A.M. and Ford, R. (1993) The changing distribution of elderly people: Great Britain 1981–91, Occasional Paper 37, Department of Geography, King's College, London.

Warnes, A. and Law, C. (1985) Elderly population distributions and housing prospects in Britain. *Town Planning Review*, **56**, 292–313.

Warrington, E.K. and Sanders, H.I. (1971) The fate of old memories. *Quarterly Journal of Experimental Psychology*, **24**, 432–442.

Weaver, T., Willcocks, D.M. and Kellaher, L.A. (1985) *The Pursuit of Profit and Care: Patterns and Processes in Private Residential Homes for Old People*. Polytechnic of North London, Centre for Environmental and Social Studies in Ageing.

Weber, M. (1930) *The Protestant Ethic and the Spirit of Capitalism*. George Allen and Unwin, London.

Wechsler, D. (1944) *The Measurement of Adult Intelligence*, 3rd edition. Williams and Wilkins, Baltimore.

Weg, R. (1983a) *Sexuality in the Later Years: Roles and Behaviour*. Academic Press, New York.

Weg, R.B. (1983b) The physiological perspective. In: Weg, R.B. (ed.) *Sexuality in the Later Years: Roles and Behavior*. Academic Press, New York, pp. 40–80.

Welford, A.T. (1958) *Ageing and Human Skill*. Oxford University Press, London.

Welford, A.T. (1976) Thirty years of psychological research on age and work. *Journal of Occupational Psychology*, **49**, 129–138.

Wells, B.W.P. (1983) *Body and Personality*. Longman, London and New York.

Wenger, G.C. (1984) *The Supportive Network*. Allen and Unwin, London.

Wenger, G.C. (1986) A longitudinal study of changes and adaptations in the support networks of Welsh elderly over 75. *Journal of Cross-Cultural Gerontology*, **1**, 277–304.

Wenger, G.C. (1987a) *Support Networks: Change and Stability. Second Report of a Follow-up Study of Elderly People in North Wales*. The Centre for Social Policy Research and Development, University College of North Wales, Bangor.

Wenger, G.C. (1987b) *Relationships in Old Age – Inside Support Networks. Third Report of a Follow-up Study of Elderly People in North Wales*. The Centre for Social Policy Research and Development, University College of North Wales, Bangor.

Wenger, G.C. (1987c) Dependence, independence and reciprocity after eighty. *Journal of Aging Studies*, **1**, 355–377.

Wenger, G.C. (1991) *Informal Care: The Bedrock of Care in the Community*. Centre for Policy Research and Development, Bangor.

Wenger, G.C. (1992) Morale in old age: a review of the evidence. *International Journal of Geriatric Psychiatry*, **7**, 699–708.

Wermal, M.T. and Gelbaum, S. (1945) Work and retirement in old age. *American Journal of Sociology*, **51**, 16–21.

Wheeler, R. (1982) Staying put: a new development in policy. *Ageing and Society*, **2**, 299–329.

Wheeler, R. (1986) Housing policy and elderly people. In: Phillipson, C. and Walker, A. (eds) *Ageing and Social Policy. A Critical Assessment*. Gower, Aldershot, pp. 217–233.

Wicks, M. (1978) *Old and Cold*. Heinemann, London.

Wicks, M. (1989) Community care: the challenge for social policy. *Generations*, **9**, 31–46.

Wicks, M. and Henwood, M. (1988) The social and demographic circumstances of elderly people. In: Gearing, B., Johnson, M.L. and Heller, T. (eds) *Mental Health Problems in Old Age*. Wiley, Chichester, pp. 57–66.

Wicks, M. and Rossiter, C. (1982) *Crisis or Challenge? Family Care, Social Policy and Elderly People*. Study Commission on the Family, London.

Widgery, D. (1991) *Some Lives*. Sinclair-Stevenson, London.

Wilcock, G.K., Gray, J.A.M. and Pritchard, P.M.M. (1982) *Geriatric Problems in General Practice*. Oxford University Press, Oxford.

Wilkes, E. (1984) Dying now. *The Lancet*, 28 April, **1**, 8383, 950–952.

Wilkin, D. (1987) Conceptual problems in dependency research. *Social Science and Medicine*, **24**, 867–873.

Wilkin, D. (1990) Dependency. In: Peace, S.M. (ed.) *Researching Social Gerontology*. Sage, London.

Wilkin, D., Mashiah, T. and Jolley, D.J. (1978) Changes in behavioural characteristics of elderly populations of local authority homes and long-stay hospital wards, 1976–77. *British Medical Journal*, **2**, 1274–1276.

Willcocks, D., Peace, S. and Kellaher, L. (1987) *Private Lives in Public Places: A Research-based Critique of Residential Life in Local Authority Old People's Homes*. Tavistock, London.

Williams, G. (1990) *The Experience of Housing in Retirement: Elderly Lifestyles and Private Initiative*. Gower, Aldershot.

Williams, R. (1986) Images of Age and Generation. Paper presented at the British Sociological Association Annual Conference, Loughborough University.

Williams, R. (1990) *The Protestant Legacy: Attitudes to Death and Illness among Older Aberdonians*. Clarendon Press, Oxford.

Williams, R.H. and Wirths, C.G. (1965) *Lives Through the Years*. Aldine-Atherton, Chicago.

Williamson, J. (1979) Notes on the historical development of geriatric medicine as a medical speciality. *Age and Ageing*, **8**, 144–148.

Willmott, P. and Young, M. (1962) *Family and Kinship in East London*. Penguin, London.

Willner, P. (1985) *Depression: A Psychobiological Synthesis*. Wiley, Chichester.

Willson, J.W. (1989) *Funerals without God: A Practical Guide to Non-religious Funerals*. The British Humanist Society, London.

Wilson, B.A. and Moffat, N. (1984) *Clinical Management of Memory Problems*. Croom Helm, London.

Winn, R.L. and Newton, N. (1982) Sexuality and aging: a study of 106 cultures. *Archives of Sexual Behaviour*, **11**, 283–298.

Wirz, H.M. (1982) Sheltered housing. In: Lishman, J. (ed.) *Research Highlights No. 3: Developing Services for the Elderly*. University of Aberdeen, Department of Social Work, pp. 87–102.

Wolfensberger, W. (1972) *Normalisation: One Principle of Normalisation in Human Services*. Leonard Crainford, Toronto.

Wong, P.T. and Watt, L.M. (1991) What types of reminiscences are associated with successful aging? *Psychology and Aging*, **6**, 272–279.

Woodberry Down Memories Group (1989) *Woodberry Down Memories. The History of an LCC Housing Estate*. ILEA Education Resource Unit for Older People, London.

Woods, R.T. and Britton, P.G. (1985) *Clinical Psychology with the Elderly*. Croom Helm, London.

Woodward, K. (1991) *Ageing and Its Discontents: Freud and Other Fictions*. Indiana University Press, Bloomington and Indianapolis.

Worden, J.W. (1982) *Grief Counselling and Grief Therapy*. Tavistock, London.

World Health Organization (1989) *Health of the Elderly. Report of a WHO Expert Committee, Technical Report Series, 779*. WHO, Geneva.

Wright, F. (1986) *Left to Care Alone*. Gower, Aldershot.

Wyvern Partnership (1977) *An Evaluation of the Group Unit Design for Old People's Homes*. University of Birmingham: Wyvern Partnership/ Social Services Unit.

Young, K. (1977) Values in the policy process. *Policy and Politics*, **5**, 1–22.

Young, J. and George, J. (1991) *Ethnic Minority Populations in the United Kingdom*. Edward Arnold, London.

Young, M. and Willmott, P. (1957) *Family and Kinship in East London*. Routledge and Kegan Paul, London.

Young, M. and Willmott, P. (1973) *The Symmetrical Family. A Study of Work and Leisure in the London Region*. Routledge and Kegan Paul, London.

Zabalza, A., Pissarides, C. and Barton, M. (1980) Social security and the choice between full-time and part-time work and retirement. *Journal of Public Economics*, **14**, 245–276.

Zacks, R.T. (1982) Encoding strategies used by young and elderly adults in a keeping track task. *Journal of Gerontology*, **37**, 203–211.

Zeisel, J., Epp, G. and Demos, S. (1977) *Low-rise Housing for Older People*. HUD-483 (TQ.)-76. US Dept. of Housing and Urban Development, U.S. Government Printing Office, Washington, DC.

Zeldin, T. (1983) *The French*. Collins, London.

INDEX

ABC analysis, 148
Abrams, M., 8, 9, 85, 249, 250, 251
abuse, 138, 241
acceptance, of death, 155, 157, 158
accident, age related, 55
Achenbaum, W.A., 322
activities of daily living (ADLs), 270–1
activity theory, 32–3, 153
adaptation theory, 135
adjustment, in later life, 15, 81, 93,
   97–132
  determinants of, 118–19
  individual meaning and, 122–31
  special aspects of, 100–12
Adler, A., 27
afterlife, belief in, 160–2
ageing, 1–3, 7, 10, 21–2
  biological theories of, 22–4
  differential, 92–4
  images of, 304–32
  predicting changes in, 6–7
  psychological perspectives of, 24–31
  sociological perspectives of, 31–40
  theories of, 100–2
  see also senescence; old age
ageism, 10, 80, 139–40, 223, 265, 323
  institutionalised, 347–9
Alexander, B.B., 90
Allon-Smith, R.D., 204
altruism, 260–1
Alzheimer's disease, 40–1, 47, 48–9, 65–6,
   315–16
Americans for Generational Equity (AGE),
   262, 348
Ames, D., 272
anaemia
  iron-deficiency, 60
  pernicious, 60, 64
Anderson, R., 140
angina, 62
anthropological studies, on adjustment to
   ageing, 124–6
anti-collectivism, 221
anxiety, 112
  retirement and, 185

appearance, 126, 310
  awareness of, 324, 325, 327
Arber, S., 3
Archer, J.L., 102, 159
Ariès, P., 152
Armstrong, D., 152
arthritis, 60, 270
Asia, increasing aged population, 2
assessment
  of cognitive deterioration, 43–4
  of need, 44
asset ownership, 289–91
Atchley, R., 190, 192
atherosclerosis, 62, 65
Atherton, J.S., 141
Atkinson, D.A., 217
attachment theory, 95
attitudes, to elderly, 10–16, 80–1, 318–22,
   331, 345, 347
  political ideology and, 344
Audit Commission, *The Community
   Revolution*, 273
autonomy, 339
aversion, 331
Avolio, B.S., 340
awareness
  of ageing, 323–6
  of death, 156, 157, 158

Baikie, E., 114
Baker, D.E., 218
Baltes, P.B., 146
Barrow, G.M., 308
Barrowclough, C., 145, 190
Bayley, M., 221
beauty, 311, 312
Beauvoir, S. de, 154
Becker, E., 153, 265
behaviour, 126–7
  disturbed, 147–8
  environment and, 133–50
  family prescriptions for, 234–5
Bengston, V.L., 80, 235, 237, 317
bereavement, 173–9
  depression and, 120
  see also widowhood

Bergman, Ingmar, 105
Bernard, M., 251
Betjeman, John, 255
Beveridge, Sir William, 299, 300, 301
biographical work, 48–9, 191
biological ageing, 53–67, 69
    effect of mental functioning, 71–3, 78
Birren, J.E., 338
birth rates, 333–4
bladder function, 61
Blakemore, K., 5, 318, 325
Blau, P., 261
Blumer, H., 36
body, and ageing, 305–18
Bond, J., 218, 219, 223, 270, 274
Boneham, M., 5
bones, thinning, 55, 60
Booth, T., 143, 146, 218, 219
Bornat, J., 317
Bowlby, J., 29
bowel function, 61
    stress and, 137–8
Bowling, A., 175, 177, 218
brain, age-related diseases of, 65–6, 73
Brayne, C., 272
Breadline Britain survey, 283
breathlessness, 62
Brenan, G., 313
British Social Attitudes Survey, 348
Britton, P.G., 143, 146
Bromley, D.B., 131, 133, 314–15
Bronte, L., 267
Brown, G.W., 119, 121, 122
Browning, Robert, 256
Buddhism, death and, 162, 164
Bulcroft, K., 249
'burden' of ageing, 187, 198, 266–8, 273,
    347, 349
Burgess, E.W., 205
Butler, A., 211
Butler, R., 104–5, 110, 157
Bytheway, W., 189

Canada, income of pensioners in, 292,
    296
cancer, 60, 67, 337
caring, 234–5, 260, 264
    community care and, 222
    for the dying, 168–73
    in institutions, 219–20
    services for, 273–6
    stress and, 138–9
    by women, 240–1, 263
Carp, F.M., 15
Carstairs, V., 270

Cartwright, A., 140, 175, 177
cataracts, 59
Cattell, R., 72
cautiousness, 90–1
cells, 21, 23
    replication of, 23, 67, 337
changes
    ageing and, 94–5, 107–9
    acknowledging, 126
Chicago Life Satisfaction Index, 99
child mortality, reduction in, 2, 7
Child Poverty Action Group, 227
Chiriboga, D., 87
chiropody services, 276
Choice, 328–30
Christianity, and life after death, 161
Christmas, elderly at, 156, 239
circulation, 62–3
city, ecological model of, 205–6
Clark, M., 311
Clark, P., 218, 257
Clark, R., 266
Clayton, V., 88
clinical depression, 115, 116
    stress and, 119–20
cognitive deterioration, 25, 43, 72–3, 95–6
    assessment of, 43–4
    death and, 112
    experimental studies in, 73–4
Coleman, P.G., 106, 155, 156
Comfort, A., 10, 21, 246
community care, 9–10, 138, 273–6
    for the dying, 170–1
    living arrangements and, 220–2
Compassionate Friends, 178
Comte, A., 31
confidants, 121–2
conflict theory, 33
confusion, 81, 166
    over family responsibilities, 234–5
congruence model, of environmental
    influence, 135
Connelly, N., 143
consumerism, 140, 325, 327–8
    and future images of old age, 330, 331
Continuing Care Project, 274
contribution condition, for social security
    benefits, 229, 301
control, sense of, 127–8, 146
Copeland, J.R.M., 115
coping styles, 82, 86, 94, 139
    with stress, 117–22
Costa, P.T., 83
costs, of elderly, 266–7
Cotier, J., 311–12

counselling, 339
Coupland, N., 308
Cowgill, D.O., 11
Crapo, L.M., 268, 337
Craven, E., 227
Crawford, M., 185, 186, 189
Cribier, F., 190–1
critical social science, 39–40
  and study of dementia, 49
cross-sectional studies, 51, 85, 187
CRUSE, 178
crystallised ability, 72, 78
Cuber, J., 246
Cumming, E., 32, 84, 153, 186

Dale, A., 213
Dant, T., 278
daughters, as carers, 240
Davies, B., 145
Davies, D., 161
deafness, 57–8, 85, 120, 270
death, 103, 159
  acceptance of, 155, 157, 158
  age of, 13–14, 151
  attitudes to, 103–4, 109–12, 152–4
  individual perspectives on, 155–60
  medicalisation of, 168
  in pre-industrial Britain, 320
  religious beliefs and, 160–3
death denial, 152–4, 155, 172
dementia, 3, 65–6, 70, 272
  care and, 138, 145
  clinical approaches to, 40–2
  psychological approaches to, 42–6
  as social death, 166
  sociological approaches to, 46–50
  treatments for, 42
  understanding of, 44–6
  see also Alzheimer's disease
demographic changes, 1–7, 230
  in twenty-first century, 333–6
demoralisation, 114, 116–17
  determinants of, 117–22
dependency, 146, 224, 235, 255–9
  disability and, 258, 268–73
  forms of, 256–64
  measuring, 265–8
  structured, 277–9
dependency ratios, 266–8
depression, 66, 85, 86, 97–8, 114, 272
  bereavement and, 120, 176–7
  determinants of, 117–22
  epidemiological studies of, 115–16
  symptons of, 115
  theories of, 20

deprivation, 283, 289
developmental psychology, 26–30
deviancy, old age as, 264–5
Dex, S., 192
diabetes, 63, 71
differential ageing, 92–4
digestion, 60–1
disability
  chronological age and, 6, 57
  dependence and, 258, 268–73
disease
  ageing and, 54–7
  effect on mental abilities, 70–1
  life expectancy and, 337–8
  see also illness
disengagement theory, 32, 84–6, 100–1, 110, 153
divorce, 9, 233–4
  and restricted access to grandchildren, 342
Dixon, S.R., 146
doctors, 273, 275
  role of in euthanasia, 165, 167, 168
domiciliary services, 276
Dono, J., 249
Durkheim, E., 46
dying, 112
  acceptance of, 110
  care for the, 168–73, 175
  fear of, 158–9
  at home, 170–1, 175
  individual perspectives on, 155–60
  institutionalisation of, 154
  in residential homes, 171–3
dying trajectories, 173

early retirement, 34, 189, 195, 198, 296, 298
Ebrahim, S., 171
education
  about ageing, 345, 349
  for the elderly, 345–6
elderly
  attitude to modern childrearing methods, 243
  as carers, 138, 245, 263
  geographical distribution of, 201–2
  proximity of family to, 238–40
  role of relatives in lives of, 240–1
  see also ageing; old age
Elderly at Home Survey, 98
elderly population, 1–3, 7
  projections of, 334–6
Elias, N., 154
Emerson, A.R., 185

employment, 185, 293–4, 340, 346
enduring grief, 175
environment, 30
  effect on longevity, 336
  influence on behaviour, 134–6, 147–50
  intellectual change and, 80–1
  requirements for institutional living,
    141–5
  shaped by older people, 139
Erikson, E. 28–30, 87, 88, 105
  concept of integrity, 102–4, 110
Estes, C., 277, 344
ethnic minorities
  ageing among, 5–6, 317–18, 343
  dying among, 171
  grandparenthood in, 237
  residential location of elderly in, 206,
    214
ethnomethodology, 38–9, 48–9
Europe, proportion of elderly in
    institutions, 215
European Federation for the Welfare of
    Older People, 166
euthanasia, 163–8
Evans, J.G., 274
Evers, H.K., 218
evolution, 22, 23
exercise, 62
expectations, and adjustment to ageing,
    125
expenditure, of pensioner households,
    282–3
experiences, 69, 78–80, 91, 122–3
experimental psychology, 24–6
extended family, 229

Fairhurst, E., 309
Falkingham, J., 266, 267
family, 226–31
  care of old people in, 8, 9, 13, 215, 222
  changes in structure of, 9–10, 231–7
  contact with old people, 238–40
  loneliness within, 252–3
  retirement choices and, 193
Family Expenditure Survey, data from,
    282, 283
family networks, 252–3, 341–2
family roles, 242–3
fear, of death, 153, 158–9
Fielden, M.A., 107
Fillenbaum, G., 146
Finch, J., 264
Finlay, D.E., 142
Fischer, C.S., 182
Fischer, D.H., 11

Fiske, M., 87
Fleming, I., 145
fluid ability, 72, 78
Folkman, S., 117
Ford, G.G., 136, 140
Forster, Margaret, 253
Foucault, M., 49
frail elderly, 215, 222
  living arrangements of, 219, 223–5
Francis, D., 124–5
Franks, H., 172
Freden, L., 128
Freud, Sigmund, 26–7, 100, 160
friendship, 250–1
Fries, J.F., 268, 337
Frisch, M. 91
fulfilment, 103, 105
functionalism, 32
funerals, humanist, 163

Galton, F., 25
Gaullier, X., 277
gender differences, 343
  in approach to death, 159–60
  in friendships, 251
  in longevity, 3–5
  in personality, 82–3, 85
  in retirement, 186, 192
generational span, 230, 231
generativity, 28, 88–9, 90
Gergen, K.J., 101
geriatric, 308, 313
Gilhome-Herbst, K.R., 120
Gilleard, C.J., 138
Ginn, J., 3
giving, intergenerational, 262–3
glaucoma, 59
Goffman, E., 37, 218, 219
Goldberg, E.M., 143
Gonzalez-Crussi, F., 312
Gorer, G., 152, 178
Graebner, W., 182
grandparenthood, 236–7, 239, 243
Grandparents' Federation, 237
Gray, B., 255
Gray Panthers, 14, 331
Greene, Graham, 100
grief, 176, 177–8
  stages of, 174–5
group living schemes, 143
Gubrium, J.F., 49, 99, 315–16
Guillemard, A.M. 189, 191
guilt, 105, 178, 235
Gumpert, M., 184
Gurland, B.J., 115, 116

Gutmann, D., 83, 88–9, 101
Gwynne, G.V., 218

Haber, C., 320
Hagestad, G., 236, 343
Haight, B.K., 107
Hanley, I., 114, 147
happiness, 32–3
Haroff, P., 246
Hartley, S.F., 178
Harwood, E., 77
hassles, 114, 117
Havighurst, R.J., 32
Hayflick, L., 23
Haynes, M.S., 319
Hayworth, Rita, 316
Hazan, H., 124
health, and quality of life, 56, 252
health authorities, 273
    care for the frail elderly, and 224
    community care and, 220
health beliefs, of older people, 139–40
health psychology, 133, 147–50
hearing aids, 58
hearing loss, 120, 270
heart conditions, 62, 270
heating, 209–10
Heincke, S.G., 83
Hemmings, S., 309
Henry, W., 32, 84, 153, 186, 326
Henwood, M., 2, 268
Heron, A., 190
Hess, B., 244, 245
Hinduism
    death and, 163
    reincarnation and, 162
Hinton, J.M., 112
hip fractures, 35, 60
Hirsch, F., 261
HIV/AIDS, 154, 334, 335
Hochschild, A., 249
Hockey, J., 172, 314
Holden, U.P., 147
Hollingshead, A.B., 46
home
    dying at, 170–1, 175
    meaning of, to elderly, 136, 204
home equity schemes, 212
home helps, 276
Home Life: A Code of Practice for Residential
    Care, 144
homeostasis, 63
hormones, 63–4
hospice movement, 154, 168–9, 172, 173

hospitals, 215, 217, 219, 274
    dying in, 170
household structure, 212–14
housing, of elderly, 136, 200, 208–14,
    346–7
    community care and, 220
    conditions of, 209–10, 283–4
    tenure of, 208–9, 223
housing associations, 211, 220, 224
Houts, P.S., 145
Howell, S.C., 136
Hoyer, W.J., 139
human body, images of, 305–7, 310–12,
    324–5
humanism, death and, 160, 163
Hunt, A., 85, 210, 238
Husserl, E., 38
Huyck, M., 247, 251
hypothermia, 63, 134, 210

identity maintenance theory, 105–6
illness, 3, 149, 270
    depression and, 119–20
    inadequate income and, 256
    morale and, 125
    retirement and, 184–6, 187
images, 304
    of human body, 305–7, 310–12, 324–5
    of middle age, 326–8
    modern, 322–6, 347
    of retirement, 328–30
    of senility, 313–18
    traditional, 318–22
immortality, sense of, 160–1
implicit privatisation, 221
income of pensioner households, 281–2,
    283, 285, 346
    and assets, 289–91
    in different countries, 295–6
    sources of, 292–6
income support, 281
incontinence, 61–2, 271
independence, 13, 141, 204, 257
    aids to, 342
inequality
    among older people, 287–9
    poverty and, 291–2
inferiority, 27–8
informal carers, 222, 261, 263
    terminal care and, 170–1
information-processing resources, decline
    in, 73, 75–6
Inquiry into Provision for Retirement, 284
Institute of Medical Ethics, 167

institutional living, 214–20, 223–4, 314–15
  see also residential care
instrumental reason, 40
integrity, 29, 83, 87, 89, 102–4
intelligence, 68–73, 82, 95
intelligence tests, 25, 71, 78
interdependence, 257–60
intergenerational issues, 237–43
intergenerational relations, 348–9
introversion, 82
Israel, income of pensioners in, 292, 295, 296
Italy, old age in Renaissance period, 11

Jacobson, D., 192
James, N., 159, 314
Japan, ageing population in, 6–7
Jerrome, D., 108, 177
Jews, understanding of death of, 162, 163
Johnson, M., 140, 267, 278
Joseph, J., 256
Jung, Carl, 27, 30, 86, 88, 160

Kahana, B., 135, 139
Kahn, R.L., 338
Kalish, R.A., 110, 111
Karn, V.A., 207
Kastenbaum, R., 111
Kearl, M., 153
Keith, D.M., 110–11, 158, 263
Kellaher, L., 146
Kent, S., 311
Kerckhoff, A.C., 190
Khan, Y., 316
kidney function, 61
kinship see family
Kitwood, T., 44, 45
Kivnick, H.Q., 102
Knapp, M., 145
Knopf, O., 328
Kohli, M., 278
Kornhaber, A., 239
Kubler-Ross, E., 110, 112, 155
Kuypers, J.A., 80, 235

labelling theory, 36–7, 49, 264–5
labour market, older people in, 199, 293, 297–8
Labouvie-Vief, G., 80
Laing, W., 274
language, 36, 39–40, 48
Larkin, Philip, 179, 255
Larson, R., 117
Law, C.M., 207
Lawton, M.P., 116, 135, 136

Lazarus, R., 114, 118, 136
learning, 76–8
Leather P., 208
leisure, 130, 198, 340–1
Lemke, S., 142
Less, L., 191
Levinson, D., 92
Liebermann, M.A., 97, 107, 126
life-death attitudes, 110–11
life expectancy, 2, 151, 325
  increasing, 336–8
life review, 105–7, 157
life–span developmental psychology, 29–31, 42, 133
  ageing in, 91–4
lifestyles, 93–4
Lifton, R.J., 160
Liggett, J., 310
Linn, M.W., 120
Lipman, A., 143
Lippman, W., 309
Litwak, E., 249
Living Well into Old Age, 144
living wills, 165
local authorities
  care for frail elderly in, 224
  community care in, 220, 222
  homes for the elderly run by, 215, 217, 273–4
Lohmann, N., 117
loneliness, 8, 13, 176, 226, 252–3
longevity, gender differences in, 3–5
Longfellow, H.W., 255
longitudinal studies, 51, 85, 87, 94, 119
  on coping with stress, 118
  on retirement, 190, 192–3
Lopata, H., 177, 248
loss, experience of, 97, 98, 113–14
Luker, K.A., 56
lungs, 62
Lynott, R.J., 49, 99

McCrae, R.R., 83
McCulloch, A.W., 108, 109
MacDonald, B., 310
MacFarlane, A., 318
McGlone, F., 270–1
McMahon, A.W., 105, 107
madness, 49
Malinowski, B., 260
malnutrition, 60
Manton, K.G., 338
marital therapy, 95
marriage, 244–6
Marshall, V.W., 158, 168, 179

Martin, J., 192
Marx, Karl, 33, 39
Marxism, 33–4
mask, ageing process as, 312–13, 316–17
Mason, J., 264
Maugham, Somerset, 103
Mauss, M., 260
Maynard-Smith, J., 21
Mead, G.H., 35–6
meaning to life, for old people, 129–31, 339
medicines, use of by older people, 140
Mellstrom, D., 176
memory, 41, 43–4, 65–6, 74–8
men
  as carers, 263
  deaths of, 159
  friendships of, 251
menopause, 64
mental illness, 46–7, 49, 270, 271–2
middle age, social construct of, 326–8
middle class
  friendship and, 251
  and migration in later life, 207
Middleton, S., 311
Miesen, B., 46
migration, in retirement, 205, 207–8, 334
Miles, W.R., 73
Miller, E.J., 218
Ministry of Pensions and National
  Insurance, 185, 280
Mitchell, A., 256
modern society, attitudes of elderly to, 107–9
modernisation, 11–12, 323, 347
Moorhead, P.S., 23
Moos, R.H., 142
moral siege, 108–9
morale, 116, 117
  health and, 125
  marriage and, 244
  reminiscence and, 106, 107
mortality patterns, 337–8
motherhood, ideology of, 242–3
mourning rituals, 178
Munnichs, J.M.A., 110, 257
Murphy, E., 119, 121
muscle power, decline in, 59–60
Muslims, attitude of to death, 161–2, 164

Nahemow, L., 135
National Federation of Retirement
  Pensions Associations, 14
National Health Service, 139–40
  see also health authorities

National Institute of Mental Health in
  America, 70
National Insurance Act 1946, 300
Naylor, G.F.K., 77
need, definition of, 301
nervous system, disfunctions of, 64–5
Netherlands, euthanasia in, 165–6
Neugarten, B.L., 123
Newton, N.A., 90
NHS and Community Care Act 1990, 215, 217, 221, 273
No Surrender (film), 315
Noble, I., 189
non-verbal skills, 71
normalisation, 147, 219–20
Norman, A., 308, 342
Norway, income of pensioners in, 292, 295, 296
nuclear family, 229
nursing homes, 200, 217, 273
  dying in, 171–3
  for frail elderly, 224
nutrition, 60–1

obligation, 263
  of family members, 228, 234
occupational pensions, 188, 198, 285, 288, 290, 294–5
old age
  association of death with, 153–4
  attitudes towards, 10–16, 318–22
  definitions of, 6
  as deviance, 264–5
  historical perspectives on, 181–3
  poverty in see poverty in old age
  stereotypes of, 265, 308–13
old age pension see retirement pension
old people's clubs, 251
Olson, E., 160
oral history, 14
Orgel, L.E., 23
Orwell, George, 109
osteoporosis, 60
owner-occupiers, 208, 223, 290

Palmore, E.B., 190, 192–3
parent-child relationship, 231, 237, 239, 240, 241
Parker, S., 188, 191
Parkes, C.M., 174, 176
Parkinson's disease, 41, 65
Parnes, H., 191
past life, attitudes to, 45–6, 105–7
Peace, S., 172, 204
peer relationships, 243–51

pension policies, 298–302
pensioner organisations, 14
pensioners' clubs, 243
Perkins, E.S., 56
permitted deviance, 86
pernicious anaemia, 60, 64
personality, ageing and, 82–91, 93, 94–5
personality development, 26–8
phenomenological research, 123–4
phenomology, 38–9
Philadelphia Geriatric Center Morale
    Scale, 99
Phillips, D., 143
Phillips Committee, 300–1
Phillipson, C., 34, 182, 189, 268, 278, 349
Piaget, Jean, 26
Pieterse, N., 307
Pifer, A., 267
Pincus, A, 142
poetry, description of old age in, 255–6
political action, 344
political economy of old age, 34–5, 194,
    223–4, 267–8, 277–8, 345
poverty in old age, 34–5, 198, 277, 280–4,
    288
    in different countries, 291–2
    official underestimation of, 284–7
    social creation of, 296–302
    widowhood and, 177
pre–industrial societies, old age in, 11,
    181, 318–19, 320–1
presbyacusis, 57–8
Prichard, J.C., 40
Priestley, J.B., 30
Pritchard, J., 138
programmed ageing, 22–3, 338–40
prostate gland, 61, 67
psychiatrists, 47
psychological ageing, 24, 25, 68–96
psychological development, 87–91, 96
psychological tests, age differences and,
    25
psychophilosophy, 130

Quadagno, J., 182
quality of life, 116–17
    measurement of, 145–7
Qureshi, H., 264

Rabbitt, P.M.A., 72, 73, 74, 76, 81, 108
racial stereotypes, 307
Raglan, Lord, 328–9
reality orientation, 147–8
Rebok, G.W., 139

reciprocity, 240–1, 260–1
    intergenerational, 262–3
Redlich, F.C., 46
reincarnation, 162
re-kindled grief, 175–6
relationships, intimate, 226–54
religion,
    death and, 111, 160–3, 177–8
    meaning of life and, 129–30
remarriage, 233–4, 248–9
reminiscence, 103, 104–7, 148
resident mix, in institutional living, 143–4
residential care, 141–5, 278
    guidelines for, 144–5
    physical environment of, 141–2
    quality of life in, 145–6
    social environment of, 142–3
    see also nursing homes; residential
        homes
residential homes, 200, 215, 218–20
    dependency and, 314
    dying in, 171–3
    for frail elderly, 224
    funding of, 216, 217
resources, of the elderly, 288–9
    effect of retirement on, 34–5
    housing tenure and, 223
    migration and, 207
    see also income
respect for old age, 11, 12, 89
response, speed of, 73–4
retirement, 85, 298–9, 324
    access to resources and, 34–5
    adjustment to, 197
    attitudes to, 183–4, 187, 198, 297–8
    compulsory, 37, 185
    experience of, 188–91
    future of, 194–9
    health and, 184–6, 187
    images of, 328–30
    pension age and, 198–9
    places of, 200, 201–4
    policies for, 296–8, 346
    preparation for, 95, 189–90
    sociology of, 181–99
    see also retirement pension
retirement pension, 262, 278, 294
    age for, 198–9
    subsistence principle in, 300–2
    value of, 285, 286
Reynolds, D.K., 111
Rhudick, P.J., 105, 107
Richardson, I.M., 185
Riegel, K.F., 26
Rimmer, L., 227

Ritchie, J., 190
Roberts, C., 192
Rome, ancient, images of ageing in, 319–20
Rose, A.M., 101
Rosow, I., 99, 101
Ross, H., 141
Rossi, A., 231
Rossi, P., 231
Rothwell, N., 143
Rousseau, Jean-Jacques, 26
Rowe, J.W., 338
Rowles, G., 136, 142
Rowntree, S., 301
Royal Commission on the Distribution of Income and Wealth, 280
Ryff, C.D., 83

Sackville-West, Vita, 95
safety, in residential care, 142
Salthouse, T.A., 73
Sanders, C.M., 177
satisfaction, with life, 33, 98, 116, 117, 118–19
  marriage and, 244
Saunders, Cicely, 168
savings, 289, 290
Schaie, K., 72, 77
Schama, S., 306
Scheff, T., 47–8
Scheidt, R.J., 134, 135
Schneider, W.F., 192
Schooler, K.K., 135
Schroots, G.F., 338
Schutz, A., 38
Schwartz, A.N., 126
Scott, R.A., 145
Scrutton, S., 265
Seabrook, J., 108
Seale, C., 169, 170, 172
self-esteem, 98, 122, 126, 128
  sexuality and, 247
self-perception, 126–31
senescence, 21, 50–1, 336–7, 338
senile demetia see dementia
senile dysphoria, 114
senility, image of, 313–18, 319
separation anxiety, 173
service planning, 1–2, 6–7, 220, 276
sexual division of labour, 193, 245
sexuality, in old age, 90, 246–7
Shanas, E., 184
Shaw, G.B., 69
Sheldon, J.H., 184

sheltered housing, 200, 208, 211, 224
  very, 217
Sherman, E., 130
sibling relationships, 249–50
Siegler, I.C., 71
Sikhism, 162–3
Sinclair, I., 136
Sixsmith, A.J., 136, 204
skin changes, 59
Skinner, B.F., 317
Sklar, R., 178
Slater, R., 143
social action, 35, 36
social attitudes, 80–1, 85
social breakdown, 80–1
social change, 108
  family and, 229–37, 340–2
social class
  lifestyle and, 343
  resources and, 287, 289
  retirement and, 191, 194
social death, 152, 166
social environment, of institutional living, 142–3
social networks, 252–4
  changing structure of, 7–10
  and decision to migrate, 208
  in the future, 341–2
social policy, future, 344–9
social security, 299–300
Social Security Act 1980, 300
Social Security Act 1986, 287
social security benefits, 198, 293, 298
  see also retirement pension; supplementary benefit
social security departments, 273, 274
society, changing values of, 89, 108
Soldo, B., 244, 245
Sommer, R., 141
Sontag, S., 256
Sophocles, 79
Spengler, J., 266
spouse carers, 245–6
stability, 82, 83, 94, 96
stages of life, 28–9, 157
'staying put', 212
Stearns, P., 180, 182
stereotypes
  in old age, 308–13
  racial, 307
  of retirement, 329
Stieglitz, E.J., 184
Stoddard, K.M., 328
Stone, L., 12
Stott, M., 14–15

Strang, P., 189
Strauss, A., 173
Strehler, B.L., 21
Streib, G.F., 192
stress, 45, 113
  coping with, 113–22
  depression and, 119–20
  effects on individual functioning, 136–9
  types of, 113–14
strokes, 65, 271
structuralism, 31–5, 46
sub-culture theory of ageing, 37–8
subsistence principle, 300–2
supplementary benefit
  older people on, 281, 282
  and payment for residential care, 216
survival curves, 53–4, 336–7
Sweden, income of pensioners in, 292, 295, 296
symbolic interactionism, 35–8
  dementia and, 46–8
Szasz, T.S., 47
Szelenyi, I., 249
Szinovacv, M., 192

Tamke, S.S., 321–2
Taylor, H., 170
technological change, 230, 341, 342
  and change in women's roles, 9, 10, 242
teeth, 60
terminal care, 154, 165, 166–7, 168–73
terminal drop, 112
Thane, P., 13, 182, 267
theory, in study of ageing, 19–21, 50–2, 100–2
Third Age movement, 278
Third World, 335
  ageing population in, 2
Thomas, Dylan, 100, 155
Thomas, K., 181, 319
Thomas, W.I., 36
Thompson, P., 156, 159, 160
Thomson, D., 302
thyroid disease, 63–4
Tinker, A., 212, 224
Titmuss, R.M., 261 264, 287
Tobin, S.S., 86, 97, 107, 126
Toner, J.A., 116
'total institution', 218
Townsend, P., 34, 189, 218, 219, 220, 223, 224, 277, 278, 288
traditional societies, psychological development in old age, 88–9

Treas, J., 237
Twycross, R., 167

ulcers, 60–1
unemployment, 286, 297, 298
United Nations, World Ageing Situation, 266
United States of America, income of pensioners in, 292, 295, 296
University of the Third Age, 345
unprogrammed ageing, 23–4
uselessness, 324

validation therapy, 148
values, 130
  changes in, 89, 108
verbal skills, 71
Vetter, N., 271
Victor, C., 170, 171, 270, 274
vision impairment, 58–9, 270
voluntary bodies, 273
  involvement of elderly in, 263
vulnerability, 55–6, 126, 135

Waldman, D.S., 340
Walker, A., 34, 146, 189, 194, 268, 277
Walter, T., 152–3
Walters, M., 311
Warnes, A.M., 207
Watt, L.M., 107
wealth, 287, 289–91
Weaver, T., 220
Weber, M., 34, 205
Wechsler, D., 71
Wedderburn, D., 220
welfare state, attitudes to, 348–9
Welford, A.T., 73
well-being, 116–17
  measures of, 99–100
Wenger, G.C., 238, 239, 240–1, 253
West Germany, income of pensioners in, 292, 295, 296
Westergaard, J., 189
Wheeler, R., 208
Wicks, M., 227, 268
Widgery, David, 171
widowhood, 174, 176–7, 247–8
Wilkin, D., 258, 278
Willcocks, D., 141, 143, 147, 218, 220, 224, 314
Williams, R., 156, 157, 158, 159, 167–8, 322
Windley, P.G., 134, 135
wisdom, 69, 78–80, 89, 339